Introduction

THIS IS THE STORY of a man who told a story. It was nothing less than his version of his people's account of the creation of the world and the beginning of their history, their equivalent of the Old Testament, the Epic of Gilgamesh, the Upanishads, or the Koran. Commonly told orally and in separate episodes depending on the traditional occasion, here for the first time it was on paper and of a piece. Although his version proved one of the most complete examples from Native America of the most important narrative that any society can tell itself about itself, it was published anonymously. Until recently no one knew the narrator's name. How it took a lifetime for this man to experience and string together this epic, its fate as a publication out in the world, the banishment that he and his family endured for being themselves and sharing such information, and their subsequent adventures and struggles for survival throughout the twentieth century are this book's story.

Edward Proctor Hunt was born in 1861 in the mesa-top village of Acoma Pueblo in western New Mexico—said to be the oldest continuously inhabited community in North America. But that was his Anglo-American name, which he discovered in a donated Bible that he received in an Albuquerque boarding school. Back at home he was known as Day Break, the identity he received when he was presented to the rising sun at the age of four days. Later he would acquire a third name, Chief Big Snake, when he performed with his family in the guise of Plains Indians on stages, in school auditoriums, and in circus arenas around the country and across Europe. Shortly after returning from Europe in 1928, he and his family stayed in Washington, D.C., where he put together the Acoma creation story for scholars at the Smithsonian Institution.

That story told of the emergence of two sisters out of the earth—one becoming the "Mother of all Indians." Hunt described the arrival of the first human beings, the incremental creation of their ecology, and established them in their high desert landscape. He related the making of their first, archetypal village, with its traditional spaces for human life, work, and ceremony. All the while he introduced their lessons for the proper conduct of social, political, and religious life. He narrated their promising and tragic experiences thereafter, as they worked through their conflicts with their guiding supernatural spirits. Finally he set his people on a migratory journey through mishaps and dramas that ultimately brought them to their present homeland.

After this telling, in estrangement from his tribe, Edward and his family learned to become self-sufficient citizens as they wove and dodged their way throughout the upheavals of a modernizing America. This book also traces the growth of Acoma as one of the world's distinct cultures and New Mexico's evolution as a multicultural state within which Edward was first a hunter, farmer, trainee as medicine man and sacred clown, and then a controversial storekeeper, culture broker, ardent Protestant, government translator, brother-in-law to a "Jewish Indian Chief," and convert to the American dream. Finally it lays his family's multigenerational story within the changing contexts of Indian-white relations from the time of Anglo arrival in the Southwest to the beginning of the twenty-first century.

Edward's life span also covered the period of the greatest displacement of indigenous peoples in world history. During this time many millions of tribespeople and peasant villagers were thrown on the road, uprooted by war, famine, greed, genocide, or extreme prejudice. The story behind the Hunt family's hegira is akin to that of refugees in general who must face anguishing decisions about staying put or reaching out for more survivable and successful futures. Many strike hard bargains between tradition and progress and wind up fending for themselves through all manner of diasporas, both external and internal. Their stories are a defining aspect of our human experience, as thousands of premodern communities produced postmodern families like the Hunts.

Although Edward Hunt never lived in his birthplace again, through the narratives he shared on the third floor of the Smithsonian's red-stone castle he returned to it in memory and spirit and paid it a high honor. Among the seventy or so songs that he regarded as integral accompaniments to his story, and that were recorded for the Smithsonian's sound archives, were some whose function was to rekindle, in words and incantations, the same magical forces that brought to life each element in the world's creation before the dawn of time.

One of them, Edward explained, was chanted by the "Mother of all Indians" herself. She sang it to instruct her Acoma Pueblo children about "the world and how it works" and their place in it. Edward called the song "How the World Moves." His son Wilbert offered this translation:

Some time ago, some time ago,
The earth, to be respected, was born.
Some time ago, the sky, to be respected, was born.
Some time ago, to be healthy, this earth was born with corn pollen.
Some time ago, to be healthy, this sky was born with turquoise color.
The earth's motion, the sky's motion,
Goes from north to west.
Look. The earth's motion, the sky's motion,
Goes from south to east.
Look around at the earth's motion, the sky's motion.
This all happened some time ago.

In the story that Edward told, the song's counterclockwise circuit reflected the centripetal movement of the early Acoma migrants as they spiraled ever inward in search of their predestined homeland. But the life Edward and his family led took a clockwise, centrifugal turn and hurled them outward into the unknown—from their home mesa at Acoma to its satellite hamlet of Acomita to the pueblo of Santa Ana to the city of Albuquerque to the nations of Europe and back to New York and then the nation's capital and Albuquerque again and finally, for at least one of them, back to the bosom of Acoma.

This book opens with the first movements of Edward Hunt's life, in the middle of winter on the large rock that his people still consider the pivot of the universe.

PART ONE

Day Break
(1846–80)

The Sun's Latest (1861)

It was my Tewa name, a thing of power. Usually such a name evokes either nature—the mountains or the hills or the season—or a ceremony under way at the time of the birth. By custom such a name is shared only within the community, and with those we know well. Thus, in the eyes of my Tewa people, I was "brought in out of the darkness," where I had no identity. Thus I became a child of the Tewa. My world is the Tewa world. It is different from your world.

—Alfonso Ortiz, 1991

ON THE FOURTH MORNING after he was born, the child received his name. With this identification he crossed his first threshold in a step-by-step progression toward full membership in his community. After this the village crier could refer to him personally as he strode up and down the dusty lanes of Acoma Pueblo proclaiming daily announcements, work assignments, and upcoming rabbit hunts or pilgrimages. His parents could get his attention from their rooftops. The village's spiritual leader and ultimate authority, the cacique, could add a pebble to his tally of those under his wing. Before long the boy would be summoned for further initiations and recruited for communal responsibilities. With this name everyone would know that he was someone and who that someone was.

The ritual began when he left his seclusion in a darkened room and was handed over to a fellow medicine man and his wife, his ceremonial godparents. They would introduce him to the world and the world to him. About an hour before sunrise that morning, this man and his wife carried the blanket-wrapped infant to the mesa rim. Nearby lay one of the rock's natural freshwater cisterns, whose overshadowing walls kept the pool of rainfall and snowmelt cool and free from algae even in midsummer.

Every tribal member was consecrated through this life-passage ritual. The tribe's creation myth provided its model. That was the distant time when the surface of the world was still unmade, damp and spongy. Crawling out from three underworlds, two sisters, Iatiku and Nautsiti, the world's first inhabitants, emerged on this earthly plain and waited for the dawn. They breathed in and prayed as the new light burnt their untried eyes. Then they sang the first Acoma creation song.

> *I am going to pray, am I not?*
> *I am going to pray to the sunrise lake in the east for life.*
> *I am going to pray, am I not?*
> *I am going to pray to the sunrise lake in the east for life.*
> *I am going to pray to the sunrise lake in the east*
> *That I will grow old.*

Later in the myth, Iatiku, the tribe's female progenitor, would do likewise for her twin boys. Four days after their birth, she presented them to the sun, with pollen and sacred cornmeal clenched in their tiny fists. When the myth mentioned the ritual this second time, it established an institution for humans to follow.

To officiate at these sun-presenting and name-giving functions Iatiku anointed a shaman from the Fire Society—one of the tribe's five groups of official curers. In the myth she spelled out the proper procedure: the parents' invitation to this shaman, his use of differently colored minerals to make a turtle-shaped sand painting on which to bless the child, holding the infant aloft to the cresting sun so that "his" rays could infuse its body, the intakes of breath from the new day, the uttered prayers for long life and formal announcement of its clan, the return to home, family, food, and final blessing.

Since parents were not supposed to present their own children to the sun, shortly after the birth the baby's father made low coughing noises outside a fellow medicine man's residence—the polite way to signal one's presence. Would this colleague do the honors? In the predawn hours, the man responded by making his presence known outside the parents' house in similar fashion.

By the light of a small fire, on a cleared floor space, he drizzled sands made from colored minerals to create the ground painting and array his ceremonial objects around it. He sang to the shaking of his gourd rattle while his wife ritually bathed the mother and child. The baby in her lap, the mother was seated on sheepskins with her husband alongside this depiction of the earth. The medicine man dipped eagle-wing feathers into a step-rimmed (symbolizing rainclouds) pottery medicine bowl and sprinkled the newborn.

Even in this rudimentary ceremony, key symbols of Acoma religion came to life and did their duty. Foremost among the medicine man's objects was the cloth-wrapped fetish of a completely kerneled ear of dried corn festooned with turquoise beads and known as a *honani*. With it was a bowl of cleansing water, feathers for dipping and blessing, pieces of chipped flint, and appropriate prayer sticks, or *hatcamun,* the Pueblo Indian medium for conveying human messages to the spirits.

These sacramental items served to draw in and focus unseen powers. For this occasion they helped introduce this child to the world. Did the father have prayer-stick offerings of his own? More good wishes for the child's health and long life were invested into these six-inch fetishes and added to the basket. Had a name been chosen, or did the parents want him to come up with one? No one remembers who proposed it, but one was ready.

Acoma mesa, "the place of preparedness."

The cold night was over; a glow spread in the east. Having turned over their newborn, the parents began their vigil back home. The name-giver and wife carried the swaddled child and basket to the rim of the mesa. Now he sang in memory of the world that was given to the first humans on earth.

When I came out, when I came out.
Who was it that was born this morning?
It was that earth, that sky,
They were first born.
When I came out, when I came out,
Who was it this morning that was first born?
It was that rainbow, the stars,
They were first born.

The medicine man directed his words toward the sun. The first rays shot past the mesa called Katzimo and into their eyes. The medicine man's wife straightened her arms and extended the infant toward the dawn. Again her husband sang.

Out from the darkness
Into the glare of life
I now present you.
What greets your newly opened eyes?
The sun, the moon, the stars, the rainbow
Are now your companions,
Your heritage of beauty,
Which is life.

The medicine man upended the basket and the prayer sticks spilled over the cliffside. He inhaled, drawing breath from the north, the west, the south, and the east. Leaning toward the baby, he blew life from the four quarters upon him. Out loud he spoke his name.

Gaire.

In short English that meant "Day Break." More specifically, it described "the first illumination in the east before the sun actually breaks over the horizon." It was a strong name in a community that relied on a delegated

Facing sunrise, eastern rim of Acoma village.

watcher who kept track of the sun's movements back and forth across the grooves and notches of a special boulder just east of the mesa so as to provide advance word on upcoming ceremonies that were linked to solstices, equinoxes, and the agricultural year.

Walking back to the infant's home, the medicine man arrived at the door. Now he referred to the baby in the third person. "Day Break, this is his home," he announced. "Here he comes. He is going to live here. May he have long life and all kinds of crops, fruits, beads. He is coming in."

"Let him enter," answered his parents from inside.

All of them drank from the brew of mixed medicines. They blessed the food and ate together. The medicine man swept up the colored sands, gathered his materials, and left the family to themselves.

Recognized as a human being, Day Break was now on his way toward becoming a social person. He was bundled and wrapped with buckskin ties onto an old cradleboard, a family heirloom made from slats split off a lightning-struck ponderosa pine that had fallen on the slopes of Mount Taylor, the tribe's sacred mountain of the north. A packet of corn from the cob fetish was tied to its left side; the rest of its kernels were kept for planting in his father's field.

Other indoctrinations lay in store as Day Break would be drawn more deeply into his people's religious practices. But of all the rituals in which he would partake, and in large measure recant, this ceremony was the one he cherished most. He would replicate it for his children and theirs in the future.

Up on Acoma mesa in western New Mexico these rhythms of life may have felt timeless and reliable. But down below, the country that surrounded it was in turmoil and its future far from certain. Only two months into Day Break's life the nation erupted against itself. One impact of the Civil War on the Southwest was the withdrawal of many Union troops from frontier outposts like Forts Defiance and Wingate. This left their old enemies, the Navajo peoples who lived to the north and west, bolder than ever.

Since the eighteenth century, the warriors of their spread-out bands and extended-family camps had been attracted to the relatively easy spoils of Acoma Pueblo and her nearest native neighbor, Laguna Pueblo, about thirty-five miles to the northeast. Wearing their skull caps of mountain lion or wolf pelts, carrying spears, bows and arrows, and heavy rawhide shields, the Navajos sneaked into their territories via the north. After rustling animals from around Laguna they often continued southwest to steal sheep, burros, and horses from corrals just below Acoma mesa, and kill or abduct any youngsters tending them.

As they hastened back around Ambrosio Lake, the raiders snatched all the extra livestock they could handle from other Laguna Pueblo pastures just west of Mount Taylor before they broke for home. At Waters Spring and Agua Blanca they watered their herds before pushing them into the rougher, wooded high country known to locals as "the Enemy Trail." Up to this point any Acoma or Laguna warriors on their tail might try to retrieve their stock, and even cut some enemy scalps. But here they pulled back, aware that by now the stolen animals were too well hidden in brush, and that they would be exposing themselves to retaliatory attack.

By the early 1860s predation by Navajos upon white ranchers and Hispano and Pueblo villages had gotten out of hand. As if sensing that his people's marauding lifestyle was ending, a well-known Navajo headman named Red Shirt led nearly three hundred warriors south from the Blue Mountains for one last strike. Around Thoreau his horsemen split up, one bunch going after any Acoma herds they found in the river basin between Mount Taylor and McCartys, the others heading by way of Ice Cave to empty any corrals they found south of Acoma mesa. Joining forces at Que-mado Canyon, they headed northwest. But at Mancos the pursuing war-riors from at least five pueblos caught up with them, and Red Shirt was killed.

It was the Navajos' last hurrah. Except for holdouts in a few hideaways, over the winter of 1864 the entire tribe was rounded up and removed to an internment center at Bosque Redondo, in New Mexico's deep southeast, where the prisoners were forced to construct their own prison, which was named Fort Sumner. By the time they were released in 1868 and com-menced their trek back home to a new reservation in the Four Corners re-gion, the tribe had lost about a fourth of their number. Their survivors gradually dispersed into local enclaves and a new life of staying put, sheep-herding, and regenerative peace.

One of Acoma's worries was starting to lift, but new ones were soon to come.

2

Born of the Rock (1861)

All Indian history is family history.

—Robert K. Thomas, 1970s

THIS CHILD WAS BORN with a secret. Not a *social* secret, like those that people keep to themselves after breaking some behavioral taboo, a vi-olation of the sort that Day Break would one day commit and suffer his first ostracism as a result. Nor an *institutional* or *religious* secret, like those with which Pueblo Indians were entrusted during their various initiations, and whose disclosures as an older man would contribute to Day Break's further estrangement from his people. Not an *historical* or *political* secret, of the kind that researchers uncover when doing oral history or ferreting in archives and that can shed revealing light on past events.

This was a *personal* secret, and it remains unclear when Day Break learned of it. For the handsome Acoma Indian farmer and sometime war chief named Juan Faustino Rey (usually just identified as Faustino), who wore a headband when he was photographed by Charles Lummis in 1888 and whom Day Break's family always identified as his father, was probably a stepfather. Nor was the Zuni man with whom his mother (whose name has been variously listed on genealogical documents as Juana or Lolita) lived for a few years in the 1860s at Zuni Pueblo, forty miles west of Acoma, his biological parent either.

In fact, the child's genetic father was probably not Indian at all, which might have explained his heavier-looking European-like features as he matured, his eventual plus-Pueblo height and girth, and who knows what other inclinations, gifts, or liabilities.

Nor was it regarded as a particularly dark secret. Day Break's braided genes linked him to the generations of bicultural offspring that emerged from the tidal wave we call colonialism. As the probable child of an His-

The Padre's Trail up Acoma mesa.

pano father and Pueblo mother, this newborn joined a mixed-race or *Genizaro* world that, over three centuries, had grown into a social and demographic force up and down the Americas. Furthermore, in Pueblo society it was the mother's brothers who oversaw much of the guidance customarily provided in Anglo-American society by a birth father. And since Faustino became the boy's functional parent for the rest of their lives, he is referred to in this narrative as his father.

We have no word about the liaison that produced him, how far the secret got out, or whether it affected his standing in the tribe or offered him greater or lesser opportunities. But apparently being part Hispano was a secret with which his life began. When people recall him as an adult they often mention his uncommon height, booming voice, and light eyes, disagreeing whether they were blue-green or brown-hazel.

Even though he went nameless for the first four days of his life, other pieces of his identity were already in place.

He was the offspring of a sandstone mesa that rose nearly four hundred feet like a gigantic pedestal in the midst of a valley bottom in what is today Cibola County in western New Mexico. From what whites call the Deadman's Rock overlook on the crest of Woods Mesa, the view of this eroding tabletop and its low-lying buildings on the summit rivals that of Machu Picchu in Peru or the fortress of Masada in Judea.

At a distance the dun-colored village looks organic to its foundation. Sliced by deep ravines and boulder-choked clefts, some sections of the mesa rim seem ready to detach and crash downhill. Surrounding the mesa is a gigantic sculpture garden of rain-eroded, wind-cut pinnacles and natural bridges. Capped by slabs of tougher Dakota sandstone, the ring of ocher-and-cream-colored Zuni sandstone crags and monoliths seem to be guarding the mesa against all comers.

Below spreads the floor of Acoma Valley. In springtime it is carpeted with grama grass and tufted with juniper and rabbit brush. In the old days it was also checkerboarded with scattered fields of native-grown corn, melons, beans, and tobacco. Among them, if you gazed a few miles to the northwest and knew what to look for, lay the ten-acre plot belonging to the tribe's "mother," the old cacique. Every tribal member was expected to help clear, plow, plant, water, and harvest those fields so as to replenish his community storage up on the mesa. That way the cacique could ration supplies to his neediest in the dead of winter or times of scarcity.

The rimrocks of Woods Mesa run northeast, bleeding into Seama Mesa. On the valley's southern boundary they merge into the cliffs of Southwest Plaza and East and Blue mesas. As the plain extends past the uplift of Katzimo, or Enchanted Mesa, these barricades narrow toward Acoma Creek. Clouds of great size and definition roll across a dome of blue sky. By turning in place an Acoma farmer hoeing his patch could check on the progress of three or more weather systems. On occasion, when blizzards or dust storms stream across the plain, only the crest of Acoma mesa is visible. That is when one can imagine the rain gods of Acoma mythology hunkering down on those cliffs, entertained by the human dramas unfolding on this rocky proscenium.

The prospect of rock, village, and craggy backdrop seem to exemplify Frank Lloyd Wright's prescription for optimal design—buildings as "companions to the horizon." Except for two bell towers that jut into the skyline, these stacks of mud boxes practically fuse into the rock. For nearly five hundred years, writers have competed for descriptions that could measure up to one of the most dramatic architectural settings on the continent.

This newborn belonged to a village composed of three parallel alleylike streets that ran in an east-west direction. Fronting them were eight stone-and-adobe houseblocks that rose to three stories and faced south. At each level they were stepped back, for full exposure to the winter sun, while offering maximum terrace space for outdoor activities in summertime. "Up and down the ladder" was a Pueblo Indian term for entering their houses. Pole ladders carried you up to each terrace, while other ladders, angling down through centrally placed smoke holes in the roof, dropped you into the sleeping and storage rooms.

Demarcating the individual house units within the blocks were vertical walls that were stepped and paved so as to serve as additional stairways. On the rooftops, from which rose chimneys of mortared-together old pots and spreads of drying fruits and hanging flakes of thin-cut meat, the people spent much of their time—working and socializing and scanning the mesas, ravines, and valley floors from five to fifteen miles in every direction.

◆ ◆ ◆

As a child in a matrilineal society Day Break was tied to his community through membership in his mother's clan. Like her, that made him a "big" child of the Sun Clan, one of the tribe's nineteen or so clans. But he simultaneously became a "little" member of the clan of his mother's current husband, Faustino. This connected him to a preeminent social group at Acoma, with whom he enjoyed another set of rights and was obligated through another set of behaviors.

Foot trail up Acoma mesa.

As a child in a village where men customarily moved into their wife's family's household, he took his first breath on the sheepskin-softened second-tier floor of his mother's family home. In this warren of rooms lived his mother and father, eventually his two younger sisters (shortly to die of smallpox), his mother's mother and father, his mother's three brothers and two sisters, his mother's eldest sister's husband, one of that man's sisters, and his great-grandmother. Around him were the soft, throaty sounds of the language that was also part of his inheritance—a western dialect of Keresan.

Of greater import than the fact that his genetic father was probably of Hispano descent was that he was born poor. Although the ideal of face-to-face Pueblo Indian communities was share and share alike, at Acoma as at other Keresan villages, subtle class divisions did exist. As a medicine man, his father devoted long hours and often all-nighters to chanting and crafting prayer sticks and making altars in the chambers known as kivas where their societies met in secret. These obligations cut into the time he could spend hoeing his fields and feeding his family. Hence the baby's parents were partly dependent upon donations from families they assisted through their healing, naming, and other rituals.

The infant's birthing room had been remudded over many years until it had acquired the softened feel of a cocoon. It was walled with shaped sandstone and adobe mortar and roofed with a low ceiling of whitened cottonwood rafters, or *vigas*. They supported a mat of yucca stalks or layering of smaller sticks, then a padding of brush topped by spread adobe mud that soon hardened. After plastering with adobe the interior was washed with a gypsum slip that left a chalky surface marked by a swooping pattern from the palms of the women who had applied it.

That winter of 1861 was especially cold. But the earthen walls preserved the combined heat from warm bodies, little lamps with wicks burning sheep fat, and a small fire crackling in the corner fireplace known in Spanish as a *fogón*. Together with the solar heat that the walls had absorbed and then radiated inward after dark, the room kept its sleepers, wrapped in their sheepskins on the floor, sufficiently warm. In those years the condominium-like units still lacked milled doorframes and glass windows. During the day illumination beamed down the ladder well or glowed from porthole-like

Plan of Acoma village.

openings that were glazed with chunks of mica (crystallized gypsum), which had been quarried twenty miles to the north.

Every day the women left and returned by means of their ladders, often while balancing one three-quart clay water jug, or *olla*, on their heads, another angled on their hips, and maybe a baby in a cradleboard on their backs. Each year, in the weeks anticipating the pueblo's annual St. Stephen's Day fiesta on September 2, when the mesa's three cisterns were brimming with water from late-summer monsoons, they replastered their house exteriors, leaving more imprints where their hands repaired fallen patches, and freshened the whitewash.

That year the village of Acoma was occupied by fewer than six hundred souls. This baby added one more. But no matter how modest its population or constrained its seventeen-acre footprint, his mesa-top village was home to one of the most unusual small-scale, preindustrial, subsistence-based, deeply historical, and fiercely independent oral cultures on the planet.

Even before Day Break received his name, the little universe of Acoma was part of him and he of it. The mesa held a foundational role in Acoma's culture, cosmology, and collective consciousness. For a thousand years or more it was the setting for ceremonies that renewed its cultural energies. But as this child would one day describe for scholars at the Smithsonian Institution, the place predated history. To this "center of the world" the female deity Iatiku had led their ancestors in an ancient journey. Here she had positioned them within the protection of four sacred mountains, initiated their social and religious institutions, and launched them into historical time.

Day Break would pay dearly for sharing such information with out-siders, and for daring to be *from* it but no longer *in* it. For now, however, as an innocent newborn, he lay in this second-floor room of a three-story house on the southeasternmost of the mesa's three streets. As soon as possible his mother buried his afterbirth down below, as if further anchoring him to this location. No matter how far his life spiraled outward from this place, or how estranged he grew from its fusion of natural and built forms, this mesa-top village remained central to his identity.

Many years later, that baby, by then known as Edward Hunt, was on the mesa with José Concho, his maternal uncle, replacing crumbled walls and restoring wooden frames at his ancestral house. Some lumps on an ex-posed doorjamb jogged the older man's memory. On the day of his neph-ew's birth, Concho recalled, he'd been chewing juniper sap, a natural gum that turns pinkish with saliva. Fashioning the puttylike mixture into let-ters and numbers, his uncle stuck them onto this wood frame to mark the arrival—"fev 61."

Following his bent for figures, Edward chose midmonth for the exact day. On the many documents he filled out over his lifetime he always wrote his birthday as the fifteenth of February, the moon his people knew as the Daughter of Spring.

Atop a World Apart (1861)

Surrounded by air, we live where
a step ends the world. Nothing
begins where we look down. We never
take that other step. A blue wall
Holds home together.
You in your home: birds weave
around you too something you
never dare touch. At night you
come in and are near: the world falls,
a long silent plunge through the sky.

—"Acoma Mesa" by William Stafford, 1977

I N EARLY COLONIAL TIMES, an Indian infant like this would have been
regarded by the Spanish as little more than a nondescript heathen, hope-
fully the child of a native guide to sources of gold, silver, or precious jewels,
potentially a domestic servant to ship off to Santa Fe or even old Mexico,
but definitely an inferior being, a colonized subject and one more number
on their baptismal rolls. With few exceptions the early Spaniards did not
possess much ethnographic curiosity. The only native traditions regarding
places, clans, social relations, languages, or cosmologies that interested their
soldiers and missionaries (and most nineteenth-century American educators and reformers as well) were those that led them to treasure or pin-
pointed the pagan customs that they wanted to wipe out.

Yet this child, soon to be known as Day Break, then Edward Proctor
Hunt, later Big Snake, and finally Dad Hunt, did fall under one Spanish
cover term that reflected his people's lifestyle. At first glance their villages
struck these Iberians as reminiscent of their rural towns, or "pueblos,"
back home. Hence he became a *Pueblo* Indian.

The word conferred a certain dignity, invoking an agricultural folk who
built permanent homes in settled communities that were organized around

central plazas where everyone got together for festivals and ceremonies. They also set aside special spaces that the Spanish called *estufas* that functioned as their own "churches"—the sacred chambers commonly known as kivas. Generally circular in form in the Rio Grande pueblos, at Zuni, Hopi, and Acoma the kivas were rectangular. Moreover, the seven Acoma kivas were embedded into the houseblocks, perhaps, some maintain, to disguise them from Catholic zealots who wanted to eradicate native rituals. Clearly these people were unlike those predatory "wild" Indians, the *bravos* like the Utes, Comanches, Apaches, and Navajos, who were always sniffing around Pueblo lands to steal their crops, livestock, and women and children.

Being labeled Pueblo Indians suggested that they were a cut above. They stayed put and cultivated their fields and fought mostly to defend themselves. Within a few generations of Spanish contact, they were breeding their own Churro sheep and short-statured mustangs. Being a Pueblo Indian credited them with loyalty to their "home village," a degree of social respectability as "a people," and a rung up the ladder toward European notions of evolved humanity.

Hence the inhabitants of the ninety or so stone-and-adobe villages the early Spanish encountered in present-day Arizona and New Mexico were lumped together as Pueblo Indians. Each of their autonomous, self-governing villages became a separate pueblo. Anyone hailing from one of their communities was a Pueblo Indian. As an offspring of such a village, this baby might be variously referred to as a Pueblo Indian from Acoma, an Indian from the pueblo of Acoma, an Acoma Indian, a speaker of a western dialect of the Keresan language family—one of the five, mutually unintelligible languages spoken by Pueblo peoples across the Southwest—or, in that lexicon of theirs, *Acume-ahne mu-dehish,* meaning "an Acoma person."

Most of the Pueblo villages became further identified by the name of the Catholic saint whom the Spanish assigned as their spiritual patron— such as the pueblo of Saint Philip (San Felipe Pueblo) or the pueblo of Saint Dominic (Santo Domingo Pueblo). Other communities, like Taos Pueblo, Isleta Pueblo, Jemez Pueblo, or Acoma Pueblo, retained versions of their own names. For reasons that remain obscure, the saint selected in 1699 for Acoma was Saint Stephen (San Estevan). His identifying symbols were a handful of rocks, to represent the stoning of Christianity's first martyr, and a palm branch, suggesting his heavenly reward for that self-sacrifice.

Acoma street with ladders, bread ovens, drying meat, firewood.

Yet the Franciscans did not make Acoma drop its ancient name. The village was called *Ha'ako,* which translates neither as "Sky City," the catchphrase promoted by the tribe's tourist program, nor "people of the white rock," as some popular authors suggest. Originally it may have meant "place of preparedness," alluding to the mesa's ability to protect its inhabitants from intruders. Or, as some Pueblo interpreters prefer today, it was "the prepared place," to emphasize its importance as a haven ready to embrace the ancient emigrants who coalesced as the Acoma people.

Shortly after the Franciscan campaigns to Catholicize their villages, each pueblo installed the carved and painted wooden statues known as *santos* in special niches within their new altarpieces. On his perch in San Estevan, the Acoma parishioners believed their little Stephen actually "lived," as the latest addition to the company of their supernatural beings. Only during his birthday fiesta on September 2 does he emerge, borne on a bier by church elders to his brush-covered enclosure in the plaza. There he is guarded all day by young men standing with .30-30 rifles, honored by prayers, blessings, songs, and colorful dances until his return to the San

Estevan altar before sunset. In the Pueblo mind the powers of these introduced icons only added to the force field already afforded by the sacred
beings that really counted—their rain-controlling Katsinas.

At the time of Spanish arrival in the mid-sixteenth century the Pueblo
Indian world extended from the cottonwood-shaded eastern banks of the
Rio Grande westward four hundred miles across the Continental Divide
to the Painted Desert. Over this dry, elevated landscape, any other distinctions drawn by the Spanish between their villages were determined by
their resistance or submission to the crown, to Spanish colonists whose
farming settlements began encroaching on Pueblo lands, and to Catholic
missionaries seeking their conversion. By this standard, the removed village of Acoma soon acquired its reputation as among the most recalcitrant
and hostile of them all.

Not for another three centuries would outside scholars draw finer contrasts
between the river Pueblos to the east and their desert brethren to the west.
Striking among the features of most Eastern, or "Rio Grande," Pueblos was
their division into two social groupings, a practice largely absent in the
west. Labeled by anthropologists as "moieties," each of these halves, or
"sides," possessed its own circular kiva, the semisubterranean, customarily
circular, secret meeting chamber for initiated members only. One side was
identified with Summer and symbolized by vegetables (its members convened in the Squash or Pumpkin kiva); its complementary other half belonged to Winter and was associated with minerals (their men met in the
Turquoise kiva).

These internal divisions were also exogamous; that is, everyone married
into the village's "across" side, thereby knitting bonds of kinship throughout the community. At prescribed moments during their ceremonial year,
these halves competed and collaborated to strengthen their collective identity. An overt symbol of their fundamental unity occurs during the last
round of their all-day annual corn dance. Held during each pueblo's main
fiesta celebration, this is when the two divisions, which alternated throughout the day in their dance performances, merge in the plaza.

Beneath the honeyed light of a late New Mexico afternoon, and hope-
fully under the downpour of a summer monsoon, the full throng of young
and old, male and female villagers display to visitors and spirits alike their
social integrity. They enact a ritual cycle that is part of the participatory

responsibility of human beings in the maintenance of the universe. These ceremonies are, as succinctly put by Jemez Pueblo scholar Joe S. Sando, "carefully memorized prayerful requests for an orderly life, rain, good crops, plentiful game, pleasant days, and protection from the violence and vicissitudes of nature."

As the Rio Grande and its tributaries provided a steady supply of water for their cornfields, villagers along the river put much of their energy into upkeep on their irrigation canals. The stream's reliability also freed them to concentrate on maintaining the sun's strength throughout the year. Through equinoctial rituals such as competitive footracing events on sacred east-west "Sun Road" racetracks, they loaned the strength of their young men so the sun could make it through its weaker, low-lying winter months and return as strong as before.

With the Western, desert-dwelling Pueblos, however, the internal structure of villages was less cohesive. The Hopi and Zuni villages were looser aggregates of migrating clans that had congealed sporadically following the abandonments of the Mesa Verde and Chaco Canyon regions in the late fourteenth century. Now they refined the dry-farming skills necessary to survive in a desert where irrigation was less reliable. Their symbols, prayers, and rituals concentrated on locating moisture in the ground and drawing rain from the clouds.

Across this landscape the pueblo of Acoma sat almost dead center. Accordingly, her social structure and worldview combined aspects of west and east. She featured an assembly of clans, following the Western Pueblo model. But her political and social systems kept community integration to a tighter degree, as found farther east. Like the Hopi and Zuni villages, she displayed multiple, rectangular kivas (seven, it is believed). But only one of these sacred chambers seems to have housed the ceremonies that drew all tribal members under one roof.

Acoma's concept of the cosmos and her reliance on rain-connected "cloud" spirits reflected Western Pueblo beliefs. But the importance she placed on shamanic or "medicine men's" societies was closer to curing practices along the Rio Grande. Her ceremonies, ritual art, and sacred chants focused on the rain-giving powers that made dry farming possible. At her "wet" farming camps, however, Acoma's irrigation canals diverted water from the Rio San Jose and other streams much as their eastern cousins drew upon the Big River and its tributaries.

For these reasons some scholars characterized Acoma as a "bridge" or "gateway" community, a sort of buckle to the crescent-shaped belt of Pueblo towns that extended from Arizona's Painted Desert on the Colorado Plateau to the Rio Grande string of Pueblo villages. Hence, she can be viewed as an "epitomizing" exemplar of what being a pueblo means. Unlike European stereotypes of what American Indians looked like, lived like, and cared about, Acoma served all this up on a single sandstone island, to the wonderment of the world.

And no less a marvel to herself. At the climax of Acoma's origin myth, as this child would put into words later in his life, here the destiny of their

Three-story Acoma house: first level for storage, second for sleeping, third for cooking.

mythic War God Twins, sons of the sun, was fulfilled. Having subdued the world's monsters, the Twins readied the big mesa for human occupation. It was selected, they said, "because they knew that Iatiku meant for the people to live on top of the rock, as it would be more wonderful and mysterious."

In September 1861, seven months into the child's life, his parents watched unfamiliar horsemen tying up their chunky horses down below. They weren't built or dressed like Pueblo Indians. They were Apaches, linguistic cousins to the Navajo and an unnerving reminder that Acoma was not alone in this native region.

Cloth headbands kept loose hair from their faces. Long breechcloths flapped over high-topped moccasins with hard rawhide soles and bobbed toes. Bandolier belts holding pistols and cartridges bounced around their long-sleeved Mexican cotton shirts. Only five years previously one of their war parties had chopped a local Indian agent to pieces and stolen Acoma's cattle.

Up they bounded on the single-file trail. Head and shoulders above the rest came a seventy-year-old man surrounded by bodyguards. His Chiricahua Apache name was "He Just Sits There," Mexicans feared him as "Fuerte," or "Strong One," but the Americans who'd invited him here for a last-chance council knew him as the legendary Mangas Coloradas (Red Sleeves). "He comes nearer to the poetic ideal of a chieftain such as Homer in his Iliad would describe," wrote one official. "The most magnificent specimen of savage manhood I have ever seen," said another, who helped assassinate him two years later. The surgeon who performed his autopsy admired "muscles that would have crazed a young and enthusiastic student of anatomy. His limbs were faultless, perfection in proportions and symmetry."

Mangas was foremost in a line of Apache guerrilla leaders who had pillaged in old and new Mexico for decades. Their Athabaskan-speaking ancestors are believed to have originated from western Canada between the eleventh and thirteenth centuries. Migrating southward down the mountain chains, in the Southwest they splintered into the multiple bands we know of as Apache and Navajo and gained notoriety as exploiters of local opportunities.

Toward the Pueblo peoples they found already residing here the newcomers developed a two-faced approach. Their agricultural skills were worth adapting, their arts and some of their religious concepts were appealing. Then they robbed them every chance they got. They sold Pueblo children into slavery, traded away or took as wives the women, rustled any livestock they could find, and made sure to strike during harvest time, when vegetables were ripe.

Day Break's parents need not have worried. Desperate to save his war-weary and decimated followers from encircling U.S. troops, Mangas was reviving a failed agreement he'd made here with white soldiers a decade before. When he broke this new pact and refused to stop marauding south of the Mexican border as well, it was the final straw. Under a flag of truce Mangas was soon captured, tortured with heated bayonets, and his head was mailed to Washington, D.C.

Wariness of outsiders was thus bred into Acoma's bones. Threats from Apache and Navajo predators produced a warrior code that coexisted with a Pueblo behavioral system that sought quietude and equanimity. Following the model of their mythic Warrior Twins, boys like Day Break were hardened from childhood. Soon enough he would begin his training at running, hunting, and vigilance.

His people had internalized the necessity for that the hard way.

4

When Cosmologies Collide (1540)

San Estevan—It creates a monumental interior space, which is one of the first and noblest to be built above ground on the northern part of the continent—a high-shadowed volume, fast and austere. . . . It is built of Indian materials, but it rejects the hived, stepped massing of Indian forms. Its verticality is uncompromised, but its horizontal axis is intensified as well. Its assertions are fierce and heroic, ultimately Hellenic in origin, and it physically introduces the divine pretensions of the European individual into the savagely innocent American land.

—Vincent Scully, 1969

A FEW HUNDRED FEET from the ladder that lifted Day Break's mother to her roof terrace rose a building so large that it sometimes blocked the sun. As he looked around while she tanned deer and antelope hides, peeled long curls of squash for drying on racks, and shucked corn, he never forgot the impression. "The church was there," he would recall, "when I first opened my eyes." A reminder of the closest his people ever came to extermination, the largest Christian church in New Mexico could look equal in sacred authority to the Acoma sun itself.

Three hundred and thirty years earlier Acoma Pueblo was but a rumor to the outside world. The first Spaniard to hint at its existence was an emaciated survivor of Indian attacks and lonely wandering who stumbled into a northern Mexican town in 1536. Farther north, reported Álvar Núñez Cabeza de Vaca, were "many people and very big houses."

Two years later Father Marcos de Niza, a priest with a tendency to exaggerate, heard from an elderly Zuni Indian about a "kingdom" called "Acus," one of an estimated 70 to 110 native pueblos spread across the Southwest. Then, in an August 1540 letter back to Spain, Don Francisco de Coronado mentioned "this settlement (Acus) and situated on a river that I have not seen but of which the Indians have told me."

But priests couldn't reform these heathen outposts on their own. "You might as well try to convert Jews without the Inquisition," Don Diego de

Wolf Robe Hunt painting—ceremonial riders approaching Acoma mesa.

Acoma looking north—church and sacred mountain (Mount Taylor).

Vargas would write, "as Indians without soldiers." Later that same August, through Spain's customary pairing of church and state in the persons of "the fighting friar," Juan Padilla and Coronado's fearless captain, Hernando de Alvarado, rumors became reality. "Thirty leagues from Cibola," recorded a scribe of the Coronado expedition, "[Alvarado and Padilla] found a rock with a village on top, the strongest position that ever was seen in the world."

Before the Spanish and Pueblo Indians could communicate through a common language, their symbols spoke for them. For many of the early, formal encounters between conquistadors and Pueblo people, that meant the Indians would first institute their ritual of protection. This entailed laying a line of sacred cornmeal before the entrance to their villages, which the Spanish were expected not to cross. For their part, the Spanish enacted their ceremony of possession. This meant reading aloud to the Indians from a text, the *Requerimiento,* which instructed every native community they encountered to accept Christianity and conquest, or expect war and total annihilation.

When the Acoma people realized that Alvarado and company had no intention of respecting their powder on the sand, instead of starting a fight they set out a spread. Before long the bulk of the initially "warlike" Acomans descended from their mesa and joined what almost sounds like a southwestern version of a first Thanksgiving. The Spanish trespassers were fed home-raised turkey, steamed corn, rolls of parchment-like bread, squash, beans, and piñon nuts, and were presented with gifts of cloth made from homegrown cotton, tanned deerskins and buffalo hides, and turquoise quarried from local mines.

Whether these were bribes to leave or invitations to visit didn't concern the impatient Alvarado. After he clambered to the summit his soldier's eye sized up the place. Like most Spanish appraisers of Acoma, he recognized its strengths as a natural fortress and reckoned that "it was a very good musket that could throw a ball as high." Any attackers faced easily defended pathways that led up narrowing crevices with pecked-in toe and finger holds as the sole means for gaining access. Nor did a rock pile at the rim escape him, "which they could roll down without showing themselves, so that no army could possibly be strong enough to capture the village."

Alvarado appreciated how the cliffs rendered the site defensible by men whose only weapons were stones, clubs, spears, bows and arrows, and clay pots sealed full of angry bees that could be thrown, like organic hand grenades, on attackers below. He also noticed an underappreciated fact of traditional Pueblo Indian architecture. These honeycombs of piled-up rooms were food factories, designed as much for the grinding, drying, processing, cooking, and storing of edibles as for human habitation. Within the coolness of Acoma's house clusters could be stashed enough dried corn, squash, venison, and other foodstuffs to last four years. The villagers need not descend for water—the large rock pools near the rim held three to five thousand gallons of fresh water, with guards making sure the area was swept clean and the water unpolluted.

Over the following decades other visitors added their observations. They commented on Acoma's extensive gardens and the farming stations that lay nearer the San Jose River. They reported on Acoma's distrust of outsiders, which only deepened once they heard of clashes between their Zuni Pueblo neighbors and these swaggering strangers. A few detected in Acoma's textiles, featherwork, jewelry, and dance regalia hints of trade relations with old Mexico. And they warned each other about the trapdoors that lay within their adobe apartments.

Around forty years later, relations went downhill. Interpreting the community's assurance of its sovereignty as "impudence," Antonio de Espejo had his soldiers put "a fine field of maize" to the torch. He commented, as if surprised, that it was "a thing which they felt a great deal." One imagines the shield-bearing warrior society of Acoma, the Opi, toughened by defending their people against predatory tribes, readying for a new threat.

Firsthand accounts of sixteenth-century run-ins with the Spanish are hard to decipher, so off-base were white and Indian interpretations of each other's behavior and so rapidly did miscommunications escalate into bad blood. Spanish accounts describe the Acomans as hospitable and compliant when, in late October 1598, Don Juan de Oñate had them sign an agreement of obedience and homage. The document has never surfaced; we have only Oñate's word on Acoma's willingness to become Spain's latest vassal.

Oñate did recount that one Acoma leader, a cacique named Zutucapan, invited him into a kiva. Taking a look at the ladder protruding from its dark recesses, "with courteous disclaimers," as one historian puts it, New Mexico's prospective governor declined. This probably saved his life. It was an old ruse: the Indians slipping out, pulling up the ladder, shutting the kiva's escape hatches, stuffing flaming brush, resinous splints, and dried chilis down the ladder well, and then hastily covering it, resulting in a blinding, stinging death for all within.

The Oñate "paper conquest" rolled west. To the Indians, its reading of the proclamation, the mimicked oaths of fealty and strange scratches on parchment, were bewildering, perhaps even amusing. During the Oñate administration (1598–1607), the Spanish added a bureaucratic layer upon the preexisting Pueblo system of leadership by religious leaders and caciques. Each tribe must appoint a governor (functioning as the tribe's secretary of state for foreign affairs), lieutenant governor, sheriff, officials overseeing the irrigation ditches, and church wardens.

To confer authority on this colonial regime, the Spanish replaced the feathered staffs of office wielded by Pueblo war chiefs in the sixteenth century with black ebony canes, capped with silver and festooned with silk tassels. Every governor was handed one, to be passed on during each midwinter's investiture of a new officeholder—as continues to this day. These were paradoxical symbols, intended to secure Pueblo Indian allegiance at the same time that they certified the crown's recognition of tribal sovereignty.

Five weeks after Oñate's close call at Acoma, Acoma invited a seventeen-member squad of Spanish soldiers led by Oñate's lieutenant and nephew, Juan de Zaldívar, to a meal on the mesa. Now her true feelings burst forth. At a signal, Zaldívar and twelve of his men were clubbed and speared to death. Four of his soldiers survived by leaping to the sandy slope below. They grabbed their horses and raced to alert Oñate and the nearest Spanish outpost at San Juan Pueblo (today's Ohkay Owingeh) on the Rio Grande.

Two months later the uncle returned to Acoma, deep in mourning and hot for revenge. Oñate's retaliation against Acoma Pueblo has gone down as the cruelest Indian defeat in southwestern history. During three days in late January 1599, his advance detachment of soldiers under Juan's brother, Vicente Zaldívar, scaled the mesa and set about leveling the village. Their chipped-rock cannonballs pounded Acoma's buildings into rubble. Roof beams, ceiling rafters, brush mats, tanned hides, woven cloths, food supplies, wooden tools—all went up in flames. "Dense columns of smoke poured forth from the windows," wrote participant Gaspar Pérez de Villagrá, in his poetic epic on the siege, "as from the mouth of a volcano." For killing eleven Spaniards and two servants nearly six hundred men, women, and children were reportedly hacked to death in the streets; an equal number were taken prisoner. Some were penned alive in the kivas beforehand, then killed and their corpses tossed off the cliffs.

Following the bloodbath came a grotesque and still-controversial epilogue. All of Acoma's men over the age of twenty-five were sentenced to have one foot cut off and twenty years of servitude. Males between twelve and twenty-five, plus females over twelve years of age, were sentenced to twenty years of servitude. More than sixty girls were sent to Mexican convents.

Few Indians knew or cared about the trials in Spain later that year. The viceroy of New Spain, King Philip III, condemned not the horrors visited upon Acoma Pueblo but the harsh behavior of Spain's commanders toward their own soldiers. Oñate himself was banished from Mexico City for four years, Zaldívar for eight, and the poet-hero of the assault, Villagrá, for six; each was fined eight thousand Castilian ducats.

The hideous episode notwithstanding, only thirty years later a remarkable new edifice rose on the rock.

San Estevan del Rey took eighteen years to build. Largest of all Pueblo village churches, the oldest Catholic place of worship in America remains the best-preserved example of a seventeenth-century mission. How its sweat and toil was exacted from the native population remains unclear. Legend paints the Franciscan who arrived in 1629 to direct the construction, Fray Juan Ramírez of Oaxaca, as the compassionate padre of Catholic folk legend, all tonsure, rope-belted cassock, and long-suffering piety.

*A procession begins:
St. Stephen's Day at
Acoma village.*

He had walked the 150 miles from Santa Fe to a shell-shocked, rebuild-
ing village with ample reason for detesting all Spaniards, and was reportedly greeted at the base of the mesa with a rain of stones. But he won their
hearts, it is said, by behaving much like one of their own medicine men. As
he walked away under yells and insults, an eight-year-old Acoma girl
slipped and fell eighty feet down the mesa. Ramírez either caught her or
broke her fall (in another *milagro* he is remembered as curing a dying
child with baptismal water). It was a sign, goes Spanish folklore, and he
was welcomed up top, where he spent the rest of his life.

Ramírez's charisma supposedly inspired his new flock to erect this earthen
megachurch in the middle of nowhere. An estimated twenty thousand tons of
earth, sand, and clay were dug below the mesa and piled into burden baskets
slung on Indian backs from tumplines stretched across their foreheads. Each
carry-up was a chore; one scholar estimates the building required ninety thousand of these loads. Two feet of earth alone were necessary to even out the
church's nearly five-thousand-square-foot floor. Tons more fill went into the

cemetery yard, or *campo santo,* so that its walled, boxlike expanse could level out the summit's slanting bedrock. To retain this extension, a forty-foot rock wall rose flush up the mesa's eastern flank. Including convent and cemetery, the new compound covered twenty-one thousand square feet.

For the church's *vigas,* or roof beams, ponderosa pines were felled from over twenty miles away (some say fifty). Trimmed to forty-foot lengths, they were de-barked and seasoned, then hefted onto the shoulders of relay teams of Indian men, a few dozen carriers per log—they were not to be desecrated, goes local folklore, by contact with the ground. Water for molding adobe bricks, mixing mortar, plaster and whitewash filled the clay *ollas* balanced on Indian women's heads that they brought from the cisterns nearly a thousand feet away.

From the Acomas who worked with a white foreman in charge of restoring the badly eroded structure in the 1920s, however, came a different story. Without coercion from Spanish troops, as Bernhard Reuter was told, the building would not exist. His Indian crew walked Reuter around the lumpy remains of what they claimed was a military garrison, within San Estevan's compound. They described forced labor by armed soldiers, workers in long files like slaves erecting Egypt's pyramids, Indians expiring in the heat, and hunger due to absences from farming and hunting.

This colossal structure, measuring 150 feet long and 40 feet wide, was the result. Some walls were eight to ten feet thick; its ceiling stood over 50 feet high. Down the hardened earthen floor ran a gutter for draining roof leaks. Native-drawn paintings on the walls depicted stylized sun, moon, and crop symbols. The priest's section featured a dramatic *reredo,* or painted wooden altarpiece, that was the building's glory. The interior served as an acoustical chamber that made every pipe and drum in the choir loft resound as if from heaven.

It is little wonder San Estevan was the first thing Day Break remembered. Today the building still looks "almost antagonistic to the adjacent rows of dwellings," in architectural historian Marc Treib's words. Despite the stories of renewed faith that enabled its rise so soon after the village's destruction, Acoma no longer trusted the Spanish. Before long the pueblo's pent-up anger and humiliation would contribute to one of the greatest firestorms in American Indian history.

Taking No More (1680)

For the Pueblo people specifically, the greatest legacy of the Revolt of their ancestors has been that they have been able to endure with their cultural integrity intact, free to speak their native languages and to perform their ancient dances. Because of a desperate, despair-born gamble on the part of the Pueblo people of 1680, their descendants have lived to find that their well-being and continued cultural integrity is regarded as essential to the well-being of all of New Mexico and of the Southwest.

—Alfonso Ortiz, 1983

AFTER FATHER RAMÍREZ'S TENURE the battered old refuge of Acoma withdrew into a period of restorative peace and relative autonomy. Lying some distance from wagon routes like the Santa Fe and Chihuahua trails, it was further isolated by miles of juniper desert, steep-walled mesas, winding canyons, and ravines gouged by flash floods. Besides, until the early seventeenth century, Spain was preoccupied with nurturing her pioneer outposts along the Rio Grande frontier, and resolving power struggles between her own religious and military authorities.

This kept Spanish meddling in Western Pueblo life to a minimum. Farther east, however, the invaders were exerting ever-greater control over Pueblo civil and religious affairs. More and more acres of Indian land were appropriated for Spanish colonists. Soldiers kept demanding higher taxes of maize and blankets. Increasing numbers of natives were conscripted to dig and haul in their silver mines. Pueblo boys and girls were seized for domestic work as servants in Santa Fe. By 1630 the Franciscans were claiming that around fifty priests were administering to a total of some sixty thousand baptized Indians in some ninety pueblos.

But when they interfered in the practices of Pueblo belief and seasonal ritual, the Spanish went too far. In 1598 the original colonizer, Don Juan de Oñate, warned a gathering of Pueblo leaders to accept baptism or face

Struck by surprise, the Spaniards retreat to old Mexico—reenactment for the film Surviving Columbus: The Story of the Pueblo People.

"cruel and everlasting torment." Two generations later priests were torturing Indians for "devil worship," and officials were executing Indian leaders for sedition. In the 1660s tensions reached a head. On the Spanish side came an intensification of what one historian has termed "the Franciscan war on native religion"; from the Indian side, the absence of rain between 1666 and 1671 was blamed on these foreign witches.

In 1675, Governor Juan Francisco Treviño made good on Oñate's threat and outlawed meetings in hidden kivas and ceremonial dances in open plazas. Backed by the military, priests prohibited Katsina appearances, and soldiers stormed into kivas, kicked apart altars, and threw sixteen hundred masks, prayer sticks, and fetishes on bonfires. Treviño's soldiers arrested forty-seven medicine men from a range of Rio Grande communities on charges of "practicing witchcraft." Three "sorcerers" were hanged in their home villages, while the rest were carted in chains to Santa Fe, publicly flogged in the plaza, and thrown into jail.

Among the beaten men was a middle-aged religious leader from the Summer division of San Juan Pueblo whose native name was "Ripe Squash"; Spanish documents register him as "Pope" or "Po'pay." Little is

Po'Pay, leader of the 1680 All-Pueblo Revolt, marble statue by Cliff Fragua of Jemez Pueblo.

known of his background, but with his charismatic leadership and die-hard antagonism toward all Spaniards he was the man for the moment. The 75 percent reduction of the Pueblo population since 1540 due to smallpox epidemics, the recent five-year famine, and increased raids by enemy tribes, made many Indians feel the end was near. The indignities of this antipagan crusade lit the fuse. There seemed little left to lose.

The pueblos lashed back and Santa Fe was caught by surprise. An army of Pueblo warriors, mostly Tewa-speaking and raised practically overnight, surrounded the capital of New Spain. Governor Treviño was compelled to release his prisoners. Set free, Po'pay hurried north, bypassing his home village of San Juan and making the kivas of Taos Pueblo his base of operations.

As the Spanish later learned from rebels and defectors they tortured and interrogated, Po'pay underwent a mystical vision of three Katsina-like spirits. "[E]mit[ting] fire from all the extremities of their bodies," they inspired him to hatch a war for freedom and told him how. Conspiring with other Pueblo leaders, Po'pay arranged for many Pueblo villages to rise up on the same day.

The strategy for coordinating this feat was to dispatch cadres of runner-messengers in relays all across the desert. At dozens of villages they delivered yucca-fiber cords that were knotted according to the number of days before they were to rise up. Untying a knot each day, when the cords were clear the villagers were to "burn the temples" that had threatened the authority of their kivas, and "break the bells" whose clocklike tolling had challenged lifeways that were supposed to be synchronized to the sun and the seasons.

So it happened on the new moon day of August 11, 1680, that the people of nearly two dozen pueblos and their roughly twenty thousand members, speaking different languages and spread over four hundred miles, rose as almost one. The first arrows flew at Tesuque Pueblo, just north of Santa Fe, killing its priest, Father Juan Pio. As the rest of Pueblo country rebelled, nearly all Franciscan churches were burned. Priests were hung beneath their belfries and their corpses were thrown on their altars. Some were forced on all fours and ridden like animals before their throats were slit. All told, twenty-one clerics were killed, and upwards of four hundred men, women, and children living in scattered Hispano enclaves lost their lives. The rest of Spain's pioneers retreated south to safety.

Evicting foreign spirits and vanquishing their symbols was just as important. The rebels burned crucifixes, smeared human excrement over the altar carvings of Catholic saints, and threw their rosaries into the fire. To purge their baptismal associations they waded into the Rio Grande and scrubbed their bodies with that all-purpose Pueblo purifier, the greasy gray suds of shredded yucca root. They burned introduced plants and seeds and butchered livestock identified with the colonists. The Corn Mothers, the rain gods, the spirits of the hearth, field, and hunt were back in force. Long term, the uprising can be considered the most successful in American Indian history.

Stories of his mesa's destruction, and his people's liberation eighty-one years later, were transmitted to Day Break without dates or books. They were conveyed through attachments to what the French historian Pierre Nora has called the "sites of memory" where the events occurred, and fragments of oral lore. Day Break was taken to the southwestern side of the mesa; under a cliff were the sooty smudges left from the great fires and Spanish gunpowder. On the rimrocks he played around the remains of a makeshift fort through whose portholes his ancestors once showered arrows upon the invaders. Whenever those days were recalled the women would break into ritual wailing over the survivors' terrible punishment. "Those poor, poor boys," they cried, tears streaming down their cheeks, as if it had occurred last year. From childhood Day Break was aware that he lived on the same uneven rocks that once soaked up his people's blood.

Anecdotes about the revolt also reached his ear. Someone pointed out where their priest, Father Lucas Maldonado, a native of Tribugena from the sherry-making region of southwestern Andalusia, was thrown over the cliff, together with his assistant. But Acoma lore added a twist that academic historians never caught. At Acoma, as Day Break later told his son Wilbert, they sealed some of the nuns whom they didn't kill into an alcove and plastered them up alive. As for those they threw over the cliff, one escaped. Day Break heard that his robe served as a parachute and landed him safely on a sandbar. Seeing this miracle, the warriors let him limp back to Mexico and report the catastrophe.

Still, native accounts of the uprising, whose effectiveness seems to have stunned the Indians almost as much as the Spanish, remained strangely piecemeal. When the Spanish interrogated the Indians, they couldn't get a straight answer. "Who was the leader of the revolt?," Jemez Pueblo historian Joe S. Sando says the Spanish governor demanded of some captured men, each speaking a different Pueblo language. "Oh, it was Payastiamo," answered the Keresan prisoner. "Where does he live?" the governor inquired. "Over that way," responded the rebel, pointing generally toward the mountains. From the Tewa speaker he extracted the name Poheyemu, and was told his home was in the northern mountains. A third man of the Towa tongue said the leader was Payatiabo and that he dwelled in the mountains, too.

Each was probably referring to an identical spirit, known in the Tewa language as "he who scatters mist before him." It was this same mythical mentor, added Pueblo Indian anthropologist Alfonso Ortiz, who was considered the keeper of plants, animals, and rituals, and whom Pueblo people regarded as a rival to the Spaniards' Son of God. A native story even has Jesus and this spirit engaging in a competition, much like a classic shaman's duel, in which the Indian wins by eating more squash, growing more corn, and uprooting a large tree.

One explanation for this conspicuous silence on the revolt references the Pueblo aversion to recollections of bad times that might haunt the future. "The Pueblo Indians have an amnesia about the revolt," Ortiz told Anglo historian David Grant Noble. "It was a very negative, traumatic event, and they put it out of their collective memory." Or as Acoma historian Brian Vallo concurred, talking with author David Roberts, "What the elders do tell the kids is our migration story. But not about the atrocities, the fights.

That doesn't give you life, it doesn't give you anything good." And Hopi scholar Peter Whiteley adds, "The possibility of good relations with Hispanos and Anglos today depends on suppressing some of the past."

Twelve years after the revolt, a three-hundred-member military expedition led by Don Diego de Vargas restored Spanish dominion over the region. Even after this *reconquista,* however, their sway was never total, their confidence never secure. The colonizers had learned a lesson articulated by photographer Edward Curtis many years later. Speaking of Acoma's resistance to Spanish oppression, Curtis wrote, "In them we see emphasized the character of all the Pueblo people. Superficially smiling and hospitable, and, as long as all goes to their liking, most kindly. Anger them, and they are fiends. A purring cat with an ever-ready claw."

Chastened like few powers in the history of European colonialism, now the Spanish closed down the 175-year-old practice known as *encomienda,* by which it had felt free to distribute large swatches of land to its colonists, along with rights to the slavelike labor and resources of resident Indians. Royal, or "crown," grants of four leagues of land, amounting to over seventeen thousand acres (known as the "Pueblo League"), were affirmed for each New Mexican pueblo. Even a public defender of sorts was assigned to protect Indian rights.

Now evolved a unique détente that "compartmentalized," as some academics have phrased it, the respective domains of the Christian church (initially Catholic, then Protestant); the chastened civil authority (first Spanish, then American), together with its mediating Indian governor and officials; and the guiding powers that the revolt restored to the traditional cacique and elders and medicine men. After this, as Santa Fe author Erna Fergusson wrote of the Santo Domingo Pueblo annual fiesta, "There is not the remotest connection between the mass for the saint and the ancient ceremony. They sit side by side; that is all; they do not touch."

Becoming Their Own Spirits (1866)

A kachina is not a god. . . . The sacred masks are handed down from gener-
ation to generation. In a kachina dance, the prayers of the people are trans-
mitted to the kachinas by the elders of the village. And the dancers, having
assumed the powers of the kachinas they're impersonating, are able to act as
messengers to our Father-Mother-Creator. Prayers are usually for rain and
snow, good crops, good health, and well-being for people everywhere. . . .
When you've been watching the kachinas all day, absorbing the rhythm of
the stamping feet and turtleshell rattles, inspired by the music of voices in
unison, muffled beneath the masks, you can't help feeling the sincerity and
dedication behind it all.

—Fred Kabotie, 1977

B Y THE TIME he was five or six years old Day Break and his age-mates
were aware that their lives were about to change. They knew it had to
do with commencing their relationship to the rain-bringing spirits known
as Katsinas (often spelled in the Hopi and Zuni literature as Kachinas).
Their initiations were scheduled for midwinter, when the war chief and
cacique had agreed for their age group to join the Katsina Society. On one
of the village crier's rounds, Day Break heard his name.

Unusually tall for his age, he was bunched with the bigger children
whose numbers had increased sufficiently over the past few years to form a
cohort. Four days before the ceremony his father sought a sponsor, almost
like another godparent, to shepherd him through the ordeal. The boy was
bathed, his head scrubbed with yucca-root suds, and he was forbidden
meat or salt.

The youngsters were stripped down to breechcloths and ushered to the
head kiva's ladder. As if reverting to a state of babyhood, they were hoisted
onto the backs of adults. This time it was wise old men and not their mothers who bore their weight. For they were about to undergo a second birth
of sorts, as new members of this inner circle of their tribe.

◆ ◆ ◆

Day Break was never fully prepared for the biannual visits from the Katsinas, one in midsummer, another near the winter solstice. Anticipating
their appearance brought a shiver of excitement and apprehension. First he
heard the throbbing of cottonwood-log drums, then the sizzle of rattles
and scraps of song. People skidded down their house ladders to claim a
view from near the Rainbow Trail. From around the corral behind the
church, the masked spirits began appearing, and soon swelled into a company of seventy or so.

Some of these Katsinas hailed from homes at far-off Wenimats, their
sacred underground lake to the west. Others were said to live around the
foot of Acoma mesa. Each had their identifying mask and body paint, attire and handheld accessories, their singular speech and whistles or chor-
tles. Their buffalo-hide masks darted this way and that, the dark eye-holes
warning onlookers to keep their distance. When one approached his
mother, Day Break shrank back. The dancer left her with a toy bow and
arrows so he would grow up brave.

A few he already recognized by name. There was Tsitsaniuts, "chief" of
this intimidating crew. He noticed the fierce War God Twins: Masewi with
his black face and Oyoyewi in his yellow mask, both gripping bows and
clubs. The Hunter spirit in his rabbit-fur headgear; another known for
throwing mud balls—whoever they struck would enjoy long life; the Run-

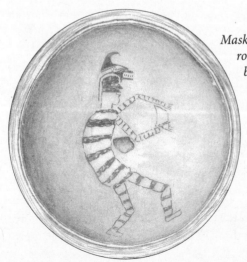

*Masking in the Southwest has deep
roots. A masked dancer on a
black-and-white Mimbres
bowl, Classic Period,
950–1150.*

ner Katsina with a bear paw painted on his face (he had once raced a bear and won); and blind Kaubat, escorted by his mother with her rattling sheep bones. Others showed up as full teams: the Good Farmers, green vines atop their dance masks; the Crow, Duck, and Mountain Sheep Katsinas; and other bands of supernatural personalities.

Their dancing commenced on the bedrock between San Estevan and the seventh houseblock, followed by a counterclockwise tour of eight traditional dancing stations spaced around the streets. It was as if they were lacing the community together through a choreography that lasted all day.

Who were these mysterious beings? At one time they were a central feature in most Pueblo mythologies and ceremonies. By the mid-nineteenth century it was only among the Western Pueblo villages of Hopi, Zuni, and Acoma where the role of the Katsinas remained most alive in story and performance.

Spirit entities of many parts, they serve as friends, allies, teachers, and divine intercessors, communicating between human beings and the cosmic forces. They are the incarnations of the deceased, the embodiments of one's bygone relatives and friends and fellow villagers. They are anthropomorphized aspects of clouds, mountains, and springs. They ride on the clouds, they are the clouds, they control the weather. They are the spiritual backbone of the people. All these meanings and more inhere in these sacred creatures.

Children like Day Break were smart to be on edge when they were out and about. Proud and quick to take offense, Katsinas always knew if you'd been bad or good. If disrespected they could retaliate by withholding rain or game or dispensing storms and earthquakes.

It is misleading, even demeaning, to term the "belief" in them as constituting a "cult," as was common in southwestern scholarship. In their otherworldly society, which runs like a parallel presence to that of humans, Katsinas enjoy a deathless existence. On their goodwill the people depend. Rather than being worshipped, they are propitiated, honored, and hosted. For they are messengers and mediators, guardians and friends, and preservers of core culture. In fact, there is no such thing as *belief* in Katsinas; they constitute an ultimate reality. To one writer they embodied "the spiritual essence of everything in the real world." But a term apparently coined by writer Charles Lummis may sum up their nature even better. He called them *The Trues*.

Whether inviting them for regular visits or in times of need, humans contact the Katsinas through cloudlike puffs of smoke from prayer cigarettes of homegrown tobacco rolled in dampened corn husks. Or they leave prayer sticks for them, as invitations laid at designated sites. As a medicine man, Day Break's father was often sending them his people's prayers for rain, good health, and long life. He carved his prayer sticks only from the branches of particular trees. He painted and clothed them variously, and deposited them at appropriate shrines. From there they would time-travel, so to speak, to their respective Katsina homes. When these actions were done properly, and the prayer sticks were strengthened with good thoughts, the Acoma people could sing about the results.

Here is one Katsina song Day Break never forgot:

Nicely again the raingods have returned.
Life-giving crops as a gift to the people they have brought.
Nicely again the raingod Nawish has arrived,
Raingods and game as a gift to the people they have brought.
Nicely the kernels of the corn turn yellow,
They form the yellow color.

Pueblo believers and Anglo scholars tell different stories of Katsina origins. To the Acoma people their "mother" deity, Iatiku, first created these beings and instructed them about their symbiotic coexistence with humans. In exchange for the happiness and support they delivered from their world— clouds, moisture, and long life—the people would provide sustenance from theirs. This meant the disembodied "essences" of such good things as corn pollen and tobacco smoke.

In a ritual that was common throughout the Pueblo world, Iatiku first "opened" (blessed) the road to Wenimats, the Katsinas' distant home, which lay beneath a weed-filled lake to the west and south of Acoma mesa. "Whenever my people want you," she proclaimed, "they will send prayer sticks like these." She carved the first samples so each Katsina could recognize the message aimed specifically to them, and ordered, "You must respond."

Along with these Katsinas, who served in summertime, she created a complementary band, the Kopishtaya, to "rule the winter clouds." They were more oriented toward male values; to them her people would pray so as "to obtain bravery and long, healthy life." Not long afterward, continued the myth, the Katsinas arrived "in a cloud" for their first gathering with humans. They danced and exchanged presents and all were happy—but only for a while.

Not until the 1980s did an archaeologist, E. Charles Adams, a veteran excavator of early Hopi sites in Arizona, present an outsider's theory about the origin of Katsinas. After comparing recurrent motifs in rock art, old pottery designs, and kiva murals found across the Colorado Plateau, Adams argued that by the early fourteenth century native ideas about weather-controlling spirits had synthesized into a new belief system. The impetus was the need for an ideology that could unify the immigrant clans who were abandoning older regions, such as Mesa Verde and Chaco Canyon, and converging in a series of larger, hastily built communities. In the past they were labeled either "Cliff-Dwellers" or, after the 1938s, as "Anasazi," from a Navajo word meaning "enemy ancestors." Now the preferable term became "Ancestral Pueblo," which acknowledged them as the parent groups of today's southwestern villages.

In Adams's reconstruction, these migrants continued southward, building and abandoning towns until they settled where the early Spaniards found them. For some of these composite communities, the Katsina system's form of priestly leadership, spiritual outlook, and associated symbols offered a kind of social glue. It overcame language differences and was not based on kinship ties or shared political styles. Plazas and kivas became the common arenas for Katsina performances, which were focused around controlling the weather, eliciting rain, and cultural survival.

So Day Break disappeared down the ladder, clinging to his sponsor's back. Awaiting the youngsters was Acoma's cacique and other elders. "I was pretty scared," he told anthropologist Leslie A. White. When one of the masked beings holding a bundle of yucca blades barged into the kiva, "I thought the Whipper Katsina was real."

After flailing at each child's back and legs, the Whipper spirit exited the kiva. Soft eagle breast plumes representing sanctifying breath were tied in each of the children's hair. Following four long days of song, storytelling, and instruction, the initiates were released. They looked exhausted and somber; their elders remained inside, praying, dancing, and singing until dawn.

The ceremony was not quite over. "They didn't show us the masks until two or three years afterward," Day Break remembered, "when we got old enough to know about such things." The masks contained the Katsinas' sacred potency, which is why the Hopi called such masks "friend." Led by their sponsors behind San Estevan Church, the initiates found the ranks of Katsina impersonators resting on the *banco* (bench) that lined the building. But this time their faces were naked; at their feet lay their buffalo-hide Katsina masks. Now the youngsters could recognize their parents, relatives, and neighbors.

With the mystery of the Katsina impersonators revealed, Day Break and the others entered a deeper strata of Acoma social responsibility. All this they were sworn never to reveal. They were told how human disrespect of Katsinas had once led to an epic war between the two that left many dead on both sides. They learned how the technique of impersonation was invented by Iatiku to make sure this rupture was never repeated. From now on the Katsinas would help humankind from a distance.

*Soon to be initiated:
Day Break's nephew and Day
Break's older brother,
Cipriano Rey.*

They were taught the perils of masking. Donning them and assuming their otherworldly personae meant more than playing a theatrical role. Impersonators internalized their particular Katsina's spirit; they *half became* what they enacted. Until the removal of these masks, the wearers existed in a shaky transitional zone between human and supernatural identities. Infraction of taboos associated with the ceremony, breaches of celibacy, or failure to use emetics properly could leave a person trapped between states of existence. At the Keresan-speaking pueblo of Zia, for instance, Leslie White heard of a long-ago couple who had sexual relations during the four-day purification period before a Katsina dance. When they tried to pull off their Katsina masks they found them stuck to their faces. The transgression led them to permanently become what they were personifying; no longer talking like humans, they could only utter the cries of their particular Katsina. Their neighbors walked them around the village, as if to offer a last goodbye. The couple waded into the Jemez River and sank out of sight.

Similar to such initiations the world over, the injunction to safeguard restricted knowledge was driven home. Whipping from yucca staves, sometimes until the blood ran, fixed these warnings into muscle memory. Speaking of such ordeals among Hopi youngsters, religious scholar Sam Gill emphasized how the "experience of disenchantment" when the masks were removed ended their innocence. For Gill this opened them up to a deeper religious awareness, and established "an agenda of religious inquiry and a keen interest in pursuing it." These revelations did not mean that their people's beliefs were a sham. The world was replete with paradoxes, ambiguities, and covert realities. These were theirs.

Day Break never divulged how this indoctrination and its revelations affected him. But he knew the demands that came with them. Eventually he was expected to don a mask, experience intimacy with his Katsina, join their dances, and remember the first Katsinas and their part in his people's origin story. Of those duties he fulfilled only the last, but he would not care whether the circumstances for sharing them were sanctioned or not.

Yet Day Break never brought outsiders to any Katsina dances. To this day whites have been excluded from witnessing the comings and goings of the cloud-and-rain beings of Acoma.

Mericanos Are Here (1846)

The total picture of the Corps operating in the West is, more than anything else, a picture of the cultural mind in action. It represents the collective absorption by a people of new knowledge, and an appreciation of the complexity of the modern world as the nineteenth century began to see it. Above all it provides a picture of man employing all his skills to arrive at a kind of ordered knowledge of his environment.

—William H. Goetzmann, 1959

DAY BREAK'S PARENTS were among the nearly naked kids who hid their laughter behind their hands on October 21, 1846, as twenty-five-year-old James William Abert and an assistant trudged up the curving burro trail and stood on Acoma's sacred roost. These white men looked different from the earlier Spanish, and also from the Mexicans who'd taken over after winning their war for independence. Above his straggly goatee, Abert's face was a pinkish color, and he spoke a hard-sounding language they rarely heard. Dropping the leather satchel carrying his note and sketchpads, Abert tried to ignore the touching, running, and jumping children who crowded around the visitors in their uniforms and heavy boots.

Abert arrived only two months after U.S. Army general Stephen W. Kearny stood in the Las Vegas town plaza to claim New Mexico for the United States. Three days later Kearny repeated his declaration in Santa Fe, again victorious without firing a shot. The bloodless victory coincided with Abert's more benign mission as the youngest officer in the eight-year-old U.S. Corps of Topographical Engineers. In anticipation of the takeover, he was assigned to take stock of any natural and cultural resources that might benefit the nation over the long haul.

That morning Abert left Laguna Pueblo, "surrounded by crowds of children who, impelled by curiosity, flooded the camp," and headed south for Acoma. His party crossed sheep paths and local Hispanos leading burros laden with clingstone peaches, watermelons, and dried fruits for

Acoma Mesa and U.S. Army Engineers Camp: James Abert drawing, 1846.

delivery in Cubero. He encountered Indian shepherds driving flocks of sheep to market in Santa Fe. Per his assignment, he took notes on the ecology: the broad leaves of cholla cacti, the pink-berried mistletoe, the harvest of peaches and apricots, the contrast between softer and harder sandstones.

After about fifteen miles Abert's party reached "our goal, the ultima thule of our advance, the magnificent 'sierra,' that raises its summits several thousand feet where they mingle with the clouds." Then he made out "high on a lofty rock of sandstone . . . the city of 'Acoma.' On the northern side of the rock, the rude boreal blasts have heaped up the sand, so as to form a practical ascent for some distance; the rest of the way is through solid rock."

Filing between a narrow passage, "the road winds round the spiral stair way, and the Indians have, in some way, fixed logs of wood in the rock, radiating from a vertical axis, like steps; these afford foothold to man and beast in clambering up." As the first official representative of the United States, Abert was the vanguard of a powerful new authority over Western Pueblo Indian lands and lives. Unlike earlier foreigners to enter their world, the Mericanos he represented were here to stay.

Once the Treaty of Córdoba freed Mexico from Spanish rule in late August 1821, Pueblo Indians were no longer royal subjects. To the silver-headed canes of office that each pueblo had received from the king of Spain was added a second group of ceremonial canes of alliance and respect from their new Mexican overlords. But this regime was less invasive. During the twenty-eight-year Mexican Period, Pueblo Indians were granted full citizenship, promised racial equality, and had their titles to communal lands confirmed.

The Catholic presence had also lightened up; in out-of-the-way Acoma clerics were practically nonexistent. Over the late eighteenth century, Franciscans stopped replacing their friars who died of old age; after the Mexican takeover, any who were Spanish-born nationals, representing the old disregarded monarchy, were expelled. Fewer than six priests remained in a region they once dominated. In the orphaned Hispano hamlets of San Mateo and Cubero north of Acoma, and similar little villages along the Rio Puerco valley, the clerical vacuum was filled by lay brotherhoods of the Cofradía de Nuestro Padre Jesús Nazareno, generally known as Los Penitentes for carrying on Old World practices of self-flagellation and intensely devout Lenten processions and Semana Santa (Easter Week) enactments. Now they assumed governing functions as well, while the heavy hand on native religious expres-

Base of Acoma Mesa, sand hill side: James Abert drawing, 1846.

James Abert drawing of the Padre's Trail, 1846.

sion was lifted. Once again the open plazas of the Indian pueblos re-
sounded with ceremonial dancing, and prayerful chants rose from the
kivas.

However, this also meant fewer protections against encroachment upon
Pueblo lands by an upsurge in Hispano homesteaders and sheepherders.
More and more Indians were bringing their complaints before local con-
stabularies and courts, to little avail. Meanwhile, the alliances that once
maintained an off-and-on peace between Spain and more nomadic tribes
like the Comanche, Ute, Navajo, and Jicarilla Apache had frayed. Adding
to the allure of slave-taking was easy pickings from the merchant caravans

that no longer paid Spanish taxes and clogged the Santa Fe, Gila, and Chi-huahua trade routes. Auxiliary warriors from pueblos like Laguna and Acoma joined local militias for protection against predatory nomads. Al-though freed from Spanish domination, and while the Americans would vow to honor their Spanish land grants, for the moment pueblo life was unstable and dangerous again.

The formal agreement between Mexico and the United States via the Treaty of Guadalupe Hidalgo remained two years and a brief conflict away. Its outcome was a foregone conclusion, but the American repub-lic wanted a better idea of what it was about to own. Across the un-charted West, Washington dispatched inquiring eyes like Abert's for a closer look.

His mission embodied the split personality of many official walkabouts. Advance men for the nation's doctrine of Manifest Destiny, the officers of his Corps were half scientific explorers, half imperialist appraisers. Gener-ally they were individuals of an adventurous spirit who reveled in the mandate to exercise their country's avaricious curiosity.

Abert's presence in this prelude to occupation and exploitation was a family affair. Back in 1838 President Van Buren had named his father, Col-onel John J. Abert, to command the new corps. The colonel turned around and assigned his son, a recent West Point graduate, to John C. Frémont's 1845 expedition across the Great Plains so as to halt Mexico's dreams of a northern empire. James Abert, a softer soul than the rough-and-tumble Frémont, was to fulfill the corps' scientific mandate. Following the model of Lewis and Clark forty years earlier, he was to take barometric readings, make astronomical observations, and record flora, minerals, fauna, fossils, and native life. A trained engineer, Abert would assess sources of gold and coal, determine the best routes for railroads and riverboats to transport raw materials, locate timber for ties for the soon-to-come railroads, and survey the optimal locations for military forts to defend the still-little-known Trans-Mississippi West.

Even though Frémont's four-month mule train expedition left him ill and recuperating at Bent's Fort, Abert did not falter from sketching Indi-ans around the trading post and collecting their tribal vocabularies. By early October he was in charge of his own team. With fellow engineer Lieutenant William Peck, Abert followed the Santa Fe Trail from Kansas to central New Mexico's Galisteo Basin. He inspected gold placer mines in the Ortiz Mountains, spun *la cuna* at Hispano fandangos with señoritas in Santa Fe, prayed beside their parents in Catholic pews, and rode south to sip homemade wine in Bernalillo. Continuing on the old wagon route leading west, he collected fossils and camped outside Laguna Pueblo. Then he tired of the pesky kids who "impeded the men in the performance of their duties" and turned toward Acoma.

After catching their breath atop the mesa, Abert and his assistant saw "one of the first objects that strikes the eye . . . a large chapel with its towers and bells"—San Estevan Church. When he wondered about the villagers' seeming inability to communicate in Spanish, his geographer reminded him of an old Spanish law that forbade whites from visiting Acoma and denied her Indians admittance to white settlements.

By the time of Abert's arrival Acoma's population had fallen to under four hundred inhabitants and was still dropping. But he was invited to walk up the partition steps to their roof terraces, where he noticed the walls "covered with festoons of bright red peppers, and strings of pumpkins and musk melons, that have been cut into ropes, and twisted into bunches to dry for winter use." The Indians arrayed basketfuls of clingstone peaches for drying on the rooftops and, "with great gladness," motioned him to "eat, eat."

In consistency their scrolls of unleavened cornbread bore "a striking resemblance to a hornets nest; it is of the same color and is thin as a wafer." After showing off their sleeping chambers, they escorted him to lower storerooms packed with "corn, pumpkins, melons and other eatables." Outdoors the Indian men were wrapped in broad-striped Navajo-woven blankets that hid baggy cotton pantaloons, bound at the knees with red cloth straps, while the women, Abert noted, stuffed their leggings with wool "which makes their ankles look like the legs of an elephant."

Upon his descent Abert returned to his task. In these final decades before the prevalence of photography, he sketched the first views the world would have of Acoma's wonders—a close-up of the trail leading up the mesa, a broader view of the sandy drifts at its base, and, from his camp tent at the valley's main spring, a panorama of the mesa entire.

Following this expedition, the quality of Abert's verbal descriptions and visual renderings quelled accusations of nepotism that had greeted his father's naming him for this plum assignment. After the Civil War abruptly ended this age of exploration, Abert survived the Shenandoah campaign to become a teacher of English literature in Kentucky.

Before the U.S. military abandoned such scientific inquiries, however, it lost its primary responsibility over Indian affairs. In 1849, the U.S. Congress turned that assignment over to its just-established Department of the Interior. This reshuffling began the paradoxical process of supposedly protecting Indians from brutal treatment by soldiers and militia while opening their treaty-protected lands to white speculators and settlers. Its ultimate goal was to hasten the day when Indians might be transformed into "self-supporting, self-respecting, and useful citizens of the United States," as a new, reform-minded Board of Indian Commissioners soon put it.

But a third initiative commenced as well. The previous year the U.S. Congress had established a national repository for the collection of natural history specimens, historical oddities, and social and religious information on the same American Indian traditions that it became so anxious to stamp out. The brainchild of a precocious young scientist named Joseph Henry, its holdings were generated in large part by voyages like Abert's into the terrae incognitae west of the thirty-one established states. The unit would be named after James Smithson, an amateur British mineralogist who bequeathed £100,000 to the United States for "the increase & diffusion of Knowledge among men."

In the spring of 1848 the Smithsonian Institution laid a cornerstone for its red-stone Castle. As its first secretary, Henry made his passion for American Indian cultures one of his priorities. The Smithsonian's first publication concerned Indian ruins in the Mississippi River valley. In 1879 the Bureau of American Ethnology was established expressly to record the languages, legends, and customs of the American Indian.

Sixty-three years later, the 135th bulletin of the Bureau of American Ethnology would be devoted to the memories and spiritual lore of the son of two of those hardly clad children who giggled at the sunburnt Mericano man taking stock of their mesa on behalf of an expanding nation.

Toward the New West (1861–66)

In 1864 Acoma was described in the same manner as it was in 1540, with houses in parallel rows, ladders used for ingress and egress to the buildings, low arch formation for doorway passages, and window plates of crystallized gypsum. There are also descriptions of a variety of fruits and vegetables, blue corn foods, herds of sheep and cattle, weaving, pottery and basketry, and evidence of Spanish silver.

—Velma Garcia-Mason, 1979

THE YEARS THAT THRUST Day Break into the world and bracketed his childhood represented a hinge moment in American history. The War between the States was followed by the last-ditch uprisings of Plains Indian tribes and final outbreaks of rebellious desert tribes. The country's population, economics, and lifestyles were dividing between the habits and heritage of a lawless, unfenced frontier and the aspirations of an emerging civic consciousness. "A journey of even a few miles in 1860," writes historian Adam Goodheart, "could take you from bucolic isolation—and most Americans still lived on farms or in small villages—into a maelstrom of ceaseless news, advertisements, celebrities and mass spectacle."

Over the next quarter century technological innovations knit America's many outbacks into a single, mostly domesticated nation. The Pony Express, which for a brief interlude carried mail thousands of miles across open country, was shortly eclipsed by the telegraph, and quickly came the telephone. The stagecoach was soon outrun by the railroad, to be followed in short order by the automobile.

With hardly a breather, the boundless Old West became fenced, sanitized, and then romanticized through the succession of dime novels, Wild West shows, and early western films. Boomtown lawlessness and violence-backed greed bowed to the spirits of hometown pride, civil society, and spreading capitalism. In the mid-1880s the Southwest was attracting its first tourists. Visitors lost no time looking back on these recent years of a raw frontier with sepia-tinted nostalgia. Another decade and the nation's door opened on a century of modernization and industrialization. Rarely in American history had Before and After stood so close.

In the late winter of 1861, when Day Break was still an infant, events nearer to home plunged his high desert into turmoil. Only forty-five miles west of his home mesa, at Bear Springs on the very day of his birth, a frustrated United States made its final pitch to suppress Navajo raiding through peaceful means.

For centuries Navajos had pillaged Spanish villages and stolen Pueblo corn and sheep. Their clans and families were in turn decimated by Spanish slavers. A state of insecurity and almost-war kept everyone's nerves on edge. But that afternoon at Bear Springs the offer of free rations and protection by U.S. soldiers induced the more progressive Navajo headmen to sign the Fort Fauntleroy Treaty and accept an accord. On paper, at least, that meant they would desist from the thievery that had become as much a Navajo reflex as roaming free and tending their sheep.

The following September the Navajo bands galloped into the fort for the promised supplies. But the local commander, a former slave hunter named Colonel Manuel Chaves, turned a minor quarrel into an excuse for murdering a dozen of them. Distrust flared back up; for three more years the landscape known as Dinetah became outlaw country again.

The reassignment of federal troops to face the Confederate threat to the east gave the more warlike Navajos, branded as *ladrones* (thieves) by their victims, free rein. They set upon more affluent fellow Navajos, known as *ricos* (rich ones), and anyone else within reach. Their younger warriors rustled from the newly expanding Mexican and Anglo stock ranches. Then the Navajos became prey themselves, as white slave hunters revived their open season on the now-renegade tribe.

This was the last straw for major general James Henry Carleton. A Maine-born, fifty-year-old infantry officer who had just defended the territory against Confederate incursions, Carleton was the antithesis of empathetic military men like James Abert or the ethnographer Major John Gregory Bourke. "All Indian men of that tribe are to be killed," Carleton had ordered in 1862, when assigned to quell Mescalero Apache marauders, "whenever and wherever you can find them. . . . If the Indians send in a flag of truce, say to the bearer . . . that you have been sent to punish them for their treachery [and] that you are there to kill them."

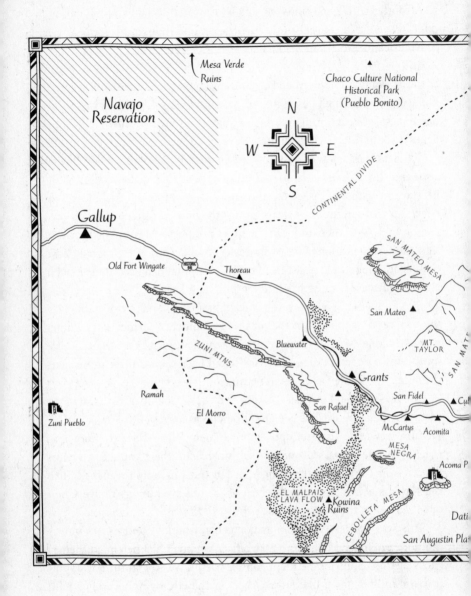

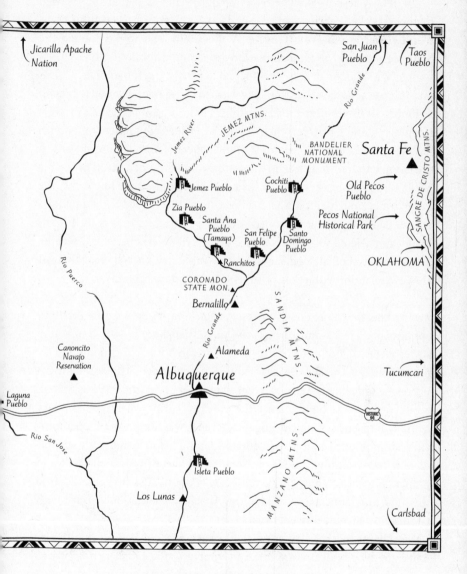

Map of Central New Mexico

In 1864 Carleton launched a campaign that was seared into Navajo memory as the "Fearing Time." Near today's Grants, he set up his command center at old Fort Wingate. A mountain man who'd entered the Southwest during the Mexican Period's mercantile heyday, Colonel Christopher "Kit" Carson of Taos, was tapped to recruit Ute Indian mercenaries and impose a scorched-earth policy. Navajos were hounded out of canyon redoubts. Resisters were killed on sight. Thousands of Navajo sheep were slaughtered and left to rot, their cornfields dispersed, family compounds and few possessions burned. Most of the tribe was rounded up and driven on a four-hundred-mile trek to the cottonwood-shrouded banks of the Pecos River in southeastern New Mexico. After what became known as "the Long Walk," much of it in the dead of winter, they joined their sometime enemies, the already imprisoned Mescalero Apaches, in a giant internment camp. Here they languished for four terrible years beset by sickening alkali water, spoiled food supplies and malnutrition, venereal disease, abrasive relations with other prisoners, and military brutality.

Meanwhile, the last bands of off-reservation Apaches in Arizona Territory continued their hit-and-run attacks on settlements, freight trains, and stagecoaches on both sides of the U.S.-Mexican border. The month of Day Break's birth witnessed the Chiricahua Apache leader Cochise's being invited to a parley with American representatives at Apache Pass. Bad blood between them was boiling since the previous spring when the legendary Mimbres Apache chieftain Mangas Coloradas was jumped by copper miners and humiliated by a bloody horsewhipping before being released. Soldiers tried something similar on Cochise for allegedly stealing cattle and kidnapping a white boy, but he cut his way out of an army tent, fled into the hills, and launched the last of the Apache wars that only ended with Geronimo's surrender twenty years later.

For Plains Indians farther north, the early years of Day Break's life signaled the bloody beginning to an inevitably tragic end. The final Plains Indian bids for freedom began with the Santee Sioux outbreak of August 1862. In an uprising on the scale of the All-Pueblo Revolt of 1680, but less well organized, some four hundred western Minnesota homesteaders were killed, while hundreds more settlers fled the region. The succession of major battles and running standoffs between a dozen or more Plains Indian tribes and U.S. troops and militias would end with the massacre of Plains

Indian Ghost Dancers at South Dakota's Wounded Knee Creek in 1890. Popular historians would seize upon that tragedy as a convenient benchmark for closing their chronicles of the American Indians. But the demise they invoked would actually prove contrary to the remarkable survival and eventual resurgence of Indians across the country.

These regional clashes rumbled within a country already at war with itself. The week Day Break was given to the sun and received his name, Jefferson Davis was sworn in as president of the Confederacy. Two months later pro-slavery rebels in South Carolina bombarded Union forces at Fort Sumter. The fight for the nation's soul was coupled with a burst of expansionism that called for removal, containment, or obliteration of any western tribes in the way.

Most Americans picture the struggle between brothers as a North-South contest. Its East-West dimensions are less understood because the West did not immediately feel allegiance to any national unity. It was difficult for Californians to feel connected to Washington when it took a voyage around Cape Horn, or three weeks on an Overland Stage facing Indian attacks, or else hopping ship-to-ship and then trudging through the Panamanian jungle and another long boat ride for easterners to even reach the place.

The Civil War's impact on Pueblo Indian country was minimal. In July 1861, breakaway Texans claimed southern New Mexico for their short-lived Confederate Territory of Arizona. Its high point came when Confederate general H. H. Sibley briefly seized Albuquerque and Santa Fe. But his defeat in late March 1862 at Glorieta Pass at the hands of Colorado irregulars sent him packing back to Texas.

Meanwhile, slower-moving but longer-lasting changes were shrinking the frontier. In 1847 fewer than five thousand pioneers made it to Oregon; four years later over sixty thousand whites headed west. Each spring their numbers multiplied, expanding the creation of mining camps and hastily erected towns across Idaho, Colorado, Wyoming, and California. To meet their transportation and communication needs, Ben Holladay bought the Butterfield Overland Stage Company in 1856; seven years later John Bozeman mapped his famous trail.

Clearly, the government's promise to protect wagon trains and stage-coach lines needed boots on the ground. In the absence of troops due to redeployments for the war, the job was filled by local volunteers and militias. With less training than regular soldiers, they had minimal sympathy for Indians. The legacy of their rampant, undisciplined campaigns against Indians meant that the postwar period of the Indian Wars was riven with the racism and brutality that President Grant's Peace Policy sought to stop.

At the same time, Holladay's "stagecoach empire" was soon upstaged by two of modernity's trademark projects. To link the East Coast with the West, in October 1861 the connections for Samuel Morse's expanding telegraph wires were hooked to Salt Lake City and then to the Coast. This meant that coordination of troops, monitoring the movements of renegade Indians, and financial transactions enabling civic progress and Indian pacification could be transmitted instantly.

More monumental and longer-lasting was the second innovation. To further bind the country, boost transcontinental travel, and haul supplies to the gold and coal fields of the Rockies and beyond, in 1862 President Lincoln signed the Pacific Railroad Act. Surveyors had already drawn up New Mexico Territory's most inexpensive routes, concentrating on north-south-running lines.

Just because that year federal officials dismissed New Mexico's Pueblo Indians as quietly pursuing "their usual avocations with their wonted industrious habits and exemplary conduct" did not mean they would stand idle while their lands were usurped. In Day Break's own future, the southwestern portion of this railroad system, cutting through Acoma and Laguna territories, would be a persistent presence. Wrapping the nation in a web of steel tracks required the cumbersome, uncertain, stop-and-go process of raising money and securing rights-of-way, especially on public—which meant mostly Indian—lands. But settlers racing to realize their western dreams demanded access to these "free" lands as well. Fulfilling another campaign promise, Lincoln in 1862 signed the Homestead Act, which offered 160 acres to settlers willing to cultivate them for five years; in 1880 Congress added public domain to acreage they could take over as well. Under the Indian Homestead Act of 1875, those benefits were extended to any natives willing to terminate tribal memberships in exchange for U.S. citizenship. But few Indians signed up.

For settlers west of the Missouri, the Homestead Act enabled the private ownership of over 1.5 million acres. Here the railroads also benefited, for undistributed lands were snapped up by corporate speculators or turned over to railroad corporations. When the original quarter-sections proved too dry and barren to support a decent living, later acts permitted farmers and grazers to increase their plots to 480 acres or more. For poor whites the act affirmed their preconceptions of an open "frontier," and participation in America's oldest vision: a nation of independent, family-oriented farmers. As settlers bent on civilizing the wilderness, they felt they shouldn't have to purchase lands into which many had already invested life savings and sweat equity. For Indians, however, the "yeoman farmer" image ignored a deeper reality. This self-same landscape was a quilt of their own unfenced and somewhat overlapping tribal territories, most of which were traditionally accepted and then legalized and protected through pre-existing treaties.

As she had for the past two hundred years, Acoma Pueblo tried to sit out these events. She remained, as historian Howard Lamar put it for the Pueblos in general, a "grandmaster of cultural isolation," exercising her arts of living as if averting her eyes from the white man's growing presence. In the Western Pueblos the Indians were largely alerted to the years "when white men fought white men" by the absence of bluecoats at Fort Wingate, which made them vulnerable to Navajo and Apache raids. At the same time the Homestead Act left them at the mercy of incoming Anglo-American trespassers, and only compounded their disputes with Hispanos over centuries of squatting on their borderlands.

But the Pueblos were not entirely ignored by Washington. Upon an aide's advice, in 1863 the Lincoln administration perpetuated a venerated formality by dispatching to Acoma and six other pueblos another, third set of silver-headed, ribbon-tasseled ebony canes. Each was engraved with the president's name, the date, and the pueblo. Every January, following selection of the coming year's "outside" officers, it became Acoma practice for the new governor to receive a Lincoln cane, his first lieutenant the Spanish staff, and his second lieutenant the Mexican standard.

In public these emblems of office would be trotted out on official functions. Otherwise they were treated as living affirmations of a new America's nation-to-nation tie to pueblos like Acoma, and safeguarded in special rooms where Day Break was permitted to glimpse them. Resting on altarlike tables, they were sustained by bowls of water and cornmeal. In years to come, one of his own silversmith sons would be honored by the Acoma governor and asked if he would repair the worn silver knob at the head of its Lincoln cane.

9

All He Had to Learn (1869)

The People were living at Cipap. They set out to separate over the world. Salt Woman said, "I shall travel anti-clockwise around the earth, circling inward spiral fashion to its center. Follow after me. Tell your children and your children's children that they will meet me again at a place called Acoma at the center of the world."

—Anonymous, Acoma Pueblo, 1930

THE REST OF AMERICA might have picked up speed, but the pueblo of Acoma was still moving at its own ancient pace. Back where it took a mesa to raise a child, this period of relative isolation allowed Day Break to undergo the world's oldest form of homeschooling. "It consisted of, first, everything about the Indian religion," he remembered, "except things that we must not know of until we came of age."

In those days they toughened their young early. "They got you up," an Acoma man told linguist Wick Miller, "wrapped you in a blanket, and put you outside, and you waited until the sun rose." When hunting, Day Break was not to drink or eat too much, at home not to warm himself by the fire, not to smoke before he grew up lest his joints crack and eyes run, and only to eat things "grown from the land."

Some training was almost play. "Our instructor was the War Chief," Day Break later recalled. He was taught "the use of the sling and the bow and arrow and the buffalo-hide bow guard." This schooling developed "endurance to run many miles, endurance to go without water. The west side of the village was used for the sham battles. All the women and small children were ordered to the rooftops to watch the warriors. Cornstalks were tied into large balls and thrown up into the air or rolled along the rock. In a few seconds they would be bristling with hundreds of arrows. But everyone could identify their own arrow."

Other lessons came as folk sayings; Acoma elders had dozens of warnings for youngsters like Day Break: Close the door if you see a dust devil approaching, it can permanently twist your body, even kill you. When a dog scratches around a house or a baby yanks its own hair, death or disease could be next. Don't whistle at night, you'll blow your life [breath] away. Don't lie down after mealtime, a flash flood might wash away your corn. Never tease ants, you'll get sores. Never cut your hair during the solstice, the sun will rest on you after you're dead. A few even offered positive advice: Put a juniper bough in the fire in summertime to get rain, in winter if you want snow.

Songs also conveyed fundamentals of life. Once Day Break was initiated into the Katsina Society, he was exposed to singing practice in the kivas. Their lyrics taught him how the rain-bringing Katsinas and human beings and their crops were bound together. Like the cornmeal strewn to bless places or the smoke from prayer cigarettes, singing was serious business. During the 1920s fad across America for Indian-themed popular songs, a Laguna Pueblo man was asked to share a tribal "love" song. "That's for white people," he scoffed, "not Indians. Indians don't sing about anything as silly as love. When we sing, we sing about things that matter: rain and sun and corn."

Dance was another chance to transmit information. Even though the reign of terror leveled by the Comanche war machine in the eighteenth century against Mexico, Texas, and eastern New Mexico never reached this far west, Acoma passed on the memory as if in solidarity with the sufferings of their Rio Grande Pueblo brethren. With their black-painted bodies, Mohawk-like crest of upright eagle feathers, and high-pitched war cries, their Comanche Dancers entertained the village shortly after Christmas just like they did among the Eastern Pueblos. This was also a time to change outfits and mimic their more immediate enemy, the Navajo, in another dance that allowed townsfolk to see how others of their kind could behave so differently.

Day Break also tapped into a form of distance-learning through hard evidence of a wider geography. On his mesa were copper bells, obsidian cores, olivella and abalone shells, yellow and red ocher, buffalo hides, bright parrot and macaw feathers. These items added to more common imports such as European livestock and metal wares. They brought their backstories of exotic origins and intertribal trade. "Distances can be dealt with," advised southwestern archaeologist Steve Lekson to colleagues trying to reconstruct cultural relationships in the early Southwest; "everyone knew everything."

No matter how parochial each Pueblo's worldview, before and after white contact there existed extensive travel networks and factional migrations that carried foreign ideas and material culture. Far-off lands might be dangerous or polluting, but hunting, gathering, or trading expeditions required one to enter them. To Acoma came goods from middlemen centers like Taos, Zuni, Pecos, and even the Chiricahua Apache; from Acoma went hunters trading for buffalo along the northern Rio Grande, hunting antelope to the far south, and finding birds, bear, and even turtles to the west.

In later years, one of Day Break's sons would recount the memories of two of his "grandfathers" who rallied comrades and their families from Zuni and Hopi communities to gather at Isleta Pueblo for a half-year trading expedition east to Tucumcari Mountain. Provisioned with bread, corn, dried peaches, pottery, and other items, a band of nearly two hundred walked and rode burros to barter for buffalo hides and horns, shields, beadwork, and bows and arrows made of strange woods from those same Comanche warriors who had ridden in from still farther east. Along the way the Pueblo party camped at favored springs and rivers; during the weeks of the trade rendezvous they feasted and traded songs while the Comanches killed more buffalo and dried their meat for them on the spot.

When the grown-up Day Break and his family drove in the family automobile to Tucumcari, his wife wept when she realized how surprised those old-timers would have been at the dirt road that now led the entire way; she was amazed that right here was where her own father had met those Plains Indians, and she mourned those who died from hardship on the way.

But story was primary. In winter, the season for storytelling, Day Break was tutored in his people's deep history and behavioral expectations. "My mother's mother (*sapapa*) and especially my mother's father (*sanana*)," he recalled, "used to tell me them. I spent a lot of time with them." They narrated the escapades of various Katsinas, fights between the War God Twins and monsters, accounts of Flint Bird, Spider Grandmother, Turkey Girl, and other fabled characters, stories of seduction and love affairs, legends of great warriors like Kasewat and Flaming Arrow Boy, and tales of giant snakes. Most of these were of the old *Hama-Ha* variety, that required listeners to respond out loud with the Keresan equivalent of "Long ago" at the beginning, and "This is the way it happened" at the end.

Through many of these narratives ran key Acoma values: Don't judge by appearances, the way some original Acoma migrants before reaching the mesa got hoodwinked by choosing the pretty egg over the drab one when deciding their future route. Remember that behind the tattered clothing and ugly mask of the folk character named Bushy Hair Youth was a generous, pious, and even handsome man. Few seemed to notice how Day Break was taking all this in; one day he would regale his children, grandchildren, and famous scholars with these same stories.

In piecemeal fashion and situations both sacred and secular, Day Break eventually heard about the origins of almost everything. Only later, like the formation of a lifetime's mosaic, would they fit together in his mind. Early on he was told how the tribe's mythical mother, Iatiku, established the universe, positioned her Acoma people in it, and magically created their homes. "She spoke some sacred words," he was told, "and all of a sudden there grew a house." In the future, she instructed, this should be a model for their dwellings. Then she "laid out the plans for the town," built up the houseblocks, and laid the ceremonial plaza, or *Kakti,* in the middle.

Even before undergoing his initiation into the Katsina Society inside the largest of the community's seven sacred kivas, Day Break knew they were not places to take lightly. He learned how, like the village itself, Iatiku first created them. She was bidding her Acoma children a final farewell when it dawned on her that she had neglected to provide a resting place for the rain-bringing Katsinas during their visits. For the roof of that first kiva she chose beams from the same four types of trees that she and her sister used as ladders to climb from the three underworlds at the time of creation. In its floor she embedded turquoise of various colors together with prayer sticks, "so the foundation would be strong and never give way." Its walls stood for the sky, the roof beams symbolized the Milky Way, the benches inside where masked Katsina dancers rested were

*Cleaning his ditch—
Faustino Rey, Day
Break's father.*

"clouds," the ladder that led inside was called the Rainbow, the fireplace was named for every medicine man's preferred guide: the Bear.

In these chambers men prepared dance regalia, instructed novices, rehearsed songs and rituals, and prayed with corn-husk cigarettes (the smoke-borne messages rising like misty clouds, pleasing the spirits). Acoma's kivas were embedded in the houseblocks, but distinguished by their oversize ladders with braces stepped like abstracted cloud formations, and identifiable by the telltale sacred cornmeal scattered around their porthole-like windows. In the chief kiva, just behind Day Break's street, was dug a floor cavity covered by a board. It stood for Shipapu, the mythic opening place in the northland from whence human life had first emerged. Stamping on it sent messages and prayers to "the powers that rule" who congregated below.

Day Break acquired respect for sensitive zones around his mesa by being shown them and walking around them. His tabletop homeland brimmed with mythological references; hardly an alley or rock formation lacked its lore. Like an actor learning his cues and hitting his marks, he internalized a choreography of everyday life. Off the eastern edge rose the sandstone pinnacles into which Acoma's superheroes had disappeared at the end of their mythical adventures—Masewi, the elder, and his brother Oyoyewi. Their reputations as monster-slayers were models for defenders-in-training. Fed and honored with cornmeal and prayer plumes, from their rocks the Twins still guarded the mesa. Boys like Day Break shot arrows at its crevices to be blessed with good aim in return.

He steered clear of the rim where, in the "Rite of Forgetting," pebbles were rolled down a groove upon a resident's death. Nor did he trifle around the "Wind's Home," a hole on the mesa's north side, where religious leaders prayed and left balls of honey as offerings when storms blew too hard. From a distance he saw where the community's sun watcher stood at dawn as the rays approached the solstice boulder in order to coordinate upcoming ceremonies. He carefully approached the natural-rock cisterns of drinking water so as not to pollute them, and never scampered over San Estevan's mounded graves. He felt similar caution around the southwest trail behind the church, where the Winter Katsinas first showed themselves, and the shrine at the mesa base where the sunrise spirits arrived from their faraway home. It became second nature to keep an eye on the arrival points where the mesa's eight trails reached the summit. That was where he greeted his mother balancing a water *olla* on her head, or waited for his father to appear, shouldering an antelope quarter after a hunt.

Radiating out from the mesa was a wider web of special springs and shrines. Homes of particular Katsinas (especially crowded around the mesa's base), mossy springs, and algae-dried sinks were rimmed with the disintegrating prayer sticks that had been deposited by pious Acomans who thereby expressed their pleas for the rainfall, of which there was never enough.

Farther out, bounding the tribe's sacred landscape, were the cardinal directions, each possessed of their own mountain, rain-making spirit, prey animal, type of tree, identifying color, and other associations. In ritual chants each was cited in the order of their creation. First came north, with Kawetsima, or Mount Taylor, which harbored Cakak, the Snow-Bringer, and its association with the mountain lion and the color yellow. To the

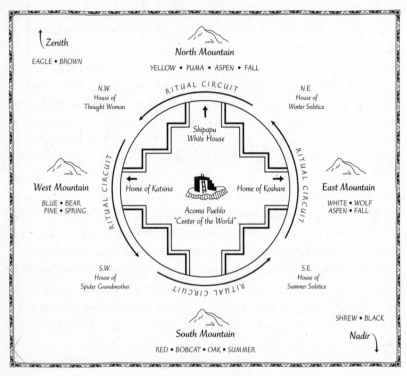

Acoma symbolic landscape.

west was Bunyakot, the Zuni Mountains, where dwelled Guicthia, the Rain-Maker, connected with the bear and the color blue. In the south rose Dautyuma, the home of Maiyatcuna, the Drizzling Rain one, tied to the lynx and the color red. To the east, at the mountain called Kutcana, lived Cuitra, associated with fogs, mist, the wolf, and the color white. In paintings on altars and ceremonial regalia or spoken in songs and prayers, these references reminded people of their hallowed landscape and their place at its center.

Outside what archaeologists would one day classify as this "Acoma Cultural Province" lay more fabled locations. Wenimats, of course, was the western spot near the Zuni Mountains where most of the Katsina spirits lived under their lake. To the north was Shipapu, the place of emergence. Closer lay White House, an important village site during the tribe's legendary years of migration prior to reaching Acoma mesa. As a Pueblo man once said of his northern Rio Grande village, so it was at Acoma: "The story of my people and the story of this place are one single story. No one can think of us without thinking of this place."

To live meaningfully in this storied and patterned landscape, to conduct oneself so as to contribute to its well-being, meant more than obeying the rules. Central to what one might call the Tao of Acoma was the imperative that every member feel that they were part of a whole. Striking out on one's own spelled disaster, not only for the loner but for everyone else. Existing in this arid, elevated universe, where years without rain and elusive game could bring hard times, famine, and death, meant learning a range of potential dangers.

More than sheer survival, there was always a higher goal, even if humans, being human, found that difficult to achieve and sustain. "The purpose of our ceremonies," said a San Juan Pueblo elder to a scholarly visitor, "is not entertainment but attainment; namely the attainment of the *Good Life* [italics in the original]." At Acoma, perhaps the most isolated, insulated, and independent of all the pueblos, the commandments that were requisite for their version of that good life emphasized egalitarianism, the effacement of individuality, and the priority of the collective.

Beyond these dictates, there was one's duty to contribute to the culturally appropriate ambience, etiquette, and level of collective awareness. From infancy Day Break absorbed the calm pace by which his relatives moved. He copied their cautious behavior with one another and modeled his speech after the soft pitch of their voices. He internalized the affective expectations that a proper Pueblo person should embody. In anthropologist Ruth Bunzel's description of the ideal Zuni Pueblo personality these included "a pleasing address, a yielding disposition, and a generous heart." A benign cheerfulness was most desireable, a mien of sadness or glumness a danger sign. Someone who appeared to hunger for power or even knowledge, or who "speaks his mind where flattery would be much more comfortable," was criticized, and even suspected of sorcery. Without being explicitly told, Day Break knew that he would be expected to embody these attitudes, gestures, and mental associations. Thoughts were deeds; one should develop a smooth and even-tempered mind. Yet this education also demanded alertness and caution, with periodic reminders of fear and awe.

◆　◆　◆

This site of what today is known as "old Acoma" remains central to the tribe's spiritual life. It is natural topography and village architecture as single shrine. In the tribe's cosmological scheme, according to Edward Hunt the rock itself was conceptualized as the butt end of a giant ear of perfectly kerneled corn. Long the mainstay of the Pueblo Indian diet, corn was also more than food. Its stone-ground meal and powdery pollen were the blessings that "opened" and sanctified the "roads" of all human endeavors. No symbol was as central to Pueblo Indian life and survival, no ceremony could take place without it.

At Acoma the principle of life-giving corn was incarnated in that holiest of ceremonial objects, the *honani*. Fashioned from the perfectly kerneled cob of "mother" corn, this fetish, in turn, was said to embody the original female deity, Iatiku. It spoke for her, and its word was law.

In the old days, when the cacique invited a newly married couple to the mesa, he was said to employ an unusual phrase—he invited them to climb "on top of his head." The formulaic wording collapsed a number of references. First was to the mesa itself as a giant ear of corn. Second was to an ear of corn as the embodiment of Iatiku, the female progenitor of human beings. Third was to himself as cacique, the male representative of Iatiku within the community and keeper of the main corn fetish that stood for her. All of them centered upon corn—their ancient "staff of life."

The cacique's invitation raised corn into the rare status that scholars sometimes call a root metaphor. It joined those key symbols that have guided human cultures, civilizations, and religions the world over—eyes, pyramids, tridents, crosses, hammers and sickles, crescent moons, or six-pointed stars. By inviting them "on top of his head," he fused all these meanings and reminded the couple they were being elevated into a sacred world.

All this was a lot to learn. After a lifetime most inhabitants of Acoma were content with knowing only the portion that assigned them their roles and rules. Day Break would be one of the few whose unusual experiences would give him a sense of the whole.

Ancient Hard Work (1867)

In the valley below they planted their patches of corn and squash. At times the harvest was slender, but by sparing use of grain the people managed well enough until the next planting season. Good years came, too, when the jars in the storerooms overflowed with nuts and seeds of many kinds. Harsh as the life seemed, the people were happy in this dim past, for Iatiku, the mother of all, lived with her children at White House. She guided their days, ever mindful of their well-being, of their houses, and of their fields.

—Henry Wolf Robe Hunt and Helen Rushmore, 1963

DURING HIS EARLY CHILDHOOD, Day Break and his family lived much like his ancestors two or even three centuries before. "There were no doors on the first floor of the houses," he remembered. "There were little mica windows, and no air, except for a little hole in the window. If there was yelling or announcements in the street my mother listened at the hole. In winter we slept on sheep pelts on the ground floor. In summer we lived on the second or third floor."

Their water came from their cisterns or springs down below; their fuel was the juniper and piñon faggots they broke to length and carried uphill. Inside their rooms they cooked over small fires; their bathrooms were the sides of the mesa; their clocks the sun, the moon, and the seasons. They preserved their food by curing it in sunlight and open air and storing it in cool dark rooms. They spun and wove their homegrown cotton and Churro sheep wool into mantas, kilts, and shirts that they decorated with embroidered designs. In older times their dyes came from plants and minerals—a rusty red from mountain mahogany, muddy yellow from clay, blue from copper sulfate; later they traded for indigo from Mexico and commercial dyes and colored yarns at trading posts. For painting bodies and murals on kiva walls they collected minerals, ground them to powder, and mixed them with animal grease. The rare family owned some Mexican trade ware, otherwise most still used their homemade clay pottery. Their ornaments were beads of shell and turquoise that they cut and polished, their feather adornments came from wild birds and the turkeys and parrots they raised.

Without matches or kerosene lamps, they made fire by twirling yucca sticks between their hands in the fire-by-friction method, and then lit the wick in a bowl of sheep fat for light. Although a few men had guns, predominately flintlocks, most relied on bows and arrows. Some families had wagons, or even buckboards—the "pickup trucks" of the Old West. But a number still employed the old wooden-wheeled *carretas,* pulled by burros or oxen, whose ungreased axles sent out tortured squeals.

One time, Day Break remembered that "my mother's father and mother went to Laguna to sell some pottery and buy some things. They brought back some wheat. That was the first time I ever saw it." Later on they traded for coffee and sugar. "Poor Mother," he added, "she was very fond of coffee, but we were poor and never had much."

By age six the boy was fully engaged with his parents in living off the land. In the last days of the month named after the root of the Daughter of

Men's work: farming below Acoma mesa.

Spring plant (February), the days grew longer. But the ground remained frozen, the animals still hid from chilling winds. Typically this was the lean season, when the family relied on dried and stored fare. Tapping the mark on her plastered wall to locate the hollow sound, his mother used her stone *mano* to crack into the cyst where she had kept nutritious, pre-parched piñon nuts from the previous fall pickings.

For late-winter meals she had packets of sun-stiffened antelope strips. Below the sleeping quarters, reached by lifting a pegged-wood hatch cover and climbing down a ladder, her darkened storage room was stacked with baked cobs still in their husks. Also tucked away were separately bundled items that included boiled/dried pigweed, to thicken a gruel made of stewed dried meat. There were also willow sticks coated with honey that were covered with dried beeplant seeds and could produce a filling hot mush. She kept packets of dried juniper berries, chokecherries, peaches, and yucca fruit that she could resoak and boil into thick, syrupy treats for children.

This had the look of a fair year. It did not appear that the people would be reduced to consuming dried soapweed hearts, roasted cactus stalks, or ground-up mistletoe berries, or, even worse, be left to drink the dirty-brown soups extracted from boiled leather harnesses.

Within a few weeks everyone breathed easier. The cacique announced that the time *when-the-ground-is-soft-like-ashes* was at hand. Wheat would be sown without fanfare, but corn was another matter. During his four-in-the-morning round in late winter, the village crier jangled his bells and rallied farmers to the chief kiva. That evening, the country chief gathered the baskets full of seed corn and led dancing and prayers around them. They sang in memory of those original seeds that were brought in baskets by their ancestors from out of the earth. Thus opened the planting season.

A long time ago from Shipapu, the underworld, they came south.
With life, with crops, carrying useful things, they came.
A long time ago, with clouds, with fog, from Shipapu, the
underworld, they came south.
The common people, beautiful and pure, carried these useful things
to nourish themselves.

As the United States emerged from warlike forces that almost ripped her apart, Acoma Pueblo clung to traditions like these that kept her together. They tightened social stability, strengthened harmony between humans and the cosmos, and fed her people from the surrounding landscape. The year revolved through seasons of growth, decay, and rebirth. As Acoma's sky watchers had done for centuries, they kept tabs on where the sun rose and fell to schedule their ceremonies, which were especially intense around equinoxes and solstices. They also kept abreast of the rising moon's swing across the night's horizon, so as to forecast that interval when it appeared in the same spot for a few nights in a row.

Western New Mexico is a tough ecology from which to wrest a living. But the high desert could support those who were trained for it and worked with it. Around the age of four Day Break's uncle started waking him in the dark, covering him in a blanket, restricting his water intake, and leaving him on the rooftop. Down below the red-blanketed village crier walked up and down the streets and called out the day's business. From a distance came the night's last snarling of coyotes, and the yowling of village dogs in response. Overhead the stars remained sharp, although dawn soon extinguished them. Once Day Break was allowed indoors he was still kept from drinking, eating, or warming himself at the hearth. To put in long hot hours in the fields, to track antelope for days, and then to face Navajos who (in the past) wanted your livestock and women, you needed to prepare yourself.

Before sunrise, he hustled down the cliff at his father's heels. They ran at a clip toward the sandy basins east of Katzimo where the man's experience told him a lens of snowmelt lay but feet below the surface. In their hands were oak digging sticks, a knob from a cut branch still protruding for pushing into the dirt with one's foot. Strung over his stepfather's shoulder was the pouch of seed corn that had been preserved from last year's harvest.

Over the winter the wind and snowstorms that swept up Acoma Creek had dismantled the shelter-half of posts and branches where they camped overnight beside their gardens. At sunrise Day Break began untangling the branches and clearing ground for reerecting it. His father sank the drills and deposited the seeds, singing to them all the while. So went early

Women's work: annual plastering at Acoma village.

spring, day after day. Up and down the canyons that branched from the main valley, other fathers, uncles, and sons were doing likewise. Was this agriculture, farming, or gardening? For families like Day Break's it was the life-sustaining activity that was initiated by their mother Iatiku at time's beginning.

The corn would not reach taller than him. With only one crop per year, each stalk produced three or four ears. Stockpiling any surplus was always in the back of their minds—well-dried and properly stored it could last up to seven years without spoiling. If necessary, their storage rooms contained enough for the village to hold out for four years. It was good as gold in more ways than one. Along with their dried melons, squash, and beans, the hanging braids of dried ears provided fare for trade with middlemen tribes who exchanged their horse-borne cargos of buffalo meat, skins, tallow, Spanish coins, and hand-woven cloth plus glass beads and other exotic trade from the Mexican and Mericano worlds.

A longer jog was necessary to reach the fields that utilized a more elaborate watering process. When Day Break ran alongside his father before sunrise on the stretch to North Valley, they were prepared to stay awhile. Other families were already there, working in teams to clear debris from the irrigation ditches that drained off the San Jose River. They repaired check dams, and chinked the hardier rock shelters that backed up to the north-facing mesa that overlooked the fertile bottomland. Cottonwoods and willows were budding, along with peach, apricot, apple, and other fruit trees. Eastward the soft hump of Flower Mountain betrayed a green blush, but further north the snowpack on lofty Kawetsima remained heavy.

In those days no white man's metals were supposed to pollute this ancient work. Rather than being nailed, their wooden plows, hoes, and shovels were pegged and lashed together with wet rawhide that hardened stiff. Wheat was sliced with sharpened cow jawbones and threshed by unshod ponies tethered to a slowly revolving central hub and walked around in endless circles in what would be called by whites the biblical method.

Day Break relished his sojourns in the North Valley camp. As he remembered it, singing was always in the air. Work breaks let him and his playmates splash around in the irrigation ditches. Overnights in the sheep camp were exciting; you never knew what beasts crouched just beyond the fire. He was always ready to join his uncles in their hunts around Mount Taylor.

As the crops grew, the prayers followed. Beseeching the clouds, Day Break's father sang out his wishes:

> You are breeding tassels, ears of corn.
> You are breeding pumpkins.
> Rain gods in the northwest and southwest,
> Rain upon the field, you are breeding crops.

Later on, with cornstalks and melon vines about to ripen, he shifted focus:

Dear corn plant maiden, you are standing in the middle of the farms,
Are you not. I sing for you.
Dear vine-plant maiden, you have spread your arms in the middle of
the farmland.
I make an offering to you,
This I sing. There, corn plant maiden, vine-plant maiden, Up Up—
begin to come out
Corn plant maiden, vine-plant maiden, up, up. Begin to bear.

Varying their diet with meat from rabbits, deer, antelope, and the rare bear presented a problem. One replenished the cultivated products of the field by selecting the following year's seed corn from each harvest. Those prayers and respectful treatment encouraged the earth to respond in kind. At harvest time Day Break was reminded by his parents how the "mother of all Indians," Iatiku, always husked her cobs with tenderness. But her sister, sometimes referred to as the "mother of foreigners," ripped the dry husks off roughly.

Given these attitudes, how was one to assure the same renewal and reciprocity from creatures whom one slaughtered, sometimes in club-wielding melees during mass rabbit or antelope drives? During each of the year's four major rabbit hunts, the entire community raced around in ever-shrinking circles to frighten their prey into tight clusters before the kill. Then all the carcasses were lined up in the plaza and blessed with cornmeal. For slain deer, ceremonial attention began as soon as they fell. The rib cage was brushed with a spruce bough. Yellow pollen was dribbled on the snout. Stone hunting fetishes were laid on the corpse. The animal was surgically butchered to avoid ritual pollution. After a feast back home, a bit of its tongue was left outdoors, together with corn-husk cigarettes. Only this way would the deer's spirits send more of their kind to grateful hunters.

By end of August the fruit trees and melon and squash vines were ready for picking, along with the first green corn. Two months later came the full harvest. Everyone pitched in to pick, haul, husk, and prepare the crop, some for storage, some for immediate consumption. With each exposure of a naked cob came close scrutiny, not only for worm damage but also in hopes of finding those unblemished ears. Set aside, they were dried and stripped and their kernels then hand ground on a series of three tipped stone basins set in the floors—coarse to medium to fine—until reduced to a bluish powder. Sometimes mixed with corn pollen, the result was consecrated by a medicine man and kept in a jar; as Day Break later explained, "this we used the way other churches use holy water."

To greet the dawn, Day Break's parents left their home every morning. At the mesa's rim they extended their arms and scattered this mixture toward the light and inhaled from the four directions. They asked the new day for strength, health, blessings, and enough resources to help them get through the coming winter.

Until the 1870s, most everyone still clung to the mesa. "No one did any farming in the Acomita valley," Day Break remembered, "the few houses down there were for people to graze their sheep." As worries eased over Navajo and Apache predation, however, their instincts for seclusion and self-protection began to relax. During the summer months a number of families moved down to the San Jose watershed to live in their farming shelters. They worked their fields on both banks of the narrow river valley, and opened irrigation channels that eventually branched from a two-mile-long "mother" ditch.

His family were among the early migrants who relocated to the outlier hamlets of Acomita (North Valley) and McCartys. Matrilocal households were giving way to nuclear family homes. They expanded the rock-and-adobe cabanas that perched on the southern bench of the shallow cliffs overlooking the river. To the northeast they could see the snows of Mount Taylor. Breaking into smaller units, freed from Acoma mesa's "constant scrutiny and supervision," plus the location's proximity to the railroad, encouraged an "independence of mind and spirit," as anthropologist Leslie White observed. On the one hand this weakened the old, conservative community spirit; on the other it deepened the symbolic importance of "old Acoma" as the tribe's ceremonial stronghold, "the home of the gods and the medicine men."

Deeper Mysteries Still (1871)

My people, the Acomas, still believe in witches and magicians, who have evil power. That is why the parents tell the children not to talk when they go in other homes, as someone might be there who is a witch, and who might lay a spell on you. That is why Indians are so quiet and just watch you, to this day.

—James Paytiamo, Acoma Pueblo, 1932

AROUND THE AGE OF TEN Day Break underwent "the misfortune I have never forgotten." He was herding livestock for his uncle a short distance north of Acoma mesa. Since the seventeenth century, the live-stock derived from animals introduced by Spanish colonists had become indispensable. Distant as Acoma was from usual routes of commerce, by now most families were accustomed to horses for riding, burros and mules for carrying firewood and other goods, some oxen for pulling carts, and sheep for food, pelts, and trade.

That afternoon something spooked his horse. "I was thrown off. He kicked at me with both hind legs. One connected with the top of my head and crushed my skull and I fell unconscious." A fellow herder draped the boy's body across his saddle and tore back to Acomita.

His crown was pouring blood. Later in life his grandchildren liked to fit their knuckles into the permanent dent under his white hair. He was out cold; everyone thought that he was dead. They stretched him out on the floor. Orienting his head toward the east, they covered him with a shroud. Bowls of water and cornmeal were readied for his spirit's journey to the northerly resting place of the ancestors.

"The next morning," Day Break said, "my mother was preparing me for burial." His relatives crowded into the small room and began to mourn. Soon they would load the body on a wood-wheeled cart and take him to the *campo santo* in front of the church. Some say his grave was already dug.

"It was about sunrise. They had laid me facing the door. I swung my arm and brushed back the blanket and sat upright. The sun was blinding. I

Acoma corral below mesa, like the one where Day Break was kicked unconscious by a horse.

said, 'I must have slept so long.' I wondered why there were so many people. My mother hugged me and cried. She was very happy. Later I was told what had happened—I was lucky."

In another sense he was not. Unlike his Katsina initiation, what happened next was not a normal step in every youngster's progression toward adulthood. Day Break's recovery from near-death had primed him for a deeper immersion in his people's spiritual life. As his father and uncle knew well, now it was nigh impossible for him not to follow in his father's footsteps and become a healer.

In contrast with less tightly organized Indian societies—in California, say, or the Great Plains, where individual shamans commonly cured their fellow tribespeople of disease, misfortune, or witchery—the pueblos often held the practitioner working solo as a shaman gone wrong, and quite possibly a witch. Their medicine men, the class of specialists whom religious scholar Mircea Eliade once dubbed "technicians of the sacred," were organized into secret societies that held collective rites for transmitting their esoteric lore.

Day Break's father and uncle belonged to one of them, the Fire Society. As in the mesa's other curing brotherhoods, its members were dependent upon supernatural allies, who commonly were animals. Channeling such powers, they administered to the sick and fought witches on behalf of the village. In former times, Day Break was told, were more societies; by around 1871, however, only the Flint, Fire, Kabina, and Thundercloud survived. Anyone living through a direct lightning strike was automatically inducted into the Flint Society; old stone arrowheads contained their curative potency. Snake medicine men were anointed by having recovered from a rattlesnake bite; but according to Day Break they never formed a full society.

Among the pueblos, sorcery was the explanation for most ailments and problems, physical or psychological, individual or communal. The combat between medicine men and evil witches was one of life's unavoidable and ongoing struggles. Witches sickened their victims by "shooting" items into their bodies, or "stealing" their hearts. The identity of the community's medicine men was common knowledge; the question of who was a witch was less certain, and the subject of suspicion and slander.

After their services were solicited, medicine men used music, gourd rattles, crystals, song, prayer, and ritual smoking to locate the life-threatening objects. These they sucked out, or removed with powers derived from eagle feathers. Ornate wood-slat altars, ground paintings drawn with differently colored crushed minerals, corn-cob fetishes, and special bowls for mixing herbs and other medicines were used for a healer's diagnosing, cleansing, and purification activities. Their cures took up to four days, during which time the medicine men were forbidden from meat or salt; for days afterward they were not permitted to wash or have sexual relations.

Rare as it was, some people elected to join their ranks. But this was uncommon; theirs was a taxing, lifelong commitment, calling for lengthy immersions in the kivas, extended periods of celibacy, meditations on behalf of the community, and a modest life. Medicine men and their families largely survived off uncertain handouts from their patients of basic foods and necessities.

There were other ways of being "trapped" into the brotherhoods. Most people were careful to avoid crossing the lines of wood ash that demarcated normal space from prohibited zones where shamans might be firewalking, sword-swallowing, or conducting sensitive rituals. Trespass those boundaries and you were likely to be conscripted. Maybe your mind was on something else and you unthinkingly accepted a corn-husk cigarette and smoked it. Commit that infraction—secularizing what should be an activity reserved for prayer—and you might be "trapped." Arms yanked behind your back, you were hustled into a kiva and kept out of sight for days. Or, as with Day Break, through no fault of your own, you might suffer some near-fatal accident or illness, and find yourself becoming a "wounded healer."

"The incident was looked upon as a mystery," Day Break recalled of his frightening induction. "So my uncle determined to make me a medicine man also, for he really believed I had some strength or was endowed with power to bring back life." Around these individuals hung a special aura;

Graveyard (campo santo) *in front of San Estevan, where Day Break was to be buried.*

everyone knew that they handled extraordinary and dangerous powers. Sometimes they displayed them in public.

Very likely it was Day Break who would tell Leslie White about the Acoma medicine man who one night invited a skeptic to the mesa's eastern rim. He pointed to a freestanding sandstone pillar about forty feet away, separated by a three-hundred-foot drop. The medicine man took off and leapt across the span. In the moonlight a chipped flint he tossed to the ground exploded in sparks. No sooner had he landed than he spun around and hurled himself back again. Another time, a medicine man sucked some toxic items from a patient's body but could not cough them back up. With a flint knife, a colleague sliced open his chest from stomach to throat. The man's guts and heart were exposed and from his innards was pulled a ball of cactus thorns. The healer rubbed the stone blade over the open wound, clapped his hands, and blew on the skin. The patient stood up and walked back over to his curing altar, healed and without a mark.

For the most part, the trainings and rites behind such displays were kept secret, especially when novices like Day Break learned the mysteries. If he did undergo a Fire Society initiation, he may have been secluded in the mesa's northwestern kiva, where that society normally met. Day Break described these experiences with such detail that it is hard to believe he was not a witness, but one cannot be sure.

Stripped to breechcloths, faces painted black, hair fastened up with corn husks, the trainees learned to use the tools of their trade—the flint arrowheads, bear paws, herbs used for mixing in special medicine bowls, eagle plumes, little stone animal fetishes, and the varieties of prayer sticks, like those he'd watched his father make, for depositing in appropriate shrines, trees, and rocky clefts, or throwing over the cliff as messages and offerings to the spirit world. They acquired the special vocabulary exclusive to medicine men. They drank awful-tasting medicines concocted from unpleasant elements and learned sleights of hand and other performative skills to awe their audiences.

In a culminating performance, the village was welcomed into Acoma's historic-period equivalent of an ancestral Great Kiva for a demonstration of their powers. The novices extracted pebbles, sticks, and string from their audience's bodies. Rubbing against freshly painted wall murals depicting mountain lions, bears, clouds, Katsina spirits, and sacred clowns, they withdrew vegetable seeds from the images and passed them around.

A grand finale took place in the street, where a fire pit had burned down to raked and smoking coals. The candidates rolled across the glowing bed, amid corn kernels that popped and stung their flesh. Eight days later they danced into the plaza to the beat of drums and swallowed long wooden swords.

Another appearance by Acoma's medicine men occurred in late February. Anticipating his people's spring departure to their fields, the cacique scheduled an all-village curing. The feast took four days to prepare, and each day the healers drank an emetic to purge themselves of impurities. Again they erected elaborate altars in their kivas; again they invoked the powers of the bear, eagle, mountain lion, and snake to create a protective cloak over the mesa and its people.

With eagle plumes and flint arrowheads they "whipped" disease from each inhabitant. In bowls of still water the medicine men "saw" witches and "fought" them to recover the "heart" of the community. Throughout the night they grunted like bears, performed curing rites, and worked to extract all and any evil. The residue they collected was thrown over the mesa. They passed around purified cornmeal to lend the people the strength and freedom from care so they could anticipate with joy the coming season in their fields.

"So I was initiated into the religious institution of my people, and into the mystics of the medicine men," Day Break testified later. After his naming ritual and joining of the Katsina Society, this initiation drew him even deeper into his tribe's secret workings. But inwardly he was troubled. "All this I learned and tried to believe with my whole heart. But somehow I could not entirely."

Despite his misgivings, one more rite of passage lay in store.

Tracks Through the Past (1848–82)

Pueblo people easily identify with any and all those places, because making distinctions about who actually lived where and for how long is not how we think. We dwell more on connections and know that even if the Hopis or the Zunis claim direct ancestry from the prehistoric Chaco people, we are all related through our common belief that we came out of the same earth. Our sense of the past is mythological and our sense of identity is ultimately dependent on knowing that we humans are but one group of the earth's progeny.

—Rina Swentzell, Santa Clara Pueblo, 2004

I N THE 1930s, when Day Break and his sons war-danced in eagle-feather bonnets at Boy Scout jamborees and public school assemblies across the American Midwest, local newspapers billed them as vestigial remnants of the ancient Pueblo "Cliff-Dwellers" who could provide a glimpse into the "traditions, customs and history of the Vanishing American." Audiences had no reason to question their claim of descent from the spectacular ruins they'd read about in *National Geographic* magazine concerning archaeologist Neil Judd's recent discoveries at Chaco Canyon.

Unlike most promotional copy for appearances like theirs, the Hunts' press release contained some nuggets of truth. But it took a while before professional archaeologists accepted modern Pueblo Indians as descendants of the ninth- to twelfth-century southwestern sites of Chaco Canyon and Mesa Verde. Since the mid-nineteenth century this blind spot prevented scholars from crediting Indians across the country with lineal ties to the "higher" civilizations of yesteryear whose remains were excavated in their neighborhoods. It was hard to believe that, for instance, the secluded, poverty-stricken remnants of Creek, Choctaw, and Natchez tribes from the Southeast, barely surviving in Oklahoma, were heirs to the architecturally sophisticated towns and temple mounds of the Ohio and Mississippi River valleys. Equally inconceivable was the notion that Indian families huddled in dugout cabins across North Dakota's Three Affiliated Tribes Reservation

A home of Day Break's ancestors: Mesa Verde ruins, southern Colorado.

derived from the dozens of plaza-centered villages of Mandan and Hidatsa Indian farmers, hunters, potters, and boat-builders whose complex social systems thrived two hundred years before along the middle Missouri River.

To explain how contemporary Indians were linked to monumental ruins, each theory was nuttier than the last: America's great archaeological sites were evidence of the rise and mysterious disappearance of "lost races"; they were constructed by remnants of vagrant Welshmen, wandering tribes of Jews, Aztec travelers gone astray, or aliens from another planet. Most far-fetched was a claim in the 1920s by a former British lancer named James Churchward that he had found and translated a cache of clay tablets documenting that the pre-Pueblo peoples migrated twelve thousand years ago from the lost continent of Mu.

For their part, this Pueblo family of traveling "Show Indians" were never motivated to refute these outlandish theories, of which they probably weren't aware anyhow. Their performances were responding to the fantasies that they had come to realize existed in their audiences' imaginations. If whites wanted their Indians both ways, as vanishing warlike Plains warriors *and* surviving Pueblo Cliff-Dwellers, few performers were better equipped to deliver the mixed message. As "Show Indians" in Europe the Hunt family would transform into the buffalo-hunting, scalp-taking angry warriors of white melodrama. Then they could hook this stereotype to a second, the "Noble Savage." Thirdly, they were also showcased as the *last* of those bygone tribes, almost cousins to such "Stone Age" tribes as still survived in the Amazon.

To this tangle of preconceptions was added the lament for the "Vanishing American." A sentimental salute to the demise of a race, the phrase reflected a pervasive belief, and often a deep-seated wish, that it was only a matter of time before American Indians disappeared due to disease, natural attrition, and dissolution into America's melting pot. The fact that these advertisements for themselves ran contrary to this family's actual civic, agricultural, and cultural roots never disturbed them. No one was getting hurt. They were teaching pride and respect for Indians and making a living the best they knew how.

During Day Break's boyhood, what *was* known about his people's deep history? Was there some inexplicable rupture between their ancient past and current existence? Where did the Acoma people themselves believe they came from?

White scholars might have been dubious about Acoma's claims to ruins like Mesa Verde and Chaco Canyon. But Day Break's elders responded by taking him there. As if retracing the footprints of their ancestors' woven yucca-fiber sandals, the linkage of Acoma's earlier shrines and marks of former residences followed migratory routes into what the whites would call "prehistory." Day Break accompanied these treks, which his elders considered their "present history." In southwestern Colorado, near the place of their Emergence, they left prayer sticks, sprinkled cornmeal, and prayed in memory of their forebears.

From here they turned southward to Kashkachu, or White House, which "may well represent Chaco," believes archaeologist Ruth Van Dyke, who quotes Acoma poet Simon Ortiz's description of his ancestors' idyllic existence here: "Animals and plants could talk to each other, and the people could talk with the animals. . . . Anytime they needed rain, they would just ask their friends and neighbors the sacred beings to bring rain from the west, and the rain would fall and nourish their plants."

Some sixty miles from Acoma, they sprinkled cornmeal at Sage Basin, an ancient campsite, then visited a series of smaller ruins, such as Tule Lake, before reaching larger village remains at Kowina and Calabash, only fifteen miles west of their home mesa. Along the way his stepfather pointed toward Wenimats, the lake near Zuni Pueblo under which most of Acoma's

Katsinas resided. They passed remembered cornfields, old sheepherding pastures, rock art sites with images of Katsinas, stars, antelope, and migration routes, and cairnlike shrines with deposits of decaying old prayer sticks.

In this way, through legends that recalled where their events supposedly occurred, generations of youngsters like Day Break were tutored in their people's past by walking through it.

The early Spanish rarely wondered about this land's human ancestry. As he traversed the jagged volcanic trail from old Zuni to Acoma in 1540, Hernando de Alvarado passed the stone-and-adobe remains of Matyata without comment. In 1694, Father Eusebio Kino paid little mind to the Casa Grande ruins, and never linked its ten-foot-thick mud walls to the heritage of the Piman villagers he saw around him. A contingent of Mexican soldiers glanced briefly at Chaco Canyon's monuments in 1823 but never drew or described them or asked Pueblo people who made them.

Once Americans entered the region, Spanish lack of interest was replaced by wild speculation. What were the origins of these abandoned

Where Day Break's forebears lived next: Pueblo Bonito ruins in Chaco Canyon, northern New Mexico.

towers, kivas, and plazas? From where had the present-day Pueblo people originated? Were there any connections between the two? In October 1846, when Lieutenant Abert saw the ramparts of Acoma, Bernal Díaz del Castillo's eyewitness account of the conquest of Mexico, with its "fortresses that were observed by the army of Cortez," crossed his mind.

One of the more well-read members of America's Corps of Topographical Engineers, Abert was the first visitor to project the Old World's romance for moss-covered Roman and medieval ruins onto the American Southwest. Only days after leaving Acoma, he delighted in an "ancient ruin" near Santo Domingo Pueblo, which "excites the speculations of the curious," and would liken the crumbling adobe walls at Tajique and Abo to Aztec architecture.

Two years later one of his corps colleagues, Lieutenant James H. Simpson, proposed a connection between the two Mexicos. Dispatched on a monthlong mapping trip through Navajo country, Simpson, who evinced distaste for the hand-to-mouth existence of contemporary Hispano and Indian hamlets, fawned over the remains he found after crossing the Continental Divide. His guide was a Jemez Pueblo elder, Hosta, his official artist a splendid watercolorist named Richard Kern. For three days they explored the nine "great house" ruins that lined Chaco Canyon's dry creekbed.

Unlike his superior, Kern was smitten by the down-to-earth villagers and tan-colored adobe villages. Still, he had "no doubt of their [the Chaco Canyon ruins] having been built by a race living here in long past ages—Its style is so different from anything Spanish." Simpson accepted without question Hosta's belief that these ocher-colored "cities" were built by Mexican ancestors, and in print he specified the Toltecs. Their appeal was reflected in one name he gave—"Painted House" (*Pueblo Pintado*), replacing the Jemez designation, "Pueblo of the Rats." The presumed Mesoamerican link would abide through such place-names in the Four Corners region as Aztec, New Mexico; Montezuma Creek, Utah; and Cortez, Colorado.

With the chaotic disruption of the Civil War and the corps' disbandment, exploration of western New Mexico was set back decades. Its final expedition scouted the rim of Colorado's Mesa Verde province. But the compact, multistoried dwellings nestled within its cliff shelters would not be discovered until 1888. In the meantime, the notion of Mexican ties to the Southwest was taken seriously by the first scholar to instigate a panoramic history of the region. Thirty years after Simpson's visit to Chaco Canyon, a self-taught Swiss-born businessman named Adolph Francis Bandelier began this project.

Balding, unpretentious, and linguistically astute, Bandelier was in his thirties when he became so entranced by Mexican antiquities that the tension between his tedious day job and his imaginative passion caused a nervous breakdown. To his rescue came Lewis Henry Morgan, the so-called father of American anthropology. An attorney from upper New York State, Morgan shared Bandelier's passion for early Indian history and their contemporary social organization. His library of travel accounts and historical memoirs was voluminous. But unlike many "armchair scholars" of his day, Morgan also traveled. In 1878 he visited his first southwestern ruins, and toured the living pueblo of Taos, but never reached the distant western villages, which included Acoma.

Bandelier shared with Morgan the documents he had unearthed and translated in Mexico. When Morgan became head of the new American Association for the Advancement of Science in 1879 he roped Bandelier into his circle. These connections netted Bandelier a dream assignment: he would join his mentor on a multiyear cultural reconnaissance of the Southwest. When ill health forced Morgan to back out, Bandelier was on his own; although temperamentally and physically unsuited for arduous fieldwork, he didn't hesitate.

Ahead lay a three-year journey of discovery, the first time the Pueblo world was the subject of such a broad inspection. At first Bandelier leaned toward the theory of Mexican origin for the ruins coming to light in the Four Corners region. But from the same white men who would one day befriend Day Break he was about to learn differently.

So far the boy's daily life had touched the white world at a remove, if at all. But he never forgot the day that its existence became a reality. He was around twelve years old and tending his uncle's sheep uprange from North Valley. Like most children of the mesa, he learned to keep his eyes open. To the east he noticed dust and movement. Until now, "I had never seen a white man." But then, "I saw a covered wagon near the place where now there is a little Mexican town known as Cubero. They were a family of Texans. Thereafter I saw many more wagons come and go. They always headed toward the setting sun."

Who Should Know What (1875)

Misinterpretation of Pueblo secrecy is partly due to differing views of knowledge. . . . In the Anglo world, knowledge is highly regarded and its acquisition is rewarded in a variety of ways, including admiration of knowledge for its own sake. . . . But that is not the case in the Pueblo world. Like the Anglos, Pueblo Indians consider knowledge to be of high value. . . . Some types of knowledge, however, are accessible only to the mature and the responsible. This is particularly the case with esoteric information that requires a religious commitment.

—Former governor of Cochiti Pueblo, n.d.

UNTIL THE AGE OF FIVE or so Day Break played with his friends around the kivas but wasn't allowed to descend into one. That changed with his initiation into the Katsina Society. Down in that overheated, cedar-scented interior the lessons about the importance of secrecy would be etched into him with lashes from a yucca whip.

"This is now real," the original medicine men stressed in the segment of the tribe's creation narrative that was always recited during this experience. As Day Break shared many years hence, the story invoked those ancient elders discussing the Katsina Society and the transformations wrought by masking and impersonation. "This mask has the *same power* as the real Katsina," they insisted.

The initiates learned that each mask *contained its own identity*. By donning one and looking through those eye-holes, one was no longer oneself. One had merged with that identity, and was looking at the world through its eyes and behaving accordingly. This was a delicate and dangerous process. No wonder those wise ones always added, "Most of all, this is going to be secret from this day on."

To the culture-keepers in most southwestern Indian pueblos, the glimpses into ritual life that intrigued Adolph Bandelier and his scholarly descendants were considered none of their business. At Acoma, secrecy was central to the air she breathed. Her mesa was practically a metaphor for this principle—guarded by its ring of sandstone pillars, her people wary and watchful whenever strangers approached below. A castle keep, she lifted her drawbridge whenever she sensed that disclosures were in the offing or inquisitive minds needed to be kept at bay.

Returning home after his initiation, Day Break sensed a shift in his familial relations. In the kiva he'd learned things for no girl's ears, which distanced him from his younger sisters and even his mother. When his father, the Fire Society medicine man, crafted his prayer sticks or set out the crystals that gave him second sight into the causes of diseases, drew

Adolph Bandelier, ostracized at Santo Domingo Pueblo for asking questions.

out his magical bear-paw gloves or picked out the flints that endowed him with the gift of flight, Day Break knew to look away or leave the room.

For most pueblos practiced two kinds of secrecy—that which must be kept from outsiders of a different religious persuasion who might attempt to repress their beliefs, and, even more important, the internal sort. If ritual knowledge was power, compartmentalizing and controlling it prevented others from being hurt by it or capitalizing on it. Acoma mesa was so riddled with secrets because its mutually exclusive religious societies had to preserve their knowledge and maintain their boundaries. Together with the trade secrets of shamans like his father, the restricted knowledge to which people acquired ownership was dispensed according to their stage of life, their gender, clan affiliation, membership in religious or hunting societies, and rules of the medicine societies. This was especially true when their private ceremonies had the power to control fate and affect life and death.

If revealed they might evaporate like smoke. Pueblo Indians could respond to a scholar's inquiry by saying that they lacked the right to share information, didn't know anything, or by confessing, "I don't even *want* to know about that." Informed on a right-to-know basis, individuals were only taught their part of a full ceremony. The whole only jelled if everyone, especially the centurions of secrecy, added their part. That way no single person could take sole charge, which seems to have been an underlying concern within this conservative, ideally egalitarian society.

So much of their mythology and society came in opposing twos. Men and women. Initiated and noninitiated. The two sacred sisters responsible for creation and the Twin War Gods skilled at destruction. The masked dancers of winter and those of summer. The season of gardening, which emphasized life-nurturing, and the time for winter hunting, which meant killing and death. Maintaining such oppositions in balance meant that people had to understand what they needed to know and what they didn't. Within the fishbowl setting of Acoma village, where everyone lived cheek by jowl, distinctive spaces like kivas, fetish rooms, council chambers, and even the corn-grinding workrooms preserved their guarded practices.

As with the men's secrets to be kept from women, women's from men, and those of the initiated from the uninitiated, so it was with the confidences that must be kept between their people and all the rest. His topography taught Day Break a fundamental separation between his universe and everybody down below. Up there, closer to the cloud spirits than perhaps any Indian village in the continent, Acomans shared the sort of collective nervous system and fellow-feeling that one finds among occupants of ocean-surrounded islands. They watch with narrowed eyes as mainlanders disgorge from cruise ships; they take their money but keep their secrets. Sometimes the line between Acoma and all others was just as literal. During sensitive times when she sealed herself from external contamination, she drew those lines of cornmeal across all entry and exit points. Then their world became the only world again.

But no lines on the ground could protect Acoma from the prying eyes of Euro-Americans. Their unrelenting curiosity raised Acoma's concern about preserving her privacy to a near-permanent state of high alert. Each brand of foreigner seemed to bring a different reason and strategy for penetrating the place. For the Spanish the secrets of Acoma religion concerned the whereabouts of shrines, masks, and "houses of idolatry" they wanted to destroy. Their campaign of extirpation would not vanish with the relative success of the All-Pueblo Revolt of 1680. Although native rebels restored their traditional dominance over community affairs, as late as 1819, Father Juan Toril, the Franciscan assigned to Cochiti Pueblo, broke into one of their kivas and burned its "idols" in the village plaza. To deflect such intrusions, one theory is that this is why Acoma redesigned her seven kivas from circular to rectangular, the better to disguise them within the apartmentlike clusters of regular domestic rooms.

The antipathy that Anglo-Americans displayed toward Pueblo secrecy would prove less religious than ideological. Something about such a "closed society" in their midst rankled them, and ran against the democratic grain. Despite its tradition of secret brotherhoods like the Masons (which would induct one of Day Break's sons), the Order of Red Men (which denied American Indians membership), or the Ku Klux Klan (which saw them as subhuman and akin to the African Americans it despised), America espoused an "open society" and free debate. And despite the "romantic inflation" of Pueblo society that abides to this day, there was something grating in how these Indians rejected the premium America publicly placed upon full disclosure and complete transparency.

On the other hand, the age of cultural exploration ushered in by Bandelier found no Pueblo practice too forbidden or intriguing. The earliest of these interlopers were relative amateurs. Their innocent queries, expressions of friendship, and readiness to merge into the tribal life raised the first alarm. Epitomizing this advance guard was Bandelier's hero, the mustached tubercular named Frank Hamilton Cushing. For nearly five years (1879–84) Cushing resided at Zuni, was introduced to the tribe's religious lore, and became a popular writer whose dispatches from the pueblo remain a landmark of lived Indian experience and revealed secrets.

The next generation of professional anthropologists, supported by museums or universities, brought a more intrusive gaze to the Pueblo Southwest. Under the banner of objective science these late-nineteenth-century arrivals did not come to make friends and refused to take no for an

Following this famous image by Edward S. Curtis, other photographers sought the location; then Acoma declared the freshwater cistern off-limits.

answer. Their fervor for esoteric information would often become an intellectual combat between aggressive scientists and increasingly withholding
Indians.

The confrontational style of early ethnographer Matilda Coxe Stevenson left native animosity and disgraced Indian friends in its wake. On the
outskirts of Taos Pueblo in northern New Mexico she established her
"Camp Defiance," where she tried to wear down her tight-lipped informants. "To distinguish between what was being withheld by my most astute informants, past masters in the art of evasion and subterfuge," wrote
Elsie Clews Parsons about Taos a generation later, "and what was merely
different, was no easy job." Yet she enjoyed its challenge. "As ever among
the Pueblos," Parsons advised, "you must know something in order to
know more." Later she almost bragged, "I never regretted paying extra for
an insight so valuable in future dealings with those I asked to incur
danger—the very great danger of visiting forbidden places or of imparting
forbidden information." Working with her favorite Isleta Pueblo female
informant, Parsons confessed, "We were friends and enemies, for we respected, even admired, each other, and our duel of wits is a high spot in my
Pueblo experience."

One colleague who took this attitude to task was the offbeat scholar
and writer Jaime de Angulo. When anthropologist Ruth Benedict asked
for a Taos Pueblo informant whom she might interrogate at a "safely
American place," he castigated his old friend. "Don't you understand the
psychological value of secrecy at a certain level of culture? Do you realize
that it is just that sort of thing that kills the Indian? . . . That's what you
anthropologists with your infernal curiosity and your thirst for scientific
data bring about. . . . They have a real, actual meaning and value, as secrets, for the members of the society. You must not rob them. You must not
sneak into their house. You wouldn't inveigle my child into telling you the
secrets of my home."

Secrets of another sort were forever circulating through Acoma. Often generated by personal jealousies, they concerned suspicions of witchcraft that
passed from rooftop to rooftop. Among the facts of life that got you on the
community's list of suspects were unexpected and sudden good fortune, the
accumulation of greater-than-average wealth, and any conduct considered
self-assertive, noncooperative, unconventional, excessive, or selfish. Behind

his back, whispered from person to person, a number of these postures and behaviors would one day be charged to Day Break. Everyone knew that he was exposed to the medicine man's secrets, but his errant, independent-minded behavior could still tag him as a possible witch. There is no record that he was ever directly accused of witchcraft. Perhaps people were afraid that by then he had become too estranged from his origins to care what anyone thought.

Finally there were the private secrets almost everyone holds to their chest. They related to buried transgressions, hidden sexual proclivities, or conflicted religious or political allegiances. In a pueblo where conformity was taken for granted, what minimized lying about one's true feelings or confidential associations was a pervasive inhibition about asking personal questions. So long as your outward, public life fit the norm, few embarrassed you by asking about your opinions, your likes or dislikes, or your dreams.

The keeping of personal secrets would not make life easy for Day Break, and he collected his fill. Some pointed to the secret of that Hispano branch in his family tree. Even deeper secrets would revolve around his cultural loyalties. "In the Keres pueblo," wrote Mary Austin, "the sacred epic is so guarded from White spoliation that it is likely to be finally extinguished with the lives of the jealous elders who dare not submit it to youth trained in the brash and stupid ignorance of the Government schools." In Day Break's case, however, story by story, and initiation by initiation, that submission was well under way.

Day Break's imminent move away from Acoma would threaten everything his mesa education taught him, and mark a turning point in his life. Because of his growing reluctance to participate in keeping his people's secrets, and for spilling them to outsiders, he would soon pay a price. To sharpen the irony, soon would come a European circus asking him to keep secret both his Pueblo and his Christian identities so they could market him as a Plains Indian chief with the invented name of Big Snake.

Serious White Men (1875–79)

I learned about racism firsthand from the Marmon family. My great-grandfather endured the epithet Squaw Man. Once when he and two of his young sons (my Grandpa Hank and his brother Frank) walked through the lobby of Albuquerque's only hotel to reach the cafe outside, the hotel manager stopped my great-grandfather. He told my great-grandfather that he was welcome to walk through the lobby, but when he had Indians with him, he should use the back door. My great-grandfather informed him that the "Indians" were his sons, and then he left and never went into the hotel again.

—Leslie Marmon Silko, Laguna Pueblo, 1996

O NE DAY IN THE LATE SUMMER of 1876, Day Break's father told him to stick around the house. As if reliving the perilous days of his own father's generation, when Acoma's Opi Society warriors geared up against Navajo or Apache marauders, he pulled from storage his bow, quiver, and rawhide shield. Painting his face, he slung a pouch containing a stone arrowhead over his neck. From the mesa rim Day Break watched as a file of men with their bows, rabbit clubs, and a few muzzle-loaders skipped downhill.

Friction between Acoma and Laguna pueblos was of long standing, and practically between cousins. Thirty years earlier they'd come close to blows when Acoma demanded the return of a supernaturally powerful oil painting of Saint Joseph that the two villages had shared since the mid-eighteenth century. Fearing they would lose their patron saint, the Lagunas had armed themselves and raced south. As the tribes confronted each other, the Acomans were outnumbered. They faced certain defeat but for the intervention of Father Jean-Baptiste Salpointe, who nonetheless decided in favor of Laguna. Although a territorial court ordered the icon's return to Acoma in 1857, that squabble exacerbated their old friction over contested boundaries.

Now siding with Laguna over a disputed parcel near Ojo de Gallo

Springs, about twenty-five miles northwest of Acoma mesa, was U.S. Indian agent Ben Thomas. His friendships with the Civil War veterans who were making Laguna their base of operations and the decision against Acoma's land claims set the villages on this collision course. It would rank as one of the rare battles between two pueblos in documented history.

Once Day Break lost sight of his father the party probably headed due west, crossing the cairn-marked trail that bisects the Malpais badlands. It customarily led Acoma traders on to the rest of the Acoma-to-Zuni trail, landing them south of today's Gallup. This time they only followed it as far as Gallo Springs.

Awaiting the Acomas with infantry and cavalry of better-trained and -armed Laguna Indians was a professional surveyor and former Civil War lieutenant from Ohio who had resided at Laguna for six years. In that period thirty-one-year-old Walter G. Marmon had made himself paterfamilias of an unusual Anglo-American foothold in Pueblo Indian country. Stigmatized as "squaw men" behind their backs, this close-knit group of former Union soldiers brought fortune and factionalism to what was officially the youngest of the Pueblo communities.

New residents at Laguna Pueblo, in Civil War military dress. Left to right: *George Pradt, Robert Marmon, Walter Marmon, John Gunn.*

◆ ◆ ◆

Once Americans took charge of the Southwest in 1848, their religions were not far behind. A magnet for a small but influential handful of missionaries, educators, and merchants was Laguna Pueblo, Acoma's closest native neighbor. Perched on her knoll overlooking the Rio San Jose, capped by St. Joseph of the Lake Mission whose ivory color stood out against pine-grizzled Mount Taylor, Laguna was named for the reed-bordered reservoir east of the village. Following the All-Pueblo Revolt of 1680 and Spanish reconquest twelve years later, she became a haven for still-resistant refugees from Acoma, Cochiti, and Santo Domingo. While the two pueblos shared dialects and religious and social practices, there was that defining exception—the uncommon welcome some Lagunans extended to outsiders.

Often assumed to be the most recently minted of pueblo villages, in actuality Laguna sat on ancient ground. Around 11,000 BC, Paleo-Indian hunters pursued mammoths in her well-watered valley. Ten thousand years later, local bands survived there on foraging, hunting, and tilling plots of tiny-cobbed corn. Then the site witnessed the customary succession of native occupants classified by southwestern archaeologists—from the Basketmaker Period (300 BC–AD 800) to Ancestral Pueblo (AD 800–1400), with the Historic Pueblo period reaching into the present.

In 1684 a Spanish land grant legitimized the pueblo's existence. Considered a satellite of Acoma at the turn of the eighteenth century, eighty years later Laguna, with her growing population, her prime location on trade routes, and a generous land allocation by the U.S. government, made the Catholic Church registry switch that around. Now Acoma was decreed to be an outlier of Laguna. Something about her boundary role betwixt Pueblo and Navajo domains, and her economic importance once the Santa Fe Railroad steamed through town, kept Laguna a crossroads for commerce, ideas, and ethnic rivalries.

Back in 1851 the first American resident in Laguna, Baptist missionary Samuel C. Gorman, found a small village hunkered down in fear of Navajo and Apache attacks. Six years later Gorman won U.S. approval to build his adobe school, chapel, and home a half mile northeast of the village's cramped plaza. The Gorman compound would become a popular stopover where Navajo-fighting generals (William T. Sherman, James Carleton, and Vincent Canby), famous Indian scouts (Kit Carson), territorial governors (Lew Wal-

Laguna Indian scouts, trained by the Marmons: Troop F, 1st Regiment, carrying .45-70 carbines, 1886, after the Geronimo campaign.

lace), scholars (Adolph Bandelier), and even outlaws (Billy the Kid) rented rooms, paid for meals, strategized war plans, or hid out from pursuers.

Trained as a civil engineer, Walter G. Marmon arrived in 1868 as a surveyor for the Atlantic and Pacific Railroad. Three years later he moved into Gorman's broken-down old mission and eventually opened a post office. Then appointed as government teacher, he oversaw a class of mostly old-timers who spoke no English, sat on log benches, shared a single book and pencil, and read by whatever light streamed through holes in the wall.

Walter ingratiated himself with a pro-white religious leader named Kwime (Luis Sarracino) who had attended a Catholic school in Durango, Mexico, but then converted to Protestantism. Marrying Kwime's daughter, he made himself indispensable as Laguna's doctor and political counselor, colonel of her Indian cavalry, and surveyor of her boundaries. In 1872 he was joined by his more outgoing younger brother Robert, also a surveyor and future Indian trader.

Soon joining the Marmons were their Ohio cousins the Gunns, another white surveyor named George H. Pradt, and, in 1875, the Protestant missionary John Menaul with his wife and brother James. All added their families to Laguna's mixed-blood neighborhood on the pueblo's northeast side. A cattleman and merchant, John Gunn would run Laguna's major flour mill and country store. Remaining at the pueblo until 1887, Rev. Menaul installed New Mexico's first printing press and began turning out copies of *McGuffey's First Reader* in the Keresan language. In years to come one of Day Break's sons would also marry into one of Laguna's eight mixed-blood families.

Through their marriages these Anglo change agents nurtured a progressive generation who would be of the pueblo but not entirely controlled by it. Sharing dim views of what they considered the medieval Catholicism of Hispano hamlets like Cubero and San Mateo, while also deploring the heathen practices of their native neighbors, they aroused opposition from Christian and native "traditionalists" alike and incited the kinds of factional rifts with which Day Break would become all too familiar.

Complementing the Anglo-Protestant foothold at Laguna was the affiliation, from the 1860s onward, between Acoma Pueblo and some Jewish merchants who hailed from a single family, the Bibos of Westphalia. Affinities between Jews and Indians had been the subject of outlandish speculation for centuries. In his Delaware Indian neighbors the Quaker William Penn saw "countenances to the Hebrew race." As early as 1824 a Christian missionary in the Southeast was struck by similarities between the Ark of the Covenant and a Cherokee Indian shrine. More maverick Christian offshoots, like the Latter-day Saints, even claimed that Indians were descendants of a "lost" Israeli tribe. Better documented are accounts, twenty years before the *Mayflower,* of Jews walking north from Mexico, crossing the Sonoran Desert, and venturing up the Rio Grande. Escapees from religious persecution in Portugal and Spain, they were either true *conversos* to Catholicism, or so-called crypto-Jews who adopted a Christian cover while observing their Sephardic rituals in private.

By Day Break's birth an estimated 150,000 Jews were in America. Of the 200 in New Mexico by 1880, most sprang from Ashkenazi migrations from Prussia, and nearly half were cousins or even closer. Earliest to set up shop in Santa Fe were the Spiegelbergs. After eighteen-year-old Solomon Jacob arrived by ox-drawn caravan on the Santa Fe Trail, one by one his four brothers shortly followed. Although he began by selling goods from a converted gypsy wagon, by the 1850s the prestigious House of Spiegelberg was established.

Winning early government contracts to supply military outposts in Navajo country underwrote this family's success. Before long their elegant Santa Fe storefront on the plaza's south side was offering factory goods from back east, taking in barter, and extending credit. Jewish immigration swelled, Santa Fe's commercial slots were soon full; incoming concerns like the Staab and Ilfeld families were dispatched to more promising outlets in Las Vegas, Bernalillo, and venues even farther afield.

Into this mix of ethnic alliances and antagonisms plowed the greatest harbinger of modern times. On its arrival in central New Mexico in 1880, the Santa Fe Railroad opened up isolated Indian villages, transformed some towns into commercial trade hubs, left others in the dust, transported the East to the West, and kick-started a tourist industry that would quickly grow into a profitable business.

From 1860 to 1880, pushing railroads through western plains, mountains, and deserts was a risky endeavor of speculation and backroom dealing. If flooding rivers, mountain barriers, and swampy or sandy bottoms didn't deter the process, then competing rail companies, insufficient finances, unsecured rights-of-way, townsfolk irate at being bypassed and demanding separate spurs, or angry and obstructive Indians would slow it down. Once Colonel Cyrus K. Holiday gained control of the Atchison, Topeka and Santa Fe Railroad in 1859, it took twenty years before steel rails could enter New Mexico. First the crews tunneled through Raton Pass, then headed for Las Vegas, Albuquerque, and beyond.

Difficult personalities could also upend the best-laid plans. One day in early 1878, Bernalillo storekeeper Nathan Bibo watched five men step out of a Concord stage and huddle across the street with local *jefe* and merchant Don José Leandro Perea. When they left an hour later, they were not happy. The railroad reps had offered $3 an acre, but the stubborn don held out for $425. Bernalillo was condemned to marginal status while Albuquerque's preeminence was assured. Yet when Catholic archbishop Jean-Baptiste Lamy learned the same year that instead of coming through Santa Fe as planned, the railroad would be diverted south to Albuquerque, the influential prelate led the drive for an expensive bond issue to fund a seventeen-mile spur into the old capital.

After the mass resettlement in late 1868 of virtually the entire Navajo tribe on their 3.4-million-acre reservation (still less than 10 percent of the land they had previously occupied), many in western New Mexico breathed a little easier. Some Chiricahua Apaches remained at large, but their last raids were concentrated safely to the far west and south. Even atop Acoma mesa, although it was still pervaded by what one writer of the period called an "air of hoary antiquity which made innovation seem almost a sacrilege," life felt less fragile and self-protective. That was when some villagers extended their summer stays beside irrigated fields in the North Valley hamlet some fourteen miles closer to Mount Taylor.

"The people went further away north to Acomita," remembered Day Break, "and settled in that little valley. Here was fine farming and plenty of water in a stream that ran through it. They began making dams and ditches for irrigating their farms." Overlooking the spindly Rio San Jose with good sheep meadows upslope, they gathered friable sandstone and constructed rock wall additions to the temporary shelters that clung like wasp nests to the north-facing slopes of Woods Mesa.

Acoma's watchfulness was especially keen on that day, eight years after the Navajo treaty, when Day Break's father and his fellow warriors headed out to confront the fighters from Laguna. Were the Acomans aware that the Marmons had fused the tribesmen into an infantry force that were armed with carbines, and that Pradt had trained a company of mounted scouts? Was the field of battle the contested Ojo de Gallo Springs, a prized water source a mile or so north of the Spanish hamlet of San Rafael, where camp followers and ex-soldiers from old Fort Wingate days still squatted on Indian land and refused to move? All we know is that the Acomans held their ground, suffered casualties but no fatalities, and retreated when U.S. agent Ben Thomas showed up from Fort Wingate with a cavalry detachment.

Was Day Break's father among the Acomas taken prisoner by Thomas and placed on wagons bound for Santa Fe? And was their arrest a hollow gesture anyhow, since en route the agent got the Acomas to forswear any more violence before letting them go? What was not resolved on the battlefield would await the courts. What we do know is that after quieting the militancy of Day Break's father's generation, Agent Ben Thomas, the Marmons of Laguna, and other influential white men and women now set their sights on transforming the future for his.

Into Their World (1880–81)

We need to awaken in him wants. In his dull savagery he must be touched by the wings of the divine angel of discontent. Then he begins to look forward, to reach out. The desire for property of his own may become an intense educating force. . . . Discontent with the tepee and the starving rations of the Indian camp in winter is needed to get the Indian out of the blanket and into trousers—and trousers with a pocket in them that aches to be filled with dollars.

—Merrill E. Gates, 1891

FOUR YEARS LATER, in 1880, a delegation of three white men traveled by wagon from Albuquerque to Acoma mesa. On the way two of them overnighted at Laguna as guests of the Marmons. There was thirty-seven-year-old Ben Thomas, then in his sixth year as U.S. Indian agent for the Pueblos. Sickly in body but a die-hard reformer in spirit, Thomas represented the breed of Indian reservation agent that was being recruited from Christian denominations under President Grant's postwar Peace Policy and placed throughout Indian country. Their mandate was to reform the Indian Bureau's corrupt bureaucracy and uplift the nation's Indians to the benefits of "civilization."

When Thomas first saw Santa Fe in 1870, his impression was of a godforsaken backwater of drunks, raucous white soldiers, superstitious and lazy Hispano Catholics, and sullen pagan Indians. They seemed proof that "this whole country [is] emphatically a possession of the devil." Yet Thomas remained grateful that its pure mountain air was extending his life. Initially assigned the thankless task of agency "farmer" to the Navajo, then failing to coax those seminomadic horsemen to remake themselves as domesticated homesteaders, Thomas was next assigned as agent to the Apache, with similarly uninspiring results. As for this third assignment, he prayed that among the "quiet, industrious, reliable" Pueblos he might yet produce "valuable citizens."

His companion, Rev. Sheldon Jackson, was nine years older, handicapped in physique and eyesight as well, but better educated and bound for national fame as a "spiritual empire builder." Born in New York State, Jackson had attended Princeton Theological Seminary, which was long associated with converting Indians. By age twenty-four he was teaching at Oklahoma's Choctaw Mission Indian School. But in 1870 he became superintendent for the Board of Home Missions of the Rocky Mountain District—an immense parish that took in New Mexico.

Described as a man of religious zeal, unflagging energy, and an effective executive, the missionary had already logged 345,000 miles of hard travel—which would amount to an estimated million miles by his career's end. He would deliver thousands of sermons, edit church newspapers, organize over seventy new congregations, and oversee the construction of nearly forty churches. He was known for peppering his sermons with his adventures—escaping a raging prairie fire; leaping from a stagecoach just before it tumbled down a canyon; surviving outlaw holdups, once with a circle of cocked pistols aimed at him; living through New Mexico's small-

On alert: Faustino Rey, Day Break's father, also an Acoma war chief.

pox epidemic of 1878; and enduring the Mesilla-to-Deming stage run during the month of its highest body count from Apache attacks. Jackson had defied Mormons in Utah and the entrenched Catholic establishment in New Mexico. When he later moved to Alaska Territory, the "indefatigable little religious tramp" challenged the Russian Orthodox establishment, founded its school system, and became the region's leading lobbyist.

Most incongruous was the party's third member, a multilingual Jewish trader named Solomon Bibo, joining as translator. Of all the Bibo brothers to open general stores in western New Mexico, Solomon ventured farthest in geographical reach and cultural distance. As he sided with Acoma Pueblo in her disputes over federal surveys of 1876 and 1877, he fell at odds with the Marmons of Laguna while deepening Acoma's dependence on his commercial connections and general counsel.

The delegation tied their wagon at the mesa base, secured water and hay for their animals, and ascended the Camino de Padre Trail. Benjamin, the bureaucrat, Sheldon, the missionary, and Solomon, the merchant, shared the conviction that Indians could not survive as Indians. Now that the Indian Wars were coming to an end, they embodied the latest generation of Anglo-American institutions to dominate the West.

Topping the list of reforms that followed America's struggle to free the slaves was transforming Indians into working, praying, and well-behaved versions of her own white selves. If the nation's banner read "An Era of Progress," the slogan over her reservations was "Civilization"; its method was "Assimilation." Among the steps that began this post-abolitionist crusade to absorb Indians and their lands into the national fold were excursions like this one up Acoma mesa.

Out of protocol the visitors probably exchanged greetings with Acoma's "inside" leader, the lifelong cacique. Quite likely Bibo urged his companions to also pay respects to the governor and "outside" regulator at the time, who was probably Martin Valle, Day Break's future grandfather-in-law. Then came visits with native parents like his own. The following are Day Break's own words about what became the most consequential decision of his life. They come from fragmentary memories typed in capital letters on onionskin paper by his daughter Josephine in 1947, shortly before his death. The ribbons of staccato phrases and full stops read like a telegram from yesteryear.

OLD FOLKS OF ACOMA WERE TALK TO ABOUT EDUCATING.
SOLOMON WAS ACTING INTERPRETER. FOR THIS MAN WHO
WANTED CHILDREN, CHIEF GAVE OVER 30 POOREST VERY
POOREST CHILDREN. MY FATHER WAS THE POOREST. HE WAS
MEDICINE MAN. WE HAD THREE SHEEP SKINS TO SLEEP ON.

Day Break was about to join a generation of Indian children for one of the most ambitious experiments in social engineering in American history. Its core vision was hardly new. After a treaty was signed in 1794 with midwestern tribes, Thomas Jefferson had proposed a "Civilization" program that would induce Indians to become "yeoman farmers," plowing homesteads and tending livestock, their womenfolk sewing quilts, dwelling in single-family frontier cabins. In 1819 Congress created a "Civilization Fund" with allocations for the retraining that would make this vision come true.

After the Civil War this call mounted into a chorus. Official after official laid down the law: Indians faced a "stern alternative," declared one, "extermination or civilization." Threatened another, "Savage and civilized life cannot live and prosper on the same ground. One of them must die." And a commissioner of Indian affairs confessed that while "this civilization may not be the best possible, it is the best the Indians can get. They cannot escape it, and must conform to it or be crushed by it."

Buttressing the campaign was a theory of cultural evolution that saw human societies like American Indians rising from savagery to barbarism to civilization, or progressing, in historian Roy Harvey Pearce's words, "from past to present, from east to west, from lower to higher." Energized by their victory over slavery, these former abolitionists, evangelical Christians, and social reformers forged new alliances to assist Indians in their ascent. They lobbied to halt brutalities against Indians. They fought to stem bureaucratic corruption on their underscrutinized reservations. They tried to insulate them from frontier vices like alcohol, prostitution, and outlawry. They wanted to redirect their pagan souls to Christianity. Loosely grouped as "Friends of the Indian," this reform movement enjoyed unprecedented influence as it designed this "final solution to the Indian problem."

Their civilization crusade had three parts.

First was the program to replace native ties to their tribes with the values of individualism, hard work, and the primacy of private property. It stressed personal initiative, elevated allegiance to the nuclear family over clan and ethnicity, and privileged the settled farm or independent ranch over a communal life and an economy based on hunting and gathering.

To accomplish this meant transforming the *external* conditions of Indian existence. As a prerequisite the reformers supported the end of nearly a century of treaty-making (1783–1871). They felt it was ludicrous for the United States to negotiate on government-to-government terms with conquered, depleted, and uncivilized Indians. The next step was the redistribution, or "allotment," of tribal lands to Indian families, and opening what was left over to white settlement.

Second was a judicial system to replace any *internal* orders of Indian existence. Its goal was to "educate these men-children into that great conception of the reign of law, moral and civil, to which they are now strangers," as reformer Merrill Gates put it. To save money by "deputizing the opposition," reservation Indian police were established in 1878; six years later tribesmen were in blue uniforms at forty-eight different Indian agencies. In 1882 the courts of Indian Offenses were created to handle such crimes as the "rites, customs . . . contrary to civilization" that President Chester Arthur delegated his interior secretary to outlaw. These included the "sun dance," the "scalp dance," the "war dance," and "feasts," "heathenish" practices of "medicine men," polygamy, sale of liquor, and abuse of property.

The third part was the extraction of Indian children from their tribal environments and their reeducation far from home. They would learn to worship the one true God and be taught principles of thrift, cleanliness, and a work ethic. They would adopt Anglo-American modes of dress and replace their tribal languages with English. They would acquire a basic education in the three Rs and gradually advance toward full U.S. citizenship sometime in the future.

But applying this paternalistic program to the Pueblo world presented some problems. First of all, just what kinds of Indians were they?

Clearly these reclusive farmers were not the "Indians" who danced in the heads of the social reformers—not those whooping, war-bonneted, horseback-riding, buffalo-hunting bands of Plains tribes who after defeats in battle and treaties signed had only just been confined to reservations.

These settled villagers of the Southwest were natives of *another* kind.

So implied the U.S. Supreme Court in 1876 when it declared that all Pueblo Indians were legally exempt from most of the laws and edicts applicable to other Indians. So agreed many knowledgeable observers: "In the sense traditionally attached to the word," wrote author of the popular novel *Ramona* and investigative journalist Helen Hunt Jackson in 1885, "they are scarcely to be considered Indian." And so concurred local Indian agents, whose minimal comments on the Pueblo Indians under their charge left the impression that their retiring existence rendered them thankfully inconsequential. Their hands were busy enough with the troublesome Navajos, Apaches, and Utes.

Persuade these Indians to slice up their reservations into individual family plots?

For openers, the pueblos already owned nearly seven hundred thousand acres, the sum of nineteen separate land grants that were not U.S. reservations but derived from first Spanish and then Mexican decrees that had been duly ratified by the 1848 Treaty of Guadalupe Hidalgo between the United States and Mexico. Second, their liminal legal status would protect them from U.S. government programs until they became officially "Indians" once again in 1913. Last, few tribal groups had such strong sociopolitical organizations and as tight a communal-religious ethos as these seemingly docile, town-dwelling people—wasn't that why they were distinguished as *Pueblo* Indians in the first place?

What about teaching them farming and animal husbandry?

A May 17, 1882, Act to Civilize Pueblo Indians released money for purchasing new kinds of seeds, fruit trees, agricultural implements, and the construction of irrigation ditches. But for a thousand years Puebloan peoples had managed to squeeze every drop of moisture out of their high desert in order to cultivate corn, beans, squash, and tobacco and breed turkeys and parrots. And since the days of the Spanish they had taken to successfully raising sheep, horses, oxen, mules, burros, even pigs.

Did they need any encouragement to be peaceful?

The archaeological record suggests that Ancestral Pueblo Indians could be almost as brutal and defensive as any other society. They fought when

*Where Day Break was
headed: the temporary
Indian school in Duranes
barrio, Albuquerque.*

their land base or spiritual values were threatened by Spaniards, Navajos, or Apaches. More than perhaps any other pueblo, warfare had played a role in Acoma Pueblo mythology and history. But by the American Territorial period all the pueblos had been greatly reduced in numbers and resources and were lying low.

What about making them build permanent homes and stay put?

These were not the seminomadic Indians whom the commissioner of Indian affairs warned in 1871 should "no longer roam over trackless regions of the country; they must settle on lands set apart." Planting themselves permanently on their own lands was what Pueblo Indians had done for centuries, the more isolated and left alone the better. Some of their villages featured stone-and-adobe apartments that had gone up when Europe was still in its dark ages. Acoma, Oraibi, and Taos pueblos remain the oldest still-inhabited towns in the Western Hemisphere.

But from a Pueblo standpoint, two items on the civilization agenda were threateningly relevant to their Southwest. Both targeted the heart and soul of Pueblo survival.

First was that pressure to "individualize," a concept that was anathema to communities, however small, that saw themselves as intact little worlds, each the "center" of their cosmos, each dependent on every member prioritizing the collective before the personal.

Second was this plan to educate their children, a threat whose social implications most parents like Day Break's fully saw. As much as the loss of working hands in fields and home, the absence of their young from village existence would interrupt the transmission of central values and cultural information. No prospect was as ominous as their sons and daughters boarding at distant schools that detached them from ways of life to which they might never return. Yet for social reformers like this threesome no item on the civilization agenda was as urgent.

Through his personal contacts with Acoma's influential Antelope Clan, Solomon Bibo may have known which parents were most vulnerable to surrendering their young. Among the poorer households he possibly earmarked as a likely source was one on the mesa's front row.

Day Break's parents were against the idea. But then Bibo apparently put it directly to Day Break. Again we have his voice speaking from the page:

> TALKED A LONG TIME OF ME BUT MY FATHER AND MA
> REFUSED UNTIL I PERSONALLY MADE MY DECISION TO GO SO
> WAS ALLOWED. AGREEMENT REACHED 30 CHILDREN AND ALL
> THE PARENTS CAME TO SEE HOW CONDITIONS WERE TO BE—

What tribal ethic about individual rights permitted this son to make such an independent decision, against the wishes of parents, tribal cacique, clan uncles, other elders, and local Catholics? Perhaps the assurance of seeing him fed and clothed caused his parents to relent. Perhaps every Acoma person past infancy and those threshold initiations was allowed to chart their own course and face the consequences. For Day Break, at least, something more than physical survival seemed at stake. How did this personal desire develop? What farther star was he following? Had Bibo a hand in this decision?

With some thirty others crammed into wagons and parents trailing along on burros, the caravan left the mesa and headed east. The trip in horse-drawn wagons from Acoma to the banks of the Rio Grande probably took about three days—one campout on the banks of the Rio Puerco, a second near the present village of Los Lunas before crossing the moonscape of West Mesa and dropping into the Southwest's longest river valley.

Their final night together they bivouacked on the Rio Grande's western bank. One can imagine Day Break looking across the river at the darkened town of Albuquerque, with few lights or fires visible, the sounds of animals bedding down, and perhaps moonlight on the mountains.

How would they cross these waters, what lay ahead, who out there wished him well?

PART TWO

Edward Hunt
(1880–1918)

PREVIOUS PAGE: *The storekeeper, Ed Hunt.*

Turned Inside Out (1880–81)

I have recently thought that the "Indian problem" may be solved by algebra. In fact, it must be solved by "elimination," and the Indian is the "factor" to be "eliminated." But how shall Mr. Lo! be eliminated? Theories are numerous, but I think most of the "short cuts" will fail to give the "answer"—civilization. When the answer to this problem has been realized and the Indian has become civilized, the Indian as a race will have passed away.

—William F. Howard, 1893

A T AROUND AGE NINETEEN, Day Break was probably the oldest and tallest of the Indian youngsters standing with their parents on the Rio Grande's western bank. Across the river a blanket of mist and woodsmoke hung above the salt cedar, willow, and cottonwood trees. Beyond were earthen roofs weighing upon protruding *vigas,* a pair of pointy steeples and the alarum of pealing roosters, braying burros, and clanging bells—hence the Navajo name for what was then known as Hispano *Alburquerque:* "Where the Sounding Things Are Suspended." Farther in the distance the Sandia and Manzano mountains were backlit by a rising sun. In its finale as a frontier crossroads, the settlement still resembled a patchwork of overlapping ranchos.

During the dry season the river ran so shallow you could roll up your pants and wade across, always feeling for dangerous quicksand. Come the spring melt or summer monsoons, however, the Rio Grande could swell into a flood of chocolate-colored waves. Day Break had never seen such a broad body of water.

Incoming boatmen pushed poles, assisting the tow rope that drew a barge of adze-squared logs. With only the makeshift Bernalillo bridge upstream, this was still how livestock, stagecoaches, and freight wagons got across. The Indians boarded and bunched up at one end. As it cast off, one can imagine their spirits tightening into hard kernels. They say you can't ford the same river twice. For Day Break this transit would be doubly irreversible.

Early class at Duranes Indian School. Edward (Day Break) in back row,
fourth from right.

Near today's Barelas Bridge they pulled into a clearing hacked out of
the bosque. Jumping into knee-deep water, the ferrymen lashed fast and
the Indians filed down a gangplank. Awaiting them were white women in
long dresses and dark-suited white men looking on. In no time Day Break
got a foretaste of life ahead. Boys and girls were separated and led to a
broken-down adobe ranch house near the Duranes plaza, only a few miles
away. Left behind, the parents camped on the river's western bank for a
week to make sure their children were safe.

As recruits for Albuquerque's first Indian Training School, Day Break
and his companions had been swept into one key strategy of America's
crusade to "assimilate" and "civilize" the nation's Indians. Parents might
be a lost cause, but their kids had a chance. The philosophy of these "industrial" training schools dominated Indian education for the next half
century. Early into his three-year stay, Day Break laid eyes on their architect. One morning the students noticed Superintendent W. D. Bryant escorting a smartly uniformed visitor around the parade ground like he was

royalty. With his thinning hair, broad brow, smallpox-scarred cheeks, oversize nose, and crisp bearing, Richard Henry Pratt was inspecting the place as if reviewing troops at the barricades.

Teaching Indians in schools run by whites had been among the "rational experiments" originally proposed by George Washington in October 1791 to extend the "blessings of civilization." Two years earlier the president had demonstrated he was serious by personally sponsoring Princeton University's first native student, a Delaware Indian named George White Eyes. Putting into practice Washington and Jefferson's commitments to educating Indian children became Pratt's lifelong mission. It meant uprooting them from home and tribal environments and enrolling them in distant institutions that blended teaching the three Rs, military discipline and drilling, religious indoctrination, and training in "manual" skills so they could support themselves in a white world.

Born in 1840, Pratt studied for the priesthood and ran a hardware store before finding his vocation during a second stint in the military. In the Civil War he had fought in over thirty engagements before being recommissioned to command the all-black "Buffalo Soldier" 10th Regiment against Comanche and Kiowa Indians in the Washita (1868–69) and Red River (1874–75) campaigns. In late 1875, Pratt found himself escorting seventy-two Kiowa, Comanche, and Southern Cheyenne prisoners of war to an old Spanish fortress in St. Augustine, Florida. Now his soldier's career answered to a higher calling as the seminarian and disciplinarian merged with the reformer. Pratt conceived of an educational approach that involved, as he notoriously put it, killing the Indian to save the man. "We have tried to take civilization to the Indian," he preached, but "the better plan is to take the Indian to civilization."

Within the damp stone walls of Fort Marion some of the warriors who'd wanted his scalp turned into his devoted students. Pratt led them through fundamental English and math, the basics of Protestant worship, and arts and crafts. He encouraged them to alleviate homesickness by illustrating with pencil and crayon their tribal lives, hunting memories, even battlefield exploits, along with scenes from their journeys by train and boat from the dusty plains of Indian Territory to the Atlantic coast.

Replacing white guards with handpicked Indians, Pratt also found jobs for promising inmates in the wider St. Augustine community, thereby initiating the widespread practice known as "outing" for integrating Indian boarding school students into local white society. Importing his radical approach to Virginia's Normal and Agricultural Institute, he intermixed twenty-two Indian prisoners with black freedmen who were learning agriculture, carpentry, and blacksmithing. But then, concerned that the Indians might attract racial prejudice by association, he persuaded the Interior Department to turn over an abandoned army barracks in Pennsylvania for an Indians-only institution.

Two years before Day Break arrived in Albuquerque, Pratt had opened his Carlisle Indian Industrial School. Wearing military-style uniforms, his eighty-two students divided their days into academic and vocational classes and marching drills. A fervent and innovative lobbyist, in his promotional literature Pratt used before-and-after photos to demonstrate his transformation of long-haired heathen boys and girls into shorn, uniformed, churchgoing cadets and junior-miss homemakers.

In western New Mexico the ground for Pratt's ideas was plowed and waiting. For years U.S. Indian agent Ben Thomas had advocated extracting Pueblo, Navajo, and Apache children from the "negative influences" of family and tribe. Like most progressive-minded Presbyterians, the cluster of Marmon-Gunn-Menaul mixed-blood families at Laguna Pueblo supported Pratt's model at Carlisle. But Thomas ran into resistance from New Mexican Catholics. They felt sidelined in President Grant's postwar policy of replacing often-corrupt civilian Indian agents with religious leaders, largely from Protestant denominations.

Then the Protestant evangelizer Sheldon Jackson got the go-ahead from Carl Schurz, Grant's secretary of the interior, to open in January 1881 a New Mexico version of Pratt's school. Jackson came to Albuquerque, organized one of the town's first Protestant congregations in a private living room, and rented the dilapidated Duranes homestead. Adapting its five acres for a school to be run by a fifty-fifty contract between his Presbyterian Board of Home Missions and the U.S. government, Jackson and Thomas then headed for Laguna and Acoma pueblos to recruit its students.

The shock of those first weeks were like a transfusion of a new blood type. Under Superintendent J. S. Shearer, the makeover began with their bodies. Day Break's headband, homemade cotton pants, baggy tunic, deerhide moccasins, and Navajo blanket were incinerated. His pageboy-style hair was scissored to the head. Buckets of cold water doused his body, and he was scrubbed with chunks of laundry soap. He was measured for a uniform, then heavy leather shoes and a Union soldier–like cap.

Six days a week went the new regimen. Sunday mornings were for church and hymn-singing accompanied by a Miss Marietta Wood on the cabinet organ. Daily life ran by clock and bell. Boys and girls were assigned separate rooms. At first clangs, 5:45 a.m., everyone fell out of bunk beds and dressed. Fifteen minutes later a second bell set them to washing faces and hands. At 6:20 all were in formation and marched to breakfast. After mouthing grace in an unintelligible tongue they sat on plank benches at long tables. The boys marched out to class while the girls cleared the tables and carried dishes to the kitchen where cook Robert Helbig and his baker wife taught them to clean and rinse.

In the "old ruined adobe house where we were crowded into three rooms," the boys spent half the day with Miss Tibbles, learning math using chalk on slates. At numbers Day Break displayed aptitude, soon adding long columns in his head; by his second year he had advanced to decimals. Next came geography, then reading and spelling, with Miss Wood holding up hammers, rocks, wood, and hats and having her students sound out their English words in unison. They learned the niceties: "please . . . thank you . . . my name is . . . how are you." With these lessons came the warning—speak Indian and you got bread and water or worse.

Day Break learned by doing, and to do as he was told. Afternoons initiated students into the Protestant work ethic. Manual labor was under Mr. Kelby. They weeded the vegetable garden, split firewood, and repaired the building, with Day Break singled out for heavy lifting because of his over-age strength. Hands-on training in "industrial arts" such as carpentry, house construction, and blacksmithing were central to Pratt's pedagogy.

Smart and "grown enough to be useful," Day Break was soon measuring and slicing *terrones* bricks with straight-edge spades from the peatlike riverbanks, and molding thick, Spanish-style adobes in wooden frames. He mixed mud mortar to restore walls, learned the rough carpentry necessary to replace window sashes and doorframes and fix the leaky roof. Meanwhile the girls learned sewing, laundering, ironing, and general housekeeping from Miss Salome Verbeck.

Food was meager. Day Break never forgot the staple—Mulligan stew.

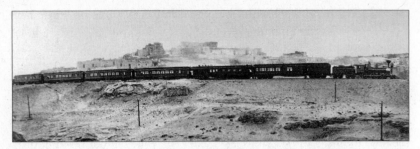

California Limited crossing Laguna Pueblo, c. 1899.

Otherwise it was mutton and bread baked in kitchen ovens and seasonal fruit from nearby orchards. Health was precarious—sore eyes were a constant, as were lung problems, which called for detested spoonfuls of cough syrup. With everyone organized into military-style battalions and companies, early evenings were for parade drills. Lights out at 9 p.m.

That first year the school held forty students. In the fall of 1882, with fresh recruits from a half dozen pueblos, it shifted to a larger site where Day Break helped raise the walls, and the student body increased to seventy-seven. The third year a contingent of Mescalero Apaches and Utes nearly doubled their ranks.

By the turn of the century Pratt's blueprint for transforming youngsters like Day Break was being replicated in nearly 150 boarding schools for twenty-five reservations in fifteen states. Over the next fifty years, thousands of Indian students streamed through these institutions, their lives altered forever. Some would shudder at the memories of their school experience—their long hair hacked off, their inherited languages outlawed, the beatings and other punishments if they broke the rules, the forced Christianity and the way their tribal traditions and identities were denigrated, the sexual abuse for some and the nights of loneliness and sickness for many.

Others would smile with nostalgia at those years. They had made new friends. Some met their future wives. The mixing of different tribes became the seedbed for pan-Indian movements such as the peyote-using Native American Church and the all-native Society of American Indians. And in lean times, where people were starving and destitute back in their home communities, their parents had the consolation that at least they were being fed, clothed, and sheltered.

"I stayed at the Mission School for three years without going home," Day Break recalled. "Sometimes men from Acoma would come down to the mission to see their sons," he added, never mentioning if they included his father or uncle. Nor did he betray worries that kin or tribe had abandoned him. Despite his unmooring from everything familiar, and this foreign way of relearning everything he'd been taught, for some reason Day Break was open to other kinds of life skills, other ways of acquiring them, and other sets of values. But would this new white world help him face the consequences of becoming one of its rare success stories?

17

City on the Cusp (1880–83)

Today the new civilization of the East is brought into direct contact with the ancient civilization of New Mexico. Today the bell of the locomotive tolls the death knell of old fogeyism, superstition and ignorance, and proclaims in clarion notes that henceforth knowledge, education, advancement and progress shall be the right of our people. Are we of Albuquerque prepared to take advantage of this opportunity?

—Judge William Hazeldine, 1880

THE YEAR DAY BREAK started school in the barrio of San José de Los Duranes the folksy neighborhoods of Old Town were slipping into second-class status. A few weeks after settling in, Day Break saw for himself the catalyst of their decline. It was a Sunday afternoon, the Indian students' only time for free play. A stroll south of school, near today's Central and 1st, brought them face-to-face with the demon that was devouring the Old West.

Years later the elders of Acoma claimed their forefathers knew it all along. "The grey-eyed people are coming nearer and nearer," Day Break's nephew, James Paytiamo, said, recalling the old prophecies. "They are building an iron road. They are coming nearer every day. You will mix with these people. You will drink black hot water and your teeth will become soft. You will smoke at a young age and your eyes will tear and your eyesight will be poor. Your joints will crack when you want to move slowly and softly. You will sleep on soft beds and not like to rise early. You will wear heavy clothes and sleep under heavy covers and grow lazy. Then there will be no more singing heard in the valleys as you walk."

Everywhere downtown was confusion, noise, digging, dust. Squads of workers were measuring and framing buildings, nailing a foundation for a boxcar to serve as temporary depot, hammering workbenches and lean-tos for storing raw materials; others were guiding earth-graders pulled by scrawny mules being whipped to the bone.

The boys leapt aside as one cacophony drowned out the rest—a wheel-clanking, metal-squealing, steam-hissing locomotive. Coal smoke billowed from its funnel-shaped stack, a single headlight beamed like a Cyclops eye, its raked grill resembled the bared teeth of an Ogre Katsina. "When we first saw the locomotive," Day Break remembered, "we nearly fainted, we were so scared. We thought it might swallow or burn or run over us." He never forgot one grinning engineer getting a kick out of coaxing the boys to come close, then yanking a cord so his steam whistle scattered them like sparrows.

Before their eyes the two western town types that constituted this urbanizing community were pulling apart. An emergent, main-drag-centered Anglo Albuquerque was leaving a has-been, plaza-centered Hispano *Alburquerque* in the dust. A generation after its founding in 1709, the Hispano neighborhood of Duranes, where Day Break later refurbished his school's crumbling adobe, had become one of a number of seats of Spanish gentry. As with today's divided perceptions about New Mexico's "impoverished" (or "historic") urban barrios, and her "run-down" (or "picturesque") rural villages, any outsider's opinion of these Hispano townships depended on the aesthetics and sentiments they brought to the scene.

For a British surveyor strolling around here in 1867, the seemingly haphazard mix of ranchitos exuded a certain charm. Getting lost in the narrow, unpaved, meandering streets amid the odors of livestock and hay, he hopped over *acequias,* or irrigation ditches banked by earthen berms, whisked at mosquitoes, and saw the coyote-stick fences and high grass that hid older and more relaxed rhythms of Hispano family and cultural life.

After navigating the pathways linking adobe casitas and their outdoor beehive-shaped *hornos,* or baking ovens, and barbecue pits, backyard ra-madas shaded by grapevines and weedy fruit orchards, the visitor arrived at the one place where he could orient himself—the communal plaza with its protective guardhouse. Here were dozing old-timers, hitching posts, and the thick-walled San Felipe de Neri adobe church topped by two wooden steeples. It evoked the laid-back "older" West of a Mexican-inflected spa-ghetti western, whose survival would one day pit community leaders and historical preservationists against a business-oriented city council and ur-ban redevelopers.

A twenty-minute walk east brought the visitor to a "collection of wooden tinderboxes and false-front adobe sheds." "This side of the tracks," com-mented one visitor, exuded "a certain perverse vitality." There were twenty boisterous saloons, seven opium dens, clamorous gambling parlors, four brothels, fleabag hotels (where the Briton was obliged to sleep), packed liv-ery stables, and other hallmarks of an aggressive township on the make. The air was ripe with animal and human manure and rotting garbage. One heard English rather than Spanish, much of that unprintable. Gun-shots rang out on Saturday nights, the occasional public hanging drew big crowds, the final caravans of ox-drawn wagons loaded with eastern goods still lumbered along the Chihuahua Trail, turning Central Avenue into a boot-sucking muck. This was brazen "new" Albuquerque, the Southwest's counterpart to a Deadwood or Dodge City.

To the fastidious neither side was terribly appealing. Probably it was the older Hispano-Catholic community a New York journalist was thinking about when he wrote that "in the heart of our worst civilization is an Amer-ican city . . . with all the signs of ignorance and sloth." Most likely it was the wild and wooly New Town a Chicago newsman was referencing when he reported that "no man of sense and sanity would go there to settle."

As with other territorial settlements in the railroad's path, during the 1880s Albuquerque's economic and ethnic divides only widened. By the time the Atchison, Topeka and Santa Fe tracks reached Las Vegas, New Mexico, on January 1, 1879, the split personality of that city, and Albu-querque's quickly to come, was unavoidable.

From eastern Kansas, a ribbon of wooden ties and iron rails followed old covered-wagon ruts to Colorado. Dropping south around present-day Boulder, the railroad hugged the Rockies' rain shadow before crossing the New Mexico border just below Trinidad. Winning its rivalry with the

Denver and Rio Grande over rights to the final stretch west, the AT&SF reached Albuquerque on April 5, 1880.

Then the rails looped south, proving a blessing for one of New Mexico's cultural treasures. Animal-drawn wagons heading west from Albuquerque might be disassembled, their wheels, axles, tang, and bed lashed on barges and ferried across the Rio Grande. Not so a thirty-five-ton Baldwin locomotive. No substantial bridge traversed the volatile river. And ten miles farther west there was the Rio Puerco to worry about, in those pre-dam days a more turbulent stream. So surveyors bent the line to reach the narrower crossing at Isleta Pueblo before lifting it northwestward and then hewing to the old Beale's Road on the 35th parallel that broke straight for Arizona and California.

The railroad's expansion and Albuquerque's boom encroached upon old Indian lands. As its detour dipped below the southern rim of Albuquerque's volcanic plateau, the AT&SF's slow-moving army of workers could not miss seeing depictions of masked faces and sheep and antelope etched by native hands into sun-varnished rock or scatters of broken black-and-white pottery and human bones poking out of old Indian burials. The slopes that drained runoff from the Sandias to the Rio Grande, and the stepped escarpments west of the river, preserved traces of Ancestral Pueblo lifeways

Scourge of the Western Pueblos: Nana, Apache raider and war chief.

that were more adapted to this high desert ecology than the Hispano colonies, Anglo cowtowns, or commercial railheads that replaced them.

Along Albuquerque's West Mesa, native ancestors of Day Break and his Pueblo classmates had hunted, camped, and created societies for upwards of twelve thousand years. Spared by the railroad's southern detour were the seventeen miles of today's Petroglyph National Monument, whose scratched images of hunted animals, sacred beings, and solar eclipses represent one of the greatest concentrations of aboriginal rock art in North America.

Less than ten miles from Day Break's classroom, a cluster of excavations in the 1930s revealed that from 8500 to 7500 BC, Indian bowmen chipped leaf-shaped stone points with a distinctive groove running their length and named for where they turned up first—Folsom, New Mexico. From long-cold fire pits also came evidence of their prey—shaggy-furred bison with huge crowns like Texas longhorns.

Following this so-called Paleo-Indian period, early Albuquerque Indians embellished their diets. Using stone basins and grinding rocks (usually called by their Spanish terms, *metate* and *mano*), they pulverized piñon nuts and grass seeds. Two thousand years before Europe's Christian era, Indian corn emerged as the Southwest's staple, cultivated by occupants of pit-house villages whose sunken floors were dug into western terraces overlooking the Rio Grande. By AD 400 squash and Mexican beans were added to a menu that included wild plants—lechuguilla, sotol, bear grass, yucca, and mesquite. Cotton for weaving and tobacco for smoking were cultivated as well.

Then commenced the steady evolution toward the Historic Pueblo lifestyle that Day Break experienced as a child. By AD 800 or thereabouts, their gardens had shifted closer to the river floodplain and were being watered via irrigation ditches. Their farmers occupied boxy houses that were walled with puddled adobe, roofed with beams, thatch, and mud, and eventually stacked up to two or more stories with shaded baskets or sunken pots serving as food lockers. The old, circular pit-house forms were transformed into ceremonial kivas.

Around 1300, from present-day Bernalillo down to Los Lunas, came the region's heyday as "the center of this old native kingdom," writes historian Marc Simmons, "which the Spaniards from the time of Coronado knew as the Province of Tiguex." Over the ensuing period, the architectural high

Pueblo Indian potters, from Acoma or Laguna, selling to train passengers.

points (at least those that archaeologists know about) were bracketed to the southwest by Pottery Mound along the Rio Puerco, with its seventeen ki-vas that contained nearly eight hundred murals, and to the north by Kuaua, or "Evergreen" in the Tewa language (today's Coronado National Monument, within the Bernalillo city limits).

Located less than twenty miles from Day Break's new school, this old village was supported by extensive gardens of corn, beans, squash, and cotton. Eventually the Evergreen community burgeoned into a twelve-hundred-room pueblo, containing three plazas, each with its own kivas. In one underground chamber archaeologists found walls that had been re-plastered eighty-five times, undoubtedly as part of key rituals. Some seven-teen of the layers, when unpeeled, featured murals depicting corn seeds, magical animals, Katsinas, clouds, and other sacred images. All of the paintings appeared directly ancestral to the visualized prayers for mois-ture, health, and well-being that Day Break had watched religious leaders like his father apply on kiva walls when he was growing up in Acoma.

In 1862, when the U.S. Congress pushed to charter the Transcontinen-tal Railroad, it openly vowed to "extinguish as rapidly as may be the Indian title" along its projected route. Now rumors reached Day Break's schoolyard about pueblo complaints over the lines cutting through their homelands. Upset when workers busted their irrigation channels and flooded their fields, at night the inhabitants of Isleta Pueblo ripped up the tracks. Irritated by the telegraph wires, Santo Domingo Indians cut them to pieces and made off with insulation fixtures. Extracting rights-of-way from Laguna and Acoma communities was not easy either. Their Anglo and Jewish advisers supported the easier access to goods, services, mail, and communication that trains would provide; the Jewish trader Solomon Bibo even hauled water for the rail crews (earning his family a lifetime free pass). But those were precisely the harbingers of change that conservative elders of both tribes opposed.

Each pueblo cut its own deal. After initially yanking out surveyors' stakes, Laguna stalled line construction through the village while it negotiated not only for a higher price but a deeper commitment from the railroad. Ultimately the AT&SF agreed to free transport for Laguna Indians, and a hiring priority for villagers willing to work for it.

The elders at Acoma were less compliant. To cripple the metal beast some medicine men buried in its path the same prayer sticks they used to magically deepen the arroyos that diverted summer monsoons to their cornfields. When Acoma's cacique learned of this he feared the maneuver would harm his people more than the monster, and ordered the sticks removed. To the Indians, Day Break recalled, "the engine and the train were supernatural," and they wondered what the beast wanted from them. "When they got the courage enough to come up close to the engine, they threw corn meal for prayers on it." Meanwhile, the rails lengthened at the rate of about a mile a day, inexorably heading toward Arizona and the Pacific.

More troubling to the Acoma and Laguna students in Albuquerque was other news. Not long after Day Break left home an Apache war party, over fifty warriors strong, slipped into Valencia County. Word was they were led by Nana, the Mimbreño raider who had taken up Victorio's mantle after his assassination in Mexico the previous year. First they hit Cienega, a half day's ride from Laguna Pueblo, and then struck Ojo Torribio and the El Rito Valley. They ransacked and burned ranches, butchered sheep to eat and scattered the rest, and killed or captured anyone in their path.

Locals like Pablo Pino, a Mexican wagoneer, and rancher Gregorio Montanio, peeked from hiding as the Apaches raised hell and moved on. At Laguna, fresh with memories of marauding Navajos, the menfolk mobilized, benefiting from the military training and new carbines provided by Colonel Marmon. But like most experienced guerrillas, the Apaches avoided open warfare. Swerving west, they murdered another sheepherder, kidnapped a Cubero woman, and took out a ranch at Cebolleta before slipping into Sonora. Day Break was relieved: Acomita had been spared, his parents were all right. No one knew it then, but this was the swan song of Apache outlawry in New Mexico.

Anglo railroad in, Apache raiders out. A modern day was dawning across the Southwest and within the worldview of one student at Albuquerque Indian School.

18

A New Secret (1881–83)

As New Town progressed, Old Town declined. The disparity between the two meant more than a New Town leaving its aging parent behind. Racial and ideological nuances permeated the split. An example of this was a statement during the early days of New Town's existence by the Albuquerque Morning Journal: *"The decadence of old Albuquerque is only additional proof of the fact that where the Anglo Saxon meets the Latin race, the latter falls behind and soon ceases competition."*

—Tomas Atencio, 2006

A T HIS DURANES SCHOOL, Day Break commenced a second series of initiations promoting the opposite of everything he'd learned back home and designed to repudiate those tribal attachments altogether. Rendered a blank slate by the loss of his long hair, homemade clothes, and as much skin tone as soap could wash away, now his body could be reinscribed with the trappings of civilization.

New identities called for new names. Day Break's came within one of the first shipments the freight trains brought to town. A trunk from Cleveland, Ohio, addressed to his school contained secondhand clothes designated for needy Indian students. In the side pocket of the coat from an especially large suit, Day Break felt a lump and pulled out a black book.

◆ ◆ ◆

In many Christian testimonies of religious conversion the inner turn-around takes effect only after what psychologist William James described as the traumatic crisis of a "divided self." This was when a struggle within the soul between the sins one knew one had committed and the confession that enabled redemption reached its catharsis. Some forms of "death" and "rebirth" were the only way out. For early Protestants committed to converting Indians, it was less personal misdeeds than the general misfortune of being born and raised Indian in the first place that required it. As in a class action suit, their brand of Christianity issued a condemnation against all Indians simply for being themselves; turning them into something else promised the only escape from their *aboriginal* sin.

Day Break's new institution, like most Indian schools, put a premium on religion. Theirs was not the laissez-faire approach that had come to characterize Catholic missions, with priests content for Pueblo Indians to go through the motions of chant, confession, and mass. Having learned from the All-Pueblo Revolt about the futility of suppressing native beliefs, the Franciscans looked the other way as parishioners disappeared into kivas that were off-limits to outsiders, held public dances at harvest time, imitated animals for hunting dances, and paid allegiance to spirit beings that controlled the weather and were propitiated by medicine men using prayer sticks and corn pollen.

Not so the mostly Protestant superintendents who oversaw many of the post–Civil War "industrial" boarding schools. No historical defeats had weakened their zealotry. Day Break said grace before meals, knelt in prayer by his bunk at bedtime, sang English hymns in choir two or three times a week. Sundays began with lengthy church services, and students were required to memorize biblical slogans plastered across classroom walls. Before this it was said that the only good Indian was a dead one; now he could be a Protestant.

In the colonial period New England clerics molded good Indians by quarantining them from heathenism and the temptations of a lawless frontier. In the mid-seventeenth century, fourteen of these islands of Christian indoctrination, known as "Praying Towns," were established in Massachusetts by pastor John Eliot. One person whose ancestors lived close by one of these compounds was Mary Rice, who would marry a Civil War veteran named Edward Proctor Hunt. The son of a farmer and prosperous real estate agent from Cleveland, Edward became a grade school

Teachers of new ways: staff at Edward's school.

teacher before enlisting in the 105th Ohio Infantry during the Civil War. Although briefly taking up law after the war, in 1865 he established a successful hardware firm that he ran for over half a century, and in 1869 he wed the daughter of a prominent local family.

Strong believers in public education and members of the Woodland Avenue Presbyterian Church, where they conducted Sunday school for eleven years, Mary and Edward Hunt sat in their pews one Sunday as a charismatic visitor, the evangelist-adventurer Sheldon Jackson, extolled his New Mexico crusade. Especially proud of a new Albuquerque Indian school, Jackson listed its needs. The Hunts went home and responded.

From his donated coat Day Break drew a Bible that contained a personal note. Whoever received this book, it said, could take its donor's name. Most of Acoma Pueblo's traditional names derived from the cycle of days and seasons and plant life. When these Indian boys were enrolled in school they were often renamed after famous generals, presidents, and other historical figures—Washington, Sherman, Grant, and Julius Caesar. His was different. From that day forward he would be known as Edward Proctor Hunt, the first public symbol of his new way of life.

The Day Break who had arrived in Albuquerque had internalized his people's cultural lessons. Back home his age-mates had been taught through the oral traditions that accompanied their tribal initiations. These were reinforced by sacred terms in their native language, place-names in the landscape, and symbolic drawings on pottery and woven garments and murals in their kivas. Back there the sun and the seasons governed life. Their importance was interpreted by experienced elders and internalized through story, song, dance, initiation, and ceremony.

Now those former teachings were submerged beneath new symbols and lessons about how to be and behave in the world. In place of a traditional universe divided into eight levels—four beneath and four above—the Protestants offered a simpler cosmology: heaven, earth, and hell. Its code was communicated through written words embodied in a sacred book. Unlike in Catholicism, every believer had access to this book, and daily worship and work would be timed through a disc on the wall that ruled the hours of the day.

Concerning Edward's *internal* conversion we have no direct testimony. In eighteenth-century New England, fresh Indian converts were pressured into publicly confessing their repudiation of Indian sins and embrace of Christianity. Formulaic expressions of faith were considered more sincere if accompanied by breast-beating and flowing tears. But Pueblo Indians appeared less prone to emotional displays, and Edward was no exception.

Later in life he possibly hinted at one strategy for coexisting in Indian and white worlds. His friend and collaborator, anthropologist Leslie White, wrote about an anonymous informant from Acoma Pueblo, who was almost certainly Hunt. The man confessed that he no longer believed in his people's Katsinas or the powers of their medicine men, and admitted following the "Cristo."

Then he shared a recent dream. He was standing before God, who was seated in an office "just as in a bank" and dressed as a successful American Indian businessman. "Where's your license," God asked, "your right to enter heaven?" When the Indian brandished his Bible, the Almighty responded, "That's not your license. This is," and held up a traditional Acoma prayer stick. The Good Book, He insisted, was the white man's "license." For the rest of his life Hunt used "breath feathers" to bless the Indian names he bestowed upon his children and grandchildren, but kept a Bible by his bed and made sure his clock was visible.

Perhaps Hunt adopted the same sort of clean separation between

Living by new rules: boys' dining hall at Edward's school.

Indian and non-Indian domains and allegiances that anthropologist Edward Spicer said was distinctive to Pueblo societies in general. This approach allowed for a tentative coexistence between contradictory political and religious systems. As a Pueblo Indian whose immediate family would one day become its own transient little world, maybe Edward was learning to do the same.

Day Break's whole or partial adoption of the Protestant ethic may have gone uncelebrated, but not Albuquerque's welcome to the modernization that it fostered. Completion of the country's second transcontinental railroad line changed everything. Whereas horse-drawn stagecoaches raced for two to three weeks to get from Kansas City to the Rio Grande, now it took fifty hours. Almost overnight, the fabled Santa Fe Trail became history.

The town's coming-out party opened on an October weekend in 1881. It took the form of a harvest and renewal ceremony that was fast becoming an American staple—the regional fair. Whether territorial, county, state, or national in scale, these displays balanced reverence for the traditional with enthusiasm for the innovative. Fairs mediated between nostalgia for a pioneering era that was hardly past and welcome to a future of such marvels as steam power, electricity, and the telegraph. At state and local levels the fairs included agricultural and livestock exhibits, competitions in crafts and athletics, and the display of living products of modernity, such as the ranks of uniformed Indian students marching in time to their school bands.

To signal their emerging commercial and political prominence, Albuquerque's civic leaders, like Judge William Hazeldine, flour mill magnate Franz Huning, and the mercantile Ilfeld brothers, had organized this Agricultural, Mineral and Industrial Exposition. Eager to attract business, highlight civic values, and hasten statehood, the affair celebrated what the Hispano families of Old Town dreaded about the Anglo presence. What complicated the self-promotion of southwestern towns like Albuquerque was that they had multiple "pasts" that looked and spoke so differently. Huning helped draft the fair's slogan: "Civilization of the 19th century and Civilization of Prehistoric Times." This foreshadowed the priority of American Indians to the region's tourist industry and the demotion of Hispanos in the pages of its written history.

Amid a thunderstorm, on October 3, 1881, Governor Lionel Sheldon opened up five days of speeches, baseball games, drills by local militia—such as the Laguna Pueblo Indian Guards under Colonel Walter Marmon—Indian dances, and footraces. Up went a public notice: those "creating a disturbance are liable to be shot on sight."

The exposition was held at the newly designated fairgrounds just north and west of today's intersection of Central and Rio Grande. At the time, only the grandstand had been built, so the exhibits of produce and livestock were housed in canvas tents that high winds soon blew into the sky. Yet the drenched visitors filled the site and packed the fence around a half-mile racetrack as sulkies and jockeys tore up the mud. By the fair's second year, the town fathers had acquired a permanent venue, just west of Old Town, along Railroad Avenue, and almost extending to the Rio Grande.

Edward Hunt joined the Indian students, wearing uniforms they'd ironed themselves, who marched before cowboys, orchard keepers, ranchers, civic boosters, Navajo, Apache, Ute, and Pueblo onlookers, bearded Hispano caballeros, Jewish merchants, thieves, drunks, and an over-dressed clutch of "soiled doves of the demimonde."

What Edward made of all this is anybody's guess. Where's the youth that doesn't love a fair or marching down Main Street? Yet the underlying values it promoted may have filtered into his consciousness and reinforced the cultural conversion already under way. As fairs were a means for new railroad towns like Albuquerque to celebrate their modernizing selves, marching in them may have meant that he internalized that progressive spirit as well.

Albuquerque was growing up. Mule-drawn streetcars ran along Railroad Avenue (today's Central Avenue), connecting the two parts of town, with a spur to the Barelas bridge. Two years later, her Anglo wheelers and dealers had an ulterior motive for raising $4,300 to purchase sixty-six acres of what one writer described as "high, dry sand which grows cactus, loco weed and is filled with rattlesnake holes" for a more permanent Indian school. Their strategy was not unlike that which had caused Spain to nail down its southwestern claims with land-grant colonies and garrison outposts. The site of the Menaul Indian School staked out a northern perimeter that allowed for the expansion of their Anglo-dominated New Town.

Bent on becoming Albuquerque's city fathers, the newcomers summoned surveyor Marmon from Laguna Pueblo to map and name New Town's grid of streets and sever them from the rambling, country feel of Catholic Old Town. An aggressive Anglo future was consigning the Hispano presence to a quaint yesteryear and poisoning the region's ethnic relations for decades to come.

19

New Tribe in the Desert (1883–85)

In 1869 I was living in Cebolleta; I had been at Ft. Wingate and was on a visit to Cebolleta, when a delegation of Indians from the Pueblo of Laguna called upon me, complaining of the great difficulty they had in their pueblo, and requested me to help them. It was kind of a religious strife. I am of Jewish descent, and they wanted to become what I was. They wanted to belong to my religion. I told them it could not be.

—Nathan Bibo, 1924

BEFORE FATE threw Edward Hunt and Solomon Bibo into the same family they were surely acquainted. Over the 1870s the Jewish merchant showed up on the mesa with increasing frequency, even before his translating role for school recruiters got Edward to his Albuquerque school in the first place. Later in life, when Edward recalled Solomon as his "first young white friend," he possibly meant his first awareness of a new brand of relationship as well.

For some Indian youth, boarding schools offered their earliest exposure to broad categories like "friend," or even "Indian." Back home a shared language and traditions made fellow tribespeople all the company and support one needed. Social and emotional needs were normally satisfied through blood and marriage. Within a tiny, tight-knit community like Acoma it was rare to find anyone who wasn't some sort of relative or affiliate in some social or religious group.

But the boarding school experience revealed that not only might one get along with members of foreign or even enemy tribes. A few could become lifelong buddies; conceivably, you could even marry one. Relying on fellow students in this alien environment also foreshadowed the broader bond they would share as "Indians" once they entered the Anglo world. That ethnic consciousness, later given the cover term "pan-Indian," provided a foundation for national movements and religious alliances in the century to come.

Day Break's older friend and future mentor was, from all accounts, a highly intelligent (which local anti-Semites would inevitably characterize as "shrewd"), hot-tempered, garrulous extrovert whose popular title would one day become "Jewish Indian Chief." Born in 1853 in Brakel, Prussia, Solomon Bibo was the sixth child of Isaac Bibo and Blumenchen Rothstein, who eventually raised eleven. A schoolteacher, the eighth generation in his family's lineage of rabbis and cantors, Isaac had good reason to worry about the spell cast over his sons by his own father-in-law's yarns. To avoid being drafted, in 1821 Blumenchen's father, at age sixteen, fled to America. He spent eight years among Pennsylvania's Quakers before returning home for his wife, who balked at further overseas adventures. But his son, Joseph, inherited his wanderlust and landed in Santa Fe, only to fall ill and be buried in the town's Odd Fellows Cemetery.

By 1865 the Bibos' onetime Prussian neighbors, the Spiegelberg clan, had cornered New Mexico Territory's postwar military market. Trains of their ox-drawn wagons supplied outlying forts like Wingate and Canby. Fifteen years later, they had advanced from being wagon barons to store princes. As Santa Fe's preeminent merchants, they operated out of a spacious two-story establishment on the plaza (and occupied a mansion a few streets away). Like so many Jewish émigrés, they utilized a transatlantic Jewish "chain" by which established families helped relatives or *landsman* (Yiddish for fellow Jews from Eastern Europe) like the Bibos to gain purchase in the Southwest. By 1850, half of New Mexico's Jews were related, and shared sufficient social, religious, and economic customs so as to create a mutual aid network.

Isaac Bibo's own boys itched for adventure. In the late 1860s the aging rabbi watched them leave home one by one. First was Simon, sailing to New York in 1866. Interning with the Spiegelbergs in New York, he learned numbers, rudimentary English, and the fundamentals of frontier commerce. Simply put, that meant raw goods derived from the hunt, the pasture, the ranch, and the mines, shipped east in exchange for manufactured goods like nails, dyes, sugar, coffee, and shovels to be freighted west.

Reaching St. Louis by train, Simon joined a wagon caravan on the Santa Fe Trail. After a second year's stint with the Spiegelbergs, picking up Spanish and becoming an efficient, courteous clerk, in 1868 he branched out. A year later arrived Nathan, the most colorful Bibo, with his adventures in Dinetah (Navajo country); riding shotgun on Concord stagecoaches, delivering corn to army forts, being rescued by Apaches from a blinding snowstorm, surviving close calls with pistol-wielding outlaws, and early ranching in the Gallup area, not to mention his penchant for gambling and eye for the ladies.

To avoid choking Santa Fe with competition—five Jewish firms, brothers and in-laws, were soon thriving there—the Spiegelbergs persuaded (or dispatched) the Bibo brothers to serve their interests farther afield. Perhaps a class distinction lurked here as well: the cultivated, urbane Spiegelbergs sending the more rustic Bibos to the frontier. Eventually, Nathan ran the Spiegelbergs' military contracts in Navajo country, which saw him blazing the Zuni–Fort Wingate Road. By 1872, however, he was set up as Bernalillo's storekeeper and postmaster, while Simon won his trading license for Laguna Pueblo in 1871, and opened a more durable home-store in Grants around 1880, where he was instrumental in arranging the rail-road's right-of-way. Toward the close of the nineteenth century, the Bibo boys were managing half a dozen trading posts along the territory's western edge.

When Solomon left Bremen, Germany, on October 26, 1869, their father's heart was breaking. Emil, last of his eleven children to go, never forgot the sight of the old man in tears behind the windowpane. During his obligatory New York City and Santa Fe apprenticeships, Solomon proved quicker at Spanish than English. In February 1875 he swore to U.S. citizenship in Santa Fe, and over the next five years schooled himself in the territory's cultural mosaic.

Learning the lay of western New Mexico meant identifying its zones of power and influence. Fundamental to the Bibos' fortunes was the business milieu centered on the Spiegelbergs in Santa Fe, which drew upon the shared trading habits of the wider coalition of Jewish family enterprises in Las Vegas, Bernalillo, and Albuquerque. As with other ethnic diasporas circulating through the global economy, when families of traders migrated to yonder shores, New Mexican Jews on the receiving end were mutually supportive. They devised ways to minimize competition among themselves while maximizing trade with other nationalities by carving out separate sales territories and clientele.

Inside the city of Santa Fe, Solomon grew aware of a second power center in ascendance in the 1880s. This was the informal network of Anglo lawyers, judges, politicians, ranchers, and newspaper magnates who were labeled, and feared, as the Santa Fe Ring. One can imagine Willi Spiegelberg tooling Solomon around the plaza, pointing out a portly, steely-eyed thirtysomething in a three-piece suit and mustache named Thomas Benton Catron.

When his background as a Confederate officer barred him from lawyering in his native Missouri, at age twenty-five Catron headed west, turned Republican, and struck gold when he realized how many old Spanish land grants he could amass by any means necessary. Private lands, village-style "common lands," mining claims, livestock pasturage, railroad shares, timber lands, water rights—his Ring wanted them all. Characterized as "crusty, blunt, energetic and domineering," Catron, and his cronies, especially his less abrasive but equally sharp law partner, Stephen

The Bibo brothers from Germany. Left to right: *Samuel, Simon, Emil, Nathan, Solomon.*

"Smooth Steve" Elkins, replaced the hell-raising gunslingers of the post–Civil War era with a breed of robber baron whose professional and political roles raised them to the level of semirespectability.

Unlike the Jewish merchants, the Ring sought bottomless wealth, overweening political power, and endless acreage. They dominated New Mexico politics and commerce for another forty years. Avarice this extreme, as Solomon probably did not need the Speigelbergs to warn him, was never a smart move for their tribe. Simmering beneath many southwestern communities where Jews carved out their mercantile and banking roles was envy and its ever-ready expression, anti-Semitism. While a visitor to Santa Fe in 1884, the professional soldier and ethnographer John Gregory Bourke, bemoaned the town's "motley crew of hook-nosed Jews," most Anglo merchants grumbled more circumspectly how competitors of the "Hebrew persuasion" undersold or outflanked them. Solomon learned to stay apolitical, but risked forgetting the other lesson about the dangers of unfettered land lust.

By the 1890s Catron had amassed over two million acres from nearly eighty land grants. This made him, rumor had it, America's largest landowner. It also positioned him as a prime candidate for New Mexico senator once it gained statehood in 1912. Shortly thereafter, a second incarnation of the Ring turned its attention to vulnerable Pueblo Indian lands.

Venturing outside of Santa Fe acquainted Solomon with a third, older source of ethnic rootedness and cultural influence in western New Mexico. This was the unorganized group of elite Hispano families who for a generation or more had presided over their small, often isolated villages or rural barrios. Wherever sufficient springs, adequate pasturage, and irrigable creek and river bottoms allowed secluded ranchos to evolve into *colonias* of Hispano-Catholic culture, he found doors open and *ricos* like Manuel Chaves of San Mateo, Ramon Baca of Cebolleta, and Monico Mirabal of San Rafael ready to invite him in.

Some of these few dozen families had overseen their enclaves for more than a century; others only settled in once Mexico took over the territory in 1822. Evacuating their homesteads whenever Navajo or Apache raids got too close, then reoccupying them when the danger passed, they shared a rich song and storytelling tradition, a folk Catholicism that included the Comanche Dance and other conquest-and-resistance dance dramas, colorful Christmas celebrations, especially the intense Semana Santa, or Easter Week, observances, and spiritual governance by the secretive, lay brotherhoods who convened in narrow, windowless structures called *moradas*.

By the late 1870s the Indian threat against these villages subsided, thanks to crackdowns by U.S. troops and their Indian allies. Visitors to these self-sufficient outposts with their adobe houses all facing small plazas, their rear walls backed like stiff shoulders against the outer world, their folk chapels, attached cemeteries, and circular *torreones* serving as lookout towers, were welcomed, like Solomon, into an Old World code of hospitality. For their part, his Hispano hosts realized that, unlike Catron and his kind, these Jewish merchants were after trade, not real estate. Thus ties of a utilitarian, even personal nature often ensued. Besides, some of these same Hispano pioneers descended from Jewish escapees from the Inquisition, who survived as outward converts (*conversos*) to Catholicism but privately preserved Judaic customs.

With a fourth power center, the cluster of intermarried Anglo-Indians based at Laguna Pueblo, the Bibos had less in common. Among these Protestant families, ethnic prejudices lay closer to the surface. Furthermore, the Marmon, Pradt, and Gunn families were likely competitors for the same local customers. Their primary alliance with Acoma's frequent antagonist, Laguna Pueblo, also put them at odds with the Bibos.

As the fifth and farthest-flung of the region's power centers, the pueblo of Acoma was regarded as the hardest for white outsiders to crack. Yet Solomon envisioned its mesa-top site as a commercial opportunity. Flying in the face of their reputation as the most xenophobic of pueblos, Acoma's elders responded in kind. Maybe this uncommon alliance occurred because Jews displayed little of the anti-Indian prejudice that marked the Southwest's Civil War vets, border ruffians, conservative politicians, and even newspaper editors. As if to equal his mentor Willi Spiegelberg, who reportedly spoke four Indian dialects, along with his native German and Yiddish, Solomon also became conversant in Spanish, broken English, Acoma Keresan, Laguna Keresan, Navajo, Zuni, and possibly Apache.

Then there was the subtle significance of what these German-accented traders seemed *un*interested in. Much as Acoma Indians had no desire to adopt Anglos into their culture, Jews were not inclined to convert them to the Torah or teach them Hebrew. After so many years of whites telling them how to live, that may have come as a relief. Lastly, Jews proved flexible about doing business the Indian way, which meant taking sheep as collateral, extending loans, bartering, and developing one-on-one trade partnerships.

These power centers intersected in tangled ways. In 1877 Pueblo Indian agent Ben Thomas tried roping Catron, then a U.S. district attorney, into siding with Laguna Pueblo against Acoma in the tribes' long-standing

A patriarch: Martin Valle, grandfather of Juana and Marie Valle, seven times governor of Acoma.

border dispute. But nine years later it was Catron who drew up Acoma's petition for reviewing and revising those very boundaries. To counter the influence of the Marmons at Laguna, the Bibo brothers lobbied on behalf of Acoma's rights and won repeated land surveys in 1876, 1877, and 1881, culminating with a supposedly definitive patent of 95,792 acres allotted to the tribe in 1884.

Solomon's on-the-job training as trader and culture broker did not neglect his personal interests. Increasingly he hung around one cluster of adobe rooms on Acoma mesa's east side. This was the family compound of Martin Valle, six or seven times governor of the pueblo, and his Antelope Clan associates, the community's leading body. Through them Solomon maneuvered the unthinkable. Despite opposition from Anglos and Hispanics alike, in April 1882 he won a trader's license and opened a general store up on the mesa.

The venue featured readier access to corrals, pack animals, and foot traffic arriving up the Padre's Trail. Intentional or not, its location was also symbolic—a vacant room on the convent's second floor attached to St. Stephen's Church. This produced quite the spectacle—frontier capitalism in perhaps its purist form as introduced by a Jewish entrepreneur now sat atop the Southwest's largest monument of pioneer Catholicism within what may have been the oldest American Indian city-state in the Western Hemisphere, which was governed by a pre-Christian theocracy. With longer stays on the mesa and Solomon's intensified role as the tribe's unofficial adviser also came his deepening interest in one of Martin's attractive granddaughters, Juana.

Such was the stew of ethnic groups, economic interests, religious affiliations, and personal alliances that surrounded Edward upon his release from Albuquerque Indian School for a summer vacation in the spring of 1884, and that Solomon was discovering around the same time. Already their paths had crossed, and soon would converge. And one wonders, as Edward watched the Bibo families successfully relying on each other over the next decade, whether a third social category joined "friend" and "Indian" in his consciousness.

Whether or not Edward ever heard the Yiddish word *mishpucha*, witnessing the Bibo brothers in action must have communicated the possibility of what it meant—extended and often dispersed families who could survive as independent units, help each other out, feel free to move about as opportunity dictated, and periodically unite to celebrate themselves and their heritage. No doubt Acoma Pueblo possessed family and clan support systems. But their powers were strongest on their rocky citadel, and diminished in proportion to their distance from it. For these Jewish entrepreneurs, at least, the operative distinction was their *mobility,* and relative freedom from any hub or homeland. For the Jew, writes George Steiner, "does well to keep his bags discreetly packed. . . . No city is not worth leaving if it succumbs to injustice." Perhaps this exposure to a survival strategy for those who believed that "the truth is always in exile" also allowed Edward to imagine that, if the necessity arose, he could create such an independent unit of his own.

20

Home for the Summer (1884–85)

Polingaysi had not been home long before she began to be restless and unhappy. Her cooking prowess was unappreciated. More often than not she was the only one who cared to eat the fancy pies and cakes she baked. . . . She had been torturing herself with questions. Did she belong in the white man's world, or should she try to cast aside her learning and return to the easy old ways? Insecure in spite of her progress in school, she wavered unhappily between her two worlds, never seeming to belong entirely to either.

—P. Qoyawayma, Hopi, 1964

ONE MORNING THAT JUNE the student who still had to think a second whenever a school official called out "Edward" tossed his secondhand suitcase onto a Santa Fe flatcar. Bouncing on the day's only westbound train, he was headed home for his first break in three years. Coming out of the smoky haze of Albuquerque the train clacked south to Isleta. Edward caught flashes of the Rio Grande paralleling the tracks as they crossed a trestle, took on water and passengers, and briefly swung north before turning west at Los Lunas.

Having been away for so long, Edward saw things with fresh eyes. With the advent of private railroads and new government policies, there were new things to see. When the whistle sounded and the train halted in the middle of Old Laguna, he witnessed the birth of a new economy. Some of the cowled women waiting near the rails he recognized by name. Through open windows they handed painted ceramic pots to strangers. In return they received not sheep or buckskins but silver coins and printed paper.

No longer bartering with fellow Indians for water-bearing *ollas* and bread-dough bowls that they hand-coiled from clay, the women began producing them as souvenirs for white strangers passing through. In a way this was a godsend. Manufactured kitchen wares from the white world, like enameled metal pitchers and bowls, were already replacing clay vessels in pueblo kitchens. Now the same railroad that imported those goods brought these customers eager for their older wares. Colloquially called "potteries" in Pueblo-English, they became central to an emergent native enterprise, and a major revenue source over the century ahead. For tourists, painted pueblo pots were proof on the mantelpiece, the glass case or the "Indian corner," that western journeys had been undertaken, real Indians encountered, and, for more discerning travelers, an ancient genre of indigenous American art discovered. It did not take long for pueblo potters to adapt to this market, turning out both more portable, smaller pots, clay figurines, and vases with long necks modeled after glassware, as well as larger, more heavily painted pots, and then exchanging the proceeds for household staples from local trading posts run by outsiders like the Bibos and Marmons.

Five times the train dropped and picked up passengers before reaching McCartys, leaving more coal grit in Edward's teeth with each stop. Eighty-five miles from Albuquerque he leapt off the train at the Alaska stop and walked to Acomita. At least here he would be buffered from the daily scrutiny of his mother mesa, about fourteen miles to the south. To ponder his new double life as the Acoma Indian Day Break and the Albuquerque school student Edward Hunt, and read his Bible without drawing critical scowls, Edward made himself scarce. The best excuse for doing that was herding his mother's brother's sheep on the east-sloping pastures of sacred Mount Taylor.

Because Pueblos stayed put and didn't raid whites, and in fact were not even officially "Indians," the government's campaign to suppress their traditions was not as intrusive as among Plains tribes. Often enjoying a certain lag time in imposition of government policies, the pueblos would not confront that threat for another forty years. Still, with Pueblo phobias about cultural contamination, acceptable penetration by foreigners was always a matter of degree. Just as Edward was steering clear of censorious tribal elders, so was the vulnerable population of Acoma, by now up to just under six hundred, increasingly nervous over inquisitive outsiders in their midst.

Two years earlier, in May 1882, Washington had allocated funds to "civilize" Pueblo Indians by hiring day-school teachers and appointing white "government farmers" who were to purchase new seeds and agricultural tools for them and oversee their work on irrigation ditches. The irony was that these agricultural agents were giving advice to Indians who had drawn life-sustaining crops out of this obstinate landscape for nearly a thousand years. Then a tougher personality, Pedro Sanchez of Taos, replaced Ben Thomas as regional U.S. Indian agent and outspokenly condemned native religion and social practices. Critical eyes were now poking into Acoma's backyard.

Juana Valle Bibo, wife of Solomon.

◆ ◆ ◆

Edward could not escape participation in all community doings, especially during summer's busy ritual season, when his father's duties as medicine man and sacred clown were in high demand. Both of these roles were supposedly secret identities, but the long absences from home gave him away. In July, during the month known as When Corn First Appears, the cacique watched where the sun rose on the horizon and set the date for the summer's Natyati Festival. This was Acoma's collective prayer for cloud-emptying monsoons, and when the mesa welcomed the fullest company of masked Katsina spirits into the plaza.

Now his father was gone for long nights in the kiva where he refurbished, fed, and smoked the Katsina masks made of buffalo hide to restore their powers. At home the corn-grinding activity stepped up, foods were stockpiled, pottery-making intensified. Four days prior to the Katsinas' arrival, his father disappeared altogether—he was celibate, fasted, meditated, prepared regalia, practiced old songs, and composed new verses.

One activity Edward enjoyed free from any internal conflict was the collective hunt for enough rabbits to fill stewpots during the upcoming feast day. He happily joined the brush-beaters as they fanned across the valley bottom. Encircling the swarms of darting, hopping creatures, like closing a drawstring purse they tightened together until they were close enough to club them senseless. Then they lined the furry carcasses on the ground for a collective blessing—the sprinkling of cornmeal and prayers of thanks.

Sleeping overnight on the rooftops, before sunrise Edward joined the rest of the crowd as they waited for the Katsinas to emerge from around St. Stephen's. Sixty or so strong, some of them milled about in identically masked and attired companies of a dozen or more, while others arrived as individuals.

At this point Edward underwent two kinds of recognition. It had been three years since his last Natyati Festival, but among the Katsina roster he could identify the knobby-masked Messengers, who joked and threatened anyone getting too close. He was familiar with the contingents of Mountain Sheep, Crow, and Duck Katsinas, and knew others by their masks, painting, attire, and regalia. Yet it was hard to ignore the identities of neighbors and relatives he could recognize from boyhood by their distinctive movements, vocal patterns, or familiar scars. He went along with the

At entrance to Acoma, Solomon Bibo presides.

performance, even when he knew that behind the sacred clown's mud-stiffened corn-husk hairdo, black-ringed eyes and mouth, and horizontal stripes of dark body paint was his own parent. For the greater good, Edward joined in the collective suspension of disbelief—or more accurately, the fullest embrace of cultural membership.

But as the Katsinas shuffled counterclockwise through the dance stations that effectively blessed all neighborhoods atop the mesa, this was no longer *his* father. Nor for that matter were any of the other impersonators anybody else's recognizable relatives. The potency of this imagined reunion of living and dead Acomans counted on unquestioned consensus by the community and absolute containment from outsiders.

Throughout the summer Edward played cat-and-mouse with his homeland. He merged with onlookers at the frantic rooster pulls of the San Juan, San Pedro, and San Diego fiestas, but went missing during their associated rituals. He was nowhere to be found when the initiated sequestered in ki-vas before the summer and fall Katsina appearances to repair masks and regalia, and was absent when clan-mates went to gather the rain-inducing spruce boughs for their dances.

His caution was warranted. Whenever Edward was in the public eye he couldn't ignore the disapproving glances at his clipped hair and laced, hard leather shoes and the half-English phrases he exchanged with Jim Miller or other school returnees. Using conspicuously loud voices, people in a crowd called him out in Keresan, "Day Break," as if by this indirect Pueblo style of public reproof they were reminding him who he truly was, or at least who he should be around here. Though few in number, his cote-rie of "schoolboys" was monitored like a cell of subversives who might con-taminate the mesa.

At the same time, outsiders like Agent Sanchez were also appraising their reentry. Sanchez worried how these Albuquerque and Carlisle schoolkids, "the pride of every man that appreciates education and desires the welfare of these Indians," would handle "the gross ignorance so deeply rooted in their people" when they returned home. Torn as they were be-tween these opposing expectations and demands, for Edward and his fel-low students something was bound to snap.

Complicating Acoma's internal affairs that summer was its debate over what to do about "Don Solomono." Were the Jewish storekeeper asked to name the year that changed his life, chances are he would have cited 1884–85. By then Solomon Bibo's standing in Acoma was high, his ties to former governor Martin Valle and his circle of clan members and supporters never stronger. So why did he get embroiled in a controversy that tested those bonds and cast a shadow over his reputation?

No sooner had Bibo's counseling efforts on Acoma's behalf helped to force the U.S. government to confirm the pueblo's rights to her full land base than the trader turned around and, under Martin Valle's approving signature, helped himself to leasing that entire territory for thirty years. He even added exclusive rights to graze animals, control water, and mine for coal. For rent Solomon would pay Acoma Pueblo $300 for the first ten years, $400 for the next ten, and $500 for the final decade, plus ten cents a ton for any coal.

Had the greedy behavior of the robber barons of the Santa Fe Ring rubbed off? Did Bibo collude with an Anglo cattle company that wanted more pasturage to pad his own pocket? Or, as the Bibo brothers argued, was it a preemptive strike against the Marmons of Laguna, who had their eye on just such a lease but under less favorable terms? Upon learning of Solomon's deal, and fearing renewed pressure on Laguna to return disputed acreage to Acoma, the Marmons cursed it as an "infernal, damnable, high handed outrage."

As a Hispano and a Catholic, Pedro Sanchez, the fifty-one-year-old man who'd replaced Ben Thomas as U.S. Pueblo agent in 1882, was an odd choice in a region where the authority of Anglo-Protestants was on the rise. Born in Acoma's Valencia County prior to the Treaty of Guadalupe Hidalgo, Sanchez had moved to Ranchos de Taos with his family when he was six. As a youth he fell under the spell of its charismatic prelate, Don Antonio José Martinez. During the Civil War, Sanchez commanded a group known as "Antelope Hunters," Union volunteers who eventually suffered defeat under Major Edward Canby at the battle of Valverde in 1862. Once the invading Texas Confederates were driven out, however, Sanchez's war record boosted him into various political offices, where he acquired some celebrity as a champion of the underprivileged.

Although it was in a Catholic ceremony that he married his first wife, Refugio, favored niece to Father Martinez, Sanchez reputedly "flirted" with Protestantism, or at least with its progressive principles. His annual reports as Indian agent suggest that this sympathy intensified between his first and second years on the job, when he bonded closer with the Marmon, Gunn, and Pradt faction at Laguna, whom his first report in 1883 praised as "business [inclined], well-to-do, honest men."

That first year Sanchez characterized the Pueblo Indians under his authority in benign terms, even citing reclusive, wary Acoma Pueblo as "in good health . . . and disposed to learn." By his next annual report in 1884, however, the tone had darkened: "I am, indeed, extremely sorry to state that these Pueblos, with but two exceptions, ie. Laguna and Isleta . . . are debased and idiotized by the effects of ignorance, indolence and superstition." Sanchez's diatribe singled out Pueblo kids "who attend no school, but are growing in idleness . . . and amusing themselves with the most obscene and repugnant dances, to the eyes of a civilized society; and this they call a 'sacred tradition' that they must carry on to their posterity untouched."

◆ ◆ ◆

As the Bibo controversy erupted that spring, Agent Sanchez grew infuri-
ated at Solomon's "complete and bold falsification" of his lease document
with Acoma. After huddling with the Marmons he called a meeting at the
other Acoma satellite, McCartys. What transpired there became grist for a
flurry of communiqués between Washington and Albuquerque. Sanchez
begged the U.S. attorney to "compel Solomon Bibo to vacate his lease and
remove his property and employees from Acoma." He told Commissioner
of Indian Affairs Hiram Price that he'd warned Governor Valle and the
sixty Acomans in attendance to "Look out for that Solomon Bibo and his
band . . . [they are] clad of sheep but rapacious wolves." Getting in Solomon's face, he ordered, "You have no right to speak, sit down! If you don't
take that lease back immediately the government will punish you severely!"

But another witness to the gathering, Solomon's brother Simon, claimed
that only half that number had attended and no interpreter was provided.
He also maintained that Martin Valle's son informed Sanchez that his father actually accepted the Bibo lease. When Sanchez produced a statement
from Valle disavowing the agreement, Simon Bibo tried another tack. Exploiting a wedge between government holdovers from the days of the Indian Wars and the softer-hearted reformers of the post-Grant era, Simon
independently contacted the Board of Indian Commissioners. Set up by the
U.S. Congress in 1869, this body of ten overseers had been charged with
auditing books and uprooting corruption across Indian country. Simon
wrote that his brother's "intentions with these Indians are of the best nature
and beneficial to them."

Ultimately winning a vote of confidence from Acoma's elders, Solomon
narrowly weathered the crisis, although he nullified his lease in 1887. Sanchez was swiftly replaced. Whatever news of the imbroglio reached young
Edward, their friendship also survived. Solomon's passion for schooling
the pueblo's young remained undiminished; he soon constructed a new
day school for Acomita and installed one of his own store clerks, Andres
Montoya, as its teacher. That summer he even hired Edward to haul rocks
for its walls, harden its dirt floor with ox blood, and with his new carpentry skills build benches for its students.

When Edward returned to Albuquerque in the fall a replacement Indian
School building funded by her city fathers was also under construction. This
called for a way of brickmaking that was new to Edward and the region—no

longer "burning bricks" in the sun but in great ovens. His new term also brought a new breed of student, Ute boys from northern New Mexico's Four Corners area whom Edward recalled as "tough guys" who wouldn't let anyone touch their long hair. Where Edward's thinking would have stood after continued exposure to such rebels we do not know, since once he returned home the following summer he never went back to that school.

As for Solomon, by following the same avenue by which his Anglo-Protestant rivals had deepened their ties and authority at Laguna Pueblo, he strengthened his at Acoma Pueblo. On May 1, 1885, in St. Stephen's Church atop Acoma mesa, a Catholic priest married the Jewish merchant Solomon Bibo and Juana Valle, granddaughter of kiva elder and former Acoma governor, Martin Valle. Witnessed by presiding Acoma governor José Berrendo, in a ceremony interpreted by Andres Ortiz, the union was verified with a postritual certificate. To leave no stone unturned, four months later Solomon and Juana rode their buggy to San Rafael where a Valencia County justice of the peace held the ceremony a second time, sealing the bond on the New Mexico Territory registry.

This alliance secured for the Bibo children clan membership at Acoma. It set Solomon up for unprecedented leadership in tribal affairs. And it brought Edward a valuable in-law when times got rough, as they surely would.

21

Return to the Padres (1887)

The white man's religion never overtook their beliefs in their Indian ceremonials. I received a very good answer to this not many years ago when I asked a Catholic priest who has said mass at the Catholic church at Acoma for over twenty years [Father Fridolin Schuster] how many of the Indians on the Acoma reservation would he consider real Catholics, and he said, to this date not one.

—Wolf Robe Hunt, n.d.

THE NEXT TIME Edward Hunt crossed the Rio Grande he was returning to a white man's school, but to a different one. In a way he was
backsliding. Not "back to the blanket," as Protestants disparaged their former students who returned to tribal communities and pre-Christian, "pagan" ways. This was only halfway back, to the earlier style of missionary
Catholicism that had been a fixture of his childhood years.

Like the Protestant recruiters who'd visited Acoma five years earlier,
now a Catholic priest from Santa Fe showed up at Acomita to make his
pitch. Quite possibly the visitor who traveled there in the fall of 1885 was
Father Joseph A. Stephan, a full-bearded Benedictine nicknamed the
"Fighting Priest" for his opposition to Protestant-run schools. He reminded the Indians of their long détente with the brown-robed friars who,
except for monthly appearances to baptize and marry Indians, largely left
them alone. Edward recalled this Catholic outreach as igniting an anti-
Protestant "rebellion" among Acoma's "old folks." Following the visit, "My
parents didn't like that the Albuquerque mission was Presbyterian. They
thought I ought to go to a Catholic school. So in I went to St Catherine's in
Santa Fe."

We don't know whether Edward traveled by train to Albuquerque, then
wagoned along the river before zigzagging up La Bajada's switchbacks to
the Santa Fe plateau, or took a backcountry shortcut by horse or wagon,
covering the sagebrush flats of the Rio Puerco valley to cross the Jemez
River before following the Rio Grande north. Whichever route got him
there, the town he entered at the foot of the aspen-and-ponderosa-mantled
Sangre de Cristo Mountains was something of a throwback.

Strings of burros blocked Santa Fe's narrow streets. Their spines bent
under lashed piles of neatly cut juniper firewood, wobbling bundles of
green alfalfa, or oaken barrels slung off their ribs. Along the Santa Fe river-
bank lines of kneeling washerwomen slapped clothes on smooth boulders.
From the traffic of buckboards and surreys came the jingle of horse livery,
from the few remaining ox-drawn, wood-wheeled *carretas* a screeching of
ungreased axles. Half-wild dogs sniffed and padded through the garbage
and manure. Strummed guitars and drunken yells rang through the swinging doors of packed saloons and gambling halls.

Life in the old capital still revolved around her plaza. On all sides were
porticos whose old columnar supports had been recently replaced by

Catholic presence at Acoma: interior of San Estevan.

whitewashed milled lumber. Its function was already shifting from marketplace to town square, with a central, open park fenced by white pickets. Shading its radiating pathways, iron benches, tin-roofed bandstand, and military memorial were locust and maple trees.

A number of recently constructed two-story buildings now faced the plaza, dominating their older adobe neighbors. They boasted cast-iron columns, brick cornices, ornamental moldings, and large showcase windows. Up side streets a growing line of gable-roofed mansions were housing the town's up-and-coming professional class. On Palace Avenue rose the half-completed, stunted towers of Archbishop Lamy's ill-fitting legacy, the granite-block St. Francis Cathedral, that would never, to the relief of architectural traditionalists to come, be crowned by the Gothic steeples Lamy had always envisioned.

Heading toward the same foothill where Don Diego de Vargas had camped during his 1693 reconquest of the city after the All-Pueblo Revolt, Edward glimpsed the waning years of Santa Fe's diverse street life, which had just been profiled in *Harper's Magazine*: "gallant Fra-Diavolo-looking Spaniards from El Paso and Chihuahua; blue and gold army officers; negro soldiers, erect and self-satisfied; dirt-begrimed bull-whackers just in from

Las Vegas or Arizona; grizzled nervous-looking miners; natty clerks with Hebrew noses; and everywhere Mexicans in every stage of slothful ease or protesting make-shift to work; troops of slender dark-eyed women; and scant-clothed Indians out of the surrounding wilds."

More laid-back than modernizing Albuquerque, Santa Fe was hurting from the loss of its freighting business to that new hub. "This by-passing [by the railroad] was one of the most fortunate things that ever happened to the Ancient City," author Oliver La Farge could write in hindsight, "but at the time its inhabitants did not think so."

After 1910, the success of southwestern tourism and the salvation that Santa Fe's high mountain air promised eastern victims of pulmonary disease would turn the demographic and economic tide. But for the moment the elders of her thinning population of six thousand inhabitants were following Albuquerque's lead by seeking a $25,000 appropriation and hundred-acre site for a new Protestant Indian school to be located two miles south of the old plaza. Along with a new State Prison and School for the Deaf, they prayed these institutions might stem her decline.

After bad-mouthing the government's public schools, Father Stephan had pictured for the Acoma parents a new Catholic institution in Santa Fe that would stand many stories high. But in a repeat of his Albuquerque experience, Edward followed Santa Fe's northern irrigation ditch about a mile to Mount Vargas only to discover a stone foundation for a building still to come. Once again he and his fellow students were quartered in a crumbling adobe house, near the old Rosario Cemetery. Once again he split his days between molding adobe bricks and mortaring walls and buttresses for classrooms he was supposed to be sitting in, and reading books and doing math the rest of the time. By one year later, the fourth half-story had been completed on what is considered to be the tallest earthen building in New Mexico.

Secretly pledged to a Protestantism that blessed with oil, Edward Hunt was returning to communicants his tribe called "wet heads" for baptizing with water. At his first school Christianity's reformers had pulled on one arm, now the faith's older denomination yanked on the other. Not only was Santa Fe supremely Catholic; since 1620 the town had served as the faith's southwestern capital.

The previous year, 1886, saw the retirement of legendary French archbishop Jean-Baptiste Lamy. During his thirty-five-year reign, the austere, determined prelate tried to clean house. He wanted to elevate the home-grown, folksy feel of old Santa Fe through European etiquette and civic design. He tried to break up the autocratic fiefdoms of entrenched overlords like Father Antonio José Martinez of Taos (eventually excommunicating him), and unsuccessfully attempted to disband the widespread Penitente brotherhoods.

At the same time, Lamy forged alliances with Anglo and Jewish power brokers who were upgrading the tone of Santa Fe's civic life. And as if to remind the adobe town what true culture looked like, he planted in its heart this neo-Romanesque cathedral of stone with its attached neo-Gothic chapel. By the time of Edward's arrival a retired Lamy was cultivat-ing grapevines and fruit trees at his Villa Pintoresca retreat a few miles north of town, while fellow Frenchman Jean-Baptiste Salpointe took his place. But the old man's personality still loomed over Santa Fe, with his opposition to Protestant-dominated education partly responsible for Ed-ward's coming there in the first place.

A bright young man like Edward must have sensed that he was a pawn in a greater and older game. For American Catholics the U.S. government's postwar campaign to educate Indians was a Presbyterian ruse to steal their flocks. Their notion of Indian education was primarily doctrinal. That meant Jesuit- or convent-run schools where children sang hymns and memorized catechisms in Latin. Less interested in transforming Indians into U.S. citizens than raising Catholics under priests who answered to the Vatican, they were inflexible in what constituted education but creatively adaptive in regard to ritual. While older forms of folk Catholicism flour-ished throughout the territory's rural Spanish-speaking hamlets, a lower-key Catholic presence maintained its diminished role in Pueblo life.

What Edward certainly did not know was how this jockeying for power stemmed from the deepest cleavage in Christiandom. By the sixteenth century breakaway sects had fragmented the Holy Roman Church, sprout-ing the Armenian Church in the fourth century, the Egyptian Copts in the fifth, and the orthodoxies of Greece and Russia in the ninth. But none shocked Rome like the day in 1517 when Martin Luther pinned his objec-tions to Catholic practices to a church door in Saxony.

In England the Reformation meant replacing older monasteries, threatening landed aristocracies, and upsetting feudal financial arrangements. In their place rose an entrepreneurial class with nationalistic ambitions. Their ascendance coincided with the rise of international colonialism, which sharpened the contrasts between Rome's vision of a religion that might fuse with local traditions, and Protestantism's all-or-nothing ideology. In the global context this also meant that the old "culture wars" between Catholic Spain and Protestant England had migrated to the Americas.

A century after Rome gained footholds in Latin America, Mexico, and the American Southwest, Protestantism imported the form of aggressive evangelism it had honed in brutal campaigns against the pre-Christian tribes of Ireland and Wales. At the same time it promulgated the anti-Catholic, luridly sensationalistic narratives that became known as the "Black Legend," concerning Spanish atrocities against Indians in Mexico and the Indies. Among the Protestant reforms was a preference for personal inspiration and testimony over rigid doctrine imposed from on high. Their antihierarchical bias seems to have lent Protestant missionaries greater effectiveness, as evidenced by their success across the country, which extended into the Catholic Southwest once the United States assumed control of these territories after 1848.

◆　◆　◆

St. Catherine, Edward's new Catholic school in Santa Fe.

Solomon Bibo (fourth from right) as Acoma governor, with his council.
Agent Pedro Sanchez, his antagonist (second from left), beside
Martin Valle, in bowler hat.

Partly to counter these Protestant inroads, in 1887 a twenty-nine-year-old heiress from Philadelphia won an audience with Pope Leo XIII in Rome. More missionaries for America's Indians, she begged. "Why don't you become one?" he challenged, and so she did. One reason why Katherine Drexel already agreed to fund construction of a Catholic Indian school was that the Santa Fe–based Pueblo Indian agent reported that Pueblo parents "did not like and would not send their children to Protestant schools."

Her project was welcomed by Father Stephan, who warned that "if we neglect it any longer, the government and the Protestants will build ahead of us schools in all the agencies and crowd us completely out and the Indians are lost." In mid-June 1886, recently appointed archbishop of Santa Fe Jean-Baptiste Salpointe set the new school's cornerstone. Arriving shortly thereafter, the physically strong, Protestant-trained Edward Hunt was among those who laid tiers of adobe brick up from there.

At Acoma, priests held mass in Latin, conducted baptisms, and consecrated marriages, but otherwise stayed out of everyone's hair. Here in Santa Fe, first the nuns, then the Benedictines, ruled day and night, but were satisfied by outward gestures of obedience and piety. If their students could recite catechisms, learn the lives of saints, chant prayers and psalms, pay attention to visual aids depicting the Catholic "roads" to heaven and hell, and make first Communion, souls would be saved and their charge would be met.

Edward never spoke about what he learned at this parochial school. With days beginning at the sound of trumpets each morning at 6:30, in some respects his quasi-military schedule at St. Catherine Indian Industrial School resembled his Albuquerque experience. Until Mother Drexel's new order, known as the Sisters of the Blessed Sacrament, could take over, Santa Fe's own Sisters of Loretto taught Edward and his classmates, under the supervision of a French priest, Father Antonio Jouvenceau. Except for classes, the genders were separated—only on Thanksgiving, Christmas, and the last day of school were doors between their dining rooms opened so boys and girls could wave to each other. And apart from hard labor on the main building, Edward's days were occupied by the three Rs and a ritual calendar almost as full as his people's back on the mesa.

No longer was developing economic self-sufficiency an overriding goal. As St. Catherine had no land to farm nor water to irrigate, Edward never worked in a garden nor tended any animals. Instead of cleaning his own clothes, the wash went to a Chinese laundry. Most meals contained no vegetables or cereals. Paid only $80 a year and unable, for the most part, to speak English, the French Sisters, complained one visitor, "have not more interest in the Indians than an old Jew in a hog."

A preoccupation of New Mexico's Catholic priests remained their tussle with Protestants. Father Stephan boasted how he had subverted Edward's Albuquerque school by purchasing the adjoining parcels. That way kids from the government school could find a priest right next door. Meanwhile, Edward kept his Protestant Bible hidden in his trunk.

His free days were mostly holy days, when the town's Catholicism repossessed her streets. In early March, outside St. Michael's Chapel, renowned as the Southwest's oldest church, Edward joined processions for the Feast of the Ascension. Come late June, during Corpus Christi festivities, he tagged along after celebrants praying at temporary shrines set up through the central city, then joined the La Conquistadora procession that celebrated the cherished female icon who was believed to bless the reconquest of his Pueblo people in 1693.

Not all processions were cyclical or sacred. One day in late May the students were drawn to a commotion downtown. Wending its way through the plaza was a weary caravan of over five-hundred Jicarilla Apaches, dragging tipi poles lashed to the flanks of their horses, their travois loaded with rawhide bundles, heading for their new northern New Mexico reservation. Edward joined the crowd as they watched mostly women and children on horses and burros, baby cradles swinging from saddle horns, their dogs slinking alongside, the entire group guarded by ten warriors and a handful of cavalry. Upon recognizing a son or daughter among the student onlookers, reported the Santa Fe newspaper, an Apache parent "walked solemnly forward to the street curb and shook hands with them, and there were tears in the eyes of the smaller girls when they shook hands for the good-bye and resumed their place among the pupils."

Despite Father Stephan's concerns about weather delays and lazy workers, construction on St. Catherine was finished the following spring. On April 11, 1887, Edward saw an aged Archbishop Lamy, leaning heavily on his cane as he walked down the aisle to preside over its dedication. But by early February of the following year, when Lamy was buried beside his cathedral, Edward was long gone.

For a month after the completion of St. Catherine, word reached him on the school grounds that he had a visitor. Outside the main building he found his mother's sister's husband, a war chief from Acoma. Two horses were tied to a tree. He had bad news. Edward's father, Faustino, had died; he was needed at home. Edward emptied his trunk into some saddlebags. Within the hour they were riding out of town, dropping down La Bajada Hill and passing the Santo Domingo pottery-clay deposits, heading for the Rio Puerco basin. Although he had been in schools for six years, all the time spent on manual labor had held him back; he never got past fourth grade. Edward's formal education may have ended, but more life lessons lay ahead.

A few days later they ascended Acoma mesa. Upon her husband's passing his mother followed custom and moved her few possessions into her sister's house. Feeling his way back into village life, Edward participated in the regular public harvest dances so as not to stand out. Now the school returnee became the man of the house, assuming responsibility for the family fields and livestock.

This also gave him a legitimate excuse for days away from the mesa and nights under the stars and time to himself. "I didn't want to go to the kiva and make prayer sticks or take part in ceremonies," he recalled. "Now I believed in the Bible. Whenever they were going to have a ceremony or a Katsina dance or do some healing or anything, I went out to the sheep camp while they were getting ready, and only came back on dance day."

<hr>

22

Enter the Authors (1884–88)

The marvelous Flower of Ancient Cultures in the Southwest can be kept alive only by appreciation; if it finds an atmosphere only of ignorant contempt, it must wither fast. And God knows we need to keep alive, somewhere among us, the Breeding and Faith of our Mexican pioneers; the Art and Religious and Social Sense of our Pueblo Indians. We Americans are wondrous smart—but we cannot create Antiquity. We can make money, but we cannot make Aristocracy.

—Charles Lummis, 1926

WHILE IT WAS NEVER their conspiratorial intent, three writers who slipped into New Mexico during the decade that Edward was absorbing the white man's ways would fuel opposition to almost everything that his new education stood for. Inadvertently, these popularizers of Pueblo Indian traditions would lay the groundwork for revolutionary legislation that repealed the assimilation agenda a half century later. Of the three, only Charles Lummis came to know Edward personally. At the same time, all their writings would do much to create the wide audience appeal on which his family's future survival would depend.

Each was eccentric in his own fashion. Frank Cushing the self-dramatizing ethnographer, Adolph Bandelier the indefatigable historian, and Charles Lummis the cocky journalist shared a passion for the cultural history of the native Southwest. Each possessed boundless energy, fearlessness, and a talent for communicating Pueblo histories, arts, and ceremonials on the page.

First to arrive was a sickly young man who'd collected arrowheads in western New York as a boy. At age seventeen Frank Hamilton Cushing published his first scientific paper on the state's Indian artifacts. Too impatient to finish Cornell University, he dropped out and, in 1879, at a time when such opportunities were open to gifted amateurs, joined James Stevenson's landmark, Smithsonian-backed expedition to New Mexico. For it he helped buy or otherwise acquire thirty thousand pounds of Zuni and Hopi pots and artifacts for shipping to Washington museums.

Frank Hamilton Cushing at Zuni Pueblo.

Desiring a fuller immersion, that September, at age twenty-two, Cushing began a four-and-a-half-year residence within Zuni Pueblo. His reverse assimilation into the world began with "hardening his meat," as the Zunis described it. His white man's clothes were removed. He was isolated, fed minimally, addressed brusquely, and made to sleep on the floor. Renamed "Medicine Flower," he then acquired the dashing buckskin outfit that became his trademark, moved into the Indian governor's home, elbowed his way into secret ceremonies, was accused and acquitted as a witch, and won admittance to the tribe's warrior Bow Society.

Admired by many for establishing the prototype of the obsessed researcher who loses himself in another culture, to others the man was a self-promoting narcissist. Cushing's archrival, the famously pushy Matilda Coxe Stevenson, wife of the Smithsonian expedition's leader and a prolific writer on the Zuni in her own right, considered him "the biggest fool and charlatan I ever knew."

After breaking with his Smithsonian colleagues and becoming the tribe's key culture broker, Cushing fought for Zuni sacred land interests, mediated disputes between Zunis and their neighbors, and lobbied for aid when famine struck. In a public relations coup, this "white war chief" then cast the Zunis into the old role of Noble Savages by escorting a contingent of six priests and elders to Washington, D.C., where he behaved, writes one historian, as their "secretary of state and of defense, as well as a public information officer."

A year after Cushing's arrival a Swiss-born scholar began poking around the abandoned Pecos Pueblo east of Santa Fe. Adolph F. Bandelier had come from scouting Mexican ruins to upper New York State in 1873, where he'd visited his friend and mentor Lewis Henry Morgan, the lawyer who drew upon his landmark Iroquois Indian studies to formulate a theory of universal cultural evolution. Gauging by the Pueblos' advanced stonemasonry and irrigation practices, Morgan slotted their villages like Zuni and Acoma as existing at a "middle barbarism" stage of development. Simplistic as Morgan's scheme looks today, under its influence fieldworkers like Cushing and Bandelier netted invaluable data.

In 1880 the forty-year-old Bandelier's investigations of defunct Pecos, very much alive Jemez, and other Indian pueblos, both bygone and flourishing, broke interdisciplinary ground. The age and complexity of southwestern Indian traditions proved amenable to his amalgam of folklore and mythology studies interlarded with archival, archaeological, and ethnographic research.

But Bandelier's first foray among real Indians got a comeuppance. Ignorant of Pueblo sensitivities, he had a Santa Fe friend take photographs around conservative Santo Domingo Pueblo, and the two bumbled into a funeral ritual. One shot that day captures Bandelier, decked out in his incongruous bowler and looking miserable, backing into Santo Domingo's kiva wall as if trying to render himself invisible. Describing what followed in a letter to Morgan, Bandelier confessed that being starved out of the village was "in consequence of one of those errors which the novice in ethnology is liable to commit."

That October he fled to nearby Cochiti Pueblo, where her governor gave him a warmer reception, loaning a room with a serape-covered bed of hay and a corner fireplace. Reflecting Morgan's characterization of Indians as "primitive communists," Bandelier praised Cochiti's collective spirit: "They began to treat me as one of their own," he wrote, "and to exhibit toward me the spirit of fraternity which prevails among them in their communism." At Cochiti, Bandelier recruited a tribal consultant, witnessed performances by their sacred clown society, and visited more cliff ruins, especially drawn to the large twelfth-century site of Tuonyi, which Cochiti claimed as its ancestral home.

Throughout the 1880s he continued his pueblo explorations, visiting Acoma among other villages. Upon his appointment as official historian for the Hemenway survey, Bandelier came to admire his new colleague Frank Cushing as "the direct successor to Morgan in the study of Indian life." Among the institutions of Zuni life to which Cushing introduced him were the ritual clowns, those outrageous flaunters of normalcy whom Cushing once described as "the delight makers of the culture," a phrase that stuck in Bandelier's head.

The third writer arrived on foot—all the way from Ohio. Five months after Edward Hunt hopped a train home from Albuquerque in the spring of 1884, a twenty-five-year-old aspiring journalist followed the same tracks in the same direction. A more blatant self-glorifier than Cushing, Charles Fletcher Lummis boasted that his hike had covered the entire continent; actually he only walked the country's "left side." Still, it was a feat: from Cincinnati to the Pacific Ocean in 143 days. The stretch of Lummis's 3,507-mile tramp that cut through New Mexico launched the greatest pitchman in southwestern history.

Charles Lummis, in Los Angeles after his famous walk across America.

Repelled at first by northern New Mexico's poverty and "indolence," Lummis soon fell for its blood-red sunsets, spectacular mesas, humble earthen architecture, chili-spiced stews, and multiethnic hospitality. South of Española, the governor of San Ildefonso Pueblo made him a houseguest. In Santa Fe he met Hispano notables like Pedro Sanchez, and the *rico* Amado Chavez, who invited him to stop by the family's San Mateo rancho, just north of Acoma. After spending two nights in Albuquerque, Lummis decried the city's modernism in a *Chillicothe Register* dispatch, whereupon an Albuquerque newspaper discounted him as "an ungrateful, conscienceless little scrub [who has] traveled farther, seen less, and lied more than any youth of his age and inches in the country." It was the kind of scrap the little bantam sparked throughout his life.

Striding on to Isleta Pueblo, he was put up by the prestigious Abeita family. Then Lummis headed for the Laguna Pueblo Christmas festivities before another hop west to take up the Chavez invitation. There, Amado's father, the legendary Indian fighter Don Manuel, greeted him in the high *haciendero* style, prompting Lummis's realization that "my whole imagination and sympathy and feeling were Latin."

Upon reaching California, Lummis looked a fright. His face was sunburnt and wildly bearded, his busted left arm lay in a homemade splint, he wore a hatband of freshly skinned rattlesnake hide, smelly coyote pelts enclosed his sinewy frame, a pair of Colt revolvers at his waist. Three years later, exhausted from his nonstop journalism, his left side paralyzed from a blood clot, and disheartened by a bad marriage, Lummis retreated to New Mexico. In February 1888, Emil Bibo picked up the broken man at the Grants train stop and bedded him down in the Chavez compound.

Half a year later and encamped at Los Alamitos, it was Lummis's turn to refresh a traveler. "In the teeth of a particular New Mexico sandstorm," Adolph Bandelier entered his clearing, a "bronzed, middle-aged man, dusty but unweary from his sixty mile tramp from Zuni," bearing "the most extraordinary mind I had met." The two became fast friends; both were admirers of Cushing, both accused Anglo-Saxon culture of stigmatizing New World Catholicism as brutal and medieval, and both avoided discussing their contrasting evaluations of Pueblo society.

Though wildly different personalities, all three had much in common. Each had arrived in the 1880s, that crack of time between the end of *then* and beginning of *now,* when Old West adventures were still to be had. Cushing witnessed one of Zuni's last witch executions, policed Zuni boundary lines against Mormon and Mexican poachers, shot at Navajo interlopers, and killed trespassing horses. As a recruit into Zuni's warrior society, he joined a war party pursuing horse thieves that killed two of them and captured the rest. Less of a grandstander, Bandelier still had his close shaves. He'd faked insanity to evade hostile Chiricahua Apaches, endured a bout with smallpox, escaped from outlaws, and rode and then walked out of a blizzard that froze his two companions to death. Lummis's escapades also piled up. After live reportage on the last Apache wars, he was shot at for secretly photographing rural Catholic rituals, and scaled Enchanted Mesa near Acoma to confirm that her ancestors had once lived there.

Amid personal crises all three became intimates of Pueblo Indian governors and enjoyed the last opportunities for Anglos to dwell inside Indian pueblos—Cushing at Zuni, Bandelier at Cochiti, and Lummis for nearly five years at Isleta.

All shared a penchant for dressing up. To one admirer, Cushing's appearance, the headband around flowing blond locks, formfitting buckskin-and-silver-buttoned breeches, silver concho belt, bandolier straps, and heavy jewelry, all signaled "no streak of eccentricity that prompts him to dress that way; no desire to make himself conspicuous." But in detractor Matilda Stevenson's eyes, Cushing's "fantastic dress" marked the man as impossibly vain. "He even put his hair up in curl papers every night. How could a man walk weighed down with so much toggery?"

Liberating his inner Hispano, Charles Lummis based his favored getup on the guitar-strumming, dancing caballeros he'd met in Valencia County—the wide-wale green or brown corduroy suit over red long johns, woven Spanish sash in lieu of a belt, bandana tied pirate fashion on forehead, weather-beaten sombrero, and cigarillo jauntily clenched between his teeth.

As for the modest man who normally dressed with all the flair of a Lutheran minister, on occasion Bandelier could look the most outlandish. Riding into Fort Apache in 1883, he drew stares for his "genuine Scottish bonnet, the Glengarry with the two ribbons hanging down behind; he wore a Norfolk jacket, knickerbockers of rough tweed, and heavy English walking shoes." Glimpsing him on an oversize Spanish saddle that covered his burro's neck to its tail, onlookers noticed that Bandelier's long legs almost scraped the ground.

Most significantly, each was a persuasive wordsmith who explored new rhetorical strategies for impressing readers with the Southwest's wonders. What redeemed much of Cushing's self-dramatizing were his detailed "you are there" accounts, which streamed into popular magazines before being compiled in 1882 in a book titled *My Adventures in Zuni*.

Frustrated that his scholarly descriptions of picturesque ruins and living pueblos were not reaching the general public, Bandelier took five years to compose an experimental novel set in the ancestral Cochiti landscape of the Jemez Mountains. He immersed readers in its pre-Hispanic culture

Scholar of Hispanic history and culture Adolph Bandelier at Santo Domingo Pueblo.

and imagined how a woman's treachery caused her community's destruction. Lummis poured exploits and images from sixteen trips into books and articles that highlighted New Mexico as a tourist destination, and coined the slogan, "See America First." In the indigenous Southwest these writers began to build the "cradle of anthropology" that scholar Peter Whiteley would claim "produced a greater volume of ethnographic studies than any other comparably populated area in the world."

Forty years later the Hunts would dress and dance for general audiences in the guise of Plains Indians. But they would also package themselves as descendants of the "Cliff-Dwellers," with Edward promoted to "Chief of the Delight Makers." Like a handful of other Pueblo Indian entertainers, they would spin the images created by Cushing, Bandelier, and Lummis into a commercial opportunity for getting through tight times.

With Divided Heart (1887)

Now it is true that most of the Indian pupils on returning to their homes have, sometimes voluntarily, more frequently under compulsion, returned to their former way of living. The same feeling against "putting on airs" or being "tony"—usually imagined—is found among the Indians as exists among their superior brethren. An educated boy or girl in a community of ignorant reds must be a truly courageous soul to succeed in taking the stand he has been taught to take by the white man against the customs of his race.

—William Howard, 1893

THE FIRST PHOTOGRAPHIC PORTRAIT of Edward Hunt, probably shot during this period of readjustment to life up at Acoma mesa, makes you want to look closer. More striking than the fact that he doesn't automatically appear Indian is something that's going on behind his eyes. Staring into the middle distance, he is lost in thought. Seated on his left knee, his little sister burrows into his chest. They look caught, not posed. Their expressions differ—his contemplative and protective, hers frightened and perhaps prophetic: she and their other sister will be dead within a year from smallpox; we will never learn their names. Both of these subjects project a sense of isolation and vulnerability in a precarious world.

In its suggestive window into inner states, the image also contrasts with most southwestern photos of the period. Whether documenting government surveys or publicizing railroad tourism, the early photographers who hefted cumbersome equipment and fragile glass plates throughout the region in the 1870s and 1880s gloried in surfaces. And what surfaces—immense skies, colossal clouds, broad mesas, juniper-studded mountains, and sculptural adobe villages. Preconceptions about Indians as stoic, distant, and noble, already planted in American consciousness, were also confirmed through these chemical stamps of authenticity.

From their very invention, cameras helped to create the public's Southwest.

After photographing Indians around Omaha, Nebraska, Civil War veteran and artist William H. Jackson worked for the Union Pacific Railroad in 1869, but did double duty as a U.S. Geological Survey photographer. Also initially employed by a railroad, the Atlantic and Pacific, Ben Wittick remained a professional photographer for hire until a rattlesnake he was contributing to a Hopi Snake Dance took his life.

Their work did not probe Indian souls, and nor did that of independently financed "art" photographers like Edward S. Curtis, Frederick Monsen, or Joseph Dixon. They often romanticized their posed subjects with gauzy moods or stagey surroundings, or they shot portraits that made them look like Roman senators, so as to feed the imaginations of viewers and potential tourists. Not even Adam Clark Vroman, whose views of Navajos and Pueblos were somewhat more realistic, would have taken a picture that depicted such uncertainty.

In later years, Edward recalled, "Solomon Bibo had a camera and took my picture." Although this image wound up in Charles Lummis's archives, one suspects Bibo swapped with him, not an uncommon practice among frontier photographers. And maybe it took a sympathetic friend to capture Edward off guard, when he was at a loss about his future. Whatever its history, the shot can be read as revealing someone in the clichéd dilemma of "caught between worlds," and his little sister in a brief interlude between life and death.

Now that he was home, Edward was constantly reminded of patterns of life that had been second nature since childhood. One day he was visiting his mother's relatives when the salt gatherers returned. Ten days earlier, on one of the rare occasions when Acoma and Laguna pueblos teamed up, the salt pilgrims had departed on a 150-mile round trip to gather minerals from their sacred lake, the naturally saline reservoir south of Zuni Pueblo. All the while their relatives had kept praying for their safety. Now the sacks in their wagon bulged with wet mash so flavorful on meat or corn that the sixteenth-century Spanish wrote home in praise of it. But even had Edward wanted to join, as a member of neither the Parrot nor the Pumpkin clans he knew he was ineligible.

He had a rough idea of their route to Salt Woman's resting place, where the mythic woman had withdrawn after her people insulted her for being unclean. A number of Western Pueblos acknowledged her parting gift, when her body was transformed into the briny lake, and scrapings from her skin left its shoreline encrusted with crystals. Upon the salt pilgrims' return every house on the mesa had its clan symbol freshly painted on the outside wall—his was the Sun. So when the salt gatherers passed by they left enough for distribution among all relatives, including his at Acomita.

Other ceremonies, even if Catholicized, presented no problem; they felt more cultural than religious. Shortly after sunset that Christmas Eve, Edward held a candle and joined the procession that wound its way into the grand interior of St. Stephen's. In every family's hands were baskets containing clay figurines of the domestic items they wanted the visiting priest to bless—tiny homes, little sheep, dogs. Crowding the altar in the flickering lights of a hundred candles, the baskets received benediction while from a choir loft the old men boomed their off-key Latin chants.

But come midnight, as Edward remembered well, the old pre-Christian beliefs took over. With the clanging of bells announcing the Christ child's birth, the singers dropped down the winding staircase as if beating a hasty retreat. Through St. Stephen's massive doors strode the drummers, followed by a chorus of fifteen or more basso-voiced men. Edward joined the onlookers pressed against the wall murals or standing on adobe *bancos* that lined both walls as the dancers entered in sequence. The deer, butterfly, and buffalo teams moved in time to drums and rattles whose sounds were amplified by the building's earthen walls.

Outside were lit the bonfires of resiny pine that burned until dawn. Over the four following days the celebrations continued—drumming in every kiva, family feasts in every home, and the Comanche Dances below the mesa. Then the Christmas celebrations were over and the pueblo turned to the down-to-earth business of electing the coming year's governor and other officials.

With spring approaching, Edward tried to lay low, but a pueblo was a hard place to do that. Everyone knew what everyone else was doing, or wanted to know, or talked about it whether they knew or not. Behind the normal scrutiny found within most small-scale, kin-based, face-to-face communities, in this elevated world an additional gallery of judgmental onlookers kept tabs. These were the religious caretakers, with watchful eyes in the backs of their heads. For them the presence of school returnees

The man who whipped the returned schoolboys.

like Edward was a threat; they kept watch on these "in-between" youth with their short hair and hard-soled shoes, who tossed around white words and questioned their old ways.

One day Edward had escaped to the eastern flank of Mount Taylor and was guarding his sheep when three riders from home located him. He was ordered to drop everything and come with them. "What's this about?" he asked; "you'll see," they said. No one spoke as they headed back, not even the rider with whom he doubled up. At his house on the mesa he slid off. When he entered, his mother ran up and "threw her arms around me and cried and cried."

Soon afterward the war chief's helpers came to the door and made him accompany them to the head kiva. As he was dropping down the ladder he felt hot air from the fire and the steamy presence of warm bodies. The kiva ladder was pulled out of its hatchway in the roof so no one could escape.

Edward recognized the other young men inside—they were branded as the schoolboys, or, as the Hopis put it, those who had "taken up the pencil." One was James Miller, who'd attended Richard Pratt's Carlisle Indian School in Pennsylvania. Unlike Edward, Miller came home with a big mouth. He called their beliefs "superstitions," made fun of ceremonial dancers, and laughed when warned that the spirits would punish him. Woken from a sound sleep that morning, Miller was gagged and trussed and dropped into the kiva, where he sat on the earth in dim light surrounded by tribal elders who smoked their prayer cigarettes and said nothing.

Then the oldest medicine man addressed him. According to writer George Wharton James, who got the story from Miller himself, the boy was told that "his irreverent words and conduct had not only deeply wounded the religious sentiments of the Acoma people, but if allowed to go unpunished would bring upon the town and its people some severe visitation of Those Above. He had been to the white man's school, certainly, but white men did not know everything. They might know what was good for themselves, but they did not always know what was good for the Indian."

A rawhide rope was fastened to Miller's bound hands and looped over a ceiling beam. Four men hauled him up until his toes just touched the floor. His blanket fell off; his groin was covered by a loincloth. A Mexican horsewhip was produced and he was lashed to the rhythm of a drum. By the time he was lowered to the floor he had passed out.

Next came Edward's turn. He and the other students received more admonishment from Acoma's acting governor for denying the efficacy of their medicine men. Each was interrogated about doubts they'd expressed to relatives. The speaker was furious, Edward remembered; saliva sprayed from his mouth. Our medicine men are so powerful they can move mountains from one place to another, he said; they can bring people back to life. Then he picked up the horsewhip. One by one, the others were brought forward, stripped of their shirts, and struck until their backs ran with blood, Edward among them.

Now would they behave properly and attend rituals in the kivas and make prayer sticks and dance the Katsina dances? "I didn't say anything," remembered Hunt, although two uncles were persuading him to accept a return to the "old way." The ordeal went on through the night, the next day, and into a second night and day. Then the underlying anxiety that was driving all this burst out. "We've got to be one people," begged the war chief, the acting governor, the cacique, and the medicine men. "We've got to

James Miller (center), *as Acoma governor (holding cane of office), later in life.*

believe in the medicine men, and believe in the Katsina, and believe in our ways." Everyone was weeping, Hunt said, "in pity over what had happened."

That evening the kiva ladder was reinstalled and the students were allowed to leave. When Hunt stepped into his home his mother and sisters and brothers encircled him with their arms and cried. He was proud that he had not shed tears so far, but his mother's wailing filled his eyes. She spread lard on his bleeding back. For three days the pain kept him awake. After many weeks the scabs fell off, then the dried skin peeled away in long strips. Later in life one of his grandsons remembered Edward removing his shirt when he was guarding them as they splashed in an irrigation ditch. Faintly visible across the old man's back was a lattice of old stripes.

After this experience Edward let his hair grow long. He attended kiva meetings and helped with the prayer sticks and joined in the Katsina dances. No one scolded or made fun of him. When word about the whippings got out, Bibo complained to authorities. The acting governor was taken to Albuquerque and jailed for a number of years. Upon his release the man confessed he had overdone it. He beseeched his people not to judge him. The "schoolboys" could wear their trousers and shoes. The older folk could urge them to "remain Indian," he said, but they should not punish them for leaning toward Mericano ways. Hunt kept his pouch with cornmeal for praying in the traditional way. But when he did so now he silently prayed to the God he had discovered in Albuquerque.

Meanwhile, the prospects for Edward's friend Solomon Bibo were looking up. Having survived his showdowns with tribal and U.S. officials, he'd married into one of Acoma's leading families. Those in-law ties and Acoma's loyalty led to an even more unlikely achievement. Some documents suggest that it was a newly appointed Pueblo Indian agent, W. C. Williams, who proposed him for the post of Acoma governor in 1888. Later, Solomon claimed to have held the position in 1885 and 1886 as well.

Whatever years they occurred, this annual investiture was customarily scheduled shortly after the midwinter celebrations. From the mesa's old cacique Solomon received the ebony cane, the badge of his new office, whose silver knob was engraved with the wording "A. Lincoln, Prst. U.S.A. Acoma, 1863." This staff was added to the other canes of office the pueblo had accumulated from Spain, then Mexico, each certifying its ambiguous status as both an independent and a vassal state. After that Solomon proudly rested the staff in the crook of his arm during the St. Stephen's Day festivities.

His role had many purposes. It served as a buffer between the pueblo and the outside world; the governor ran the tribe's "foreign policy," as it were. He upheld Acoma's interests during interactions with Catholic missionaries, Protestant government officials, and schoolteachers. His office also shielded the community's true and traditional governing authority by the cacique, the war or "country" chiefs, and the ranks of medicine men. Perhaps a multilingual Jew with inside and outside connections was a good choice. The appointment also meant that now Edward had at least one friend in a high place.

The Last Hunt (1887)

These people had abilities to control the weather, to bring rain, to make it cold or warm. We do not possess their abilities or their knowledge now, and for this reason it makes it hard to believe. Some of us even have genuine doubts that those people had these powers, especially nowadays when we are living a completely different lifestyle. People today cannot really understand this.

—A contemporary Hopi, quoted by Peter Whiteley, 1988

S EIZING ANY OPPORTUNITY to blend in, Edward next participated in one of the world's oldest techniques for killing lots of game. To Acoma people the sanction for the "surround" form of hunting came in their creation myth. Some scholars suggest the method was part of a cultural kit their Pueblo ancestors received from Great Basin peoples of present-day Nevada. However early it began, the "drive" allowed Indians to collect a stunning amount of protein in one fell swoop.

By distributing the person-power of a village into spread-out circles of brush-beaters who tightened their orbits so as to converge at crude corrals, box canyons, or rocky cul-de-sacs, herds of deer or antelope could be bunched within easy range of arrows, javelins, or clubs. To assure that no hunter sprang out of turn and spooked the game required the same kind of submission to a central authority demanded by managers of irrigation systems who coordinated many hands to clear debris and open and shut ditch gates.

Usually the hunt leader partnered with medicine men who oversaw the rituals that made sure their prey were treated with respect. Game animals were beseeched to "give" themselves; once slain, their spirits—what whites called "souls"—were fed. Sometimes one hunter behaved as "bait." Wearing antlers, masked in a dried deer snout, carrying a hide with its legs drooping over his shoulders and back, he mimicked the deer's jerky head movements and cautious steps to draw the curious herd closer. If the surround involved many beaters whose thrashing of grass and setting of fires drove animals toward the constricting center, they were warned not to rack up a high count just to impress the girls.

When he was around ten years old, Edward's first experience on a group hunt was more of a training exercise. Conditioning for manhood stressed running down deer or antelope on foot, but Day Break was not ready for that. On this trip he joined as a helper, gathering firewood, packing supplies, preparing light meals, and watering and feeding horses or burros. After scouts located the animals, the war chief sent out his strongest runners in tightening circles, starting with a radius of twenty to twenty-five miles, then compressing the animals into a natural alcove where a high corral lashed together from poles awaited them.

The war chief walked quietly among them, searching for the smallest female. Pulling her out, his hunters laid hands upon the hot, trembling

Leaving Acoma: the route to antelope country.

body, prayed their thanks, and set her free so as to assure the animals' return in greater numbers the next go-around. The others they culled and slit their throats to save the blood. "Everything of their bodies was precious," Edward remembered. There the hunters camped and quartered the carcasses and roasted some of the delicacies. They packed the meat on burros and came home the next day.

Of all Edward's hunting memories, his second expedition was the most unusual. It took place some years later, around midsummer. A drought had stretched so long that there was no harvest. Their food stores were used up and the older people's skin began to split. They were reminded of earlier hard times—bone-dry riverbeds, shriveled cacti, empty larders, dying dogs, and sheep carcasses everywhere. His family remembered one stretch during his grandmother's lifetime. Everyone fled to Zia Pueblo, where they ate roots and made stew from animal bones dug out of old trash piles.

Normally the monsoons of When Corn First Appears (July) and When Corn Beards (August) brought the landscape back to life. Not this year. The high desert could turn deadly very fast. You thought you had enough water and then you didn't. Day after day the people searched for rainclouds above Mount Taylor. Only wisps were seen, and they disappeared. Bad luck or improper behavior had made the rain gods withhold their benevolence. The people felt abandoned.

Hunting was not customary in midsummer, for fear the meat would spoil. Now they had no choice. A party of about fifty men was assembled, led by the medicine men with their hunting fetishes. Again young Edward was in tow. For days they walked toward the southwest. The sun rode hot and high. Pack animals with protruding ribs fell over and kicked but could not stand back up. The travelers grew weaker. Their supply of parched corn and antelope jerky ran out. The water in their pottery canteens was rationed.

They moved toward the San Augustin Plains. Seeing no animal signs, they struck on. When they started out the medicine men said they would move from spring to spring. But at the first spring, they found it dry and caked. Then one man said, I know another one. When they got there that spring was dry too. For three more days this continued. Their canteens were empty; the situation looked hopeless.

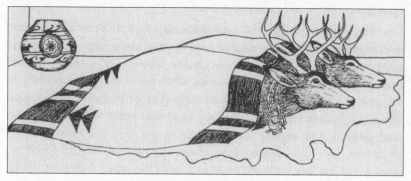

Pueblo honoring of slain deer.

The medicine men stopped everything. Although they were passing the Datil Mountains, and could see the range's trees and shade cover, they gathered everyone at an open, hot, barren place. They wanted the spirits to witness what they were going through.

All the men came together, the remaining animals huddling with them. From sunrise to sunset they prayed under the sun. They took spruce boughs they had cut, the same lengths that were worn by the rain-bringing Katsinas during their dances. As one medicine man ended his prayer he threw them on the fire and dared the rain spirits to put it out.

They squeezed into a tighter circle. When it rains, the lead medicine man said, I want everyone to have their canteens and gourd cups ready. He didn't say *if,* Edward always stressed when telling this story. He said *when.*

Hungry and exhausted, they lay down. Twilight faded into night and then a little breeze picked up from the southwest. When it blew stronger everybody woke up. They wondered if the medicine men had angered the storm spirits, and got scared. The wind became intense and they felt wetness. But it wasn't rain, it was snow.

They rose to their feet and began eating it. So did their animals. The medicine men explained that the "Great Spirit" knew better than to send rain, since they wouldn't have been able to catch it all. This way we can melt some, they said, and fill our containers. Then we will roll snowballs into low depressions, so when we get back there will be water. It snowed about half a foot. In the darkness they rolled snowballs as high as a man's waist and left them in sandy basins.

Next morning they were very tired. We will sit and stay here all day and thank the "Great Spirit," said the medicine men. They kept the fire burning throughout the day and prayed around it and gave thanks. By the time they left the next morning the melted pools of water were protected under thin seals of sunbaked sand.

The hunters found the herds of antelope and surrounded and killed lots of them. They sliced the meat into thin slabs and jerked it over ropes tied between trees. Each burro could carry the dried meat of about six antelopes. On their way home they broke into their buried water basins and drank and filled the canteens.

They'd been gone a week. Waiting nearer home, runners were on lookout for the band and reporting regularly to the mesa. Everyone was worried that they had died of thirst. Then the hunters were spotted and on the mesa the people gathered to watch them approach. The meat was divided among all the families. Edward saw all this and never forgot it.

By coincidence his third and last expedition occurred around the same time that Washington sought to end Indian freedom to roam and hunt at will. In early February 1887, the U.S. Congress passed the Dawes Act, also known as the General Allotment Act. A momentous piece of legislation, it ordered all federally recognized Indian tribes to disband as semisovereign nations. Their lands, as measured and supposedly secured in earlier treaties, were to be broken up into 160- or 320-acre parcels ("allotments") and distributed to male heads of Indian families so they could farm like white homesteaders. Acreage left over went to the highest bidder.

Motivating the bill was a desire to destroy the complicated allegiances that made Indian tribes stick together. Now they were to think of themselves as stay-at-home families and individuals who must learn to survive in American society on their own. The fact that just after bringing in their fall harvest the cream of Acoma's manhood set out from their land-grant village on a communal hunt suggested the limited degree to which these policies had influenced the Pueblo Indian world so far.

Again the hunters headed south for the San Augustin Plains. Now pueblo elders found Edward's bilingual skills useful. He was still a lowly helper, but he could interpret for the white Datil postmaster who owned land in the vicinity. As the tribe's largest and last communal hunt, this was a veritable safari. The party included seventy-four hunters, four cooks, and eight burro handlers. Edward's uncle loaned him a percussion-cap rifle he'd brought from California. At Datil he asked the postmaster if they could overnight near his spring.

"All right," the man replied, "but not too close."

"The burro tenders built a big corral," Edward remembered, for pack animals and mounts. Killing and butchering a pronghorn, the cooks built a fire and they ate together. Afterward the hunt leader laid two fetishes beside the fire that were made from ears of corn. One represented the old cacique up on the mesa, the other belonged to the hunt leader.

In their medicine pouches each hunter kept his fetishes of the animals he wanted to hunt, accompanied by cornmeal to nourish them and beads and other items. Now they pulled them out and laid them by the fire. The hunters sat close together until the middle of the night, singing hunting songs so as to meditate and pray over what lay ahead.

At first light they ate again and, carrying their hunting fetishes, started out. Some of them dressed like antelope, with painted faces and stuffed animal heads tied above their hair and wearing shirts the color of antelope hides. Edward stuck by his uncle. Soon they came upon a large herd. That day, he remembered, they surrounded and killed 744 animals. One man got 34 all by himself. Then they skinned the carcasses and sliced up the meat.

All the old rules were observed. They cut out the hearts and dipped their fetishes in the blood to feed them before returning the little sculptures to their pouches. "If the animal were female," Edward recalled, "the hunters took out her stomach, cut it open, and then placed the vulva in the stomach and sprinkled them with sacred corn pollen. If the animal were male, his penis and testicles were similarly placed in the stomach and sprinkled with the pollen." All this was done to respect the animals and please their spirits so they would increase.

"We stayed out there about two weeks," Edward remembered. "We spent a lot of our time cutting up and drying the meat." As the piles of dried meat grew it was clear their burros couldn't haul it all. The war chief sent some boys riding back to Acoma for more animals.

Meanwhile they continued to hunt in the surrounding mountains. Edward was paired with an older hunter, a member of the Kabina medicine men's society. Climbing a small rise, the man said, "I'll go down this way, you go that, we'll meet down there," and trotted off. After sitting for a moment, "pretty soon I heard something coming, making cracking noises." It didn't take long to realize what it was. "He was eating acorns—you could hear him cracking them. He came up close, but didn't see me." Edward froze. "I'd never seen a live bear before."

He'd heard of the oversize grizzlies that still hung around Mount Taylor. He was told how brown bears like this one stood on their hind legs like people when they pulled piñon nuts or peaches out of the branches. When skinned, their carcasses supposedly resembled human bodies. Perhaps this was why, among Rio Grande Keresan pueblos, anyone killing a bear was automatically welcomed into the warrior society, just as if he'd slain an enemy.

Of all the land creatures, bears were considered the most sacred. They were the sole game animal that Pueblo men hunted and ate but that, like human beings, also hunted and ate its prey. They were revered as benefactors to medicine men who healed and to warriors who killed. To show respect to a slain bear, its skull was buried under rocks, bits of food were mixed with its bones and thrown into a river, and hunters prayed for its spirit to have a safe journey onward. In Acoma's origin myth, the War God Twins once killed a bear and skinned it, but left the paws whole. They cleaned out the smaller bones and meat so the paws could be worn like gloves when making medicine. Following suit, Acoma's shamans wore their leg-skins and paws with claws still on, to impart their powers to kiva altars and to fight witches.

After a moment's uncertainty over whether to stand or run, Edward fired. It was a lucky shot, penetrating liver and lungs. The animal roared, heaved its body into the air, then turned in circles. Edward took off. Hearing the blast, the medicine man rushed back. Bloody patches showed where the bear had slumped here and there. When they found it curled in a cave they poked it with a stick, but it did not move. They saw it was a female.

Do not skin below its "elbows," warned the medicine man. Keep the lower leg-skins intact and peel them from there. They cut through a thick layer of fat and around the stomach. Upon extracting the bear's heart the medicine man made Edward leave him alone. When he returned the stomach and heart were gone.

Stripping off the rest of the hide and saving two fatty ribs for food, they carried everything to camp, where the medicine man extracted bones, tendons, and muscle from the bear's forelegs and paws and filled the cavities with hot sand. After they were sufficiently dried he replaced the sand with stuffed grass. The next morning they loaded the rest of the meat on fresh burros.

Back home Edward gave the bear hide to a medicine man who belonged to the same Fire Society as his deceased father. From now on it would cover a stool for warriors of the Opi Society to sit upon during the scalp ceremony—the same ceremony that, to his dismay, Day Break was expected to oversee very soon.

<hr>

25

Becoming a Delight Maker (1888)

The leader who was a visionary man chose this way of reminding his people that they have only their worldly ambition and aspirations by which to gain a spiritual world of eternity. He was showing them that we cannot be perfect in this world after all and if we are reminded that we are clowns, maybe we can have, from time to time, introspection as a guide to lead us right. From this beginning when we have been resembled to clowns we know that this is to be a trying life and that we will try to fulfill our destiny by mimicry, by mockery, by coping, by whatever.

—Emory Sekaquaptewa, Hopi, 1979

ABOUT A YEAR after that big hunt, the young man still called Day Break around home was torn between his loyalties to community and his closeted Christianity. To escape Acoma's expectations of him as a member of the Katsina, medicine men's, and now warrior societies, again he left the mesa and lost himself tending his uncle's sheep in the pastures around Mount Taylor. By day he roamed through the piñon and juniper. At night he read his Bible by the fire.

One day out with the animals, Edward heard yells and gunshots. Drawn to the commotion, he came upon Acoma men in war paint, racing back and forth. They were shouting war cries and firing muzzle-loaders at what resembled the kind of brush shelter that Navajos erected in summer-time. Out of the structure ran someone waving a patch of dried skin from which dangled long hair. Later he learned it was a mock attack. Elderly men, members of the nearly defunct Opi warrior society, were honoring their trophies.

The origins of American Indian scalping is an old debate. Was it a traditional practice of Indian tribes, or an introduction by Anglo-Europeans in colonial times, with scalps demanded as proof before Indian allies were paid bounties for dead enemies? At Acoma Pueblo, at least, it is also described in their creation narrative. Cutting a small patch from a dead enemy's head was a way to honor one's foes. Respectful care and "feeding" of scalps kept their "ghosts" from haunting tribal warriors.

Acoma children were told how the fearless Hero Twins began scalping. The ghost of a Navajo woman they had killed would not let them sleep. She dogged them until they were exhausted and losing weight. Digging up her corpse to make sure she was dead, they cut a circle of flesh and hair from her head. They vowed to dance, purify themselves with emetics, and abstain from sexual intercourse. Assisting them through the exorcism ritual were the original Koshare, the sacred clowns. During the four days that they danced and sang in the kiva, her scalp hung from a pole in the plaza. Their final performance ended around the pole, and the scalp was left in the Twins' care. Her ghost never returned.

Conflicts with Navajos hadn't taken place for years, so any Opi warriors with firsthand memories of their fights were down to a few. But they had turned up an old scalp and fabricated the mock Navajo shelter and reenacted the Twins' mythic experience. It dramatized the alarms when Navajos began attacking Acoma shepherds, the retaliatory attack on their brush homestead, and the Acoma warriors' triumphant homecoming. A few weeks later the Koshare were expected to play their part. Since there were so few of them left too, it was decided to initiate certain young men in place of their deceased fathers.

Edward's father was among their number. On his deathbed, apparently, he declared that he wanted his oldest son to take his place. One night a messenger showed up at Edward's door. He had no choice but to comply. With six other initiates he was led to the head kiva, not far from his family house on the mesa.

"Will you become Koshare?" asked the headman. "We can't make you unless you agree."

"If I don't," Hunt asked, "will you let me go?"

"No," was the reply. Perhaps fearing another horsewhipping, Hunt submitted.

Whether in story or ceremony, most Native American societies feature these irreverent, independent, and cunning characters who talk and act in every worst way. In oral narratives they manifest through various Trickster figures—Rabbit in the Southeast, Glooskap in the Northeast, Raven in the Northwest, Spider-Man in the plains, Beaver in the Great Lakes, and, most ubiquitous of the bunch, Coyote, who seems to prowl almost everywhere.

In social and ritual contexts the functions of the Trickster are fulfilled by ritual clowns—the phallic-nosed Boogers of the southeastern Cherokees, the Heyoka of the Plains-dwelling Sioux, the Mudheads of nearby Zuni Pueblo. Granted license to be outlandish, subversive, licentious, rude, gross, and inappropriate (but never outright evil), by their words and deeds they paradoxically wind up reinforcing how to properly behave. For a society whose members prided themselves on personal modesty, self-discipline, and public decorum, these characters also provided an escape value for any societal tensions produced by the behavioral rules and expectations they were overtly flaunting. At the same time they let people laugh at themselves and the absurdities and solemnities of their self-important social worlds.

Given Pueblo Indian tendencies to institutionalize their ceremonial roles, it is little surprise to find among them entire ranks of sacred clowns. During Edward's four-day induction into this brotherhood he heard how Iatiku created the first Koshare. "He was kind of crazy," Edward described that primordial fun-maker, "picking around, speaking loudly, using garbled speech, talking backwards, wise-cracking and overly self-confident." Once he'd learned, with alarming rapidity, all his tribe's rituals, even Iatiku wasn't sure what to do with this uncontrollable character. "You have done your work faithfully," she said, "but you are not acting normally enough to be here with the people. You are not going to be afraid of anything or to regard anything as sacred."

Then Edward talked about the clown's inner nature. He was different from other people, he said, "*because he knew something about himself.*" Over the years this cryptic phrase has intrigued cultural commentators. To folklorist Barbara Babcock, Edward's words evoked the kind of performer who could "transcend himself: in his laughter is detachment, and in his detachment, freedom."

To be sure, Pueblo clowns had their formal responsibilities, too, mediating at serious ceremonies between the unseen spirits and ritual officials, announcing when the rain gods were coming, and even summoning the powers of creation itself. At the same time they had that ability to flip the world on its ear, mock its social conventions, and unmask human pretensions. Thus, Agapito, a famed clown from San Ildefonso Pueblo of the mid-twentieth century, took no prisoners. Decked in his necklace of white man's doughnuts, he jiggled his impressive belly through the plaza to parody overweight tourists. He bullied Spanish-American visitors, pretended to read English magazines backwards, pantomimed archaeologists digging up pots, and teased the shy Navajo and Apache visitors. Everything was fair game for his withering humor and overplayed hospitality.

The sexually graphic nature of some clown performances frequently aroused white condemnation. But as a Hopi once responded, "Well, white man, you think [this] business is vulgar, but it means something sacred to us. This old Katchina is impersonating the Corn maiden; therefore we have intercourse with her so that our corn will increase and our people will live in plenty. If this were evil we would not be doing it. You are supposed to be an educated man, but you had better go back to school and learn something more about Pueblo life."

Accepting his fate, Edward and the other initiates entered the kiva. Numerous times Edward would describe what happened next—to Edward S. Curtis's assistant in 1912, to Leslie White in 1926, and to Matthew W. Stirling in 1928. Becoming a sacred clown steeped him in the esoterica of Acoma, and represented his greatest departure from the good Christian he aspired to be.

Although Edward was never hesitant about discussing what happened, details of the symbolic actions that transpired over the following week in and around that chamber are best left alone. Besides satisfying a certain prurient curiosity, what positive use and meaning would they possibly

Wilbert Hunt at his father's kiva at Acoma.

have to nonparticipants and nonbelievers, what efficacy to the world that most non-Indians occupy today? Keyed to narratives of creation, Edward's lengthy initiation utilized a wide repertoire of Pueblo ritual practices. Those days and nights involved invocations of spirit beings, crafting ritual objects and regalia, donning proper attire, hours of sacred narration, and chanting and prayer. All was done with admonishments and memorizations, amid darkness and the pungent mixture of human odors and woody incense. As a kind of public finale, the newly minted clowns then paraded into the open streets and alleys. In their faces their parents, relatives, and fellow villagers saw the consequences of the teachings and expectations that had been imparted to them.

The same year that Edward faced the prospect of thus fulfilling his father's deathbed wish, Adolph Bandelier was residing in Santa Fe and translating into English from German his first stab at a piece of fiction about Pueblo Indians. In a remarkable coincidence, the Keresan-speaking protagonist of his emerging novel was dreading the prospect of filling his father's desire that he take on the mantle of a sacred clown. Like Edward, one suspects, this invented young character harbored misgivings about the role's requirements.

Bandelier had just finished living in Cochiti Pueblo for nearly a year. In his new book he sought to meld his experiences there and at Santo Domingo, Santa Clara, and San Juan pueblos with his study of Cochiti's ancestral ruins at El Rito de los Frijoles. To reach general readers he hoped fiction might be more effective by "clothing sober facts in the garb of romance." This was a bit inconsistent, since Bandelier's hybrid of archaeology, ethnology, and fiction was adopting an approach he had formerly criticized—castigating James Fenimore Cooper, in particular, for exemplifying the "romantic school in American aboriginal history."

Bandelier cribbed its title, *The Delight Makers*, from a phrase by his hero, ethnologist Frank Cushing, who characterized clowns at Zuni Pueblo as "makers of delight for the people." His creative turn was also akin to that of the muckraker Helen Hunt Jackson, who followed her underappreciated exposé of U.S. Indian policy, *A Century of Dishonor* (1881), with the more popular romance *Ramona* (1884) about the plight of Southern California's Mission Indians.

To this Catholic convert and proper gentleman, one of his most shocking experiences at Cochiti included an "exhibition of obscenity" he'd witnessed in November 1880 by black-and-white-painted Koshare clowns, with their black-circled eyes and tall horns fashioned from corn husks. Bandelier felt "terribly ashamed" to witness "sodomy, coitus, masturbation, etc . . . performed to greatest perfection . . . to the greatest delight of the spectators." Missing the point of these enactments, in his story Bandelier portrayed the Koshare fraternity as standing for everything he found disreputable about Pueblo society.

The Pueblo scholar Alfonso Ortiz once told of a boyhood friend, a high school dropout from San Juan Pueblo (today's Ohkay Owingeh), who had a vivid dream. It featured a ritual clown, only three feet high and covered in body paint. After consulting with the medicine men, the boy's parents were told the dream meant that their son must join the society or suffer ill health or even worse. As had Edward's mother, they mourned the lifelong commitment that lay ahead, as the youth began nearly two years of celibacy and training. Yet like many a mendicant's immediate family, they rallied in support, accumulating the gifts and food he was expected to donate to the clown fraternity and his village at large.

During his first public appearance, Ortiz watched the young man cavort with the other clowns during the Turtle Dance that fall. After having fasted for four days in seclusion and learned the brotherhood's secrets, he was publicly taunted and humiliated, required to guzzle a disgusting brew, kick apart outdoor baking ovens, break glass windows, fling his arms around women, and commandeer any food in sight.

As he watched, Alfonso knew he had lost his friend for good, and inwardly said goodbye. Having become "an expert in nothingness," as he wrote in his field notes, his old playmate had joined a "world of immense solitude, but also a world without fear."

Was Edward about to dwell in that other realm as well?

Keresan clowns at San Ildefonso Pueblo. At left is the famous Agapito.

Love and Marriage (1889)

When I got married, then one of my uncles said, "Why you want to marry that boy? He's just a fisherman, fishing in the river, killing bird, or catching bird. He's no farmer. He doesn't know anything about farm. He doesn't know any work or anything. I don't know why you want to marry him." I didn't say anything. But when he asked me again, I say, "I love him." That's the way it happened.

—Maria Poveka Martinez, 1970

T HE TURN OF EVENTS that liberated Edward from participation in Katsina performances, the onerous duties of medicine men, the crude and irreverent behaviors of sacred clowns, and everything else his Christian teachings condemned as blasphemous, was not only that he fell in love. It was with whom.

In a piece of family lore passed on by his descendants, Edward was no more than ten years old. With his father a full-time medicine man, the family was largely dependent on donations from patients and relatives. To supplement their rations, his mother ground corn for a well-to-do household, the Valles, and was paid in kind. Walking with her son in the morning darkness from their home on the mesa's southernmost street, she cut across the small dance plaza before being admitted into a door at the northeast end of the middle street. In a corn-grinding room located in the rear, kneeling over a worn granite *metate* basin tipped into a wooden box, his mother pushed and rolled the *mano* to pulverize the dried kernels. Her torso moved back and forth in unison with other kneeling women to the rhythms of two or three standing male singers chanting corn-grinding songs. The meal was passed from rough to medium to fine stones, ultimately turning into a powdery flour ready for mixing into a blue-gray batter. Spread by gliding fingers over a pitch-cured, wood-heated, spitting-hot stone griddle, it sizzled, cooked, and was quickly rolled into a scroll of unleavened, parchment-textured, highly nutritious bread.

One anecdote has young Edward hearing a just-born baby crying—the girl who would become his future wife. Another has them both some years older, her watching the hungry boy as he surreptitiously scooped meal that dribbled to the floor and crammed it into his mouth. A third has her noticing him stealing eggs from the Valle chicken coop, but saying nothing. She was Marie Valle (or Vallo), daughter of Juan Diego Antonio and his wife, Barbarita, a member of the large Sarracino family of Laguna Pueblo. The child had a sister named Juana, while her grandfather was the famous Martin Valle, who had served some seven terms as Acoma's governor. The little girl, it is said, pitied the hungry boy and never forgot him.

Ten or fifteen years later, that older but still poor young man not only fell for that same girl from a privileged family and distracted his conflicted heart, he probably added a melodramatic twist by making her pregnant. While that was not usually grounds for disapproval in their generally tolerant, nonpuritanical society, another aspect of the affair was. For both of them, it is said by some today, belonged to the Sun Clan, practically making them siblings and their union symbolically akin to incest. Maybe that was just the excuse an upper-status family needed to object to their daughter marrying a commoner. Whatever was the case, Edward and Marie became a couple for good.

It would have been unusual for Edward not to have known the attractive teenager who was baptized in 1868 at St. Stephen's Church as Marie Valle. A better example than Acoma of what anthropologists call a "face-to-face" society would be hard to find. Everyone knew most everyone else all their lives, and most were also related by ties of kinship, clanship, and societal membership. Barely a month went by without everyone seeing everyone else and knowing their relationships.

Whatever moral, clan, or class lines the lovers had crossed, they shortly learned its cost. When Marie's father showed up on horseback at Edward's door one morning, she was on a horse beside him. Heavy bundles were lashed to their saddles, and her father led a third mount by the reins. The three rode to a chapel in the hamlet of San Rafael where, on November 24, 1889, a Father Bruno married them. After the quick service they remounted and headed eastward toward Acomita, then veered to a sandstone cliff not far from a sprawl of tar-colored, cinderlike ground cover. Scoured hollows near the base showed the work of wind and rain. One cavity looked shoulder high. Dismounting and lugging the bundles to the cliff could not have taken long. There is no record if her father said anything to the new husband and wife. When he rode back alone to the mesa, the other two horses went with him.

Of the courting that led to the Hunts' sixty-three-year-long marriage the family record is also silent. Romance and sexuality rank among taboo topics to discuss with outsiders in Pueblo country. This appears less out of prudery or guilt than respect for modesty and privacy; Indians see little reason for strangers nosing around in their interpersonal lives, whether for scientific or literary reasons.

Like most rural kids, Edward and Marie knew where babies came from. All around were dogs, burros, sheep, oxen, and other animals mixing it up. Graphic accounts of seductive women and male seducers spice Acoma tales and legends. Frisky teenagers could always figure out ways to get together. At some pueblos everyone knew that an attachment had begun when they saw a girl combing a young man's hair with a bristle brush. "The youth of Zuni," wrote a Boston newspaperman after visiting Frank Cushing there in 1881, "are just as sentimental, just as 'spooney' in their love affairs, as fond of moonlight rambles and whispered nothings, as any lover well can be."

Edward's only recorded memory of such intimacies occurred on that trip home from St. Catherine Indian Industrial School immediately after his father's death. Riding from Santa Fe to Acoma with his uncle, he dropped down La Bajada Hill to sojourn for the night at Santo Domingo Pueblo, where they had in-laws. "They were glad to see us," Edward remembered. "When an Acoma or Zuni Indian comes to Domingo they believe that it's sure to rain, because we live near the Katsina."

The next day, attending a Katsina dance, Edward was struck by the village's strict code of behavior. Unlike back at Acoma, no one was allowed to watch from the rooftops. They were forced to stay put in the plaza, "and you had to *stay* there, too; you were not allowed to leave until the dance was over. If you had to relieve yourself, you had to use a pottery bowl."

But this conservatism did not spill into private affairs. As he turned in a second night at the relative's house, "There was a girl who took a fancy to me. I stayed with her that night, as she invited me, but the next morning we left. She went along with us until we got out of the pueblo about a mile.

*Garcia Mesa, near the cliff shelter where Marie Hunt bore their
first three sons. The Calabash Village ruins, home of early
Acoma migrants, are at upper left.*

She was nice and pretty, but I did not think I was old enough to get married yet."

Had circumstances been different, and Edward and Marie married more traditionally, the process might have entailed mutual agreements between the bride's and groom's parents. Perhaps he would have sewn Marie a pair of moccasins cut from the tanned hide of a deer he killed, a keepsake for the rest of her life. Relatives would have convened in the bride's family home for her shower, each bringing a special old pot, some smoothly tanned buckskin, or strands of evenly matched, hand-milled turquoise beads. A clan elder or uncle or even the mesa's cacique might have blessed them and, when their firstborn arrived, added a pebble to the pot by which he kept count of all his children.

Such was not this couple's fate. No family gathering, no smiling witnesses, no rejoicing or support. They were on their own.

◆ ◆ ◆

Marie Valle Hunt, wife of Edward.

The blackened outback near which Marie's father dropped the newlyweds represented the most recent lava deposit in North America. Located in a valley south of today's Grants, so forbidding and impenetrable were the thousand-square-mile remains of nearly seven hundred thousand years of successive eruptions from a hundred or more volcanoes that the Spanish aptly dubbed the place El Malpais—"the Badlands."

The most recent layer, the McCartys Flow, flowed less than four thousand years ago and left an inky surface that congealed as jaggedly as a coral reef.

When Antonio de Espejo's third expedition traveled through here in 1583 the crusted rocks cut and twisted their horses' hooves, slowing movement to a careful walk. The layer of frozen lava was fifty feet deep and created a blasted landscape dotted by spiky green plants and spindly wildflowers.

The badlands formed a natural barrier between the lands of the Acoma and Zuni Pueblo peoples, and over the centuries the Indians blazed a few foot trails—one seven-mile stretch of the Acoma-Zuni footpath is still marked by old cairns. Within the Malpais were serpentine lava tubes, rippled rocks that resembled oil-blackened shorelines, dark fissures, burst lava bubbles caught in freeze frame, and caves with ice that never melts.

With its overall feeling so primeval and mythic, how could such a landscape not breed stories? Everywhere lay evidence—remains of earlier Indians who had created secluded compounds and shrines away from their enemies, bone-filled recesses bearing witness to outcasts and outlaws seeking hideaways, rusty pots, sun-cracked harness belts, and crude shelters left by treasure hunters.

Every tribe had its explanatory tale about this anomalous mass. To the Navajo it was the coagulated blood of a mythic monster that their Hero Twins had killed farther north, its flow spilling southward like dark syrup, its head solidified into Cabezon Peak. For the Zuni the blasted expanse was also attributed to the days of the War Twins. Leading the proto-Zuni

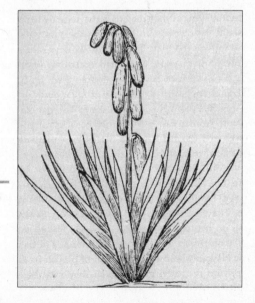

Yucca: the life-supporting, all-purpose plant.

wanderers across this unformed ground, with monsters threatening them on all sides, they called upon their Sun Father. His lightning strike hardened the ground, wiped out the monsters, and darkened the rocks with their burnt blood.

As children, Edward and Marie heard Acoma's explanations for its unearthly appearance. A mean-spirited gambler seduced a girl and left her with twin boys. Eventually finding their father, the boys wagered and won a hide-the-ball game, grabbed their winnings, and then plucked out the gambler's eyes. In a rage he felt around for his fire drill, spun a blaze, and fed it pine splints. As he sang, oozing pitch melted over the countryside, torching everything in sight. Barely outrunning the river of flame, the boys prayed to the cloud spirits. "It rained for four days and four nights before the fire was out," as Edward later told it. "The pitch became hard and cold, you can see it near the town of Grants today." Even now the crusty Malpais reminds Acomans of this story, as do two stars said to be the gambler's eyes, and the masked dancers who portray him and his long-suffering mother.

Banished to the ends of their society's known earth, given no decent interval to become acquainted as newlyweds, within a day the Hunts were a couple dependent on one another for survival. At the same time, they found themselves in closer proximity to their tribe's origins than any of their kinfolk back home. For their cave shelter—which they remodeled into what archaeologists term a *cavate,* or cliff hollows with crudely constructed extensions that enlarge the living space—lay hard by Cebolleta Mesa, whose archaeological ruins of Calabash and Kowina are the last sites occupied by Acoma's early migrants before they ascended the mesa and blended with earlier occupants to form the Acoma ethnicity of historic times.

Still older is a spot on the western flank of Cebolleta Mesa, about ten miles from where Maria's father dropped them, where some ancestors of today's Acoma people lived even longer. Labeled as LA24D on archaeological maps, it has all the virtues of a superb village location. The wind-cut and rain-eroded cliff indents beneath a broad overhang of Mesa Verde sandstone, shielding it from winter winds. Nearby is a small grove of ponderosa pines. About a mile down Spider Canyon a green grassy patch amid the surrounding gray ground cover marks the spot where an underground aquifer pumps clear water to the surface year round—a more common phenomenon here in earlier centuries.

After the Acoma people gave Alfred E. Dittert and Reynold J. Ruppe their blessing to dig at this site from 1947 to 1952, within its rooms, great kiva, and remnants of the Chacoan road system the archaeologists found pottery fragments that they estimated to be over a thousand years old. But the shards lay atop a still older occupation level, which, although barren of pottery, revealed stone scrapers, wood choppers, hammer-stones, and pressure-flaked knives. Indians had continued to sleep, work, hunt, and build here well after the Spanish arrival, penning their sheep below and raising children. Dittert's photos of the field site, with its sockets where upright posts once stood, and storage pits and sitting benches sculpted out of sandstone in the rear cave portion, were not unlike the Hunts' new home. Although their audiences never knew it, when in later years the title of "Cliff-Dwellers" advertised the appearances of Edward and Marie Hunt and their children at Indian shows around America, the billing carried a certain credibility. For their *cavate* bore a similarity to those half-cliff dwellings carved out of the soft tufa walls of Los Frijoles Canyon in the fourteenth century that had inflamed Adolph Bandelier's imagination— and caused the environs to be preserved as Bandelier National Monument.

It is hard to imagine that the experience of a couple's banishment for transgressions of social norms did not ring a deeper bell. The sole book that Edward carried into the wilderness began with its parallel: a couple expelled from paradise and condemned to hide their nakedness in a wilderness. Edward had won his freedom, but at a price for which his future family would pay as well. Cast out of the garden, the couple faced the promise and the terror of a new beginning. How can one not envision them as some Native American Adam and Eve, tumbled from cultural grace, banished near-naked to this no-man's-land? How can one not see their exile as a break with everything that had given their lives cultural meaning and social stability, while at the same time invigorating them— or Edward at least—with an unprecedented sense of possibility?

Already Edward had undergone significant rebirths, but none this stark and perilous. Whether or not the Hunts survived out here, at least they would not have to answer to anyone again.

Brother Bibo Steps Up (1889–1910)

One day Solomon Bibo's Acoma Indian wife, Juana, came into the living room, bawling her eyes out. Through her sobs and tears she told Solomon that somehow, because of disease or storms or something they ate, she'd just learned that all her sheep had suddenly died. And she still owned a lot back in New Mexico, thousands and thousands. All gone. He just snapped at her and said, "Gayate, l'osico. Lo que tiene, pierde." (Be quiet, old one. He who has, loses.)

—Abe Peña, 2005

HOW THE HUNTS COPED in that half-cave, they never said, as if wanting to put those rough years behind them. One imagines that being raised at Acoma held them in good stead. They'd been schooled in plant knowledge, older foraging practices, hunting, and camping. By their age they could handle knives, hatchets, needles, scrapers, hammers. Marie could fix clothing out of hand-me-down scraps. Edward benefited from vocational skills he'd picked up in Albuquerque, shaping sandstone, making adobes, mortaring walls, banging together benches, a table from scrap wood. Relatives must have brought blankets, tools, axes, pots, possibly a rifle. From nearby Black Mountain—least known of the Southwest's three or four "Black Mountains"—he cut and hauled ponderosa timbers for roofing the extension to their cave.

Springs and feeder creeks to the San Jose River provided water for their clay jugs and gourd canteens. Wild animals abounded, from mountain cottontails to black-tailed jackrabbits, squirrels, prairie dogs, mule deer, and the occasional antelope, among others. Edward knew how to snare birds and smoke beehives. With his throwing club he got small mammals. Deer and the rest he stalked with bow and arrow or rifle, making sure to drink first the Oregon grape tea that prevented the contracting of sickness from any hooved creatures that he wounded. They could have eaten fried grasshoppers, mesquite beans, wild onions and wild celery, juniper berries, boiled acorns, among other natural foodstuffs. But whenever Acoma's feast days came around, with their giveaways of surplus food, someone probably dropped off pots of stew and blue cornbread. In late summer bags of extra local peaches, apricots, and apples would have come their way.

Their drug and grocery stores were the outdoors; on this borderland that drew upon volcanic and desert ecologies they were well stocked. Yucca was a special lifesaver. Crushed and soaked leaves and roots of the *Makani* yucca made body soap, its pounded leaf fibers were woven into rope, its ripe fruit, gathered at the moons of Corn in the Milk (September) and Mature Corn (October), could be consumed off the plant. A harsher soap that was better for washing hair came from *Haasha* yucca roots (sometimes mixed with *Siucha* grass to boost follicle growth). That plant's stalks were also used for fire-by-friction drill kits. Its soft heart shoots could be eaten outright or brewed into one of the hundred or more teas Acoma people made from wild plants, each targeting a specific affliction. Its chewed spiny leaves made fine-line brushes for painting pottery. And after baking to remove its skin, yucca fruit was boiled down to an inch-thick jelly, dried on scaffolds, and rolled into loaves, whereupon it could be resuscitated into a drink, a syrup, or a spread.

Adding to their winter larder were boiled Rocky Mountain bee seeds that were then dried and stuck to willow withes until the time came to mix them into hot mush. Boiled and dried shoots of pigweed were similarly stored for the cold months. Split-open, dried joints of cane cactus were preserved for winter consumption, while the plant's woody stems could be lit like candles for illumination. Cactus thorns served as needles, and their pith alleviated ear problems. Also stashed away for later consumption were dried chokecherries, buckthorn berries, hackberries, and pre-parched piñon nuts that might last for years.

When Marie bore the couple's first child, Ervin, her sister Juana or another female relative probably came to midwife. With spring water suffused with wormwood they freshened her bedding so as to repel bedbugs. Bundling together brome grass stems, they brushed her hair. When her labor got too hard they boiled a ragweed tea, and following the birth applied a lip fern douche. So it was with Alfred, the second son, born two years later, and then Allen, in mid-March 1894. After each birth, they probably helped wash Marie's head and provided a cedar emetic for cleansing her system. As nursing progressed, she brewed dogbane or milkweed teas for richer breast milk and then massaged the crushed leaves directly on them to encourage its flow.

So they survived.

Meanwhile, as Edward and his family were barely existing on the rim of the badlands, about ten miles away Marie's sister and Solomon's fortunes were looking up. From the roof of his cramped one-room store above St. Stephen's old convent, Solomon could gaze over the farther mesas and valleys like a lookout in a crow's nest, and feel just as isolated. His advocacy for Acoma's rights and marriage into the Valle family had insinuated him into its bosom.

But eventually this location proved a poor place to grow a business. Except for established, well-controlled public occasions, Acoma's inhabitants were as wary of outsiders as superstitious seamen or xenophobic islanders. With his ties to Acoma solid once again, in 1887 Bibo shifted to a more promising venue just outside the Spanish-speaking border town of Cubero.

Popular historians love gunslingers and sheriffs, cavalry fighters and rebel chiefs. But the role of lowly storekeepers like the Bibos and the Hunts in humanizing the West has been undersung. Initially peddling out of wagons at mountain passes or setting up shop at crossroads during seasonal fur rendezvous, the earliest traders were thrust into the role of multilingual culture brokers. Through links of kinship their Indian wives often tied them to a native clientele. The frontier's quintessential "contact zones," their more per-

Solomon Bibo's trading post at Cubero, where Edward worked.

manent, tent-roofed or log-cabin house-stores that came next functioned as destination points and resupply depots for government diplomats, official surveyors and explorers, wastrels and bandidos, maverick artists and tourists.

As trails, roads, military forts, family farms, new towns, and railroads edged toward the Pacific over the nineteenth century, these stores were replaced by more permanent trading houses. And they exchanged more than goods; every sack of flour, bolt of calico, Indian-made pot, or New York–manufactured screwdriver imported its expectations of new usages, changing values, upscale appetites, and new roles in somebody's domestic life, both white and Indian.

As critical as their economic function was in exchanging goods through the lingua franca of economic exchange, so were these establishments' offer of human discourse, if often rough-hewn and shorthand. These trading posts were forums where representatives of different cultures, nationalities, and stations of life faced and felt each other out, learned about local happenings, and got tips about regional dangers, incoming storms, and the availability of game. In such an offhand way they also helped to minimize the risks of misunderstanding and potential trouble.

Customers, neighbors, and hangers-on exchanged world news, talked shop, argued politics, made future appointments, located missing persons, gambled and played games, smoked, gossiped, joked, repaired gear, fed and rested livestock, and provisioned for setting forth again. Along with military posts, frontier schools, sheriff's offices, and new town halls, trading posts and country stores civilized the frontier—never more so than in this most multicultural corner of the American West.

For decades now, Solomon's brothers had traded in the Cubero–Grants–Fort Wingate region of Valencia County. Situated on a pre-Spanish Indian trail and named for a seventeenth-century territorial governor, Cubero was a weathered hamlet. By Solomon's arrival the little settlement suffered an outsized notoriety as a hangout for Mexican slave traders, Anglo bootleggers, and gunrunners. Its Navajo name meant "water in a crevice," referring to the perennial spring nearby, a good reason for Solomon to open here. Another virtue was that its location snagged valley traffic on the wagon trail from Laguna to Grants, overnighters from the Santa Fe Railroad, and shepherds descending Mount Taylor to barter grass-fattened animals for coffee, sugar, flour, and bacon.

Within his new compound, Solomon maintained corrals for watering and feeding visiting mounts, sheds for surplus tools, barns stocked with hay and wool, and counters for tallying goods and writing letters. Villagers from the surrounding Spanish hamlets of Marquez, Cebolleta, and San Mateo became regulars. His having been Acoma's governor also lured friends, family, and clan members from the mesa, Acomita, and McCartys. Competition from Anglos at Laguna and his brothers' stores denied Solomon a total monopoly, but after his lease debacle, one might imagine that one of Solomon's *dichos* might have been, *bastante es*—"enough is plenty."

At Bibo Mercantile one ran into Canoncito Navajos, Hispano villagers, Mormons from Ramah, comparative shoppers from Laguna Pueblo stacking Bibo's prices against the Gunns' store back home, Zunis visiting in-laws at Acoma and Laguna, shepherds and cowboys passing through, and any religious missionaries or governmental officials catching up on who was who and looking to influence them. Plus there was the occasional exotic who wandered in—a Jicarilla Apache from the northeast, skittish gypsies asking to camp along Cubero Creek, a pale-faced eastern painter with a portable easel strapped to his back, pioneer photographers heading for the Hopi Snake Dance, or Zuni priests down from depositing prayer sticks for rain in the "lightning hole" at Mount Taylor's summit.

To interact with this customer base called for a movable skill Solomon's tribe held in high regard. For a Jew to flourish in the Diaspora, says George Steiner, he must become "a guest among men. . . . He learns the languages of his hosts, but may strive to speak them better." Before and after religious or social feast days at Acoma, Laguna, Cubero, or San Mateo, around Bibo's potbelly stove, sheep pen, loading dock, or dinner table crowded with visitors, could be heard a southwestern Babel, and Solomon conversant in it all.

Whether on his own or provoked by his wife, Juana, or her sister, Marie, Solomon must have extended a proposition to his banished brother-in-law. One assumes that Edward's apprenticeship began with watering and feeding the sheep, stocking goods, sweeping, and keeping the store and warehouses free of rodents. Edward watched as Solomon maintained his inventory of coffee, sacks of sugar and rice, packages of lard, locally dried peaches and apricots, cans of preserved fruit, bolts of cloth, work shoes, harnesses for horses, light wagons that were kept out back, and patent medicines—all items that by now were found in Indian and Hispano homes alike. During this training Edward learned to mix the pure spirit of Solomon's stripped-down form of capitalism with the Protestant work ethic hammered into him at school.

Solomon's dealmaking braided together three different styles of exchange. The oldest mode of obtaining exotic goods Edward had imbibed in his mother's milk. For thousands of years southwestern Indians trafficked in raw materials and handcrafted objects over hundreds of miles on the long-distance trade routes that crisscrossed the Southwest and tied together old Mexico, the Pacific Ocean, and the Mississippian Southeast. As New Mexico's most isolated village, Acoma generally received these rarities from Zuni Pueblo, but also traded with the Rio Grande villages.

Many items were received through informal, local exchanges or as gifts from foreign guests during intergroup feasting. Some were part of a ceremonial redistribution or more formal sit-downs between established "trading partners." This sometimes meant that reciprocity was "delayed"; one could wait to make good on a transaction until the next season came around. Even though Solomon was running a profit-making enterprise, with his in-laws, relatives of officials, and old friends from Acoma and Laguna he probably had no choice but to give and take through such highly personalized gift exchanges.

Edward's first clock, which accompanied him wherever he set up shop. Clock time, introduced by the railroad, reinforced by the boarding school schedule, replaced diurnal time.

To this tribal tradition of drawn-out trade Solomon grafted the Hispano form of economic partnership known as the *Partido* system. In a region where Churro wool was the basic currency, he paid shepherds in advance to feed and protect his stock over the winter. In spring they would be sheared, the rough outer coat separated from the finer inner fleece, the lucrative "clip" stuffed into long cloth bags. Upon receiving this semiprocessed material, Solomon subtracted the cutting costs and a percentage of the original loan. To his shepherds fell the burden of keeping his animals healthy and replacing any that died. Although Anglo traders who bought into this system claimed the collateral of Hispano ranches and farms if droughts or hoof-and-mouth disease prevented the borrowers from returning all the animals, Bibo probably found other ways to balance accounts with his local "partners."

With a third style of doing business that relied on Jewish connections in Albuquerque and Santa Fe, Solomon must have felt most comfortable. These contacts benefited him in many ways. Located within sight of the Santa Fe Railroad, Solomon's new post at Cubero was easily replenished by their shipments and, by extension, their eastern suppliers. By example the Spiegelbergs also taught him financial planning. Keenly aware of the prejudices that could rend the cordial veneer between Jews and others, they also showed him how to steer clear of direct competition.

With his Cubero store proving a moneymaker in its local niche, Solomon followed the lead of other frontier Jews who set enough aside for an upgrade. While the Spiegelbergs relocated to New York, in 1898, Solomon and Juana, with daughters Irma, Clara, and Celia, chose the opposite coast. Although Juana wanted her husband to sell off his New Mexico interests, Solomon balked, enjoying his frequent trips back at shearing and lambing times (they still owned the twenty thousand sheep and retained interest in various Valencia County stores).

Upon moving to San Francisco, Solomon invested in real estate, but storekeeping remained his forte. His co-owned, fine-quality grocery at the corner of Polk and California streets, Bibo, Newman & Eichenberg, provided an outlet for imports from New Mexico as well as more distant suppliers. Until mid-April 1906 it gained goodwill and flourished. But after the San Francisco earthquake reduced it to matchsticks, the fire department dynamited what was left to prevent a three-day inferno from spreading.

In only a few days the relationships of a decade earlier had turned around. Now it was the Bibos who had to create a new life in a charred wasteland, while back in the region they had vacated, the Hunts' prospects were on the rise.

28

New Merchant in Town (1900–10)

Cultural intermediaries have contributed to the history of North America in significant, albeit largely unheralded ways. Across the centuries, from the colonial era to the present, they have endured hostility as well as danger, but their persistent curiosity about the "other side" has given them the incentive to thrive on that supersensory awareness necessary for moving between and among different worlds. They have stepped outside, while others have remained within.

—Margaret Connell Szasz, 1994

WHILE SOLOMON BIBO turned most of his Cubero operation over to relatives and relocated in San Francisco, Edward scouted around for a place of his own. Like his mentor's first trading post, his would lie within the reservation boundaries. Instead of atop the mesa, however, Edward eyed a promising spot in Acomita, on the reservation's northern border. Although it was not his intention, this marginal location would position him as another culture broker, an unofficial role for which his study of Solomon's social interaction with a wide range of customers surely prepared him. To the increasing dismay of the more conservative of his fellow tribesmen, over the next seventeen years he would become Acoma's major meeter-and-greeter.

The location of Hunt's store was also a reflection of his ever-precarious status, as someone who would benefit from being *of* the traditional community but was no longer willing to pay the price of being fully *in* it. In

The Hunts' new home in Acomita village, northern satellite of the old pueblo.

hindsight, the prospects for a permanent berth at Acomita were forseeably dim. Given the estrangements with elders and in-laws that the Hunts had already suffered, how could they not expect that such a high-profile role would not lead to another, even more decisive rupture? But Edward was a struggling householder, with little ones to feed and few alternatives. This was the next best step.

At the foot of Acomita's boulder-strewn mesa, squeezed between its wagon road and the southern lip of the San Jose River basin, Edward and his sons scratched out the main structure's twenty-by-forty-foot outline. Its advantages were undeniable. For his immediate neighbors in Acomita it offered the convenience of staples like coffee, flour, sugar, and matches within walking distance. Facing the sole dirt road, it caught traffic bound for Acoma mesa and travelers heading east for Laguna Pueblo, the Rio Puerco villages, Los Lunas, or Albuquerque. Overlooking the fertile river bottom, it was a short footpath from Edward's cornfields and fruit orchards, which did well in the floodplain soil. Proximity to the San Jose offered easy irrigating—"Hunt's Ditch" runs there to this day. The site also put him within a few hundred yards of the river and the AT&SF tracks, which meant that Edward could add a post office's appeal and clientele. And the location offered a panorama of sacred Mount Taylor to the north, whose changeable cloud cover could be monitored throughout the day like a weather forecast.

While mixing, molding, and sun-drying adobe bricks, Edward and his boys, probably assisted by his brothers and brothers-in-law, collected wood for rafters, windows, and doors. After raising two-foot-thick walls, they roofed a shallow gable frame with corrugated metal sheeting, then plastered inside and out. With its shell up, next came bringing the place to life.

From his clerking at Cubero, plus innumerable visits to the Bibo and Marmon brothers' posts, and even one side trip to Lorenzo Hubbell's legendary compound in Ganado, Arizona, Edward had a template for his store. As one entered from Acomita's dirt street, there was a long L-shaped wooden counter at the rear, lifted chest high to deter a scoundrel from grabbing at the till and, over the years, scraped hollow from use. It held an embossed metal cash register and a glass jar of hard candy. Underneath were stashed tools and a protective firearm. A hinged break let Edward lift and squeeze out to greet visitors, cart in new supplies, shoo out unwanted dogs. Behind the counter rose shelving for the usual necessities: canned fruit, matches, salt, dried yeast, flour, tackle, Arbuckle coffee cans, needles, shears, plug tobacco, coal oil, and more, often depending on individual requests.

On the left was Edward's half-enclosed post office nook and the desk where he kept accounts and sorted mail. To the right was a darkened storage room with bins for flour sacks, dried corn, stacked sheep hides, and wool cuttings. All around the main room were more shelves for bolts of calico, tin cups, and enamel cookingware, locally made Acoma and Laguna ceramics on consignment, hooks for bridles and livery, a few saddles propped against the corner, and a hanging pole displaying Navajo blankets.

Dominating the rough-planked floor space, the "bull pen," stood the room's potbelly stove, its metal stack rising through the roof, split juniper and piñon firewood piled beside it. Against the wall were a few straight-backed chairs that could be hauled close to the heat in winter. Among the sensations upon entering the merchandise-stuffed interior was a swirl of smells—aromas of sage, piñon, and cedar; saddle-soaped and oiled bridles and leather livery; dust from crushed hay and boot-stuck manure; sweaty horsemen and wagon drivers; mutton fat; and odors that escaped from Marie's chili-roasting, lamb-stewing, bread-and-pie baking, and coffee-brewing back in the house kitchen.

Interrupting the shelving behind the counter was the door to the family's private quarters. Here was their large dining room with cookstoves and pantries to the left, a walled-off bedroom to the right, and an extra-large table for midday feasts in the middle. Another door opened to a screened-in rear porch, where the family slept on a sheepskin-padded floor in summertime. In line with the dropoff to the river plain Edward planted a row of cottonwoods. Nearby, Marie tended their extensive corn, bean, squash, and gourd gardens, fed by his new ditch. A few hundred yards east Edward spaced his apple, peach, and apricot trees. Far to the south, as well as on open pasturage along the upper base of Mount Taylor, they ran their cows and sheep.

The crocodile tears shed across America over the widespread lamentation that the country's Indians were a "vanishing species" were in flood as the nation approached its new century. The year the Hunts moved into Acomita, the total number of American Indians in the United States was down to around 238,000, and still falling. This meant an overall population loss of over 96 percent since Columbus's arrival. The decline was due to four centuries of disease, famine, poverty, warfare, murder, forced removal, and collective depression.

Coupled with these crises was the drastic diminishment in Indian landholdings. As a consequence of the 1887 General Allotment Act and its fragmentation of treaty lands and allocation of plots to individual Indian householders, by 1890 tribes had lost well over seventeen million acres, or about one-seventh of their remaining properties across the country.

Painters, sculptors, and photographers exploited the nation's distress over the plight of the Indian by portraying broken warriors fading into sunsets, riding alongside train tracks or telegraph wires, or slumped over drooping horses. Such was the sentimental image satirized by newspaper editors and cartoonists as "Poor Lo" (from "Lo, the Poor Indian"). What no political or social forecasters were willing to admit was how this pathetic vision caused inner sighs of relief. If everyone remained patient, natural attrition and what some called "the normal replacement of one race by another" would solve the "Indian Problem" all by itself.

As so often, the situation with Pueblo Indians did not fit into this picture of Indian malaise, and defied predictions of imminent demise. Their populations remained fairly stable, if consistently low. And nowhere, ironically, was the spirit of American optimism and insurgent capitalism stronger than on a small piece of ground in the hamlet of Acomita where Edward Hunt was preparing to fill some of the economic vacuum left by the departure of Solomon Bibo.

Perhaps Edward thought that, as an Acoma Indian, he could do better

Edward's store, the new commercial hub of Acomita.

among his own people than in Cubero. Here was a customer base whose cycle of ceremonial requirements, food preferences, and basic needs he knew firsthand. Whether he had sufficient savings or Solomon grubstaked him, we have no record, nor do we know when he opened for business. One assumes he won the approval of the Acoma cacique, whose ancient office, like the community "mother" for whom the man was a stand-in, "owned" all the pueblo's lands and held the power to grant house plots everywhere on the reservation. But it's a good bet that Edward was the first *native* Indian trader in western New Mexico, if not across the territory.

Setting up his own shop offered a chance to reinvent the white man's system. Apart from his cottonwoods and fruit orchards, what Edward planted at Acomita, more durably than Solomon ever accomplished up on the mesa, was an outpost of "pioneer capitalism" pared to the basics. Everything but the land would be privately owned. For the white reformers who aspired to "individualize" the Indian on a national level such free enterprise would have been considered a powerful measure of success, even as it was anathema to Acoma's collective ethos. Because Edward was Indian he needn't apply for a trader's license on the reservation; in this out-of-the way venue he didn't worry about non-Indian competitors.

At the same time, free of regulatory controls, Edward could exercise a monopoly over pricing, which meant his cost structure was flexible enough to absorb the ups and downs of weather conditions and uneven availability of goods. Perhaps he also persuaded his suppliers in Albuquerque to offer him exclusive rights on the reservation, so long as existing outlets in Laguna, Cubero, or Grants were not threatened. Promotion, advertising, markups, and modes of exchange were his to create on an informal, ad hoc basis, since in this outlier there was little oversight other than community gossip and maintenance of goodwill.

With his unique accumulation of previous on-the-job experiences, intelligence, charisma, and ties to extended blood and in-law families and like-minded "progressives," and energized by the spirit of homespun entrepreneurship, onetime pauper Edward Hunt was positioned to become the region's first native patron.

To his compound Edward added a barn for his mules, horses, wagons, and livery. He built a chicken coop for a regular supply of eggs to cook and sell. To cross the San Jose and its marsh he nailed together a spindly footbridge;

Along with the clock, the book: Edward's first Bible also accompanied him everywhere. Here shown by son Wilbert Hunt.

as Acomita postmaster he needed this in order to reach the north bank of the railbed before 10 a.m. That was when, each morning, he hooked a three-foot-long outgoing canvas sack onto a mail crane for its pickup, and awaited the incoming sack, kicked out of the speeding train car's open door, to carry back to his store for sorting.

By 1900 Edward was doing so well that he expanded his interests. Near Alaska, one of the AT&SF railroad stops a few miles west of Acomita, where the San Jose River funneled through rocks to produce a sufficiently powerful flue, he imitated his Hispano neighbors and constructed a small *molino,* or flour mill. It was powered by a wooden waterwheel, its two circular grinder rocks shaped from volcanic boulders dragged by Edward's mule team from the Malpais badlands. Near Needle Rock, at the base of old Acoma, he established a smaller, gable-roofed outlet to serve visitors on feast days, and a ranch where his retainers, working off debts, ran his growing cattle herd. At various pasturages, near Dripping Springs and north to Mount Taylor, others looked after his quickly multiplying flocks of two- (and sometimes four-) horned sheep.

In Albuquerque Edward's wagons became regular visitors to Putney's all-purpose supply at First and Railroad, which had catered to Indian tastes since 1880. Creating working relationships with the succession of "boss farmers" who were appointed as agricultural advisers by the Pueblo Indian agent located in Albuquerque to help the Indians improve the variety and yield of their farmlands, Edward took on the transportation of coal and other official supplies from the city.

As if to keep up with her husband's expanding domain, Marie maintained a steady production of the couple's children, eventually bearing a dozen. Two years after Allen's birth, in 1896 Evelyn became their first girl, arriving in their Acomita bedroom. Two years later came her little sister Cecelia. The new century was marked by Clyde's birth. Next came Henry Wayne, born in mid-November 1902, followed by Ida Pearl in 1904, and Wilbert Edward on October 22, 1907. Their last three were girls, Mary, who died in infancy in 1908, Josephine Viola, born in 1910, and Florence Angeline in 1914.

From each delivery, Marie rolled the afterbirth in a cloth wrapping. As soon as she could walk a few steps, she buried it at the base of the cottonwoods that lined the raised bank of the San Jose floodplain. No matter where they moved after this, a piece of her body and theirs would remain in the land. After another four days, Edward made sure a relative or medicine man held each of their little bodies up to the sun. Then he and Marie bestowed an "Indian name," in their Keresan language, likewise tying them to their people and its history.

<hr>

29

Around the House (1911–15)

The dinner was a mixture of many traditions. Down the center of the table matzohs, unleavened bread, alternated with guayave, *the unleavened ceremonial bread of the Acomas. Chicken and farfel, a tiny noodle of German origin, was served with deer jerky brought from the pueblo. It was a happy crowd and although the languages spoken were as varied as the food, the laughter was universal.*

—Bobette Gugliotta, 1974

A T AGE THREE, Wilbert Hunt, the family's ninth child, started first grade at the same Acomita day school that was established by Solomon Bibo, only a stone's throw from Edward's home-store. About five years later he was sent to St. Catherine in Santa Fe, the boarding school Edward had helped to build nearly thirty years earlier. When Wilbert returned for his first summer vacation, in 1915, his father was at the height of his prominence as the village's richest citizen.

Wilbert's recollections of those Acomita holidays, which lasted until Edward's high profile precipitated the crisis that exiled his family from Acoma, remained the sharpest of his life. No Indians saved journals or daybooks in those times, and his father's store records were never archived. The fragmentary memories that Wilbert kept until he was almost a century old sprang to mind out of chronological sequence. But they were always vivid and usually brought smiles and wonderment as they recalled another American way of life.

First was his physical memory of returning each summer to the puppy pile of brothers and sisters. All were quickly growing up, their distinctive personalities emerging. After starting, like Wilbert, at the Acomita day school, Edward's first three sons had been sent to Haskell Indian School in Lawrence, Kansas. Like Albuquerque Indian School, this institution was modeled after Pratt's Carlisle school and opened in 1884 to a multitribal clientele.

But now, a generation after the Indian boarding school idea was launched, the thinking in Indian education had degenerated. The importance of the three Rs and humanities became secondary to instilling practical skills in "the Indian child" who, in the estimation of Estelle Reed, President McKinley's choice for national Indian education director, "is of lower physical organization than the white child . . . his very instincts and modes of thought are adjusted to this imperfect manual development . . . his face seems stolid because it is without free expression." Once the basics in reading, writing, and arithmetic skills were over with, Indian boys should concentrate on learning to become cobblers, field hands, and factory laborers, the girls seamstresses, lace-makers, and domestics.

Aside from the pleasure the Hunt boys found playing clarinets in Haskell's school marching bands—an Indian school staple everywhere, with its appeal of being outdoors, traveling with sports teams, and wearing nifty uniforms with fancy piping—the discrepancy between this dreary prospect and the more open futures envisaged by their entrepreneurial father may have caused them to quit after a few years. Ervin was maturing into a quietly obedient, serious young man, possessed of a strong work ethic, the same with Allen. As for Clyde, a cutup who'd do anything for a laugh, he was the only brother whom Wilbert remembered his father chasing around the house with doubled-up rope.

More worrisome was Cecelia, who returned from Haskell with a case of tuberculosis, a not uncommon result of school dorm life. To quarantine her from contagious contact, Edward built a shack a few hundred feet from home, where food was left outside her door every day. Next were the problems Edward was having with Alfred because of his susceptibility to enticements

Success allowed for Edward's second store (upper right), open during feast days and special events below Acoma mesa.

from old-timers on the mesa. He would disappear for days and nights, return stone-faced and uncommunicative, often unavailable at home whenever secret religious doings took place. Was Alfred succumbing to the clutches of those Edward and Marie now referred to as the tribe's "black magicians"?

The greater Edward's economic success, the more intense grew community pressure that his boys be initiated into the kivas. They were wanted not only for the fiesta dances but for what the progressive Acomans like their father disparaged as "the old religion." Edward's opposition to his sons joining these activities stirred grumbling around the village about his excessive wealth and gossip about his comfortable rapport with outsiders.

Let those remain his dad's worries; young Wilbert was too busy with summer fun. By now the cottonwoods his father had planted near his store's hitching posts were leafing out at forty feet. Edward's orchards, a few dozen peach and apple trees, were heavy with fruit. Men paying off store debts were tending his growing cattle herd near the Patoche Butte just southeast of Acoma mesa. Others were pasturing his thirteen thousand head of sheep on the southeastern slopes of Mount Taylor.

On summer mornings Wilbert loved sitting on the roof waiting for the westbound train. As soon as it pealed its whistle at the Alaska crossing he cranked his forearm up and down. The conductor threw him a wave and a few extra toots as he screamed toward Grants.

The two-week stretches Wilbert spent under the sky and the stars with Clyde looking after sheep on Mount Taylor's eastern flanks were the most delightful hours he would know. Anything could happen out there, anything might be seen. Brown bears, rattlesnakes, coyotes, eagles, ants working and sheep mating. Hispano shepherds sometimes shared their coffee. After the rainstorms the desert was radiant with rinsed light and the earth smelled fresh and ripe. The nights were cool and sometimes swept with meteor showers. Once they were out there, enjoying an after-lunch siesta, his older brother Clyde absorbed in the latest Zane Grey novel, when they made out three horsemen in the scrub, silently sitting on their horses and staring at them. The boys got to their feet. With stately formality two of the riders egged their horses toward them. Bundles sat over their saddle horns. Beneath their eyes ran streaks of red paint.

They were Acoma's war chief and his cooks, on pilgrimage to Mount Taylor. The bundles carried prayer sticks for depositing into the shrine orifice at the summit. Ritually cleansed with smoke, fasting, and celibacy, the men were to be given a respectful distance. Edward had earlier alerted his sons that if they showed up to give them what they wanted. The riders halted about thirty feet away and addressed them in low voices and declared what their father had promised. The visitors were permitted to cull a ewe, butcher her in the trees, and then they disappeared up the mountain.

Because of his school year's late-spring schedule, Wilbert was not on hand when Cubero's chapter of Los Hermanos Penitentes conducted their physically exacting Holy Week devotions. Their processions accompanied the year's choice for Christ as he hauled his full-size cross down a rock-marked path to the hillock serving as Calvary and tied him to it. The cross was raised among other crosses as fellow Penitentes sought to identify as intimately as possible with their Savior's pain and passion. In this fairly live-and-let-live multicultural region, as some have written, "eyewitness accounts do not tell of [Pueblo] Indians rubbing elbows with Anglos in the underbrush" to spy on these rites; Acoma had enough problems protecting its own ceremonies from the intrusions of outsiders to trespass on others. And Wilbert knew the trouble his father's friend Charles Lummis got into after photographing the Brothers at San Mateo.

But one mid-August day, Wilbert did crawl in the scrub within eyesight of the Cubero brotherhood's adobe *morada*. From hiding he watched the file of Corpus Christi celebrants heading back up that hill. Old gilt-fringed cloth banners featuring painted saints whipped in the wind. Biers bearing carved *santos* were carried on shoulders uphill to the slow rhythms of shrill flutes and ponderous drums.

One morning there was a clattering and coughing outside the house. Waiting for their caravan of three engines to cool down were the Hunts' Osage Indian in-laws. They'd just arrived on their annual excursion from northern Oklahoma for the Albuquerque fair. Amos Hamilton had married into a branch of the Valle family after meeting his future Pueblo wife at Carlisle boarding school. Thanks to oil strikes on their reservation, his tribe had gained notoriety as the richest per capita community in the world. The Osage poured their dollars into hiring white carpenters to build elaborate mansions, filling them with imported furniture, then mostly abandoning them as they preferred tipi living in their backyards or camping in extensive family compounds out in the bush. There they retired during summers, hosting hundreds in huge guest halls, roasting beef quarters over large brick pits, and conducting all-night meetings of the peyote-using Native American Church in jewel-box-like wooden "church houses" that they also hired white carpenters to construct.

With the caravan of Hamilton cars came their African-American servants and trunks overflowing with fancy western clothing. Each summer Wilbert and the rest looked forward to riding in their latest Cadillacs. He remembered the Osage as physically overpowering, hospitable beyond belief, their wall-tents and large barbecues open to all, and he and his siblings falling asleep to adult laughter in their ears.

Another summer highlight was mid-June's chicken pull, the spectacle of Acoma men on twisting and falling horses, bloodying each other as they fought over a cock buried to the neck on the sandy bank just below the

The three oldest Hunt boys—born in a cave—in the Haskell Indian School marching band, Lawrence, Kansas. Left to right: *Allen, Ervin, Alfred.*

Padre's Trail. Their father wouldn't let his boys join in, which especially rankled Alfred. But they could watch the morning footraces, in homage to both Santiago (Saint James), impersonated in the plaza by the little horse puppeteer, and to Chapiyu, the black-dressed horseman who joined the little horse as it pranced around the plaza. Then, following prayers to the dwelling places of all horses, the war chief let Acoma boys choose mounts from the St. Stephen's corral and ride counterclockwise around Lonesome Rock four times before the actual tussle over the chicken. Soon they'd torn it to shreds and dispersed its parts, as in a sacrifice, to the four directions.

One summer's pull was especially memorable. Among the riders maneuvering their horses up the sandy drift was Pero, a man Wilbert knew had served time in New Mexico state prison for cattle rustling. He was tough and had enemies. One was the same religious leader who'd horsewhipped Edward in the kiva years before. His quirt handle was weighted with lead. As the riders rammed their mounts into each other, grabbing at the mess of bloody feathers and rooster flesh, this one sought out Pero. In the whirling no one saw him turn the quirt around and crack Pero's skull. Wilbert remembered him falling dead in the sand.

◆ ◆ ◆

Then there was joining his father on buying trips. Wilbert hitched a brace of mules to the buckboard for the three-day run to Putney's supply in Albuquerque. They camped the night on the banks of the Rio Puerco, not far from the Canoncito outpost of off-reservation Navajos who'd holed up there for nearly a hundred years. Far to the east twinkled Albuquerque's distant lights, where they arrived the next day. After hours of bargaining, buying, and socializing, they tarped their wagonload and set off. They rekindled their riverside campfire from the previous night and reached home the next evening.

After they opened their second store below the mesa for St. Stephen's Day and other fiestas, it was Wilbert's assignment to wrap their grandfather clock in quilts for the bumpy wagon ride from Acomita. Along with his Bible and money box, it accompanied Edward everywhere. Like talismans of his business persona, the three were by his side as he sold odds and ends to a community that preferred teaching through oral tradition, time-counting by the sun, and exchanging goods and services rather than using white man's currency.

But Edward was not against having a good time. Besides, it was good business making his store a community center. This included sponsoring gambling, dances, and competitions. Card games took place on blankets spread on the store floor, the men cross-legged and smoking, throwing coins into the central pot. More elaborate was the betting over foot- and horse races. Setting the date weeks in advance allowed people to save up money, jewelry, whatever they wanted to place behind their teams. On the appointed day wagons and horses packed the roadside. On two Mexican blankets out front the wagers were piled. Agreements were made over equivalent items—a silver concho belt for a saddle, and so forth—until all were satisfied.

Readying themselves, the runners took up starting positions behind the cornmeal line on the ground between the piles of goods. At a pistol shot, the two teams of runners, each kicking their marked kick sticks, headed across the main Acomita bridge. Then they turned north, running along the old wagon road to the seven volcanic humps outside today's Sky City Casino. Their bare feet kicked at the sticks, keeping them sailing through the air. All told they raced perhaps a dozen miles before returning to Edward's store. Then the winning bets were distributed.

The races over, around noon it was Edward's custom to take a look around before locking the front door. Whoever was still inside was welcome at their table spread with pails of chili-spiced lamb stew, pots of beans with gourd ladles, boiled squash and roasted ears of corn, home-brewed, honey-sweetened Indian teas, loaves of leavened bread and rolls from Marie's outdoor oven, and fruit pies for dessert.

So fell the golden seasons of a storekeeper's son.

30

The Noose Tightens (1917–18)

One whose eyes or lids look red is always regarded with suspicion here, for witch-people are supposed not to sleep at night, but to change themselves into animals and roam over the world. Eccentric actions also lay one open to accusation; and when I first came here I was dangerously near being classed with the witches because I imitated various animal cries to their great edification, but to the various serious doubts of their elders. The fact that they doubt whether Americans know enough to be first-class witches was largely instrumental in saving me from serious danger.

—Charles F. Lummis, 1891

O NE WILD NIGHT confirmed for Edward that his family's days at Acomita were numbered. That a witch had not attacked earlier was testimony to the protective aura of his independent and forceful personality, economic success, and increasing importance as a cross-cultural communicator. But those same traits also placed him under suspicion. Unless he was a witch, how else could a single family accumulate such wealth?

For many Keresan pueblos the sacred clown's outlined eyes and black-banded, white-spotted body paint that had once covered Edward as an initiated Koshare were close to what rumors said witches looked like. Together

with his nonconformist, go-it-alone attitude, he was prime sorcerer material. So when a witch finally came, it was possibly a preemptive strike.

Edward's immersion in the ways of shamans and clowns may have also
given his enemies pause. Acoma's healers, after all, worked the same terrain as her sorcerers, only to positive rather than negative effect. The shopkeeper's manifest powers were such that none dared target him directly.
Instead, the evildoer went after one of his family's youngest and most vulnerable members—seven-year-old Josephine.

Around midnight, with everyone wrapped in blankets on floor mattresses, the child shot upright. She was delirious, her body convulsing, then
she began crying uncontrollably. There was nothing Marie could do. At the
same time a racket drew Edward to the back window. A shape like an oversize dog was scratching at the screen. Most members of the pack of half-wild
pets that roamed Acomita he recognized on sight—but not this creature.

Pulling on trousers and boots, Edward slipped into the front room and
reached beneath the counter. Normally he was averse to firearms, not even

Old method: winnowing wheat by hand at Acoma.

carrying one on the long wagon rides through open country to restock from Albuquerque suppliers before feast days. You keep guns around, he told his boys, you attract gunfire. But he'd been advised to have something to protect his post office against thieves. As he stood under the stars, the Henry .44-40 rifle in his hands, there was enough illumination to see paw prints in the sand.

The tracks wound this way and that before dropping into the shallow river basin. Ahead was the animal, at the narrow footbridge across the San Jose, not moving, just looking back at him. Steadying the barrel against a wall, he pulled the trigger. He heard a cry. It was not a dog's—more like a young girl's, but he couldn't see a body.

Back in the house his other kids were still asleep. They hadn't heard their sister's cries, the scratching dog, the gun blast, or the scream. He rousted everybody. "I shot a dog," he told his brother Cipriano. "Did you hear it?" They lit lanterns, borrowed another rifle, and returned to the bridge. Blood was smeared on the planks. Droplets led past the tiny hut where Cecelia was quarantined, past the gardens, along Hunt's irrigation ditch, and into the darkness. Edward called a halt and they went back to bed.

At sunup, after folding the bedding and rolling mattresses against the walls, they retraced their steps. Flattened grass indicated where the injured thing had lain down before moving on. They reached the railroad tracks and followed them west. Now wherever there was open ground instead of dog pads they saw the footprints of a small person.

Edward, like everyone around Acoma and most other pueblos, was raised within a climate of anxiety about witchery. Trouble was never random or neutral; it had to be personified, demonized, and fought. Disease epidemics, unbroken drought, tragic accidents, plagues of caterpillars or grasshoppers—someone must have done something to someone with malicious intent. Unhappiness, grumpiness, depression, or anger, attitudes considered antisocial; selfishness, independence, arrogance, nervousness, unexplained absences from the community; a preference for competition over cooperation, a tendency toward solitude—all were danger signs that witches were afoot.

How shape-shifting witches conducted their nasty business under cover of night was the subject of accounts that usually followed a script.

Some malevolent animal or being mysteriously showed up; a wolf, rat, owl, frog, or hitchhiking stranger, even a fireball in a lightning storm. Just as spookily, the ominous arrival then disappeared.

Often there ensued a chase; the creature was killed or dismembered in gruesome fashion. Coincidentally, someone else was discovered dead or injured. In the cosmic balance of good and bad, Acoma's medicine men, their culture's countervailing force to evildoers, tried to bring them around, usually without success. Finally, some revelation about the dead person explained their turn to the dark side.

Local talk about witches was drawing close to home. "It's a wonder that they haven't done anything to me," Edward had said one evening, "as much as some of them hate me."

Then his son Wilbert's Acoma schoolmate from Albuquerque Indian School committed suicide by jumping off his dorm's third-story roof. Just beforehand, a siege of whooping cough had infected the mesa; there were casualties. Late one night, people heard drumming in Acoma's streets; it sounded like a throat hacking. The medicine societies set up a rock crystal altar that directed them a few miles west of Acoma.

They found a saddled horse and recognized Bessie, the Albuquerque student's animal, and nearby they trapped a "witch man." As they were lowering their captive into a kiva, he turned into a rat and scampered across the dirt floor. After beating and burning it to death, the shamans declared the student a witch. The next day the local Indian agent and Edward's friend, Philip T. Lonergan, got the phone message about the boy having killed himself the previous evening. A cause-and-effect narrative having been pieced together, the boy's "two hearted" identity was confirmed, for which his marginalized status as a uniform-wearing, English-speaking boarding school student surely made him eligible (as Edward had been, and for which he'd been given that horsewhipping, the identical punishment afforded a caught witch). With this verdict, the student's corpse was denied burial in the St. Stephen's cemetery.

And there was the recent day when one of Edward's nephews had helped chase a wolf-witch. A fellow pursuer confided to the boy that the night before, he'd dreamt about a feral cat entering Edward's store. The storekeeper unlocked his door for the search party. They looked everywhere, to no avail. But the site was clearly marked in Acoma consciousness as a den of potential trouble.

◆ ◆ ◆

After coming on those human footprints along the San Jose river bottom, Edward headed for Acoma mesa to consult an old medicine man and silversmith. The signs came from a witch in training, he said, and Josephine had been her test. If Edward hadn't shot, his child would have died. In three days, predicted the old man, you'll know who she was. On that date a girl who lived down the tracks between Acomita and McCartys refused to get out of bed. When she died they found rags hiding a bullet hole in her side.

Edward, a standout success, had become the focus of jealousy and suspicion. His flocks numbered almost twenty thousand sheep, and his second store below the mesa was a moneymaker. His Albuquerque outlets kept him well supplied. He made no secret of siding with government agents on issues of schooling, modernizing farming practices, helping the railroad, and getting Acoma's youth to sign up for World War I. He even rented a home to a government "farmer." By 1917 he'd become Acoma's preeminent example of a Pueblo progressive, a friend to whites and Hispanos alike, a model for tomorrow's Indian.

People wondered, how was he doing so much better than everyone else,

New method: Edward Hunt (right) and sons using government-issued gas-driven threshing machine at Acomita.

and was he revealing tribal secrets to those outsiders who kept showing up at his store? It became harder to ignore the frozen faces when some towns-folk, even neighbors and relatives, walked by his door without even glancing in. Some made a point of traveling the extra miles to trade in Laguna, Cubero, even Grants.

Had these tensions affected him alone, Edward might have stood his ground. A courageous and stubborn man, he had a thick hide by now. But much as white educators were willing to abandon Indian parents as a lost cause and pour their energies into assimilating their children, Acoma's religious officials may have given up on Edward and his progressive cohort. Instead they went after his sons, their community's future. Nineteen-year-old Alfred, a composer of songs and eager participant in public dances, was already slipping under their spell.

With matters coming to a head, and not quite ready to join Albuquerque's handful of pioneering "urban Indians," a term that wouldn't enter common usage for another quarter century, that July the Hunts began scouting for a new home. Marie had a Laguna relative who was drilling wells for Sandia Pueblo, a small Tiwa-speaking village of fewer than a hundred members that had survived through seven centuries of abandonment and resettlement. In the past it had provided sanctuary to Pueblo refugees, notably from the Hopi mesas. Maybe, her cousin suggested, it would do the same for them.

Located north of Albuquerque, Sandia, with its proximity to Berna-lillo, had a Hispano flavor. The brush-covered sand hills promised good hunting. Access to the Rio Grande meant her fields were so well watered that there was even a danger of seasonal flooding. Then they learned how deeply conservative Sandia actually was; its small population was no defense against the Pueblo susceptibility to fractious politics, no fellow Protestants resided there, and according to Marie's cousin-in-law Robert Marmon, "the people are very jealous and always fighting."

Instead, Marmon urged Edward to consider Santa Ana Pueblo, only fifteen miles to the northwest of Sandia. Known to its people as Tamaya, the old village was located on the Jemez River beneath the basalt wall of San Felipe mesa. Like Acoma, she was a Keresan-speaking village, with a familiar cosmology and clan system, which meant the Hunts could con-

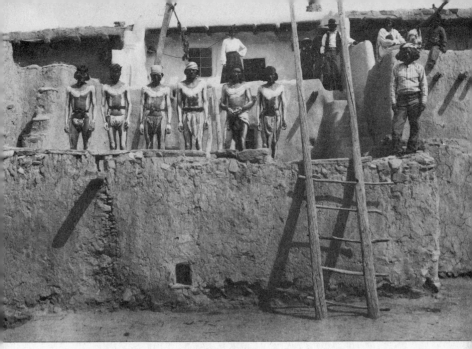

As if watching the Hunt family go: traditional runners standing atop one of Acoma's kivas.

verse "in Indian" and rely on Sun Clan "relatives" to smooth their acceptance by the community.

Santa Ana resembled Acoma in a third respect as well. The crumbling old central village became a virtual ghost town for much of the year as townsfolk occupied the satellite community of Ranchitos, with access to a steadier supply of irrigation water. Although a hundred years earlier there had been enough tillable land close by, changing creek patterns and the encroachment of sand dunes had left most of its acreage unfit for farming. Buying up large tracts and small, Santa Ana was able to provide plots between Bernalillo and Algodones that drew upon the reliable Rio Grande. As at Acoma, for key festivities and kiva rituals everyone repaired to Santa Ana's old ceremonial center.

There was also a mythic symmetry to the move. In one account of their epic wanderings after emerging out of three underworlds, the ancient Santa Anans undertook a wide circular migration, which even brushed against Acoma's rocky mesa. Discovering people there who spoke a mutually intelligible language, one of the party lingered behind and was taken in by the village, while his fellow tribespeople resumed their search for Tamaya. Much as Hunt's own destiny spiraled out from Acoma, he was almost asking Santa Ana to return the favor.

Taking a first step, Edward and Marie rode the train to Bernalillo and paid a formal call on the old village, which had been described not long before by Archbishop Jean-Baptiste Salpointe as "the most desolate and barren spot of all the Indian pueblos of New Mexico. There is no vegetation but a single solitary cottonwood tree, which is the remnant of what was once a rich productive land. Indians live there because it was the cradle of their forefathers and through respect for the past traditions."

Meeting with Santa Ana's governor, Joe Garcia, and tribal officials, Edward asked if his family might be "adopted." That night Garcia talked it over with his people. Then the Hunts were interrogated about their background, intentions, and religious affiliation. However Edward responded (he did allow he was a Roman Catholic), the family was voted in. A scenario for their ritualistic arrival and "adoption" into the village was worked out.

En route home to close up shop, Edward stopped in Albuquerque. His old confidant Agent Lonergan expressed surprise that the Santa Anans would share their land. Then came the return to Acomita and a final negotiation. The way the family recalls this break, it was less a banishment or eviction than a mutual recognition that things had gotten out of hand. The incompatibility between Christian entrepreneur and his community of origin could not be mediated or ignored. The Hunts had to go, needed to go, had no recourse but to go.

Acoma's leading cacique, Francisco Candelaria, the pueblo's "mother," was there, along with his wife, and Edward's female cousin and the woman's grandmother. Edward wanted them as witnesses, but no papers were signed or record made. Edward declared he would sell his Acomita house and store to the grandmother, but retain rights to his farms and orchards along the ditch. "I want my fields left alone," he said, "maybe one day one of my sons or daughters will come back and they can have that land."

The process took all night. To soften the pain and show respect for their home pueblo, Edward and Marie hung blankets over the shoulders of the cacique and his wife. All held hands and blew their breath on them. For a member of such a community to pull out for good was akin to an amputation, even a death of sorts. By morning all were in tears, as if at a wake. Some of this emotionalism was pro forma. Having been left in the Malpais to fend for themselves once already, the Hunts would let nothing cut that deep again.

On November 1, 1918, they finished emptying the house, store, and barn. They sold some sheep and Wilbert's favorite horse, named for President Wilson. With help from Marie's five brothers and Edward's brother Cipriano, they loaded about eight wagons, their buggy, and their buckboard for the overland trip to Santa Ana. West of Cubero the caravan passed Encinal and turned east. The Hunts were on their own once more.

PART THREE

Big Snake
(1918–30)

A Second Chance (1918)

This village is as fine an example of human adaptation to a barren environment as could be found in searching the world over. . . . Not many miles away are opportunities in agriculture and industry that would seem to beckon them to a more abundant life. But Santa Ana sticks to its sand hills and watches the world tearing by on the east and south without the slightest desire to participate.

—Adolph F. Bandelier and Edgar L. Hewitt, 1937

ONCE AGAIN Edward Hunt stood on the banks of an unfamiliar river facing an uncertain future in an unknown community. But this time he was not an Indian boy heading for a white school in Albuquerque. This time he was a grown man who was responsible for the wife and six of his children standing beside him. His family stepped down from the wagon and dismounted from horses and looked across the Jemez River at Santa Ana Pueblo, their future home.

The sacred mountain of Edward's birth was less than sixty miles away. But community and family had reached a mutual acceptance that they no longer fit in. Their umbilical tie to Acoma Pueblo was cut, probably for good. After being shipped off to Albuquerque as a schoolboy, then exiled with his bride to the Malpais wilderness, it was Edward's third time as a castaway—the worst of Pueblo Indian nightmares. One version of Acoma's origin myth, collected by anthropologist Florence Hawley Ellis, tells of early refugees from Acoma and Santa Ana pueblos joining forces to create the present-day Laguna Pueblo. Could this displaced family similarly rebuild their lives with their old ally?

They were standing nine miles upstream from the river's release into the Rio Grande. To the east the winding Jemez was spanned by a home-built single-lane bridge. In earlier days Santa Ana farmers paddled to their fields in dugout canoes that they hollowed out of cottonwood trunks. Up ahead the pueblo's one- and two-story adobe apartments seemed "to lean," as Adolph Bandelier put it in 1892, "against the craggy wall of the extensive mesa of San Felipe." Fifteen miles to the northwest, the mountain wall of the Jemez chain rippled low and darkly forested along the horizon. Roughly the same distance behind them rose the steeper, granite-and-limestone Sandia and Manzano ranges. All around lay clumps of cactus, swaths of grassy chaparral, and rolling sands dotted with two-needle juniper and piñon. As it was early November, a fringe of gilded cottonwoods and reddish willow shoots marked the meandering Big River.

Pressed between the old Bernalillo land grant to the south and San Felipe Pueblo to the north, Santa Ana Pueblo was better known to its occupants as Tamaya, which Edward translated as "Place of the Notch." To its Tewa-speaking Pueblo neighbors, however, the quiet old town was known as "Village of the Dancing Place." Like most of the dozen or so Indian pueblos strung up and down the Rio Grande, Tamaya was a theocratic, autonomous, self-sufficient, linguistically singular city-state. In existence since at least the fourteenth century, the cluster of humble earthen homes and animal corrals remained the geographical and spiritual heart of her 22,400-acre, square-shaped land base. By the year of the Hunts' arrival the pueblo's population had dwindled to under three hundred, the lowest on record. This may have widened her welcome to linguistically and socially related refugees who could bolster her numbers.

Awaiting the Hunts up the road stood a sizable contingent of those villagers, looking expectantly their way.

In the 1890s, around the same time that Acoma Pueblo spawned its outlier hamlets of Acomita and McCartys so as to allow her farmers easier access to the San Jose River, Santa Ana Pueblo families took similar advantage of their tribe's El Ranchito Grant addition. Temporary field camps gradually combined into the year-round, utilitarian settlement known as Ranchitos. Here their separate adobe homes stood conveniently closer to narrow rectangles of individual fields whose irrigation channels drew upon the Big River.

Santa Ana's "mother ditch" ran just north of Bernalillo's "Mexican Ditch," which was kept clean and fast-flowing through the upkeep of Hispano villagers. Then the Indians' waters fed through a network of trenches to their corn, squash, bean, and melon fields. As it turned out, the largest of Edward's plots, still known in Santa Ana today as "Gaire's Field," or "Day

Across the Jemez River, Santa Ana Pueblo, the Hunts' new home.

Break's field," was squeezed between these two parental canals—as if the man really needed another metaphor for his liminal status in the region.

Most Santa Anans lived year round in Ranchitos, but they never abandoned their beloved home village. As with so many adobe communities dotting New Mexico's backcountry, its abandoned appearance was misleading. No matter any loss of population, old Tamaya retained its prominence as the ancestral hearth and sacred center-place of the Santa Ana universe. Only here lay its southern plaza and navel shrines. On this moccasin-pounded ground the cycle of solstice, harvest, and other dances sprang to life. Open sightlines to the southeast lifted the gazes of her dancers toward the community's high holy places.

Only at old Tamaya stood the two tawny-colored, circular kivas associated with the Turquoise and Pumpkin social sides, or moieties, and the meeting chambers assigned to medicine societies, Katsinas, and sacred clowns. "Generation after generation of people live their lives out upon these desolate hills," wrote Adolph Bandelier and Edgar Hewitt in 1937, "in all the contentment of a prairie dog town."

Facing west from the north plaza stood the community's adobe church, dedicated in 1706 to Jesus's grandmother Anne, patron saint of female equestrians and book lovers—for it was she who taught her daughter Mary to read. With its roofline parallel to Black Mesa and seemingly mimicking that skyline, to architectural scholar Vincent Scully the religious structure "stretches out before the mountain and under the clouds, and its façade is kept flat in elevation and so is subordinate to that wonderful stretch, as of some fine animal or simply the special force of nature that it is."

During the cycle of ceremonies that united Santa Ana as a social and religious body, all these venues did their duty. Only old Tamaya was the proper arena for greeting ancient spirits like the Katsinas, or embracing new arrivals like the Hunts.

By November the autumn harvest was in. A handful of key ceremonialists bade farewell to their Ranchitos kinfolk before walking, riding horses, or rocking in wagons on the rough dirt road back to the old village. To the untutored eye in wintertime the place resembled a ghost town—"the cats alone remain," wrote a myopic census taker in 1894, "prowling like specters over the roofs and through the deserted streets." But in the same way that a skeleton crew of war chiefs and retainers served old Acoma Pueblo up on the mesa between the equinoxes, amid cedar smoke and snowdrifts these Santa Ana caretakers kept a human presence alive and kiva rituals on track. Meanwhile, back at Ranchitos, most Santa Anans chinked drafty holes, repaired window frames, packed larders with jerked venison, dried peaches, and heaps of corn, stacked firewood, and readied themselves for the cold months ahead.

Those were the same ritual leaders who'd put their heads together after Edward Hunt came in search of a safe harbor. "I have come to this place to get to be adopted with my family into your Pueblo," he told them. What would prove a mixed blessing at Santa Ana may have been Hunt's prior acquaintance with progressive-minded, Christian families like his who already resided there. For now, however, he downplayed those connections.

Following a prearranged script, on November 4, Edward, with his wife and youngest daughter, took the train out of Albuquerque. Meanwhile his sons, brother, and brothers-in-law headed overland with wagonloads of furniture, tools, clothing, household gear, and food, leaving Mount Taylor behind them and moving at the pace of their mixed herd of remaining livestock across the broad Rio Puerco valley.

A Santa Ana elder, among those watching Edward Hunt's impact on his village.

"When we arrived at Ranchitos," Hunt remembered, "we moved into a house that they had fixed up for us. They said we could live there until we could build one for ourselves." A week later a tribal official showed up and announced the community was ready for the formal adoption. "We hitched up the wagon and buggy," Edward remembered. "My wife and I and our six children started out. Some of the boys rode horses. When we got close to old Santa Ana all the people came out. In the lead was the cacique, with the medicine men and other officials. Then the cacique raised his hands, put his palms forward, and brought them down to his breast as if he was drawing us in. They told us to step down."

With some solemnity the family was escorted into town. "There were groups on either side, the medicine men joining us, the officials ahead, the people walking behind." The procession led them into the cacique's house, where they offered sacred cornmeal and prayers before a stuffed antelope head that hung in the northwest corner.

"And so they adopted us. They had brought our wagon and horses over and unhitched them." At another house the women brought in different foods each one had cooked—mutton stews, loaves of outdoor-oven leavened bread, folds of wafer-thin unleavened cornmeal bread. "First the cacique prayed, offering food to all the spirits. Out came the stools, we sat down to eat for a long time. We had more than we wanted. I told them, 'You help us eat this—we can't eat it all.' But they said to us, 'You eat first, then we'll eat.'" Leftovers were packed into baskets and cloth-wrapped pots to feed the Hunts in their new home. So it was that they began to merge into the larger community.

As a new tribal member, Edward was not entirely surprised but remained diplomatically noncommittal when Santa Ana elders hinted that his boys might participate in their kiva rituals. Joining the annual fiesta and July 26 corn dance was all right. But wasn't their refusal of any deeper role in native religion one of the reasons the Hunts had split with Acoma? A familiar wariness reentered the family's nervous system.

The following month they attended midnight Christmas mass at old St. Anne's. Over the next days they joined crowds of onlookers at the Deer, Buffalo, Mattachine, and Comanche dances. In low, respectful voices they murmured Keresan greetings whenever they were addressed and softly shook and breathed upon hands in Pueblo fashion. When they learned of the annual appointment of Santa Ana's new officials for the coming year they kept their own counsel.

They also paid silent attention when neighbors alluded to the retreat of the coming year's "ditch boss," as he left the old village to pray alone in the eastern hills to the spirits of the waters and the lesser supernaturals that inhabited the irrigation channels. They were alert to his announcement to ready their picks and shovels in anticipation of opening the ditches. Edward and his boys watched the ditch boss and the sacred clowns pray and ask these invisible beings "to take everything that was dear to them" and peacefully depart so they could irrigate. From the ditch head down through all the gates they saw the clowns sweep the bottoms and sides of the channels with eagle, turkey, duck, and warbler feather brushes.

Four days before ditch work began, they heeded the call for volunteers. Edward and his boys accepted their assignments to clear their stretches of the ditch, which were measured by the ditch boss using his shovel held lengthwise. Over four days their pitchforks removed branches, trash, and leaves. They replaced rotted sluice gates, repaired dams, shored up fallen berms, and regraded branching channels, all to the accompaniment of ditch-cleaning songs that addressed the water spirits and the sacred directions. They stood by as Santa Ana's religious officials and sacred clowns deposited prayer sticks and fed the water spirits. They planted the four acres assigned to them with corn and beans and squash. They tried to fit in and not arouse comments by behaving differently than anyone else.

What desperate or self-deceiving thoughts convinced Edward that his family could make it in a village that he must have known was just as conservative as the one that had just more or less kicked them out? Had not the Pueblo memory bank transmitted the abiding attitude of Santa Ana's conservative faction toward the non-Indian world, as illustrated by her behavior right after the pueblo killed its priest and burned his chapel during the All-Pueblo Revolt of August 1680?

That was when the mixed-blood rebel leader from Santo Domingo, Alfonso Catiti (whose Spanish half brother fought on their enemy's side), perched himself across a Santa Ana banquet table from the revolt's firebrand, the man we only know as Po'pay. In the kind of symbolic reversal that was normally the license of sacred clowns, the two hoisted the Communion chalices they'd confiscated from Santa Ana's church before burning it down.

"To your Paternal Reverence's health," toasted Po'pay. "To your Lordship's, Sir Governor," responded Catiti. After this little burlesque, commented a Spanish scribe, "there remained in all the kingdom no vestige of the Christian religion; all was profaned and destroyed."

Was Edward so reluctant to break with his Keresan-speaking roots that he blocked out everything he knew about the depth of Pueblo suspicion toward apostates like himself? Hadn't his painful experiences taught him that sooner or later Santa Ana would resent his commitments to Christianity, capitalism, and individual liberty? And for its part, was the Rio Grande pueblo of Santa Ana so removed from her western cousins that the moccasin telegraph had not communicated rumors of this independent-minded family of Christian progressives? How could they not have included hearsay about this controversial Acomita storekeeper, friend to

Jews and Hispanos alike, married into one of Acoma's most prestigious families, who broke with his homeland because he wouldn't let his boys be initiated into its Katsina and medicine men societies?

How could both parties not foresee that the contradictions between Anglo-American and Pueblo Indian worldviews would blow up in their faces?

32

Storms Far and Near (1918–21)

They have also been able to protect their young people in large measure from familiarity with some of the less desirable habits of the European races which have attempted to reduce them to the practices of civilization. . . . This has been no Utopia, communistic or otherwise, yet in four hundred years nobody has reported chronic poverty nor apparent wealth, and there have been no appeals for individual or public charity. . . . Behind it all, perhaps explaining much of it, is the fact that they do not tell how it is done. It is the apotheosis of those who mind their own business.

—George Parker Winship, 1926

L IKE THE WINTER OF 1861, the year that Acoma Pueblo embraced the just-born Day Break as one of her own, when she parted with him fifty-seven years later the country was again at war. Only now the fate of all Europe, not just a divided nation, was at stake. Much of America had a dim view of joining the global conflict. But the patriotism that inspired New Mexicans to volunteer in overwhelming numbers against the kaiser was probably fortified by their pride in having achieved statehood only five years before. Of the nearly eighty thousand residents who signed up from the thinly populated state in the spring of 1917, more than seventeen thousand wound up serving in all branches of the military.

Also stiffening New Mexico's antagonism toward any thought of foreign invasion was Jack Pershing's recent thrashing of Pancho Villa for fording the Rio Grande and killing seventeen New Mexicans in the border town of Columbus. This was the clash in which a young George S. Patton Jr. cut his military teeth, as he would regale for Edward Hunt's youngest son, Wilbert, when the famous general occupied his barber's chair during the next world war.

With Pershing and Patton accompanying the American Expeditionary Forces overseas, back at the hamlet of Acomita the current Pueblo Indian agent, Philip T. Lonergan, sought out Edward Hunt for help in translating his recruiting pitch into the Keresan language. "Lonergan and I had a hard time to make the people, the Governors and officers understand," Hunt remembered. "I had four of my boys register, but because I was following the orders of President Wilson I was criticized," which only added to Hunt's reasons for leaving the village. For their part, some non-Indians scoffed at the value of raising Indian troops, considering them "inept" and "under-motivated." But a Santa Fe historian argued that "hundreds of them might have responded if they had been invited to enlist." And any lingering prejudice against Indians serving in the military would evaporate during the next war.

Of the well over twelve thousand American Indians who did sign up (nearly 20 percent of the adult male Indian population), only a hundred or so from New Mexico saw combat—mostly Apaches and Navajos—with the few Pueblo soldiers hailing from the Laguna, Acoma, and Isleta communities. Among the twenty-three from Laguna Pueblo were offspring of the Marmon, Gunn, and Pradt mixed-blood families. From Acoma went five men whom Edward knew well: a few fellow students from Albuquerque Indian School, one even his relative. Most Indians comported themselves proudly, even though, as more than one historian pointed out, they swore "to defend the constitution without possessing any rights under it." Yet their participation in the Great War changed that, as offering full citizenship to all American Indian veterans in 1919 seemed the least a grateful country could do.

During Pershing's stand against the Germans at St.-Mihiel Salient, an army captain from Santa Fe leapt into a trench and onto the back of a machine gunner from Laguna Pueblo, who remained "as stolid as if he were an onlooker at the Zuni Fire Dance." A cousin of Edward's own wife, Frank White of Company B, 305th Infantry, limped home after being shot in his right leg. Near Fismes, on August 26, 1918, another soldier from Acomita, Amado Garcia, with Company K, 110th Infantry, crawled with two buddies under three hundred yards of barbed wire toward a six-man machine-gun nest. Advancing against steady fire from only thirty feet away, he personally killed three Germans. Using rifles as clubs, the three drove off the rest and recovered German weaponry. For this feat, plus being gassed at the Vesle River and losing his hearing from an exploding shell, Garcia was among the U.S. Army's 150 Distinguished Service Cross winners and one of ten Indians on whom France bestowed its Croix de Guerre. Upon his return the medicine men decontaminated him from the ghosts of the enemies he'd slain.

But most pueblos, Acoma included, remained allergic to white men's wars, although a few supported the troops in quieter fashion. A dance troupe from Cochiti Pueblo carted their Mattachine Dance regalia thirty miles in horse-drawn wagons to Santa Fe's Museum of New Mexico to offer benefit performances for the war effort. A Santa Clara elder sold handmade war bonnets for the cause. Conservative villages like Santo Domingo

The firebrand: John Collier, U.S. Indian commissioner, with Hopi village chief and son.

and San Felipe allowed the Red Cross to set up fund-raising booths during their annual corn dances. And patriot Hunt must have been especially gratified to learn that along with the $200,000 in Liberty Bonds raised from New Mexico's Indians, every family in his adopted pueblo of Santa Ana bought a Red Cross membership.

By then his son Wilbert was in school. On November 11, 1918, he remembered the bells ringing in celebration of Armistice Day. That war was over; he would not escape the next.

The 1920s proved a landmark decade for Indians everywhere. For one thing, their prospects for sheer survival were looking up. For the first time in a half century, reported U.S. Indian commissioner Cato Sells in 1917, native births exceeded deaths. With nearly twenty-one thousand Indians in New Mexico alone, no longer could they be eulogized as a "dying" or "vanishing" race, as "Friends of the Indian" reformers had mournfully predicted. But when Sells added his excitement at the coming "revolution in the administration of Indian affairs," he had no idea how profound it would be nor the unexpected direction it would take.

Over fall and winter of the following year, however, the demographic upswing was threatened by the scourge of Spanish flu, which infected a full quarter of the nation's American Indians. Often leading to the pneumonia to which Indians were especially vulnerable, between October 1918 and March 1919 the virus "killed people off so fast in San Juan Pueblo," recalled San Juan member Alfonso Ortiz, "that some days the church bell never stopped tolling, day and night."

Meanwhile, a cast of strong personalities were staking out positions in looming battles over Pueblo Indian land and religious rights. Well before the United States entered the Great War a transformative fervor, with tremendous political, social, and cultural ramifications, gripped the Western world. In turn-of-the-century America, a rebellious idealism, an internationalist spirit, and a fired-up social conscience swept over the urban clusters of American writers, artists, radical utopians, and labor and social organizers.

They were energized by the success of the abolitionist movement, invigorated by the struggle for women's rights, toughened by the fight for workers' causes amid the grim working conditions produced by the Industrial Revolution, and inspired by revolutionary manifestos and uprisings that were sweeping Europe. Some of these progressive-minded networks seized upon the issues of American Indian land rights and cultural free-doms. And it was hard to find a more compelling group of Indians on whose behalf to fight than the picturesque Pueblos.

Enabling this enthusiasm for Pueblo Indian causes was the migration to New Mexico, from around 1910 onward, of influential, articulate, and often wealthy and mostly eastern artists, writers, poets, architects, and so-cial activists. Some arrived dying slow deaths from lungs afflicted with pulmonary disease, seeking in Santa Fe's thin desert air the space to save their lives. Others arrived by happenstance, and felt they'd stumbled upon an environmental and cultural Shangri-La. The range of personal temper-aments and political allegiances that streamed into the Santa Fe–Taos axis fused into one of the most unified lobbies in the history of the American left. Characterized as "Yearners" by writer Oliver La Farge, "Moderns" by historian Tisa Wenger, and "Cultural Nationalists" by art historian Molly H. Mullin, their members fought among themselves over politics, art, women's rights, and sex. But one cause that united most of them was the protection of what they understood to be Pueblo Indian territoriality, reli-gious expression, and traditional arts.

While the wealthy anthropologist Elsie Clews Parsons emerged as the major funder and dominating practitioner of southwestern cultural stud-ies, another East Coast heiress, equally intelligent and comparably driven, became queen bee of its artistic and activist milieu. By the time Mabel Dodge, born in 1879 to a wealthy Buffalo, New York, family, first saw Taos Pueblo in 1917, she had already lived three lifetimes, each with a husband in its wake. Mabel's energy, romanticism, and penchant for collecting cultural luminaries had emerged in upstate New York, flourished in Flor-ence, Italy, and deepened in Greenwich Village before she relocated to the American Southwest.

In mid-December 1917, Mabel escaped from New York for a short vaca-tion to Taos. A week later she attended the Christmas dances at Santo Do-mingo Pueblo. "I heard the singing and drumming as soon as we reached the Pueblo," she later recalled, "it drew me strongly and I left the others and ran hurriedly towards it with my heart beating. . . . I heard the voice of the One, coming from the many."

From her palatial adobe mansion overlooking Taos Pueblo she wrote old friends about this "garden of Eden inhabited by an unfallen tribe of men and women." Not content with the surface of Pueblo Indian life, she

*Supporters of Indian rights: Tony and Mabel Dodge Luhan,
Taos, New Mexico.*

married into it—her fourth and final husband was Antonio Luhan, one of
Taos Pueblo's prominent members. To this Bohemia West wended a stream
of international stars who mingled with her cadre of local painters, writers, and eccentrics.

None in Mabel's orbit left as enduring a mark on American Indian
history as the thirty-two-year-old firebrand who visited in December 1920.
Mabel knew John Collier from New York, where he'd spent over a dozen
years community-organizing in New York's impoverished Lower East
Side. Born in 1884 to a wealthy and progressive-minded Atlanta family,
Collier was sent to unconventional schools, went wandering in Europe on
his own, and honed his writing skills while becoming a social worker.

Burned out by organizing in New York, Collier was en route to California to teach when he took a layover at the Luhans'. Three days after he saw

the Christmas Eve ceremonies in Taos Pueblo's San Geronimo Church he witnessed the Red Deer dance in its plaza and underwent an epiphany much like Mabel's three years before. Its impact would alter the course of American Indian history and make him the principal architect of President Roosevelt's Indian New Deal.

The dance's spirit, Collier wrote later, entered "into myself and each one of my family as a new direction of life—a new, even wildly new, hope for the Race of Man." His life's mission was cast. "They had what the world has lost," Collier claimed. Despite a lifetime of setbacks, he never wavered from that belief. "They have it now," he continued. "What the world has lost, the world must have again, lest it die." A bureaucratic messiah was born.

In California, Collier met another woman destined to become an equally central, if less flamboyant, player in American Indian affairs. A native of Minneapolis, Stella M. Atwood was an educator, feminist, and advocate for Indian rights in Riverside. Good-humored, bright, and liberal, she made Indian welfare a key issue for her influential General Federation of Women's Clubs.

Opposing this left-liberal lineup in upcoming battles over Pueblo rights were equally forceful personalities. Some, like Thomas Catron, were carryovers from the earlier "Ring" of well-heeled professionals who belonged to Santa Fe's Republican upper crust and had amassed fortunes by swindling Hispanos out of their land grants. Now their successors formed what some critics considered a second-generation "gang" of pro-development, anti-Indian politicos.

With the installment of fellow Republican Albert Bacon Fall as secretary of the interior, the prospect of resolving land disputes in their favor brightened. Enjoying high status among this conservative clique, Fall was Hunt's age-mate. A Kentucky transplant, he rose from cowboying and mining to newspapering and lawyering before becoming a New Mexico senator in 1912. From him would come the term "fall guy" for his disgrace during the soon-to-come Teapot Dome scandal. In Washington he cozied up to President Warren Harding, who reciprocated in 1921 by naming him head of his Interior Department.

That promotion left Fall's Senate seat vacant. A special election filled it with a like-minded colleague, fifty-year-old Holm Olaf Bursum. Born to an Iowa farming family, Bursum moved to New Mexico in 1881, where he enjoyed a successful career as a freighter, sheepherder, rancher, and sheriff before becoming active in territorial politics around 1899. A strong advocate for Indian assimilation, he attained his senatorial high point during the 67th Congress with his controversial proposal for settling the seventy-five-year-old disputes over Pueblo Indian land titles.

Sharing Fall's and Bursum's determination to open Indian lands to mining, drilling, and ranching, and to stamp out "pagan" traditions, was Charles H. Burke, a New York–born lawyer and realtor who became a South Dakota congressman in 1895 and stayed in national politics until Fall named him U.S. Indian commissioner in 1921. His sentiments toward Indians were reflected in his 1906 sponsorship of the Burke Act, which crushed prospects for granting Indians citizenship. Burke's opening pledge as commissioner was to allot Indian lands so as to hasten "a departure from old communal traits and customs to self dependent conditions and to a democratic conception of civilization with which the Indian must be assimilated if he is to survive."

The Hunts didn't know it, but by relocating to Santa Ana they found themselves at ground zero in the clash between these constituencies. Although triggered by predominately Pueblo Indian issues, the outcome would revolutionize the status of Indians everywhere. In 1920 the handful of Pueblo veterans who returned from France found their tribes' land and religious freedoms under threat as never before. Instead of Navajo raiders, armor-clad Spaniards, or Bible-bearing missionaries, their new enemies were these assimilation-minded politicians and the bureaucrats who did their bidding.

Nor could the Hunts have foreseen how this period would test their family and toss them on the road again. As ditch waters trickled into their gardens at Santa Ana that spring, Edward kept his head down, steering clear of rising tensions between the pueblo's progressive and conservative factions, while focusing on farming and adding a new room onto his Ranchitos home.

Threats to Pueblo Lands (1922)

The Acomas held here, this 13th of November, at Acomita, in the year 1922, a meeting: there met the Chief of Acoma and all his principal men and his officers. Willingly we will stand to fight against the Bursum bill, which by this time we have discovered and understood. Our White brothers and sisters: this bill is against us, to break our customs, which we have enjoyed, living on in our happy life. . . . Therefore we are willing to join to the others our pueblo, where we may beat out the Bursum bill for the benefit of our children and of our old people and of all our future.

—Chiefs of Acoma, November 13, 1922

AFTER HIS CLOSE FRIEND the Franciscan priest Fridolin Schuster visited Ranchitos and relayed the shocking news of what had happened to an Acoma shepherd, Edward knew how easily the tragedy could have befallen his own boys. Guiding their flocks through sagebrush and scrubby piñon beneath a big blue sky, pastoralists ambled in a time zone all their own. Gauging their "when" by double-checking the position of the sun and their "where" by periodic glances at Mount Taylor, how could they avoid drifting across invisible lines of old land grants, unfenced pastures, and contested land claims?

Resentments between Pueblo Indians and Hispano squatters and trespassers were getting ugly. "Some day there will be bloodshed" over these encroachments, warned Santa Fe attorney Francis C. Wilson, a smart, fair-minded legal assistant to the pueblos. During U.S. Senate testimony, Pueblo Indian agent Philip Lonergan's successor, the former Hopi agent and short-story writer Leo Crane, confessed that it was "a mystery that one-half of the pueblos are not on the warpath and the other half in jail." By then it was April 1924, only two months before the Pueblo Lands Act stood to resolve all long-standing disputes to pueblo lands. Out in Valencia County, its verdicts could not come too soon.

As Father Schuster reported the incident, twenty-two-year-old Francisco Salvador, a native of Acoma, together with his younger brother, were herding along the pueblo's western border. Out of nowhere rode a local Hispano, the son of Juan Barelas, a prominent Valencia County *patrón*. Barelas's dog scattered their sheep, the man screamed "trespassers" in Spanish, and raced at them. Bending low, he swung at Salvador with his quirt. Francisco stumbled for cover, gripping his rifle. As he did so, it was later determined at his trial, he zigzagged across the reservation's boundary line. Tumbling down an arroyo, he wheeled, drew bead, and dropped the rider. Tried without witnesses by an all-Hispano jury, Salvador, who spoke neither Spanish nor English, was promptly convicted of murder and sent to prison.

Like members of every southwestern pueblo, Edward knew the backstory. Boundary disputes between Indians and Hispanos erupted soon after Spain first apportioned land grants to both her own colonists and Indian pueblos. As "crown vassals," the Indians expected the king to protect their territories. But land surveys of the seventeenth and eighteenth centuries were notoriously vague and often ignored native boundary markers. Broad expanses were demarcated by uncertain lines drawn between highly local points of call—an unreliable spring known only by a native term, old petroglyphs hidden by brush, a pile of rocks that was easily kicked apart, some mesa that bore a similar name to two others. Before long it was more length of occupancy, force of habit, and local authority that held sway than Spanish documents or geographical boundaries dimly recalled from times past.

This fostered the bullying style of trespass-and-stay-put practice that twenty-first-century academics would characterize as the crudest form of "squatter sovereignty," a subset of "settler colonialism." Informal land takeovers were absorbed into local norm and custom, leaving few able to reconstruct just when a given village lost land bit by bit, or how temporary interlopers had become permanent residents. Unlike territory acquired by military conquest or authority imposed top-down by imperial decree, this usurpation rose from the bottom up and was harder to uproot. After Mexico took over from Spain, a more aggressive breed of Hispano pioneer entered the picture. Sweeping Indian claims or complaints aside, they built homes and ran sheep and cattle wherever they found water, and freely dispensed riverside plots to relatives and friends.

Their uncertain status in the white man's world made the Pueblos especially vulnerable. Outsiders were still hard put to culturally and legally pigeonhole these "atypical" natives whose looks and lifeways didn't fit their preconceptions of how Indians ought to behave, live, or worship. When the United States took over the region in the late 1840s, it sidestepped the knotty problem of these Pueblo-squatter disputes and tackled the prior question. How should one categorize these town-dwelling, non-aggressive, farming and pastoral natives who governed themselves by an intricate weave of social, political, and religious principles? Were they even "Indians"?

In 1869 New Mexico's territorial court had approvingly contrasted their "law-abiding, sober and industrious" lifestyle with that of "wandering savages" whom laws like the Non-Intercourse Act of 1834 were designed to protect. But if the Pueblos were not "wards" like most other tribes, and still not "citizens"; if they were well-behaved farmers like homesteading whites, yet denied the right to vote, the question arose again, what type of human *were* they?

In 1876 the Pueblo Indian's anomalous status was only reinforced by

Pueblo leaders unite against threats to Indian lands and ceremonies.

the U.S. Supreme Court. A Hispano homesteader near the Colorado border named Antonio Joseph wanted title to a ten-acre ranch that sat on Taos Pueblo lands in northern New Mexico. The Court acknowledged that Pueblo people physically resembled "true" Indians, like Navajos or Sioux. But the ensuing *United States v. Joseph* decision decreed that they were too "civilized" and "superior" to be designated as such. Besides, they appeared to "hold land in common like Shakers and other communistic societies." Still not Indians, but certainly not white Americans, Pueblo people remained in a definitional limbo, which left their ancient lands, riverside farms, and sacred mountains more vulnerable than ever.

By 1913 well over three thousand non-Indians were freely running cattle and sheep, planting and harvesting on Pueblo Indian lands up and down the Rio Grande valley and farther west. That year the new state of New Mexico finally flexed its muscle. The deciding case came when a Hispano bootlegger named Felipe Sandoval was charged with selling liquor on Santa Clara Pueblo land. By winning for Sandoval on the basis that he was not Indian and hence not subject to laws pertaining to Indian reservations, his lawyers set the stage for an appeal that would resurrect the jurisdictional conundrum over Pueblo lands. In deciding this second case, *United States v. Sandoval,* the Supreme Court finally overturned the earlier *United States v. Joseph* decision. After seventy-five years, Pueblo people like Edward Hunt found themselves officially American Indians once again.

Despite their "inclinations" to "peace and industry," wrote Justice Willis Van Devanter in this official change of heart, the Pueblos' "superstition and fetishism . . . [and] crude customs inherited from their ancestors" were evidence that they were "a simple, uninformed, and inferior people" and thus certainly "Indians." Overlooking what anthropologist Edward Dozier criticized as Van Devanter's "condescending, ethnocentric and racist language," now at least the Pueblos had a beachhead from which to fight for their lands. Almost overnight, thousands of trespassing New Mexicans, most of them Hispano farmers, found themselves on shaky ground.

In quick response ranchers and farmers fenced their suddenly precarious holdings. Indians retaliated by tearing out the fenceposts and running off livestock. The troubles predicted by lawyer Wilson and Indian agent Crane were coming to pass. Landowners like the one whose son would chase down Francisco Salvador prepared to defend their spreads in rough-and-ready fashion.

To resolve the volatile situation once and for all, on June 20, 1922, New Mexico rancher and U.S. senator Holm Bursum introduced Senate Bill 1938, henceforth known far and wide as the Bursum Bill. It was drafted by land-grant expert Alois B. Renehan, attorney-historian Ralph E. Twitchell, and Interior Secretary Albert Fall, all members of what one historian calls "the old Santa Fe Ring reincarnated." The legislation would legalize the non-Indian claims of title to Pueblo lands that dated up to ten years before 1912 and return to federal courts the authority to adjudicate Pueblo water rights and land disputes. In sum, it proposed the biggest usurpation of Indian lands of the twentieth century.

John Collier caught wind of the bill while vacationing in New Mexico, and alerted his friends Mabel and Tony Luhan. The Bursum initiative upended Collier's life plans; destiny was calling. Among New Mexico's pueblos he had glimpsed a "red Atlantis" that might lead America into a higher societal and spiritual incarnation. But beneath that romantic vision ticked the brain of a relentless organizer. Collier's lobbying began by drawing America's attention to injustices that had festered for nearly a century. Abetted by prior court cases and land survey maps, he explained to government officials and magazine writers how an estimated twelve thousand non-Indians came to reside illegally on Pueblo Indian property. The dollars lost to Indians by this land grab were calculated at nearly $12 million, with some three thousand outstanding land claims backlogged in the courts. These statistics were given flesh when Collier, with his flair for public relations, relayed Indian accounts of near-starvation, land takeovers, and Pueblo fears of cultural extinction.

At Tesuque Pueblo, just north of Santa Fe, hundreds of disputes over encroached-upon farmlands remained unresolved. Poverty-stricken families from Cochiti Pueblo, just south of the capital, were barely surviving off a half acre each. Laguna and Acoma farmers had less than an acre per capita to feed their households. Illegal squatting at San Juan Pueblo up the Rio Grande had left tribal members there with fewer than 600 tillable acres, a net loss of 75 percent of their prime corn, squash, and pumpkin fields. Although the original grant to neighboring San Ildefonso Pueblo amounted to some 12,000 acres, only 1,250 acres remained irrigable; of that amount tribal members now retained around 250 acres, a net loss of 80 percent. At Santa Ana Pueblo, as new resident Edward Hunt could see for himself, more than thirty squatters now enjoyed permanent residence. Every day Hispanos from Bernalillo tilled and watered prime plots within walking distance of his new Ranchitos home. Translated into cash, this meant that by the early 1920s, income at San Ildefonso Pueblo was estimated at thirteen dollars a year per capita, sixteen dollars at Tesuque Pueblo, and at San Juan, the most well-off community, twenty-two dollars.

Under the proposed Bursum Bill, granting automatic title to non-Indians on the basis of only prima facie evidence of rights to land (and denying Indians any opportunity to appeal) would strip New Mexico's nineteen Indian pueblos of an estimated sixty thousand acres. When they heard the bill would compensate them, the Indians put two and two together. "If the land does not legally belong to us," they asked, "why should we receive compensation? And if it does belong to us why should be forced to part with it?"

The second prong of Collier's strategy to defeat the Bursum Bill yielded one of the most effective and unanimous protests in the history of the American left. In a display of solidarity rarely found within this fractious network of writers, artists, activists, and intellectuals, the U.S. Congress and national media were soon flooded with petitions, letters, and newspaper and magazine articles. Most important, Collier organized the Indians themselves. His clarion call for an all-pueblo gathering at Santo Domingo Pueblo was designed to activate "the living, undiminished continuum of a democracy older than the Saxon folk-lore and probably older than the Athenian democracy." It was both the right thing to do and a brilliant stroke of community organizing.

In kivas and council chambers throughout the Pueblo world, elders worked toward unanimity within their own tribes. After an all-day huddle between the Acoma cacique, officials, and governor in the Acomita schoolhouse, everyone inked their thumbprints on a paper below words written out by Edward's old friend, translator James Miller: "Willingly we will stand to fight against the Bursum Bill," it stated.

So it went, with pueblo after pueblo signing up.

Whatever problems Edward began having with Santa Ana traditionalists, on the Bursum Bill debate he stood foursquare with his fellow villagers. Upon Collier's call for the emergency meeting he joined seven other Santa Ana delegates for the twenty-five-mile wagon ride north to Santo Domingo, largest of the Rio Grande villages. On a cold November evening

Widening its road, repairing its church—Acoma slowly opens up.

in 1922 they met 121 other representatives from all nineteen pueblos for what Collier would always broadcast as the first example of united Pueblo resistance since their 1680 revolt against the Spanish.

Taking notes was Hunt's mentor, Father Fridolin Schuster, with Charles Kie of Laguna presiding. "Through a day and a night they sat in the council room," went Collier's typically inspirational account of the landmark gathering, "a long chamber with whitewashed walls, where through blue smoke wraiths glowed bright blankets, the ceremonial costume of the governors, the stately, white-draped figures of the Taos delegates. Silver and turquoise ornaments flashed amid the bright eyes of the Indians. There the terms of the Bursum bill were interpreted in the five tongues spoken by the tribes."

After Collier summarized this "appeal to the American people," his draft was read in English, Spanish, and the native Pueblo languages until all reached consensus. To him this constituted America's first true treaty with Pueblo Indians. It affirmed U.S. promises, originally made in 1859, to uphold "Pueblo rights to maintain their own customs and democratic self-governing institutions." It also represented, as Collier later told a U.S. Senate committee, "the fully awakened consciousness of the Pueblos to the present menace which confronts them and is a token that henceforth they intend to stand together for mutual aid."

Then Collier carefully stage-managed a follow-up jaunt to Washington by a few dozen of the Pueblo leadership. Ever the ringmaster, he advised Acoma Pueblo, "Should a representative be sent with the delegation, I trust that he, with all the other delegates, will go in his usual Indian costume, blanket and all. I am making this suggestion to all the Pueblos."

So the Bursum Bill went down in flames, but Pueblo lands remained illegally occupied. To address the abiding Indian grievances, new bills were drafted and promptly rejected. Finally, on June 7, 1924, a three-member Pueblo Lands Board was created whose researchers quickly estimated the total loss to the pueblos from centuries of trespassing, squatting, and sales at over forty thousand acres (worth roughly $2 million). However, the actual awards were cut to $600,000. Indian title minus any compensation was awarded to about half that acreage, and no funds were appropriated for the purchase of additional lands.

Addressing that inequity would await John Collier's further rise to power. Still and all, by 1938 most non-Indian squatters had been ejected from Pueblo country. "For the first time since late in the seventeenth century," summarized historian Herbert O. Brayer, "the Pueblo Indians of New Mexico are free from land controversy."

This was overly optimistic, as proved by future fights to restore Pueblo lands. To many the board offered pitiful satisfaction. After a five-year study of Santa Ana Pueblo's convoluted land transactions, for instance, it appeared that only a fraction of the pueblo's original holdings and water rights were recovered. Meanwhile, stinging from his bill's humiliating defeat, Indian Commissioner Burke prepared a more ideological assault at the heart of Pueblo identity.

Little of this legislative maneuvering mattered to Francisco Salvador, the Acoma shepherd then serving a life sentence in Santa Fe Penitentiary. Staying in his cell and refusing to speak, he earned the superintendent's respect as a "model" inmate.

Children of the Railroad (1922)

It was like a little Indian reservation, and we had our own governor and people, and they told us to behave, and you know, told us to be courteous and be polite, and don't get into fights. Indian camp was just a whole bunch of rows of boxcars, six on the south side and six on the north side. They gave you the amount of boxcars you needed because of your family, so we had two together.

—Mary Toya, Laguna, 2012

IN THE SPRING OF 1922, Wilbert Hunt returned from Albuquerque Indian School to an unusually silent house. With expectations of a summer's fun ahead, he'd half run the four miles from the Bernalillo depot to Santa Ana Pueblo. Eighty years later, he still winced at what he'd then found. Allen's and Clyde's sleeping places were vacant, mattresses rolled against walls, their bedding, clothing, boots, toothbrushes—all gone. "I was beside myself. I didn't behave well. I was angry, I didn't understand it, I couldn't accept it."

His brother Allen's disappearance was tough enough. But Clyde's, with whom he was closest, was almost unbearable. Ever since the family's days back at Acomita, it was always the Hunts against the world. Summers were a time to celebrate the reunion of the family, like parts of a body reassembling and breathing as one again. Wrestling, teasing, laughing at home; working, rabbit-hunting, and helping Dad Hunt outdoors. Nights and days meandering through pasturage north of Cubero, reading by the campfire, sleeping side by side at the sheep camp. Summers banked their collective intimacy against the fall when they had to break apart again and return to their respective boarding schools.

Seven years older than Wilbert, Clyde was the family jester. "Uncle Loco," his nieces and nephews would call him, always affectionately, with rolling eyes and forgiving shrugs. Of all Edward's sons, he displayed the least interest in school. Had Clyde gone too far again? He had indeed, but this time with dad's blessing. Clyde was on a big adventure. From feeling bereft, Wilbert turned jealous.

Contrary to stereotypes about the Puebloans as homebound, provincial farmers, these villagers also relished the open road, changes of seasons and scenery, a break from routine. Spring moves to summer "field camps" nearer their plots of corn and other vegetables combined work with play—swimming, hunting, herding, and a looser lifestyle. But some Pueblo journeys ventured farther. Edward told his boys of ancient Acomans who upped and disappeared to the south, a story he wove into his version of the creation story.

Nor were Allen and Clyde's trips the first time a Hunt relative lit out for the territory. Far-off lands might be dangerous or polluting, but a hunting, gathering, or trading expedition required one to enter them. And there was always that adventuresome soul who just wanted to see the other side of a mountain. One was Day Break's favorite uncle, José Concho, who was sent into Mexico with other Pueblo children to learn to read and write at a Catholic seminary and brought back stories of a colony of Keresan speakers still surviving in Mesoamerica. Around 1869 about forty Cochiti, Santo Domingo, and other Pueblo men passed through Acoma, hoping to work in the California sheep camps and make enough money to bring horses back home. That night young Edward heard the bunch carousing through Acoma's streets, happily singing a Comanche Dance song: "California, I am going out there." After their departure early the next morning, Edward suffered his own surprise: his uncle had gone with them, not to return for another decade.

Like some new god, the railroad took and the railroad gave. It confiscated Pueblo lands, penetrated their protective isolation, accessed Pueblo natural resources, and brought land speculators, bureaucrats, exotic seekers, do-gooders, and other meddlers to their doors. In questionable compensation, it introduced cultural tourism, opened new markets for their homemade wares, and in Clyde and Allen's case, found them jobs. Wilbert's brothers' disappearance was due to the national crisis known as the Shopmen's Strike of 1922; they'd hired on as scabs for the Santa Fe Railway Company.

Once the armistice was signed, the newly elected Republican president, Warren G. Harding, turned against labor. In a backlash against wartime unionism, which had enjoyed support from Democratic president Woodrow Wilson, the Harding administration backed the companies that sought to reduce wages, change work rules, weaken job security, and plan layoffs. As it had threatened, the Railroad Shopmen's Union, with its million-plus workers, called a national strike for July 1. For the Santa Fe line alone that meant six thousand carpenters and metalworkers stayed home.

Desperate for strikebreakers, it was natural for the railroad, thanks to one of the unlikeliest alliances in American Indian history, to turn to Laguna Pueblo, and through it, to Laguna's friends and in-laws at Acoma. The railroad's unusual association with Laguna began in 1880, when the village became furious over surveyors plotting its westbound rails directly through town. In an unwritten gentleman's agreement, known to Lagunans as "the Flower of Friendship," a compensatory deal was sealed with a handshake and honored for nearly a century. The AT&SF railroad promised priority hiring for the pueblo's men and offered Laguna Indians free travel passes in perpetuity.

Every year thereafter, a pueblo delegation visited the line's corporate headquarters in Los Angeles to reaffirm this relationship. Their annual pilgrimage was called "Watering the Flower." Soon Laguna officially designated the workers' camps that began springing up along the major westbound depots—at Grants, Gallup, Holbrook, Winslow, Barstow, and up to Richmond, California—as "Colonies of the Laguna Pueblo in New Mexico."

When Laguna exhausted her available hands—around a hundred or so—they turned to Acoma for additional workers. As Stella Atwood testified in Congress that year, Indians everywhere were hurting, you grabbed anything at hand. Hearing about the opportunity from relatives, Clyde and Allen packed up for Richmond, just across the bay from San Francisco.

When the Hunt brothers arrived on Pennsylvania Street, across from Richmond's railroad tracks, they bunked and ate in a firehouse. Soon they joined a remarkable kind of urban pueblo in the making. As the Indian men brought their families to join them, two households would create a makeshift duplex composed of two wooden boxcars, erected on sidings, with a middle passage linking them. One served as a sleeping room, some packed with a half dozen children. The other was for eating and cooking

"Boxcar baby": Edward and Marie Hunt's grandson Wallace, at the Richmond, California, "Indian village."

on wood-burning stoves. A single window looked out on a commons. Painted window frames, vegetable gardens, and picket fences soon lent a neighborhood feel to the impromptu village.

The "Richmond Colony" adopted a leadership structure that paralleled the one back at Laguna Pueblo. Every year after Christmas they elected their own "governor," and followed a ceremonial cycle that ran concurrently with their parent pueblos in New Mexico. At most of the growing number of these Laguna "colonies," which were pitched along the Santa Fe line between New Mexico and California, one or two boxcars were designated as a meeting hall, which also served as a sort of kiva. For sacred Katsina dances the Richmond compound was declared off-limits to whites, and curtains covered the windows.

Over time the two participating pueblos differentiated their living quarters at Richmond—Laguna boxcar homes were repainted yellow, those of the Acomans red. Newborns were referred to as "boxcar babies." Teen clubs, all-Indian brass bands, their own "Redskin" baseball teams, and Christmas pageants joined with traditional rituals, butterfly dances, and "grab days"—when, just like back home, gifts and candies were tossed from boxcar roofs to outstretched hands below. Before long Hunt family cousins, from both Laguna and Acoma, were serving as culture brokers for the Richmond Colony with the outside media, functioning much like the "outside chiefs" back in their New Mexican pueblos.

Shortly after his arrival in California, Clyde was assigned to the Santa Fe's "operating crafts" workshop, but that didn't last long. By September 1923, the last major strike of the World War I period had collapsed. Allen decided to stay in the East Bay, marrying an African-American woman and beginning a lifelong career in the Richmond shipyards. Whether or not he was fired as a scab or retained per the old agreement, eventually Clyde felt the pull back home. He'd become handy repairing wooden boxcars, but with the rise of America's hunger for Indian crafts his earlier apprenticeship as a silversmith offered better prospects.

To the railroad also went much of the credit for the rising fascination with southwestern Indian creativity and culture. It began with Pueblo women carrying their ceramics to sell at railroad sidings and depots. Painted Pueblo Indian pottery was a tradition that went back millennia, but silverwork was a more recent commodity.

Traditional post-Christmas Comanche Dance, at the "Indian village,"
Richmond, California.

Well before his California adventure, Clyde discovered his gift for crafting metal up at old Acoma. Mother and Dad Hunt may have suffered estrangement from their homeland, but for Clyde, Henry, and Wilbert the mesa remained an inspiration all their lives. Their father's opposition to his boys entering the labyrinth of Acoma religion may have even freed them to explore the mesa as their personal playground, without entry fees or enveloping obligations. Over the long term such liberation from societal obligations was unsustainable; no culture countenances players who do not pay their dues. While it lasted, however, Clyde and his brothers relished the best of both worlds. Of Acoma but not enmeshed in it, they could be pampered by blood and clan relatives, play hide-and-seek in pictograph-covered caves, chase jackrabbits, and absorb the daily dramas while exempt from traditional activities.

Each boy pursued his own bent. For rebellious Alfred it had meant defying his father and exploring those smoke-thickened kivas where medicine men and sacred clowns prepared ritual paraphernalia and chanted for hours. For Henry Wayne it had meant exposure to rock art near the mesa and access to the storytellers and dancing traditions that would inspire his later paintings and writings. For Wilbert it had meant basking in the company of cousins and playmates, oblivious to the tensions that swirled around his father's store. For fun-loving Clyde, the mesa had been a school where he could observe the few, like Juan Luhan, who pounded on crude anvils cut from train rails alongside beehive-shaped adobe furnaces where they heated metal in order to hammer out the large silver earrings favored by Acoma men.

Standard histories of southwestern metalwork have early Navajos first admiring bridles and jewelry made by Mexican silversmiths in southwestern New Mexico and the upper Rio Grande. Initially they worked with scrap iron, then copper and brass, and finally beat or melted the silver from Mexican pesos. Following the tribe's freedom from imprisonment in southern New Mexico in 1868, craftsmen in hogans sprinkled throughout the nation's largest reservation were turning out bridles, rings, bracelets, and circular conchos strung on belts.

Decorating their work with handmade stamps, these smiths also invented new forms, such as the repoussed, silver *ketoh* bow guards worn at the wrists and the squash-flower-shaped (actually pomegranate) beads that festooned necklaces from which dangled the crescent-shaped *naja*—a symbol taken from the Spanish who'd borrowed it from the Moors where it was an Evil Eye–deterring talisman worn on the forelocks of their horses.

Yet Clyde's older brother Henry Wayne always contended that Acoma silversmiths learned their craft a good century before, from Mexican *plateros* in nearby Cubero. Despite his claim, most sources have the craft passing to Acoma around 1870, possibly via the same Mexicans who'd taught the Navajo. At first they only turned out those simple loop earrings, sometimes adding single silver beads. From their necklaces occasionally was suspended the double-cross silver pendant, an Acoma trademark that was tipped with a sacred heart.

Soon notable Acoma artisans, like Juan Luhan, José Platero, and Vicente Chavez, were beating the impressions of decorative stamps into their work, which was an innovation Navajos apparently adapted from tooled leatherwork. They also began pouring melted silver into tufa-stone molds for the cast bracelets and belt buckles. Whichever of these early craftsmen taught Clyde, he was a quick learner. For the time being, however, it was a skill stored away for a later day.

One can imagine Clyde chugging home from California, noticing at each town junction evidence of the "Indian curio" business that would soon become part of the Hunt family's stock-in-trade as well. Once the AT&SF railroad exposed tourists to Indian pueblos south and west of Santa Fe, with the narrower-gauge Denver and Rio Grande doing much the same for villages along the northern Rio Grande, travelers couldn't get enough of *anything* Indian. "What curious people these Americans are," exclaimed an old Pueblo woman in 1881. "One just bought the [draft-regulating] stone that covered my chimney. What could he want with it?"

By the mid-1920s southwestern Indians had become the darlings of the decade. Railroad tourism created an opportunity for visitors to take a piece of them home. The Santa Fe outlets for native baskets, pottery, and Navajo, Chimayo, and Saltillo blankets and rugs that brothers Jake, Abe, and Aaron Gold opened in the late 1870s culminated in 1883 with Jake's colorful "original" store at San Francisco Street and Burro Alley. Another forty years and the Indian trade had grown into a major cottage industry across New Mexico and Arizona.

In a short time modifications in the production and marketing of Indian arts and crafts came to reflect a hierarchy in taste and value. At the lower end of the quality spectrum the size of claywares and their designs conformed to tourists' preference for smaller novelties and items with stereotypical "Indianist" symbols that they could easily pack home. Although considered "debased arts" by Santa Fe elites, figurative pieces such as the Cochiti "circus acrobats" and Tesuque "rain gods" were turned out by the hundreds.

Meanwhile, interactions between early archaeologists like Jesse Walter Fewkes and the next generation of Santa Fe–based scholars and cultural leaders elevated the status of certain potters and encouraged a revival of earlier techniques and older designs. The income from their products helped to stem a decline in the quality of homemade ceramic wares that had been caused by the preference in Pueblo Indian kitchens for less breakable tin and enamel cookware. At the same time it elevated in status and cost a "new-old revival pottery" and lent prestige to innovations by the cadre of "master potters" who had been anointed by museum officials. Now some of those same craftswomen who were still turning out two-spouted wedding pots, ashtrays, and amusing animal effigies for the tourist trade began putting time into exquisite pieces for Santa Fe's collectors, who courted them and supported the Indian art competitions held by the Laboratory of New Mexico, the Gallup Inter-Tribal Indian Ceremonial, and other organizations.

Little of this commercial promise was lost on the Hunts. Besides his skill with silver, Clyde had another talent. Even in a family possessed of abundant people skills, his gregarious personality earmarked him as an outstanding shopkeeper. As silversmiths and painters, the Hunt family would swim this tide along with hundreds of other Pueblo Indians. But they would become pioneer native marketers as well, and extend the range of this lucrative trade into urban centers like Albuquerque, Carlsbad, and Tulsa, Oklahoma. Their family was coming into its own at a period when public fascination with Indians, especially in the Southwest, was peaking. In a time of limited economic opportunity for anybody, Indians especially, they would make the most of it.

Entrepreneurs in the Making (1902–24)

Clearly the west was "won" when it reached a point of marketability, when it could be sold to Americans living in the rest of the country. The bulk of the civilizing salesmen were ordinary citizens who displayed extraordinary drive and originality in pursuing an amazing array of jack-of-all-trades careers. . . . The West as we know it today was built by such individuals, men and women who responded to the myth as perpetuated in dime novels, railroad propaganda, and journalistic hype.

—Nancy Peake, 1991

H ENRY WAYNE, the fifth of Edward and Marie's twelve children, was born in his parents' bedroom in Acomita, New Mexico, on November 12, 1902. Following custom, four days later he received his Indian name, "Growing Plant." Entering the new century, Indian tribes across the country were still losing whatever lands they had left; their populations continued to drop, and poverty and disease remained pervasive on their reservations. But in this hamlet of a few hundred souls, Growing Plant's childhood was fairly free of concern.

He was swaddled in a cradleboard on his mother's back throughout infancy, and his parents then sent him across the street to a day school at age three and to Albuquerque Indian School three years later. But in summertime the lad soaked up the comings and goings of a bustling home that doubled as country store. Being underage, living near Acoma's sacred mesa but not constrained by its rules and expectations, indulged by relatives, he savored the best of both worlds.

Like any Indian kid, Growing Plant wanted a stronger weapon than a throwing stick. Each year his mother's brothers carved a new, longer bow to keep height with his rising shoulders. Per their warnings he never shot his arrows at buzzards lest he find out that any rabbits he shot after that would prove sick or impaired; under Acoma's beliefs about *like* rubbing off on *like*, that would make him, like those carrion eaters, more scavenger than hunter. When it was not in use he kept his bow unstrung, away from the fireplace, and "alive" by frequent rubbing with animal fat.

Upon his first kill he had every intention of smearing it with the animal's blood as he had been instructed. But one day when he was around eleven, bow and quiver slung on his back, Henry glanced down to see what looked like the pad imprints of a mountain lion. His feet did not stop running until he reached the safety of the sheep camp.

Two years later it was a different story. Herding for his father on Mount Taylor's well-grassed eastern spur, Henry noticed the silhouette of an oversize coyote on a rocky ledge. It was stock still, head tipped down, zeroing in on his sheep. "It was a ways off. That day I had a .45 revolver in a holster. It was so heavy I had to hold it in both hands. I closed my eyes and pulled the trigger. When I opened them the animal was still in the air and then fell into a ravine. I walked around my flock and went over there. Sure enough, it was a wolf." The predator Henry had killed with a lucky shot through the neck was probably one of the last Mexican gray wolves to venture this far north from Mexico's Sierra Madre.

Knowing how to skin and cure, he dragged the carcass back to camp. With care not to puncture it, he sliced loose the hide from the carcass, stretched it out, and began scraping away the flesh, fat, and membranes. He hoped his father would turn the pelt into an arrow quiver. Meanwhile that skin became so precious to him that he slept with it. A few days after he returned home his mother was feeding him breakfast when someone showed up at the door.

"Usually, when you visit someone's home," Henry later recalled, "you let them know you're outside by calling out, *Kuwatse*. But when you hear someone say *Kaya*, that's a ceremonial greeting. You'd better pay attention, because it's a tribal officer." His mother suspected as much before she greeted the visitor. He said, "I understand we have a son here." Although a woman, she knew the Eagle, Bear, Mountain Lion, and Wolf were considered her people's earliest hunters and teachers. Aware that her boy had recently killed a wolf, she answered, "Is he the one you want?"

"Yes, we're going to initiate him today." She told Henry that they would take him to Acoma mesa, into the chamber of the Hunters Society. Four times they would whip him with a stiff yucca leaf—on his shoulder, waist, thigh, and ankle. "Usually they hit pretty hard," remembered Henry, who

*Now a San Francisco hostess:
Juana Valle Bibo.*

got scared. But since he was still young, his mother reassured him that somebody would probably grip his hands while it happened, and try quieting the man delivering the blows.

In the special room a diorama-like shrine was suspended from the *vegas*. On its little platform stood foot-high carved effigies of the Warrior Brothers, Masewi and Oyoyewi, patrons to hunters, each gripping their miniature bow and arrows. The boy was frightened but obedient. An uncle led him to the altar where a masked "whipper" danced around him four times, giving him a whack down his body with each encirclement. "Then they gave me another name. They called me Wolf Robe because they knew I used to sleep with that hide."

As a Pueblo lad with artistic and entrepreneurial leanings, Wolf Robe Hunt couldn't have grown up in a more auspicious place and time. His youth and America's postwar love affair with the exotic Southwest developed in tandem. Rarely in the nation's history would a single region be subjected to such adoration. By 1915 an estimated four hundred painters, nearly all emigrants, were ensconced along the Taos–Santa Fe corridor. Equally unusual was the coalition that sprouted behind Pueblo Indian rights. Archaeologists and anthropologists stood alongside writers, painters, and social activists in studying and protecting ancient ruins as well as Pueblo land and religious causes. Over these decades their influence founded a host of cultural institutions that enabled them to do so. Starting with the New Mexico Historical Society Museum (1885), they included the School of American Archaeology (1907), Santa Fe's Fine Arts Museum (1917), the Indian Arts Fund (1922), the Spanish Colonial Arts Society (1925), the Laboratory of Anthropology (1927), and the Navajo Museum of Ceremonial Art (1937).

Like religious converts at a suddenly popular shrine or miners hitting a fresh vein, recent arrivals wrote old friends back east: *It's happening here.* Coincident with the well-to-do professionals coming to recover their health were tourists drawn by a sophisticated advertising campaign. Exploiting the commercial possibilities of photography and recruiting top-flight writers, the Santa Fe Railroad hooked up with hotel magnate Fred Harvey to turn vacationing passengers into cultural explorers. Among the region's must-see wonders, Pueblo Indians topped the list. The public adulation of Pueblo Indian culture and their southwestern surroundings came into full flower.

Now a San Francisco merchant: Solomon Bibo.

The targets of this adulation hardly knew what hit them. First came the question of how to decipher the ravenous curiosity that energized these eager white faces. It was such an about-face from even a generation before, when disdain, even disgust, for Indian religion, social practices, and pace of life was palpable. What range of desires lay behind this new scrutiny, and why were they being questioned about beliefs and practices these whites once found so abhorrent?

Then Indians experienced the subjective and changeable ranking that whites imposed upon the handmade merchandise on which their livelihoods depended. Old pots that early archaeologists dug out of ruins at Bandelier, Coronado, Pueblo Bonito, and Mesa Verde were *artifacts* when shipped to East Coast museums. They became *relics* or *curios* on the shelves of Jake Gold's, Solomon Bibo's, or Edward Hunt's funky shops. Everyday *utensils,* such as the dough bowls and water-carrying *ollas* that nineteenth-century fieldworkers acquired by the barrelful were sold as *souvenirs* when travelers purchased them at pueblo railroad sidings. But at Fred Harvey's gift shops, where visitors were treated to living Indians stamping silver or weaving rugs so the maker's name and tribe lent prestige to the price tags, they were marketed as *crafts*—a somewhat loftier category. Two products might even ascend to the level of *art*—the new categories of fine pottery and the genre of "flat" Indian painting then being promoted in Indian schools. With each shift in status, of course, came an adjustment in economic value. Without formal appointment, Santa Fe's salons of aesthetes, artists, and scholars became the new arbiters of authenticity and quality. "It is the artist," proclaimed painter Marsden Hartley, "who is most of all privileged to celebrate the scientific esthetic of the redman."

Upper-crust bohemians became aficionados of *their* Pueblo village, visited *their* Indian family on feast days, and patronized *their* favored artisans, all the while looking down upon the popularizers and peddlers who had created this Indian trade in the first place. As if following the sartorial excesses of anthropologist-gone-native Frank Cushing, Santa Fe denizens became noted for their mix-and-match costumery—reservation Stetson hats, Navajo silver concho belts, Pueblo shawls, long Spanish-style skirts, and high-top moccasins.

Attendance at Pueblo festivities was de rigueur: "Failure to appear on a sunny roof on every Saint's day," remembered regional booster Erna Fergusson, "marked one as soulless and without taste." Some patrons favored Indian artists who were more "traditional"; others championed innovators. With exceptions like writers Charles Lummis and Mary Austin, many of these new tastemakers betrayed a preference for Pueblo cultural products over those stemming from New Mexico's Hispano legacy.

A smart family like the Hunts could ride this wave of Indianism for years. Working for Solomon Bibo introduced Edward Hunt to the hunger of Anglo tourists for something authentically "Indian" to take home. Some created entire "Indian corners" in their East Coast homes, glassed cupboards jammed with dusty Kachina carvings, Navajo wedding baskets, and Apache jugs waterproofed with pine pitch.

When Henry "Wolf Robe" Hunt got to Albuquerque Indian School he played sports, especially football. At home he picked up silverwork from Clyde, and studied his father's comfortable way with customers. To his school Wolf Robe brought a familiarity with making things; at home "we were always interested in art because my mother used to make pottery and we would help her." After Marie built up her pots with coiled clay, then thinned and smoothed their moist walls for the characteristically fine

*Family reunion: brothers-in-law Solomon Bibo and Edward Hunt (*left to right: second and third standing*) in San Francisco.*

Acoma ware, Wolf Robe and his siblings would dip yucca fibers into black paint to add the delicate scrollwork prior to firing.

In later years Wolf Robe attributed his pictorial influences to locations right around Acoma. "Like most merchants in those days my father was by necessity a rancher, because he had to take cattle to close out some accounts. That made me a cowboy riding the range for him. And that took me all around the mesa cliffs where pictographs by the old cliff dwellers are found." Hard by his great mesa were sandstone alcoves containing house ruins, and rock-face panels of scratched-in circles, marks on a line as if counting days or moons, and humanlike figures, possibly Keresan ancestors, that dated back hundreds of years.

He was especially taken with other panels, also within a stroll of Acoma, featuring check-patterned rectangles (possibly depicting pre-Hispanic textiles), snakes (perhaps connected with prayers for rain), animal figures (maybe hunting magic), and corn plants. One even showed what looked like a buffalo, perhaps recording an Acoma trip to the east. "Some were colored in ground-up rocks," Wolf Robe remembered, "others in natural colored clay. My love and admiration for these rock paintings are what made me an artist, rather than any study of academic principles."

He also had some art education. As best we can reconstruct it, his Indian School teacher, Isis Harrington, encouraged her students to draw their traditional lives back home. Wolf Robe was around eighteen years old when the Indian School was visited by a beautiful woman with a gleaming smile and owlish eyeglasses. She was Nina Otero-Warren, grandniece of the state's first Hispano governor, a promoter of Hispano culture and Pueblo Indian assimilation, and equally conversant with the old *rico* world, Anglo Republicans, and Santa Fe's artistic crowd. Apparently she took an interest in Wolf Robe's talents, and arranged for his work-study service at the studio of Carl Redin, a Swedish modernist in his mid-twenties, who'd moved to New Mexico to recover from tuberculosis.

Perhaps this mentor's looser brushwork influenced Wolf Robe, whose own pictures were freed from the fine-line primness of the so-called Bambi style of studio painting that was being imposed by Santa Fe's Indian classrooms. Like them, however, his pictures were a few steps removed from their origins. When he painted Apache Crown Dancers, for instance, there is no certainty he had seen them for himself—perhaps he improvised from pictures he'd been shown. At first his stiff, two-dimensional figures, usually in profile, stood against white backgrounds with few hints at setting or landscape. He painted generic Indian dancers, or nostalgic scenes of an idealized Indian existence that their non-Indian viewers wanted to remain in the past but preserve in frames on the wall. In the triple bind between realistically depicting their authentic tribal selves, painting the stereotypical (mostly Plains) Indians their customers would recognize, and perhaps longing to experiment with modernistic approaches that their white teachers considered ethnic betrayals, Indian artists would be stuck for the next half century.

Longest-lasting of Wolf Robe's influences was watching his dad's skill with his hands, how he was open to new tools and ideas, congenial with customers and other ethnic groups, and still honored his own heritage. To those tendencies Henry added his knack for networking. Parlaying contacts into friendships, and friendships into new introductions, he kept thick appointment books and a web of prospects for appearances that would sustain him, and his entire family, throughout their lives.

From his dad Henry also learned how to be the Indian his clientele wanted him to be. That this was often as not a Plains Indian was no secret; before his premature death from tuberculosis even the photogenic darling of the Santa Fe set, the San Ildefonso Pueblo painter Crescencio Martinez, was asked to perform as a "Sioux" Indian for guests at the School of American Archaeology in Santa Fe.

One day the school disciplinarian made an announcement in Wolf Robe's class. A Boy Scout camp in Little Rock, Arkansas, was looking for an Indian arts and crafts teacher for the summer, to instruct in leather- and featherwork, dancing to the drum, and singing Indian songs. "You know how timid I was?" Wolf Robe recalled. "I only raised my hand a little over my shoulder. But he saw me and put me on a bus." For eight weeks, "I taught them dancing, some leather work, I talked about our customs, and I was paid a good wage. But they taught me other things, too, how to sell—the beginning of my being a merchant."

36

Troubles at Santa Ana (1922–25)

If all of Santa Ana's neighbors, Indian, Mexican and American, should be suddenly obliterated, or removed to a distance of five thousand miles, Santa Ana would carry on. They are quite capable of completeness, self-sufficiency, and independence. And, the writer feels sure, the predominant spirit in the pueblo is one that would just like such a situation as this—one in which the pueblo could go its own way, alone, undisturbed, and in peace.

—Leslie A. White, 1942

WHEN THE PUEBLO of Santa Ana opened its arms to the homeless Hunts they were given their starter farm for free. "Part of it had been cultivated some fourteen or fifteen years ago," Edward remembered, "but nobody was working it and it had all got raw again."

A hundred years earlier, whenever high waters from the spring snowmelt subsided, Pueblo farmers whose irrigation ditches drew upon the Rio

Grande and its tributaries could raise their vegetables on upwards of
twelve to fifteen thousand fertile acres, with few worries about watering
them. But by the 1910s, the number of farmers statewide had tripled, and
demand for water skyrocketed accordingly. At the same time, years of silt-
ing from the heavy runoff caused by overgrazing and timber cutting in
northern New Mexico (the trees going into railroad ties, mineshaft supports, and steam engine fuel) had transformed almost a third of the arable
Rio Abajo shoreline into marshland. The river bottom became ribbed with
sandbars and quicksand sinks; both banks of the Rio Grande were a mo-
rass of thick cattails, stinky mud, and rotting tules that bred clouds of
malaria-carrying mosquitoes.

Santa Ana Pueblo asked white officials to reclaim the precious acreage
by draining the Rio Grande's waterlogged western shore. The same surveys that exposed the extent of potential land loss to Pueblo Indians if the
Bursum Bill had passed into law also revealed that, up and down the Big
River, Indian families were barely making it. Squatters from Bernalillo
surrounded Ranchitos. Thirty or so non-Indians were tilling and watering
within sight of Edward Hunt's new home.

After clearing, plowing, seeding, irrigating, and weeding, his little plot
was actually doing so well that he wondered if any Santa Anans wanted to
sell or lease any more land. Word got around; soon he was working twenty-
two acres. His Hispano neighbors inspired him to put in a nonnative
crop—alfalfa—whose three or four "cuts" a year he sold through Julius
Seligman's mercantile outlet in Bernalillo. His neighbors watched as Edward erected a barn and introduced a gas-powered thresher that worked
far more efficiently than the older method of walking livestock in endless circles over the stalks—*if* efficiency was what one wanted. Santa Ana
saw the ease with which Edward bantered and bartered with his Hispano neighbors and sensed his impatience with their traditional ways.
They began to wonder what kind of cultural Trojan horse they'd invited
into their midst.

Well before the Spanish first appeared, Pueblo farmers had diverted water
from seasonal streams as one of a number of desert farming techniques.
Even though at Santa Ana the Hunts could count on a steadier supply of
river water than they had ever enjoyed before, their hosts still kept their
eyes on the skies. As at Acoma, the Santa Ana "conception of beauty in a

Early spring: everyone helps repair the "mother ditch," Isleta Pueblo.

landscape," observed Edward's anthropological friend Leslie White, "was a cloudy day." But gratitude for any moisture the spirits provided from above was matched by the necessity to draw the most from what coursed below.

With the spread of Spanish settlements in the seventeenth century came centralized irrigation systems for transforming the Rio Grande valley into what environmental historian Richard White calls an "organic machine." The Hunts' personal migration from the arid west to the middle Rio Grande enrolled them into the kind of "waterwork society" that some anthropologists at the time, extrapolating from Asian agricultural practices, saw as necessitating a centralized authority. Projecting this theory onto the pueblos, they argued that the degree of social coordination required by "hydraulic farming," with all parts working together to fairly distribute water over a communal area from a single source, called for some individuals to be in charge and others to do as they were told. No longer only "dry farmers," the Hunts were now expected to adopt the irrigation practices and rituals of their new riverside home.

For New Mexico's pioneering Hispanos, the duties of collective irrigation were spelled out in the *Recopilación* of 1706, which drew upon agrarian practices that hailed from Spain and North Africa. Across the dispersed villages of colonial New Mexico, yearly maintenance of the *acequia* (irrigation ditch) system was a hallowed institution. Only by summoning all hands for a spring cleansing of the ditches could the "mother ditch" (*acequia madre*), the smaller channels, check dams, and headgates function like a healthy arterial system, circulating water throughout everyone's fields.

Early each spring, a week or two was set aside for a communal *zansas,* the collective fulfillment of irrigation duties by each ditch beneficiary, known as a *pariente,* under the direction of a "ditch boss," or *mayordomo,* who carried out the wishes of an elected village commission. That was when the previous year's accumulated debris of branches, leaves, and tumbled-in banks was shoveled out. Channels were realigned, and *atarques,* or diversion dams, and *compuertas,* wooden sluice gates, were restored. Finally the local Catholic priest "opened" the cleansed ditches with prayers. Parishioners carried out their carved household *santos* for renewal. With thanks to Isidro Labrador, saint of farmers, and Nepo, patron of irrigation, plowing and planting could commence.

At the Indian pueblos along the Rio Grande, however, the customs of ditch maintenance were less bureaucratic. They were a culture, after all, not a corporation. They had myths, not bylaws. They shared surplus crops, they did not disperse paid dues. They preserved the important decisions of their lives in their collective oral memory and did not keep written minutes of monthly meetings.

Besides, Pueblo Indians already possessed ample socioreligious mechanisms for maintaining community cohesion. Instead of invoking saints, during the ditch-opening rituals their shamans and clowns placated the pre-Christian spirits-of-place that were so rudely disrupted by all this digging and cleansing, especially the Horned Serpent that controlled gravity flow in the Big River. Offerings of corn-and-bean meal, fish scales, and prayer sticks, as well as special ditch-cleaning songs, accompanied every phase of the work. Tribal ditch bosses made sure any water users cleansed and patched their assigned stretches.

A number of farms in the Ranchitos community, like Edward's own wedge of topsoil, lay between the Hispanic and Indian mother ditches and the differing cultural systems in charge of them. That first summer of 1918 the Hunts complied with Santa Ana's ditch duties while ducking entreaties to join her more private, traditional rituals. But no matter how inconspicuous they tried to be, any withdrawal within a society already dedicated to withdrawal placed them under scrutiny.

Each January's change of governors also meant a more conservative regime could take action. "Every year everyone made about five trips to old Tamaya [the old Santa Ana village] for their religious meetings," Edward remembered years later, "but my family worked steadily on the farm and never went. The people began to think I was not a good Indian. They became jealous and criticized me. When an official asked why I did not attend ceremonies my excuse was that I did not know their beliefs."

Over the next couple of growing seasons these tensions ratcheted up. Edward sidestepped indirect suggestions, then outright insistence, that his boys participate in Santa Ana's kiva ceremonies. These went beyond the public harvest celebrations of Santa Ana's July 26 fiesta, which the Hunts joined willingly. They painted their faces, tied feathers in their hair, held sprigs of pine needles, and danced from noon to sundown in weaving formations to the drumbeats and resonant baritones of headband-wearing singers. Where Edward drew the line was deeper involvement in Katsina ceremonies, medicine men's initiations, curing rites, and the transgressive antics of sacred clowns that he knew well.

But for communal prayers to be effective, healing rites to cure, fields to produce bountiful harvests, and women to bear healthy children, Santa Ana had to function as a single unit. A pueblo had no time for part-timers or withholders. Also, the underpopulated village needed fresh blood from the generation of Edward's sons to fill key roles in its Flint (medicine men–healers–exorcists) and hunting societies, to take on the three-year terms of war chief and cooks, to assist initiations as sacred clowns, and to hold other ritual posts. "I told them that I had my children educated in another way besides your old customs. I cannot make my children, who are growing up and have been to school with the government, believe as you do."

Before long these conflicts thrust Edward before two different tribunals. First he was called on the carpet by Santa Ana's newly appointed conservative governor, who held progressives like the Hunts in low regard. "They stood me in the center of the Santa Ana Pueblo meeting house," Edward remembered, where he was surrounded by community elders. What were his religious beliefs back at Acoma? they wanted to know. "I did all the old initiations and rituals," he replied. Then why not perform them here as well? they asked. "Don't you believe in the powers of the rain-bringing Katsinas, the medicine men, or the old customs?" How could his or any family possibly remain healthy, and profit from corn and wheat harvests, without their help?

After so many struggles with pueblo officials and personal reversals of fortune, little submission to any creed or status quo, whether Christian or Pueblo, remained in Edward's makeup. "Don't you remember," he shot back, "only one god made the heaven, the earth and people. He is the only one to pray to." This met a mocking retort. "So let's watch Mr. Hunt," challenged a Santa Ana elder, "and see if his God can produce corn and wheat in front of this altar here to take home?" When another Santa Anan was more sympathetic, reminding everyone of a painting in their Catholic church that sympathetically portrayed Nautsiti, one of their mythic spirits, as the "mother of whites," he was told to be quiet. The mood forbade any accommodation between Indian and Anglo lifeways.

Then Edward's wife, Marie, and son Alfred were escorted into the room. She responded as had her husband—"maybe even better when she told them about God," Edward later allowed. And despite Alfred's attraction to the old tribal ways back up at Acoma, in this face-off he remained loyal to father and family.

A few days later, Edward recalled, "I was told that I was no longer needed in the Pueblo. I could plant in the dry field, but not use their irrigation ditch. I was shocked and hitched my team to report to the Indian agent." Since Edward's largest plot lay between Santa Ana's "Indian" ditch to the east and Bernalillo's *acequia madre* to the west, instead of drawing on the Indian water he petitioned the "Mexican" ditch *mayordomos* in Bernalillo. "They said whoever worked their ditch had a right to water. They measured how many yards I needed to keep in repair, and for the next three years I did that."

Living within an Indian community but irrigating from an Hispano ditch was an untenable situation. It got even dicier when Edward's family stayed reluctant to participate in Santa Ana's political and cultural life. Within a few years another conservative became Santa Ana's governor, and a new Indian agent of the pro-traditional persuasion assigned during the Collier regime replaced Edward's more progressive old friend, Philip Lonergan.

One morning Edward woke to the pueblo's ultimatum. Whether or not he used the Indian water, he had to join the crew working on their ditch. When he resisted doing more than his share, "The governor came to my house and told me I was no longer fit for the Pueblo. I must get out and look for somewhere else with my family." In defiance, Edward asked him to "think these things over." They did so overnight, but the next day "they threw me out like I was a strange man. I stood there with my shovel and said, what shall I do?" You can bring in one more harvest, they told him. Then the Hunts had to leave Santa Ana for good.

Edward was never shy about complaining to authorities, and his file in the Pueblo Indian agent's office had grown. Around this time he was summoned before a second panel of inquisitors. Whatever information he had already aired, it gained new currency within the loosely knit group of conservative Anglos who were still seething from the resounding defeat of their Bursum Bill. So on April 10, 1924, Edward took his wagon to Santa Fe to plead what he thought was his case against Santa Ana Pueblo.

The old town at the foot of the Sangre de Cristos had modernized since Edward molded and mortared adobes for St. Catherine School thirty-five years before. Wooden timbers replaced stone boulders in the bridges across the Santa Fe River, gratis of Santa Fe's previous mayor, Arthur Seligman. Only a handful of washerwomen pounded clothes on the river bottom anymore. Buckboards, buggies, and even some automobiles outnumbered burros in the streets, although the firewood-packing animals still clogged the unpaved byways between them. No beef or sheep carcasses swung for sale in the shadow of the plaza's portals. Fewer bars and brothels enlivened the nights on lower San Francisco Street. And by now, after sundown the glow from electric streetlights surrounding the plaza almost obliterated the stars.

As he entered downtown, one glance at the relatively new art museum may have caused Edward a double take. Its two towers, façade, and proportions were modeled after Acoma's old St. Stephen's Church. It demonstrated the enduring impact his Pueblo culture would have on the town's new architectural aesthetic. Edward's destination was the Federal Building, which had recently been moved on rails to its new location at Marcy and Washington.

In a first-floor meeting room he found himself across the table from some of the state's power brokers. Chairing the session was former New

Acoma's influence: Santa Fe Museum of Art (1916), modeled after San Estevan del Rey Mission.

Mexico territorial governor Herbert J. Hagerman. Son of a pioneer Pecos valley developer, the fifty-two-year-old Cornell graduate and former diplomat to Russia was handpicked by Interior Secretary Fall to serve as commissioner to the Navajos. An intimate of the Santa Fe Ring old-timers, Hagerman was an advocate of Indian assimilation, and antagonistic to John Collier's reforms.

Oldest of the Anglo faces was sixty-five-year-old Ralph E. Twitchell, a year shy of his death. A pillar of the city's political and academic establishment, Twitchell was a staunch Republican, railroad attorney, prolific historian, and crony of the Santa Fe Ring. A drafter of the Bursum Bill, he advocated an English-language-only movement and put down Pueblo Indians as "primitive" and "pagan." As special assistant to the U.S. attorney general for Pueblo land titles, he was advising Indian agents C. J. Crandall and Chester Faris. Finally, there was the same Adelina (Nina) Otero-Warren who had befriended Wolf Robe, a Republican, suffragette, and strong advocate for Indian education.

Twitchell opened by asking for a summary of the Hunts' sojourn at Santa Ana, but quickly focused on what was really on his mind. "What, if any, ceremonies were held in connection with your being received [at Santa Ana] at that time?" After recalling the welcome in November 1918, Edward described how relations had soured. Twitchell fast-forwarded, "In what ways did they trouble you?"

"The governor came to tell me at my house that I am not fit for the Pueblo any more, that I must get out and look for somewhere else with my family. I did my part on the Bernalillo ditch, then about a week later the Governor called me to his office. I did not want to go. I thought that was all. But I was afraid they might ask me questions about the medicine men."

Hagerman got impatient. "You have not said anything as to what were actually the customs or ceremonies they tried to impose on you. What did they want you to do or say you believed in?"

"They wanted us to believe in their pagan beliefs, that we must believe the same as their families, as they were taught as little children."

"What were some of these customs or beliefs?"

"I don't want to mention them."

As if to help Hunt out, Crandall tried to explain to the others, "These things are Masonic to an Indian. A man's life is in jeopardy who would disclose them."

But Otero-Warren pressed. "Did you believe these practices were harmful?"

In response, Hunt revealed the lasting impact of his personal experience so many years before. "Yes, after what my children learned at government school, they might be hurt. When I returned from school they wanted us to take our American clothes off and live as Indians, and they beat us."

Following Hunt the Santa Ana officials were brought in. The panel tried to get the governor to reveal the real reason the Hunts were being harassed. Was it because of their refusal to do ditch work, or their unwillingness to join "private ceremonies"?

"Would you require him to take part in the pagan ceremonies as part of this community work?"

"Beside the ditch work he would have to take part in these ceremonies," replied the governor, "as he agreed to when he came to the Pueblo."

One imagines an uneasy family returning to Santa Ana. How could they remain in the midst of such friction and animosity? Had they no inkling that their testimony might help to restart one of the white man's oldest threats to American Indian hearts and traditions?

Threats to Pueblo Spirits (1922–25)

Much has been written about the advancement of these Pueblos in civiliza-
tion and religion, but, as a matter of fact, the situation is an anachronism—
a relic of the dark ages. Collectively speaking, they are little short of
barbarians, clinging tenaciously to their old customs and stubbornly resist-
ing any governmental measures along progressive lines. . . . They have, it is
true, been surrounded by a form of civilization, but largely of the Mexican
variety, which is practically no higher than their own.

—Matthew K. Sniffen, Indian Rights Association, 1921

FOR THE TIME BEING Edward took the stony looks from his Santa
Ana hosts in stride. He had more pressing worries—maintaining his
spread, feeding his family. His corn, wheat, and alfalfa fields needed planting, weeding, irrigating, and harvesting. Marie and the kids pitched in.
Apple, peach, and pear trees had to be pruned, picked, and watered. There
was fruit to dry, sheep and livestock to feed, a half-built barn to finish,
brush to clear from the Bernalillo ditch.

Edward suspected that his hassles with village elders over community
obligations—on the irrigation ditch and general upkeep—were covering
their deeper displeasure over the family's resistance to embracing their
ceremonial life. In this tension between civic and religious responsibilities
he was not alone. By now every southwestern pueblo had its dozen or more
returnees from government boarding schools whose progressive ideology,
like a vaccination, had taken. Avowedly Christian and antipagan, they
were proud of their ability to read and write. They supported technological
changes in farming practices where they cut time and costs. They embraced the ethics of American individualism and "furthering themselves."
Most of them wanted to maintain a contributing presence in their home
pueblo, but not remain beholden to its religious order.

Some had already butted heads with their conservative elders. At Santa
Clara Pueblo, Vidal Gutiérrez and his progressive cohort complained

when their family members whom they thought ought to be in the kitchen or in school were told to sweep the streets along with everyone else. It was also unfair, Gutiérrez argued, to recall nonfarmers holding down jobs in the outside world to work in the village's irrigation ditches when they weren't benefiting from their produce. But like Hunt, he discerned the underlying conflict. "It all goes back to their pagan rites," insisted Nina Otero-Warren, who translated for Gutiérrez to Santa Fe officials. "The ditch question has nothing to do with it." And Gutiérrez added, "We can all dance like everybody else, of joy, if we want to. But we do not want to be forced."

San Juan Pueblo's self-described "little bunch of progressives" begged officials for protection, "otherwise there is nothing left to the progressive Indian to do except fall back into the old pagan way of living, or to suffer all kind of petty persecutions . . . or else to leave the Pueblo and live elsewhere like a white man." At Cochiti Pueblo, two leading progressives, Juan Pedro Melchor and his Haskell Institute–educated son, Joseph, complained that although they drew water from the "Mexican ditch," the tribe's governor insisted they shovel the Indian channels, and even boasted, "I can drive you around just as you drive your cattle." Joseph's fencing was torn up, his posts and wire tossed into a corral. When he refused to join the Christmas dances, his wife was allegedly stripped naked in a freezing room.

These progressives also shared an antipathy for the traditional "cacique system" of pueblo leadership, with absolute power wielded by a holy elder chosen secretly for life. Their school exposure to American politics made them want voting rights, U.S. citizenship, and a greater say in tribal governance.

Nor were their issues unique to New Mexico. On the national stage a multitribal organization, the Society of American Indians, was organized in 1911 for those with similar educational backgrounds and "Americanized" points of view. Most of its membership were products of Richard Pratt's Carlisle institution, or the similar boarding schools it spawned. Unlike their more working-class Pueblo counterparts, a number had even become professional doctors, lawyers, educators, artists, and writers. Until internal dissension splintered its ranks in 1925, this elite Indian body published its own journal, *The American Indian,* and lobbied for equal employment, cultural respect, voting rights, and American citizenship.

Uproar over the Bursum Bill was dying down. Santa Fe was returning

Edward Hunt (sixth from right) hosts Progressive Pueblo Indian Council at Santa Ana, with visitors from the assimilation movement: Matthew K. Sniffen of the Indian Rights Association (second from right), Nina Otero-Warren (third from right), and Ralph E. Twitchell (eighth from right), among others.

to whatever the notoriously unconventional town considered normal. The victory of Collier's coalition of Pueblo spokespeople and petition-signing artists, writers, and activists against Republican-led efforts to legitimize squatters on Pueblo lands had not been perfect. Indians would only retrieve a portion of the lands they'd lost. But with encroachments halted and the worst of the bill's provisions thwarted, the pro-Pueblo camp took a breather.

Then Indian Commissioner Charles H. Burke caught them off guard. Reheating the forty-year-old post–Civil War crusade against Indian traditional belief systems, he condemned Plains Indian tribes for a slew of social and ceremonial practices. But he also singled out the "immoral" and "vulgar" Pueblo rites, especially the "lewd" clowning with which Edward was familiar. Some interpreted Burke's edict as a vindictive response to his Bursum Bill's embarrassing defeat. But Burke had ignored how intimately land and religion were linked in Pueblo Indian consciousness and underestimated the staying power of John Collier's lobby.

He further undermined his crusade by resorting to intimidation. In a February 24, 1923, letter, a "Supplement to [the 1921] Circular No. 1665" addressed "To All Indians," Burke threw down a gauntlet. "I could issue an order against these useless and harmful performances," he warned, "but I would much rather have you give them up of your own free will." The Indians were given nine months to cease and desist. Otherwise, Burke finger-wagged, "some other course will have to be taken."

The pueblos were taken aback. "The letter [from Commissioner Burke] threatens us about our dances and religious ceremonies," protested the Zuni. "We were feeling relieved about our religious liberty and our right to our old good customs because the Bursum Bill which would have destroyed them had been defeated. But now we are again thrown into great trouble . . . we dance and worship in order to have more rains."

This time around the Anglo community was split. Although less influential in stature and numbers, a vocal minority flipped the religious freedom argument around. It was their school-educated, progressive Indian friends who were suffering persecution by Pueblo traditionals for their rejection of "degrading and degenerating" rites. As a counterweight to Collier's All-Pueblo Council, Hunt and his network formed their own Progressive Pueblo Indian Council.

Old allies faced off. For years Nathan and Solomon Bibo had aired concerns over the plight of families like their brother-in-law's, the Hunts, who "had civilized teachings and have been trying to live according to American life and Citizenship." And like Nina Otero-Warren, the Bureau of Indian Affairs investigator and champion of Indian health and education, they found themselves at odds with their mutual friend Charles Lummis, who hated Indians being bullied, whether into attending government boarding schools or forswearing their pre-Christian ceremonies. Celebrated photographer Edward S. Curtis, whose twenty-year career made the most of photos of many of the rites under threat, sided with the progressives. Yet the editor of Curtis's own twenty-volume masterwork, anthropologist Frederick W. Hodge, signed petitions against Burke's initiative.

To Indians the spasmodic nature of the white man's antipagan campaigns had always been bewildering. Unaware how they were driven by sectarian rivalries half a world away, they also had to contend with the unpredictability of official personalities closer to home. Early-sixteenth-century Jesuits living among the Yaqui of northern Mexico had blended native and Catholic ceremonies with relative ease. But in eastern Canada seventeenth-century Catholic hard-liners outlawed animal sacrifices associated with Indian burials.

A century or so after Spain's pioneering families learned to survive in the high desert, the Spanish Inquisition followed them across the Atlantic. While sixteenth-century padres of New Spain pursued a rather live-and-let-live policy, the Franciscans to follow condemned the Pueblo use of cornmeal in place of holy water, wearing Katsina masks to benefit crops, the salacious antics of their ritual clowns, dancing with poisonous snakes, and "devil worship" in secret *estufas* (kivas).

In contrast to the Spanish heavy hand, New England Puritans preferred psychological coercion. Guilt-inducing the Algonquian-speaking Indians they cooped up in America's first Indian reservations, the so-called Praying Towns, they extracted tear-drenched promises to put their paganism behind them. From such "confessions," reported Increase Mather in 1684, "it is known that . . . oftentimes at their Dances the Devil himself appears in bodily shape." Particularly fervent evangelists railed against "witch doctors," known as *pawwaws,* who nonetheless retained their influence well into the early eighteenth century.

From generation to generation, region to region, and priest to preacher, the intensity of these antipagan campaigns fluctuated. A functionary might get zealous about rooting out idolatry and have his soldiers drop an iron hand. As a consequence, some practices died out, others found cover as social gatherings, and many merged with Christian rites or even waited underground for a brighter day.

Once Mexico broke free of Spain in 1822, it had enough on its hands without worrying about any regressive Indians north of the border. Left to their own devices, terrorized by Navajo and Comanche raiders, the orphaned Hispano villages hunkered down and relied for self-governance on lay Catholic brotherhoods—the Penitentes. When the United States took control more than a quarter century later, she had a Civil War and irksome Navajo and Apache marauders to overcome before President Grant's Peace Policy could refocus on confining Indians to reservations and saving their souls.

The American hard line did not come until December 1882, when Interior Secretary Henry M. Teller created his courts of Indian Offenses, and a year later formulated the Religious Crimes Code. Forty years before Burke's edict, he targeted Plains tribes, whose "Sun Dances, Scalp Dances, polygamy, the influence of medicine men, and customs of giving away property," popularly known as giveaways, were all considered "hindrances to the civilization of the Indians" and "repugnant to common decency and morality." Tribe after tribe shut down their sun dances, ending with the Kiowa in 1890 and the Ponca in 1908, although a few fulfilled their skin-piercing vows out of sight and disguised their "old heathenish dances and rites" from the prying Indian agents, native police, and their on-site spies, the "boss farmers" who were delegated to teach Indians modern farming. Between 1880 and 1930 the shadow of bureaucratic surveillance and religious suppression descended on Indian country.

Around 1915 complaints over "old pagan customs," "general immorality," and an epidemic of witchcraft first emanated from Zuni Pueblo. Edward's old friend Philip Lonergan, then head of Pueblo schools, warned the Indian Bureau about "Immoral Dances" and "disgusting practices" whose "particulars [are] so bestial as to prohibit their description." His alarm germinated the government's "Secret Dance file" that supposedly documented reprehensible pueblo practices. Over the next decade the Indian Bureau built a case of rumor and misrepresentation against their religion. In 1921 Commissioner Burke issued his Circular 1665, followed by the inflammatory 1923 challenge. The Rio Grande valley was in crisis mode again.

In early May 1924, Hunt and other Pueblo progressives were summoned for a second time before a delegation in search of damning testimony about ritual practices. Led by old-school reformer Matthew K. Sniffen, director of the Philadelphia-based Indian Rights Association, the team roped in the usual local conservatives—retired Indian schoolteacher Clara True from the Española Valley, Nina Otero-Warren, who translated from the Spanish, and historian Ralph Twitchell.

During his earlier testimony, Edward had tried sticking to his dispute over irrigation, seemingly reluctant to delve into esoteric matters. But as star witnesses five months later he and his wife were unable to sidestep the religious interrogation. In him the visitors saw a model example of their "new Indian"—Christian convert, shopkeeper committed to economic independence, enterprising farmer open to modern methods, and a man with firsthand knowledge of these immoral behaviors.

First they were asked for corroboration that moments in the ritual year sanctioned free love. "What about the young girls when they return from school?" As progressive Indians from Taos and Cochiti had already testified, Edward allowed that there were intervals of sexual license. "I did these things when I was young," he said, "and was encouraged to do so by elders."

For one ritual Edward remembered being forced to strip and run cross-country. "By the time we get on top of the mesa, we were shivering," he said, "[I was] practically naked and let everybody see them—full exposure. I got a licking for not believing in these things."

He detailed the initiations of medicine men and sacred clowns, described esoteric curing ceremonies and effigies that served as scapegoats and secret altarpieces, and recalled the so-called phallic rites when clowns pantomimed sexual acts. None of the testimonies the team collected were placed into any cultural context that might make them understandable within the logic of Pueblo religious thought and worldview. Without explanatory concepts, such as the symbolic parallels between these actions and producing healthy children and generating bountiful crops, or the intended opposite consequence when sacred clowns mimicked transgressive

Wilbert Hunt (front row, far right), soon to run away from Albuquerque Indian School and join the Wild West show, and future wife, fellow student Vedna Belle Eckerman (middle row, second from left).

sexual behaviors that people were supposed to avoid, their anecdotes simply turned into titillating glimpses of primitive debauchery.

Then Edward's testimony took a turn; one imagines his interviewers exchanging quizzical looks as he veered off script. Growing less interested in what his interrogators appeared to find perverse or repugnant, Edward simply tried to record them accurately. Toward some masked dances he even expressed affection, especially the "four or five times a year" when the rain-makers (Katsina dancers) visited and prayed for his people. "When they dance they bring all kinds of good things to eat and pass them to their friends. This part was very nice, and the people were expecting something good of it."

As if noticing his listeners' lack of interest in this tack, Edward was reminded of his earlier effort at sharing "these old time stories" with photographer Edward S. Curtis's field assistant, the University of Washington teacher Charles Strong, but "I do not know what became of him, and I have heard nothing of it." He continued to deflect their prosecutorial agenda by staying with the more scholarly inquiries into his people's ceremonies. "If the government wants these things," he offered, "I would like to be taken to Washington and have all them made, everything they want of me." But he added, "I want to be paid and be protected so as not to be injured or any of my people, because there is always a danger in every direction I turn."

When Collier learned of Burke's latest threat again he swung into action. Defending Pueblo rituals was as dear to his heart as protecting their land base; for the second time in two years, he rallied his circle. The deluge of letters to editors, newspaper columns, and protests that fell on Washington had their impact. Even quicker than the Bursum Bill, "Burke's manifesto may be considered dead," Collier soon announced. "The Indian Office didn't want to be denounced for its many past persecutions of Indian religion and its politically-intended threat of greater persecutions to follow." Years later its demise even turned in Edward's favor, as summarized by historian Margaret D. Jacobs: "What moral reformers initiated as a campaign to eradicate the 'immoral' dances of the pueblos evolved instead into a defense of those Indians [like the Hunts] who did not wish to dance or to clean their pueblo's community irrigation ditch."

For their key witness, however, that defense was too little too late.

Edward Hunt was fed up with Santa Ana Pueblo. For three years he'd drawn water from the Bernalillo ditch every summer and cleaned his assigned stretch every spring. Less than a year after he'd been called before the Sniffen committee, the pueblo appointed a new water boss. "Early one morning, before I got up, he came to tell me to work on the Pueblo ditch." Edward said he'd already been denied rights there and had made other arrangements.

Unlike his predecessor, the new Indian agent, C. J. Crandall, took the pueblo's side. "He condemned me because I was disobeying the Santa Ana Governor and their religious ways." Edward had enough. "I told the Indians if they bought my property and paid for the improvements I'd leave. As soon as I said that to the Governor they immediately consented. The whole Pueblo had to put money in to pay me."

Eventually Santa Ana raised about $4,000 to buy him out. What the family could not pack on twelve wagons they sold to Hispanos in Bernalillo. On October 28, 1925, their caravan rolled into Albuquerque. With their Santa Ana settlement Edward purchased a lot on North 4th Street, in the Monkbridge Division beside the Santa Fe Railroad tracks. He and his sons laid adobes for a brand-new home. From now on they would make it as an extended family, through a growing network of external friendships and relatives, rather than count on fellow clan members.

Now they would have neighbors, not co-villagers. They would buy from grocery stores, not trading posts. Their streets would be paved. They would attend churches, not kivas, but on fiesta days they would still visit relatives and friends at Laguna, Acoma, and even Santa Ana pueblos. Outside their windows they now heard car horns and church bells, not drums. For the rest of their lives they would hoe their vegetable gardens in a series of backyards they owned themselves, not larger plots on Pueblo land held in perpetuity by the community. They would come to have inside bathrooms, not outhouses; electric lights, not kerosene lanterns; and experience a new kind of privacy, not constant exposure to neighbors, gossip, and sharp looks. In this urbanizing world, they would be on their own for good.

Indians as Global Icons (1927)

How can we save the American Indian if the Indian Bureau is permitting special privileges in favor of the wild-west Indian shows, moving-picture concerns, and fair associations for commercializing the Indian. . . . We see that the showman is manufacturing the Indian plays intended to amuse and instruct young children and is teaching them that the Indian is only a savage being.

—Chauncey Yellow Robe, Society of American Indians, 1914

ONE DAY in the late summer of 1927, Wilbert Hunt was guiding his father's two-horse wagon up 4th Street toward Bernalillo when a woman flagged him down. His older brother Alfred had been among the road crew that recently paved the major artery to Santa Fe. Rains spilling off the new blacktop left the roadbed high-centered. Without culverts, the earthen gutters had turned into gushing ravines. She had a hard time getting in and out of her property. Would he get some gravel and fill them in? Wilbert spent the day hauling three loads of gravel and leveling her access. Her husband had died recently, she said, and his black Dodge was collecting dust in the barn. She didn't drive. If he could start it up it was his.

Wilbert was familiar with combustion engines from trucking coal between the railroad terminal and his Albuquerque school furnaces. He checked the plugs, yanked the choke, turned the crank, and it sputtered to life. "How did I ever get that car?" he always wondered. "I never got that poor woman's name, never even a sales slip." That summer and fall his classmates pitched in for gas. Indian kids on the go, they hit events in Bernalillo or headed south for the Isleta Pueblo fiestas, bringing back bread hot from adobe ovens and freshly picked melons, and parking behind the school barn.

Then Wilbert got word of an astonishing decision made in his absence, worse than Clyde's departure three years before. Father and Mother Hunt, together with brother Henry and Philip Sanchez, a Santa Ana orphan the

Hunts had taken into their fold, had signed with a Wild West show. How that connection was made he never knew. After some training in northern Oklahoma, they wrote him a letter, the family would be off to perform in Europe.

Wilbert's status at Albuquerque Indian School had risen. There had been one lapse—a failed runaway attempt with a fellow student from Isleta Pueblo. Otherwise he was a model student, a favorite of writing teacher Isis Harrington, a dorm monitor, and set to graduate from twelfth grade. More coach than disciplinarian, as a drill instructor Wilbert was recognized for winning students' obedience through patient encouragement. He felt conflicted, but not for long.

This time he kept his plan a secret, even from his sister Josephine, Harry War Bow, his best friend, and his girlfriend, Vedna Eckerman, daughter of a white surveyor and his Indian wife back at Laguna Pueblo. At a used car lot Wilbert sold his car for $75, went to the depot, and bought a one-way ticket to Marland, Oklahoma. That night he packed and stashed his suitcase under his bed. "I just forgot everything else. I wanted to go with my father to Europe. I wanted to see the world."

After bed check he reported all boys accounted for and switched off the lights. For a half hour he lay on his bunk, dressed and awake. When the boys were sound asleep he pulled out the suitcase and walked into the night. At the Alvarado station he boarded the first of three trains that finally dropped him in Marland. The Miller Brothers 101 Ranch, he was told, was not far.

Wilbert lifted his suitcase and caught a ride about three and a half miles north. The first thing he saw was a gleaming southern plantation-style mansion known as "White House." From its broad balconies the owners, George Jr., Joseph, and Zachary Miller, could peruse their 110,000-acre spread and scan the Salt Fork River valley, the Arkansas River, and the blue Osage Hills beyond.

Wilbert asked around and soon his family found him. "When my father and mother and Wayne saw me they were surprised. My dad didn't like it that I had run away and didn't graduate. But he couldn't change it. Besides, they needed more Indians."

The Hunts had landed in what claimed to be the largest and most diversified and self-sustaining ranching, experimental farming, and entertain-

Headquarters of Miller Brothers 101 Ranch, Marland, Oklahoma. Famous "White House" to extreme right.

ment operation in the world. Wilbert saw Brahma bulls, Jersey cows, work mules, and a fraction of the 101 Ranch's hundreds of working, racing, and trick-riding horses. Out of sight grazed Texas longhorns, a large bison herd, zebras, elephants, ostriches, anteaters, and Karakul sheep, plus wild animal pens and cages for chimpanzees. Into the distance ran fruit orchards, vineyards, and fields of alfalfa, corn, and wheat, among dozens of other crops. Closer to headquarters were farm machinery, equipment sheds, plus a slaughterhouse, packing plant, hide tannery, fruit cannery, oil refinery, filling station, laundry, twelve-thousand-seat rodeo arena, company store, and trading post.

Moving between barns, corrals, and mess tents were Mexican vaqueros, Russian Cossacks, bulldoggers, bronco busters, western cowboys and cowgirls, Indians from local and South Dakota tribes, trick riders, sharpshooters, rope twirlers, former buffalo hunters, and Indian fighters. Above the far-off trees Wilbert made out the tips of oil derricks and sprays of tipi poles.

This operation had begun in 1871 when a pro-slavery Confederate colonel named George Washington Miller left Kentucky and drove his first cattle herd through the free-for-all that was Indian Territory. Miller ingratiated himself with local Indians so effectively that he opened the ranch on their lands in 1893, and continued to lease, buy, and wrest more land from Ponça and Quapaw tribes. By the time "the Colonel" died in 1903, his three sons, Joe, Zack, and George Jr., owned a 172-square-mile ranch that covered four counties. It attracted presidents, politicians, and European royalty, generals, business tycoons, and movie stars, and featured the occasional marquee western performer—Lillian Smith, Bill Pickett, Hoot Gibson, and Tom Mix. For a half century the Millers were the premier hosts, experimental breeders, agricultural innovators, and entertainment promoters of the southern plains.

Simply by being themselves, whenever Indians traveled outside their home communities they often felt onstage. It was never enough that they *were* Indians, they always had to *be* them as well. That meant satisfying old preconceptions and stereotypes. For many self-described progressive Indians that presented a problem. They wanted to be taken as equal citizens and were insulted to be expected to deck themselves out in feathers and furs, or to have to explain why they didn't feel like doing so. Some, like Iroquois archaeologist, museum director, and writer Arthur C. Parker, and his colleague, the prominent Sioux educator Chauncey Yellow Robe, a graduate of Carlisle Indian School and relative of the famous Sitting Bull (who needed only "be" his notorious self when he accompanied Buffalo Bill's 1885 national tour), agreed with white supporters like Indian Commissioner John Oberly: "The effect of traveling all over the country among, and associated with, the class of people usually accompanying Shows, Circuses and Exhibitions, attended by all the immoral and unChristianizing surroundings incident to such a life," Oberly wrote in 1889, "is not only the most demoralizing to the present and future welfare of the Indian, but it creates a roaming and unsettled disposition."

Yet Edward was as removed from the opinions of Society of American Indians progressives like Yellow Robe and Parker as he was from the strictures of Acoma's old conservatives. He was not bothered that the theatrical roles Zack Miller expected of his family distilled the experiences of upwards of four hundred Indians who had performed in almost two dozen different Wild West shows for nearly fifty years. With few employment options, this job offered income, status, adventure, and a chance to turn the experience to his family's longer-term advantage. *Being Indian* would become their trade.

In Oklahoma the Hunts learned to dramatize the stereotypes. One, detested by progressives, which fit *hostile* Indians into the nation's centennial festivities, had been the drawing card during Arizona Indian agent John Clum's tour of twenty-two Arizona Apaches during 1876–77. The recent annihilation of General George Custer's command on the Little Big Horn was still in daily newspapers when Clum's "red thespians" leapt at white actors with mock scalping knives in Washington, D.C. But six years later, when Frank Cushing escorted six Zuni elders to the nation's capital, it was *noble* Indians who enthralled onlookers. As the blanket-wrapped elders from New Mexico laid prayer sticks in Boston harbor, journalists covered them as if they were a delegation from the Vatican. When Lakota Indians from South Dakota reenacted in London their tribe's doomed Ghost Dance and *their* recent massacre at Wounded Knee Creek it was the *vanishing* Indian image that gripped audiences.

These were the kinds of Indians craved by the public. But the Hunts were short-haired, peace-loving Pueblo Indians who bore Christian names and weren't vanishing anywhere. As Wilbert knew, "People in Europe wouldn't recognize you as Indian if you were from Acoma, New Mexico." The Dresden-based German circus with whom the Millers had subcontracted ordered long-haired, warlike Sioux Indians with "Indian" names. When the Millers began to rebrand them the Hunts considered it a lark. Was this profession's license to pretend that different from the kind of personal reinvention for which Edward's life lessons had prepared him? In his family's generally optimistic, tolerant, and self-confident view, this additional way of *being Indian* never prevented them from being who they were. Besides, they were having fun.

By attaching themselves to the Miller Brothers show the Hunts caught the tail end of an entertainment phenomenon that gripped America for half a century. Before their appeal was eclipsed by motion pictures, Wild West shows bridged the old and new frontiers. The same year that Frank Cushing escorted his Zuni friends to Massachusetts, the Nebraska-born former buffalo hunter for railroad workers and army scout named William F. Cody launched his "Wild West Show" in Omaha, Nebraska.

Cody's show was the first business to take full advantage of the nation's new rail system—one season his show was seen by 130 different communities. In its heyday, Cody required three trains to move hundreds of performers and laborers, cooks, harness-makers, and tent-erectors. He also was a pioneer in mass advertising, blanketing towns large and small with lithographed posters under an annual promotional budget that eventually peaked at $100,000. After the notices were up his customized trains arrived with horses, wagons, buffalo, circus tents, trick riders, sharpshooters, Mexican charros, and a small army of Plains Indians.

Over its thirty-four-year life span, his Wild West Show was on the road half of every year. Before it folded, Buffalo Bill's extravaganza had been seen by an estimated fifty million people—in 1893 by an estimated six million alone. The industrial era's most popular spectacle, the Wild West Show inspired a few dozen knockoffs; but none enjoyed the longevity of the Millers' operation.

First off, however, the Hunts needed new names. Henry's "Wolf Robe" could stay; it even duplicated that of a prominent Southern Cheyenne warrior. But for bloodthirsty Indian hostiles screaming after white men, those charming Pueblo names associated with plants and the seasons were too tame. The Millers borrowed Wilbert's from a recently deceased young Ponca man—Raymond Blue Sky Eagle. Edward required something more fearsome. Already on the Millers' payroll was the Hawkins family, Sioux Indians from Pine Ridge, South Dakota. To replace James Hawkins's boarding school name, Zack Miller dug into local lore. Best known of the old Poncas on whose appropriated land his ranch resided was Chief Standing Bear. The chief's refusal in 1877 to accept a reservation had led to one of Indian America's most famous courtroom dramas. Joining him in jail was his brother, Big Snake, the respected leader of a Ponca military society. So Hawkins was redubbed Big Snake, but the Millers found their headliner a homesick complainer. Feeling they needed a backup, they gave Edward that name as well. For the rest of his life he bore it proudly.

Next came wardrobe. The Hunts knew how Pueblo Indians lampooned yet admired their onetime Plains Indian enemies, enacting them after Christmas in their Comanche Dances. Here in northwestern Oklahoma they were surrounded by the real thing. Topping all Show Indian outfits was the obligatory, full-fanned Plains Indian war bonnet of eagle-tail feathers. At first Edward balked at this key symbol; then it became his pre-

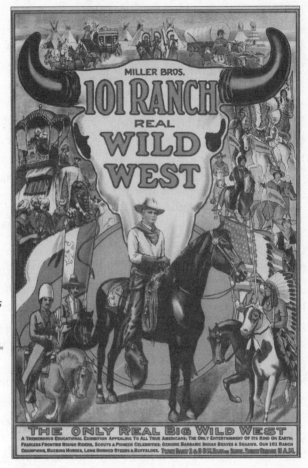

In Oklahoma the Hunts learned to look like Plains Indians (lower right) and attack stagecoaches (upper left), as this 101 Ranch poster advertises.

ferred headgear. Shirts were of tanned deerskin with beaded shoulder strips, or vintage cotton smocks. Next came buckskin leggings, beaded vests and glove cuffs, decorated breechcloths, beaded moccasins, and bandanas around the neck.

Over time the Hunts added touches from home: Pueblo-style shirts bearing yarn-embroidered symbols, Navajo silver bow guards at the wrists, silver bracelets and rings, necklaces of grizzly bear claws, antler tips, and trade beads. One wants to respect the contemporary Indian claim that the word "costume" denigrates the often spiritual nature of the natural materials and iconography that make up traditional regalia. In the case of the

Hunts, however, its use seems justified. During Edward's final years as a showman his feather bonnet was embellished with cow horns, adding a Viking touch. An embroidered Pueblo tunic, beaded and flared leggings, silver concho belt, squash-blossom necklace, beaded armbands, and a fox-pelt bow carrier and quiver slung from a furry bandolier were coupled with a Navajo medicine pouch ornamented with handmade silver buttons. Tall, with broad shoulders and a booming voice, Edward in his multitribal ensemble came to resemble an Italian opera's fantasy of a native potentate from the golden West.

Named and clad afresh, the Hunts learned to move anew. As Wild West Show Indians they were given four speeds. First was neutral. Years of depictions in paintings and photographs had produced a lexicon of iconic Indian postures. Stern-faced, feathered and breechclothed, arms crossed in front of chest (stoic defiance). Still expressionless, but one hand up, palm out (friendly "How"). Arm extended, finger pointing (Indian guide indicating to pioneers the route ahead). Gazing meaningfully at dawn light (spiritual longing). Raising straight arms to sky (prayer to Great Spirit). Staring meaningfully at far horizons and setting suns (accepting fate—vanishing, extinction). Leather-skirted maidens entranced by reflections in still pools (demure Indian princess).

To *act* as Indians, their next gear was a stately slow motion as they rode in regal parades and waved poles from which rippled their conqueror's flags. Third speed was fast and noisy, whether on the ground performing the Plains Indian–style toe-heel, head-bobbing Grass Dance to wailing song and thumping drum, or on horseback shrieking their war whoops and galloping in circles after stagecoaches or covered wagons. When they learned to tumble safely as if shot from their horses, Wilbert and Henry replayed the death throes they had perfected as youngsters playing cowboys and Indians outside their father's store. It also meant copying more experienced Sioux colleagues as they raised tomahawks against white captives tied to stakes and then scattered like frightened birds when the Miller Brothers' posse or cavalry rode to the rescue.

Borrowing from Buffalo Bill, the Miller Brothers marketed their Indian appearances as "authentic" and "educational." Offstage, in mini–Indian villages of cloth tipis or around the log cabin the circus erected at every stop, Show Indians practiced a fourth gear. During these interludes, normally around midday, they remained in costume but became more approachable, responding to questions in the clipped "Indian English" familiar to moviegoers. Their audiences milled around, the kids sat cross-legged on tipi floors, their wide eyes rising to the smoke hole, the parents buying bits of beadwork. Hidden from public view should be any Indian familiarity with modern machinery, fluency in German or French, enjoyment of reading novels or newspapers, propensity for writing complaining letters to government authorities, pleasure in dressing in suits and ties, smoking cigarettes, taking naps, drinking liquor, or joking or flirting with coworkers.

With reserved smiles, and new metal badges that gave them free access and meals in the mess hall, the Hunts accepted their conditions of employment. These skills of impersonation, of separating their public from their personal lives, would help them survive outside the tribal fold.

At the same time, they were overjoyed when their Osage in-laws from Hominy, Oklahoma, learned they were nearby and insisted they visit as honored guests. At Pawhuska and other Osage hamlets, the Hunts entered huge dance and council roundhouses, saw the beaver coats, fine clothes, marriage outfits, and brand-new furniture these wealthy Indians stockpiled in the two-story mansions they rarely occupied, met the tribe's great chiefs, Bacon Rind and Lookout, attended all-night rituals where peyote was the sacramental medicine, were smothered in gifts of blankets and paper money, and found every meal a feast with African-American cooks and servants bringing out endless platters of eggs, turkey, venison, and corn fritters.

Their makeovers in Oklahoma complete, they packed for the grand tour. Onto the train in Marland they loaded the Millers' much-repaired Deadwood stagecoach, eighteen black-and-white paint horses, and trunks of gear. It was a four-day journey to New York, where they stayed at the Hotel Astoria and performed in Grand Central Station. Together with eighty other Indians they boarded the three-year-old SS *Deutschland,* a twenty-one-thousand-ton ocean liner, bound for its home port of Hamburg. Wilbert watched the city skyline recede. The vessel's steam whistle pierced through his body—he never got used to it. After thirteen days at sea they saw the German coast and prepared to disembark.

Joining the Circus (1927)

Suffice to say here that German Indianthusiasm is basically a nineteenth-century construct, an expression of colonial desires and fantasies, that it has escapist and self-aggrandizing tendencies, that it is narcissistic in that it constructs Indianer as people who love Germans, and that it is a by-product of the nineteenth-century invention of an essential German nation.

—Hartmut Lutz, 2003

Aꜰᴛᴇʀ ᴛᴜʀɴɪɴɢ ɪɴᴛᴏ the Elbe River at Cuxhaven on February 14, 1927, the steamship *Deutschland,* bearing Southern Cheyenne Indians from Clinton, Oklahoma, for the Krone Circus in Munich, and the Miller Brothers entourage of Sioux, Seneca, Creek, Arapaho, and Pueblo Indians bound for the Sarrasani Circus in Dresden, crawled the next sixty miles to the port of Hamburg. From there the Hunts and the rest disembarked and registered at Emigrant Hall, across the river. Two days later their contingent boarded a train that cut nearly three hundred miles across northwestern Germany. During their six-hour ride the Indians watched the cultivated hills, estates, vineyards, and churches of old Saxony rattle by until they stopped near Dresden. Then cowboys, Cossacks, Indians, horses, stagecoach, and gear were transferred into circus cars for a final lap to "Florence on the Elbe."

Dresden was long famed for its baroque architecture, its churches, theaters, and famous museums for painting, jewelry, and porcelain concentrated in the Altstadt district on the river's south side. To allow more public venues and revitalize the neglected Neustadt quarter on the river's north bank, around 1910 Dresden's city fathers permitted a circus clown named Hans Stosch-Sarrasani to add to Germany's roster of the "theaters of the world," where visiting American Indians frequently performed.

From Max Littmann, a highly regarded architect, Stosch-Sarrasani commissioned a dome-roofed performance space to be located in the Königin-Carola-Platz, a crossroads for this emerging neighborhood. It cost a million marks, and its electrically lit interior accommodated five thousand spectators around a circular arena. Except for expensive boxes in the front row, all seats cost the same—first come, first served. Stosch-Sarrasani felt that the Ringling Brothers' "three-ring" idea distracted from central events. Wilbert Hunt recalled how its arena spotlighted the boss himself, gleaming in his white outfit, turban glittering with diamonds, whip and hook in hand, a dozen elephants at his bidding.

Born in Poland in 1873, Hans Stosch had caught the circus bug early. By age ten he was a stable boy on a traveling circus, then gained fame as a clown. One reason he likely had no problem with renamed Indians was that he'd appropriated Italy's clown tradition by rechristening himself Giovanni Sarrasani. Moving to the Dresden suburb of Radebeul when he was twenty-eight, he opened his circus two years later. By the time of the Hunts' arrival the Zirkus Sarrasani enterprise employed 800 people and included 250 horses, 100 wild animals, 22 elephants, and 175 vehicles. Under its immense traveling tents, upwards of 10,000 spectators saw Sarrasani's *Revue der Welt* ("Festival of Nations") every year. The acts included Bedouins, Ethiopians, Chinese, and Japanese, along with Cossacks, cow-

When performing at the Sarrasani Circus home base in Dresden, Germany, the Hunts lived in the alcoves of their monumental arena.

boys, and, most popular of all, American Indians—preferably Sioux, whom Buffalo Bill had made Europe's tribe of choice.

Whether caught and coerced or voluntarily signing on, American Indians had been showing up in Europe for centuries. After Hernán Cortez brought Aztecs to pose and juggle for the court of Charles V, every thirty years or so came fresh arrivals. In the sixteenth and seventeenth centuries Indians were displayed as spoils of war and chattel for European slave markets, or as exotic curiosities to be exhibited before royal and scientific circles. In the eighteenth century they visited as diplomatic teams, engaging their European counterparts on issues of trade or military alliances. By the late nineteenth century, with most Indians established on reservations, Wild West shows became the more common opportunity.

Their experiences were mixed. For some like the Hunts, the trip abroad was a sport and a pastime; for others, it was a descent into loneliness, ex-

Inside the single-ring stage, the Hunts joined the Sarrasani's "Festival of Nations"—at extreme rear right, along with other "Sioux" Indians.

ploitation, and abandonment. After Christopher Columbus introduced Taino natives to Spanish royalty, on his second voyage he abducted fifteen hundred of them to be sold in Seville. Some Indians underwent the gamut of emotions in a single tour. In 1719 a pair of native "princes" from South Carolina, probably Creek tribesmen, displayed their full-body tattoos across France and Germany. Three years later, the novelty worn off, they were abducted to Italy and disappeared.

In Le Havre, France, crowds greeted six Osage visitors as celebrities in July 1827; five months later they were begging on the streets of a Paris suburb. Displayed as freaks in Belgium, two died from smallpox (which, along with consumption and tuberculosis, was a common danger for Indian travelers), then the survivors were left on their own in Italy before returning to America as paupers in 1830.

Wild West shows chalked up their casualties too. In 1892, a Buffalo Bill performer, Lone Wolf, died and was interred far from home in London. A leading Sioux from one of Stosch-Sarrasani's early troupes, the much admired Edward Two Two, died in July 1914 and was given a Catholic funeral in Dresden. International politics could entrap Indians, like the Sarrasani performer who was beaten by a mob on suspicion of spying for Russia, or the Indian crew who, lacking passports, were arrested in Hamburg for espionage at the outset of World War I. They fled to Denmark before wending their way to freedom in London.

With their Pueblo background, the Hunts could sympathize with one drawback for Indians visiting Europe. If you didn't hail from a Plains Indian tribe, you could be branded "the wrong Indians." That happened to nine Bella Coola tribesmen from the Northwest coast whom entrepreneur Carl Hagenbeck brought over in 1885. "They are not those proud, red-skinned figures," complained a German journalist, "with cunningly bowed eagle-noses, dark-black, shimmering bushes of hair, and colorful feathers, which school boys reveling in Cooper and *Leatherstocking* like to dream about."

Revealing what some Indians must have felt but hesitated to express was the inspired pushback by a Micmac Indian from Nova Scotia performing in France. When promoters assigned him to kill, cook, and eat a deer before an audience, he added a step. After tracking the animal around the arena, killing it with bow and arrow, then butchering it, cooking it, and eating a portion, "To take a mischievous revenge upon them for making an exhibition of him," wrote the Reverend Silas Rand, "he went into a corner of the yard and eased himself before them all."

Of all the countries that Indians visited over these many years, none maintained its passion for Indians as steadfastly as Germany. Later academics would have a field day unpacking what scholar Hartmut Lutz characterizes as *Indianertumelei*—the yearning, fascination, and "romanticizing about a supposed Indian essence." Some cite Germans' appreciation for Indians as due to their "love of nature" and "anti-civilization critique of culture," or as historian Eckehard Koch puts it, "the intense desire for freedom, change, adventure, and escape." Others reference more recent history and explain this German passion as a sign of a proud people's efforts to revive indigenous traditions that might, like their understandings of wrongs suffered by American Indians, rekindle patriotism after their humiliating defeat in the Great War.

Even a racial affinity was concocted. Following his teacher, the German folklorist Max Müller, Charles Leland alluded to the Aryan-like features of the Algonquin Indians he'd studied in Canada. This idea flowered when Adolf Hitler issued his declaration that the Sioux were actually of Aryan extraction. Injured nationalism, the search for a racially pure virility, a roots-based militancy, and the inspiration of Indian rebellions like Tecumseh's against invading forces—all these elements conspired toward this enduring fascination.

It was reinforced by the work of painters like George Catlin and Karl Bodmer, who'd visited the upper Missouri Plains tribes in the 1830s, and German writers inspired by James Fenimore Cooper. A success throughout Europe, Henry Wadsworth Longfellow's 1856 prose poem *Hiawatha* had opened the readership for Cooper's bestselling Leatherstocking novels, especially *The Last of the Mohicans,* which established an archetype for white-Indian complicity: the maverick white hero and his noble sidekick. But no one would milk this scenario as successfully as a small-time thief born into poverty in a Dresden suburb in 1842 named Karl May.

Since its early hospitality toward the visiting Cherokee "princes" of the early eighteenth century, Dresden had displayed a soft spot for Indians. By locating there, Stosch-Sarrasani was building on its status, firmly established by May's influence, as Europe's capital of the American West. May, a sickly boy and then ex-convict, turned his gift for self-invention to writing imaginary melodramas about American frontiersmen, Arab sheiks, and Indian guides. "Don't tell the truth," May once advised, "if you have something more interesting to say."

The protagonist of three of the novels that appeared between 1876 and 1893 was a noble red man from the Southwest, Winnetou, who was best buddy to May's alter ego, Old Shatterhand. Nearly every Sarrasani ticket buyer had read his May, whose books were boyhood favorites of Albert Schweitzer, Albert Speer, Albert Einstein, Hermann Hesse, Franz Kafka, and Adolf Hitler. Translated into forty languages, his hundred or so titles would sell more than a million copies and make May a national luminary.

When the Sarrasani Circus subcontracted with the Miller Brothers, it requested the older, long-haired Plains Indians, and was put off by the 1927 contingent. But it was a trade-off. The short-haired, softer-faced Acomas were reliable, already trained, good-humored, and willing to don wigs, while the braided and weathered Sioux were prone to despondency and *feuerwasser*, alcohol. No matter to them, the Hunts happily joined Hindus, gauchos, Bedouins, Boers, Ethiopians, jugglers, clowns, and magicians in Western Europe's greatest show on earth.

Aboard caravans of specially outfitted vehicles that could transport their animal and human menagerie, the Hunts toured France, Italy, Germany, and Belgium from spring to late autumn, sleeping in trailers or tents. During the month they spent in Berlin they stayed in the kaiser's palace, and were so popular that their parades throughout the city were stampeded by fans. When the circus wintered in Dresden, they were quartered in the vertical bays that bordered the theater's grand entrance and ate in the circus canteen. As Sarrasani learned during his first season with hired Lakotas from South Dakota's Pine Ridge Reservation, to avoid problems with liquor and misbehavior he needed rules. Visits with locals were restricted to those morning demonstrations of "the Indian way of life." They might ride in city parades, stand like feathered statues at formal visits with city mayors and other dignitaries, answer briefly at press conferences, or attend Catholic churches. Otherwise they were largely isolated. Some still found ways to haul schnapps to their windows with long ropes, or rappel down to meet local girls and get invited to their parents' for meals.

As for sightseeing, the Hunts didn't stick to the circus grounds or grouse about going home. Changing into suits and greatcoats, combing back their glossy short hair like movie stars, they enjoyed wandering the

"Big Snake" (Edward Hunt), with Karl May's widow, Klara, overlooking
the other Big Snake (Jim Hawkins), Hans Stosch-Sarrasani, Patty Frank, Wolf
Robe Hunt, and unidentified Indian following a January 1928 visit to
the tomb of Karl May and the opening of the Karl-May-Museum,
Radebeul, Germany.

narrow cobblestone streets. One of Wilbert's delights was crossing the
Elbe, marveling at the bridge's sculptural carvings, and strolling through
old Dresden—especially the broad steps leading up to the sandstone-block
church, the Zwinger museum complex, and city hall.

Sarrasani offered afternoon and evening performances lasting nearly
four hours each. After the circus parade, the audience saw its fourteen acts
in brisk succession: the "wildest horsemen" from Europe's steppes, Circas-
sian and Cossack trick riders racing their mounts; "the world's only camel
school"; trained Japanese actors in a *Mikado* medley; an exhibition of
horse dressage; the display of Hans Stosch's personal bodyguard of gor-
geous women from around the globe; a sea lion trainer from Canada; a
"Fata Morgana" performance with knights, snake dancers, and Congolese
driving zebras, camels, and hippos; the predator show featuring polar
bears, lions, and tigers; acrobatic acts; the turbaned Stosch with his Indian
elephants; classical equestrian displays; and the "sizzling Orient" with
three different Chinese groups.

Topping off the program were its ever-popular "Wild West" reenactments. Tearing in with the rest, the Hunts dug their moccasin heels into tough, springy pinto ponies. After mad-dash circuits to arouse the crowd, they dismounted for a four-"scene" drama. The set featured mountainous backdrops and a water tank through which the horses could ride. At points the Indians danced, enacted rituals, and climbed the rocks. American cowboys and Mexican vaqueros lassoed and trick-rode some of the hundred horses running around the arena.

Lastly came the Indian attack on the Deadwood stage that the Hunts had perfected during their Oklahoma boot camp. They killed and scalped, women screamed and saved their babies, whites rode to the rescue. The place went dark, the lights came up, all took a bow. Good times for a family from New Mexico.

Their sojourn ended on a high note. To commemorate the opening of the new Karl May *Indianermuseum,* on January 17, 1928, the show's Indians danced in procession the three miles from Dresden to May's hometown. Led by the (Sioux) Big Snake and Edward, his (Acoma) understudy, together with sons Wilbert and Henry, they reached the Radebeul cemetery and May's mausoleum, a mini–Greek temple. With Klara May, the writer's widow, and American consul G. P. Wallace in attendance, they laid flowers and sang funeral dirges. Standing between white columns, Jim Hawkins/Big Snake addressed the spirit of Karl May in his native Lakota, as translated later: "You dear friend. You built our dying nation an enduring monument in the hearts of youth of all nations . . . never has the Red Man had a better friend than you."

The procession continued to Villa Shatterhand, the log cabin that served as May's research library and writing studio. A local character joined them, cowboy buff and May enthusiast Ernst Tobias, who'd renamed himself "Patty Frank" and bunked in the cabin. Not to miss the occasion was his friend Stosch-Sarrasani. They posed for photographs with the widow May presiding, and Frank, Stosch, and Hawkins Big Snake looking reflective. Standing near Klara May like bodyguards were Wilbert and Henry Hunt, war paint slashing their cheeks. Watching it all from the rear was an expressionless Edward Hunt.

Had the family any idea what was brewing around them? Adolf Hitler was still licking his wounds from his failed 1923 putsch and subsequent incarceration. Although his racist tract, *Mein Kampf* (1925–26), was still virtually ignored, with each rally he stirred up virulent anti-Semitism and built support toward the world-changing 1933 German elections. To one Sarrasani show came Paul von Hindenburg, the Weimar president, who shook Edward's hand. Looking back, Wilbert recalled boys in the town squares drilling with wooden rifles; through the train window he always claimed to have glimpsed artillery and tanks hidden in the woods.

According to Hunt family lore, and supposedly seen by a family member serving in Germany in the 1990s, there is yet another notable photo. Shot during the Hunts' tours with Sarrasani, it is said to hang in a Berchtesgaden beer garden. It shows Edward Hunt shaking hands with the thirty-eight-year-old orator—his toothbrush mustache, forelock swept to one side, and hypnotic eyes.

40

Another Greatest Story Ever Told (1928)

The old myths tell this story over and over again. In fact, genesis is the very soul of any myth. To understand the world, the story of its genesis has to be told. To understand the gods, the study of their genesis has to be told. Cosmogony and Theogony are the primary subjects of any myth. . . . An enterprise of this kind does not make much sense unless one relates everything ultimately to beginnings, which make any genesis possible. These are precisely the mythical origins. They contain, of necessity, these two elements: the Male and the Female.

—Jacob Klein, philosopher and educator, n.d.

INTO THE WELCOME SHADE of the Smithsonian Castle's portico stepped the Hunts. Tallest was Edward, barrel-chested, full-suited, and clearly the patriarch; he could have passed as Latin American or Mediterranean.

At his side stood his diminutive wife, Marie, clothed in traditional home-spun cotton skirt, calves thickly wrapped in whitened, high-top Pueblo women's moccasins, a customary woman's flower-print and fringed manta cowling her head. Of the three younger men, Philip Sanchez, the Santa Anan who'd been adopted by the Hunts when he was an orphan, presented the most stereotypical visage with his deep-set eyes, sharp nose, and angular cheekbones. The other two, Hunt's sons Henry and Wilbert, had softer faces and almost looked southern European, especially the photogenic younger Wilbert, with his dark eyebrows and glossy hair evenly parted and slicked back like a matinee idol.

Perhaps in America's capital the Castle's medieval-style towers and notched turrets looked out of place, but the showy edifice did not seem strange to them. Europe had opened their eyes in many ways. They'd grown sophisticated about other styles of life and gained confidence about living on their own. Most important, they'd picked up a profession for doing so. Over the past year and a half the Hunts had become expert at portraying the storybook warriors their audiences wanted to see. It would provide them with a livelihood for years to come.

But that wasn't who they were or why they were here that day. No longer was the family following Joe Miller's instructions in Oklahoma or performing under Hans Stosch-Sarrasani's command. Germany and France had introduced them to Old World culture, a cultivated landscape of stone monuments, elegant cities, and white man's prehistory. Now they were in *their* old world; Edward was ringmaster of this show. For the coming nine weeks or so he and his family led their listeners into the Southwest's mountains, canyons, and ancient villages—and into America's deep culture. They had taken the train from New York to the nation's capital in order to tell how their homeland of Acoma Pueblo in western New Mexico once became the power center of its world.

To their right rose the Washington Monument, an axis mundi that nailed the city's prominence to the sky. To their left, like a command center, the Capitol dome held sway over the fifty-acre green Mall. Folded in trunks back in their hotel were their stage outfits—eagle-feather bonnets, beaded shirts, and leggings and moccasins. For this occasion Edward, Wolf Robe, Wilbert, and Philip Sanchez wore white man's suits. Only Marie remained in her Pueblo woman's traditional best.

Passing through the Smithsonian's massive metal doors, they traded

In street clothes, Edward Hunt, Wilbert Hunt, and Philip Sanchez outside the Smithsonian Castle, Washington, D.C., 1928.

open sky and late-summer humidity for marbled coolness and an aura of institutional superiority. Their shoes clicked on the polished floor. A guard took their names and directed them to stairs leading to the east tower's third floor.

For American Indians the journey to Washington was a time-honored pilgrimage. Ever since five Iroquois chiefs met George Washington in 1789, streams of Indian delegations had beaten a path to the door of the Great White Father. They came to affirm political and economic relationships, receive gifts and benefits, and often to party on the side. Initially, government officials put up with the visits to secure political submission and land cessations from the Indians, and to impress them with white America's overwhelming numbers of people, her technological superiority and military power. For over a century, appropriations for these meet-and-greets had been slotted into Department of Interior budgets. The protocols of photographing native delegates, looping medals of friendship over their necks, and gossiping afterward about missing Indians who had misbehaved became part of capital folklore.

Treaty-making between the U.S. government and native tribes ended in the 1870s. America's attention turned away from conquered, quarantined, and presumably disappearing Indians. The annual treks to Washington became antiquated, the talks increasingly hollow and ceremonious, the travel funds scarcer. In the early twentieth century, the occasional appearance of a feathered chief striding through congressional halls might still startle tourists. Special appearances, such as the visits by Pueblo delegations that were orchestrated by John Collier to fight the Bursum Bill, might resurrect some of the old clout. But maintaining any pretense that tribal delegates retained negotiating authority, or that stilted expressions of mutual respect carried any follow-through by government action, was harder to pull off.

If Indians were lucky or their concessions of land or minerals were at issue, they might enjoy a token tour of the White House. Once the rounds of handshakes and formal photographs at the Capitol were done, a secondary ritual often saw them hustled over to the Smithsonian, where their heads would be cast in plaster, their tribal vocabularies written down and sign language illustrated, their likenesses in full regalia were studio-photographed, their songs recorded, their musical instruments inventoried by museum curators, and their tribal histories and myths of origin transcribed. Well fed but wrung dry, they were thanked and packed off, back to the poverty and powerlessness of their home reservations.

Briton James Smithson's half-million-dollar bequest created the Smithsonian Institution in 1846 "for the increase and diffusion of knowledge among men." Nine years later the fortress became the first structure on Washington's central park, its turreted ramparts resembling something seen along the Loire rather than the Potomac. Along with botanical, biological, and geological specimens, all manner of donations and queries wound up here. Farmers dropped off dinosaur vertebrae and fossils of ferns, schoolboys brought arrowheads and shark teeth, hoaxers presented dried bear fetuses as evidence of alien visitations. Letters from across the country requested samples of exotic seeds, rocks, animal parts, and historical photographs. But topping the Smithsonian's expressed agenda was collecting knowledge about "manners and customs of the various tribes of aborigines of the North American continent." To its "mother stuff of the universe" the Hunts were about to add their own offering.

As scientific surveys and military explorations traversed the West, their notebooks, drawings, paintings, and photographs, as well as the archaeological artifacts and Indian tools, arts, and regalia they collected, also ended up at the Smithsonian. Soon these crowded every available nook, shelf, desktop, and floor space. In 1879 the adventurer-ethnologist-geologist Major John Wesley Powell, a national hero for losing his right forearm in the battle of Shiloh and being first to boat down the Grand Canyon, took over the new Bureau of Ethnology (which was renamed the Bureau of American Ethnology five years later). Now began the cataloging and shelving of this eclectic trove.

The bureau soon found itself in competition with anthropology departments and city museums that began amassing their own Indian collections. Most valued of the Smithsonian's "heterogeneous collection of Indian lore" were tribal narratives, ritual accounts, and oral traditions gathered by its first generation of fieldworkers. This work could put government employees in a bind. Alice Fletcher's personal convictions made her a champion of assimilating Indians, breaking up tribal lands, and their conversion to Christianity. At the same time she worked with Pawnee and Omaha elders to preserve their religious lore and tribal rituals. The Irish nationalist James Mooney sympathetically documented the Sioux Ghost Dance during the same decade that government troops were suppressing it.

Their focus on Indian stories and texts as windows into native belief systems and social organization intensified once Franz Boas, a German-born anthropologist-geographer then at New York's Columbia University, entered the American scene. Boas, who collected narratives in Laguna Pueblo and possibly Acoma in the early 1920s, raised the bar on documenting native grammars and producing interlinear translations. His influence on the country's next generation of ethnographers, especially its complement of female scholars such as Elsie Clews Parsons, Ruth Bunzel, Ruth Benedict, Margaret Mead, and Esther S. Goldfrank, imposed those standards on their Pueblo Indian transcriptions.

◆ ◆ ◆

At its inception, the Southwest could be described as the Bureau of American Ethnology's pet region. The Smithsonian's earliest leaders, Major Powell, Frederick W. Hodge, and Jesse W. Fewkes, cut their teeth on her archaeological and ethnographic treasures. Over American anthropology's "Golden Age," from the 1880s through the 1920s, the Southwest's dramatic vistas, well-preserved remains, and accessible Indian pueblos and Navajo hogans attracted the bureau's most colorful "army of fieldworkers."

Helping the Smithsonian's scholars as collaborators were unsung ranks of American Indians. Like the Hunts, many of these "informants" acquired their bicultural awareness and linguistic facility by virtue of mixed-race parentage, education in government boarding schools, or personal intelligence and curiosity. Of the stripe today termed "organic intellectuals," their multilingual skills and scholarly interest in their own cultures proved of inestimable value. Often they were the coauthors, even authors, of classic monographs, but the title pages rarely bore their names and too frequently their work remained unacknowledged.

By showing up in Washington, the Hunts turned that relationship around. Rather than a white fieldworker coming to New Mexico, they brought a cultural treasure to the nation's doorstep. Although many students of Acoma and Laguna passed through Edward's store, and he'd provided invaluable service to Elsie Parsons, Edward Curtis, Leslie White, and others, how they connected with the bureau remains unclear. Possibly the go-between was John P. Harrington, the eccentric genius of American Indian linguistics, who was said after his death in 1961 to have amassed the largest archive of any scholar in any discipline in American history. One of five of the bureau's in-house ethnologists, Harrington surely knew the Hunts, and kept a correspondence with them well after their D.C. sojourn. Whatever the preamble, Washington officials had some prior appreciation of the Hunts' value.

By now the Smithsonian had already archived lengthy, often patched-together examples of origin myths from the Iroquois of the Northeast, the Cherokee of the Southeast, and the Pawnee and Omaha of the Plains, to name some of the best-known texts. But the account of the Acoma creation narrative would prove one of the most accessible of all. Fourteen years later, when it finally appeared in print under the byline of the bureau's director, Matthew Stirling, Edward's sequencing of stories and fragments he had learned since childhood would join the world's library of culture-guiding myths and national epics.

Its transcription in Washington telescoped into a few months the sort of effort that took other sacred texts of creation and culture-making from around the world decades, centuries, and even millennia to complete. And some would say they are never finished, as subsequent generations revise, update, and add on to them.

To compile such narratives of great magnitude, at least three processes are generally at work.

First comes synthesis. Some gifted individual of capacious intellect and prodigious memory, or a select group of seers, chanters, or priestly elites, must summarize and sequence a wealth of oral narratives, liturgical fragments, prayers, songs, prophecies, and sayings. The sum total of these stories provides, as anthropologist Bronislaw Malinowski famously put it, a "charter" that will govern societal, economic, and political life as well as human relationships with the unseen, the cosmos, the spirits, and the birth of everything alive and dead. As final arguments and ultimate arbiters for all questions, human and divine, these creation myths carry the authority to hold their cultural worlds together.

The second process is their conversion from spoken recitations to some medium of inscribed symbols. Whether marked on stone, leaf, bark, or paper, in this transformation some elements are dropped and some added. This process, too, can take a long time. For better or for worse, no longer would listeners need to experience a specialist's gift for adapting the mythic to the moment, for an audience around the campfire.

Sometimes the old values of retaining multiple oral versions is mimicked in the written work, as with the New Testament's multiple accounts of the same events. And texts like these are surely embellished and amended over the centuries. Revisions can be imposed to clarify or update diction and vocabulary or to enhance their exclusiveness and sanctity. Spontaneity and flexibility often wind up being sacrificed for durability and perpetuation. Now everyone can hold in their hands an all-governing text, and explore it in private, at their leisure, and without mediation by any religious authority. In reality however, those who control the published version often hold power over those who don't.

In full regalia, the Hunts at the Smithsonian, 1928. Left to right:
Philip Sanchez, Wilbert Hunt, Edward Hunt, Marie Hunt, and
Henry Wolf Robe Hunt.

The third process is dissemination. Belief systems, as institutionalized into religions, can seek to extend their authority by translating their foundational narratives into other tongues. In these proselytizing efforts subtle changes and emphases often infiltrate the narrative. Sometimes the changes update an archaic text into a more contemporary and accessible vernacular. These alterations can also result from intercultural contact, as the culture of the recipient language becomes associated with a different religion or theology that the text is then modified to accommodate.

Why was Edward Hunt so ready and willing to undertake this time-consuming job, and resurrect his personal memories, some of which had to be painful? His detractors would accuse him of self-aggrandizement, compensating for being unrewarded at home by winning attention, prestige, and possibly wealth among whites. Even though Edward's name would not be found on the resulting publication, accusations of financial windfalls in the white world always beset successful Indians. In the case of a handful of Pueblo potters, carvers, or painters, there was sometimes truth in this, and so what? From all accounts, however, the Hunts always lived hand-to-mouth, surviving by their wits and helping each other out in lean times.

Maybe after being abroad so long Edward needed a return to origins; possibly summarizing his people's creation stories was the strongest way to do so. The Pueblo scholar Alfonso Ortiz once suggested that that was why Pueblo Indians often narrated and discussed the myths of their homelands when they were so far away, as a means of bringing their sacred centers to their side. When the feisty Hopi traditionalist, Yukeoma, left Arizona for Washington in March 1911, the most convincing case he could make to President William H. Taft and Indian Commissioner Robert H. Valentine against sending Hopi kids to the Keams Canyon school was to launch into his tribe's emergence myth and its prophecies. He had hardly begun before he was promptly sent over to the Smithsonian Institution to be photographed and interviewed.

Or perhaps Edward had to strip away the past years' saturation in an ersatz Plains Indian identity with the most emphatic declaration he could offer of his Pueblo roots. Then again, he might have realized he might never again enjoy the combined resources of his text-translating son Wolf Robe, his song-translating son Wilbert, the beautiful singer Philip Sanchez, and the temporary residence his wife maintained that freed them to put together this offering. Most likely, however, Edward's prior conversations with eastern scholars had lent Washington, and the Smithsonian, a certain prestige as the premier repository for what he had bottled up for so long. One writer has characterized the Smithsonian and its landmark building as a "repository of enchanted objects around which the narrative of our history has formed." Few offerings would be as enchanted as the one these visitors were about to share.

The Hunts climbed the stairs, located the "Bureau of American Ethnology" door label, and knocked.

Telling the Myth I:
Iatiku's World (1928)

*Edward Hunt insisted that the entire account should be given in its proper
sequence just as it was taught to him during his period of initiation as a
young man. Every social, political and religious institution is so deeply
rooted in this fundamental cosmology that it seemed best to present it
chronologically. . . . According to the native concept, everything in the culture must harmonize with this tradition. When new institutions are
adopted, no doubt they are carefully fitted into the scheme.*

—Matthew Stirling, suppressed portion of Acoma myth introduction, 1942

I N AN OCTAGONAL OFFICE illuminated by tall windows that gave onto
the Mall, the family found themselves surrounded by paper-piled desks,
Navajo rugs, overflowing bookcases, and color lithographs of eighteenth-
century Indians. In one corner leaned a ladder that led to the east tower
loft where owls were known to nest. From her chair rose May Clark, secretary to thirty-two-year-old Matthew Williams Stirling, the "chief" of the
Smithsonian's Bureau of American Ethnology, who was just settling into
his new job after two years of hacking his way through the jungles of Dutch
New Guinea. Edward, hat in hand, was confused at first when she led them
to a wooden desk in another hidden corner. He smelled the archaeologist's
cigar before the smiling-eyed, mustached little man stood up and extended
his hand.

Having been only a few weeks at the government post he would occupy
for nearly thirty years, Stirling was not exactly qualified for this assignment. With a master's degree from George Washington University, the archaeologist had extracted artifacts from the ground, not stories from the
living. And his early American digs were confined to Florida and South
Dakota, not the Southwest. As he was removed from Franz Boas's ethnological influence, the urgency of transcribing narratives in their native
tongue was never drilled into him. Even Miss Clark, whom he'd inherited

from Jesse Fewkes, was better informed. She
knew the priority that Stirling's predecessor
placed upon oral traditions, and she was also
familiar with Keresan pueblos, having shot
photographs by flashlight of kiva altars at New
Mexico's Zia Pueblo for Matilda Coxe
Stevenson—the strong-willed anthropologist
whom Zuni Indians called "Big broad but-
tocks like a mesa" behind her back.

Even by the standards of its day the transcription process was woefully incomplete.
No effort was made to record Hunt's stories
in the original language, whether through
some orthographic system on paper or by
voice recordings on wax cylinders. Stirling
had no clue that Acoma's oral lore was separated into genres of prayer, chant, tale, myth,
legend, and song, each earmarked for particular occasions, whether ritual or social.
Hence, he had no way to know if and when
Edward was taking creative license in splic-
ing them together.

Matthew W. Stirling,
Bureau of American
Ethnology "chief" at the
Smithsonian, who
transcribed the myth that
Edward Hunt narrated and
Wolf Robe translated.

No vocabulary list was compiled. As Edward talked, no documentation
was made of his hand gestures, body movements, and facial expressions,
his alterations in volume and pitch, elongations of words and whispers,
mimicry of different characters, emotional tone or use of esoteric or old-
fashioned words—all techniques used by Acoma storytellers. Also lost
were conventions and habits of poetic rhythm, phrasing, breathing, paus-
ing, and analogizing. Minimal record was kept of instances when narrator
Edward and translator Wolf Robe huddled over a problematic section or
discussed some term that was either archaic or part of "ceremonial" or
"kiva" language. Such specialized knowledge was one way Pueblo elders
kept their secrets from those who were not privy to—or not ready for—
them. No log was kept of the narration's day-by-day progress. Nothing has
turned up in the Smithsonian archives of the family's financial, transportation, or room and board arrangements.

◆ ◆ ◆

After coffee and Dr. Stirling's tour of the Castle came logistics. The old "Indian House" on 3rd Street, where visiting tribesmen were put up in the past, was shuttered in 1910. Apparently a rental was found just over the Virginia line. We imagine the Hunts got bus schedules, unpacked, visited local markets. But on the appointed morning for launching the project, instead of Stirling himself the Hunts found a pale, handsome, wavy-haired young man of twenty-six who addressed them in an almost incomprehensible accent.

His diploma in prehistoric archaeology from London's University College hot in hand, C. Daryll Forde was an ethnographic greenhorn. His only field experience had been a summer's survey of megaliths in Yugoslavia, Romania, and Hungary, as assistant to the mysterious spy-archaeologist V. Gordon Childe, one of the presumed models for filmdom's favorite scholar-adventurer, Indiana Jones. Now on a postgraduate Commonwealth Fellowship, Forde was paying a courtesy call at America's clearinghouse for Indian studies. Then he was heading for the lower Colorado River to study how its Yuman-speaking tribes fit into their desert ecology. Perhaps to delay his own daunting assignment, Stirling put the visitor to work in his place. Forde was smitten to be amid genuine Indians. But he had little appreciation that here was some kind of major narrator about to deliver his people's greatest story ever told.

Forde coaxed Edward to begin.

Accustomed to rolling with the unexpected, and having tried unsuccessfully to deliver the full creation narrative to white listeners before, Edward may have paused to clear his throat. What channeling of childhood memories, bricolage of origin stories, folktales, and ritual incantations, and thoughts about sequencing them, began to congeal in his imagination? He never divulged his creative process. Stirling would recall that although Edward was an avowed Christian, he "apparently put himself completely into the spirit of the pagan beliefs at the time he was recounting the narrative, and gave what seemed to be undoubted evidence of hesitancy and even fear in recounting certain passages."

Over the next two months Edward hypnotized himself into this state of concentration and remembrance every day. He opened with the world's first beings.

In the beginning two female humans were born. These two children were born underground at a place called Shipapu. As they
grew up, they began to be aware of each other. There was no light
and they could only feel each other. Being in the dark they grew
slowly. After they had grown considerably, a Spirit whom they afterwards called Tsichtinako spoke to them, and they found that it
would give them nourishment. . . . So they waited a long time, and
as they grew they learned their language from Tsichtinako. When
all was ready they found a present from Tsichtinako, two baskets of
seeds and little images of all the different animals there were to be
in the world. The spirit said that they were sent by their father. They
asked who was meant by their father, and Tsichtinako replied that
his name was Uchtsiti and that he wished them to take their baskets up into the light, when the time came.

With each choppy utterance, Wolf Robe translated in rhythm with the
incoming Keresan phrases, pacing his English responses so Forde's pencil
could keep up. Occasionally he signaled for his father to pause while he
searched for the right words.

That opening sentence gave a hint of Edward's process. The biblical resonance of "In the beginning . . ." was understandable from one so versed
in the black book that brought his Anglo name and Christian affiliation
forty-eight years before. Other Old Testament characters and themes were
hinted at: a tempting evil serpent, expulsion from a tranquil gardenlike
habitat, the mention of "sin." Was Edward fusing two traditions that both
his conservative Pueblo elders and his intransigent Presbyterian teachers
agreed were irreconcilable? Like the recollections of a Lakota seer and
Catholic catechist from South Dakota that, transcribed at around the same
time by a Nebraska poet, would produce the classic 1932 autobiography
Black Elk Speaks, did Edward hope that some form of blended theology,
marrying the best of Indian and white belief systems, might be his legacy?
We will never know.

That opening sentence finished, however, by restoring an indisputable
Pueblo authorship to this remembered world. Have no doubt, it reminded
us, this creation was vested in the female domain. Yet in Edward's telling,
Acoma's cosmology was still overseen by an all-male creator, Uchtsiti, even
though this Supreme Being quickly became a *deus otiosus,* the mysterious

Supreme Being who withdraws from human affairs, leaving creation's actual managers to be quickly identified—Tsichtinako and the sacred sisters.

At this point the inexperienced Daryll Forde may be forgiven for getting his Pueblo deities, not to mention their genders, mixed up. Many searching for a common theology among New Mexico's Keresan-speaking pueblos have faced this dilemma. Was Edward making a concession to his Protestantism or non-Indian readers when he identified the tribe's Prime Mover as a male "father" and gave "him" the name that other pueblos often reserved for the oldest of the two sisters? Or did this reflect the deeper, bi-gendered nature of a supreme "god-goddess" in ancient Keresan cosmology?

Whichever was the case, Hunt now introduced the wondrous Tsichtinako, variously translated as "Thought Woman," "Prophesying Woman," or "Our Mother," whose mental activities "were always carried into action," as Franz Boas learned at Laguna Pueblo. Native feminists hold her in special regard. To part-Laguna novelist Paula Gunn Allen she is "a puzzling figure commonly referred to as Old Spider, Grandmother Spider, or Spider Woman. Spider Woman's Keres name is translated as Thought Woman (it can be better understood as Creating-through-Thinking Woman)."

Hunt's opening sentence also gave no explanation concerning the parentage of the first of his narrative's three sets of siblings: Iatiku, "mother of all Indians," and her sister, Nautsiti, progenitor of whites. As Edward was describing how their "father" wanted them to carry baskets of plant seeds and animal fetishes up to the earth, he interrupted himself for an exchange with Henry. When the sacred sisters asked Tsichtinako why it was so dark, she replied that it was because they were under the earth. "Under the earth?" Henry repeated uncertainly. And Forde asked, "How do you say that in Keresan?" Then Edward employed a Keresan term that was unfamiliar to the son—*Nuk'timi*—and Henry repeated it, suddenly becoming a student of his own heritage as well.

As Edward cobbled together his version, these sisters shouldered the details of world-making. Using speech infused with sacred breath, they imbued each item with its life force. The more non-Indian sister's basket yielded items from afar: white man's wheat, nonnative plants, hard metals, and "something written."

But Edward's account concentrated on the more Indian sister, Iatiku, whose centrality as her people's "Corn Mother" took over. His narrative

Edward's version of his people's creation story tells how the earth was made and human society developed on it.

became a descriptive catalog of creation; her basket produced the indigenous seeds for trees, corn, tobacco, and native plants. Her breath on stone fetishes gave life to kangaroo mouse, rat, mole, prairie dog, mountains, plains, mesas, canyons, and "game" animals along with the "prey" animals that hunted them. She established her human children's twenty or so original clans, the ruling spirits for the four directions, their seasons, colors, and sacred mountains.

Iatiku taught them to send prayer sticks to these spirits to maintain the yearly cycle of moisture, warmth, ripening, frost, and spring planting. All her actions repeated the correct sequencing and ritual movements for creative activity—north to west to south to east; these earliest stirrings became the model for human rituals yet to come.

◆ ◆ ◆

Day after day broadened and deepened Edward's unfolding story. Forde hung in for about a week, then he had to leave. Stirling let this section become the young scholar's first academic publication. But that meant that Forde missed the most intimate of all Acoma's sacred beings.

> **With dirt from her basket Iatiku gave life to the spirits known as Katsina. She told them to go to Wenimats, a place under a weedy lake to the west and south. There is where they should live. Whenever the people wanted the Katsinas they were to communicate by means of prayer sticks, and she showed them how to make them. She gave the Katsinas songs to bring happiness to the people. "Your people and my people will be combined," she said. "You will give us food from your world and we will give you food from our world. Your people are to represent clouds, you are to bring rain."**

Now it was Stirling who was told how Iatiku created Acoma's cosmic intermediaries, the Katsinas. They were a multisided company of anthropomorphic beings. If treated respectfully Katsinas could be the best friends a culture could have. If not, as Stirling soon learned, their anger could be devastating. Edward shared how Acoma divided these sacred beings by season: the summer Katsina proper and the winter Kopishtaya.

Iatiku seemed to be making it up as she went along. As if it just dawned on her that interactions between human and spirit beings might require special precautions and procedures, she instructed her people on how to invite the Katsinas using prayer sticks. To secure their base on earth her magical words called forth domestic and civic architecture. This brought houses for families related through the female line, a plaza with its appointed stations where visiting Katsinas were supposed to dance, and the kiva chambers, rich in symbolism, for hosting them.

Iatiku spelled out the rituals to ensure successful expeditions by members of the Hunters Society, and what the Bear, Eagle, Weasel, Flint, Fire, Giant, and other medicine men's societies needed to know to achieve effective cures. Making altars, using prayer sticks, handling fetishes, preparing sand paintings, mixing medicines, learning songs, and matching ailments with practitioners trained in treating them required exactitude. A misstep, a broken taboo, even a bad thought, and more suffering might ensue.

After so much methodical instruction, Iatiku felt her people needed some entertainment. For this she provided the stick-racing game, the ball-kicking game, and the gambling-guessing game. To let them laugh at their own foibles while remembering how to behave correctly, and for a guide through sensitive rituals, she instituted the paradoxical role that Edward's father had passed on to him.

Iatiku had three more things in her basket, the third she did not know so she brought it to life to see what it was. At her words it came alive in the form of a man. It was Koshare, who acted kind of crazy, was active, picking around, talking nonsense, talking backwards, and behaved like he knew everything. He accompanied the most serious men everywhere, using garbled and loud speech, making fun, and self-confident. "You will be called at times to help the people," she told him. "You are not going to be afraid of anything or to regard anything as sacred. You are to be allowed everywhere."

Into his narrative stepped that crazy-walking, wild-talking, hilariously misbehaving principle of disorder—Koshare, sacred clown, the first "delight maker." Telling this part of the myth surely brought back memories. It was Stirling's impression that Edward's knowledge of the origin myth had largely occurred during his traumatic initiation as a clown. Certainly he'd grafted that lengthy account onto other stories acquired over many years. And becoming one of these institutionalized outsiders may have also foreordained his own success in the non-Indian world. For as Edward memorably said of those who became a sacred clown, "they knew something about themselves." One wonders when it first dawned on Edward that his fate was to be an outsider as well.

As he was to narrate next, the clown's mythic role would be critical once the human weaknesses of Acoma's fledgling tribe threatened to wipe them out.

Creation's Sights and Sounds (1928)

In nearly every Indian myth, the creator sings things into life. . . . To the Indian, truth, tradition, history, and thought are preserved in ritual of poetry and song. The red man's song records the teachings of his wise men, the great deeds of his heroes, the counsel of his God. If all things Indian must, indeed, pass away under the white man's ban as being "pagan" and "uncivilized," then will be lost to the red man not only his whole unwritten literature, but also, and sadder still, the realm wherein his soul aspires.

—Natalie Curtis, 1907

MAKESHIFT THOUGH IT WAS, the Smithsonian's documentation of Edward's story would have lost a lot more had he come all by himself. Not only was elder son Wolf Robe able to do his translating, but the twenty-two-year-old was a budding artist. He could illustrate in pictures much of what his father was putting into words. Although primarily the behind-the-scenes Pueblo woman, feeding, clothing, and cleaning for her family, his wife, Marie, shared ethnographic tidbits (once describing how her people inspected a horse's eye for the tiny splashy growths, called "trees," that indicated the animal's character; one "tree," and it was likely to be ornery, more and it was probably gentle). Also on hand to translate the songs that punctuated his father's narrative was younger son Wilbert, while Philip "Silvertongue" Sanchez sang them for the Smithsonian.

"Now they prayed to the sun as they had been taught by the Spirit," Edward said, "and sang the creation song." Forde was too busy scribbling the myth's opening passages to notice Edward leaning into the older son's ear. Signaling a break, Henry drew Philip close before they could continue. At this point Edward hummed to Sanchez the melodies and words which he would then record on a wax cylinder machine.

When Iatiku first bestowed life upon the elements of the world, they sprang into being at the command of sound. An Arctic shaman who talked with

Philip "Silvertongue" Sanchez, adopted member of the Hunt family, recorded for the Smithsonian the many songs associated with the myth.

Danish ethnologist Knud Rasmussen best described this process. Back in mythic times, he said, "the human mind had mysterious powers. A word spoken by chance might have strange consequences. It would suddenly come alive and what people wanted to happen could happen. All you had to do was say it." Whether a wordless vocable or an incantatory melody, prayerful music transcended the mechanical, bypassed the ordinary, and provided a wavelength for powerful forces. Music did more than accompany reality. Acquiring its spirit in the heart, its purified strength through the lungs, and its intent from the focused mind, songs switched on a kind of electric current. They made life light up, so the words they bore could make things real. "My friend," a Pueblo man from Santa Ana confided to anthropologist Leslie White, "without songs you cannot do anything."

Thus it went for future generations. "The boys like to sing," Edward told Stirling. "They sing often in the evening while riding through the valley or at some house. New songs are frequently composed. Sometimes the young men gather at a house in the evening to practice songs." For nearly every occasion and purpose there were songs. In the days of Edward's youth, singing rang across the Acoma and San Jose valleys. It was public, accompanying planting and harvesting festivities; it was private, and commonplace, to hum to oneself. Men like Philip Sanchez and Edward's son Alfred were forever composing new songs. "Melodies are always in my mind," Sanchez told ethnomusicologist Frances Densmore. "I make up songs when I am by myself, in a sheep camp or some such place."

When you were on the road or far away, songs also provided a touchstone to home. "I started painting when I was at Santa Fe [Indian School]," remembered the Hopi Indian artist Fred Kabotie. "And naturally when you are away from your people you think about your people. When there's breeze in the mountains back of Santa Fe you hear that Katsina music among the trees and it's that music that inspires you to start painting. . . . As I paint the Katsina dancers I would hum that particular Katsina music because you're just involved with all that and you're bound with that and you can't help but sing very softly as you paint." For the Acoma poet Simon Ortiz, "Sometimes I sing the songs just when I'm running. It just helps to keep the rhythm, for one thing. And to provide, I think, a kind of structure that is somewhat symbolic and spiritual. It's not to get something, but to be included in it, within the process of your life."

It was Jesse Fewkes who initiated the recording of American Indian music in 1896 by preserving Passamaquoddy Indian songs from northern Maine on wax cylinders. Now Philip Sanchez began his back-and-forth to Anthony Wilding's sound studio downstairs in the Castle to preserve nearly seventy songs associated with Edward's recitation. They included songs of creation, hunting songs, Koshare songs, medicine men's songs, corn-grinding songs, Katsina dance songs, and animal dance songs, among others. Lamentably, no one queried Edward about the distinguishing characteristics of these different genres. Their recording sessions were so improvisatory that the Smithsonian's resident carpenter had to handsaw something resembling a traditional rasping stick, with its gourd resonator, which Sanchez modified to sound more authentic.

Around the turn of the century, America's appetite for everything Indian was broadening, and native-inspired music gained a following. Since the 1880s, high-end composers had been producing Westernized adaptations of what they considered Indian-influenced rhythmic patterns and drum-beats, in such works as Frederick R. Burton's opera *Hiawatha,* Theodore Baker's *Indian Suite,* and Charles Cadman's songs based on Ojibwa musical transcriptions. On the pop culture side, around 1903 a genre of ragtime known as the "Indian Intermezzi," with lots of brass and 3/4 time, enjoyed popularity among consumers of sheet music. A spate of books alerted general readers that Indian music and poetry were in fashion. In this period, ethnomusicologist Natalie Curtis mined the songs and liturgies collected by the first wave of Smithsonian ethnographers for her 1907 *The Indians' Book,* an anthology of American Indian myths and song-poems. She epitomized popularizers of the time who lifted lyrical passages from the Bureau of Ethnology's publications but underplayed their ritual contexts and literary complexities.

In his later anthology of Indian literature, editor Bill Brandon defended editing out repetitive phrases by admitting his lack of interest in any original purpose. "In the buffalo songs," he wrote, "it would not only be

Wolf Robe said his art was based upon the landscape and sights where he was raised. This painting depicts his people's Gambler God.

wearisome to follow faithfully all the magic numbers, but we might also, who knows, materialize a buffalo. We don't really want the buffalo. We only want the *feeling* of the earnest repetitions, the *feeling* of the hypnosis, of the marvelous emerging, the *feeling* of the magic. Let the ethnologists keep the rest." That was fine for whites, but perhaps Indians didn't want strange scholars and distant institutions to keep the rest. Maybe there were good reasons for not losing their ancient magic or authorial claims. An Acoma woman proudly told Franz Boas, "The corn people have a song too. It is very good. I refuse to tell it."

Within six months of their work at the Smithsonian, the greatest scholar of American Indian music, Frances Densmore, would become the first of many to pore over the Hunt materials for her own publication on Pueblo music.

When he began illustrating the Katsina masks, altars, and ritual items that appeared in his father's narration, Wolf Robe was unaware that he was in the wake of a second ethnographic technique pioneered in North America by Jesse Fewkes. After he saw in Madrid the drawings made by Aztec artists for the sixteenth-century priest-archaeologist Bernardino de Sahagún, Fewkes was inspired to suggest the same to Hopis he met while excavating at Sityaki ruin, located on Black Mesa, three miles north of the tribe's oldest village. Around 1900, he engaged three of them—White Bear, his older uncle and better artist than the nephew, and a former boarding student named Winuta—to paint their full complement of Kachina spirits.

Fewkes's monograph, picturing 260 pencil and watercolor drawings of their Kachina pantheon, included their thumbnail biographies. First but certainly not last of such projects, these two-dimensional depictions were a logical extension of the "dolls" or figurines that the Hopis carved from cottonwood roots for instructing the young in their spirit world. Not only was his work a boon to students of Pueblo Indian religion, but it is also credited with initiating the modernist tradition of Pueblo Indian painting.

Fewkes's experiment was an extension of what early Puebloans had already done by drawing corn, clan, and water symbols and Katsina faces on pottery and scratching or painting them on rock walls. Aniconic societies are rare—most peoples want to *see* their spirits and saints. That way they can keep them around and transact with them. This calls forth art.

Katsina images began appearing on sandstone cliffs in the middle Rio

One location back home that inspired Wolf Robe. With him, his wife and daughter.

Grande region around AD 1275–1325. Another fifty years or so and they were on kiva murals, possibly applied during annual rituals. At the village called Kuaua, near Santa Ana Pueblo, archaeologists unpeeled more than eighty of these superimposed paintings from a single kiva wall. Was secrecy always part of these depictions, with only initiates allowed to gaze upon them, whether in hallowed spots in the wider landscape or in these subterranean chambers?

Other Indian painters adopted the Fewkes approach. Defying his elders' ban on painting Katsinas, around 1918 an anonymous Zuni artist produced a suite of spirit-beings. Working there ten years later, anthropologist Ruth Bunzel disguised the identity of an artist who drew 126 Katsinas for her writings on Zuni religion. Back at Hopi, one of the most gifted Pueblo artists, Fred Kabotie, trained at rendering the kiva murals uncovered at Awatovi by Harvard archaeologists before painting his own roster of Kachinas. But Kabotie was always careful to represent them in outdoor settings and during public dances.

When Wolf Robe drew his pictures we do not know if he was aware of prohibitions against such depictions, or whether he cared. The family's European interlude may have lessened their concern about keeping community secrets. Most likely he was uninformed about the consequences to artists in other villages who did so. Kabotie's caution about not portraying esoteric dimensions of Hopi ritualism was out of respect; but he was also aware that once the work of Fewkes's artists circulated around Hopi country, they fell under suspicion of sorcery.

Worse were sanctions imposed at Isleta Pueblo when the identity of a local artist who supplied Elsie Clews Parsons with over a hundred drawings of community life was revealed. The man found himself in a cultural limbo described by one of Parsons's colleagues, Esther S. Goldfrank—a profile that could have stood as a cautionary tale for Wolf Robe. The Isleta artist's life became, Goldfrank wrote, "the story of a talented artist astride two cultures. In neither of them did he find fulfillment. Until his death he remained in the pueblo of his birth, haunted by the knowledge that what he was doing not only transgressed its most valued lifeways but also if discovered, threatened his very life. The world outside, while offering him a living of sorts—work on a railway, in an art shop, and collaborating with Parsons—gave little hope of a satisfying integration. He remained in his pueblo, a 'kindly' man as one anthropologist said, generous in making gifts, particularly to children, and participating, insofar as he was permitted to, in village activities."

Now, a decade after the family's relocation to Santa Ana and three years after moving to Albuquerque, Henry found himself in Washington painting a gallery of the face-masks of Acoma's spirit world. When he took breaks to outline and watercolor these drawings is not clear, since he was simultaneously translating for his father. He also drew a map of the Acoma village, indicating its access trails, meeting halls, kiva locations, and spots where Katsina dances took place. When his father recited how Iatiku created the medicine men's societies, Henry depicted their altars. When she established the naming ritual for newborns, Henry drew their ground paintings. He added illustrations of prayer sticks, wood assemblages for exorcisms, corn and stone fetishes, musical instruments, kiva wall symbols, gaming items, ceremonial robes, and drums. One sketch showed the groove down Acoma's cliff where a pebble was rolled upon a tribal member's death.

Pooling the family's talents lent an interdisciplinary density to the gift that the Hunts were transferring from one corner of America to another.

Telling the Myth II:
The War Gods' World (1928)

Those two fellows sometimes are referred to as twins, but they really aren't twins because one is older and one younger.... In a couple of stories you hear [they] are always up to some kind of mischief.... They play jokes on people—often on their grandmother—and spend a lot of time playing shinny. But these boys have another aspect. They are creators and warriors, and they use thunder and lightning as weapons.... The two Pokangs, as they're sometimes called for short, attacked the giants and monsters and drove them out or killed them off.

—Albert Yava, Hopi, 1978

WEEKS INTO HIS STORYTELLING, comfortable with the freedom he felt in Washington to string his stories together as he saw fit, Edward spliced into his master narrative a crucial piece of domestic drama.

At this point Iatiku's job of creating the world was nearly over. Now her human children began to use the gifts and apply the practices and lessons she'd bestowed upon them. So here Edward introduced two brothers to assist her people in their transition from the world of myth to that of history. Typical of the universal Hero genre, their story began with a miraculous birth.

After the famine at White House there was a woman living with her daughter. One season there were many piñon nuts and the daughter asked her mother if she could gather some. When she went alone to pick the cones Sun Youth met her. He gave her two piñons and after he left she ate them and became pregnant. On their own the piñons in her basket increased into a large pile. Time passed and she gave birth to two children. They were named Masewi, the older, and Oyoyewi, the younger. The babies were small and not handsome, but they grew rapidly—crawling, walk-

ing, speaking, then leaving the house and wandering off to hunt
birds and small game. Their grandmother made them a bow and
arrows and taught them to shoot. Their father, the Sun, secretly
gave them powers to kill bigger animals, even bears.

Counterbalancing the female co-creators who dominated his myth's
opening, here were male co-destroyers who would protect the proto-
Acomans during their forthcoming travails. Unlike their appearance in
origin stories from neighboring Zuni Pueblo, at Acoma, according to Edward, these pairs were not true twins. Whether it was the sisters Iatiku and
Nautsiti, the two sons of Nautsiti who fathered Indian and white races re-
spectively, or Masewi and Oyoyewi themselves, one came out ahead of the
other.

The boys' magical birth and unusually small stature, their impetuous-
ness, aggressiveness, and hunting prowess, were similar throughout all
Pueblo mythologies. And their destinies as heroic pairs endowed with
warriorlike powers due to those legendary births even had echoes beyond
American shores, like the brothers who wound up establishing Rome.

Every society admires its superheroes but often grows ambivalent about

An ancient story in Pueblo Indian mythology, the Warrior Twins who destroy monsters—like this Cloud Swallower—and ready the world for human habitation. Depicted on a Mimbres pot from the Classic Period, c. 950–1150.

them. Whether they are twins, brothers, or loners like Hercules, Paul Bunyan, and their modern-day counterparts Superman, Rambo, and the Incredible Hulk, for the young they present models of might and invincibility; for the powerless they offer the promise of overcoming dominating forces. For popular audiences they provide the entertainment of dramatic tests and action-filled feats. For vulnerable communities just starting out they inspire an initial gratitude at being protected.

Adding to popular appeal are their cocky attitudes and the melodramas caused when the human side of their backstories distracts from their heroic destinies. Masewi and Oyoyewi were models of masculinity for boys to emulate. One wonders if the following chapter in their biography held special meaning to this narrator who may have wondered about the identity of his own genetic father.

After they grew a little older the boys heard other children speak about their fathers. They went to their mother and asked why they did not have someone to know as father. She told them he did not live here. The boys asked where he lived and she said at the place where the sun rises. The next morning they got up and talked together and decided to go to their father. They started walking but when they reached the crest of the first mountain range they saw other mountains as far away from them as the first had been.

So began Edward's rendition of a southwestern twist on the classic quest scenario: the journey of single-parent offspring to reconnect with a distant, unknown father. After badgering their mother for information about their origins, the twins are told how Sun Youth impregnated her through the eating of the piñon nuts.

Now they gird themselves for the kind of ordeal not usually considered part of Pueblo tradition. This coming-of-age experience seems more customary among Plains tribes, where accounts of solitary vision questers on lonely mountaintops established patterns for adolescents to follow. Pueblo youth, by contrast, usually achieved their socially recognized maturity through peer-group initiations in the kivas. But these were the War Brothers, whose proclivity for hunting and killing already made them anomalies among their Pueblo brethren. They had to traverse dangerous landscapes in order to fulfill their destinies and ready themselves for the Samurai-like tasks ahead.

So far they lacked the magical accessories to do this on their own. They had to search for proper mentoring, and for the superhuman powers and special weapons to compensate for their diminutive stature. Already one "grandmother" encouraged their hunting activities and provided tools—bow and arrows for slaughtering rabbits, deer, and antelope, and the double-pointed stick for jamming into the open mouth of an attacking bear. But to guide them the rest of the way they need their grandmother's multilegged avatar, Spider Woman.

While they were talking about this someone spoke to them. It was Spider Woman. She said to them, "My grandchildren, are you going to visit your father?" They looked in that direction and saw a spider on a bush. "Oh, is that you, Spider? Do you speak?" Then someone spoke. It was Spider Woman. The Sun already knew they were coming and sent her to instruct them how to reach him. So Spider Woman told the boys to follow her. When they came to her house, Spider Woman said, "This is my house, come on down."

In myths, as in dreams, identities often merge, disaggregate, and reassemble. This Spider Woman or Grandmother Spider is also the "grandmother" we've already met, as well as the original Thought Woman. As a spiritual guide, she now lent the boys their protective medicine, and helped them descend in a basket that hung from a ball of spun spiderweb until they were "completely lost and did not know where they were." Landing at the base of a ladder leading up to a house—like house ladders up at Acoma mesa—the boys reached Sun Youth's home and entered his kiva.

When Sun Youth announced to his brothers that his sons had arrived, they scoffed and demanded verification of their identity.

So one of the men asked if it was true that those boys were his sons. "If that is so, place them in the north den where the lions are and see if they come out alive." So their father put them in with the lions. The boys were used to lions and were not afraid. Soon the lions began to lick them and act friendly. The boys played with the lions.

One of the men got up to see if they had been eaten, and reported, "No, they are playing with the lions." So they were brought out.

Here the boys underwent the requisite tests. They survived lions in the north den, hungry bears in the west den, a bobcat in the south den, and a nest of bees in the east den, and emerged unscathed. In a tasty sidelight, while surrounded by angry bees they cracked open their bodies and sucked out the honey.

One challenge remained. Thrown onto hot coals, instead of being killed they were cooked and transformed by the blistering heat into "full grown men, as handsome as their father." This convinced their father's brothers to behave as Pueblo uncles should. They outfitted their nephews with more magical weapons and curative medicines. Their old bows were strength-

Wolf Robe Hunt paints the Warrior Twins of Acoma mythology defeating a giant bear.

ened with sinew backing—perhaps reflecting that period in early Pueblo history when hunters shifted from using the javelin-throwing sticks we call *atlatls* to adopting the stronger Plains Indian–influenced bows. Their arrows were given new stone points and bunched in newly made lion-skin quivers, each containing a pocket for the ceremonial staff that would identify them as "country chiefs."

To complete their supernatural equipment, their father added the curved rabbit-killing throw club that was their badge as "representatives of the Sun." Used with an arrowhead, its overwhelming power to bring the dead back to life should be applied with care lest, the boys were warned, it "destroy something." Then they were granted "access to all the sacred places." Lastly came their new outfits: beaded moccasins, waist sashes, armbands, turquoise and shell bead necklaces, red paint around the eyes, a fetish-festooned shoulder bandolier, and special headdress to tie in their hair.

"I have given you all that you need for bravery, good luck, and power," said their father. The following morning, just before dawn, he took them to his perch in the sky and showed them the wide world. Again Spider Woman's sons secured them in the basket, their father lowered its silken cord, and, "As before, the boys were lost, not knowing how far they had come."

They returned to their house. Their grandmother and mother had been praying for them and feared they were lost and the lions had gotten them. They looked everywhere for them but could not find them. They were not recognized by their mother as they were now handsome grown men. The boys took off their costumes and hung them up, for they had been told not to wear them until they needed them. They made up ordinary costumes for themselves, and they continued to live as common people in the villages.

The first forecast of the troubles that would test the Twins' powers began before their birth, when the people were still living at Shipapu, the origin place. Inspired by the gambling game that Iatiku had the Katsinas teach the people, some men invented a hide-the-stick game to play in the kivas, using the same short sticks they kicked in their competitive foot-races. Enthralled with it, before long they were neglecting their ceremonies, joking about women, insulting other men's wives, and even making fun of their Corn Mother.

This angered Iatiku and she said, "All right, I'll let you go on your own, and see if it is not due to my instructions that all has been going well." She told them she was going to keep quiet and they would not hear from her anymore. She said she was going to stay at Shipapu and will wait for them to come back to her at the end of their lives. This was the first mention of death. Then she disappeared.

Before abandoning her people, Iatiku set them on the first leg of their journey in search of Ha'ako, their ultimate home and resting place. First they moved to the site known as White House and erected a new village. But almost immediately the trials of real life descended on them. Drought dried up the land, their harvest was meager, famine followed. For a while the people quit the gambling game, but then brought it back.

Meanwhile the Katsinas were visiting the village on a regular basis. After one of their appearances a certain Katsina lagged behind and secretly overheard some of the gamblers in the kiva. They were mocking his fellow spirits and imitating the different ways they danced. One wobbled around like the bowlegged Katsina, another made fun of the Katsina with the offset lips. They were all laughing—"Is this the way the clouds look?" they joked.

When the spy reached his Katsina village at Wenimats and shared what he'd seen, the entire throng were beside themselves. Boiling with rage, they snuck back into the village one night. Sensing something was amiss, the village leaders used prayer sticks and last-minute pleas. But the Katsinas were too angry to halt the flow of events.

The Katsinas picked up clubs and hardwood sticks and attacked the village and killed many people. The War Gods, sons of the Sun, saw their people dying and got angry. Putting on the special regalia from their father, yelling their powerful yell and throwing their magical clubs, they decapitated most of them. Although both sides confessed they had done wrong, and the War Gods used their sacred staff and arrowheads and special herbs to work in secret and bring most of the Katsinas back to life, it was agreed they would live separately.

In all the creation myths recorded from the Southwest, no other pueblos or tribes relate this Armageddon-like episode. It was as if two cosmic realms, heaven and earth, had clashed, with cataclysmic consequences. In a terrible set of ironies, the first noteworthy actions of the people's closest allies, the Katsinas, were turned against them. And the War Twins' first opportunity to demonstrate their newfound powers was leveled against their people's best friends.

All this was unthinkable. Before their social lives had even begun, human wickedness and impiety had imperiled their future. The recently acquired medicines of the twin brothers had saved part of the day. But everyone was dumbstruck and paralyzed by the enormity of what had transpired. At this point the leader of the Katsinas came up with a solution whose brilliance would change the nature of Pueblo ceremonial life forever.

So to protect both sides he decided that the Katsina should not come any more, as they might be angry. "You will not see us any more, but we will still help you from Wenimats and we will always be waiting for you there. You have received the presents of the regalia of the Katsina. From now on you are going to imitate us. In that way we will help you from Wenimats. You have seen how we are painted up, you have seen how we are dressed. You know how to make our prayer sticks. When you have picked out the regalia of the Katsina you are to represent, his power will come to you and attach itself while you represent him."

In this way, the Katsina leader promised, "We will help you spiritually." Before the procedures for teaching people how to impersonate sacred beings and initiate them into their societies could begin, some repairs were in order. Great damage had been done. Confessions of culpability were needed, from both sides. Prayers must be exchanged. Thirty-day fasts were imposed on the Katsinas when they left for their home at Wenimats. Only then could they be reborn.

As for the dead human beings, the War Twins were unsuccessful at restoring them to life. That task was left to the new orders of medicine men. They began by instituting among human beings the "planting" of the dead.

In this way the people learned to borrow what they had learned from Iatiku about treating the end of life. They oriented the corpses with their heads to the east and returned them to the earth "so that they would be reborn."

The people had learned hard lessons. They had made mistakes, broken rules, and were facing the consequences. Perhaps the Acoma code was still so new, untried, or implicit that it called for Iatiku's tough love. Their rupture with the spirits had echoes in world mythology whenever humans and gods got too close and their worlds collided. Had Iatiku not lent human beings free will and big appetites the trigger for the series of events that followed Acoma's "War of the Titans" might have been avoided. But here they were, on their own as never before.

44

Explaining the Pueblos (1928)

Benedict deemphasized the role of the Pueblo individual and presented an unreal calm and unruffled picture of Pueblo life. Every pueblo had and has its outspoken aggressive individuals and much of the dissension and turmoil in Pueblo life is brought out by such individuals. . . . In ceremonial organizations and activities, the Pueblo individual may choose to submerge his individuality and he may also oppose nomination or election to a ceremonial office; but there are too many examples of individual deviants to assume that Pueblo culture does not also produce rebels.

—Edward P. Dozier, Santa Clara Pueblo, 1970

A YEAR AND A HALF EARLIER, in the spring of 1926, when Edward and Marie had been in Albuquerque and between lifestyles, a bespectacled stranger knocked on their door. Behind them was the bitter ouster from Santa Ana Pueblo. Ahead lay the trip to Oklahoma, and their European adventures after that. When the man said he was Leslie White from the anthropology department at the University of Chicago, Edward had a good idea what he wanted.

Ever since Solomon Bibo had introduced young Edward to white outsiders and train-riding tourists at his Cubero trading post, he had been aware of their growing curiosity about Pueblo villagers, and American Indians in general. Over the years he'd come to discern which newcomers superficially merged the two, and which were after deeper understandings. Journalistic types, like Charles Lummis, George Wharton James, and Charles Saunders, were satisfied with "retelling" Indian tales into versions with tidy beginnings, middles, and ends. Then came professional scholars who had done their homework and were developing theories about Pueblo social patterns and religious principles.

Edward was usually ready to open up about Acoma. Maybe now someone would get it right. Before the family left town they squeezed in many sessions with White for his foundational profile of Acoma Pueblo, which the Smithsonian published in 1932. That work began his thirty-one-year immersion in Pueblo studies and propelled one of American anthropology's more cantankerous careers.

Although White was circumspect about naming informants, big chunks of his information clearly derived from these visits with Edward Hunt, Marie, and the contacts they facilitated at Acoma, Acomita, and Laguna. In part his caution was to protect the Hunts against recrimination, in part to ensure that they could provide him with information in the future, and in part because it was common practice of ethnographers of the period to mute the degree to which their writings and careers relied on the generosity and intelligence of their native collaborators.

Born in 1900, Leslie White had his first exposure to Indians on Wisconsin's Menominee Reservation in the summer of 1925, and the experience left him hungry for more. When he became restless in graduate school, his mentor, the linguist Edward Sapir, prescribed a "real field trip." After connecting through Sapir to the eminent father of American anthropology, Franz "Papa" Boas, White won financial backing from Elsie Clews Parsons, the benefactress for many of Boas's mostly female disciples. But when White broached the possibility of Acoma Pueblo as a field site, she tried to head him off; Boas also worried that Acoma was too "difficult" for a greenhorn. Impatient and risking Parsons's wrath, White took off anyway. When he explained his mission to Father Fridolin Schuster in Albuquerque,

Cliff-Dwellers return: Marie (left) and Edward Hunt (second from right) visit a rock shelter at Los Frijoles archaeological site (Bandelier National Monument) much like the cliff shelter they once occupied on the rim of El Malpais.

the priest laughed in his face "and said he did not envy my task," but passed him on to the Hunts.

By the time the family returned to the United States two years later, White's account of life at Acoma was inching its way through the bureau's editorial process. After that fieldwork White would pen increasingly dense profiles of her Keresan-speaking sister villages—San Felipe (1932), Santo Domingo (1935), and Santa Ana (1942)—while acquiring a reputation among Indians as an aggressive questioner, and among anthropologists as a fiery polemicist.

Their paths did not cross in Washington, but White would reappear in the Hunts' lives to ask for more from them. And perhaps it was correspondence between Stirling and White around the publication of his Acoma profile that alerted the Smithsonian to Edward's value as a willing narrator in the first place. What neither White nor Stirling fully appreciated, however, was the degree to which the disciplines dedicated to understanding Pueblo Indian culture-history—anthropology and archaeology—were in transition.

In anthropology the Boas doctrine that prioritized the documentation of supposedly disappearing cultural practices from endangered tribes still held sway; universal theories could wait awhile. Meanwhile, with White's poor opinion of Franz Boas a notable exception, the discipline's founding figure himself remained revered. Colleague Alfred Kroeber said that he was "a self-disciplined Titan" and that "the epithet of greatness describes him better than that of genius"; anthropologist Robert Lowie added, "There was in him no petty vanity, no messianic strutting; only the Work was sacred as it was to a Michelangelo or a Beethoven."

Boas was adamant that language was a major key to culture. Edward had heard of him when his friends Edward and Elizabeth Eckerman hosted Boas at their Old Laguna hotel in 1919. That was when Boas began recording Keresan stories using a "scientific" orthographic method with interlinear translations, returning each summer until 1922.

Despite being sixty-one when he first came to Laguna, Boas was unstoppable. He climbed Mount Taylor to see the sacred pit where Acoma medicine men deposited prayers sticks. With student Esther Goldfrank he hiked up Acoma mesa for a visit she never forgot: "Memories of my day in Acoma, so removed from the usual manifestations of modernity, so alone above the desert sand, are still vivid. More than any other 'living' pueblo that I have seen, it has given me a sense of what life must have been like many centuries ago in this momentously beautiful—but often harsh— environment."

Another of Boas's disciples was a shy, poetically inclined graduate of Vassar College. A latecomer to academic anthropology, Ruth Benedict joined Boas during his 1923 summer at Laguna, and soon ventured east to Cochiti Pueblo on the Rio Grande. Her patient demeanor won her enough trust to gather stories for a hefty collection of its folklore. Wending her way to Acoma, she also spent time with Edward Hunt's nephew James Paytiamo, transcribing a handful of its folktales.

All the while a wider agenda was forming in her mind. It would underwrite one of the most popular anthropological books of all time. It was probably at Vassar that Benedict read Frederick Nietzsche's influential book *The Birth of Tragedy* (1872). As simplistic ways of lumping cultures are wont to do, the dichotomy that the German philosopher drew between opposing Apollonian and Dionysian tendencies in ancient Greek civilization lodged in her consciousness. It remained there as Elsie Parsons recommended her to Boas at Columbia University, where Benedict completed a "library" dissertation on Plains Indian vision questing in record time.

The same week that Edward was narrating the opening portion of the myth in Washington, a few hundred miles away, at the twenty-third annual meeting of International Congress of Americanists in New York,

Benedict retooled the Nietzschean paradigm as a way to categorize American Indians. In her address, "Psychological Types in the Cultures of the Southwest," she proposed that tribes like the Pueblos exemplified an "Apollonian" sense of calm, personal harmony, and balanced notion of beauty, while the Plains and Northwest coast tribes evidenced a "Dionysian" disposition that was expressed by ecstatic dance, trance music, and "passionate excess." In her bestselling 1934 book *Patterns of Culture,* she gave the world an anthropology that seemed to make sense.

Given Benedict's "concern with coherence" of cultures, according to Sidney W. Mintz, she "got aesthetic satisfaction out of closure in her descriptions of culture." Yet her facile dichotomy shut the door on further inquiries. As anthropologist Clifford Geertz once mocked Benedict's reduction of cultural groups into such camps, "the Plains Indians are ecstatic, the Zuni are ceremonious, and the Japanese are hierarchical."

In fairness, Benedict's profiles were more nuanced than that. And what she would say about the Zuni offered an equally tidy summary of their Acoma neighbors: "The Zuni are a ceremonious people, a people who value sobriety and inoffensiveness above all other virtues. Their interest is centered upon the rich and complex ceremonial life. Their cults of the masked gods, of healing, of the sun, of the sacred fetishes, of war, of the dead, are formal and established bodies of ritual with priestly officials and calendric observances. No field of activity competes with ritual for foremost place in their attention."

By moving from Boas's atomistic view of culture as a collection of endless "traits," to a perspective that focused on broad cultural "themes" and "configurations" that bound human societies together, Benedict was stretching her ties to Boas; she was also helping to introduce the importance of theory, at grand and smaller scales, into her discipline. Before long her approach began sounding static and devoid of the winds of historical change. Pueblo culture, Benedict did admit, possessed "a long and homogenous history behind it," but she held little hope that anthropology's sister discipline could reveal it. "Unfortunately," Benedict wrote, "archaeology cannot go further and tell us how it came about."

How wrong she was, argued many younger members of that profession, especially in the Southwest. Its founding generation may have been a crusty, independent-minded lot whose squabbling often rivaled that of the faction-ridden pueblos whose ruins they studied. But even some of these veteran excavators now agreed that the region's well-preserved remains did offer that rare opportunity to piece together a continuous chronology from pre-Hispanic times to the present.

Southwestern scholarship was growing more systematic. Newly established university departments in Arizona and New Mexico, and the Laboratory of Anthropology in Santa Fe, were professionalizing. It was high time, urged Harvard-trained Alfred V. Kidder, for his colleagues to take stock. His own field site of Pecos Pueblo, an old crossroads for trade between Pueblo and Plains territories, seemed the perfect venue.

Of all his sons, Edward worried that Alfred (middle, with drum) would return to traditional medicine and the old, pre-Christian ways.

Kidder began digging there in 1915; after seven seasons of work the levels of Pecos's occupation had produced textbook examples of what made the region's excavations so compelling. He found sixteen kivas, clear evidence of intertribal commerce, and even one old resident still alive. In the stratigraphy of Indian life at Pecos lay a chronicle of cultural continuity from the twelfth century to nearly the present.

Over three intense, argumentative days in late August 1927, nearly fifty scholars slept in canvas tents in a broad river valley just southeast of Santa Fe. Beside the roofless ruins of the old village's mammoth church they hammered out an overarching timeline for most of New Mexico, southern Colorado, and eastern Arizona. Like some United Nations summit, after the Pecos accord, in archaeologist Steve Lekson's words, "A necessary apparatus of any report, then and forever after, was a full page box chart (sometimes a foldout) with a half dozen or more vertical columns. Each divided by horizontal bars like a slot machine spinning the sequences of rival chronologies, and a single column to one side (often in bold) labeled 'chronology in this report.' In that game, the house always wins."

But structure also won. At Pecos and other long-occupied sites, Kidder and associates were able to unpeel layers of successive settlement at continuously inhabited sites and create well-documented timelines. Two years later A. E. Douglas perfected the approach known as dendrochronology, which more or less locked in the dates for pre-Hispanic pueblos. By slicing the tree trunks used for building material in ancient dwellings and exposing their growth of seasonal rings, one could count back to when the timber was harvested and the buildings made. The combination of the Pecos chronology and tree-ring dating turned archaeology toward a more "scientific" approach to the ancient Southwest.

Sidelined in this upgrade were any Indian accounts and interpretations of Pueblo antiquity. Although Jesse Fewkes's roughshod early excavations were held in low esteem, his efforts to correlate Hopi clan-origin legends for a more holistic picture of that tribe's gradual cohesion—its *ethnogenesis*—were ahead of their time. One imagines an ailing Fewkes back in Washington wishing to join that first Pecos Conference—it still meets every year. But most of its attendees would have dismissed his idea that Indian oral narratives of the sort Hunt was providing had anything to offer their reconstructions of southwestern antiquity.

Without Stirling or the Hunts realizing it, for the time being these developments cast a shadow over their Acoma creation story before it was even published. Edward's account of Pueblo aggressiveness, warfare, jealousy, and friction ran counter to Benedict's simplistic profile and to the romantic view of the peaceful Pueblos that was cultivated by white enthusiasts. With archaeology spurning the contributions of Pueblo traditions, the utility of his narrative to any historical chronologies, especially the migration sagas, was weakened for the time being.

Yet Stirling and the Hunts soldiered on. Edward was not thinking about where his work might go from here. His storyteller's mind was focused on getting his chosen people through their twisting journey to their promised land.

45

Telling the Myth III: Into This World (1928)

After mankind had been created, after he had emerged from the underworld, he was still forced to wander about the earth until he found his center. The image refers to the omphalo *[world navel] certainly, but more important it indicates a search for stability and balance which can only be achieved in the true home where one's heart lies.*

—Hamilton A. Tyler, 1964

E DWARD'S NARRATIVE was moving from myth into legend. The mysteries of creation were yielding to the uncertainties of migration. Now his account of a blossoming cosmology turned to the stop-and-start giant steps of human chronology. In the first section he'd talked of miracles; now he chronicled events. Creating a people and the details of their world had opened the curtains. The human drama began.

Of the general outline of southwestern antiquity a professional, up-to-date archaeologist like Matthew Stirling was surely aware. After the Pecos Conference the appreciation of the role played by migration in linking the prehistory of ancestral peoples to contemporary Pueblos only deepened. But reconstructing the uprooting of Ancestral Pueblo communities and their movements out of the Four Corners remained one of American archaeology's greatest challenges. That investigation would remove tons of earth, incite hundreds of doctoral dissertations, start many careers, spark fierce debates, and finally force scholars to revisit native accounts like those the Hunts were offering.

No one disputed that the period had witnessed major population shifts. But what German scholars called the "shining questions," whose answers might lock in why and how those migrations transpired, remained open. What assortment of instigations prompted them, what combinations of evidence explained them, what various routes, stops and starts, and reversals took place during them, what splinterings of social formations and ethnic creations were produced by them, what part did climactic patterns and ecological changes play in them, what Pueblo languages diversified because of them, how did native peoples themselves describe and explain them— indeed, how many *thems* were there in the history of the epochal southwestern population adjustments of the twelfth and thirteenth centuries?

While the responsibilities of fine-tuning a viable culture and sustainable way of life fell to Iatiku's children, the intemperate War God Twins remained at their side, for better in the beginning and for worse as time went on. To establish the people's priorities and find their predestined place on earth they had a moral compass—Iatiku's teachings and prophecies. Above all that meant interacting properly with the rain-bringing cloud people, the Katsinas. Only their assistance granted humans an edge in this tough, uncertain environment.

No sooner had Edward's story established the idealized relationship between these spirit-beings and the original Acomans than it blew up in the bloodbath between the two. The community at White House was left in an anxious state. Quarreling and defections ensued. To make things right, the time-consuming work of human ceremonialism replaced the instantaneous solutions of divine intervention. With Iatiku no longer around to work her miracles, and the War Gods' magical ability to change the

As Edward Hunt's version of the origin myth described, Iatiku, "Mother of all Indians," created the first Acoma kivas. They are in use today.

human condition neutralized, human beings were left to their own ritual devices.

As if switching from a wide-angle to a close-up lens, and sharing his people's oldest instructional manual, Edward began detailing for Stirling their newly learned techniques for putting the past behind them. The ritual solution of impersonating the Katsinas allowed them to receive their blessings without their physical presence. But those performances were precarious enactments, surrounded by stiff rules. Disrespect toward the sacred masks or infractions of ritual protocols could create backlash and more havoc.

Following the "planting" of the dead for burial, a "rite of forgetting" saw the people's cacique release pebbles down from the mesa's summit, one for each victim, so sorrow could be left behind. After Edward told

Stirling about this practice, Wolf Robe drew his picture of it—the cliff face with its blown-up detail of the well-worn groove that carried the pebbles to its base. More elaborate were the prayers, utensils, and altars by which trained medicine men sought to heal their patients. As a medicine man's son, and someone who had once "died" when he was kicked by the horse, Edward had inside knowledge of that. At his father's direction Wolf Robe pictured their altars, the medicine man's bear-paw gloves, the fetishes, and other sacred paraphernalia.

Another set of rituals involved exorcism, a means for detaching people from a polluted or disagreeable past and expunging any ghost-haunted spells that might cause illness or death. With sickness, drought, and famine the ever-present dangers since their fall from grace at Shipapu, the people needed these protections. To the burial, healing, and forgetting ceremonies were added rites of purification. Walking over ground paintings that symbolized the hills and plains they had already traversed, and stooping through a doorlike frame made of four yucca-leaf spines, the people purged themselves from the weight of their past.

Once he had them leave Shipapu, Edward described how the people moved on to White House (Kashkachu, possibly Mesa Verde), where they instituted the winter and summer Katsina impersonations.

> For a long time all was well. Then a sickness came to White House. The people got blisters all over and were dying too fast for the medicine men to help. Even the Twins could do nothing. They remembered that Iatiku had told the people to go south to the place known as Ha'ako. "Maybe this sickness is a sign that we should move on." So they went through a curing ceremony and left the sickness behind them.

After creating these exorcism rituals, the people felt free to undertake another lap in their journey, on to Sage Basin (Wash'pashuka, possibly Chaco Canyon). As they trod across the countryside they produced collective memories, good and bad. Whether Edward's descriptions of periodic eruptions of factional quarreling, internecine killing, disease epidemics, and debilitating droughts would ever be correlated with hard evidence of famine, homicide, and abandonment was a question for the future. But just as Jesse Fewkes argued on behalf of Hopi oral traditions, his accounts were leaving a legacy for such a synthesis someday.

They went to Sage Basin, where they dramatized the battle with the Katsina in order to remind people how to behave. Then they left for Tule Lake, where they made altars and experienced a great flood.

Progressing southward down present-day western New Mexico, the ancestors of the Acoma people blazed a sacred circuit for those mobile classrooms in the future that we call pilgrimages. Subsequent generations might retrace, retell, and relive their ancestral histories, restake their claims to an already traversed landscape, and renew its boundary shrines.

At Sage Basin the human propensity for misbehavior resurfaced. As if human beings never learn anything, some gamblers mocked the Katsinas a second time. Terrified of a repeat of the awful bloodshed before, their leaders instituted yet another piece of ritual theater to remind themselves of the heavy price of impiety. Those playing the role of the Katsinas wore animal intestines filled with animal blood that gushed during the enacted fight. Held every five years and conducted under the watchful supervision of sacred clowns, it would dramatize the great battle at White House.

Then the people decamped for Tule Lake (Ashthinahawai-sha) where, as at the earlier stopovers, "they lived happily for a long time." But before long, sickness, derived from contamination by ants this time, to be followed by famine and starvation, dogged them there.

Meanwhile, the War God Twins, who had kept up their rapacious hunting and readying the world for human presence by clearing it of ferocious monsters and giants, were getting on the nerves of the Katsinas and the rain-makers of the sacred directions. Impetuous and irreverent, they tempted fate and goaded the spirits, who retaliated by dispatching the Water Snake. In the form of a mighty world-consuming flood, he chased all living things up a mountain sanctuary for safety.

When the War Gods killed the snake with their arrows, the waters subsided and the people's journey could resume. From the location called Lake (Kawaika), to Hardwood Pass (Dyaptsiam), to Braced Cliff (Katsima)

Iatiku also established the first Acoma plaza. It remains the place for the village's public ceremonies.

they traveled onward, sometimes stopping, sometimes just passing through. Until at long last they arrived at the great rock.

At its northeast end Country Chief called out, "Ha'ako." When the echo came back clearly all agreed this must be the place. The people built a village at the base of the rock. But the War Twins kept travelling and bringing back scalps so the spirits of the four directions decided to punish them. Now the Twins felt bad, and finally disappeared into a rock atop Acoma. That left the people to carefully establish their village up there.

With the people's arrival at this destination, the War Gods' duties were done. The tamed world could be turned over to human beings. But the semidivine parentage of the War Gods rendered them incapable of conforming to the rhythms of normal Pueblo life.

Much as every society wants their superheroes to clean house, once that's done they often want them out of the house. The same powers that saved the people in times of crisis can threaten social stability when life calms down. Ostracized as freaks, the superheroes have no place in the human community that their overkill helped to stabilize. Public opinion turns against them, as in western movies, when the gunfighter who saves the town leaves too many bodies in his wake. Stories of their unbridled fury and skill with weaponry lose their thrill, and end with the dawning of collective maturity. The quieter values of basic decency and civil society look good again. Everyday heroes who restore the human-scale virtues of moderation and endurance must take their place.

So it went at Acoma. Fantasy figures for the young, fierce avengers in stories told around winter fires, the War God Twins and their grandmother melded into the rock. They chose this place hard by the mesa, Edward told Stirling, "because they knew that Iatiku meant for the people to live on top of the rock, as it would be more wonderful and mysterious."

Sorely missed by the people, but surviving in the Acoma imagination, the Warrior Brothers became models for the war chiefs and the Hunters Society. Their legends reminded everyone of the strength needed to ensure Acoma's safety and insularity, while also warning of irreverence and excess.

At last Edward got his forefathers and mothers to their elevated sacred zone, a homeland almost above the clouds. Their ascent was conducted with solemnity and grace.

> First they removed from the summit centipedes and snakes and planted prayer sticks. They blessed the plaza area. Clan by clan they built their houses and cleaned out the cisterns where water could be stored. After brushing disease from everyone, the medicine men led the procession up the Rainbow Trail. Along the way they prayed. The move took two days, for every ceremonial detail was observed for each clan and each society. Finally they initiated the kivas and established guards around the mesa. Here they lived for a long time, year after year going through their ceremonies.

Had Edward thought whether his family's wanderings mirrored Acoma's journey in search of a resting place? Did he feel any kinship between what his tribe had undergone in their ordeals to reach their homeland and their adventures from Acoma to Acomita to Santa Ana to Albuquerque to Oklahoma to Europe to Washington and back to New Mexico?

No one knows. Edward was not an especially introspective man, Leslie White would claim one day, asserting it as a generic Pueblo condition rather than a personal trait.

One day in late October, Edward turned to his son and Henry translated his words.

"This is as far as the tradition is told."

PART FOUR

Dad Hunt
(1930–2007)

PREVIOUS PAGE: *The family patriarch, Dad Hunt.*

Back to the Present (1928–30)

Being an Indian in the world is the loneliest kind of existence. At least, such is the case when one leaves behind the comfort and security of family and tribe for the wider world of modern societies, such as the metropolitan areas that now dominate the American landscape. Even before the Americans completed their colonization of the "frontier," Indians often found themselves as the proverbial—certainly ironic—strangers in a strange land.

—David Martinez, 2009

O N FEBRUARY 7, 1928, after an eleven-day voyage from Hamburg, the SS *Deutschland* brought the Hunts into New York harbor. From all we know, at this point the family wasn't contemplating any visits to Washington or the Smithsonian just yet; their time with Matthew Stirling was still about eight months away. But neither was there any compelling reason to rush back to New Mexico. Seasoned travelers by now, Edward and Marie Hunt and their sons walked down the gangplank open to whatever opportunities came their way. In their improvisational lives, as well as in the face of America's incoming troubles, this was wise.

Absent from loved ones and reservation homes for so long, their fellow Sioux and Ponca performers wasted no time catching trains back to Oklahoma or South Dakota. "They were homesick," Wilbert Hunt remembered. "But we wanted to stay." And none of the Indians thought to take the ferry to the Statue of Liberty or peek into the city's stock exchange. Had they gone to Wall Street they would have probably considered its yelling, arms-waving brokers out of their minds, even without anyone realizing they were driving a bull market into a brick wall.

What the Hunts found waiting on the pier were booking agents. As with their entry onto the last years of Wild West shows, for a second time the family grabbed the tail end of an entertainment phenomenon. Right off the boat they had jobs. Signs were promising that they might support themselves through the years ahead by continuing to perform as the kinds of Indians that they were not.

Whether it played upon Chinese eyes, African-American lips, Jewish noses, or Irish hair, vaudeville theater left few racial stereotypes unexploited. But aside from oddball acts, like the touring Yakima Indian, Chief Strongheart, or Cherokee Jack Macurio's Indian vaudeville show, American Indians were largely exempted from that vulgar roll call. Eclipsed by the novelty of motion pictures, vaudeville, along with Wild West shows and the Indian-themed popular music craze, was on the wane. For its valedictory tours, the Keith-Orpheum circuit sent some high-value shows up and down the East Coast. Signing on as feathered, dancing fillers during movie intermissions or marquee appearances by Fanny Brice, Al Jolson, and Edgar Bergen and Charlie McCarthy, the Hunts traveled down to Florida, back to New York, covered New England, and had a great time.

The month that the family returned to America marked the beginning of the greatest reversal in U.S. Indian policy since the decision after the Civil War to assimilate Indians instead of annihilating them. The new turnaround was signaled by the delivery, in late February, of an 842-page report to the Department of the Interior in Washington, D.C. Subcontracted by the Brookings Institution and funded with a $125,000 grant from John D. Rockefeller, the Institute for Government Research turned in *The Problem of Indian Administration* on schedule. It would be known as the Meriam Report after the forty-five-year-old Harvard-trained public administrator Lewis Meriam, whom soon-to-be Indian Commissioner John Collier had lobbied to oversee the project. Meriam's nine-person team used a year and a half to take a realistic slice of American Indian life from across the country.

Due to the predictable hoops of Washington bureaucracy, action on the report's recommendations was not immediate. That action was inevitable was tribute to the Meriam panel's prestige, its litany of hard facts, and public acknowledgment—galvanized by Indian Commissioner Collier's well-publicized campaigns on behalf of Pueblo land and religious rights—that the American Indians' day had arrived.

Earlier assessments had come and gone. Commissioning reports that counted and categorized native populations in preparation for the bureaucratic tasks of controlling their lives and appropriating their resources was common to colonial regimes the world over. Until the Meriam survey, however, most of the American versions marginalized the Pueblos.

When geographer-geologist Henry Rowe Schoolcraft produced his seven-volume, government-subsidized overview of Indian tribes in 1855, for instance, he spotlighted the Great Lakes and Plains tribes he knew personally. Where he discussed the Southwest, Schoolcraft had learned

Greeted By a Chief

As Chief Big Snake, Edward greets the most prominent Indian of his day, newly elected thirty-first vice president Charles Curtis, a part Kaw Indian from Kansas.

— Times Staff Photo

IN WAR REGALIA AND ALL

CHIEF BIG SNAKE, of the Pueblo tribe, was on hand with other Indians and hundreds of Washingtonians to welcome Senator Charles Curtis, Republican Vice Presidential nominee back to the Capital. Senator Curtis came to Washington direct from the notification exercises at Topeka, Kan.

enough from frontier correspondents like Colorado territorial governor-trader Charles Bent to condemn the "wild" and "aggressive" Navajos for their attacks on "an interesting semi-civilized people living in villages called pueblos."

The omission persisted for a number of reasons. Pueblo Indians were not confrontational, kept to themselves, shared the same tribal enemies, occupied isolated areas without (so far) desirable resources, seemed generally self-sufficient, and didn't fit prevailing images of how Indians looked, lived, or suffered. A decade after Schoolcraft's survey, a five-member congressional team led by Wisconsin senator James Doolittle traveled to Kansas, Colorado, Indian Territory, and the Southwest to investigate corrupt reservation officials and cavalry massacres of Plains Indians. His report, *Condition of the Indian Tribes,* also revealed the hellish plight of Navajos at New Mexico's Fort Sumner, where nearly the entire tribe had been incarcerated since 1864. Among additional problems, Doolittle mentioned brutality, diseases, and alcoholism. Left out of the picture again were their quiescent neighbors, even though Pueblo Indians were suffering from disease and poverty as much as Indians everywhere.

Those reservation scandals also sparked a self-funded investigation by muckraker Helen Hunt Jackson. Her 1881 exposé *A Century of Dishonor* excoriated broken treaties, government misconduct, dishonest Indian agents, and settlers who treated Indians like animals and dispossessed them. But she overlooked the Pueblos because they seemed "distinguished from all other aborigines of the continent" by a "high degree of civilization."

Seven years later, anthropologist Alice Fletcher turned in her U.S. Senate–commissioned survey on *Indian Education and Civilization.* An advocate for allotting tribal lands and absorbing Indians into the American mainstream, Fletcher praised the boarding schools operating in New Mexico, without mentioning the peaceful Pueblos, perhaps because they staunchly opposed the very assimilation she was promoting. And who was listening to these early exposés anyway? wondered many Indians. "Our Great Father sends big men," complained a nineteenth-century Ojibwe leader from the Great Lakes. "They come up—find condition on Indians. Make many papers for benefit of Indians. When they go back papers never come up."

Over the next quarter century, Indian problems returned to the back burner. Preoccupied by rapid industrialization, attendant labor struggles, and the Great War, Washington relegated its native "wards" to missionaries, scholars, and do-gooders. Not until the early 1920s would their problems arouse public interest again. G. E. E. Lindquist's 1923 *Red Man in the United States* was a faith-based fact-finding mission. The 461-page publication wound up promoting automatic Indian citizenship (which did occur a year later), underscoring the abysmal state of Indian health, and promoting Christian education, but only devoted a few pages to the Pueblos. The "proselytizing book" disgusted John Collier as "crowded with defects, invidious toward the Indian religions and saturated with religious persecution sentiment."

Collier had higher hopes for a blue-ribbon panel of reform-minded scholars, politicians, and elite Indians created by Interior Secretary Hubert Work and known as the Committee of One Hundred. Yet its membership was split by contradictory agendas. Old-style reformers wanted assimilation and frowned on paganism, while younger progressives fought for coherent Indian communities free of religious restrictions or bureaucratic oversight. Collier appreciated the fact that at least one of its members, California anthropologist C. Hart Merriam, suggested that "Indians have more to teach White folks about religion and the art of sweet wholesome living than the White man has to teach them." But native opinions on the best way forward were similarly divided, reflecting the "traditional" versus "progressive" division that was weakening tribal solidarity everywhere.

As officialdom kept assigning these surveys and updating its statistics, Indians remained skeptical of the entire process. Too often it seemed a way of sweeping problems under the rug. "We are puzzled as to what useful end all this writing serves," said some Indian court judges to anthropologist Clark Wissler. "The white man can't even remember his papers after he gets them written. For although there are many papers in Washington upon which are promises to pay us for our lands, no white man seems to remember them."

But this new document would not be buried. A straight arrow of a man, Lewis Meriam brought a reputation for strict impartiality and running a

tight ship. Where earlier surveys gave the Pueblos short shrift, Meriam
bookended his investigations with personal visits to the Southwest. Unlike
Collier, he was no flaming liberal; in the next election he voted Republican. His colleagues were an economic historian, two specialists on Indian
health, an agricultural economist, a sociologist working on family statistics, and an eminent Ho-Chunk Indian, Henry Roe Cloud, noted for his
educational expertise and a onetime pillar of the now-defunct Society of
American Indians.

In late November 1926, Meriam's teams visited reservations and
schools across New Mexico and Arizona. After the Christmas break, they
dispersed to Idaho, the Pacific Northwest, and California. From November 1926 through June of the following year they covered twenty-five thousand miles and visited ninety-five Indian reservations, agencies, hospitals,
and schools around the country. Before the 1927 Christmas break Meriam
walked around Santo Domingo Pueblo with its Indian governor. The fol-

Solomon Bibo as stereotyped in Yiddish theater. When newspaper stories reached New York about the "Jewish Indian Chief," Edward Hunt's brother-in-law became a character for popular sheet music and performance.

lowing April he visited the Zuni and Hopi villages. In the Santa Fe living room of Pueblo attorney Francis Wilson he interviewed Anglo fighters for Pueblo rights.

Meriam's final report didn't mince words. America's natives were "extremely poor," their conditions of life "deplorable." Due to insufficient food supplies, pervasive malnutrition, crowded and filthy living conditions, inadequate medical care, skyrocketing infant mortality, poorly staffed hospitals, and widespread tuberculosis (highest in the nation), whooping cough, measles, trachoma, pneumonia, and influenza, their survival seemed again at stake.

Indian education, especially the boarding school system, was "broken." Illiteracy in the Southwest alone was nearly 70 percent. Compulsory attendance was unknown. Parents kept children home to add to the workforce, or because they feared the schools' miserable diet, overcrowding, rampant infectious disease, insufficient medical services, physical abuse, reliance on student labor, and dismal teaching.

Most revelatory of the Meriam findings was the massive extent of Indian land loss. Between the General Allotment Act of 1887 (when individual Indian families first were granted 160- or 320-acre homesteads, with any remaining tribal lands auctioned off to whites) and 1934 (when this policy was abandoned), nearly two-thirds of treaty-granted Indian territories across the country slipped into non-Indian hands. As estimated by the Meriam survey, some sixty million acres of onetime Indian land were gone for good, and one-third of their seventy million remaining acres was rocky mountainside, swampy marshland, or arid desert. Among Meriam's recommendations was restoration of natural resources so tribes could recover some economic independence. But that goal would take a long while to meet, if ever.

Meriam was calling for "understanding of and sympathy for the Indian point of view" and hoping that Washington "will recognize the good in the educational and social life of the Indians, in their religion and ethics, and will seek to develop it and build on it rather than to crush out all that is Indian."

Had the Hunts not been touring Europe at the time, they would surely have been among the thirty-six "Indian migrants to urban areas" whom

Meriam counted as living in Albuquerque in 1927. Their reputations and language skills might even have marked them as promising interviewees. But among his report's more unexpected disclosures was the plight of city Indians much like them. Adding to Edward's identities as an American Indian, an Acoma Indian, a Pueblo Indian, a boarding school Indian, a progressive Indian, a Show Indian, and a pan-Indian, this report identified him as a "Migrated Indian" as well.

Life wasn't easy for these urban pioneers. As anthropologist Gene Weltfish later described the odds against them, "There are only two types of employment open to them: work based on their Indian background, and common labor. They can go back to cities like Albuquerque or Flagstaff and get jobs making Indian jewelry or weaving—still not really in the mainstream—or they can get work on railroad section gangs, construction projects or road building." Even ignoring the racial prejudices that kept Indians from becoming policemen, firemen, clerks, or even garbage collectors, "Their training has not fitted them for better jobs," wrote Weltfish, "or if it has, the competition is quite likely to be too strong for them." Yet the Meriam Report was peppered with praise of their reliability and manual dexterity, even if supervisors commented that Indians tended to work at their own steady, unpressured pace.

In late October 1928 the Hunts wrapped up their storytelling at the Smithsonian Institution. A few blocks away the Bureau of Indian Affairs was still reviewing Meriam's findings. Lingering in their Virginia rental over the winter holidays, the family was unaware of the impending reforms this survey had begun or the approaching fiscal cataclysm that would make them all the more urgent. After an exhaustive donation of their people's spiritual heritage in the nation's capital, they were preoccupied with booking their next performance.

Some Indians Survive (1929–32)

Some of you might think that reservation communities were so depressed that the fall in the stock market and subsequent economic crash would not have any effect on them. Actually the reason was quite different. There was really very little need for cash on a day-to-day basis. Those families that did not have wage earners traded corn, strings of red chili, and wheat in the nearby store for things they could not trade for with neighboring Spanish-Americans and other Pueblo Indians, or which they did not grow themselves.

—Alfonso Ortiz, 1986

RIGHT OFF THE BOAT the Hunts realized they'd returned to America with something to sell. Their Smithsonian collaborators let them interrupt their myth-narrating so they could test it out in Virginia and the District of Columbia. Their raw material was their own lives *as* Indians plus what they'd been taught about *being* Indians in Oklahoma and overseas. They'd learned to redesign themselves so as to appeal to multiple audiences. For ethnologists they shared their Pueblo heritage with *its* deep authenticity; for the general public they turned around and blithely performed *their* imagined Indian reality.

Edward's first hint of the commercial benefits of merely *being Indian* had probably come from watching white visitors to Solomon and Simon Bibo's trading posts staring with big eyes at the Indian customers standing beside them and buying their wares. The looks of awe and fascination were repeated when he interacted with whites at his Acomita outlet. They stripped his shelves of Indian-made pots and rugs and peppered him with questions about the dates of harvest dances and pueblo fiestas.

All the Hunts were familiar with the Comanche Dances, every Pueblo's burlesque of the Plains Indian stereotype, which they commonly performed after Christmas. From Zack Miller in northern Oklahoma they learned to embody this product for wider audiences. They became adept

Hunt brothers four. Left to right: *Wilbert, Wolf Robe, Clyde, Allen.*

at the fast-stepping, foot-stomping "war" dances and high-pitched singing, derived from northern-style "Omaha" or "Grass" dances that were already a staple of the pan-Indian powwow scene. The younger Hunts could safely spill off of horses as if shot while enacting Indian attacks on stagecoaches and covered wagons. In offstage intervals they fell into the statuesque poses that wordlessly communicated *The Indian*'s innate pride and nobility. Upon this training Hans Stosch-Sarrasani imposed the discipline and efficiency necessary to make their acts pay on the road; their vaudeville stint only confirmed its appeal.

This supply chain from pueblo plazas to American stages did not emerge out of any marketing strategy. The Hunts' business plan, such as it was, grew organically, through a mixture of lucky timing, personal history, fortunate connections, and their inviting personalities. Over time they had become bush-league capitalists. Soon they realized that their consumer base was broader and more durable than they imagined.

Perhaps it was Stirling, or other contacts around the nation's capital, who sparked this realization. Perhaps their government associates, compensating for the fact that they weren't paying them for the origin myth, arranged local performance venues so they might pick up a few dollars. And perhaps that is also why Stirling felt compelled to wrap up their fall 1928 storytelling sessions with one of the family's first "To Whom It May Concern" bona fides. His letter of endorsement praised their "knowledge of native customs and traditions, together with their dance and song renditions [as] both interesting and authentic . . . [and] educational." And maybe he was slyly saluting their sense of salesmanship by adding, "Their knowledge of civilized customs enables them to present the native philosophy and view point in an entertaining and thoroughly understandable way."

However Wolf Robe picked up the trick of exploiting such references to hopscotch from one job to the next three, it worked. His address book and file of written testimonials and fan letters thickened. "No entertainment given our Sunday School in recent years has made such a 'hit,' both financially and educationally," wrote Pastor Selden of Norfolk, Virginia's First Baptist Church in one of their earliest recommendations. For three weeks, in daily performances each afternoon and evening, "the company composed of Chief Big Snake, Princess Morning Star, Wolfrobe, Blue Sky and Rattlesnake [gave] an entertainment that is refined, amusing and educational; and enter into their performances with zest and conscientiousness."

When the Hunts finally returned to Albuquerque in early 1929, their four-room home on the working-class west side became a base camp for pursuing this strategy. Meanwhile, they read the newspapers and prepared for trouble. America was falling to its knees; in less than a year she'd be flat on her face. But on Black Thursday, October 24, 1929, as the stock market crashed and a fourth of the country's workforce was about to lose their jobs, the Hunts were tucking into dinner at a Pueblo, Colorado, boardinghouse before the next day's paid performance at St. Patrick's Church.

In New Mexico, where sons Alfred and Ervin held down the family's little fort whenever the others were out on tour, they saw the Depression up close. Albuquerque lay midpoint in the potholed pathway of a bedraggled migration that led from the hopeless wasteland of Dust Bowl Oklahoma to the illusory paradise of California. After 1930 the Hunts got accustomed to begging families knocking on their front door, a shanty-town springing up on Albuquerque's south side, and furtive campfires glowing underneath the Rio Grande and Rio Puerco bridges.

On Central Avenue the sight of beat-up jalopies and pickups with mattresses, chicken coops, water jugs, and gas panniers lashed on with baling wire became commonplace. Behind the Alvarado Hotel, where the Hunts still occasionally danced for visitors at the train station, hobos stared from empty freight cars. A number of the haggard nomads in threadbare clothes were fellow Indians—among them Dorothy Thompson, the handsomely gaunt Cherokee woman from Oklahoma whom photographer Dorothea Lange made the iconic face of the decade.

Commenting on the period, poet Langston Hughes reminded Americans that whatever devastation the Depression brought to the country at large, minorities were hit twice as hard. At the peak of the Jim Crow era, with limited job openings in the best of times, African Americans were already dying from disease and starvation; eight hundred thousand were on their way north. Racist editorials argued for easing the country's burdens by shipping four hundred thousand Mexicans, many U.S.-born citizens, south across the border.

For Indians these years only compounded the preexisting crisis that had been exposed by the Meriam Report. Living conditions were unspeakable—skyrocketing death rates from disease epidemics, near-starvation-level food supplies, official restrictions on freedom to hunt and forage for themselves, housing reduced to drafty shacks and canvas tents, a paralyzing sense of hopelessness and despair. In 1928 the national emergency only added to Indian suffering—an estimated 55 percent of them existing on less than $200 per capita per year. Only 2 percent—including the Hunts—were earning more than $500 annually. Such was everyday reality even before the stock market crash. But now, like the Civil War that diverted attention from Indian sufferings during Edward's childhood, obscure maneuverings in the larger white world had caught the tribes unawares once again.

Hardscrabble New Mexico, with her population of nearly twenty-three thousand Indians, third highest in the nation, looked especially vulnerable. Already suffering from a prolonged drought, the state found its railroad and mining jobs drastically cut back and tourism in decline. Out in

Valencia County the Bibo families were forced to close trading posts and sell their livestock.

But thankfully, two things weakened the Depression's impact here. Roosevelt's New Deal earmarked the especially needy, semiarid West for its public projects. Having Clyde Tingley, the state's folksy governor, as the president's personal confidant didn't hurt in funneling Civilian Conservation Corps (CCC) and Works Progress Administration (WPA) funds to New Mexico. Unemployed blue-collar workers were paid to build tourist facilities and revamp roadways. Artists (a few were Pueblo Indians, Santa Clara's Pablita Velarde, among them), photographers, writers, musicians, and architects were hired for a raft of cultural preservation projects. They painted murals in post offices, courthouses, and libraries, collected oral histories and folklore from Spanish villages, and researched local histories

Edward and Marie Hunt give Indian name to granddaughter Lo "Punky" Wayne Hunt, daughter of Henry Wayne Wolf Robe and Glenal Hunt, while Marie has the girl inhale life-force from eagle down. Left to right: Edward, Lo Wayne (seated), Wolf Robe, Marie.

for the state's first guidebook. Under a portion of the initiative known as the Indian New Deal, reservations became a special focus of CCC and WPA work crews. Whether Acoma conservatives liked it or not, her progressive governor made her the only Pueblo village to be measured and drawn, foot by foot, by out-of-work draftsmen and architects attached to the Historic American Buildings Survey, while hundreds of pages were collected on the tribe's folklore as well.

Also softening the Depression's impact were old habits of self-sufficiency. Based on sheep, the Navajo economy (whose erosion-producing impact on the Southwest's desert ecology was only starting to hit home) still offered a steady meat supply. Falling back on networks of relatives and systems of gift exchange, Pueblo Indian families could rely on native and Spanish neighbors and bartering at rural stores to meet basic needs. In exchange for surplus vegetables from their gardens, the extra venison, rabbit, and birds they hunted at every opportunity, and the surplus piñon nuts, cactus fruits, and firewood they gathered seasonally, they received cloth, tools, canned goods, or commercial medicines.

Additionally, Indians sewed their own clothing, pruned, irrigated, and harvested their own fruit trees, repaired and reroofed their own houses or built new ones out of homemade adobe bricks and ax-shaped blocks of readily available sandstone. These skills augmented whatever a family's single wage earner might bring from cleaning houses and serving meals in Santa Fe, or peddling painted pots or jewelry at local hotels and curio shops. When anthropologist Alfonso Ortiz asked fellow San Juan members about the Depression's toll, "The reply, to my surprise, was no impact at all."

Estranged from their home reservation, the Hunts were not under this safety net. But on Black Thursday they had jobs. The next morning, after a warm welcome from Pastor Joe Higgins in Pueblo, Colorado, Edward Hunt introduced the troupe. Encased in the showman's trappings of his alter ego as "Chief Big Snake," he described his birthplace high on a distant sandstone mesa in mysterious New Mexico. He mentioned the Katsina spirits and their society into which he was initiated. He described the secret Koshare, the sacred "delight-maker" brotherhood into which he was also inducted. All the while, Philip "Silvertongue" Sanchez rumbled his hollow cottonwood-log drum for dramatic emphasis.

Before each act Big Snake gave its thumbnail background, buying a minute or two for setup or change of gear. Wolf Robe illustrated Indian ingenuity in making fire without matches by the old friction method, fast-rubbing a bow drill between his palms until a curl of smoke rose from the tinder. Blue Sky stuck his arms into the sleeves of his eagle-wing dance outfit and imitated the bird's soaring flight. After all of the performers joined in a war dance, Blue Sky held up his hulalike hoop, kicked it into the air, jumped through it, and added another hoop with each go-around, all in time to rapid drumbeats.

Vedna Belle Eckerman, Wilbert Hunt's bride-to-be, walking to her government office in Albuquerque.

Without a tight rein on their timing, as Sarrasani and the vaudeville circuit had hammered into them, the Hunts could not have fit into the diverse venues they would face in their hundreds of performances across the south-central United States. At the same time they had to remain flexible; anywhere from fifty to ninety minutes might be allowed onstage. Before each display they edited out this animal dance or added that scalp dance story or description of crafting bows and arrows to adjust to the given time slot.

A large measure of the family's success was due to their attractive, even multiethnic appearance. Cameras enhanced the skin tone, bone structure, and Latinate look of the Hunts' faces. Not wearing their hair in braids was probably a plus; that might have seemed *too* Indian for those who wanted their natives authentic but approachable. Nor were they sullen, withdrawn, or monosyllabic like some of the long-haired Plains Indian performers from South Dakota who couldn't hide their discomfort at being paraded around Europe like exotic specimens. The Hunts smiled warmly, enjoyed enacting the Indians they were thought to be, answered questions in soft voices, and flavored their ease in public with an almost aristocratic reserve.

They delivered the thrills of seeing costumed and war-painted Indians in the flesh (especially those attired like fearsome Plains Indian warriors) with the sense that audiences were also being educated in their tribal backgrounds. Here were Indians who seemed incontrovertibly *Indian* but whom outsiders felt good being around. The fortuitous combination of their handsome looks and unique life experiences made them perfect mediators for all the contradictory ideas and symbolism that swirled around the paradoxical images of The Indian—as savage and noble, solid friend and frightening foe, enemy other and congenial ally, rapist and spiritualist, border-town drunk and wilderness mentor.

Furthermore, the Hunts were unique in representing themselves as an Indian nuclear family, which made them all the easier to identify with. Had fate added the literary exposure that propelled other popular embodiments of Indianness, like Charles Eastman or Luther Standing Bear, who wrote bestselling memoirs, the Hunts' marketable package might have "gone national," whether on the Chautauqua circuit or in Hollywood films. But that was not to be, and the family had no regrets.

Their performances climaxed with a group song, louder drumming, the clanging of anklet bells. Their presentations were successful because they left their audiences hungry for more. Ten minutes or so remained for one-on-one exchanges. Lingering onstage, the family answered questions from wide-eyed youngsters who fingered their buckskins, drums, rattles, and fire drill.

Once the family were back in street clothes, Wolf Robe asked Pastor Higgins for a favor. Would he mind writing a letter to a fellow pastor recommending the group? "This will introduce Chief Big Snake and his family," Higgins immediately typed in a note to his contact, Father Raher, in La Junta, praising this troupe, "who gave a very enjoyable and instructive program at our school today. Sisters and pupils alike were charmed by the Indian dances and history given."

The Hunts moved on to the next venue.

A Family of Freelancers (1930–40)

The Indian is the lusty youth of humanity. He is always ready to undertake the impossible, or to impoverish himself to please his friend. Most of all he values the opportunity of being a minute-man—a Scout.... Let us have more of this spirit of the American Indian, the Boy Scout prototype, to leaven the brilliant selfishness of our modern civilization.

—Charles "Ohiyesa" Eastman, 1914

So THE FAMILY had their product and packaging, but where was their market? To the Hunts' surprise, a pool of around eight hundred thousand consumers was eager for dances, stories, and homegrown inspirations like theirs. That was the number of youngsters who had joined the Boy Scouts of America by 1930. For some of them, and their parents, learning about Indians offered a romantic retreat in lean times and a magical entry into an ancient and more authentic America. The commodity that the Hunts found themselves uniquely prepared to deliver fell under the cover term "Indian Lore."

Unlike with other forms of popular entertainment, whose audiences had dwindled during the Depression, adherents of this pastime were only growing; for some it became an avocation. Two or three generations removed from the raw immediacy of real Indian attacks, the children of parents who'd flocked to Wild West show reenactments yearned for more benign and motivational dimensions to the Indian experience. Angry, fighting Indians they could watch in the movies. What many sought instead was the spirituality and beauty that they sensed in Indian art, poetry, music, and religion. Rather than attracting passive spectators, a distinguishing feature of this new offering was its invitation to *participate* in those loftier and earthier dimensions of Indian life.

These boys and girls longed to craft Indian tools, sew their moccasins, bead regalia, and make drums. Others wanted to go further and dress and dance like Indians. A number tried to adopt what they believed were native values about animals, the environment, and achieving manhood and womanhood. And a few, through a kind of cross-cultural symbiosis, even dreamt of *becoming Indians.*

While encapsulating this range of desires, Indian Lore was also strengthened by a grassroots resistance to modern times; it offered a curative for its supposed ills. Fortunately for marketers like the Hunts, a large portion of this fan base had segmented into hundreds of Boy Scout troops since the organization's founding twenty years earlier. With its military-

Johnson City Chronicle

Combined with Johnson City Staff News

JOHNSON CITY, TENNESSEE, SUNDAY, MARCH 19, 1933.

Decendants of Cliff Dwellers To Appear Here

—News-Sentinel Photograph.
Mrs. Wayne Hunt, left, wife of Wayne "Wolf-Robe" Hunt; Blue Sky Eagle and Telles Medicine Star, center, Wolf-Robe (Wayne Hunt), right.

Pueblos Will Entertain At Local Schools For Four Days

Traditions, Customs, etc.,
"Vanishing American"
to Be Portrayed For the
Benefit of Students

*The Hunts can portray them all—Plains Indians, Pueblo Indians,
cliff-dwelling Indians, and vanishing Indians.*

like hierarchy, Scouting's network was effective for endorsing and spreading word of presentations like the Hunts and booking their dates.

For these Boy Scouts, Indian Lore blazed two paths. One was reflected in the official Boy Scout Indian Lore merit badge whose requirements, spelled out in 1932, drew outdoorsy kids who loved camping, hiking and nature, arts and crafts, making fire without matches the old Indian way, identifying animal tracks and following them without making a sound. The other path was pursued by those American youth with historical or cultural imaginations, or who were not impervious to the rebellious sentiments of their nonconformist parents. This direction drew on the Old English root of the word, *laere,* which connoted knowledge and wisdom and evoked Indian philosophy and religion. Rather than pursuing a hobby like stamp collecting or building model airplanes, they engaged with Indian Lore as a kind of sacramental practice that merged body and spirit in the Playing of being Indian.

With their uncanny timing, the Hunts were positioned to nourish the "intangible yearnings" of this niche market, because their lives and careers combined the two, supposedly opposed poles of American Indian cultural experience that had recently been popularized by anthropologist Ruth Benedict's dichotomy. She'd contrasted the Dionysian, sensation-seeking Indian tribes and their ecstatic, often individualistic vision quests in the wilderness like those practiced in the Great Plains and the Northwest coast to the more ceremonious, communal, and harmony-seeking Apollonian tribes, like the Pueblos.

In Edward's opening remarks at Pueblo, Colorado, he'd turned the southwestern Pueblo side of their native origins, which both the Miller Brothers and German promoters sought to downplay as nonstereotypically Indian, into an advantage. His romantic description of Acoma mesa was no exaggeration, nor was his evocation of the picturesque cliff dwellings from whence his forefathers had migrated over a thousand years before. From personal experience he could recall Katsina dances, antelope hunts, killing a bear, scalp ceremonies, and clown performances. His people's fights with Navajo raiders were reminiscent of Plains Indian wars. The troupe's eagle-feather war bonnets, beaded outfits, rapid drumming, keening song, and fast dancing only reinforced that fierce image. His listeners couldn't care less about finer distinctions between Plains and Pueblo lifestyles, or what mythologist Joseph Campbell termed the mutually incompatible "ways" of the Animal Powers and the Seeded Earth. In both their personal experiences at Acoma and their stage roles here and abroad, the Hunts overrode those categories and embodied what fascinated their audiences about Indians and what many wanted to emulate.

When the Boy Scouts of America opened its Washington, D.C., headquarters in 1910 its founding foursome held differing visions of American manhood and where Indians fit in. From England came Lord Robert S. S. Baden-Powell, a British general known as "the Hero of Mafeking" for his leadership in South Africa's Second Boer War. The boys' organization he founded in 1908, whose members he dressed in military-style uniforms, was influenced by the tracking skills of scouts he'd watched in action. An American, Daniel Beard, created the Sons of Daniel Boone in 1900 so boys could practice the camping and handwork skills of legendary mountain men and frontier scouts. His vision of Christian boys following a code of honor harkened back to explorers like Lewis and Clark, with a pinch of Buffalo Bill Cody's work with railroads, hunting buffalo, and escorting Indian-fighting troops thrown in.

From Canada came their philosophical opposite, a rangy, walrus-mustached, naturalist, artist, writer, and guru named Ernest Thompson Seton. Author of engagingly written and humorously illustrated popular books, Seton saw wild animals and Indians as natural teachers for adventuresome boys. He stressed the Indian's oneness with the outdoors, their hunters' familiarity with animal behavior, and Indian philosophy. Seton's Woodcraft League of America, founded in 1902, was Scouting's most direct prototype.

A few of Seton's mentors who kindled this passion were Indians themselves. When the Hunts began their performing tours, Dr. Charles "Ohiyesa" Eastman, a Santee Sioux author from western Minnesota, was perhaps the best-known Indian of his day. Born in a buffalo-hide tipi in 1858, he fled with his family to Canada after his people's 1862 uprising—the conflict that kicked off the twenty-year Plains Indian wars. After attending mission schools, Eastman earned his BA from Dartmouth College, and a medical degree from Boston University in 1890. Then he married a white nurse on the Pine Ridge Reservation who shared his love of writing and belief in the inherent wisdom of Indian traditions.

Eastman's popularity exploded with his 1902 memoir *Indian Boyhood,* after which came nine other books that appealed to this new sympathy for living, learning, and even worshipping what he idealized as the Indian way. His fourth, *Indian Scout Talks* (1914), converted those life lessons into outdoor activities for non-Indian kids. Soon a sheaf of popular writings about Indian song, dance, and culture—including Natalie Curtis's *The Indians' Book* (1907), Arthur Parker's *Indian How Book* (1927), Julia Buttree Seton's *Rhythm of the Redman* (1930), and Mary Austin's *The American Rhythm* (1930)—supported this national passion.

For a few years Baden-Powell's militarism, Beard's patriotism, and Seton's mysticism maintained an uneasy truce, thanks to the organizational skills of Scouting's fourth wheel and national chief executive, a New York lawyer named James E. West. Before long, however, Seton bristled at Baden-Powell's martial emphasis and Beard's nationalism. Turning away from Boy Scouting won him the freedom to foster, with his wife, Julia, a more Indian-inflected alternative, the Woodcraft League, and its female counterpart, the Camp Fire Girls.

But Indian Lore remained a fixture in the Scout movement. Native mysticism may have been underplayed, but the Boy Scouts' official organ, *Boys' Life,* carried columns on making Indian crafts and ads for mail-order outlets where hobbyists could obtain their feathers, sinew, bells, and beads. To satisfy Eagle-rank scouts who desired to embody Indians more profoundly, in 1915 an elite brotherhood, the Order of the Arrow, was established. With its initiations and officers modeled after American Indian rituals, the group sought a corporeal connection with Indians through dance and concocted ceremony.

Some carried this enthusiasm into adulthood, with teachers and writers like Ralph Hubbard, Julian Harris Solomon, Bernard S. Mason, W. Ben Hunt, and others creating a national Indian Hobbyist movement that persisted throughout the twentieth century. In March 1931, during the annual Boy Scout "circus" held in St. Louis, Edward Hunt, the initiated Koshare clown from Acoma, hobnobbed with the organization's national leaders. Also in attendance was Colorado scoutmaster James "Buck" Burshears, who was inspired to kick the Indian Lore movement up a notch by forming his own, possibly Hunt-influenced Koshare Indian Dancers. Based in La Junta, Colorado, Burshear's ardent devotees, wearing tan makeup and dressed in homemade costumes, recreated traditional Indian dances and secret Pueblo rituals and built a museum-kiva home base modeled after the ancient rotunda at New Mexico's Aztec ruins.

The chapters of Charles Eastman's *Indian Scout Talks* read like a playbook for the repertoire of dances, tribal crafts, camping skills, and generic Indian spirituality that the Hunts compressed into their performances. As

Wilbert and Vedna Hunt: the romantic Indian couple, one of their many publicity photos.

the family hopped from one appearance to another over the next fifteen years, Wolf Robe's notebooks of mailing addresses were crucial to their survival. To cinch contracts they built upon endorsements from Boy Scout executives, Indian Bureau officials, and Smithsonian Institution scholars. That they dramatized Indian lifeways far different from what they'd shared in Washington never troubled them. They knew who they were.

Under Wolf Robe's guidance, the mobile Hunts, traveling in a succession of vehicles, performed before Boy Scout gatherings, circuses, troops, and jamborees, school assemblies, church gatherings, and civic festivals. They joined a handful of little-known itinerant Indian "acts" who became dancers at roadside trading posts, appeared with small-scale circuses, and even found bit parts in movies—although the Hunts, for some reason, never worked in that industry. Their success, longer than most, came from a convergence of factors.

Theirs was a mutually reliant family that traveled well together. They packed their succession of used Cadillacs and Haines touring automobiles with routine care; four suitcases fitted into special racks on the running boards—one per performer, containing personal effects and stage outfit. The drum was always tucked into the same corner in the rear; only Wolf Robe or Wilbert at the wheel. Their performing skills also meshed: Edward the patriarch, Wolf Robe the planner, Silvertongue the singer, Wilbert the handsome frontman and sometime car mechanic, and Marie the silent matriarch, in her still, watchful demeanor remaining perhaps the most "authentic" of all. The family took to heart their boarding school lessons about personal grooming, clear English, clean clothes, good manners, careful bookkeeping, a strong work ethic, and punctuality so as to prosper in the old Show Indian trade that those same schools deplored as backsliding and barbaric.

Indian entrepreneurs like them could never have flown so successfully from the tribal nest without strong women who became full partners in the enterprise. Aside from Edward and Marie, now married for forty years, there was the younger generation. Wilbert and Vedna Eckerman from Laguna Pueblo, childhood sweethearts from Albuquerque Indian School, were married in 1936. Daughter Josephine and a Navajo from Arizona, Johnny Johnson, were also schoolmates at first. Initially the old antagonism between Acomas and Navajos kept Edward from granting the couple his blessing. Over time, however, the old man came to respect his son-in-law and his skills as a silversmith, and they all posed for formal pictures together at the Inter-Tribal Ceremonials at Gallup, New Mexico.

The base of their touring years shifted after 1931 when Wolf Robe, still living in Albuquerque, met Glenal Davis, a summer art student from Tulsa, Oklahoma. After they married in 1932 and moved to her home state four years later, Wolf Robe kept touring throughout the decade, but now with Glenal, often in Indian dress, by his side.

Not a performing member of the family, Clyde Hunt opened his Indian curio shop, the War Bonnet, in downtown Albuquerque. One day a stunning Texan redhead named Estelle Shirley walked through his door; during the Sandia Pueblo fiesta in 1939 she became his second wife. Nor were Clyde and Wolf Robe the only marginalized Pueblos entering an interracial romance. Following in the mold set by the Sioux Indian Charles Eastman and Mary Eastman, and the Taos Indian Antonio Luhan and Mabel Dodge, in 1926 Hunt cousin James Paytiamo married La Rue Payne, an Indian Lore aficionado and devotee of Ernest Thompson Seton's salon of Indian Lore outside Santa Fe. After he left the Hunts' traveling company around 1930, Philip Sanchez (now known as Ray Silvertongue) fell in love with a customer, Natalie Blair, and the two also made a living off of his performing gifts.

Often their husbands' fervent promoters, these spouses contributed energy, business smarts, and family connections that added to the Hunts' success on the road. And they were on the road a lot. Between 1926 and 1943, according to Wilbert's calculations, he spent fewer than five Christmases in New Mexico. The quadrant their troupe favored was the Southeast; they found enough bookings without trying the Northeast, the Great Lakes, the northern plains, or the West Coast.

These were the glory years. As Universal Indians, the Hunts were constantly in demand and on parade.

Do Individuals Exist? (1930–40)

If I seem to say a lot about myself, it is really my times that I am thinking about. I am merely the person who happened to be there at a particular time. It is hard to put down something with myself as a center of interest— that is, to say I did this or that. It makes me out to be important, which isn't the way I see it. We Tewas and Hopis don't think of ourselves that way.

—Albert Yava, Hopi, 1978

IN THE SPRING OF 1934, while the Hunts were on break from touring, their thirty-four-year-old friend the anthropologist Leslie White paid another visit. Over the past eight years White had climbed the academic ladder to become a tenured professor at the University of Michigan. He was popular with students, prickly to colleagues, and passionate about fieldwork. For Edward's own protection, White never divulged the old man's help with his 1927 University of Chicago dissertation on Pueblo medicine men's societies, or Edward's heftier contributions to White's early, amateurish, but still unsurpassed 1932 ethnographic profile of Acoma Pueblo.

White's scholarly career lasted from 1926 until 1957. Following the proprietary attitude of his day, in scholarly circles the Keresan-speaking villages of New Mexico became known as *his* territory. And given their suspicious and xenophobic reputation, White's colleagues were probably happy to let him have them. Each of his publications fleshed out a similar laundry list of topics, each bore the signature of a meticulous fact-finder, each was an improvement in level of detail if increasingly out of theoretical fashion, and each helped to make the southwestern Pueblos one of the most written-about cultures in the world.

One suspects that studying more easygoing tribes, with Indians readier to share their culture, would have felt to White like shooting animals in a zoo. A "summer bird," he dropped into the Southwest for six-week visits during academic breaks. He was never the full-time "participant observer" like the discipline's legendary models, Frank Cushing at Zuni Pueblo or Bronislaw Malinowski in the South Pacific. White never roomed in a pueblo, never spoke the languages, and never witnessed the yearly agricultural and ceremonial cycles or seasonal appearances of the Katsina pantheon.

Trapped on campus where exercising his skills as a riveting and theoretically ambitious lecturer in classrooms offset his distaste for institutional authority, White longed for summertime and its opportunities for cross-cultural espionage. As he noted in his journal after visiting the Hunts in 1939, "Old man Hunt told me of the strife at Acoma, Santa Ana and Jemez—the same old story! the Progressives vs the Conservatives. On up to Ranchito, passing Sandia Pueblo on the way. The old feelings which always accompany my ethnological field work—the eager search, the hunt for informants, the scheming and planning—again possessed me; I felt like settling down and trying once again to penetrate the secrecy with which the Sandias surround and protect themselves."

Edward and his anthropologist, Leslie A. White.

Like a covert operative in a spy thriller, White slipped into villages to recruit compliant, preferably elder assets. With Elsie Clews Parsons as his distant control and local hotels his safe houses, he isolated his sources for debriefings, sometimes, Indians say, oiled by shots of whiskey. In duels of wits he extracted all he could about witchcraft, healing rituals, and initiation secrets. Following Parsons's guidelines, he provided witness protection by not revealing to one Indian what he learned from another, and maintained their deniability by never sharing anthropological publications or discussing the ultimate purpose of his interrogations.

With Edward living in Albuquerque, however, there was less

need for clandestine arrangements. Here was a knowledgeable informant whose doorbell White could ring and whose kitchen turned into an interview room—no inquisitive neighbors peering through windows. Renting a room in the Monkbridge Manor, a onetime mansion at 4th and Veranda streets, White could stroll over to the Hunts'. Nor was he dissuaded by Elsie Parsons's purist attitude that Edward's information was somehow tainted by his Christianity and easy accessibility. In fact, White sprinkled the old man's comments throughout his writings. Upon returning from this trip he began work with Parsons on editing Edward's origin myth for release to the public.

White's studies of the Keresan pueblos were but one facet of his professional profile. Outwardly a conventional ethnographer, spin the man around and you found a grumpy, opinionated, but brilliant theorist who was deeply ambivalent about his profession. "For many things—people, books, theories, customs, I have, and have had for years, a profound, if not bitter contempt, a feeling of loathing and hatred," White confided in his 1939 journal. "I despise the cheapness and shallowness of what passes for learning—especially in what are called the social sciences. I have nothing but contempt for the pretentious show made by petty 'scholars' which they call 'research.'"

Aiming high in his scorn, White targeted the legend who had almost single-handedly created modern American anthropology. Most social scientists of the day idolized Franz Boas, the German expatriate then holding court at Columbia University, as the ultimate ethnographer. A committed cultural relativist, Boas, with his utter repudiation of nineteenth-century theories that the world's societies evolved at different rates up the same cultural ladder "from savagery to civilization," drove White mad. Instead, White promoted what some called neoevolutionism, which introduced the effective use of energy as a universal measurement by which very different societies could indeed be compared.

It wasn't just White's zeal to create this more sophisticated update of the discredited theories of cultural evolution that marginalized him in anthropological circles. It was what many felt was his condescending way of dismissing "Papa Franz." In a typical outburst, White complained to fellow anthropologist Alfred Kroeber, "[Boas] was quite muddle-headed, incapable of creative imagination and philosophic synthesis, and at many points directly opposed to the spirit and procedure of science."

To buttress his alternative, White harkened back to the nineteenth-century work of Lewis Henry Morgan, the famous student of Iroquois culture whose writings on "primitive communism" had inspired Karl Marx and Friedrich Engels. The Russian connection also hinted at a private reason for White's identification with Morgan. Like the pueblos he studied, White kept certain affiliations close to his chest. A 1929 trip to Russia confirmed him as a socialist. Although he never officially joined the Communist Party, throughout the 1930s his pseudonym, John Steel, appeared regularly in *Weekly People* articles that extolled Soviet economics, predicted the collapse of capitalism, and envisioned communism as its evolutionary replacement.

Despite White's disdain for academics, his feud with Boas, and his closeted radicalism, he apparently kept abreast of intellectual fashion. This was probably why he was at Edward Hunt's door. He knew that influential colleagues like the brilliant University of Chicago linguist Edward Sapir and Columbia University's celebrated Ruth Benedict had grown impatient with "normative" studies of other cultures, much like the one White himself was completing on Santo Domingo Pueblo.

To any implication that *the* Santo Domingos behave this way or that, Sapir now argued that there were as many cultures as there were individuals. And even though Benedict claimed that "culture is personality writ large," she'd had enough firsthand experience with a range of Indian individuals to know that their personalities were, to the contrary, more than their cultures writ small. Under the influence of these humanistic scholars emerged the subfield known as culture and personality studies.

Its proponents might ask, for example, to what extent did the people of Santo Domingo or Acoma pueblos tolerate individualism, eccentricity, self-reinvention, stretching the rules, or even defying them? A society could try to impose its cookie-cutter mold of beliefs and behaviors on its members, but didn't it inevitably create "individuals"? How far might a man or woman stray from acceptable behavior before he or she lost the benefits inherent in tribal membership? "Why does one person bow before authority," White himself had already wondered in a 1925 article, "whereas another asserts aggressively their independence."

In Edward Hunt's case, to what degree was he reflective of what these anthropologists, increasingly influenced by psychology, termed Acoma's "modal" or typical personality? Or was White correct when he emphasized "environmental and situational factors"? If ever there was someone who didn't fit his tribal pattern, it was Edward. Yet hardly was there an Acoma tribesman who'd participated in more aspects of its traditional life. And wasn't Edward the one who had just narrated all the basic elements that created his village's idealized sense of herself in the first place?

In searching for a database to address such questions, anthropologists developed a fresh appreciation for an old genre, the autobiography, although they preferred a more scientific term, "life history." Parsons had written White about an Apache life story she'd just read. "If you are short of material on anybody and if any school bred Hopi is available," she suggested, "you might consider autobiography." White apparently felt obliged to join this new trend, with Edward as his most available and obvious subject.

Whether on their own initiatives, or through "as told to" intermediaries, for years Indians had put their lives in print, often because they had specific cases to make. When William Apess, a Pequot from Connecticut, wrote in 1829 of his experiences as a slave sold at nine, a runaway, a drummer boy, an ordained Methodist minister, and a political activist, it was to castigate American society for its cruel Indian removals and neglect of human rights.

On the opposite coast, however, Pablo Tac, a Luiseno Indian and teenage convert at Southern California's San Luis Rey Mission, offered a sanitized description of life at California's largest Catholic mission. The happy case he made for relentless toil as laborer, craftsman, gardener, and cowhand helped win him a trip to Rome, where he promptly died of disease. Tac had no ax to grind against Catholicism—quite the contrary—but the strict regime of prayer and work he described was not one his readers would have embraced.

More for popular consumption were "as told to" autobiographies elicited from famous chiefs, starting with Antoine LeClaire's 1833 life of Black Hawk, the Sauk and Fox hero of the war named for him, continuing with journalist S. M. Barrett's 1906 transcription of the memories of the Chiricahua Apache guerrilla leader Geronimo, and on through popular historian Frank Linderman's 1930 account from Crow leader Plenty Coups.

Usually embedded in these works about famous warriors and sages were arguments about their people's sufferings and struggles of spiritual survival.

With the 1920 publication of a partial life history from Sam Blowsnake, however, a Great Lakes Indian convert to the peyote-using Native American Church, came the more anthropological form of life history. As its transcriber Paul Radin wrote, "No attempt of any kind was made to influence [Blowsnake] in the selection of the particular facts of his life which he chose to present." Over the next twenty years hundreds of American Indian life stories were published, allowing readers to identify with a range of tribal, historical, and psychological Indian experiences from the inside out.

In his own house and broken English, Edward led White into an Acoma world that had hardly changed for centuries. Back in the early 1860s, "the church was there when I first opened my eyes," but the pueblo's war chiefs ruled with an iron hand. Before Protestant inroads, Edward remembered, "the Catholic priest and the people had a fight and the priest was about to be killed, so he ran away nearly before sunrise one morning." During Katsina appearances non-Indians were detained in their rooms.

Edward recalled his handmade sandstone-and-adobe three-story home with its comfy sleeping chambers where everyone bundled in sheepskins, back rooms stacked with dried corn or reserved for corn-grinding stones embedded in the floor, mica-glazed window holes, pottery lamps burning sheep tallow, corner fireplaces, and ladders for entering and leaving through the smoke hole. When food was scarce they ate raw clay mixed with wild potatoes and pear cactus.

With his father a medicine man, the days were full of healing ceremonies, chanting, crafting prayer sticks, and making altars. "I was scared," he remembered of the constant talk about supernatural affairs, "they telling us about witches killing people, the medicine men fight the witches, they looking through [clairvoyant] rock crystal."

There was that ferocious beating that the boarding school boys received, coupled with warnings never to abandon Acoma ways. Edward detailed his people's last communal hunt, his killing the bear. Clearly he could have continued, but unfortunately here the narrative stopped short, as if White had only scheduled a day or so for the task and was anxious to get going.

Edward and daughter Josephine Hunt leading the Inter-Tribal Ceremonial parade in Gallup, New Mexico.

Attributed to an anonymous Indian, Edward's story boiled down to eleven pages for an obscure Smithsonian collection that appeared nine years later. "Indians are not individualists," White wrote, as if excusing its brevity, "and autobiographies are all but impossible." As he later put it, a Pueblo Indian's life "is analogous to a great ocean liner at sea. And as the personal and subjective experience of the individual is irrelevant to the conduct of the ship, so is the personal and subjective experience of the Pueblo Indian irrelevant to the conduct of pueblo life. The autobiography of a Pueblo Indian is about as personal as the life story of an automobile tire."

But one might also interpret Edward's discretion as modesty, circumspection, or even a form of passive resistance. This centering of the self in autobiography, writes Georges Gusdorf, "expressed a concern peculiar to Western man, a concern that has been of good use in his systematic conquest of the universe and that he has communicated to other cultures." The danger for Gusdorf was that native subjects like Edward "will thereby have been annexed by a sort of intellectual colonizing to a mentality that was not their own."

When Elsie Parsons saw White's short piece, however, she appreciated its details. "You make too much of the objective mindedness of the Pueblo," she countered to White. "The Maine 'natives' [where Parsons had a summer estate] would be quite as lacking in introspection and so would many other circles of White Americans."

The truth is more likely that White's heart wasn't in the project. Anxious to continue his cross-cultural sleuthing, he wasn't interested in requesting follow-up interviews or extracting Edward's fuller story. A true misanthrope, White was not only blaming the person who helped enrich his anthropological career for his own shortcomings as an interviewer. He was holding extroversion as a universal measure of an evolved personality and implying that Pueblo Indians were underdeveloped as self-conscious human beings.

White's half-baked effort to stay in the game had yielded one more publication based upon Edward's knowledge and experience that his informant would never hear about. But the family lost no sleep over it. Visitors like White had come and gone from their lives for years.

50

Another Native World (1936–45)

One day in Memphis a little boy braver than the others, came close and I say, "This sure is a nice day, ain't it?" to get him friendly, but he get back behind the tree. Pretty soon he peeps out and says, "Are you a wild Injun?" and I says, "No, they made me go to school." "But how many scalps did you take when you was wild? Do you eat raw meat?" And then I could see he was serious, so I says, "My little friend, do you really want to know these things?" And he says, "Sure, Chief. Will you tell me?" And out he came from behind the tree. Then I says, "Well, you call your little friends and tell them I am not a wild Indian and we will sit down here under this big tree and we will talk."

—Wolf Robe Hunt, 1936

WHEN WOLF ROBE and his wife drove from New Mexico in 1936 to resettle in her hometown of Tulsa, they faced a tide of old cars and trucks streaming in the opposite direction. Across the southern plains giant windstorms had thrown a hundred million acres of prime wheat-growing land into the sky. Starting in 1932, over a quarter million Dust Bowl evacuees, dirt-poor farmers, but also middle-class townsfolk, were pulling up stakes. On the makeshift linkage of concrete lanes and unpaved detours that was America's first "national highway," they were fleeing the most maligned and misrepresented region in the country.

For most Indians, however, over the previous century what was formerly Indian Territory had grown into the most tribally diverse and ceremonially thriving hub in the country. As author George Wilburn observed, "Oklahoma is to sociology as Australia is to zoology." In the forty-sixth state lay the nation's biggest refugee camp, where nearly a hundred thousand Indians maintained their distinctive ethnic identities and languages, retaining many of their varying social and religious customs, and staking out singular, if considerably shrunken, territories.

They included over twenty Plains-style cultures, some resident, some inmigrated, largely occupying reservations on the state's western prairies. In the eastern hill country lived descendants of the so-called Five Civilized Tribes who had been forcibly removed from the Deep South in the 1830s during the Jacksonian era. Some were brought as prisoners of war, like the Chiricahua Apaches, originally from the Southwest. Trickling in after decades on the road were remnant groups of Huron from Canada, Kickapoo from northern Mexico, Delaware from back east, Modocs from California, Seminoles from Florida, as well as a slew of mixed-blood French and African-American Indians. Acknowledging their common recreational pastimes and historical predicaments as Indians, this array of communities might join together in multitribal powwows, hand games, church services, peyote meetings, and political rallies. But separately most of them also perpetuated the private customs that preserved their specific tribal identities.

Anticipating statehood for Indian Territory, some 182 Indian representatives even held a constitutional convention that lobbied for an all-Indian "State of Sequoyah," named after the Cherokee polymath who'd invented the tribe's own syllabary (in which its Cherokee-language newspaper, begun in 1828, was still published). When that didn't pan out, in 1907 the new state's name still affirmed the region's Indian soul—"Red People," or *Okla Homa* in the Choctaw tongue.

By resettling in Tulsa, Wolf Robe had landed near the intersection of Osage, Cherokee, and Creek tribal lands. The trading posts, county fairs, and Indian "doings" of the Tulsa–Oklahoma City axis attracted Indian dancers, traders, artists, and travelers from across the region. But as with many Indians from elsewhere, this was not foreign country to him. Most Indians anywhere knew some other Indians from Oklahoma. That female cousin of the Hunts', for instance, had married her schoolmate from the notable Hamilton family of the oil-rich Osage tribe from around Pawhuska, just north of Tulsa. Their own apprenticeship under the Miller Brothers 101 Ranch in nearby Marland, onetime Ponca Indian territory, had introduced them to the state's tribal mosaic nearly ten years earlier.

Wolf Robe left the middle Rio Grande, where sophisticated white patrons, elite academics, and a rowdy array of transplanted bohemians patronized their favorite Pueblo tribes and promoted their handpicked native artisans. Now he found himself in a more relaxed environment along the Verdigris River where newly rich oil barons and local Indian politicos ran things. The social prestige that Santa Fe's arts practitioners and patrons felt was their due by birth, education, talent, or old money, these self-made tycoons, like Waite Phillips and Thomas Gilcrease, believed they could buy.

Tulsa may have been as surrounded by archaeological sites just as rich and old as any around the Rio Grande. But its numerous pre-Columbian temple mounds, ceremonial plazas, and artistic treasures were hidden under slumping grassy hills and innocuous pastures. For exciting tourist imaginations they couldn't vie with the sandstone ruins and photogenic canyons of Mesa Verde, Chaco, or Acoma. Beneath the surface, however, Oklahoma extended a warmer welcome. Its atmosphere may have been clammier and folksier than the Southwest, but Wolf Robe probably found its cultural climate freer and even something of a relief.

After they returned from Europe and became self-employed, the Hunt family's success and survival would have been impossible without affordable automobiles and the road system they spawned. As the open prairie

Wolf Robe Hunt and brother-in-law Hugh Davis finishing their newest trading post off Route 66 in Catoosa, Oklahoma.

transformed into the open road, cars allowed these outcast Puebloans to release the inner Plains nomadic spirits their stage personae had perfected. White photographers would mock the apparent incongruity between early automobiles and the Indians they'd conquered, like Geronimo in a top hat, whom they posed behind the wheel, or jammed together, all feathers and buckskins, in a convertible's backseat. But why shouldn't Indians respond to this new freedom of movement, shiny chrome and growling power, the wind in the hair and cuddling in the backseat, any less than anyone else?

No one's love affair with Detroit rivaled that of the First Americans, and highway tourism responded in kind. Product trademarks and Indian motifs would proliferate throughout car culture: makes of cars like Pontiac, logos for gasoline empires like Standard Oil, and designs for motel courts with cement stucco tipis. As cultural critic Philip Deloria was first to underscore, in songs, stories, and cultural practices Indians created amusing ways of making gas-driven vehicles intrinsic to their half-modern lives. Whether they were buying them, trading them, singing about them, fixing, crashing, or trashing them, cars intensified the pan-Indian web of family, community, and intertribal communications. Along with linking together the nation, automobiles only enhanced the frolic, passion, and pride of being Indian in America.

At Indian school Wilbert had learned to drive and fix trucks. He was spellbound when his future father-in-law picked up his mail-order boxes at the McCartys train stop and hand-assembled his first vehicle. All the Hunts envied their Osage in-law, Amos Hamilton, when his large family drove from Oklahoma every summer for the Acoma feast day or the Albuquerque fair.

One would think that professionalizing his skills as an army motor mechanic in World War II would have given Wilbert his fill of gasoline engines. But what he would miss most while overseas was singing "You Are My Sunshine" with his wife as they drove the road from Albuquerque to Laguna Feast Day, and car-camping with her during August's Gallup Inter-Tribal Ceremonial, where they slept in a pup tent alongside their protective old Chevy. Nearly every month he gently badgered her from Germany to see whether she'd checked the baldness of the tires or changed the oil. Since the family's return from Germany in 1928, none of them were without their wheels. Almost overnight, cars became America's great equalizer. No longer leery of high railroad fares and fixed rails, middle-class citizens could speed between Oklahoma and New Mexico and points farther west. Even though, as New Mexican Indians, they were still not permitted to vote, the Hunts relied on the fast-expanding road network more than most of their franchised fellow Americans.

Cars also allowed Wolf Robe to hop from the commercial crossroads of Albuquerque–Santa Fe to its strongest competitor for Indian trade in the nation. His new store in downtown Tulsa counted on tourist traffic along Route 66, just as would Clyde Hunt's curio shop in downtown Albuquerque. Out-of-towners booked into Wolf Robe's Grotto Motel nearby, just as they would into Wilbert and Vedna's Lazy-H Motel, also facing Albuquerque's Route 66, in the postwar period. That same artery took their own cars every weekend to visit relatives in Laguna Pueblo, Acomita, and McCartys, to the summer ceremonial in Gallup, and carried their California relatives to them during the summer and fall fiestas. In their eyes, they pretty much owned this road.

◆ ◆ ◆

Keeping family ties.
Back row: *Wilbert*
Hunt's in-laws,
Grandpa and
Grandma Eckerman;
Wilbert Hunt;
unknown; Edward
Hunt; Vedna Hunt.

Few were as commercially imaginative about the transcontinental highway's possibilities as the family into which Wolf Robe had married. By age twenty-seven, Glenal's brother, Hugh Davis, was a local celebrity. Born in Kansas, two years after graduating from a Tulsa high school in 1928 he became director of Tulsa's Mohawk Park zoo. Fearless, fun-loving, handy with tools, a good photographer and lifelong booster of Boy Scouting, Davis didn't let his curatorial responsibilities stifle his zest for adventure. As photographer and cinematographer he joined one of Osa and Martin Johnson's last African safaris, traveled to Burma to capture animals for his zoo, and in 1938 married Zelta, who shared his passion for animals, especially reptiles.

By moving to Tulsa, Wolf Robe had extended his family's commercial reach eastward. Barely ten years in operation, Route 66, known here as the Will Rogers Highway after the legendary part-Cherokee Indian humorist, ran right by Wolf Robe and Glenal's front door downtown. Once moved into their apartment, he and Glenal wasted no time resuming their hectic performing schedule.

He renamed their troupe Indians of the Greater Southwest and added Glenal, dressed in her "Indian Princess" outfit. They continued touring throughout the 1930s and into the 1940s. To replace Ray Silvertongue, who'd sometimes worked at Charlie Eagle Plume's trading post in Estes Park, Colorado, before he got married, they recruited a handsome performer from Taos Pueblo, Teles Medicine Star. And Wolf Robe could always count on brother Wilbert "Blue Sky Eagle" to hop over from Albuquerque to join them, usually hauling Dad and Mother Hunt as well.

Constantly updating their contact lists, they advance-mailed handbills advertising their shows and headlined with endorsements from the Smithsonian Institution, the U.S. Indian Bureau, and the Boy Scouts of America. As they tacked between Scout troops and school auditoriums, their file of recommendation letters expanded, their itineraries intensified. Ten dollars' pay and a boardinghouse here, fifteen dollars and a spare room there, they took what the traffic would bear and danced hard for it.

Wherever they found themselves, Wolf Robe, Blue Sky, and a changing cast of accompanying Indian performers remained available whenever locals wanted authentic Indians in full regalia for mounting the nationally popular *Song of Hiawatha* play, a Thanksgiving pageant, or to provide the mandatory Indian seal of approval when a new public building, movie theater, or department store was opening, a visiting dignitary was being honored, or the annual Gallup Inter-Tribal Ceremonial was under way. They had no qualms about serving as Indian symbols on call.

51

Wilbert's War (1942–45)

Men of all ages, from every state, in all parts of the world, standing around at "Mail Calls." I've seen them, including myself, standing in snow at 40 below, in knee-deep mud, in rain, at all hours of the day and night, waiting for our names to be called, each man's face a study for any artist. The frankly eager ones who usually edge their way to the front of the group and hungrily eye each letter as it is passed out. The more reserved ones who stand idly about the edge of the crowd trying to appear not too anxious, yet each man's ears strained to catch the words of the voice of the mail orderly. The young P.F.C. who stood with me barely within earshot one evening, told me that he hadn't heard from his wife for over a month. Praying that he will hear his name soon but afraid that he will.

—Wilbert Hunt to Vedna Hunt, May 23, 1943

A s soon as his parents learned that Wilbert, their youngest son, was heading for war, they took him into the backyard. His father held his old Bible. They bowed their heads and prayed for his safety. Then Edward pulled from his pocket a buckskin pouch. Hanging from it was a scallop shell, inside was red war paint, a stone arrowhead, baby eagle claws, and cowrie shells. Acoma warriors carried this for protection, Edward said. Keep it with you, and Wilbert did.

Even without America's call-up after December 7, 1941, when Japan attacked Pearl Harbor, Wilbert's days of nonstop touring as Blue Sky Eagle were winding down. Happily married, he and Vedna were settling into domestic life in Albuquerque. She liked her stable job as a Bureau of Indian Affairs clerk in the Federal Building. Meanwhile, Wilbert made the occasional dance appearance, crafted jewelry, drove for a long-distance car delivery outfit, and kept his options open. He was resourceful and something usually opened up.

Then everyone's world turned upside down. Concerned for his aging parents, Wilbert delayed heading to the Santa Fe recruiting office until early June 1942. The magnitude of the German threat was inescapable: Nazism reigned from Crete to the Arctic, the Black Sea to the Atlantic. A few months after the Hunts' departure from Germany thirteen years before, a rally by Hitler's National Socialist Party filled Dresden's Sarrasani amphitheater where Wilbert had been riding horses and war-whooping.

A day after signing up, Wilbert found himself in Fort Bliss, wearing a winter uniform beneath a blistering Texas sky. A two-day train ride took him to basic training at Fort Warren, Wyoming, under a freak snowfall. At Albuquerque Indian School he'd been militarized; for the next four years he again lived at the mercy of superiors. "I'm in the army now," he wrote Vedna. "I shall be brave and do everything that is expected of me in the service of our country, our homes and loved ones like you, my angel."

He got typhoid shots, chose an upper bunk, hiked, drilled, attended lectures, wept under tear gas, trained as a heavy vehicle mechanic. He learned clutches, brakes, carburetors, steering mechanisms, and map reading, and joined long-distance truck convoys. In off-hours he began his nightly habit of writing letters to Vedna, his parents, her parents, Clyde and Estelle, Wolf Robe and Glenal, and other family members in fine cursive, rarely missing a day. He enjoyed a trip to Cheyenne Frontier Days,

Wilbert Hunt signed up, then Alfred Hunt joined to protect his little brother, but never found him.

read every *Albuquerque Tribune* sent by his wife, and finally had a brief furlough with her in September.

In mid-November, after rumors flying "thick and fast like this dust," he was relocated to the country's "best training ground," as its famous overlord, General George S. Patton Jr., liked to boast.

Although Indian Commissioner John Collier successfully opposed the formation of Indian-only units, as urged by segregationist generals, he was unprepared for the massive turnout of native volunteers. That might have been expected from warrior tribes, like the Crow of Montana. But even in the pueblos, where pockets of pacifism or antigovernment resentment held firm, forty-five hundred Indians registered within the war's first three months.

Wilbert had joined an estimated 44,500 American Indians who enlisted in every theater of the war. They represented over 10 percent of the country's native population; nearly 20 percent if one adds Indians in the homeland defense industry. About 99 percent of eligible Indian males registered; among some tribes 70 percent of their men were in uniform. With his off-reservation Albuquerque address, however, Wilbert was not counted among the fourth of all the Pueblo men between the ages of twenty and fifty in service or the sixty soldiers from Acoma. He became a solitary speck in a global storm.

After the war, some asked why a people who once were being wiped out by their government were ready to die for it. A doughboy in the previous war, Alex Cadotta, gave the answer Indians repeated again and again: "Because I wanted to hold up my flag which we and every one of us love so much. All that was in me was to save my Country for democracy, and I am a true American." A half century later, Cheyenne Indian and Korean war vet Ben Nighthorse Campbell reiterated: "We are proud of our military heritage and our country and, like our fellow native brothers and sisters in uniform, we will always be in the front ranks when our nation needs us, which is only right since we are the 'first' Americans."

Equally patriotic was the Indian home front. An estimated forty-six thousand tribesmen, like Wilbert's brother Allen, left home to build ships, manufacture airplanes, repair trucks, and crank up farm and ranch production. Indian women sold war bonds, organized air raid units, and served in the Red Cross, and a few hundred were in uniform as WACS and WAVES. From July 1942 until January 1943, one native group, the All Soldier Indian Dance Show, composed of Kiowa and Cochiti performers from the 45th Infantry Division, took thirty crates of dance regalia across Europe, entertaining troops and locals abroad and then selling war bonds and war savings back home.

At Desert Training Center, near Indio, California, whose eighteen thousand square miles made it the largest training facility in military history,

Wilbert ready to ship out, but rarely told where.

Wilbert joined Patton's armored divisions readying for tank battles across Libya, Tunisia, and Morocco. Of desert life they got a rich dose: flourlike dust infiltrated teeth, bedrolls, tents, and M-1 rifles, while temperatures reached 130 degrees at noon (inside a Sherman tank they rose to 180 degrees). An advocate for saber-slashing horsemen only fifteen years before, Patton underwent a conversion after witnessing the speed and agility of mechanized cavalry. Wilbert remembered him as a foulmouthed taskmaster. "Kill all the sons-of-bitches," Patton exhorted, "rape their women, skin them alive." Respected but despised, he sought to instill "magnificent hate" against the "dirty Nazi bastards." About proper maintenance of his tanks, trucks, and support vehicles, he was a fanatic.

Wilbert was shocked at the incessant hectoring; he felt that wasn't the best way to motivate young men. Yet when superiors noticed his ease with military discipline, internalized at Albuquerque Indian School, they assigned him as a drill instructor. While complying, he refused to adopt scare tactics. In a low, steady voice he explained, demonstrated, and won loyalty. In later years the family's "legendary memory" headlined Wilbert's role in D-Day and the Bulge, neither of which he thankfully ever saw. But Patton probably did sit in his barber's chair before the outfit left for North Africa.

Instead of his joining Patton's Operation Torch, however, the whims of military decision-making surprised PFC Hunt yet again. In mid-January 1943, Wilbert exchanged the triple-digit heat of Southern California for another hush-hush assignment, to the 45-degree-below-zero atmosphere of northern Alaska. To transport emergency troops and supplies from the United States to Alaska, a seventeen-hundred-mile transcontinental roadway, the Alcan Highway, had just been patched together. From Dawson Creek in British Columbia it wound over boggy, rocky, often precipitous and frozen terrain to Delta Junction, Alaska. Due to fear of possible Japanese attacks through the Aleutians, American troops were to protect its unpaved sections, log bridges, and jarring corduroy-road connections. Every time they relocated, they were ordered to burn whatever they left behind.

In all his postings, Wilbert was a good soldier who did his duty. He kept his hair short, uniforms clean, bunk and trunk trim. He smiled uncomplainingly when addressed as "chief" or "Geronimo." He wore fur-trimmed winter coats and slept in Arctic-tested sleeping bags, cleaned thousands of pots and pans, performed thousands of off-hours haircuts at thirty-five cents a head, read Willa Cather's *Death Comes for the Archbishop* with its evocations of home, hummed Indian chants or church hymns to himself while marveling at the Northern Lights during nightlong guard duty. He endured forced marches, regularly attended chapel, drank only the occasional beer, and took in a movie on off-days. He was buddies with Frankie, a Chinese from Grass Valley, California, and other fellow soldiers until one day the arbitrariness of upper-echelon planning meant that suddenly they weren't there anymore. Throughout the war he received hundreds of letters and care packages from parents and brothers and sisters and responded in kind. Especially he wrote Vedna, often twice a week, paying off their mortgage in small checks, effusively thanking her for visiting his parents, commiserating on illnesses of relatives and friends, recalling their first kiss, their picking piñons together, and their family reunions during the Laguna, Acoma, and Gallup celebrations. Every one of his more than 350 neatly handwritten love letters ended with the phrase "your husband and pal."

Not until July 1943 did he leave the far north, for a Tennessee post where training got serious. Wilbert stuck bayonets into dummies, threw hand grenades, earned a marksman's ribbon, crawled between land mines and under barbed wire, took all-day full-pack hikes. Finally, in November, he alerted Vedna of a news blackout. Next she heard, six months after D-Day her husband found himself "somewhere in England." He had crossed the Atlantic on the *Ile de France,* zigzagging to avoid U-boats and their torpedoes, and now was sleeping on a straw mattress in a castle near Liverpool and visiting Stonehenge. Then he sailed to France, enduring the sea-sickening landing in a Higgins boat.

His Arctic detour had deprived Wilbert of joining Patton's tank duels against Field Marshal Rommel in North Africa, and the subsequent fight against the Italian Fascist leader the Navajos called "Gourd Chin." Instead, he was soon also playing catch-up on the campaign against the German mastermind the Navajos knew as "Mustache Smeller." Based on his personal experiences, Wilbert told his buddies of the pedestal on which Germans put Indians—especially the Sioux. So deeply had their warlike image penetrated German popular culture that even Wilbert didn't fully appreciate its impact. On the one hand some German soldiers trembled at the prospect of screaming warriors wielding scalp knives; on the other,

Wilbert Hunt with German children in Bremerhaven at war's end. Some of their parents had seen him dance fifteen years earlier.

through the personal edict by the Karl May fan Adolf Hitler, who distributed thousands of the author's books to his troops, that tribe was not only admired, it was of Aryan stock. From the standpoint of this particular Pueblo Indian, having your enemy *already* afraid of you meant that, once again, it paid to be considered a Sioux Indian in Germany.

Returning to Europe caused another cramp in his heart. Fond memories rushed back. But in the heat of a world war, where black was black and white was white, it was best to keep to himself his distress at the crushed remains of remembered German cathedrals, once-walked bridges, and demolished town squares, not to mention the begging children and their emaciated mothers; few fathers were left around. "The leaves on broken limbs of trees were still fresh and green," he wrote his wife, "for it was only thirteen days that the fighting came to an end, as though a terrible storm had swept through." More than once he knelt down in the rubble and wept.

Always located just behind advancing troops, he repaired trucks, tanks, and ambulances from France to Belgium to Holland and into Germany. But somewhere in there the war caught up with him. A sniper hung behind and sent a bullet through the soft tissue of his left thigh. Laid up for only a week, he was soon in Bremerhaven watching Allied bombers blow its German submarine pens to bits. Finally, in Antwerp, Belgium, he boarded a small freighter called *Lord Delaware* with twenty fellow soldiers. Out of the English Channel they ran into a gale. Some days they made less than thirty miles. It took nearly three weeks to reach Philadel-

phia. They rode in Pullman cars to Texas, reaching it three days after the
V-E Day celebrations. He was safe.

Wilbert Hunt mustered out in mid-November 1945 at Fort Bliss. He was
among the 21,767 Indians still in the U.S. Army; 550 Indians had died for
their country, five received the Medal of Honor. When he and Vedna finally saw each other they embraced, then held hands and cried. "No group
that participated in World War II made a greater per capita contribution,"
wrote official army historian Thomas D. Morgan, "and no group was
changed more by the war."

In Wilbert's duffel bag were a few souvenirs. The Pueblo people were
never considered "warrior" tribesmen, but in the old days they did defend
their homes and take scalps. Unlike Plains Indian practice, such deeds in-
curred an obligation, as Wolf Robe Hunt explained to a Smithsonian Institution historian. One of the extended Hunt family's older veterans did
return with a German scalp. "Taking a scalp carried responsibilities with
it," Wolf Robe said. "The spirit of the person who had been scalped will
always be hovering around. He had to feed it cornmeal and say the proper
prayers so the spirit of the scalp owner did not harm him."

Wilbert brought home the fresh scar on his leg. From his Eisenhower
jacket hung ribbons for the American and European theaters, good conduct, marksmanship, and the Allied victory. He had some German Iron
Cross medals and a Nazi flag. Still intact was his barber's kit, and a tuft of
Patton's hair—perhaps a scalp of sorts.

For the man with the reedy voice still haunted him. Patton's bloodlust
clashed with the terrible parts of the war he did see. From France onward
those final weeks became a tormenting blur of mopping dried blood and
splattered brains and body parts from twisted vehicles. Once, when questioned why he couldn't recall the sequence of his final days through Europe, Wilbert shot up from his chair, arms shaking, fists clenched, tears
running. "Patton yelled at us, again and again. Kill, kill, kill those German
bastards," he said. "My people always told me, about everything, plants,
animals, human beings—live, live, live. What was I supposed to do?" He
threw out his hands, fell into his chair, and stopped talking for the day.

What Place for Indians? (1945–50)

In stimulating traditionalism and acculturation the war provided the frame-work for most of the major issues that concerned the Indian community for the next forty years. And in raising the hopes and aspirations of Indian peoples it set a new agenda for Indian programs in the twentieth century—for economic betterment, for access to education, for social mobility, for civil rights, for racial consciousness and a distinct identity, and for racial pride.

—Gerald D. Nash, 1985

S OON AFTER WILBERT got home his parents took one look at him and knew what to do. There was no denying the strained face and weakened presence. Anxious as he was to stick around his house, they drove him up Acoma mesa and turned him over to the medicine men. He was kept in the kivas and they did what they did. In most pueblos other veterans were undergoing similar purifications and exorcisms; the same went for Navajo vets sung over by masked *Ye* spirits during their nine-day Beautyway ceremony and Apache soldiers treated by their *Gans,* or Crown Dancers. Their traditions had taught them how to treat tormenting memories and critical transitions with care.

Wilbert never described their work on him. "They had Katsina dances," was all a Zuni veteran would disclose of his reentry, "and make us forget the situation we had been in." One imagines Wilbert's entailed days and nights in darkened chambers, praying with corn-husk-rolled cigarettes, chanting amid cedar smoke and incense, perhaps the ritual tending and feeding of old Navajo scalps, and other practices that would help put behind him fearful images or spirits of dead Germans and return him to normal life.

But a longer-lasting kind of postwar pollution worried pueblo elders. These veterans returned worldly wise, with Anglo buddies, accustomed to drinking, meeting foreign women, exposed to weekly Christian services, impatient with the pace of village life, aware of national politics, interested in foreign affairs, unafraid to enter white towns, ready for wider job opportunities, and demanding their rightful place as voting citizens of the country for which many of their comrades had fought and died.

Besides that, Wilbert had returned to a nation in flux. Even before the war ended, three events signaled a sea change in Indian affairs. One was noted by his father with some relief. Edward never approved of John Collier's promotion of old Indian ways. In January 1945, after one of the most radical tenures in American political history, in which a leftist, poetic visionary became part of the U.S. government's inner circle, Collier resigned as commissioner of Indian affairs. Not surprisingly, his departure was shortly followed by yet another about-face in Indian policy.

Marie Hunt in her garden at "the ranch," Alameda, in north Albuquerque.

Rather than enhancing the Indians' cultural importance and strengthening their legal status as semisovereign peoples to whom the U.S. government still owed treaty obligations, an anti–New Deal Congress wanted "out of the Indian business." This tougher incarnation of the nineteenth-century assimilation campaign sought to "free" Indians from federal controls, terminate "special relationships" between tribes and federal government, and encourage rural Indian families to relocate in cities.

But the third development in Indian affairs, one of the enduring by-products of Collier's regime, stood in opposition to this threat. Composed of the young native politicians whom his Indian Reorganization Act had groomed across Indian country, the National Congress of American Indians (NCAI) was formed in the fall of 1944. Many of its members shared a special bond as returned veterans. As their lobbying expanded and connected with other native groups, the menace of termination met its match.

Back in Albuquerque, Wilbert also found himself in a city on the make. Its economic upswing after the war was spurred by the transformation of wartime production into peacetime industry, especially around the Sandia laboratories on the city's east side. Between 1946 and 1950 Albuquerque's municipal footprint tripled, her population more than doubled, new housing was going up everywhere, and tourists returned to curio shops and Indian pueblos. To capitalize, he and Vedna soon opened their Lazy-H Motel on Central Avenue, now a commercial section of Route 66.

Postwar recovery was slower in Oklahoma, but thanks to his new family network, Wolf Robe began diversifying his operation. Just as Edward Hunt had a brother-in-law—the Jewish storekeeper Solomon Bibo—who supported his entrepreneurial tendencies, Wolf Robe took commercial inspiration from his in-laws. Especially encouraging was his brother-in-law Hugh Davis, who introduced him to Tulsa's business community, with its lodges, fraternities, and connections.

Shortly after renting their first apartment, Wolf Robe and Glenal turned it into a retail outlet stocked with Indian "curios" they'd carted over from New Mexico. First they handled silverwork and ceramics from out of Clyde's storefront in Albuquerque. With the Depression and World War II behind them, Americans could stretch their wings. Initially the

Wolf Robes also tried to maintain a touring itinerary. Their efficient packaging of dances and lectures for Indian Lore enthusiasts continued to find venues for Boy Scout groups, grade school assemblies, and intensive summer camp sessions throughout the 1930s and early '40s.

But before long the uptick in tourist traffic and personal spending money encouraged the Wolf Robes to scale back their bookings and invest more money and time around Tulsa. They borrowed $60 and rented a storefront in the Spanish Colonial–style building owned by Skelly Oil at the corner of Harvard and 11th. Wolf Robe had become one of the select Indians in the country to run his own shop. With his brother-in-law's help, he installed Hugh's handcrafted glassed showcases with their Indian tipi and sunburst symbols and ranch brands burnt into massive, thickly varnished, knotty pine frames. Named the Chief Wolf Robe Indian Trading Post, his establishment was soon a drawing card for local Indian artists, Indian buffs, Boy Scouts, and tourists. Even more genial and verbally adept than his dad, Wolf Robe was tailor-made for storekeeping, with his equally entrepreneurial wife, Glenal, a full partner.

In their store one could find Pueblo and Navajo silverwork, Osage beadwork, and ceramics from Acoma and Laguna. Wolf Robe also catered to local native craftsmen who needed buckskins, ribbons, beads, feathers, claws, and laces for making powwow and ritual regalia. Before long he added a mail-order service for Indian hobbyists, Boy Scouts, and Order of the Arrow members farther afield.

Wolf Robe continued to branch out, splintering his public persona. With Hugh's and Glenal's encouragement he expanded his role as wise elder and Indian Lore expert and copied the outreach of popularizers of native wisdom like Charles Eastman, Ernest T. Seton, and W. Ben Hunt. Inspired by pieces on Indian topics in *Boys' Life,* over 1937–38 he tried out a weekly column for the *Tulsa Daily World.* Under the byline "A Wild Injun" he wrote gentle, amusing pieces about Indian craft and culture in the manufactured Indian English dialect that other Oklahoma Indian writers sometimes affected. One miniseries on archery went through selections of woods, carving of bows and arrows, and their use. Another described making fire by the old-fashioned friction method. His accounts of rabbit hunting and the use of prayer sticks were derivative of his Acoma upbringing, yet he greeted his readers with a Navajo welcome, "Ya-Tah-Hey."

In fact, Wolf Robe was often vague about exactly which tribal tradition was being conveyed. With Glenal's help, he spent long nights on these assignments. For material he drew from their reading and research, his mother's and father's stories, and what relatives told him. This confronted him with the abiding dilemma of his family's unique position—was he communicating specific Acoma tribal knowledge or blending traditions, personal memories, and book research so as to represent "Indian Life" as a generalized production?

As he ran out of generic topics, Wolf Robe came to rely more and more on his father's esoteric information from Acoma. This might have played with scholars like Elsie Clews Parsons, who complained about never getting enough secrets from Edward. But it probably bored or confused regular readers who wanted more stereotypical information about Indians. The column only lasted a year.

One place where Wolf Robe and the whole Hunt family were royally in their element was Gallup, New Mexico. Due to their troubles before Europe, then their time abroad, their participation in that town's Inter-Tribal Indian Ceremonial, one of the Southwest's most controversial blends of the traditional, stereotypical, and commercial, came late. If the Hunts couldn't be Acoma Indians again, they wouldn't miss any opportunity to project their idealized kind of Everything Indian. During four days every summer, Gallup became the perfect place for that. After 1930, the Hunts turned the occasion into an annual family reunion.

The town began as a key watering hole on the Southwest's main route to California. Gallup's prime position on this wagon trail, then roadway, then railway, and finally Route 66, foreordained her commercial success. In the 1870s it gained notoriety as the Blue Goose stagecoach stop, store, and saloon. Twenty years later it boasted a railroad depot with a paymaster, David L. Gallup, and took his name. Alongside the tracks a "colony" of Laguna and Acoma Indian railroad hands occupied their boxcar village. By the 1930s its sidings were jammed with coal cars that Italian and Welsh miners were filling and sending off. In western New Mexico Gallup became the place for gassing up, spending the night, buying jewelry, making money, and raising hell.

A cultural crossroads, her streets featured rows of noisy bars, dance halls, trading post–pawnshops, brothels serving miners and cowboys, and buckboards full of Zunis, Navajos, Apaches, and Acomas bringing pottery and jewelry to sell to train passengers and car tourists. By 1923 two of the Fred Harvey hotel operations were open for business. To exploit its proximity to Indians and tourists, a former Santa Fe Railroad employee and local Indian trader named Mike Kirk had already won railway and hotel backing for an Inter-Tribal Indian Ceremonial. The idea was to channel this multicultural and mercantile energy for an annual event that would "preserve the purity and integrity of native customs and culture . . . through staging of an annual Ceremonial."

With its merchants agreeing on a half-day holiday, Gallup townsfolk pitched in to fix up the fairgrounds. The Ceremonial opened in August 1922. For the first night's Navajo Fire dances, a ring of car headlights illuminated the dusty arena. In these early years the event was by Indians and largely for Indians and great fun was had. Amid racing horses and bucking broncs were goofier competitions—backwards sack runs, tugs-of-war between women teams, apple-bobbing contests, chicken pulls, and footraces.

By the late 1920s the Inter-Tribal's popularity had grown and commercialism crept in. Extended to three days, the Ceremonial offered cash prizes for competition winners in arts and crafts and agricultural products. Short programs provided cultural background on the participant tribes. Each day began with a parade, then afternoon sports. Soon the sales booths stood shoulder to shoulder in one big exhibit hall; they displayed arts and crafts along with goods made by Indian boarding school students. Kirk was a master marketer; word got around and more tourists showed up.

Joining the fun at Gallup around 1932 or so, the Hunts made up for lost time and rarely missed a year. For each of the Inter-Tribal's mornings a river of Indians in full regalia, every tribal contingent bunched together and, waving their identifying placards, marched through downtown. Like war-bonneted potentates on horseback, the Hunts led each day's parade.

In Edward's hand was the Sun Boy standard, a sacred symbol used in plaza dances that he had somehow recreated and whose origins went back to the time of Keresan creation. A cluster of green parrot feathers fluttered atop its gourdlike "head," while eagle-tail feathers dangled from the long rectangular embroidered cloth banner affixed to its long pole. Astride his prancing large paint, with his multitribal outfit, regal bearing, and Sun Boy staff held aloft like a flag of state, he was a natural figurehead.

After many lives: Edward Hunt nears the end, 1948.

At Gallup the dispersed Hunt family caught up with each other, camped together, and posed for photographers on the site's famous red rocks. Soon their likenesses were appearing on Ceremonial publicity, local postcards, and Gallup restaurant menus. Although rarely acknowledged by name, the Hunts became the family faces of the largest gathering of Indians in the Southwest.

In early 1944, when Wilbert was still on duty in Alaska, he learned that his parents had decided to sell their ten acres in Alameda, north of Albuquerque. Much as Edward and Marie prized their independence and loved their garden, they weren't getting any younger. In April they found a smaller place near daughter Josephine and her husband, Johnny, both of whom were hammering and stamping at workbenches for Maisel's, the famous Indian jewelry shop on Central with its flamboyant Pueblo-Deco façade. Aside from government offices, it was one of the few places where Indians found steady work in those days.

From Edward's old Albuquerque school the older Hunts leased a little land to renew their garden. Always grateful for the trickle of dollars provided by their children, they reciprocated with melons from their latest crop.

In early 1948, Edward began having trouble keeping down food. His weight loss was rapid. Diagnosed with stomach cancer, he was given a short time to live. One last photo shows the old man with hollowed cheeks decked out in his tribal best. He was gone within a few weeks—on Thursday night, February 12, 1948, in his bed at home.

After all Edward Hunt had endured to become the self-reliant, Christianized, culturally progressive, and kindly citizen that whites had wanted, it was a pity he didn't live another six months. That was when the impact of the sacrifices made by veterans like his son Wilbert bore fruit.

It took a brave government school teacher, an ex-marine and member of Isleta Pueblo, to make the move. That spring Miguel J. Trujillo went to Las Lunas to register to vote. As an untaxed Indian, he was turned away, and his attorneys, the famed Indian law expert Felix S. Cohen among them, promptly took Valencia County to court.

On August 3, 1948, a three-judge panel declared the ban unconstitutional. After thirty-six years of statehood, New Mexico was required by law to give all its Indians full franchise. In peevish retaliation for his activism, the Bureau of Indian Affairs relocated Trujillo from his home state to Salt Lake City, Utah, where he taught until his retirement.

If anyone deserved to know he finally enjoyed the full rights of American citizenship, especially this franchise, it was Edward Proctor Hunt.

53

Legacy of a Narrative (1948–70)

I can hardly describe my emotion at this find. That these sacrosanct volumes, representing most of what will remain known about the American Indian, could actually be bought and privately owned was something I had never dreamed of. To my mind they belonged rather to the same irredeemable past as the beliefs and customs of which they spoke. It was as if the civilization of the American Indian had suddenly come alive through the physical contact that these contemporary books established between me and their time.

—Claude Lévi-Strauss, 1966

ONE MORNING IN 1943 an item in the Tulsa newspaper caught Wolf Robe's eye. Just published by the Smithsonian Institution was a creation story from Acoma Pueblo under the byline of Matthew W. Stirling. Over the previous fifteen years no one thought to update the Hunts on where their old storytelling lay in the government's pipeline toward publication. This had to be his dad's account, the same one he'd translated day after day in Washington. Such was par for research in those days. After they'd delivered the cultural goods, Indians rarely heard from their white collaborators or saw any publications that resulted.

So Wolf Robe contacted his old friend, Smithsonian linguist John Peabody Harrington. Could he have copies for himself, his parents, who were quietly gardening outside Albuquerque, and "my younger brother Blue Sky Eagle Wilbert, who is with the army somewhere"?

Some years later, unaware that Edward had died in the meantime, Harrington contacted Wolf Robe. For his part, Wolf Robe did not know that in yet another book the family was never told about, famous photographer Edward S. Curtis in 1926 had publically named Edward Hunt as "the only Pueblo informant with whom it was not necessary to work in seclusion and under a pledge of secrecy." Responding to Harrington, Wolf Robe still hoped no one would reveal his family's assistance at the Smithsonian. "As for myself," Henry wrote, "I am away from home, and have been for a number of years, although I visit each year." And then he added, "Of course we know no one can hurt Dad now."

When the *Origin Myth of Acoma and Other Records* appeared in December 1942, printed on cheap paper in an obscure government bulletin with a drab gray cover and a thirty-five-hundred-copy press run amid the tumult of a world war, it is little surprise that it fell between the cracks. So few knew of its existence that one of its own editors had to write its first

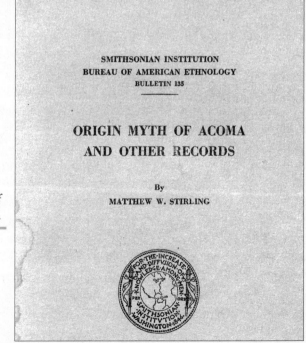

Finally, in 1942, Edward's book of genesis appeared.

review: "It enables us," said Leslie White in the *Journal of American Folk-lore*, "to see custom, ritual and paraphernalia in the perspective of the Indians' own philosophy."

As it happened, anthropologists like Parsons and White, the Smithsonian Institution scholars, and photographer Edward Curtis were not the only outsiders pursuing ancient myths about Acoma from inside sources. Unknown to the Hunts, over the thirteen years that it took to ready Edward's narrative for publication, a rival project to compile a mammoth document on Acoma's religious heritage started around the same time that Edward began working with the Smithsonian.

The instigator was a middle-aged, German-born building contractor from Pecos, New Mexico, named Bernhard Reuter. His first exposure to Acoma Pueblo was in 1923, when he was hired by Santa Fe architect John Gaw Meem to oversee yet another restoration of the pueblo's famous San Estevan Church. During its original construction in 1699 this big building pushed its organic materials beyond their normal limits; even mudding and chinking its thick walls and repairing its heavy roof every year would have been insufficient. Replastering their own homes and kivas took Acoma's residents time enough, subject as they were to the rhythms of summer rainfalls and seasonal ritual. Much as it had become a fixture and major tourist attraction on their mesa, Acoma's people retained mixed emotions about everything the gargantuan structure stood for. Now it was in disrepair again. Washed-out adobe plaster exposed dislodged stones underneath. Its bell towers were close to collapse, its convent melting under decades of monsoon rains.

In Germany the Indian-themed novels of Karl May had primed Reuter to make the most of his parents' move to Cheyenne and Arapaho country in western Oklahoma, and to his subsequent resettlement in New Mexico. This San Estevan restoration was not without the misunderstandings that often beset well-intentioned but Anglo-initiated projects among Pueblo Indians. But Reuter's successful results and rare compatibility with the Indians positioned him as a culture broker between Acoma and the outside world. This was a moment in the early twentieth century when the divide between passionate amateurs and academic professionals, especially in Santa Fe, was permeable. Equally smart and steeped in

Wolf Robe Hunt creates a stage set for a Boy Scout jamboree.

native culture, both groups could also be similarly territorial and mutually suspicious.

In 1927, Reuter became the point man for famed filmmaker Robert Flaherty in his doomed attempt to shoot one of his docudramas at Acoma. For the WPA he next distilled hundreds of pages on Acoma's stories and history for the state's first guidebook. In 1932, Meem named Reuter his go-between with the pueblo for the Historic American Buildings Survey documentation of the town. In gratitude, Reuter funneled carved ceiling beams and pintle doors from Acoma's antique church and convent into the architect's private stash for installation in Santa Fe's upper-crust homes.

Behind the scenes, with the aid of an old Acoma religious leader whom Reuter would only identify as Naic'ti'a, he began recording creation stories, songs, and ritual practices. The compilation was remarkably similar to what was being collected from Edward at the Smithsonian—verbal notes on origin myths, songs recorded on wax cylinders together with

English translation, and a portfolio of paintings of Acoma's pantheon of Katsinas by the elder's boarding-school-educated son.

Reuter's project sputtered along until 1935. He sought funds through Meem and a Santa Fe think tank, which loaned him an Ediphone recording machine and brought support from forty-three-year-old musicologist Helen H. Roberts and her contacts with the Rockefeller Foundation and Yale University. But as rumors about the project spread throughout the scholarly community, word of Reuter's "paranoid" temperament and "amateurish" approach grew worrisome. As in a southwestern preview of rivalries over the Dead Sea Scrolls, Reuter was said to have built an earthen dugout in Pecos where he was hoarding 473 wax recordings and a thousand-plus pages on Acoma myths, history, and songs.

Then Roberts went to Washington to size up the Hunt material for herself. Seeing its breadth, quality, and progress toward publication, she lost steam on the Reuter venture. Funds ran out and the fragmentary notes, incomplete translations, wax cylinders, and paintings wound up as one more archived treasure to await rediscovery.

Although it won that round, recognition for Edward's efforts still took years. First off, some of its songs that Franz Boas had reworked were incorporated into a 1957 publication by Frances Densmore, the sixty-two-year-old music scholar who was midway into her half-century association with the Smithsonian. Single-mindedly devoted to the "salvage ethnography" of preserving American Indian music, over her long career Densmore visited seventy-six tribes, collected 3,353 songs, and produced twenty books and over a hundred articles. Every publication had the songs and lyrics embedded within a cultural context.

Densmore had no mind for theory. But a second review of the published Hunt myth did allude to one conceptual debate of the day. Anthropologist Richard Long's short mention in a British scholarly journal emphasized that Hunt's "excellent" version "is not only an account of the origin of the people but is the authority for ritual practices, and the relevant parts of it are repeated before undertaking the performance of the rituals."

For over a century this chicken-and-egg question concerning Indian creativity carried on. Which came first, the myths that provided the divine sanction for the rituals to follow, or the rituals that may have been retroactively interpreted to validate the myths that came afterward? According to Clyde Kluckhohn, a famous scholar of Navajo lore, the two cultural expressions were so intertwined that responding to the issue depended on where one stood. From the position of a tribal member, clearly the Hunt version of Iatiku's mythic creation of the purification, healing, life-restoration, scalp, and "forgetting" rituals functioned as ceremonial scripts for her human children. But historians of religion, supported by whatever symbolic references might turn up in rock art or buried caches of ritual paraphernalia from the ancestral Acoma homeland of the Four Corners area, could argue that some rituals antedated their occurrence in Edward's narrative, and hence suggested the opposite.

As the 1960s and '70s unfolded, with their resurgence of popularity for Indian literature, arts, and political militancy, some editors and writers seeking understandings of Pueblo Indian life from the native perspective found Hunt's creation narrative compelling. The accessibility of its language, the clarity of its through-line from creation to migration that had dismayed earlier seekers of the esoteric, made it perfect for anthologies on Indian myth and religion. Without its narrator and translator ever identified, Edward and Wolf Robe's version became one of the most referenced of Pueblo texts. Teachers and scholars of Indian literature and southwestern

Brothers in silverwork: Clyde "Sunny Skies" and Henry Wolf Robe Hunt.

folklore taught and cited it. Archaeologists found its account of Pueblo migration useful. It helped land claims researchers nail down the geographical breadth of aboriginal Acoma territory.

One appropriation of Edward's story raised Pueblo hackles across the Southwest. Setting up his 1991 overview of three centuries of miscegenation, sexual mores, and class conflict in colonial New Mexico, the "new western historian" Ramón Gutiérrez chose Edward's account for his opening chapter's synthesis of Pueblo worldview. In his provocatively entitled, prizewinning *When Jesus Came, the Corn Mothers Went Away*, Gutiérrez described the rampant but instrumental sexuality of Pueblo women from a native culture in which "erotic behavior in its myriad forms (heterosexuality, homosexuality, bisexuality) knew no boundaries of sex or age." He claimed they used these energies as a means of establishing authority during the colonial period. For Pueblo Indian intellectuals Gutiérrez's imaginative interpretations were an intolerable invasion of privacy and a slap at the integrity of the one principle that held their societies together: descent through the female line (matrilineality) and residence in the wife's family's home (matrilocality). By impugning their women's sense of morality, venturing into the fraught and forbidden histories of Indian personal intimacies, and misrepresenting secret, sexually symbolic rituals for regenerating the earth and its vegetable and animal products, Gutiérrez had stepped over the line; the Corn Mothers were still around and talking back.

By the time of the Gutiérrez controversy, however, a deeper engagement with Edward's book had already come and gone. It began in the spring of 1941, when a thirty-three-year-old Jewish fugitive from Vichy France named Claude Lévi-Strauss escaped to New York City. Only recently returned from fieldwork among Indians of the Brazilian Mato Grosso, the young émigré was drawn to fellow bohemians and surrealistic artists in Greenwich Village and the used bookstores on lower Broadway with shelves bearing large green volumes with gold lettering published by the Smithsonian Institution's Bureau of American Ethnology. Years later Lévi-Strauss would affirm that this body of annual reports and occasional bulletins had "lost none of its glamour, and I still feel towards it an admiration and respect which are shared by innumerable scholars the world over." Though he was on a tight budget, he bought them by the armful.

So began one of the most academically influential immersions of modern times. As he read these texts late into the night, their plots and symbols, themes and personalities began to hold a seminar in Lévi-Strauss's mind. "For over the next twenty years," he recalled, "I would get up at dawn, drunk with myths—truly I lived in another world . . . with all these peoples and their myths, as if I were in a fairy tale."

Upon his return to postwar Paris, at his famous courses at the École pratique des hautes études, the now Professor Lévi-Strauss shared his passion and these readings with a generation of exceptional acolytes. Tribe by tribe, they were assigned to delve into the mythic narratives collected by Alice Fletcher among the Pawnee, James Dorsey among the Cheyenne, Francis La Flesche among the Omaha, Frank Cushing among the Zuni, Franz Boas among the Kwakiutl, among many others. How did their plots mirror, resist, or invert the kinship structures, environmental settings, subsistence practices, male-female relationships, and worldviews of the tribal peoples that held them dear? What kinds of contracts did they communicate between their human bearers and their notions of creation? How did their symbols work at a deep, structural level?

Among his students was a precocious eighteen-year-old named Lucien Sebag. In the 1960s the Tunis-born ethnographer conducted fieldwork among Indian groups in Bolivia and Paraguay. Then in 1964 he wrote a well-received text on Marxism and structural anthropology. His main application of Lévi-Strauss's method of myth analysis, however, grew out of a seminar assignment to dissect Keresan Pueblo creation narratives. Under Sebag's X-ray lens, the inner world of Edward Hunt's version of the Acoma creation story, with its proliferating twins, was laid bare.

Following a torturous love affair with fellow student Judith Lacan, stepdaughter of French psychoanalyst Jacques Lacan, Sebag committed suicide. Left on his desk was a book-length manuscript on Keresan creation stories; the handwritten document only lacked its title. When it was published posthumously in 1971, Lévi-Strauss himself supplied that: *The Invention of the World Among the Pueblo Indians*. Never translated into English, the 478-page structural analysis relied substantially on Hunt's narration. To Lévi-Strauss this myth was a prime example of the creativity of oral cultures that he would champion all his life.

"The day will come," Lévi-Strauss prophesied in 1966, when the last small-scale societies "will have disappeared from the earth, compelling us to realize that the fundamentals of mankind are irretrievably lost." And he added, in one of the cerebral master's rare bursts from the heart, "If ever we succeed in enlarging our narrow-minded humanism to include each and every expression of human nature, [and] thereby perhaps ensuring to mankind a more harmonious future, it is to undertakings such as those of the Bureau of American Ethnology that we shall owe it." Among the forty-eight annual reports and two hundred bulletins he was celebrating was this synthesis of the origin story of one of the world's tribal societies. Although it was published as the work of Matthew W. Stirling, its author was Edward Proctor Hunt.

54

Acoma and Its Inheritance (1920–70)

It was five years ago that my father served as War Chief. Our Governor asked me to collect [the fees] when the people come up to see Acoma. When they arrived they signed their name. White people pay, but the friends of the Indians just come in. The white people are very inquisitive; they keeping asking everything, about where we get our water and how the Acomas make a living. And where the children go to school, and if the government pays us. They ask all these questions. After they seen everything at Acoma, they buy pottery when they go down.

—Acoma tourist guide, c. 1956

I T TOOK THE PUEBLO of Acoma a lot longer than it had the Hunts to learn to market themselves to the wider world. When anthropologist Leslie White first climbed up the mesa to stroll the seemingly deserted village in 1926, that year's governor, Bautisto Rey, appeared out of nowhere to request the usual dollar. Nearly forty years later, when anthropologist Nan Smith was hired by the state of New Mexico to take stock of New

Mexico's tribes, the fee to walk around Acoma's windblown streets remained the same. "Yet here is Acoma, literally the Enchanted," wrote a frustrated tourism booster in 1915, "unlike anything else in the whole wide world. . . . Is it any wonder that Europeans live on the opportunities Americans throw away? If Acoma were in Germany, they would be diverting the Rhine round that way so you could see it by moonlight."

Unlike the Hunts, the pueblo would forever be in a bind about exploiting her commercial possibilities. Anxieties about outsider penetration ran as deep as the dark clefts in her rocky mesa. In the past Acoma had three ways of dealing with visitors. During Saint's Day and Christmas fiestas, they were categorized as guests, to be welcomed and even fed. When they showed up unannounced in twos, threes, and small groups, they were warily tolerated, but ignored if they were friends of a tribal member, especially an official, who was escorting them around. When the Katsinas made their biannual visitations, however, strangers became a dangerous, alien species, to be banned outright.

As the traffic in tourists increased, friends of the pueblo suggested that Acoma should upgrade their accommodations. This only intensified the pueblo's discomfort about attracting total strangers to their sanctuary in the first place, and their concerns over monitoring their movements once they got there. Even thinking about the prospect of more strangers milling about made some tribal leaders want to spread the protective label "sacred" around the limited mesa top, a process for expanding the zones where tourists must not go.

Also hampering any imaginative ideas for self-promotion were Acoma's modest expectations for what had traditionally been their subsistence economy. Turning their conservative village into the equivalent of a business enterprise was, at the time, still inconceivable. Adding to this resistance to self-exploitation was the pueblo's strong egalitarian and communal ethic, its closed system of compartmentalized knowledge that opened most of its tribal affairs to initiated members only, and the traditional function of the sacred old cacique, the pueblo's "mother," as custodian of any surplus—which he/she would stockpile for the indigent or times of scarcity. These self-protective attitudes and conservative practices undermined any gestures toward open markets, small-scale capitalism, and cultural promotion, be they ever so partial or hesitant.

◆ ◆ ◆

But the pueblo was not unfamiliar with the art of dealmaking. In the spring of 1928, when the Hunts were performing as between-act fillers on the vaudeville circuit, Acoma became the site for a duel between rival motion picture projects. Situated on its wide sandstone pedestal in the midst of a vast panorama of multihued mesas, the place held obvious cinematic appeal. In a precursor to the competition for creative preeminence between commercial studio movies and independent art-house films later in the century, Robert Flaherty, director of popular "realistic" films like *Nanook of the North* and *Moana,* was backed by the Fox company to shoot a similar "educational and instructive" treatment of Acoma. At the same time, Elizabeth Pickett, author of *Navajo,* which was described as a "modern Indian novel," sold the book's film rights first to Fox, then bought them back and resold them to Paramount. With encouragement from Indian Commissioner Charles Burke, she hoped to shoot in Taos, Acoma, and Navajo country.

Using Bernhard Reuter as the go-between, initially the pueblo of Acoma voted to go with Flaherty. Then Taos Pueblo took issue with Pick-

Shooting Redskin *at Acoma, 1927: Richard Dix plays a returned boarding school student, caught between worlds.*

ett's script for portraying a Taos maiden abducted by Apaches, and backed out anyway. Pickett turned to Acoma for her major location. At this point the government became in effect Acoma's theatrical agent and set up a bidding situation that turned out to be a maneuver so both the commercial and the educational outfits could make their films, and the pueblo double its profits.

First Flaherty made his pitch, offering Acoma $3,000, promising a new house on the mesa for film work, and fair wages to Indian extras. He upped that to $5,000, but drew the line at the idea of both films. When attorney Francis Wilson suggested that the Indians decide, a council convened atop the mesa. Pickett and Reuter, Flaherty's representative, faced off. The pueblo governor reiterated that they favored the Flaherty project. At that point government officials met privately with the Indians, who reemerged with a change of heart: both films could shoot there.

To Flaherty the decision felt conspiratorial and underhanded. For years he'd lobbied for this project. But for lawyer Wilson, who knew the tribe, Pickett's two-month shooting schedule sounded less disruptive than Flaherty's proposed year and a half, even if it did provide longer work for the Indians. No one has been able to uncover Flaherty's trial footage of Indian women with water jugs balanced on their heads, walking single-file to the mesa summit; regardless, he was out of the picture.

When Pickett's 1929 movie appeared under the title *Redskin*, it starred heartthrob Richard Dix and was not half bad. The Navajo and Acoma landscapes lent a vivid sense of place. Unlike the formulaic cowboy-and-Indian pictures shot in California from the 1930s onward that perpetuated one-dimensional stereotypes about savage Indians, this earlier, silent movie joined pioneering examples of other location-based, Pueblo Indian movies of the time that dramatized such complexities as interracial romance, reverse assimilation, and the psychological problems for returned boarding school kids. Acoma would continue to draw location scouts, even if they were often looking for a cheaper stand-in for the Sahara Desert. Acoma's dubious reward for resembling North Africa was a new studio-funded road twisting to its summit that brought more sightseers.

By the tens of thousands, American Indian veterans had returned from the European and Pacific campaigns and didn't like what they found. Despite modest gains during Collier's Indian New Deal, rampant poverty remained. The makeshift shanties and poorly clothed children on their reservations reminded some of the camps of displaced persons they'd seen in Europe. Tuberculosis and trachoma were still widespread, along with smallpox and other infectious diseases. Indians were excluded from most jobs, couldn't drink in bars, and in Arizona and New Mexico were still not allowed to vote and hence ineligible to sit on jury panels. Despite having signed up and sacrificed for their country, they felt little improvement in that ineffable category called *respect*.

Their worldly-wise generation was fed up with this status quo. The first convention of the National Congress of American Indians met in Denver in 1944 with native delegates from twenty-seven states. High on its agenda was stemming the loss of Indian lands, obtaining financial redress for outstanding land claims, and adding acreage if possible. These knotty issues were part of the unfinished business of the 1928 Meriam Report. Finally, eighteen years later, in its last piece of New Deal legislation, the U.S. Congress created the Indian Claims Commission (ICC).

Among the ICC's outstanding questions: Had the old nineteenth-century treaties fairly evaluated the extent of each tribe's geographic range and territorial boundaries, or had ineptitude or outright fraud deprived Indians of fair compensation for their aboriginal lands? Had claims over sacred places and the extended ranges used for seasonal hunting and gathering been taken into account? What historical sources, antique maps, oral testimonies, and new research techniques might be available to provide a more accurate picture of onetime tribal territories?

To answer them the ICC Act of 1946 appropriated funds for a generation of American historians, archivists, geographers, folklorists, and ethnographers to work with hundreds of Indian tribal leaders, traditional elders, storytellers, and consultants and write American history anew. Through this interdisciplinary stock-taking was born a new academic discipline, Ethnohistory, with its own professional journal. Over its thirty-two-year life span the commission redrew the aboriginal land bases for hundreds of tribes, underscored the value of exhuming archived accounts of explorers, missionaries, trappers, and early scholars, legitimized the claims of miniscule, ignored, or marginalized Indian communities to becoming federally recognized tribes, and utilized native testimony and oral traditions to compile a more Indian-centered view of the past.

◆ ◆ ◆

Before Acoma Pueblo could professionalize selling itself it needed a clearer public picture of its history and territory and any money it might be owed by the federal government. The main historian for ICC Docket 266, the case for the pueblo of Acoma, was Dr. Ward Allen Minge, a free-lance Albuquerque scholar and architectural preservationist, who amassed documents about the tribe's territorial arguments with Laguna Pueblo, its land loss to the railroad, and the murky dealings of former governor and Edward's brother-in-law Solomon Bibo. Contributing to its dossier were archaeologists Alfred E. Dittert and Reynold J. Ruppe. In tracking the origins of Acoma-connected ruins on and around Cebolleta Mesa between 1947 and 1952, they surveyed nearly three hundred sites, excavated about a hundred, and verified human occupation there back to the time of Christ.

To interview Indians they hired Florence Hawley Ellis, a well-respected, exceptionally hardworking archaeologist-ethnographer from the University of New Mexico whose close relations with Pueblo peoples were critical to mapping what they now called the Acoma Cultural Province. Of the tribal elders working with them in 1948 the closest to Ellis was probably sixty-two-year-old Syme Sanchez, who lived between Acomita and McCartys. A member of the Antelope Clan, retired railroad worker, and former tribal governor, Sanchez learned Acoma myth and history from his traditional-ist family and was liked by the Hunts.

As a teenager in the early 1900s, Sanchez remembered his grandfather and two religious leaders, probably war chiefs, loading burros with prayer sticks and turquoise offerings and heading north. Their 240-mile pilgrim-age through the tribe's major shrines took weeks. The men carried the food and water, Sanchez emphasized, not the animals, because their bur-dens were more sacred. Walking some eighty miles, they arrived at Chaco Canyon where their ancestors once lived, and prayed and left offerings.

On they continued into southern Colorado, leaving prayer sticks at Jackson Butte, a sandstone pinnacle marking an ancient foot trail into a Mesa Verde canyon. At the base of Mitchell's Butte, they deposited more offerings. Two days later took them to Sleeping Ute Mountain, outside the present town of Cortez. Most important, they would never get physically any closer to Shipapu, where the sacred sisters, "mothers" of all people,

Redrawing the Acoma Cultural Province.

emerged from the interior of the earth. After final prayers and offerings, they returned home.

Hearing his story, Florence Ellis asked Sanchez to retrace the old pilgrimage—essentially the tribe's original migration route in reverse. Its outlines accorded with her close reading of Edward Hunt's already published creation myth, and with Sanchez's account that she'd recorded during an early May 1957 tribal meeting. Accompanied by two Acoma religious leaders and their families, she headed north. So altered by farming and construction was the landscape that her companions became lost, but they did locate an old Acoma shrine near Yellow Jacket Ruin, a two-day walk north of Mitchell's Butte.

Ellis and her fellow archaeologists also interviewed a blind Acoma elder who'd memorized the Spanish land-grant records. They heard of the tribe's pre-Spanish custom of segregating lands allocated for farming from larger expanses for hunting and gathering (later for cattle and sheep grazing). Compiling a list of about thirty "boundary points"—shrines, rock art sites, and Acoma-connected ruins—they drew lines between them, thereby establishing the perimeter for an Acoma Cultural Province. Such was the extent, they argued, of Acoma's traditional territory. This was what they wanted back.

As in most of the commission's final decisions, however, no acreage initially changed hands. By its termination in 1978, the commission had adjudicated more than 670 cases and awarded over $818 million in final settlements to various tribes, but restored little land. For its part, in a final judgment on May 16, 1970, Acoma received $6.1 million in compensation. Getting dollar value for lost lands was a non-Indian kind of solution; adding to their land base was more to their liking. The Claims Commission may have been satisfied with its cash-for-acres resolution, but Acoma was not.

Despite the ICC Act's insistence that the settlement closed efforts at further compensation, Acoma tried to recover her stolen lands on her own. Among the five major purchases and donations after 1972 that more than doubled the reservation's territory, two could be construed as retribution for an ancestor's misdeeds. Arthur Bibo, son of Solomon's brother Emil, became one of the pueblo's strongest advocates. To the pueblo he willed his library, a museum/visitor center, the Kowina Foundation that he'd built to celebrate the tribe's history, and his land, including a sacred spring.

Then the pueblo used part of its land claims bounty to buy from Marie S. Bibo her discounted 236-acre ranch located on the other side of the I-40 freeway from Acomita. It seemed further poetic justice that upon this parcel would rise the industrial park, hotel, casino, and entertainment center that allowed Acoma to open its arms to the general public so as to keep its mesa more sacred and secure than even before.

By Whose Hand (1960–80)

And the fact is that many Americans, with their creative minds destroyed by the effect of factory products, can come even into this mountain country whose clear air should clean their taste, and prefer Indian jewelry made wholesale in factories in Denver or Albuquerque or in petty factories set up by white traders where Indians sit in small rows and fabricate jewelry under white direction, with arrows and swastikas and thunder-birds provided in stamps by the factory keeper.

—Witter Bynner, 1924

TIRED OF THE WEAR AND TEAR of touring, around 1965 Wilbert Hunt sought steadier work closer to home. His options weren't great. Albuquerque still had no Indian police, no Indian firemen or garbagemen, no Indian movie ushers or bank tellers. There was his wife's government service network at the Indian Bureau, but he had no clerical skills. With his mechanical training he might have tried a local garage. But he didn't need reminders of twisted vehicles and damaged bodies troubling his sleep.

For one prospect, however, Wilbert didn't have to look far. Aside from dancing, drumming, singing, and performing sign language before audiences, another family skill called for sitting down, saying nothing, maybe humming a buffalo dance song under one's breath, and concentrating over a workbench. In hammering, soldering, and inlaying silver the Hunts were mentored by Clyde, the family's in-house professional at the art that he'd picked up from old masters on the mesa.

Like craftspeople from Isleta, Santo Domingo, and other Pueblo villages near Albuquerque, Wilbert peddled his skills to cottage industries in town. His search ended in a building on Central Avenue, near Old Town's eastern border. Here, beneath the Bell Trading Company's two-story tower, he joined the trade that had launched his brother Clyde, his Navajo brother-in-law Johnny, and even his sister Josephine. He began the nine-to-five job that he would hold for the next thirty-one years.

Bell Trading joined a well-established market for Indian-made arts that had grown in Santa Fe and Albuquerque for half a century. Even before the Santa Fe Railroad brought fascinated customers in the 1880s, dealers in Indian "curios" were packing burros at Indian pueblos with pots, baskets, blankets, and other crafted items. Some of the earliest buyers were field collectors for eastern museums.

The caliber of Indian goods and displays stepped up considerably in 1902 when the Fred Harvey hotel chain's Albuquerque flagship, the Alvarado, opened its Indian Department. Under a savvy and discerning manager, Herman Schweizer, a museum, salesroom, and storeroom soon catered to all manner of customers, from high-end, knowledgeable patrons to wide-eyed middle-class tourists. This venue remained the gold standard until the appetite for cheaper fare, like the stamped metal trinkets decried by the poet Witter Bynner, swamped them in the 1930s.

In its early years the market for Indian crafts and curios was full and fluid, with new shops opening and closing or shifting location. After apprenticing at the Alvarado Hotel, Charles Wright opened his El Curio outlet in 1907 on 3rd and Gold; under various owners his establishment would move seven times over the next almost-century, with his signature building on 4th and Gold, which resembled an overblown pueblo, becoming a tourist attraction in its own right. Before the war this crowded field was joined by what may have been the city's first Indian proprietors—Wilbert's brother, Clyde "Sunny Skies," made jewelry and peddled lesser wares at his War Bonnet on Central, while brother Wilbert tried his hand at storekeeping with his Blue Sky Eagle Curio shop.

Jack Michelson, the proprietor of Bell's and Wilbert's new boss, started Albuquerque's most mechanized of all the town's Indian jewelry-making shops in 1935 above a clothing store on Central Avenue. Eleven years later he added this city landmark, the large workshop that Wilbert would oversee, with its southwestern-style portal and mission church–like bell tower to honor, it is said, Michelson's wife, Mildred Bell.

But some Albuquerque proprietors looked enviously west, at the advantages enjoyed by their counterparts in the unapologetically working-class boomtown of Gallup. The only mercantile town for miles around, it bustled with Navajo and Zuni jewelers, pawnshop proprietors, trading post shoppers, and weekend hell-raisers. By 1940 Mike Kirk, prime mover

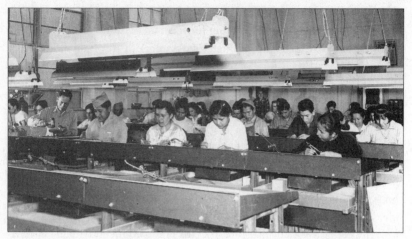

*Wilbert Hunt on the Bell Trading Company assembly line (*three rows back on right, in khaki shirt*).*

of the Gallup Inter-Tribal Ceremonial, was employing a hundred Navajo and Zuni smiths in his factory.

Back in Albuquerque, Jack Michelson knew that Maurice Maisel was his main competitor. The musical instruments and Indian arts store that Maisel opened in 1923 faced the railroad tracks and the Alvarado. Watching the hotel's booming business impressed him with the financial benefits of selling Navajo silverwork and Pueblo pottery over trumpets and clarinets.

In 1939 Maisel moved to Central Avenue; four years later Route 66 began its redirected run through downtown Albuquerque and by his door. Recognizing that successful Indian stores now required eye-catching singularity, he hired John Meem, the region's most renowned architect, to design its almost sculptural Pueblo-Deco façade and add large display windows, and then commissioned local artist Olive Rush to supervise eleven Indian painters from the Santa Fe Indian School to cover 108 feet of it with murals. He introduced the open basement workshop for shoppers to watch his jewelers—who numbered up to three hundred by the late 1940s—from a wraparound viewing balcony. With cloth headbands around their brows, they bent over their asphalt mats turning out daily quotas of rings, bracelets, necklaces, brooches—all with the sun, roadrunner, diamond, and other designs that signaled "Indian" to the world.

Along with Indian hands at Albuquerque's other cottage industries, Wilbert knew that at Bell's he was working in the aftermath of a controversy from which the dust had not settled: Could or should jewelry made by benches full of Indian workers in assembly-line fashion, using machine stamps and copper metal, legitimately be labeled "Indian Made"? Complaints had focused on claims of "authentic" for the pins and brooches listed in mail-order catalogs. A 1936 court case determined, in fact, that Maisel's lacked the right to this stamp of approval, but that did not end the debate. As Dad Hunt griped, here was one more instance of lawyers and government meddling in Indian lives. Whenever they tried to make an honest dollar, Indians ran into some new law that evolved from outsiders' ideas of how they should better themselves.

For applying at Bell's both his manual skills and personal experiences at directing men that he'd developed at school and in the army, Wilbert was eventually named office manager. He knew the difference between older, shapable Mexican pesos or sterling silver ingots that needed to be hammered thin by hand, and these lighter sheets of nickel silver from which Michelson wanted his workers to stamp out their blanks. He could differentiate between the old Navajo designs and the faux-Indian symbols decorating the flimsier, "imitation" items that ordinary tourists could afford. But like a good soldier, Wilbert never objected to mechanical punches and drop presses and happily oversaw lines of men sitting elbow to elbow and passing their work from hand to hand.

Despite his personal misgivings about the reduced quality of mass-produced fare, anthropologist John Adair described the process in neutral language. "One smith makes the shanks of rings; another applies the plate and the bezel and possibly fastens on the raindrops; a third files and finishes the piece. . . . Silver can be produced at a much lower figure [and faster rate] by these methods and the manufacturers are able to undersell the competition."

But the purists of Santa Fe were appalled by the tacky, tourist stuff coming out of Albuquerque and Gallup. Around town they proudly wore their 1890s collectors' items of old Navajo silver, and encouraged the 1930s revival among silversmiths of the classic styles of sandcast bow guards, heavy squash-blossom necklaces, and thick moccasin buttons. Henry Mera, a well-known specialist on southwestern silverwork, saw the bright side. "The flood of cheap, machine-made 'Indian silver' (despicable though

Bell Trading Company on Central Avenue, Albuquerque.

it be)," he suggested, might still offer tourists "an inexpensive introduction to a hitherto unknown subject," and create a broader market for the finer work.

Such debates flew over the heads of most Indian families who were struggling to make a living. When Vedna retired from the U.S. Indian service, Bell hired her for the accounting skills that she'd acquired from that government job. Once again the Hunts were exemplifying the sort of transformation that the old assimilationists had in mind. Even after Wilbert left Bell's in 1985, the firm used his handsome, war-bonneted image in advertisements that hawked faux-Indian moccasins made by Oglala Sioux at their factory on South Dakota's Pine Ridge Reservation to shoppers in Genoa, Italy. For the fourth time in his life it paid to look like a Sioux in Europe. As for the jewelry imbroglio, he was free to practice his craft the old way at home.

Over in Tulsa, Wolf Robe's relocation had allowed him to achieve one goal of the American dream; unlike his younger brother, he became his own boss. With stiff competition from Anglo shopkeepers, and the upper crust looking down their noses at curio shops, that would have been difficult back in New Mexico. Now he was free of their scrutiny and debates over "authentic" Indian-made products. As jeweler, painter, and Indian Lore promoter, Wolf Robe enjoyed the comradeship and freedom of Oklahoma's resourceful Indian artists who, in critic Mark White's words, "played with style as well as cultural subject to meet market demand, and no one felt tribally appropriated. At least from the 1920s to the 1950s, no one is recorded as complaining—suggesting a lack of contentiousness."

And it was easier to change locations and expand in the Tulsa area. Wolf Robe and his brother-in-law Hugh Davis took that step after 1952, when the new Will Rogers Turnpike routed tourists around downtown Tulsa. To widen their net, Hugh and Wolf Robe moved their sales operation a little east, to Catoosa, hard on Route 66. In a larger, concrete-block store they reinstalled his six massive showcases. They added a southwestern-style portal to the front and bolted iron grilles on the windows, which Hugh welded in zigzag patterns inspired by Navajo blanket designs.

Then Hugh's wife, Zelta, who had helped run the trading post, pushed for a venue of her own. Hugh built her a big plywood Noah's Ark across the highway from Wolf Robe's post, and added pens for the alligators and snakes they both loved. With this larger home base and ample storage space at their store, Wolf Robe and his wife grew their modest mail-order business in feathers, beads, and felt crowns for the Indian Lore enthusiasts they had met when they toured. Every summer they loaded up his silver-work and drums for the run to the Gallup Inter-Tribal Ceremonial.

It had not taken long for Wolf Robe to make himself an indispensable member of a loose-knit network that was analogous to the native art circles he had watched emerge in Santa Fe, Taos, and Albuquerque. But there were significant differences, both socially and aesthetically. Living here freed him from their Anglo-dictated standards and incessant arguments over fine arts; Tulsa lacked the pretensions of Santa Fe's community of upper-class patrons and their handpicked Indian painters and potters.

Before long Wolf Robe also fell in with a more convivial group of painting buddies. According to White, "Acee Blue Eagle, Woody Crumbo and Wolf Robe Hunt were master style shifters, dancing in, and out of, and between the emerging regional conventions coming to be known as Native American painting. . . . It was here that the foundation was laid for a peaceful coexistence and comingling between what was old and what was new, what was traditional and what was modern, what was tribal and what was individual."

The birth of Indian gallery art in Oklahoma is usually credited to Oscar Jacobson, a University of Oklahoma professor who told one of his prime students and soon Wolf Robe's close friend, Acee Blue Eagle, "Of course I can't teach you the art. The knowledge of the Indian art and spiritualism and religious symbols is yours . . . but I will help you concentrate all your efforts in becoming a great artist." That was the approach Jacobson took with his famous "Kiowa Six" painters in 1928, whose work first appeared in a book published in Europe to considerable acclaim the following year.

Wolf Robe's new circle belonged to the next half generation, a number of them products of Jacobson's classes at the all-Indian Bacone College. They included soon-to-be-renowned figures like the Creek/Potawatomi Woody Crumbo, the Southern Cheyenne Dick West, the Navajo Quincy Tahoma, and the Creek/Pawnee Acee Blue Eagle, among others. All were multitalented, vivid personalities, fun to be around. Like Wolf Robe, Crumbo once led his own dance troupe on a government-sponsored tour, made and played flutes, and had a weakness for adventuresome pursuits like gold mining. A Cheyenne from a reservation near Darlington, Richard West was long associated with Bacone College, which became an incubator for a number of the state's native artists.

Although just as wealthy as their Santa Fe counterparts, the Anglo sponsors of Indian art in Tulsa were industrialist friends, not high-art or academic types. Openings at two of their institutions, the Philbrook Art Center and Gilcrease Museum, provided occasions where both groups could mingle and share ideas. Arriving too late to come under Jacobson's wing, Wolf Robe took a class at the Philbrook with artist Frank von der Lancken, an Arts and Crafts movement aficionado who'd moved to Tulsa in 1926.

The differences between their mostly watercolor, exceedingly "flat" scenes of idealized Indian life—their "Oklahoma regionalism," as it would be characterized—and what was coming out of Santa Fe were subtle. Naturally they didn't portray pueblo Katsinas, lines of identical corn dancers, or piled-up blocks of mud architecture. From Oklahoma one saw more physicality—racing horses, flamboyant manes in the wind, prancing war

Wolf Robe Hunt, a regular at the Gallup Inter-Tribal Ceremonial exhibition hall (on left, standing, third up behind glass case).

dancers, and more skin. Another set of images was certainly unique to here: the waterbirds, cactus buttons, tipi shapes, metal water drums, feather fans, and gourd rattles that were symbols of the Native American Church, which used the hallucinogenic peyote as its sacramental food. By the time of Wolf Robe's appearance, this religion had been a fully accepted and officially incorporated part of Oklahoma's pantribal landscape for nearly half a century.

While a little more freedom of artistic experimentation was accepted, there was definitely greater ease and sociability. Rather than gathering at any central bar, salon, or coffeehouse, these artists, nearly all male, hung out for meals or coffee in each other's backyards, barbecuing, teasing each other, and talking art while their wives or women visited in the kitchen.

Another location where they ran into each other was Wolf Robe's store. He proudly hung their pictures, they bought his beads and feathers for their regalia, and all sang Indian songs together. His was an Indian-run trading post, a novelty anywhere; his friends liked leaving their money with him, and whatever they had to pawn or trade. Maybe things also jelled because they did hail from different tribes; what they shared was essential to the state's pan-Indian spirit. Their venues didn't cure you or correct your behavior, but they formed a kind of kiva.

In Oklahoma Wolf Robe got away with things that would have caused talk back in New Mexico. The 1963 book of his dad's stories and his illustrations, *Dancing Horses of Acoma,* that he coauthored with University of Tulsa teacher Helen Rushmore, would have been criticized as dumbed-down by folklorists and visually inept by art highbrows. When he enacted a solemn rite he called "The Last Arrow" during the burial of his friend Acee Blue Eagle in 1959, then repeated it three years later at Tulsa legend Thomas Gilcrease's funeral, someone in New Mexico would have exposed it as what would be called an "invented tradition." Worst of all, had he staged back there an "authentic snake dance," like his performance with Creek Indian chief W. E. Dobe McIntosh and live rattlers at Anadarko's American Indian Exposition in 1964, he would have been as reviled as were the Prescott, Arizona, businessmen who dressed up as Hopi Indians and committed the same sacrilege each year from 1923 to 1991.

Here he could be any Indian he liked. One more native refugee, by all accounts Wolf Robe had come as close to home as he would ever get.

56

Yet Another Conversion (1964)

"The Lamanites, while increasing in numbers, fell under the curse of divine displeasure; they became dark in skin and benighted in spirit, forgot the God of their fathers, lived in wild nomadic life, and degenerated into the fallen state in which American Indians, their lineal descendants, were found by those who rediscovered the continent." In keeping with this conception of their origin, the Mormons believe that it is wrong to destroy the faith of the Indians, which is viewed not as a false but as a degenerate form of the "true" religion.

—Evon Z. Vogt, 1966

ABOUT FIVE YEARS before Edward Hunt's death, when he and Marie could still get around and raise corn, beans, squash, and melons on their ten-acre "ranch" just north of Albuquerque, the recently appointed Catholic priest in Alameda dropped by. He was young and eager. He hadn't seen them at mass. Harder to walk around at their age, Edward explained. With son Wilbert overseas, they relied on his wife, Vedna, and she couldn't always make it. But they were loyal Christians. As proof Edward held out the Protestant Bible he'd gotten at the Menaul School back in 1881. He showed how his English name had come with it. Every day, he said proudly, he read from it.

The visitor knocked the book out of his hands. That's not your right, he said, and shook his finger at them. Never do that. Only a priest can read and interpret the holy book. You'll go blind. That's why it's in Latin.

Estranged as Edward was from pueblo religion and its responsibilities, he was still a product of its history. This exercise of priestly authority might have cowed Hispano parishioners, but not a man whose people had fought such treatment for centuries, nor one who had paid a price throughout his life for his right to keep this book. It was one of the few times, his son Wilbert said, that he heard of Dad Hunt blowing up. "Get out of my house," he said, and told the man to stay away. His parents never set foot in church again.

In the American Southwest, tribal conflicts, interethnic tensions, old factionalisms, and doctrinal animosities die hard. Like plant spores or fiber sandals preserved in dry desert caves, their molecular memories tend to stick around. At any time, current events can coax them back to life. New Mexico remains a land of open wounds.

No one knew this better than Vedna Eckerman Hunt, Edward Hunt's daughter-in-law, who was born in Laguna Pueblo to an Indian mother and a white father. Even by New Mexican standards, few communities featured such a web of mutually exclusive creeds and cultural identities. What glued Laguna together were the deeper relationships that connected people through crosscutting ties of blood, marriage, and forms of fictive kinship.

According to legend, Laguna's legacy of religious complexities began in the thirteenth or fourteenth century. Some quarrel over sacred objects up at Acoma prompted one ceremonial leader to quit the mesa and take his sacred fetishes with him. He led his followers to an old beaver pond where he established the hundred-room village that archaeologists call Punyana, near present-day Laguna. In the upheavals and relocations after the 1680 All-Pueblo Revolt, migrating clans and splinter groups of Hopi, Zuni, Jemez, even Navajos came together here, each guarding their fetishes. To help integrate the village were some medicine men's societies that were composed of healers from each of these constituencies.

Upon this impasto of Indian histories was added a sequence of Christian sects. Once the fires of the revolt cooled off, in 1699 the Franciscans established their St. Joseph of the Lake Mission. By the time of the American Civil War, when Vedna's

Wilbert and Vedna Hunt, new members of the Church of Jesus Christ of Latter-day Saints.

own grandfather, Colonel Marmon, conducted his survey for the railroad, the outpost of Baptists had already come and gone. Although Marmon arrived with a Quaker background, he soon became a Protestant.

Progressive and entrepreneurial, his friends also married into notable Laguna Indian families. Like Solomon Bibo over at Acoma, both of the Marmon brothers even served terms as tribal governor. To entangle matters further, in the 1860s Walter's Indian father-in-law, the progressive leader named Luis Sarracino, somehow obtained from Zuni Pueblo the rights to the mask-wearing Chukwena ceremony. When Sarracino sought to initiate his white son-in-law into its rituals, a cadre of Laguna conservatives got upset. Fissioning from their home community, they founded an offshoot village at nearby Mesita, much like an earlier group of religious exiles that left Laguna for Isleta Pueblo.

Reared in the center of this religious and ethnic maze, in a splintered village that even had segregated cemeteries, Vedna was given to the sun for her naming, baptized a Catholic, had Protestant relatives, but still sensed something missing in her life. A child of two cultures, she knew firsthand the cleavages and gossip that split families, created factions, and incited departures. Around 1946, both Vedna and Wilbert "suddenly felt a great need for religion in our lives." For two years they undertook a quest for the right one.

"My wife and I investigated eight different denominations," Wilbert said. When a return to Catholicism didn't take, they visited a number of congregations. "We then attended the Presbyterian Church," Vedna remembered, "next the 'I Am' cult, then the Baptist Church, and also the Episcopalians. We couldn't find what we were looking for in any of them. So we decided to just be 'Indians' and go back to the old religion they taught, as it seemed more sensible than any others."

Like everyone in western New Mexico, the Hunt and Marmon families were familiar with Mormonism. Between Acoma and Zuni lay the farming and ranching community of Ramah, with its cultural quilt of Zuni, Navajo, Hispano, Texan, and Mormon residents. Arriving in the early 1870s, the first Mormon missionaries were soon depleted by a dreadful smallpox epidemic, but they resurfaced in the mid-1880s. To this little village they borrowed a name from the Old Testament—Ramah, or "the high place."

Without American Indians the foundational myth of the Mormon faith could hardly exist. Rather than a "lost tribe" of Israelites, they became essential to the religion's long-term mission on earth. Much as Edward narrated the story of his people's migration to their predestined homeland, almost a hundred years earlier Joseph Smith's Book of Mormon described the exodus of an Israelite population out of Jerusalem, around six centuries before Christ. Then they split into two groups—much the way the ancient Keresans in Edward's story went their separate ways after choosing between the blue (Crow) and white (Parrot) eggs.

A certain similarity carried still further. Like Acoma's original sacred sisters, the more Indian Iatiku and the more Anglo Nautsiti, and the Old Testament's brothers Cain and Abel, those two pre-Mormon groups were at odds. The Nephites associated with a stay-at-home urban lifestyle, while the other bunch, the Lamanites, descendants of Jacob, were wanderers. By falling away from the fold they had been punished by a darkening of the skin. Only a second coming of Christ, which duplicated in many respects the first, brought a fleeting peace between them.

Ultimately, the bad character of the duskier Lamanites emerged. The religion's guiding text went on to describe their descendants undertaking the transpacific voyage to the New World, where they dispersed into the many different groups of American Indians. Although regarded as an "inferior" part of the faith's extended family, these fallen kin were destined to rejoin their original people in a divine circle of true believers in a "latter day." Only after a "return to God," went the belief, would they recover their lighter skin color and the full grace of God.

Thus Indians occupied a unique place and heightened expectation of salvation in Mormon theology. Their recovery would open the way to the faith's ultimate epiphany. Together with their mandate to encircle the globe with emissaries on their yearlong missions, it was especially incumbent on the church's outreach program to carry the Mormon message to these long-lost "brothers at home."

Once the wagons of pioneer Mormons began their treks west, however, reality intruded. Concerns that Mormons were inciting American Indians to violence dogged the sect. As they passed through the Midwest, other Christians took a dim view of such practices as reading from golden tablets, talking in tongues, experiencing visions on old Indian burial mounds, and the Mormon doctrine that out of intermarriages between their elders and "Wives of every tribe of Indians" would come "a White & delightsome people" who would join with the angels to bring on the millennium.

When Wilbert and Vedna were still living at South 8th and Coal, a cousin of Vedna's from Montana dropped by. They chatted and somehow got into singing a few old hymns. Vedna was struck that the woman "searched my face for several seconds" before disclosing that she'd joined the Mormon faith. This led to local representatives of the Latter-day Saints making home calls, a private way of worship that some Indians found more congenial than sitting in pews and being talked at rather than with.

In 1948, the year that both Wilbert and Vedna lost their fathers, they decided to be baptized. Four years later, they received what Mormons called their "endowments," and then "sealed" their marriage for eternity in the Salt Lake City temple. Throughout its teachings their new church stressed the centrality of succession and genealogy. So in 1970, when Wilbert was ordained a high priest, he acquired the Mormon expertise in tracing his "line of authority" five priesthoods back to Brigham Young, in 1860, then three more priesthoods back to the faith's revealer, Joseph

Wilbert Hunt, in rabbit-fur blanket, performing as Cliff-Dweller medicine man, in promotional film for Zion National Park, sponsored by the Mormon Church.

Smith, in 1829, who claimed his from the apostles Peter, James, and John, whose directives came from God.

Wilbert saw parallels between his Acoma upbringing and Mormon values. When LDS members contributed to build a community hospital he was reminded how Acoma villagers hoed, planted, and watered the fields set aside for the tribe's leading cacique, the community's "mother," in order to stock his food bank for distribution, in lean times, among his neediest "children." Anointing heads with oil and water seemed familiar, as did ritual admonitions never to say *if* but always to say *when* before undertakings of importance, so as not to weaken positive thoughts and vows. So Wilbert learned to anoint the sick, dedicate gravesites, wear the sacred undergarments, pay his tithes, and look to Salt Lake City as his Vatican.

In southern Utah, where the Mormon religion established its domain, her early pioneers created a sacred or "double" geography. Ignoring Paiute Indian designations of place, they renamed mountains, valleys, and rivers so as to consecrate their newly found world of Zion, the "place of peace." This impulse at territorial takeover would inadvertently initiate a recurring projection over the following years, not just from Mormons, of Old Testament topography onto the Southwest. Popular writers and romantic artists often evoked comparisons to the Middle East and Palestine, inspired by the kind of New World "Orientalism" that anticolonial academics would castigate a century later. In the center of this sectarian world would be created, in 1918, Zion National Park, near a river that early Mormon settlers renamed Kolob.

Some years later, through their Mormon network, Wilbert and his nephew Eddie Hunt, brother Alfred's son, would be contracted to come to Kanab, near Zion, and take roles in a promotional film by Mormon producers about Zion Canyon and its appealing environs. For nearly two weeks they were put up in the park's famous hotel. They were costumed as old Anasazi, ancestral Pueblo "Cliff-Dwellers," much as Wolf Robe's flyers had promoted the brothers back in their touring days. Wilbert portrayed a wise elder and medicine man, Eddie one of his breechcloth-wearing followers. They were filmed in sandstone caves and rock overhangs not far from favored locations for shooting westerns in the 1940s and '50s.

In Indian garb, heavy makeup, and wigs, they spent most of their time in trailers and deck chairs while cameras were shifted around and other scenes were set up. When *Zion Canyon: Treasure of the Gods* finally appeared in 2001, only glimpses of them remained. But Wilbert Hunt had made it into the movies, near the river that Mormons had named, following their scripture, "heavenly place nearest to the home of God." And the location was also probably the closest Wilbert would ever get to Acoma's own site of origin, the mythical emergence place known as Shipapu, supposedly located near Ute Mountain less than two hundred miles due east.

Return to Europe (1965–70)

A simple explanation for the reasons of the special relationship between Europeans and the native populations of North America is that no such relationship exists. Under closer scrutiny it becomes apparent that all that interested and still interests Europeans is "Indians," a wholly fictional population inhabiting the Old World mind rather than the New World land.

—Christian F. Feest, 1989

DURING THE MID-1960S, when American Indian outrage began to erupt over racial discrimination, cultural stereotyping, insulting sports logos, police brutality, ongoing land loss, reservation corruption, and everything officialdom represented, the U.S. Department of Agriculture invited Wolf Robe to return to Germany and hustle American farm produce at a food exhibition in Hamburg. Three years later the U.S. Department of Commerce paid his reconstituted dance troupe to promote other "Made in America" products across Europe.

The same year of that German junket, an articulate young firebrand named Clyde Warrior, a Ponca Indian college student and organizer of the new militant National Indian Youth Council, wrote a biting essay. His traditionalist parents had taught him to dance on the same Oklahoma land where the Miller Brothers turned Wolf Robe into a Show Indian. Warrior's piece profiled five of his own Indian stereotypes—slob, joker, sellout, ultrapseudo, angry nationalist. Which kind, he challenged Indian readers, are you?

There's little doubt that Warrior would have slotted Wolf Robe as number three. Not that the Indian storekeeper and performer would have cared. Wasn't selling themselves what had allowed his family to survive once they'd been forced out of Acoma so long ago? Forty years later, Wolf Robe leapt at the chance to revisit those countries. By now he'd become a local celebrity in his own right, his Catoosa trading post a commercial fixture and meeting ground.

◆ ◆ ◆

By recruiting "Chief" Henry Wayne Wolf Robe Hunt to put an internationally recognizable stamp of authenticity on its trade mission to Germany, the U.S. government was reviving an association between images of American Indians, long-distance marketing, and nature's bounty that harkened back to the frontier. At the same time it was employing a shining example of an economically successful and culturally assimilated Indian for precisely the sort of stereotypical role that it had condemned as regressive and shameful only a century before.

In the 1800s, when traveling peddlers and showmen with wagons and carts still plied the American frontier, a popular entertainment was the Indian medicine show. Instead of black-painted faces these minstrel shows used brown, feathered ones. They never pretended to "educate" the public, in the way that artist-writer George Catlin's Indian Gallery or even Buffalo Bill's Wild West Show sought to dignify their productions.

The hook in these mildly racist entertainments was health, one of the earliest exploitations of Indian spirituality. Sometimes the Indian component joined a slate that included puppetry, pantomime, and a painted lady.

Wolf Robe Hunt in the port of Hamburg, Germany, promoting sales of American corn.

Against a cloth backdrop depicting tipis, snakes, and buffalo, a so-called medicine man often sold a murky herbal potion that promised to cure all ills. For some reason the Kickapoo tribe, which had split into communities in Kansas, Oklahoma, and northern Mexico, was frequently associated with these patented "cures."

By Wolf Robe's day the association between images of Indians and commercial products was everywhere. Automobiles, brands of gasoline and oil, and sports teams drew upon them. "I'm sort of a roving Indian ambassador," Wolf Robe laughingly told reporters, without a hint of irony at the questionable tradition he was resurrecting.

About thirty-five years after a major American brand associated its Land O'Lakes product with an Indian maiden kneeling before still waters, the Pueblo Indian–associated commodity that Wolf Robe hustled at the Hamburg trade fair in 1964 was maize. In full stage regalia he greeted dignitaries, beat his hand drum, danced, and was photographed grinning broadly alongside bins of yellow grains.

More importantly for Wolf Robe, the trip allowed a detour to Bad Segeberg, in time for the annual German and Austrian Karl May Festival. Then in its twelfth year, the celebration was drawing tens of thousands of Indian enthusiasts to the old Nazi amphitheater, carved out of a chalk mountain, where scenes from the German author's western dramas were dramatized in full costume for the public.

For Wolf Robe this appearance became something of a homecoming, due to his family's old association with Dresden and the Zirkus Sarrasani, their visits throughout Europe in the late 1920s, and his rudimentary German. To his surprise, the German passion for Indians had spread to Poland, Czechoslovakia, France, Turkey, Sweden, and Italy, all of whom had representatives at Bad Segeberg.

So tenacious remained the grip of Indian images on the German imagination that hundreds of Indian clubs, designated as separate "tribes," ran their summer encampments along the Rhine and Elbe rivers. Most of Karl May's books were still in print. Businessmen and hobbyists alike spent weekends wearing Indian outfits that were so über-authentic, with brain-tanned hides adorned with lazy-stitched beaded strips using saliva-softened sinew and old-time greasy yellow seed beads, that any nineteenth-century Indian Grass Dancer would have been proud to wear them.

At the annual Karl May Festival, Wolf Robe meets German actors playing the parts of Old Shatterhand and Winnetou, German novelist Karl May's most popular heroes.

After a few years' hiatus, Wolf Robe was sent overseas again, this time for an "American aid sales promotion" for a different arm of government, the Department of Commerce. Joining him was a larger troupe of Indians in their performers' regalia: a Shawnee, Larry Daylight; a Quapaw, Robert Hyatt; an Osage, Julia Lookout; plus a few cowboys and his brother Wilbert Blue Sky Eagle, whom he lured from Albuquerque. For the next three years they went every selling season to France, Italy, Ireland, Israel, and seven other countries.

In Dublin, Paris, and Tel Aviv, Wolf Robe crowned prime ministers with war bonnets and brought feathered pomp and buckskin circumstance to department store openings. Once again they were playing on the associations between Indians and national products of broad appeal and western resonance. Whatever their political or religious persuasion, one of those products was now craved by youth everywhere. Whether wrinkled and sun bleached as an opportunity to identify with working cowboys, or starched and pleated in designer mode for eastern fashion plates, blue jeans were becoming one of America's few uncontroversial gifts to humankind.

The crowds and acclaim that greeted the dancing Indians who were hustling them reminded the brothers of audience responses before the war. They stretched out this swan song as long as they could. Abroad, they were delighted to find that Indians in full dress were still prime attractions.

Returning home to Tulsa, Wolf Robe found fame and respectability. His popular Catoosa store just outside Tulsa lent him peace to paint and make jewelry. He regaled customers, many of whom had attended his arts and crafts workshops in the 1950s at Tulsa's Philbrook Art Center, with the same sort of embellished stories he'd put into his short-lived newspaper column. Every August he and Glenal packed up their wares and tools for New Mexico's Gallup Inter-Tribal Ceremonial, where he reunited with family; his work station in the cavernous exhibition hall was a regular stop for old friends and Indian fans alike.

His downtown motel, the thirty-one-unit The Grotto, housed Route 66 tourists from across the country. Around Tulsa his status as an elder statesman was further cemented by induction into the Scottish Rite chapter of the local Masonic Lodge, over whose Akdar Shrine's Indian Patrol he presided. He liked catering to the rich and prestigious. The great German portraitist Winold Reiss collected his work. He treasured letters of gratitude for the bolo ties and belt buckles he gave to Oklahoma notables like baseball manager Branch Rickey and Cherokee chief W. W. Keeler. Through old Boy Scout contacts he made an eagle-feather bonnet that wound up on the head of President Dwight D. Eisenhower.

Equally important to his reputation was his ongoing participation in the Indian art scene. He ordered supplies for fellow painters, framed and hung their work, and occasionally juried a show. In 1967 he won the Grand Award at the Philbrook Art Center's twentieth annual Indian Art exhibition for his *Dancing with Snakes*.

Meanwhile, Wolf Robe's neighbor and brother-in-law was not sitting still. Always busy with his hands, this time Hugh Davis expanded his side of the Catoosa operation. Across the highway from Wolf Robe's store and near his big Ark with its cartoonlike cutouts of animals he added a new attraction. In 1970, on their wedding anniversary, he walked his wife,

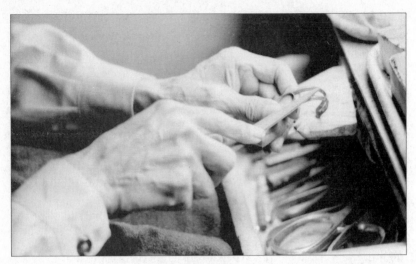

Wolf Robe Hunt, now a double amputee, still at his Catoosa, Oklahoma, workbench.

Zelta, over to their spring-fed lake from which he'd banned her for months previous with an air of expectation.

Hugh's weakness for roadside kitsch—what architectural scholar and champion of the vernacular David Gebhard once praised as America's "programmatic" creation of commercial buildings shaped like fish, coffee cups, Egyptian pyramids, and ice-cream cones—had pushed him to new heights. On the north side of Route 66 he unveiled a most unlikely addition to the family's trading post, gas station, café, inland Ark, and its accompanying park and picnic grounds. Rising halfway out of the water, its split tail lifted gaily into the air, swam a hundred-foot-long sperm whale.

Sky blue was its rebar-and-cement body, portholes lined its torso, and across its wide open walk-through mouth, complete with gleaming white teeth, spread a joyful grin. Soon Hugh opened a water slide from its belly into the lake; a diving board extended from the tail, and a snack stand was available for picnickers at the concrete tables Hugh positioned around the lake, along with giant toadstools he had made out of concrete pillars and old tank turrets. Entertainers at heart, the Wolf Robes also loved Hugh's roadside attractions. Although going through its ups and downs over subsequent years, Catoosa's Blue Whale would remain a fixture in nostalgic books and new tourist maps about old Route 66.

In the early 1970s Wolf Robe's diabetes worsened; soon both legs underwent successive amputations until they reached his torso. Yet visitors always commented on his great spirits, his kindly manner, his gentleness toward their children wandering around his shop. And although his art seemed increasingly out of date, the honors kept coming. In 1970 his painting *Acoma War Dancer* won first prize at the Gallup Inter-Tribal competition; in 1973 he was named the state's Outstanding Indian of the Year, and the following year received the Philbrook Art Center's Victory Trophy for helping fellow artists.

When Wolf Robe Hunt died three years later, it was widely considered that a piece of old Oklahoma was no more.

58

Changes on the Mesa (1980–2004)

Po'pay's name was of the summer moiety. His role after the Revolt is unclear, but the event that he led in 1680 was vital to the survival of the New Mexico Indian pueblos and as historically significant as the first American Revolution.

—Herman Agoyo, 2005

The truth is that the Pueblo Indians in general were loathe to rebel [in 1680] for many reasons; they did so because of mass hysteria whipped into a mad frenzy by their voodoo witch-doctors who saw the poor aborigines fast slipping away from their own grasp.

—Fray Angelico Chavez, 1949

DURING THE YEARS of the Red Power movement, with Indian blockades of dams and roads back east, "fish-in" demonstrations in the Pacific Northwest, and occupations of historical sites like California's Alcatraz Island and South Dakota's Wounded Knee battlefield, the Pueblo

Indians mostly lay low. When their time to protest finally came, it was subtle and embodied a deep sense of history. Its message of tribal renewal was carried by Pueblo people for Pueblo people. Everyone else, went the implication, was an interloper.

Like his dad, Wilbert Hunt closely followed the news, clipping articles, taking notes, underlining passages, scribbling in margins. He saved obits of old classmates, fellow Mormons, and coworkers at Bell Trading. He collected stories about his people's ancestry, from Mesa Verde to the Galisteo Basin's old San Marcos Pueblo, and repatriations of Indian bones and sacred objects, as well as tips on just-published Indian books and the successes of friends like Acoma poet Simon Ortiz and Laguna photographer Lee Marmon, father of famous novelist Leslie Marmon Silko. Of special interest was the doomed fight of schoolmates and Acoma governors Merle Garcia and Stanley Paytiamo to recover portions of the Malpais badlands, and shrines that established pathways for rain clouds to sail across Zuni Salt Lake, the Malpais, and the Berryhill area to the old mesa. He never missed the weekly *Tribune* columns by Paguate villager Katherine Augustine covering everything from Zuni Salt Lake to the Navajo "Long Walk" of 1868, and followed Santa Fe's endless arguments over which ethnic community was being properly or improperly represented in local museums.

Certain news stories touched a nerve—banishments of pueblo members for infractions of religious rules, alleged discrimination against non-Indian wives of tribal members, struggles within villages over banning tourists from once-open ceremonies, and yearnings by long-absent relatives to return to their pueblo fold. New Mexico's penchant for self-celebrating and opening old grievances provided constant fodder for newspaper debates over the protests that vented them.

When an anonymous protestor in 1974 chipped out the word "savage" on Santa Fe's centrally located monument to white Indian fighters, Wilbert tore out the item, as he did during the controversy leading up to the celebration of the four hundredth anniversary of Don Juan de Oñate's conquest of New Mexico and the midnight vandalism in January 1998 of the conquistador's $1.2 million equestrian statue at Alcalde near Española—his bronze right foot removed with an electric saw in retaliation for the same punishment he reportedly inflicted on Acoma's menfolk in 1599.

But Wilbert was taken aback in early August 1980 by a back-page men-

Edward Hunt's great-grandson Emmett Hunt Jr., joining the Tricentennial Run of 1980 to honor the All-Pueblo Revolt of 1680.

tion in his morning *Tribune* about the creative way that Pueblo Indians were commemorating the All-Pueblo Revolt of 1680. Organized by Hopi painter Fred Kabotie for the Western Pueblos and Santa Clara Pueblo elder Herman Agoyo representing the Eastern Pueblos, a reenactment was planned of the relay-running mission that triggered the uprising. To set it up, teams of runners bearing time-counting devices had secretly visited every pueblo beforehand, alerting them to rise up on the very same day. Three hundred years later, reenacters from nearly every pueblo in the Southwest would retrace their hypothesized route.

Nor was Wilbert alerted that his great-nephew Emmett Hunt Jr., a thirty-one-year-old cross-country coach at Laguna-Acoma High School, would bring the family's name into the event by joining its Laguna-to-Acoma

leg. Without fanfare, police alerts, or press releases, fast Indians in running shoes took over the map. For six days early in August dashing from
pueblo to pueblo, strung out on freeway curbs, single-lane roads, and unpaved fire lanes, relays of runners, young and old, boys and girls, distributed sacred pouches, ears of corn, and messages of freedom to their own
communities across New Mexico and Arizona. "I didn't know what to expect when it began," recalled Emmett Hunt, "but as I ran, as it continued,
I felt like the past was inside my body, like I was with my ancestors, and it
was wonderful."

The optimism of the Tricentennial Run of 1980 coincided with a revolution in American Indian fortunes that blindsided the entire nation and
transformed Acoma Pueblo's in the near future. The previous year, the
Seminole Indians of Florida won the right, as a sovereign tribe, to open a
high-stakes bingo hall on State Road 7 in their reservation at Hollywood,
Florida. Five years later Acoma Pueblo became the first New Mexican reservation to adopt the idea and bankroll a similar operation, Sky City
Casino.

One by one, communities jumped on the gaming bandwagon, as Indians suddenly stood to gain from the same sort of greed that had once dispossessed them. To impose order on what some described as a "Gold Rush
in reverse" the U.S. Congress passed the Indian Gaming Regulatory Act of
1988. It affirmed the legal basis for sovereign tribes, who were exempt from
state taxation, to exploit their federal status to promote economic development and governance through gaming. Their enterprises would be overseen by a newly established National Indian Gaming Commission that
approved and regulated revenue-sharing "compacts" with states.

The 1988 act, commented legal scholar William Eadington, "triggered
the most significant economic and social change to affect American Indian tribes since the founding of the Nation." Fifteen years later the commission reported that 19.5 million Americans had visited one or another
of the 223 tribal gaming operations that were spread across twenty-eight
states and drawing in $18.5 billion for American Indians.

Outsiders were admonished not to characterize this turn of events as a
"windfall," or the Indians' "new buffalo," a cosmic payback that produced
horrendously overblown Las Vegas–style architecture and cut dearly held
idealizations of Indians down to size, or as probable magnets for orga-

Acoma runners in the Tricentennial Run of 1980, being prayed over and refreshed after arriving atop Acoma mesa.

nized crime, reservation corruption that only fed the gambling addictions of people who could least afford them. Rather, this financial revolution had come about by Indian citizens exercising their legal sovereign rights and, for the most part, using their lawful profits to fix roads, pay police, train and hire tribal employees, create senior citizens' centers and Meals on Wheels programs, and otherwise benefit their communities.

For Acoma Pueblo, the new financial income meant that a community that had counted its total cash assets in the early 1970s at little more than $137,000 could add the land claims award of $6.1 million to its coffers as well as its portion of the $3.5 billion tourist industry that the state's twenty-two tribes were soon pulling in, predominately from casino revenues. In 1994, Acoma enhanced its gaming investments with Class III, or casino-style, tables in a new casino constructed on a parcel purchased from Marie Bibo with claims money, located hard by the I-40 freeway. Upon legal advice it established its own Acoma Business Enterprise bureau to wall off these increasingly complicated fiscal operations from regular tribal government operations. On the old Bibo ranch the Business Enterprise underwrote in 2001 a new 150-unit Sky City Casino hotel and conference center complex, together with an expanded trucking court.

With these opportunities for financial investments, increased tribal employment, and new tourist facilities came the need for sophisticated public relations. But outside consultants could get it very wrong. In 1963, for instance, an earlier, government-initiated proposal had urged the tribe to install a mechanical elevator to the summit of Enchanted Mesa (Katzimo). This monolith figured in Acoma lore as a place where their ancestors, under great duress, once sought sanctuary. A few venturesome whites, like Charles Lummis, proved it could be scaled, to the dismay of the Acoma people who counted it, as with most ruins of former residence, a shrinelike marker of their history. The proposal that tourists might step off a mechanical lift and buy snacks and curios at shops atop the mesa did not sit well with them.

Equally inappropriate was the invitation, which beamed from highway billboards and casino dinner mats in the mid-1990s, to "Explore Acoma." Whichever hired gun came up with that misguided slogan provided a textbook lesson on why Pueblo Indians should never outsource their advertising. For most Acoma war chiefs and other traditionalists, unsupervised poking around the mesa, its rim, or the caves and boulders around the base was the last thing they wanted. "You travel a thousand years in a day" was an improvement. But a more candid welcome than either might have been, stick to the path, consider yourself lucky to be here, stay within earshot of your tour guide's voice, ask your one question, be thankful you have the choice of taking the tram or walking down on the ancient footpath when your forty-five minutes up here are over, accept deep ambivalence as an Indian reality wherever whites are concerned.

Wilbert Hunt followed these developments with heightened interest. He played the slots, so he looked forward to patronizing the tribe's own casino and eating Sunday brunch at its buffet. He had no problem with gambling, knowing how the Indian passion for competitive sports and games of chance was sanctioned by oral tradition. In his father's creation story, the guardian spirit of their sacred South Mountain, Gaukapuchume, was admired as a quick-witted gambler and skilled kick-stick player.

Their pueblo's sacred mother, Iatiku, instituted social dancing, competitive running, and a form of bowling to offset "the continuous solemnity of the secret ceremonies." When the men added their "hidden" gambling games, players bet their livelihoods. That was when their disre-

New construction on Acoma mesa's eastern rim; Katzimo, or "Enchanted Mesa," in the distance.

spect forced Iatiku's departure, and her Acoma children lost paradise and entered history.

Horse racing, the rooster pull, footraces, hand games, even card games became favored Pueblo pastimes. The heaping of stakes in front of his dad's store before the weekend kick-stick races left a vivid impression on young Wilbert. "They'd bet blankets, concho belts, and necklaces, rings, bracelets. They even bet horses. You'd see two piles of blankets and mantas, sash belts and all kind of trinkets."

Another reason Wilbert stayed abreast of breaking events back at Acoma was closer to his heart. He found himself thinking about his real home, his natal place, where more than memories remained.

Housing all her people was always a problem for the hard-up village. Overpopulation was partly what had turned the seasonal farming outliers of Acomita and McCartys into permanent communities, where Wilbert's own paternal grandparents had settled. Now those villages, situated on inclines, with narrow purchase on the banks of the San Jose River drainage, could not support the kinds of new homes her people desired.

Up on Acoma mesa, with its lack of zoning codes, some members were freely planting single-family, one-story summer homes around the rim, using nontraditional materials like asphalt-impregnated, machine-made adobes trucked in from Albuquerque and covered with cement stucco that did not allow the walls to breathe. Further changing the look of the pictur-esque old village, and its collective massing and rhythmic progression of similar, set-back houseblocks, was the eclectic accumulation of concrete block, firebrick, aluminum storm doors, garbage cans, propane tanks, stovepipe chimneys, exposed gas canisters, metal drainpipes, prefab doors with bright brass knobs, and Christmas lights strung along the eaves. In-dividualism was creeping in.

Some tribal leaders wanted to follow architectural historian Bainbridge Bunting's detailed advice in 1965 about how to rehabilitate the three streets of classic, south-facing, stepped houseblocks, but how to pay for it back then? They did substitute septic tanks for the outdoor privies that had be-come a thicket of smelly eyesores on the talus slopes. Out of nostalgia or piety outsiders might be moved to raise money for the periodic renova-tions of San Estevan Church, and Acoma was generally grateful.

But upkeep on their falling-down domestic architecture, whose adobe surfaces required annual remudding and other forms of regular mainte-nance, was less appealing. Furthermore, it was unrealistic to expect that kind of handwork from modern-day villagers who would have to com-mute to nine-to-five jobs many miles away, and who mostly lived outside the old village anyhow. Who could fault them for not wanting to stay in a time capsule and for desiring the same modern conveniences and lifestyle as everyone else?

Wilbert was well aware that in the 1960s the tribe had won Housing and Urban Development (HUD) funds to open a new forty-eight-unit housing development, known as Skyline One, on the windblown flats just above the slopes of old Acomita, near the tribal headquarters. Some of his own rela-tives were eligible to move into its low-rent prefab homes. But construction had proven shabby: doors and windows didn't fit, nails popped out of wall boards, repairs took forever.

Around 1993, during the governorship of Wilbert's old friend and for-mer classmate Cyrus Chino, the pueblo applied for a second grant, amounting to $6.2 million, for Skyline Two. It would fund sixty-one homes west of the earlier subdivision and south of the Tribal Office. Unlike the earlier venture, its residents were promised better workmanship and offered a greater say in selection of roof types and floor plans.

On one of his occasional drop-ins at Chino's office, Wilbert learned of this latest project. Then Chino wrote him a letter, and backed it up with a personal phone call. "You can come back," he said.

59

One Came Home (2004)

The Pueblo of Acoma people retain vested interest in these lands considered for a [Malpais] national monument. These lands always remain Acoma's aboriginal lands in spite of its designation as Bureau of Land Management land and/or as state school lands. Federal and state laws may take away our lands under newly instituted laws but our people remain intact with the land, as our Acoma elders say, "We are already underneath the land."

—Acoma governor Stanley Paytiamo, 1986

WHEN WILBERT HUNT was asked why the sudden interest in resettling on the reservation, he'd answer, "My water bag is calling me." Shortly after he was born his mother had wrapped up his placenta and carried it out of the house. She buried it under one of the cottonwoods that Edward had planted in a row by the irrigation ditch. He needed to join that part of himself, Wilbert said. There was another reason, too. "I want to see Mount Taylor in the morning."

Back in late 1976 the Acoma governor's office had mailed out the tribe's annual request for updates to the tribal census. Wilbert made sure his family's information was current, with recent addresses of his surviving brothers and sisters, and even cousins. Now that Vedna had retired from Bell Trading, in 1982 the couple sold their Placitas Street home and purchased the five-year-old single-wide trailer at The Meadows, a mobile home park hard by the I-25 freeway to Santa Fe.

Three years later Wilbert retired from Bell's as well and the two began an enjoyable retirement, attending every local pueblo fiesta, visiting relatives in Laguna, taking the occasional trip to Salt Lake City. Off the kitchen Wilbert set up his jewelry bench, his gas bottles and torch to one side, log-based anvil on the other. In a green gambler's eyeshade and with the radio tuned to country music or right-wing radio, he created necklaces, brooches, bracelets, and rings and clipped from his magazines and newspapers.

Then, in early 1992, after fifty-four years of a strong marriage, Vedna's health deteriorated. Over the last decade she had grown steadily weaker from a combination of heart problems, diabetes, and a thyroid condition. On March 8, 1992, at the University of New Mexico Hospital, she died of complications from pneumonia. Little more than a month after that painful loss, Wilbert's nephew, brother Alfred's son, Joseph "Eddie" Hunt, together with his wife, Shirley, moved from Ventura, California, where Eddie had recently retired from forty years as a repairman for Toledo Scales.

For the next ten years or so, the three of them rekindled the cycle of Wilbert and Vedna's retirement activities. They never missed a fiesta on the local circuit of pueblo celebrations—the annual dances at Acoma, Laguna, Santa Ana, and any others they could fit in. They always hit the Albuquerque fair, and the openings and subsequent annual celebrations at Albuquerque's All-Pueblo Cultural Center and Acoma's own museum-restaurant complex. The annual Albuquerque Balloon Festival and the city's NASCAR races were special draws, and they attended every special occasion at local Indian casinos. They lived by a stacked calendar of fun local events but also relished long-distance drives to old friends and former performance venues as far away as Texas, Oklahoma, and North Carolina.

At the same time, amid these pleasures of retirement, a deeper dream came true.

Governor Chino's encouragement to consider the "right of return" wasn't disturbed by Wilbert's memory of an almost identical overture to his family more than a half century before. It hadn't turned out well, but that was back then. Hadn't those memories cooled by now; how could they possibly impact the wider family?

In 1932, Louis Haskaya, the part-Navajo governor of Acoma Pueblo at the time and one of his dad's old friends, often stopped by their 8th Street

Wilbert Hunt at the site of Solomon Bibo's old trading post at Cubero;
Mount Taylor in the distance.

house in Albuquerque. "Like my father," Wilbert said, "he held both tradi-tional and non-traditional ways, but he always admired my father's prog-ress. You're still an Acoma person, he'd say. Why don't you come back? Everything looks good for your return." On a small piece of property just behind St. Anne's Church that Edward had rented to the government farmer, he hired some men to start construction on a rock foundation.

But word got around. Tribal officials showed up and halted the work. Edward wasn't wanted here, they said. An emergency meeting was sched-uled. One evening Wilbert drove his parents back to Acomita, dropped his mother with relatives, and parked beside the meeting house. Only men were inside, including the old cacique, who had come off the mesa. One of Edward's own nephews spoke harshest against him. If he comes back, their side argued, he's going to talk about changing this or that. The fireplace was stoked throughout the meeting; it got stifling. Back and forth they talked all night, continued throughout the following day, and went on un-til around three or four the next morning.

By then Edward had heard enough. "Well," he said, "I love my home, I was born and raised here. My ancestors and grandmothers and grandfa-thers were born here. Some of you were maybe born in California, yet you accuse me of not being worthy of living here. I guess we're not ever going to be related again and live together. I wasn't coming back to bother anything. Some of my relatives, and friends that grew up with me, invited me." But they all knew, Wilbert said, that his father would never take part in their secret ceremonies nor let his children, either. That was what they still held against him.

"Once I left before, for the same reason," Edward reminded them. "May you live in peace all by yourselves," he finally said, "and I'll go live in peace." By then everyone was in tears, the cacique, their relatives, the people speaking for and against him. They were weeping and embracing. Wilbert and his dad got into their Chevrolet, picked up Marie, and drove back to Albuquerque. A cord was cut for good.

His father had not secured his "right of return," but Wilbert's new hope for it was undeterred. Of course the memory of their struggle did not sit well, but that was out of filial sympathy. His situation was different. Unlike his father, he was never initiated into the Katsina, medicine men's, or sacred clown societies, and hence was ignorant of and ineligible to partake of those rituals. He was an old man, honored for his years, and too weak to be expected to endure the yearlong austerities of an appointment as one of the community's war chiefs. The range of mixed-blood tribal members had increased; he had the virtue of being a full-blood, a fluent speaker of the language, and interested in researching genealogies that always lent a respected depth to his conversations with other tribal elders. Furthermore he was an honored veteran, was known as a silversmith, and did not proselytize his Mormon faith. His caretakers, Eddie and wife Shirley, could look after him in their new house on his old homeland.

So Wilbert signed up for a possible berth in Skyline Two. While his blended family at the trailer park continued to travel and attend functions, the wheels of tribal government and federal paper-pushing slowly turned. Wilbert's check-ins at the Acoma Housing Authority's office became a familiar occurrence. Its staff got accustomed to his humble, kindly presence at the door. He shared the census data and language information and family histories he was accumulating. Their life in The Meadows flowed smoothly. Off the kitchen he was at his workbench by six every morning. After an afternoon nap and his half hour of KKOB radio news, he returned to his metalwork until turning in around eight.

Thus it went until early in 2001 when assurances finally came that their low retirement incomes had met the requisite 80 percent level of the na-

Acoma's Sky City Casino and Hotel complex.

tional median income. They were poor enough; they would have their house. Beside themselves with joy, they reviewed the plans and, fearing that the more traditional-looking one might leak, chose a gable over a flat roof. Again more delays, while they dutifully attended the Housing Authority's participant meetings on "understanding your property" at the casino's Piñon Room, where they were lectured on preventive maintenance for heating and cooling systems and insurance issues; Wilbert saved articles on traditional ways to bless a new home. At long last, on Monday, January 22, 2001, their spade joined others in breaking the frozen ground for a three-bed, two-bath unit.

It took a long year of construction before they could move in. But on Thursday, April 11, 2002, the Acoma Housing Authority handed them the keys, led them through the rooms, and demonstrated the fixtures and appliances. A week or so later Wilbert Hunt dressed up in his regalia and war bonnet and met with their friends and neighbors to say goodbye in The Meadows recreation room. To piano accompaniment he bobbed and wove and performed his Indian sign-language version of "How Great Thou Art" and "You Are My Sunshine," as they sang along. They ate cake and ice cream. On May 2, Wilbert wrote in his journal, "In our new beautiful home on our Acoma Reservation—wonderful new day."

They wasted no time adding new rhythms to their old. The reservation school bus let out the kids up the street and they watched them scatter to their homes. The wind never let up and every morning a little bank of sand had to be swept from the front and back doors. It was impossible to grow a lawn; they were content with an array of unusual rocks and cactus huddled

The dancing continues: St. Stephen's Day at Acoma fiesta.

close to the walls around their entrance portico. They began attending regular veterans' meetings and watched the moon and the stars in this darker, larger sky. Whether they were coming or going the casino became a regular stop. A stray dog with a shaggy pelt started hanging around; they named her Princess. Relatives and old friends and new friends dropped by. They found themselves busier than ever.

In his short-brimmed gray Stetson, homemade turquoise bolo tie, and creased pants, and with his erect bearing, whenever Wilbert took visitors up to the summit of the mesa he stood out. Then he'd speak in perfect, even old-fashioned, Keresan, and locals often did a double take. He was always friendly and respectful to them, and chairs were pulled out for him, coffee poured, invitations to eat at the next public gathering extended. With old classmates of the Albuquerque boarding school and St. Catherine, familiars from the milieu of Laguna and Santa Ana pueblos, fellow U.S. military veterans, and old friends and long-distant relatives he hadn't seen in years, he found much in common.

For the rest he was a curiosity. Wisps of the old rumors and suspicions about his father, indeed surrounding their entire family, even the distant connection to Bibo, remained in the air and made him an odd celebrity.

One glance and you recognized a member of a wider world. He was cordial but confident, perhaps once one *of* them, but no longer entirely *with* them. Moreover, they seemed to know that Wilbert knew things he was smart enough not to talk about. For his part, he respectfully left the place alone when it was shut to outsiders, and he stayed out of religious talk and tribal business.

But Wilbert could not help noticing all the differences from years past. At first he was still allowed to drive up to Acoma mesa whenever he wanted and bring his white friends without their having to go through the fifty-minute guided tour. Eventually that changed. Strolling around, he lamented that he was prevented from showing them places of particular interest—the hole where honey offerings placated the wind spirits, the rocks that stood for the War God Twins, the freshwater north cistern where so many famous photographers, like Ben Wittick, Edward Curtis, and Ansel Adams, had positioned the shawl-cowled female water carriers with their traditional painted pots beside the glassy pool.

There were many little signs that Indians were in charge here and be on your best behavior—no photographing, recording, unsupervised walking. You encountered the warnings just after the freeway turnoff before you entered Acomita, at the dramatic overlook where you first saw the mesa in its panoramic glory, at the visitor center below the mesa, and at the disembarking stop for the tourist tram atop it. Next were all the smaller, hand-made "No Trespassing" alerts, positioned like scolding fingers at every opening along the prescribed tourist path. It seemed as if to move any-where was to risk trespass, to inquire was possibly to do harm, and to freely look around was prelude to theft, of the material or spiritual sort didn't matter. Did they want you here or not? Who knew?

Wilbert kept to himself dismay over what he perceived as inaccuracies in the tour guides' remarks. Those ponderosa church beams hadn't come from Mount Taylor, he believed, they were more likely from Black Mesa, which lay closer to the west. John Wayne never filmed here, nor ever made a film called *African Sunset*. Wilbert wished he could have shown his out-of-town visitors the older houseblocks, the interiors where his father had been raised, the old hingeless *sambulo* doors that swing on pegs in holes in their frames, the corn-grinding rooms.

And much had changed. New colors brightened doorframes and win-dow sashes, second-story outdoor *horno* bread ovens were almost a thing of the past. The old, set-back massing of adobe cubicles was nearly gone, with sheer second stories in their place. The lines of Home Depot doors and new buttresses of stabilized adobes holding up the recently remodeled north sides of old units created an alien uniformity.

The Hunts were regulars at the casino restaurant, and the waitresses greeted them by name. One day in the lobby they passed the raffle for a navy blue SUV Ford Explorer. They bought tickets and over subsequent weeks touched its shiny metal hood. Following Wilbert's admonition about thinking *when* not *if,* they would say, "This *is* going to be our car." They stood beside it and drew in its breath. On October 6, 2006, the drawing was held and the vehicle became theirs.

60

Moving On (2007)

I go back each year for a short visit with my mother at Acoma. The moon comes up over the Enchanted Mesa, and turns to silver the church of the Spanish Fathers. The valley below gleams with an unearthly beauty. Hills and spires of rock in fantastic forms are smoky blue in the distance. The tom toms in the kiva beat deeper and deeper into my heart. Gone is the white man's world, back steals the world of my forefathers, and once more I am a little Pueblo boy, waiting for the masked dancers to come.

—James Paytiamo, 1932

SIX WEEKS SHORT of his hundredth birthday, in late September 2007 Wilbert Hunt took what he did not know would be his final drive to Albuquerque and back. He and Eddie had been ignorant of the fact that going up to Santa Fe in 2005, paying respects at the graves of both of their wives, would be their last visit there. Nor that attending the Acoma fiesta on September 2 that year, Eddie pushing Wilbert's fold-up wheelchair through the crowds and over the rocky surface, would not happen again.

As usual, Eddie, or "Sonny," as Wilbert affectionately called him, was at the Explorer's wheel. For a year or so now the old man had eaten less and less and was losing weight. He was frail, hardly talked, and could no longer browbeat Eddie with driving directions. He couldn't chew, could barely see, and his hearing was shot. They visited old friends, Donna, and Dale, the night manager at their old trailer park. Eddie had a dental appointment at the Veterans Hospital and didn't like leaving Uncle Will in the house that long.

Those stops over, in late afternoon they began the drive home, passing signposts of family memory that covered more than a century. It was a clear day. Where I-25 lifted before the turnoff onto I-40 west there was the faintest outline of Mount Taylor's crest, fifty miles away. The massive wall of the Sandias behind them, a mile or so later Wilbert glanced over the roadway's eastern barrier.

There stood the old boarding school that Dad Hunt helped build, then was forced by pueblo elders to leave, and the replacement building where Wilbert himself learned a lot, met the gawky Laguna girl who would become his wife for half a century, learned to write under his favorite teacher, felt the flush of praise for schoolwork, obedience, and skills as drill instructor. Perhaps he also remembered running away with his Isleta Pueblo buddy, punished that one time, successful the second time in the dead of night. He knew he'd been bad, but that was compensated by the excitements of Oklahoma, first of his grand adventures.

The new bridge crossing the Rio Grande was so wide, and his crumpled, safety-belted old body so low, he only caught a sliver of sparkling water upstream, near the Duranes crossing, where his teenage father had first crossed on a barge, or waded in knee-deep water. Which was it? Stories of others' stories told so often and so long ago were so unreliable. Memories came and went. His family's stories, sometimes he wondered, who cared? On the opposite bank they climbed West Mesa—now a subdivision's sea of identical roofs—where his grandparents had camped for weeks, checking on young Day Break until it was time to return home.

Heading west, the sunburnt flatlands, tight fists of dark green piñon, the evil "robber" mountains hazy to the south, flat miles of chamisa and sagebrush until the gradual drop into the Rio Puerco basin, once a robust stream, now barely a trickle. How many times on two- or three-day wagon trips for restocking to Las Lunas, or farther, to Martineztown, had they camped near that spring just north, fire sparks rising to the sky, coyotes shrieking as they mutilated rabbits in the dark, the security of his burly father snoring close by?

They passed the old Canoncito turnoff (now known as the *To'Hajiilee* segment of the Navajo Nation), sanctuary to an isolated group of Navajos since the eighteenth century, where escapees from the 1864 roundup of the tribe hid out. And then the stretch to Laguna's fine hill, her bone-white church perched against the mountain backdrop, the hundreds of trips back and forth with Vedna. Her embracing family, their happy reunions, surrounded by all those mountain-driven rainclouds, windstorms, white-out snowfalls. Where was all that laughter now?

Toward Flower Mountain off to the left, the mesa pedestal with its separate mound crowned on top, like a round-topped hat. Did it earn its name when he was young? Didn't he remember it green all summer, that mound full-flowered in spring? Today all light brown and ash dry.

Closing in on the sharp Acomita turnoff at Sky City Casino—the seven rocky humps close by the Interstate that the kick-stick runners used to encircle for the home stretch to his father's store where the piled-up winnings, the saddles, silver concho belts and blankets, awaited the victors. Every weekend they raced, and all visitors eating in relays in Marie's steaming kitchen, and hand-feeding his father's lambs, the eternal smells of mutton, juniper smoke, and old leather, Clyde making him laugh.

Past the lone rocky pinnacle—drunks had knocked off its peak—where wild-eyed horses raced and turned for their home stretch, the appointed guards making sure they didn't cheat, the riders quirting each other without mercy. Across the railroad tracks, Dad Hunt hooking the mail bag every day and returning with his incoming pouch. Curving right around Acomita's mesa base, up those rocky slopes the camouflaged ruins of his grandparents' first home, their shaped sandstones then recycled for the newer dwellings below, then abandoned or sold as some residents began moving into the modern housing developments up above.

Remnants of Dad Hunt's hardworking hands—the big ditch, on some maps still bearing his name, the neglected four peach trees left in his one-time orchard, gnarled and forlorn without pruning, those last two shaggy-barked old cottonwoods near the onetime store, looking over the fallow lands where Edward once farmed, he not long for this world, one of them with *him* underneath. The old store location itself, where Dad Hunt launched his annual San Lorenzo festivities, his sons enacting their grand-fathers' trading expeditions with the Comanches, much as their tribe's great "mother," Iatiku, once introduced recreational pastimes for her Acoma children back in mythic times: so they could have fun. Some of the store's old adobes had gone into the run-down shelter that replaced it today—could anybody occupy such a wreck?

Past the shuttered, weedy Head Start building, more tumbled-down rock walls from earlier habitations popping out of high grass, their decrep-itude allowed its own sweet time to merge into the reddish earth—one more Pueblo way of respectfully coexisting with the past. There—the ru-ins of the home of the man who striped his father's back with the Mexican horsewhip. Then—the old graveyard with his sister Cecelia's name carved by his father with a kitchen knife into the sandstone. And farther down the valley, the home of "the man who was sewn together," his body map of scars frightening boys like Wilbert, the church school where his school-mates watched the nun change into her nightclothes behind a shroud backlit by a kerosene lantern, the site of Dad Hunt's stream-powered grain mill, and all those hidden spots with their rumored caches of dinosaur bones, Spanish chalices, veins of raw gold, and burrows for snakes so gi-gantic they swallowed lambs whole.

Wilbert "Uncle Will" Hunt, at his new home in Acomita, 2007.

All those stories, all those memories, all those dear ones, where they lived and where their lives and thoughts took place.

Uphill and the pull into Skyline Two. Fourteen miles farther on, Acoma mesa—he'd never see it again. And looming behind the wonderful new house toward which Eddie helped his uncle slowly shuffle in his aluminum walker—Mount Taylor.

He was home.

On Columbus Day 2007, Wilbert wouldn't take his medications, refused to eat, and gasped for breath. An ambulance took him to ACL Hospital, the Acoma-Canoncito-Laguna Indian facility on the border of Acoma Reservation and San Fidel. There he lingered for five days until around noon, on Saturday, October 13, he whispered to his nephew, "Goodbye, Sonny, take care, I'm going." He closed his eyes and died.

The viewing was held in the Mormon church in Grants the following Tuesday. On Wednesday his home on Skyline Two was the site of a traditional wake with an open casket. He was clothed in his Mormon underwear, then a suit with the medicine pouch his father had given him before the war. Some blessed cornmeal speckled on his body. When the medicine men arrived around eleven that night, non-Acoma outsiders were asked to leave. Burial was at Santa Fe's federal cemetery on Thursday morning. He was interred atop Vedna's body so the grounds could save space. Cornmeal and turquoise were sprinkled on his casket before the operator of a chugging backloader filled in the grave.

The last of Edward's children was gone. But where?

Eddie and I were back in the housing development near the tribal center complex overlooking the San Jose wash and old Acomita. Princess had died but other dogs with hungry looks and mudballs clotting their fur slinked under cars or wandered the dusty streets and grassless yards that separated the single-family units. Without Uncle Blue Sky propped up in his dining nook, nothing felt the way it should.

The empty chair at the breakfast table looked in mourning. The interior was cold and inhospitable, as if the place wanted time of its own. There was no assuaging the unforgiving reality of his absence. But the impulse to do so prompted the rudeness of my question. Where did Eddie think the old man was now?

That dropped him into an uncharacteristic moment of reflection. Looking up as from a nap, he made a gesture that said, what a thing to ask. Or maybe it was impatience that I should understand by now about how his people organized their world and afterworlds and what went on between them. He was quiet for a bit.

Buried in the file cabinets of a western archive is a colored drawing by an Acoma schoolboy that brings his people's cosmos to life. Produced in the late 1920s, it was sketched in pencil, then watercolored. It is simple and literal, almost like a pedagogical aid meant to clarify relations between humans and Katsinas and their respective realms. It could even be interpreted as a Pueblo response to the "Ladder" scrolls that both Catholic and Protestant missionaries used as visual aids to teach Edward Hunt, his classmates at Albuquerque and Santa Fe, and thousands of other Indian children across the country, the series of moral lessons and right choices they must climb in order to reach the Christian heaven.

Except for its stylized sun the drawing bears little resemblance to customary Pueblo symbols for multileveled cosmic worlds—the stepped pyramidal mountains and horned snakes that we see on old kiva murals and paintings. From the high left corner beams a golden sun with its slit eyes. Descending from it to a two-story adobe house is a yellow stairway. Down it stride two figures, one masked. The chimney emits smoke within which ghostly flowers and a deer's head soar upward. As if we are watching sequential episodes from a single drama, another masked Katsina-like figure is already standing before its door and greeting three human occupants. Leading up from this scene is a second stepped ladder, this one red and tipped with an arrow point, suggesting lightning. Striding down this staircase toward the house are three more Katsinas, as if in procession.

The right side of the picture appears to communicate its main message. On an equal plane with the stylized sun is a large, realistic face and upper torso. Appearing with naked arms and shoulders, it is androgynous-looking, but probably female, and seems to be presiding over it all. Her tresses extend horizontally, almost transforming into the all-embracing, soft mountainous backdrop. As in a classic Pueblo blessing, she is exhaling a tremendous breath for us to inhale. Lines emanate from her open mouth and blow the sacredness upon a brownish oval that dominates the central scene. A world all its own, this oval plane lies within a fencelike orbit of thirteen mounded gray clouds, all of this dreamy stage floating above a huge fuzzy cloud.

This suspended realm is clearly Wenimats, the Pueblo "heaven." Lying to the west of Acoma, near Zuni country, here is the home of the Katsinas from which the community's prayer sticks summon these spirits to visit Acoma at key moments in her ceremonial year. That is when the spirits are impersonated by initiated members of the Katsina Society. The origin of rain-bringing clouds, Wenimats is the same mythical place that one is intended to be peering toward through the little hole one notices in the rain-worn adobe wall that encloses the old graveyard in front of San Estevan Church.

That Wenimats is a fertile, well-watered place is emphasized in the picture by the surrounding clouds, and the three ropelike dangles that drop from them. Tipped with arrowheads, they are obviously lightning strikes. Hanging on to each of them, like trapeze artists with legs hooked around thick descending ropes, is a sacred clown, naked but for breechcloth and yellow corn-husk headgear. All three lean jauntily off their lightning bolts and stare directly at us, almost showing off.

The cultivated products of this unearthly realm capture our attention. Prominent to the right are four mature cornstalks, ripe with tassels and cobs, two fruit trees, vines alongside a heap of freshly picked melons, and squash, bean, and possibly tobacco plants as well. More Katsinas and clowns mill about to the left; other clowns haul more harvest in a deerskin. Behind the fruit trees two other clowns tote another skin that holds a pile of dead rabbits. The overall impression is of plenty, as if the Katsinas are supplying the customary menu on ceremonial days for the feasting that punctuates the dancing, as if this is a form of sympathetic magic to influence what the Acoma people are hoping these powers-that-be will enable them to supply for themselves on such ritual occasions.

Rain, breath of life, corn, cooperation and conviviality between earthly and sacred realms, a world that survives thanks to the complementary blessings of sun, earth, and the good things they provide. These this drawing documents, in addition to the reassuring knowledge that the dead do not die.

This is the residence of the Pueblo dead, of all their ancestors, who have automatically and universally become rainclouds and Katsina spirits and will live forever.

"I once heard one of their preachers say," a Plains Indian judge told anthropologist Clark Wissler, "that no white man was admitted to heaven unless there were writings about him in a great book."

But this was Pueblo heaven. No books, no final judgments—everyone got in.

Eddie finally answered my question. Where is he now?

"Uncle Will shows up there and his dad, grandpa, and grandma are there, and his brothers and sisters, the whole family, and the Katsinas."

What happens then?

"They're dancing. They're dancing together."

Mount Taylor, Acoma Pueblo's sacred mountain of the north.

Postscript

DURING WORK on this narrative it became clear that my reconstruction of the Hunt family story would suffer from two limitations. My best opportunity to elicit the female side to their history was gone with the death of Vedna Eckerman Hunt, Wilbert's Laguna-born wife, on March 8, 1992, about a year before I began the project. From all accounts of her personality, intellect, and memory, she could have provided an important and lively contribution from that perspective. Without Vedna's account, and with the general reluctance of other female family and community members to provide details, dates, or impressions about the Hunt family, this was going to be a mostly male-centered narrative.

Second, as I pursued the family's movements with Edward and Marie as my focus, and with the understandable emphasis on Wilbert as their last surviving child and my principal interviewee over many years, I wound up focusing on the lives and travels of Wilbert, Henry, and Clyde, at the expense of the rest of the Hunt children. Already my canvas was so broad, and the diverse contexts of encompassing historical periods and events over a century and a half so complex, that a fuller portrayal would have weakened the momentum of the central storyline. In an effort to do some justice to the full family produced by Edward and Marie, here is brief recap, filling in some blanks and a testimony to their lives. They all knew each other, it must be mentioned, and relished the get-togethers they did manage. As John Johnson Jr., son of Josephine Hunt and her Navajo husband, Johnny Johnson, told me, "My uncles and aunts were always so kind and loving with me, they were fun to be with and I remember them all so fondly."

Ervin (born November 18, 1890), the first of their children, became a small rancher, farmer, and trucker in the Grants, New Mexico, area. He and his wife, Esther (Romero), had four children. Ervin died in 1987 in the progressive community of Casa Blanca, New Mexico.

Alfred Lewis (born April 12, 1892) lived in Albuquerque, where he worked as a custodian for Albuquerque Gas and Electric. Before divorcing, he and Frances (Vigil) had four children. During the war he served in the U.S. Army as a gunnery instructor. For most of his life he remained in and around the Albuquerque area but, according to relatives, "became a kiva man again" at the end of his life. He died in 1977.

Allen Jackson (born March 12, 1894), last of the Hunts' children to be born in the rock shelter on the edge of the Malpais badlands, went to California to work for the Santa Fe Railroad in 1922. First he lived in the famous "Richmond Colony" of boxcars that formed a virtual pueblo. Then he married Rose (Cox) and eventually moved to Berkeley. Shortly after his wife died he remarried, and died in Albuquerque in 1980. He is remembered for his love of music and clarinet playing.

Evelyn (born November 27, 1896) moved to California with her husband, Andrew Paisano, from Laguna Pueblo, where he became a crane operator in the Richmond shipyard. Her second husband was Theodore Orcutt, a Hupa Indian. The couple stayed in California. She died in 1993.

Cecelia (born 1898) was born in Acomita and attended local grade schools. But after she contracted tuberculosis at Haskell Indian School she had to remain at home, where she died in 1917.

Clyde (born September 10, 1900) does appear in this book. He married Estelle Shirley and died in Carlsbad, New Mexico, in 1972.

Henry Wayne (born November 12, 1902) is well profiled in these pages; he died in 1977.

Ida Pearl (born July 3, 1904) married Joseph Eduvigan of Santa Ana Pueblo. They continued to live in the pueblo while he worked for most of his life for Bernalillo Mercantile Co. They kept a sizable garden whose produce all family members enjoyed. She died in 1985.

Wilbert Edward (born October 22, 1907) is also well profiled in these pages. He died in 2007.

Mary (born 1908) died in infancy.

Josephine Viola (born March 10, 1910) married a Navajo, John Bahe Johnson, who was a silversmith and worked for various stores in the Albuquerque area, especially Maisel's and Bell's. They had two children, Thelma and Johnny. She died in 1993.

Florence Angeline (born 1914), the "baby" of the family, attended Albuquerque Indian School until around the seventh grade when she contracted tuberculosis. She died in 1930.

ACKNOWLEDGMENTS

THIS BOOK grew out of a conversation during a coffee break at the Smithsonian Institution's National Anthropological Archives in the spring of 1993. While researching another project, I wondered if Jim Glenn, then chief archivist, had any idea who had recited the Bureau of American Ethnology's Bulletin 135, *Origin Myth of Acoma and Other Records,* which the Smithsonian had published in 1942. In the work itself its narrators were described as "a group of Pueblo Indians," whose "chief informant" had learned it during his initiation as a "sacred clown." Like many other writers on the Southwest, more than once I'd quoted from that remarkably accessible but anonymous narrative and remained curious about its origins.

Jim thought BAE Bulletin 165, Frances Densmore's *Music of Acoma, Isleta, Cochiti and Zuni Pueblos,* published in 1957, might help. Its frontispiece photo, by the Smithsonian's De Lancey Gill, featured some of Densmore's Acoma musicians, the Edward Hunt family from Acoma Pueblo, decked out in their Plains Indian–like Show Indian regalia. The photograph's date of 1928, and other tips in Densmore's text, coincided with the year that the Acoma myth had been transcribed. Jim also realized that the Smithsonian had just received about eighteen still-unprocessed boxes from Glenal Hunt, the Oklahoma widow of Henry Wayne Wolf Robe Hunt, one of Edward Hunt's sons.

A dip into this material confirmed Edward Hunt as the myth's narrator and Wolf Robe as his translator, and also turned up the Albuquerque address and phone number of Henry's younger brother Wilbert "Blue Sky Eagle" Hunt, who was with his family in the nation's capital that year. Upon my return to Wisconsin where I was teaching, I called Wilbert and a few weeks later flew to New Mexico to begin the conversations that led to a simultaneous reissue of my re-edited origin myth and this biography of the Hunt family, which we agreed would revolve around his father's remarkable life. In fact, shortly after the recent death of his sister Josephine, her daughter and Wilbert's niece, Thelma, wrote him, "We all need your remembrance of your father, our mother, your own grandfather, your mother and grandmother, so that we can tell our children and grandchildren the story of where we came from. It is an oral history that must not be lost" (Thelma Johnson to Wilbert Hunt, April 20, 1993).

My primary gratitude, therefore, is to Wilbert Hunt, who entrusted me with this story, and to whom I pledged I would make it into a book. Until his death on October 22, 2007, Wilbert "Uncle Will" Hunt never hesitated to share his sharp memories and personal archives, all of which, together with other materials collected for these books over the past twenty years, are deposited in the University of New Mexico's Center for Southwest Studies as the Hunt Family–Peter Nabokov Collection, Accession #2007-06-28. My deepest regret is that I could not put my reissue of his father's version of the Acoma origin myth and this family biography into his hands.

I am profoundly thankful to my agent, Susan Bergholz, and her husband, Bert Snyder, for their critical and unflagging encouragement over the years; to my editor, Paul Slovak, for his steadfast support, great patience, and deep book knowledge; and to my wife, Linda Feldman, for her editorial assistance, technological expertise, moral support, and loving friendship.

I am deeply indebted to Joseph Edward "Eddie" Hunt, Wilbert's nephew and son of his brother Alfred. With his late wife, Shirley, Eddie looked after Uncle Will before and through their move to Acomita and his final years. Eddie remained constantly available with photographs, memories, and a myriad of helpful tasks. Other Hunt family members, close, extended, and through marriage, who made themselves available for remembrances include the late Thelma Velez, Johnny and Nancy Johnson, sisters Lois and Nevlyn Eckerman, Mary Garcia, Elsie Johnson, Lorenzo Hunt, Elmer James Hunt, Emmet Hunt Jr., Terry Hunt, Carl and Elma Lorenzo, Henry and Karen Vallo, Mary Lowden, Vincent Gonzales, and Veronica Hunt. I am extremely grateful to them all.

For research assistance in New Mexico I am indebted to Mo Palmer of Albuquerque, who has been of inestimable value to this project and who believed in it; to Ken Wade, ace librarian of our American Indian Studies Library at UCLA, also of phenomenal assistance over the years; and to artist Shirin Raban for her illustrations. Other archivists, librarians, curators, scholars, and writers who helped with research include Mike Kelly, director of the Center for Southwest Research at the University of New Mexico; Kim Walters of the Southwest Museum, Autry National Center; Daniel Kosharek, photo archivist of the New Mexico History Museum; Catherine Baudoin of the Maxwell Museum of Anthropology at the University of New Mexico; Martha and Joseph Leibert of Bernalillo's Valencia County Museum; Kevin Proffitt of the American Jewish Archives, Cincinnati; Tomas Jaehn of the Chavez Historical Library at the Palace of the Governors; Laura Holt, archivist of the School for Advanced Research; and Diana Bird of the Laboratory of Anthropology.

Early support for this work came from Marta Weigle and Mary Powell of the former Ancient City Press, who encouraged me to pursue the Acoma myth republication and Hunt story after they were introduced to this material through our work on *Architecture of Acoma Pueblo* (Santa Fe: Ancient City Press, 1986); historian/editorial writer Abe Peña for stories of Solomon Bibo and the Grants–San Mateo area; Scott G. Ortman for unpublished word lists from Keresan linguist Wick Miller; Ted Jojola for sources on Albuquerque Indian School and his family's memories of Edward Hunt; Genie Gerard of Special Collections at the Young Research Library for access to files on the Bibo family; Audrey Dittert for memories of her husband, "Ed" Dittert Jr.; Bob Roland for information on the Calabash and Kowina ruins, Arthur Bibo, and the Malpais, and to Professor Greg Schachner for explaining their significance; Professor Clyde Ellis for great help with the Indian Lore movement and Wild West shows; photographer Lee Marmon for images and information on Laguna Pueblo; J. T. Michelson for memories of Wilbert and Vedna Hunt's years at his Bell Trading Company; Professor Kurt Peters for research and stories about the "Richmond Colony"; Professor Mick Gidley for tips on the work of Edward S. Curtis; William J. Peace for information on the career of Leslie A. White; Quinta Scott for copies of her interviews with Zelta and Hugh Davis and Wolf Robe's Catoosa trading post; Tisa J. Wenger for information on the 1920s dance controversy; Kurt F. Anschuetz for articles and information about western New Mexico archaeology; Director Rick West Jr. of the Autry National Center for his memories of the Tulsa, Oklahoma, Indian art circle.

For contacts and assistance with the Hunt family's German experiences I am grateful to my cousins Nathalie and Constaine Fasolt; Ernst Günther, historian of Dresden's Sarrasani Circus; Robin Leipold, director of the Karl-May-Museum in Radebeul, Germany; Hartmut Rietschel of Dresden; and the UCLA Fowler Museum's Agnes Stauber for translations from the German about the circus and German writings about American Indians in general.

To others I am in debt for professional advice, responses to queries, and useful materials: Brian S. Collier; historian and writer Marc Simmons; William Deverell; Margaret D. Jacobs; David Bergholz; John J. Grabowski; Gloria Tabacchi; Will Wroth; Mary Alice Waugh; Steven M. Karr; Gina Rappaport, archives specialist at the Smithsonian Institution's National Anthropological Archives; Jonathan Batkin of the Wheelwright Museum; Al Regensberg; Sarah Rivett; Louis A. Hieb; Michael Elias; Paula Fleming; Jean O'Brien; Jeanne Snodgrass; Al Hurtado; Marlene and Christopher Baker; Dennis P. Trujillo; Tawney Lim; Jay Miller; Carter Blue Clark; Rennard Strickland; Alfred Bush; Patrick Polk; Don Cosentino; Ramona Kaplan; Helen V. MacLeod; Joseph Nagy; Carolyn Schwarcz; Tim Taylor; John Hughes; Karl F. Kumli; Linda McCormick; James Snead; William Truettner; Richard White; Paul Kroskrity; Ernie Bulow; Peter Whiteley; and, as always, Raymond J. Fogelson.

For research, writing, and editing time on both the origin myth republication and this family biography I am grateful for: a Guggenheim Foundation fellowship (2008–9); a Mellon Residency at the Huntington Library, San Marino (2007–8), and strong support from then director of research Roy Ritchie; the office of State Historians Program short-term fellowship, State Records Center and Archives (2007), and support from its then director, Estevan Rael-Gálvez; a Stewart Fellowship in Anthropology, Princeton University (2006), with special thanks to Professor Isabelle Clark-Decès; and the UCLA Institute of American Indian Cultures (2003–4).

The gallery of bygone supporters for my work includes John Collier Sr., who kindly critiqued my first effort to put an American Indian life history into print; Bob Bunker, Bertha Dutton, and Anne M. Smith, who first introduced me to Santa Fe; scholars and friends Alfonso Ortiz and Vine Deloria Jr., whose personal advice and written works have been formidable influences; William C. Sturtevant, who showed me Matthew Stirling's old office in the Smithsonian Castle; and my stepfather and mother, William and Constance Darkey, who found this story fascinating.

SOURCES AND NOTES

THE DOCUMENTARY BEDROCK of this book are the few recorded instances when Edward Hunt talked about his personal background, and conversations with his and Marie Hunt's last surviving of twelve children, Wilbert Edward Hunt, between the spring of 1993 and October 2007.

Early on I suspected that anthropologist Leslie A. White's anonymous fragment, the eleven-page "Autobiography of an Acoma Indian" (in *New Material from Acoma*, Smithsonian Institution, Bureau of American Ethnology, Bulletin 136, Anthropological Papers no. 32 [1943]: 326–37), was actually Edward Hunt's story. My hunch was confirmed in White's handwritten field notebook for summer 1934, deposited in Ann Arbor's University of Michigan Library, Special Collections. On page 37 are White's penciled notes from Hunt: "I got my name at Albuquerque Indian School. They called me Gai're before that time. I got bible at that time. 1883. Didn't go to school 1885–86." Material from this source will be cited below as EPH-1.

Then family members brought me an eleven-page, single-spaced transcript (transcribed in 1947) on onionskin that Josephine Hunt apparently copied from her brother Clyde's translation of an interview conducted with their father about his life. Although incomplete, this added or confirmed important details. Material from this source will be cited as EPH-2.

In addition, the *Origin Myth of Acoma and Other Records* (Smithsonian Institution, Bureau of American Ethnology, Bulletin 135, 1942) that Edward narrated to the Smithsonian in 1928 contains much information that provides the model for various ritual procedures and other practices in this book. Periodically I have drawn upon it in this account; it will be referred to in these endnotes as EPH-3.

Other interviews and direct quotes from Edward Hunt and family, such as comments to Sophie Aberle or the semiofficial interrogations of Edward cited in chapters 33, 36, and 59, will be referenced individually. Finally, between 1993 and 2012, I visited New Mexico and talked with Wilbert Hunt and other members of the extended and descendant Hunt family. All these materials, tapes, and photographs will be archived in the Hunt Family–Peter Nabokov Collection, Accession #2007-06-28, at the Center for Southwest Research (CSWR) at Zimmerman Library, University of New Mexico, Albuquerque. Interviews with Wilbert Hunt will be cited below as WH, with the date of the relevant interview. Interviews with others will be listed by full name, with their dates in parentheses.

Other information on Edward Hunt's life experiences is piecemeal and inconsistent. Where it was absent I took liberties in creating contexts, building transitions, even using all available research to imagine *what might have been,* so as to produce a full-bodied narrative. In these notes I tried to be candid about these instances and to cite the best sources I could find to reconstruct their experiences. An example is chapter 26, when Edward and Marie lived in a shelter overhang for a number of years where she bore their first three children.

For some events and situations I had two different and incomplete anecdotes, which had become oft-told and almost stereotypical pieces of fixed family lore. For this book I sought what seemed the most factual version, but I could have been wrong. In the following notes I try to suggest whenever an alternative account exists. Aside from Wilbert Hunt's tape-recorded memories, the early records for a single American Indian family from an oral culture in rural New Mexico with minimal early contact with the white world are few. Even as the twentieth century opened up, the Hunts' paper trail remained thin. Only from Wilbert's and Wolf Robe's personal notes and their collections of newspaper clippings, datebooks, and photographs have I been able to patch together this chronicle.

In my text and selection of illustrations of this book I have sought to respect Acoma sensibilities where highly specific verbal accounts and detailed visual images of sensitive religious or social matters are concerned. Therefore I have omitted the proper names of some private individuals involved in troubled aspects of the Hunt story and included none of the ethnographic artwork that Wolf Robe and others produced for various institutions. I have also occasionally omitted or only generalized about ritual procedures that are not a part of public record or that Edward detailed in unpublished portions of his interviews with Charles Strong (fieldworker for photographer Edward S. Curtis), Sophie D. Aberle, Leslie A. White, Matthew W. Stirling, Nina Otero-Warren, and others.

To supply cultural and historical contexts I have drawn again and again from the following basic sources about Acoma Pueblo and the Southwest. When I cite from them I will only use the author's last name and the publication's date. This working shelf list includes: Velma Garcia-Mason, "Acoma Pueblo," in Alfonso Ortiz, ed., *Southwest,* vol. 9 of the *Handbook of the North American Indians* (Washington, DC: Smithsonian Institution, 1979), pp. 450–66, and other pueblo profiles and essays in that volume; Ward Alan Minge, *Acoma: Pueblo in the Sky,* rev. ed. (Albuquerque: University of New Mexico Press, 2002); my own *Architecture of Acoma Pueblo: The 1934 Historic American Buildings Survey Project* (Santa Fe, NM: Ancient City Press, 1986); Edward S. Curtis, *The Tiwa. The Keres,* vol. 16 of *The North American Indian* (Johnson reprint, 1970 [1926]); Elsie Clews Parsons, *Pueblo Indian Religion,* 2 vols. (Lincoln: University of Nebraska Press, Bison Books reprint 1996 [1939]); and Leslie A. White, *The Acoma Indians,* 49th Annual Report of the Bureau of American Ethnology (Washington, DC: Smithsonian Institution, 1932). For a regional overview: Howard R. Lamar, *The Far*

Southwest, 1846–1912: A Territorial History, rev. ed. (Albuquerque: University of New Mexico Press, 2000 [1966]); Edward H. Spicer, *Cycles of Conquest: The Impact of Spain, Mexico, and the United States on the Indians of the Southwest, 1533–1960* (Tucson: University of Arizona Press, 1962); D. W. Meinig, *Southwest: Three Peoples in Geographical Change, 1600–1970* (London: Oxford University Press, 1971); Marta Weigle and Peter White, *The Lore of New Mexico* (Albuquerque: University of New Mexico Press, 1988); and Don D. Fowler, *A Laboratory for Anthropology: Science and Romanticism in the American Southwest, 1846–1930* (Albuquerque: University of New Mexico Press, 2000). For local cities: Marc Simmons, *Albuquerque: A Narrative History* (Albuquerque: University of New Mexico Press, 1982), and Chris Wilson, *The Myth of Santa Fe: Creating a Modern Regional Tradition* (Albuquerque: University of New Mexico Press, 1997). For regional personalities: Don Bullis, *New Mexico Historical Biographies* (Los Ranchos, NM: Rio Grande Books, 2011). Especially valuable for less familiar historical figures and their role in the state's history has been the Web site and online biographies from Santa Fe's New Mexico Office of the State Historian.

To this list I add lesser-known works unusually close to the Hunt family story: Helen Rushmore and Wolf Robe Hunt, *The Dancing Horses of Acoma and Other Acoma Indian Stories,* based on Edward's stories and illustrated by Wolf Robe (Cleveland: World Publishing Co., 1963); James Paytiamo, *Flaming Arrow's People,* by a nephew of Edward Hunt (New York: Duffield & Green, 1932); Bobette Gugliotta, *Katzimo, Mysterious Mesa,* a novel by a descendant of the Bibo family covering one season, the summer of 1925, in the lives of Carl, the "half-Jewish, half-Acoma boy," and his Indian cousin Wilbert (New York: Dodd, Mead & Co., 1974); and John M. Gunn, *Schat-Chen: History, Traditions and Narratives of the Queres Indians of Laguna and Acoma,* by an Anglo resident married into Laguna Pueblo (Albuquerque: Alright & Anderson, 1916).

Along with this list, the following chapter-by-chapter notes are the references that I consulted, or quoted from, for this book. Songs cited in this book are selected from Hunt family materials that were sung, recorded, and translated for the Smithsonian Institution, Bureau of American Ethnology, in the fall of 1928. Currently they are archived in the Smithsonian's National Anthropological Archives together with the BAE Bulletin 135 papers and the Frances Densmore collections. In addition, handwritten versions of some lyrics are with Stirling's handwritten version of the myth in the archive of the myth's coeditor (along with Leslie A. White), Elsie Clews Parsons, at Philadelphia's American Philosophical Society.

All of Edward Hunt's quotes in this book are either from the sources cited above, are from other scattered firsthand materials and interviews that he gave to outsiders or family members, or are derived from Wilbert Hunt's memories of what his father said.

Introduction

1 **Shortly after returning:** Although I asked on numerous occasions over the years, Wilbert Hunt retained no memories or documentation concerning how his family gained their entrée into the Smithsonian or any details of where they lived or how they got to and fro in the nation's capital. Nor could Smithsonian archivists and historians uncover any financial records or logistical information concerning the Hunt family's working sojourn over September and October 1928. My information on this here and in chapter 40 is partly based on my being shown Matthew W. Stirling's old office by William C. Sturtevant in 1995, on Stirling's various obituaries and accounts of his life such as in the delightful Gordon R. Willey, *Portraits in American Archaeology: Remembrance of Some Distinguished Americanists* (Albuquerque: University of New Mexico Press, 1988), pp. 243–64 (which describes the experience of reaching his personal office), and on contextual information of personalities like J. P. Harrington who were operative at the time. For instance, there is a November 27, 1928, letter from Edward Hunt to John Peabody Harrington (probably written by his son Wolf Robe Hunt) in which the elder Hunt opens his request that Harrington add a sentence to a prior letter of recommendation for their troupe's cultural presentations, with the following comment: "I wish to thank you for the most encouraging letter you wrote to me. Also for the favor you done, when you spoke to Mr. Stirling for me, and I am in hope that we can work together in the future. Because I do not know of any one for whom I would rather work than you" (Hunt to Harrington, November 27, 1928, J. P. Harrington Papers, National Anthropological Archives, Smithsonian Institution).

3 **Edward called the song:** When hypothesizing about the all-important rituals led in the great kivas by priesthoods among the Chaco Canyon forebears of the Acoma people that drew the entire community together, anthropologist Jay Miller has written, "The thrust of all these priestly efforts, then as now, was to 'keep "the universe moving"—the general and typical Pueblo concept of relatedness in the universe,' as noted by Edward Dozier . . . a Santa Clara anthropologist." Jay Miller, "Keres: Endangered Key to the Pueblo Puzzle," *Ethnohistory* 48, no. 3 (2001): 503. The words to the song that Edward entitled "How the World Moves" are from "Song 9-C," National Anthropological Archives Collection #4533, the trove of recordings and handwritten lyrics collected during this ethnographic episode in Washington. In the Smithsonian files this song is described as "sung sometimes by the *chiani* or medicine men during the *chiani* ceremony," and is filed among "Acoma songs sung by Philip Sanchez, translated by Wilbert Hunt." It was recorded by Anthony Wilding in October 1928, and deposited in the Bureau of Ethnology archives by M. W. Stirling in December 1957.

Chapter 1: The Sun's Latest (1861)

For material in this chapter: EPH-1; EPH-2; WH—9/2/94.

7 **"It was my Tewa name":** Alfonso Ortiz, *National Geographic* 180, no. 4 (October 1991): 6.

7 **On the fourth morning after:** My reconstruction is based on the Pueblo naming ceremony as communicated by Edward Hunt to various interviewers: Leslie White (White 1932, pp. 132–35); Edward S. Curtis or his fieldworker (Edward S. Curtis Collection, Seaver Center for Western History Research, Natural History Museum of Los Angeles County, Box 16, Folder 3[6]); Matthew W. Stirling, as part of the Acoma origin myth (EPH-3); and again in White 1943 for the anonymous autobiography (EPH-1).

12 **Up on Acoma mesa:** These and subsequent chapter details (chapter 17) on Navajo and Apache raids in Acoma and Laguna country are from ethnohistorian Florence H. Ellis's field research, as summarized in chapters 8–14 of her *Archaeologic and Ethnologic Data: Acoma-Laguna Land Claims,* vol. 2 of five volumes of evidence for the Indian Claims Commission (ICC), Dockets 266 (Acoma) and 227 (Laguna) (republished and repaginated in New York: Garland Publishing, 1974). For more on the ICC work with Acoma and Laguna see chapter 54 and its notes. On Navajo travails and the Long Walk period, see Lawrence Kelly, *Navajo Roundup: Selected Correspondence of Kit Carson's Expedition Against the Navajos, 1863–1865* (Colorado: Pruett Publishing Co., 1970), and Ruth Roessel, ed., *Navajo Stories of the Long Walk Period* (Tsaile, AZ: Navajo Community College Press, 1973).

Chapter 2: Born of the Rock (1861)

For material in this chapter: EPH-1; EPH-2; WH—7/3/93.

13 **"All Indian history":** Quoted in Raymond J. DeMallie, "Kinship: The Foundation of Native American Society," in *Studying Native America: Problems and Prospects,* ed. Russell Thornton (Madison: University of Wisconsin Press, 1998), p. 345.

13 **This child was born:** Regarding Edward (Day Break) Hunt's parentage, in 1937 anthropologist Leslie White wrote Elsie Clews Parsons that "Father [Fridolin] Schuster, who was at Laguna when I was out there, told me that Ed Hunt had some Mexican blood in him, but he did not know the details. I never asked him or his sons about it. I do know that he lived in Acoma from his birth or at least early infancy. If his father was Mexican, I do not believe that he lived at Acoma. I am quite sure that he was brought up at Acoma as any Indian child there was reared" (White to Parsons, August 13, 1937, Elsie Clews Parsons Papers, American Philosophical Society, Philadelphia). Apparently it was no longer a secret for Hunt, for as Matthew Stirling wrote Parsons the same year, "All I know about Hunt's Mexican blood is what I have learned from Leslie White. Although when Hunt was here he told me of it without going into detail. I did not like to question him too much about it at the time" (Stirling to Parsons, September 22, 1937, Elsie Clews Parsons Papers, American Philosophical Society, Philadelphia). Somehow Edward Curtis got the impression that "He belongs to the sun clan, but has Mexican blood from his grandfather" (Edward S. Curtis Collection, Seaver Center for Western History, Natural History Museum of Los Angeles County, Box 16, Folder 3[6], "Acoma," p. 57). But since Charles Lummis's photographs of the man whom family members identify as the "Faustino" who served as his father hardly

looks old enough to have a son that mature, I have opted for the genetic father—since no other candidate appears in the documents—as being unknown, probably of Hispano origin, and not the grandfather. Was his genetic paternal grandfather possibly Hispano? I asked Wilbert Hunt. "Could be," he replied coyly.

16 **This newborn belonged:** During the decade (1860s) of Day Break's childhood, according to Acoma author Velma Garcia-Mason, "Acoma was described in the same manner as it was in 1540, with houses in parallel rows, ladders used for ingress and egress to the dwellings, low arch formation for doorway passages, and window plates of crystallized gypsum (selenite). There are also descriptions of a variety of fruits and vegetables, blue corn foods, herds of sheep and cattle, weaving, pottery and basketry, and evidence of Spanish silver" (Garcia-Mason 1979, p. 459).

17 **This connected him:** See Elizabeth Brandt on how social distinctions in historical Pueblo villages might be *upstreamed* to interpret their pre-Hispanic antecedents: "Egalitarianism, Hierarchy and Centralization in the Pueblos," in *The Ancient Southwest Community: Models and Methods for the Study of Prehistoric Social Organization* (Albuquerque: University of New Mexico Press, 1994).

20 **Many years later:** The discovery of Edward Hunt's birth date on the doorjamb is one of a number of well-oiled Hunt family legends. Sometimes it is a carving into the wood of the "fev 61" date (February 1861), sometimes the date was formed out of spruce sap gum. The uncle in question learned to read and write during his years of Catholic training in Durango, Mexico. This appears to be the same well-traveled uncle who ventured east to Tucumcari in his early years to trade with Comanches, and later west to find work as a sheepherder in California.

Chapter 3: Atop a World Apart (1861)

21 **"Surrounded by air":** William Stafford, "Acoma Mesa," *The Nation*, October 8, 1977.

24 **Beneath the honeyed light:** Jemez Pueblo historian Joe S. Sando quoted in Alfonso Ortiz, *The Pueblo* (New York: Chelsea House, 1994), p. 45.

26 **For these reasons:** My invocation of anthropologist Fred Eggan's "Keresan Bridge" concept is a loose use; it was famously challenged by Robin Fox—see summary of this debate in Elizabeth A. Brandt's "Egalitarianism, Hierarchy, and Centralization in the Pueblos," in *The Ancient Southern Community*, ed. W. H. Wills and Robert D. Leonard (Albuquerque: University of New Mexico Press, 1994). Yet the formulation is still useful to communicate the notable environmental, and to some degree sociological, way that Acoma summarizes so many generic Pueblo characteristics across the Southwest.

27 **In September 1861:** The council with Apaches at Acoma is in John Grenier's journals, published in Ralph E. Twitchell, *Old Santa Fe*, vol. 3 (1916). On Mangas Coloradas's visits to Acoma mesa, see "A Treaty at Acoma," in Edwin R. Sweeney, *Mangas Coloradas: Chief of the Chiricahua Apaches* (Norman: University of Oklahoma Press, 1998).

Chapter 4: When Cosmologies Collide (1540)

28 **"San Estevan—It creates":** Vincent Scully, *American Architecture and Urbanism* (New York: Viking, 1969), pp. 27–28.

29 **A few hundred feet:** EPH-1. On San Estevan del Rey Mission: while the customary feast day for Saint Stephen is December 26, to avoid confusing this first Christian martyr with the Hungarian Saint Stephen, the celebration was reset at Acoma to September 2. For background on the famous mission and its multiple restoration projects since 1922, see L. A. Riley, "Repairs to the Old Mission at Acoma," *El Palacio* 18, no. 1 (January 1925); Kate Wingert-Playdon, *John Gaw Meem at Acoma Pueblo: The Restoration of San Esteban del Rey Mission* (Albuquerque: University of New Mexico Press, 2012), and Beatrice Chauvenet, *John Gaw Meem: Pioneer in Historic Preservation* (Santa Fe: Museum of New Mexico Press, 1985), which contains tidbits on the Acoma go-between and amateur folklorist Bernhard A. Reuter of Pecos. On the church's materials that wound up in Mr. Meem's collection, see rafters and doors pictured in *Pueblo Treasure: From the Silverman Museum* (Santa Fe: Silverman Museum, 2005).

29 **Three hundred and thirty years:** For background and quotes on the Spanish period (1540–1822): Ralph E. Twitchell, *The Leading Facts of New Mexican History,* 5 vols. (Cedar Rapids, IA: Torch Press, 1911–17), Twitchell, *The Spanish Archives of New Mexico,* 2 vols. (Cedar Rapids, IA, 1914); and historian Ward Allen Minge, who turned his research document for Indian Claims Commission Docket 266 (*Historical Treatise in Defense of the Pueblo of Acoma Land Claim,* September 19, 1957) into the book *Acoma: Pueblo in the Sky,* rev. ed. (Albuquerque: University of New Mexico Press, 2002 [1991]). While some dispute whether Vicente Zaldívar's infamous sentence against the survivors of his destruction of Acoma was actually carried out, Wilbert Hunt (9/3/98) said that his people just wanted to forget about it. But he did recall hearing from family members about one "old grandpa" who had lost his leg from the sentence walking around with his stump and making "bump, bump" sounds. "It was lots of work," Wilbert said, "because they have to help him get into bed, to get up, and everything else. You know how it would be—no crutches, no wheelchairs, made a lot of grief for the whole family. A lot of men died from gangrene. That's all I ever heard."

30 **Before the Spanish:** For a comparative survey of the English (imposed environmental transformation—gardens), French (pomp and imposed language learning), Dutch (coastal cartography), Portuguese (grid mapping), and Spanish (formal spoken ultimatums) preferred modes of expressing and exercising their colonial wills, see Patricia Seed, *Ceremonies of Possession in Europe's Conquest of the New World, 1492–1640* (Cambridge: Cambridge University Press, 1995). On Pueblo land history: Malcolm Ebright, Rick Hendricks, and Richard Hughes, *Four Square Leagues: Pueblo Indian Land in New Mexico* (Albuquerque: University of New Mexico Press, 2014).

32 **To confer authority:** On the background of the Pueblo ceremonial canes of office from the Spanish, Mexican, and "Lincoln" (American) periods, see Martha LaCroix Dailey, "Symbolism and Significance of the Lincoln Canes for the Pueblos of New Mexico," *New Mexico Historical Review* 69, no. 2 (1994), in which she

debunks the anecdote that President Lincoln personally gave them to Pueblo leaders in Washington, and Joe S. Sando, "The Silver-Crowned Canes of Pueblo Office," in *Telling New Mexico: A New History,* ed. Marta Weigle (Santa Fe: Museum of New Mexico Press, 2009), which mentions an additional set of canes given to Pueblo governors by New Mexico state governor Bruce King in 1980 in affirmation of Pueblo sovereignty, and a second set of Spanish canes presented in September 1987 by a visiting king of Spain. In his interview with University of Utah historian D. Corydon Hammond, Wilbert Hunt recalled being asked to repair the cane's worn silverwork (August 19, 1967).

Chapter 5: Taking No More (1680)

36 **"For the Pueblo people":** Alfonso Ortiz, "Po'pay's Leadership: A Pueblo Perspective," *El Palacio* 86, no. 4 (Winter 1980–81): 22.

37 **Among the beaten men:** Charles W. Hackett, *Revolt of the Pueblo Indians of New Mexico and Otermin's Attempted Reconquest, 1680–1692,* 2 vols. (Albuquerque: University of New Mexico Press, 1942), which contains this self-contradictory statement: "Acoma played no important part in the events as related in the Spanish documents of 1680, since it was too far away to cooperate successfully with the valley pueblos. Otermin, however, learned from the Indian besiegers of Santa Fe that all the Spaniards there were dead" (vol. 1, p. xlvii). A noteworthy account is poet-conquistador-participant Gaspar Pérez de Villagrá's thirty-four-canto tome *History of New Mexico* (Los Angeles: Quivira Society, 1933). To Adolph Bandelier the author was a terrible poet "but a reliable historian so far as he saw and took part in the events himself." In addition: David Roberts, *The Pueblo Revolt: The Secret Rebellion That Drove the Spaniards Out of the Southwest* (New York: Simon & Schuster, 2004), which contains the quotes from Acoma tribal historian Brian Vallo (p. 91), San Juan Pueblo anthropologist Alfonso Ortiz (p. 148), and anthropologist Peter Whiteley (p. 232); and Robert Silverberg, *The Pueblo Revolt* (Lincoln: University of Nebraska Press, 1970). David J. Weber also discusses the dearth of native oral tradition on the revolt in "Historians and the Pueblo Revolt," from his selected and introduced anthology *What Caused the Pueblo Revolt of 1680* (Boston: Bedford/St. Martin's, 1999). Alternative discussions of the uprising are in "The Great Pueblo Revolt," special issue, *El Palacio* 86, no. 4 (1980–81), with five scholars of different persuasions weighing in, and the more partisan *Po'pay: Leader of the First American Revolution,* ed. Joe S. Sando and Herman Agoyo (Santa Fe: Clear Light, 2005). On the revolt's coordinators, see Stephanie Beninato's intriguing case for a mixed-blood instigator: "Pope, Pose-yemu, and Naranjo: A New Look at Leadership in the Pueblo Revolt of 1680," *New Mexico Historical Review* 65, no. 4 (October 1990).

41 **Speaking of Acoma's resistance:** The Edward S. Curtis quote is in Mick Gidley's collection of the photographer's mostly unpublished writings, *Edward S. Curtis and the North American Indian Project in the Field,* ed. and introduction by Mick Gidley (Lincoln: University of Nebraska Press, 2003), p. 51. It deserves mention that Edward Hunt contributed mightily to Edward Curtis's coverage in vol. 16 (*The Tiwa. The Keres,* 1926) of his monumental "project," as Curtis ac-

knowledged in the volume. Thanks to Mick Gidley, author of the definitive *Edward S. Curtis and the North American Indian, Incorporated* (New York: Cambridge University Press, 1998), for written guidance (4/24/2008) through the Curtis material that pertains to Acoma and the Southwest, enumerating Curtis and associates' visits there (1903, 1904, possibly 1905, possibly 1906, briefly during 1907–20 field trips, and 1920–25 when his two Pueblo volumes were actually researched and written). A University of Washington teacher, Charles Munroe Strong, was a key Curtis fieldworker during the 1909–10 period. As Edward testified on May 3, 1924, to Indian Rights Association investigators collecting information about Pueblo religious practices, "I spent one week in Albuquerque some time ago with a man named Strong. I gave all these old time stories from the beginning, all through, where they came from, and it took eight days to end of it. I gave the songs of medicine men for a record, and then I sung a Mask Dance, and I make the prayer sticks, and I made the mask, and I do not know what became of this man, and I have heard nothing of it any more" (E. S. Curtis Collections, #C 1–3, Braun Research Library, Southwest Museum, Los Angeles).

41 **After this, as Santa Fe:** Erna Fergusson, *Dancing Gods: Indian Ceremonials of New Mexico and Arizona* (Albuquerque: University of New Mexico Press, 1931), p. 57. On the Santa Fe Fiesta that dramatizes in highly symbolic fashion the aftermath of these events, Ronald L. Grimes, *Symbol and Conquest: Public Ritual and Drama in Santa Fe* (Albuquerque: University of New Mexico Press, 1976), and the later critique by Sarah Bronwen Horton, *The Santa Fe Fiesta, Reinvented: Staking Ethno-Nationalist Claims to a Disappearing Homeland* (Santa Fe: School for Advanced Research Press, 2010).

Chapter 6: Becoming Their Own Spirits (1866)

For material in this chapter: WH—9/4/94.

42 **"A kachina is":** Fred Kabotie, *Fred Kabotie, Hopi Indian Artist* (Flagstaff: Museum of Northern Arizona Press, 1977), p. 123.

42 **By the time he:** For these Keresan supernaturals I use the "Katsina" spelling rather than "Kachina," as predominately employed in writings about Zuni and Hopi pueblos. Among the latter tribes, words and pictures of Kachinas, by tribal members, non-Indian illustrators, and photographers, are ubiquitous. Among Rio Grande and Keresan communities, however, they are banned and rare. I like Peter Whiteley's definition: "Katsina is a triune concept, referring to spirits of the dead, to clouds, and to personated spirits who appear in ceremonies" (*Hopi Histories*, pp. 25–26); also Barton Wright's succinct description in *Pueblo Cultures* (Leiden: E. J. Brill, 1986), pp. 10–16. Among the many books on these cloud-spirit-beings: Polly Schaafsma, ed., *Katchinas in the Pueblo World* (Albuquerque: University of New Mexico Press, 1994), which contains, among other disciplinary perspectives, E. Charles Adams's summary of his theory on Kachina Society origins and functions. On popularizations of Kachina images, Zena Pearlstone et al., *Katsina: Commodified and Appropriated Images of Hopi Supernaturals* (Los Angeles: Fowler Museum of Cultural History, 2001).

43 **Day Break was never:** Edward Hunt's accounts of Acoma Katsinas and his own initiation are in EPH-1, Leslie White 1932, and Edward S. Curtis, *The Tiwa. The Keres,* vol. 16 of *The North American Indian* (1926). During his fall 1928 sojourn in Washington, Edward oversaw the recording of a number of Katsina, or "Rain God," songs, which are in the National Anthropological Archives; see chapter 42 for music references.

45 **To the Acoma people:** EPH-3 and White 1932 offer the origins and varieties of these Acoma supernatural personalities.

48 **At the Keresan-speaking pueblo:** A frequent motif among American Indian masking traditions, this version of the "stuck mask" is in Leslie White, *The Pueblo of Sia, New Mexico,* Bureau of American Ethnology, Bulletin 184 (Washington, DC: Smithsonian Institution, 1962), p. 253.

48 **Speaking of such ordeals:** Historian of religions Sam D. Gill develops this theme of "disenchantment" in "Hopi Kachina Cult Initiation: The Shocking Beginning to the Hopi's Religious Life," *Journal of the American Academy of Religion* 45, no. 2 (1977): 447–64.

Chapter 7: Mericanos Are Here (1846)

49 **"The total picture":** William H. Goetzmann, *Army Exploration in the American West, 1803–1863* (New Haven, CT: Yale University Press, 1959), p. 437.

49 **That morning Abert:** I am calculating that Edward's parents would have been youngsters when Abert arrived, hence my creation of this scene, based on his comments about bothersome kids, which were echoed by Lieutenant John Gregory Burke after climbing Acoma mesa on May 16, 1881: "chased by a parcel of white-toothed, bright-eyed children whose voices rang out in musical laughter as they emulated each other in frolicsome attempt to overhaul us." In "Bourke in the Southwest, VIII," ed. Lansing B. Bloom, *New Mexico Historical Review* 8, no. 1 (January 1943): 107. Abert's own quotes are from Senate Executive Document no. 23 (30th Cong. 1st Sess., Serial 506), republished in *Western America in 1846–47: The Original Travel Diary of Lieutenant J. W. Abert, Who Mapped New Mexico for the United States Army,* ed. John Galvin (San Francisco: John Howell, 1966). For more on Abert, early southwestern art, and the Corps of Topographical Engineers, I drew upon William A. Keleher's admiring introduction to his career in *Turmoil in New Mexico, 1846–1868* (Santa Fe: Rydal Press, 1952), and Martha Doty Freeman, "Creation of an Artistic Tradition," *New Mexico Historical Review* 49, no. 1 (January 1974). For me the most useful text for the American period remains Brian W. Dippie's *The Vanishing American: White Attitudes and U.S. Indian Policy* (Lawrence: University of Kansas Press, 1982).

51 **During the twenty-eight-year:** In his "American Westward Expansion and the Breakdown of Relations Between *Pobladores* and *'Indios Barbaros'* on Mexico's Far Northern Frontier, 1821–1846," historian David J. Weber sheds useful light on this confusing interim; in his *Myth and the History of the Hispanic Southwest* (Albuquerque: University of New Mexico Press, 1988).

55 **In 1879 the Bureau of American Ethnology:** Neil M. Judd, *The Bureau of American Ethnology: A Partial History* (Norman: University of Oklahoma Press, 1967).

Chapter 8: Toward the New West (1861–66)

56 **"In 1864 Acoma":** Garcia-Mason 1979, p. 459.

56 **The years that thrust:** Adam Goodheart, *1861: The Civil War Awakening* (New York: Vintage, 2012). Also Robert M. Utley, "Indian-United States Military Situation, 1848–1891," in Wilcomb E. Washburn, ed., *History of Indian-White Relations*, vol. 4 of *Handbook of the North American Indians* (Washington, DC: Smithsonian Institution, 1988).

56 **With hardly a breather:** I take it this is what Jonathan Lethem also means when, talking of Keith Carradine's death scene in Robert Altman's film *McCabe & Mrs. Miller*, he suggests that it stands for "a farewell to . . . the Western tradition (which was practically always saying farewell from its beginning, anyway)." *The Ecstasy of Influence* (New York: Vintage, 2011), p. 164.

62 **More monumental and longer-lasting:** See chapter 14 for railroad citations.

Chapter 9: All He Had to Learn (1869)

For material in this chapter: WH—7/20/98; WH—4/11/94.

64 **"The People were living":** Ruth Benedict, "Eight Stories from Acoma," *Journal of American Folklore* 43 (1930): 59, from tales probably obtained from James Paytiamo, Edward Hunt's nephew.

64 **The rest of America:** In EPH-2, Edward Hunt began describing his childhood with the comment, "Our schooling consisted of, first, everything about the Indian religion." The quote is from "Growing Up in the Old Days," in Wick R. Miller, *Acoma Grammar and Texts* (Berkeley: University of California Press, 1965), pp. 245–47. Other material here draws on *Pueblo Mothers and Children, Essays by Elsie Clews Parsons, 1915–1924*, ed. Barbara A. Babcock (Santa Fe: Ancient City Press, 1991), and Florence Ellis, "The Woman's Page: Laguna Pueblo," *El Palacio*, February 1959.

64 **Some training was:** For background: "Learning to Work Was Like Play," from *Sun Chief: The Autobiography of a Hopi Indian*, ed. Leo W. Simmons (New Haven, CT: Yale University Press, 1942), among other Pueblo life histories. Also, by a Santa Clara Pueblo teacher, "Indigenous Knowledge: The Pueblo Metaphor of Indigenous Education," in *Reclaiming Indigenous Voice and Vision*, ed. Marie Battise (Vancouver: UBC Press, 2000).

65 **Other lessons came:** "Acoma Superstitions," in James Paytiamo, *Flaming Arrow's People* (New York: Duffield & Green, 1932), pp. 153–58; the Wolf Robe Hunt papers at the Smithsonian also contain twenty-one Acoma sayings or "superstitions" related to behaviors at home and on the hunt, in Wolf Robe's handwriting, some duplicating Paytiamo's list, others not.

65 **During the 1920s fad:** Quote in Erna Fergusson, *Dancing Gods: Indian Ceremonials of New Mexico and Arizona* (Albuquerque: University of New Mexico Press, 1931), p. 275.

65 **Day Break also tapped:** Katherine A. Spielmann, *Farmers, Hunters and Colonists: Interaction Between the Southwest and the Southern Plains* (Tucson: University of Arizona Press, 1991).

69 **Farther out, bounding:** For Acoma worldview and symbolic organization of their landscape, Leslie A. White, "The World of the Keresan Pueblo Indians," in *Primitive Views of the World*, ed. Stanley Diamond (New York: Columbia University Press, 1960), pp. 83–94. Also Kevin Blake, "Sacred and Secular Landscape Symbolism at Mount Taylor," *Journal of the Southwest* 41, no. 4 (Winter 1999); Leslie Silko, "Landscape, History and the Pueblo Imagination," in *The Norton Book of Nature Writing*, ed. Robert Finch and John Elder (New York: W. W. Norton, 1990); and James E. Snead and Robert W. Preucel, "The Ideology of Settlement: Ancestral Keres Landscapes in the Northern Rio Grande," in *Archaeologies of Landscape: Contemporary Perspectives*, ed. Wendy Ashmore and A. Bernard Knapp (Oxford: Blackwell, 1999); David G. Saile, "Many Dwellings: Views of a Pueblo World," in *Dwelling, Place and Environment: Towards a Phenomenology of Person and World*, ed. David Seamon and Robert Mugerauer (New York: Columbia University Press, 1989.)

70 **Acoma symbolic landscape:** This graphic is adapted from material in Leslie A. White, "The World of the Keresan Pueblo Indians," in *Primitive View of the World*, ed. Stanley Diamond (New York: Columbia University Press, 1960); Franz Boas, *Keresan Texts* (2 vols., *Publications of the American Ethnological Society* 8, 1925–28); and Edward P. Dozier, *The Pueblo Indians of North America* (New York: Holt, Rinehart and Winston, 1970).

70 **As a Pueblo man:** Quoted in *Indian Voices: The First Convocation of American Indian Scholars*, ed. Jeannette Henry et al. (San Francisco: Indian Historian Press, 1970), p. 35.

71 **To live meaningfully:** Much of the material in Edward's version of the Acoma origin myth (EPH-3) can be considered a dramatized lesson plan for expressing and teaching Acoma Pueblo's preferred values and code of conduct. I am grateful to UCLA undergraduate student Tawney Lim for analyzing it as such. As Florence Ellis was told at Laguna Pueblo about such life lessons: "How to reach a good old age: on the way to it, always keep a happy heart. Do your work the best you can, and think good thoughts. Say only what is honest. Then you will live a long life. You will not become ill at the end, and suffer, but you will just go to sleep, and your father will take you home again." Florence Hawley Ellis, "The Woman's Page: Laguna Pueblo," *El Palacio*, February 1959: 20.

71 **"The purpose of our ceremonies":** "The Raingod Ceremony of San Juan [Pueblo]: A Ritual Drama," in Vera Laski's underappreciated *Seeking Life* (Philadelphia: American Folklore Society, 1958), p. 2.

72 **In the old days:** These interrelated metaphoric concepts are suggested in Leslie A. White, *New Material from Acoma*, Bureau of American Ethnology, Bulletin 136 (Washington, DC: Smithsonian Institution, 1943), p. 321.

Chapter 10: Ancient Hard Work (1867)

For material in this chapter: WH—7/20/98.

73 **"In the valley below":** Helen Rushmore and Wolf Robe Hunt, *The Dancing Horses of Acoma and Other Acoma Indian Stories* (Cleveland: World Publishing Co., 1963), p. 35.

73 **During his early childhood:** Edward Hunt quotes from EPH-1.

74 **By age six:** On traditional Pueblo farming practices: James A. Vlasich, *Pueblo Indian Agriculture* (Albuquerque: University of New Mexico Press, 2005); for Acoma work life and territoriality: Robert L. Rands, *Acoma Land Utilization: An Ethnohistorical Report,* submitted to Land Claims Commission, Docket 266 (New York: Garland, 1974); William E. Doolittle, *Cultivated Landscapes of Native North America* (Oxford: Oxford University Press, 2002); George F. Carter, *Plant Geography and Culture History in the American Southwest* (New York: Viking Fund Publications in Anthropology, no. 4, 1945). On Pueblo life skills: Ruth Underhill, *Workaday Life of the Pueblos* (Washington, DC: Bureau of Indian Affairs, Department of the Interior, 1954), and *Pueblo Crafts* (Washington, DC: Bureau of Indian Affairs, Department of the Interior, 1944). On Acoma plant knowledge, gathering practices, and cooking and curative uses of natural resources: George R. Swank, "The Ethnobotany of the Acoma and Laguna Indians" (MA thesis, University of New Mexico, 1932), based on fieldwork with older Acoma Indians in 1931–32.

79 **For slain deer:** See Paytiamo 1932.

80 **Until the 1870s:** Of relocations off the home mesa to Acomita ("North Valley") and McCartys ("North Gap"), information is scanty. L. A. Riley reported in "Repairs to the Old Mission at Acoma" that by the 1920s, "the young men, in fact, most of the Acoma families, no longer live year round at the old pueblo on the mesa but are scattered in small settlements along the San Jose River near the railroad line at Acomita and elsewhere: with this spreading out has come a certain loss of community spirit" (*El Palacio* 18, 1925). White also mentions it: "Forty years ago there were a few little huts scattered among the farms in the Acomita valley. Men went down there during the growing seasons and tended their crops. A little later some women went down to help; then the huts became lager. The children came with their mothers, and homes made their appearance along the little stream, and (later) the irrigation ditch. The tide swelled until almost every family at Acoma had a home in the new territory. At the present time there are houses strung out along the stream and the ditch for a distance of over 2 miles. Families now have more privacy than they ever had before, and this freedom from constant scrutiny and supervision can hardly fail to exert an influence upon freedom and independence of mind and spirit. At first the families came down to the valley from Old Acoma for the summer season only. Then they began to spend the winter in Acomita and McCartys, going up to old Acoma only for ceremonies. . . . There is a psychological disintegration taking place; the pueblo is tending to break into family groups. Then, Acoma is the home of the gods and the medicine men" (White 1932, p. 58).

Chapter 11: Deeper Mysteries Still (1871)

For material in this chapter: EPH-2; WH—4/1/98.

81 **"My people, the Acomas":** Paytiamo 1932, p. 125. Paytiamo was a nephew of Edward Hunt, who married an Anglo woman, La Rue Payne, a devotee of Ernest Thompson Seton's salon outside of Santa Fe. According to Leslie White, his book was actually "written by James Paytiamo's white wife La Rue . . . I knew them both—although La Rue only slightly. She is, according to many reports, a 'devil'"

(White to E. C. Parsons, April 17, 1933. Correspondence file in E. C. Parsons Collection, American Philosophical Society, Philadelphia).

82 **In contrast with:** As it was one of her major interests, the monumental Parsons 1996 is replete with information on Pueblo medicine men and their practices. Leslie White discusses Keresan medicine men initiations, curing traditions, and public displays of extraordinary abilities in "A Comparative Study of Keresan Medicine Societies," *Proceedings of the 23rd International Congress of Americanists* (1928): 604–19, and throughout his Acoma monograph (1932). The best summary of Pueblo medicine men and witches remains Florence H. Ellis, "Southwest: Pueblo," chapter 8 of *Witchcraft and Sorcery of the American Native Peoples,* ed. Deward E. Walker Jr. (Moscow: University of Idaho Press), pp. 191–222. Also Leslie A. White, "A Ceremonial Vocabulary Among the Pueblos," *International Journal of American Linguistics* 10, no. 4 (October 1944).

Chapter 12: Tracks Through the Past (1848–82)

87 **"Pueblo people easily":** Rina Swentzell, "A Pueblo Woman's Perspective on Chaco Canyon," in *In Search of Chaco: New Approaches to an Archaeological Enigma*, ed. David Guant Noble (Santa Fe: School of American Research Press, 2004), p. 49.

87 **Unlike most promotional:** Thanks to Kurt Anschuetz for the interview (12/14/2007) on Acoma archaeology and the landmark Dittert/Reynold studies in the region. Within the range of basic southwestern archaeology references, upon the advice of archaeologist James Snead I privileged Don D. Fowler, *A Laboratory for Anthropology: Science and Romanticism in the American Southwest, 1846–1930* (Albuquerque: University of New Mexico Press, 2000); I also consulted Stephen H. Lekson, *A History of the Ancient Southwest* (Santa Fe: School for Advanced Research, 2008), John Kanter, *Ancient Puebloan Southwest* (Cambridge: Cambridge University Press, 2004), and Arthur H. Rohn and William M. Ferguson, *Puebloan Ruins of the Southwest* (Albuquerque: University of New Mexico Press, 2006).

88 **To explain how:** For an entertaining overview of ersatz archaeological theories: Stephen Williams, *Fantastic Archaeology: The Wild Side of North American Prehistory* (Philadelphia: University of Pennsylvania Press, 1991), and Fowler 2000, pp. 54–56.

89 **To this tangle:** See Brian W. Dippie, *The Vanishing American: White Attitudes and U.S. Indian Policy* (Lawrence: University Press of Kansas, 1982).

91 **Two years later:** See James H. Simpson, *Navaho Expedition: Journal of a Military Reconnaissance from Santa Fe, New Mexico, to the Navaho Country Made in 1849*, ed. Frank McNitt (Norman: University of Oklahoma Press, 1964).

92 **Balding, unpretentious, and linguistically astute:** On Adolph Bandelier: Charles H. Lange and Carroll L. Riley, *Bandelier: The Life and Adventures of Adolph Bandelier* (Salt Lake City: University of Utah Press, 1996), and *The Southwestern Journals of Adolph F. Bandelier,* ed. Charles H. Lange and Carroll L. Riley, 4 vols. (Albuquerque: University of New Mexico Press, 1966–76); also Jack Schaefer's (author of *Shane*) *Adolph Francis Alfonse Bandelier* (Santa Fe, NM: The Press of the Territorian, 1966), and David Grant Noble, "The Repatriation of Adolph F. Bandelier," *El Palacio* 77, no. 2, 1972.

Chapter 13: Who Should Know What (1875)

93 **"Misinterpretation of Pueblo secrecy":** Quoted in Claire Farago, "The Sacred, the Secret, and the Ethics of Historical Interpretation: What I Learned from the *Santos* of New Mexico," in *Medieval and Early Modern Devotional Objects in Global Perspective: Translations of the Sacred*, ed. Elizabeth Robertson and Jennifer Jahner (New York: Palgrave Macmillan, 2010), p. 235.

95 **Together with the trade secrets:** Concerned about protecting the "spiritual health" of their community, the Hopi, anthropologist Peter Whiteley explains, pay special attention to "secrecy and the attendant social care and respect accorded to esoteric knowledge [which] guarantees both authority conferred by initiation and instrumental efficacy when the power and knowledge is activated." Peter Whiteley, "The End of Anthropology (at Hopi)?," *Journal of the Southwest* 35 (1993): 139. Therefore it is misleading, agree many writers, to think of secrecy as a "simple us-them barrier, Puebloans versus outsiders. Rather, the very fabric of Puebloan society, with its cross-cutting moieties, clans, societies, and kiva groups, requires an intricate network of internal secrecy to keep it from collapsing." David Roberts, *The Pueblo Revolt: The Secret Rebellion That Drove the Spaniards Out of the Southwest* (New York: Simon & Schuster, 2004), p. 158. Also see the useful discussion in Cynthia L. Chavez, "Negotiated Representations: Pueblo Artists and Culture" (dissertation, University of New Mexico, 2001). Speaking of Keresan Pueblos in particular, Charles H. Lange concurs: "An already developed faculty for keeping ritual secrets even from their own people who did not belong to a particular [priesthood] was readily transferred to their concealment from Europeans, who attacked them as being both pagan and immoral" (Lange 1928, p. 21). Often what Elizabeth A. Brandt calls "the polished evasion of questions" is to ensure that religious leaders "retain their internal control over the community." From "On Secrecy and Control of Knowledge: Taos Pueblo," republished as "The Role of Secrecy in Pueblo Society," in Thomas C. Blackburn, ed., *Flowers of the Wind: Papers on Ritual and Myth and Symbolism in California and the Southwest* (Socorro, NM: Ballena Press, 1977).

96 **And despite the "romantic inflation":** See Richard H. Frost, "The Romantic Inflation of Pueblo Culture," *American West* 17 (1980), and Leah Dilworth, *Imagining Indians in the Southwest: Persistent Visions of a Primitive Past* (Washington, DC: Smithsonian Institution Press, 1996).

98 **Working with her:** Elsie Clews Parsons, *Isleta, New Mexico*, 47th Annual Report of the Bureau of American Ethnology (Washington, DC: Smithsonian Institution, 1932), p. 202.

Chapter 14: Serious White Men (1875–79)

100 **"I learned about racism":** Leslie Marmon Silko, *Yellow Woman and a Beauty of the Spirit: Essays on Native American Life Today* (New York: Simon & Schuster, 1996) pp. 104–5.

100 **Friction between Acoma:** One wishes for more on this 1876 clash between Acoma and Laguna pueblos than brief mentions of the "pitched battle" (in Gunn

1916, pp. 99–100), and in Benjamin Thomas, *Annual Report of the Commissioner of Indian Affairs for the Year 1877*, Report of Agents in the New Mexico Office of the Pueblo Indian Agency, Santa Fe (Washington, DC: Government Printing Office, 1877). Aside from a Diego de Vargas mention in 1692 that the Zunis were at war with Acoma, this appears to be one of the rare recorded clashes between two pueblos in historical times.

102 **Once Americans took charge:** Transcript of interview with Vedna Eckerman Hunt by D. Corydon Hammond, University of Utah (8/19/1967). The Anglo-American intermarriages and influences in Laguna Pueblo deserve a book of their own. For background on the Gorman, Marmon, Gunn, Pradt, and Eckerman settlers, see Gunn 1916. Although not the focus of this narrative, the saga of the interrelated Anglo-Americans of Laguna Pueblo is in Laguna author Leslie Marmon Silko's multigenre *Storyteller* (1981); more recently her father, photographer Lee Marmon, provided information for his coauthor Tom Corbett's text in *Laguna Pueblo: A Photographic History* (Albuquerque: University of New Mexico Press, 2015); Gunn 1916 has written of the family, as has his well-known literary descendant, poet and essayist Paula Gunn Allen; and anthropologist Elsie Clews Parsons described them in her writings on Laguna, especially *Laguna Genealogies* (Anthropological Papers of the American Museum of Natural History 19, no. 5, New York). Add the related Eckerman family archives, the family into which Wilbert Hunt married, and one has a 150-year-plus history of this community's complicated, bicultural history.

104 **Complementing the Anglo-Protestant:** General citations for the Jewish role in western New Mexico are in chapter 19. The best general history of the Bibo family is Floyd S. Fierman, *The Impact of the Frontier on a Jewish Family: The Bibos* (El Paso: Texas Western College Press, 1961), which Dr. Fierman revised for a 1988 publication (Tucson: Bloom Southwest Jewish Archives, University of Arizona). Other treatments include: Sandra Lea Rollins, "Solomon Bibo, Jewish Indian Chief," *Western States Jewish History* 1, no. 4 (July 1969); Gordon Bronitsky, "Solomon Bibo: Jew and Indian at Acoma Pueblo," Southwest Jewish Archives, University of Arizona, 2008; Jerry Klinger, "Solomon Bibo: The Jewish Indian Chief," *The Jewish Magazine*, December 2011; and Taos high school student Maria Montoya's "From Brakel to Acoma" (n.d.), based on interviews with Carl Bibo in April 1977. Also useful was a seven-page typescript summary of his family's deep history by Arthur Bibo, "Over the Carpathian Mountains into Hungary and on to the Rocky Mountains in New Mexico and to the Coast Range in California by the Golden Gate," December 1, 1968, and other unpublished Arthur Bibo materials, such as "History of the Bibo Trading Posts and Mercantile Stores" (August 1967); plus Dr. N. B. Stern's unpublished interview with Solomon and Juana's children, Mr. Leroy Bibo and Mrs. Max Weiss, February 21, 1969, at Charter Oak, California.

105 **On its arrival:** Among sources on the railroad and its impact on the Pueblos: Vedna Hunt's interview with D. Corydon Hammond (8/9/1967); Mening 1971, chapter 5; David F. Myrick, *New Mexico's Railroad: A Historical Survey* (Albuquerque: University of New Mexico Press, 1990); Marci L. Ruskin, *The Train Stops Here: New Mexico's Railway Legacy* (Albuquerque: University of New Mexico Press, 2005); James H. Ducker, *Men of the Steel Rails: Workers on the Atchi-*

son, *Topeka & Santa Fe Railroad, 1869–1900* (Lincoln: University of Nebraska Press, 1983); William S. Greever, *Arid Domain: The Santa Fe Railway and Its Western Land Area* (Berkeley: University of California Press, 1994); T. C. McLuhan, *Dream Tracks: The Railroad and the American Indian, 1890–1930* (New York: Harry N. Abrams, 1985).

105 **Difficult personalities could:** Bernalillo's loss of the AT&SF railroad line is described in Marc Simmons's *Albuquerque: A Narrative History* (Albuquerque: University of New Mexico, 1982), pp. 214–16.

Chapter 15: Into Their World (1880–81)

For material in this chapter: Thelma Johnson interview, 3/10/97; EPH-2; WH—7/3/93; WH—5/10/97.

107 **"We need to awaken":** Merrill E. Gates, Indian commissioner, 1896, quoted in Francis Paul Prucha, ed., *Americanizing the American Indians: Writings by the "Friends of the Indian," 1880–1900* (Cambridge, MA: Harvard University Press, 1973), p. 341.

107 **When Thomas first:** On Benjamin Thomas, Sheldon Jackson, and Solomon Bibo, see citations in chapters 16 and 19. Also "Roster of the Albuquerque Indian School (Menaul school), 1881–1891," *New Mexico Genealogist* 14, no. 4 (December 1975).

109 **The following are Day Break's own words:** Quotes from EH-2.

110 **After the Civil War:** On post–Civil War Indian policy reformers and responses: Henry E. Fritz, *The Movement for Indian Assimilation, 1860–1890* (Philadelphia: University of Pennsylvania Press, 1963); Frederick E. Hoxie, *The Final Promise: The Campaign to Assimilate the Indians, 1880–1920* (Lincoln: University of Nebraska Press, 1984); Tom Holm, *The Great Confusion in Indian Affairs: Native Americans and Whites in the Progressive Era* (Austin: University of Texas Press, 2005); Frederick E. Hoxie, ed., *Talking Back to Civilization: Indian Voices from the Progressive Era* (Boston: Bedford/St. Martin's, 2001).

111 **These settled villagers:** For a review of vacillating legal definitions and the special case of Pueblo Indians qua Indians, see Felix Cohen, "Pueblos of New Mexico," chapter 20 of *Handbook of Federal Indian Law* (Albuquerque: University of New Mexico Press, 1982 [1942]), and Gerald Torres, "Who Is an Indian?: The Story of United States v. Sandoval," in *Indian Law Stories,* ed. Carole Goldberg et al. (New York: Foundation Press, 2011), pp. 109–45. One of the earliest regional expressions of the problem of grouping the Pueblos with other Indians appeared in 1869 when the Supreme Court of New Mexico Territory decided the *United States v. José Juan Lucero* case, which contrasted the Pueblos—"peaceful, quiet, and industrious people, residing in villages [who lived] by the cultivation of the soil"—against the "general class of Indians" who were "wild," "half naked," "wandering savages," and hence could not be treated as Indians for legal purposes—as quoted in Eva Marie Garroutte, *Real Indians: Identity and the Survival of Native America* (Berkeley: University of California Press, 2003), p. 64. In the same vein is the Helen Hunt Jackson quote, from her *A Century of Dishonor: The Early Crusade for Indian Reform* (New York: Harper & Row, 1965 [1881]),

p. 443. Agreeing with her in the *United States v. Joseph* case (1896), the U.S. Supreme Court wrote of the Pueblos, "They are peaceable, industrious, intelligent, honest and virtuous people. They are Indians only in feature, complexion, and a few of their habits . . . forbid the idea that they should be classed with the Indian tribes" (*United States v. Joseph*, 94 U.S. 614, pp. 616–17). The sense of Pueblo exceptionalism would extend into the twentieth century. "They had one large-scale rebellion against the Spanish but no more," wrote anthropologist Ruth M. Underhill in 1939. "Instead, their policy has been withdrawal and secrecy. . . . The process has been conscious. Far from amalgamating like the Five Civilized Tribes or rebelling like the Plains people, they have withdrawn to the little patches of land which they often own by Spanish grant and there they have proceeded to keep alive the life of a bygone century." "Some Basic Cultures of the Indians of the United States," in *The North American Indian Today*, ed. C. T. Loram and T. F. McIlwraith (Toronto: University of Toronto Press, 1939), p. 28. Yet this same non-Indian status fed into the justifications of non-Indian squatters, for it denied the Pueblos their territorial protections as American Indians under U.S. law. Occupying this "ethnological middle landscape in the American national imagination," as characterized by historian Curtis M. Hinsley, the Pueblo Indians in their uncertain categorization also sparked an early dispute between scholarly giants. "Neither savage nor civilized," Hinsley continues, "the Pueblos' in-betweenness inspired a vigorous debate between [Herbert Howe] Bancroft and [Lewis Henry] Morgan over their historical and ethnological status in the decade after 1875. The controversy, which burned intensely until Morgan's death in 1881, initially focused public and ethnographic attention on the Southwest." In Hinsley's "Zunis and Brahmins: Cultural Ambivalence in the Gilded Age," in *Romantic Motives: Essays on Anthropological Sensibility* (Madison: University of Wisconsin Press, 1989), p. 174. Each in their own way, American Indians, the Pueblos, Acoma Pueblo, and the Hunt family can be seen as sharing in telescoping predicaments of "in-betweenness" within the American sociopolitical-cultural system. This may have been another way the Hunts were unintentional pioneers: one is reminded of postcolonial scholar Homi Bhabha's comment that "in-betweenness is a fundamental condition of our times." It is their unintentional predicament as forerunners that has led me to characterize the Hunt family saga as a story of how a premodern village produced a postmodern family.

112 **The archaeological record:** A good summary of this archaeological research on violence, unwelcome to some: Glen E. Rice and Steven A. LeBlanc, *Deadly Landscapes: Case Studies in Prehistoric Southwestern Warfare* (Salt Lake City: University of Utah Press, 2001).

Chapter 16: Turned Inside Out (1880–81)

117 **"I have recently thought":** William Forrest Howard quoted in Jo Ann Ruckman, "Indian Schooling in New Mexico in the 1890s: Letters of a Teacher in the Indian Service," *New Mexico Historical Review* 56, no. 1 (1981): 59. Also, *Menaul School Centennial* (Albuquerque: Menaul Historical Library, 1981).

118 **As recruits for:** General introduction: Margaret Connell Szasz and Carmelita Ryan, "American Indian Education," in Wilcomb E. Washburn, ed., *History of Indian White Relations,* vol. 4 of *Handbook of the North American Indians* (Washington, DC: Smithsonian Institution, 1988). The best historical overviews of Richard Pratt and the Indian boarding school system he launched are: David Wallace Adams, *Education for Extinction: American Indians and the Boarding School Experience* (Lawrence: University Press of Kansas, 1995); Jon Reyhner and Jeanne Eder, *A History of Indian Education* (Billings: Eastern Montana College Press, 1989); and K. Tsiana Lomawaima, "American Indian Education *by* Indians versus *for* Indians," in *A Companion to American Indian History,* ed. Philip J. Deloria and Neal Salisbury (Malden, MA: Blackwell, 2002). On the daily school routine at Albuquerque, see Ruckman 1981. For the period's general estimation of the Pueblo Indian student's potential one need only note the title of Frank Spencer's 1899 doctoral dissertation from New York's Columbia University: "Education of the Pueblo Child: A Study in Arrested Development" (and to show how attitudes change, thirty-seven years later the same institution's teacher's program approved Henrietta K. Burton's dissertation: "The Reestablishment of the Indians in their Pueblo Life Through the Revival of Their Traditional Crafts: A Study in Home Extension Education").

119 **Born in 1840:** On Pratt's life and career: Robert M. Utley, *Battlefield and Classroom: Four Decades with the American Indian, 1867–1906* (New Haven, CT: Yale University Press, 1964); "Pratt, the Man with a Slogan," in Flora Warren Seymour, *Indian Agents of the Old Frontier* (New York: D. Appleton–Century Co., 1941); while the *Albuquerque Journal,* August 16, 1881, records Pratt's stay in town to recruit students for Carlisle.

120 **In western New Mexico:** The career of Indian agent Benjamin M. Thomas, a staunch Presbyterian, is profiled in Dan Thrapp, *Encyclopedia of Frontier Biography,* vol. 3 (Lincoln: University of Nebraska Press, 1991) and Ralph E. Twitchell, *The Leading Facts of New Mexican History,* vol. 2 (Cedar Rapids, IA: Torch Press, 1912).

120 **Then the Protestant:** On Sheldon Jackson, see Robert Laird Stewart, *Sheldon Jackson: Pathfinder and Prospector of the Missionary Vanguard in the Rocky Mountains and Alaska* (New York: Fleming H. Revell Co., 1908); J. Arthur Lazell, *Alaskan Apostle: Life Story of Sheldon Jackson* (New York: Harper, 1960); Norman J. Bender, *Winning the West for Christ: Sheldon Jackson and Presbyterianism on the Rocky Mountain Frontier, 1870–1880* (Albuquerque: University of New Mexico Press, 1996); and C. Hinckley, "Sheldon Jackson: Gilded Age Apostle," and Mark T. Banker, "Presbyterian Activity in the Southwest: The Careers of John and James Menaul," both in special issue, "Religion in the West," guest editor, Ferenc M. Szasz, *Journal of the West* 23, no. 1 (January 1984).

Background on Protestantism in general: R. Pierce Beaver, "Protestant Churches and the Indians," in Wilcomb E. Washburn, ed., *History of Indian-White Relations,* vol. 4 of *Handbook of the North American Indians* (Washington, DC: Smithsonian Institution, 1988); Clifford Merrill Drury, *Presbyterian Panorama: One Hundred and Fifty Years of National Missions History* (Philadelphia: Board of Christian Education, 1952); and Mark T. Banker, *Presbyterian Missions and Cultural Interaction in the Far Southwest, 1850–1950* (Urbana: University of

Illinois Press, 1993). For Catholic responses to their prime competitor for Indian students, see Francis Paul Prucha, *The Churches and the Indian Schools, 1888–1912* (Lincoln: University of Nebraska Press, 1980), and discussion throughout his *The Great Father: The United States Government and the American Indians,* 2 vols. (Lincoln: University of Nebraska Press, 1984).

120 **The shock of those:** I thank Ted Jojola of the Architecture and Urban Planning Department at the University of New Mexico for an interview (2/21/2008) based upon his empathetic research into the early history of Albuquerque and its Indian School. For further background: Lillie G. McKinney, "History of the Albuquerque Indian School" (MA thesis, University of New Mexico, 1934); Penny Quintana, "Albuquerque Indian School: Early Years, 1879–1928" (MA thesis, Arizona State University, 1992). A description of Edward's new school, its staff and daily teaching and working schedule, is in *Albuquerque Journal,* October 28, 1882, while bidding for plans and construction of a replacement facility is in *Albuquerque Journal,* October 2, 1883. As for a comparison of Pueblo and Anglo-Protestant pedagogies and ethics, see Dolores J. Huff, "The Tribal Ethic, the Protestant Ethic, and American Indian Economic Development," in *American Indian Policy and Cultural Values: Conflict and Accommodation,* ed. J. Joe (UCLA American Indian Studies Center, 1986).

Chapter 17: City on the Cusp (1880–83)

123 **"Today the new civilization":** Quoted in Simmons 1982, p. 220.

123 **Years later the elders:** Quote from Paytiamo 1932, pp. 149–50.

124 **Before their eyes:** On Albuquerque history I am indebted to city historian and Web researcher Mo Palmer, who tracked down many obscure references for me, such as material on Albuquerque's First Territorial Fair where I felt fairly confident that Edward marched with fellow students (Wade McIntyre, *State Fair: The Biggest Show in New Mexico,* 1995), the impact of the Great Depression on Albuquerque and environs, and brickmaking in early Albuquerque, not to mention my benefiting from Ms. Palmer's skills at historical photo research. My description of Albuquerque in the late nineteenth century draws from Simmons's city biography (1982, especially chapters 7, 8, and 9); also Victor Westphall, "Albuquerque in the 1870s," *New Mexico Historical Review* 23, no. 4 (October 1948). I also delved into Howard Bryan, *Albuquerque Remembered* (Albuquerque: University of New Mexico Press, 2006); V. B. Price, *Albuquerque: A City at the End of the World* (Albuquerque: University of New Mexico Press, 1992); Debra Hughes, *Albuquerque in Our Time: 30 Voices, 300 Years* (Santa Fe: Museum of New Mexico Press, 2006); Donald A. Gill, *Stories Behind the Street Names of Albuquerque, Santa Fe, and Taos* (Chicago: Bonus Books, 1994); Paul W. Bauer, Carol J. Condie, Richard P. Lozinsky, and L. Greer Price, *Albuquerque: A Guide to Its Geology and Culture* (Albuquerque: New Mexico Bureau of Geology & Mineral Resources, 2004); and Nina Veregge, "Transformations of Spanish Urban Landscapes in the American Southwest," *Journal of the Southwest* 35, no. 4 (Winter 1993). On the role of such a hub city in the social geography of the Southwest: D. W. Meinig, *Southwest: Three Peoples in Geographical Change, 1600–1970* (New York: Oxford University Press, 1971), and cultural geographer Meinig's incisive section, "New

Mexico: Hispano, Indian, Anglo," in *Transcontinental America, 1850–1915*, vol. 3 of his *The Shaping of America: A Geographical Perspective on 500 Years of History* (New Haven, CT: Yale University Press, 1988).

128 **Now rumors reached Day Break's:** For additional references to Pueblo Indian responses to the railroad, see chapter 14. A solid study is Gilbert Ortiz, "Acoma Pueblo Lands and Railroads in the Southwest," in *Native Views of Indian-White Historical Relations*, ed. Donald L. Fixico (Chicago: Newberry Library, D'Arcy McNickle Center for American Indian and Indigenous Studies, 1989). On the railroad's wider impact, see James A. Ward's wonderful essay "On Time: Railroads and the Tempo of American Life," *Railroad History*, Bulletin 151 (Autumn 1984).

Chapter 18: A New Secret (1881–83)

130 **"As New Town progressed":** Tomas Atencio, "Old Town," in *Albuquerque: Portrait of a Western City*, ed. Mary Kay Cline (Santa Fe: Clear Light, 2006), p. 101. Even though his work focuses on one community, some of the same interethnic tensions mentioned here—usually kept under polite wraps—were exposed in John Bodine's seminal essay "A Tri-Ethnic Trap: The Spanish-Americans in Taos," in *Spanish-Speaking People in the United States*, Proceedings of the 1968 Annual Spring Meeting of the American Ethnological Society (Seattle: Distributed by the University of Washington Press, 1968). More recently, scholars such as Sylvia Rodriguez, Pablo Mitchell (*Coyote Nation: Sexuality, Race and Conquest in Modernizing New Mexico, 1880–1920* [Chicago: University of Chicago Press, 2005]), and Michael L. Trujillo (*Land of Disenchantment: Latina/o Identities and Transformations in Northern New Mexico* [Albuquerque: University of New Mexico Press, 2009]), have addressed these long-simmering undercurrents.

130 **New identities called for:** See Adams 1995, pp. 108–12. Thanks to David Bergholz and historian-archivist John J. Grabowski of Cleveland, I was able to obtain the story behind Edward Hunt's new name in *A History of Cleveland and Its Environs: The Heart of New Connecticut*, vol. 3, *Biography* (Chicago: Lewis Publishing Co., 1918).

131 **In the colonial period:** On early Indian conversion: Neal Salisbury, "Red Puritans: The 'Praying Indians' of Massachusetts Bay and John Eliot," in *The American Indian: Past and Present*, ed. Roger L. Nichols, 3rd ed. (New York: Alfred A. Knopf, 1986), and Jean M. O'Brien, "The Praying Indians of Nantick, Massachusetts, 1650–1677: The Dynamics of Cultural Survival," in *Native Views of Indian-White Historical Relations*, ed. Donald L. Fixico (Chicago: Newberry Library, D'Arcy McNickle Center for American Indian and Indigenous Studies, 1989). On this spiritual crisis, Karen Armstrong writes, "The radical conversion had been characteristic of Western Christianity since the time of Augustine. Protestantism would continue the tradition of breaking abruptly and violently with the past in what the American philosopher William James called a 'twice-born' religion for 'sick souls.' Christians were being 'born again' to a new faith in God and a rejection of the host of intermediaries that had stood between them and the divine in the medieval Church." *A History of God* (New York: Ballantine, 1993), p. 281.

133 **Then he shared:** White 1932, p. 32.

Chapter 19: New Tribe in the Desert (1883–85)

136 **"In 1869 I was":** Nathan Bibo, "Testimony of Nathan Bibo" (of Bernalillo). Supportive testimony during 1924 hearings chaired by Herbert Hagerman on behalf of Edward Hunt, probably March or April, transcript in *Pueblo Indian Collection* (Santa Fe: New Mexico State Records Center and Archives).

137 **Day Break's older friend:** For background on pioneer Jews in New Mexico I thank the Harriet Rochlin Collection of Western Jewish History and her Collection of Photographs of Western Jewish Life at UCLA Charles E. Young Research Library, Department of Special Collections. In New Mexico, recent work on the Jewish presence has tended toward the more fashionable "crypto-Jewish" experience; my chronicle deals with the more overt role of her mercantile families. General sources: Tomas Jaehn, ed., *Jewish Pioneers of New Mexico* (Santa Fe: Museum of New Mexico Press, 2003); Henry J. Tobias, *A History of Jews in New Mexico* (Albuquerque: University of New Mexico Press, 1990); Floyd Fierman, *Guts and Ruts: The Jewish Pioneer on the Trail in the American Southwest* (New York: KTAV Publishing House, Inc., 1985); Rachel Rubenstein, *Members of the Tribe: Native America in the Jewish Imagination* (Detroit: Wayne State University Press, 2010); and M. L. Marks, *Jews Among the Indians* (Chicago: Benison Books, 1992), with chapter 6 on "The Strange Case of Don Solomono." In addition to the Fierman pamphlet on Solomon Bibo cited above, see Frank McNitt, *The Indian Traders,* chapter 8 on Solomon Bibo (Norman: University of Oklahoma Press, 1962), and articles by Dr. Gordon J. Bronitsky. On Nathan's own account of his adventuresome life: Nathan Bibo, "Reminiscences of Early New Mexico," *Albuquerque Sunday Herald,* June 4, June 11, June 18, June 25, and July 2, 1922.

138 **By 1865 the Bibos':** See "The Spiegelbergs of New Mexico: Merchants and Bankers, 1844–1893," *Southwestern Studies* 1, no. 4 (Winter 1964); William J. Parish, "The German Jew and the Commercial Revolution in Territorial New Mexico, 1850–1900," *New Mexico Quarterly* 29 (1959); and Tomas Jaehn, "The Unpolitical German in New Mexico, 1848–1914," *New Mexico Historical Review* 71, no. 1 (January 1996).

139 **Inside the city:** On the Santa Fe Ring: Lamar 2000, chapter 6, "The Santa Fe Ring, 1865–1885"; Ruben Salaz Marquez, *The Santa Fe Ring: Land Grant History in American New Mexico* (Albuquerque: Cosmic House, 2008). For a less critical biography of the Ring's mastermind: Victor Westphall, *Thomas Benton Catron and His Era* (Tucson: University of Arizona Press, 1973).

144 **For the Jew:** George Steiner, *My Unwritten Books* (New York: New Directions, 2008), p. 121.

Chapter 20: Home for the Summer (1884–85)

144 **"Polingaysi had not":** P. Qoyawayma, *No Turning Back* (Albuquerque: University of New Mexico Press, 1964), pp. 75, 79.

146 **Then a tougher personality:** On Pedro Sanchez's life, editor Guadalupe Baca-Vaughn's profile of Pedro Sanchez in *Memories of Antonio José Martínez* (Santa Fe: Rydal Press, 1978), and Sanchez's own changing attitudes as Pueblo agent in

Annual Report of the Commissioner of Indian Affairs to the Secretary of the Interior for the Year 1884 (Washington, DC: Government Printing Office, 1884), p. 138–39.

149 **Complicating Acoma's internal affairs:** Solomon Bibo's controversial interactions with Acoma are well covered in Minge 2002. Even Bibo's own nephew, Arthur Bibo, had to concede that, upon researching the record, "At the National Archives I had access to a file in the Indian Department relative to the investigation about the thirty-year lease my Uncle Solomon executed with the tribe ... the material tends to show that Uncle did something unethical or illegal. One must know all sides to the story to understand what really took place, and as I am familiar with the main facts I would advise you not to draw too hasty conclusions." Arthur Bibo to Rabbi Floyd Fierman, quoted in Fierman, "The Impact of the Frontier on a Jewish Family: The Bibos," *American Jewish Historical Quarterly* 59, no. 4 (June 1970): 475–76.

Chapter 21: Return to the Padres (1887)

For material in this chapter: WH—9/3/98.

152 **"The white man's":** Wolf Robe Hunt, in a handwritten manuscript entitled "The Sept. 2nd Feast at Acoma," p. 2, from the Wolf Robe Hunt papers, Box 7, National Anthropological Archives, Smithsonian Institution. More nuanced on how Pueblo people have navigated their belief systems is Don L. Roberts: "A strange duality has evolved and, as one of my Pueblo friends asserts, it is now possible for a person to be a good Indian and a good Catholic, a good Indian and a bad Catholic, a bad Indian and a good Catholic, or a bad Indian and a bad Catholic. The Mass preceding a Corn Dance is a Catholic ritual, but the Corn Dance, even if there is a shrine for the santo, is an indigenous ceremony. In sum, it can be stated that there are many gods in the Pueblo pantheon and one of them just happens to be the Christian god." In "Calendar of Eastern Pueblo Ritual Dramas," chapter 6 in *Southwestern Indian Ritual Drama,* ed. Charlotte J. Frisbie (Prospect Heights, IL: Waveland Press, 1980), p. 109.

153 **Strings of burros:** For background on Santa Fe at the time Edward first arrived: Wilson 1997 and La Farge 1959; the excellent *Santa Fe Plaza: Cultural Landscape Report,* prepared for the City of Santa Fe, Engineering Division, January 2006 by Morrow Reardon Wilkinson Miller, Ltd., Landscape Architects, guided by landscape historian Chris Wilson; Henry J. Tobias and Charles E. Woodhouse, *Santa Fe: A Modern History, 1880–1990* (Albuquerque: University of New Mexico Press, 2001); Richard Harris, *National Trust Guide: Santa Fe* (New York: John Wiley & Sons, 1997); John Pen La Farge's delightful oral history, *Turn Left at the Sleeping Dog: Scripting the Santa Fe Legend, 1920–1955* (Albuquerque: University of New Mexico Press, 2001); and Paul Horgan's *The Centuries of Santa Fe* (New York: E. P. Dutton, 1956), which, like all of Horgan's popular southwestern histories, never wears its research on its sleeve.

155 **"This by-passing":** In Oliver La Farge, *Santa Fe: The Autobiography of a Southwestern Town* (Norman: University of Oklahoma Press, 1959), p. 96. Pulitzer Prize–winning author La Farge's selection and commentary on dispatches from

the *Santa Fe New Mexican* newspaper, starting in November 1849 and continuing through December 1953, is also a vibrant introduction to the history of nineteenth- and twentieth-century New Mexico.

155 **After bad-mouthing:** Thanks to Brian S. Collier for his dissertation, "St. Catherine Indian School, Santa Fe, 1887–2006: Catholic Education in New Mexico" (Arizona State University, 2006). For more on St. Catherine I am grateful for the research of Mo Palmer, who obtained Corrine P. Sze's useful history of the school written for the Office of the New Mexico State Historian, and the summer 2003 *Bulletin of the Historic Santa Fe Foundation* that featured an extensive study, "Gone but Not Forgotten: St. Catherine Industrial Indian School." Also John Sherman, "Kate Drexel and Her School," *New Mexico Magazine,* September 1980, and the *New Mexican* newspaper articles around her 1988 beatification.

156 **A bright young man:** On Catholic-Protestant tensions, see references in chapter 16.

159 **His free days were:** On Santa Fe and its rich and contested history of collective representations, religious and civic, see Wilson 1997, chapter 6, "From Fiesta to Fourth of July"; also Sarah Bronwen Horton, *The Santa Fe Fiesta, Reinvented: Staking Ethno-Nationalist Claims to a Disappearing Homeland* (Santa Fe: School for Advanced Research Press, 2010).

159 **Not all processions:** The Jicarilla Apache appearance in downtown Santa Fe on May 28, 1887, is from the *New Mexican* newspaper account in La Farge 1959, p. 131.

Chapter 22: Enter the Authors (1884–88)

161 **"The marvelous Flower":** From Charles Lummis, "The Golden Key to Wonderland," in *The Multicultural Southwest,* ed. A. Gabriel Melendez et al. (Tucson: University of Arizona Press, 2001), p. 10.

162 **First to arrive:** General introduction to Cushing's life and work: *Zuni: Selected Writings of Frank Hamilton Cushing,* ed. Jesse Green (Lincoln, NE: Bison Books, 1981), and Curtis M. Hinsley, "Zunis and Brahmins: Cultural Ambivalence in the Gilded Age," in *Romantic Motives: Essays on Anthropological Sensibility,* ed. George W. Stocking Jr. (Madison: University of Wisconsin Press, 1989), pp. 169–207.

163 **A year after Cushing's arrival:** See Charles H. Lange and Carroll L. Riley, *Bandelier: The Life and Adventures of Adolph Bandelier* (Salt Lake City: University of Utah Press, 1996); Jack Schaefer, *Adolph Francis Alphonse Bandelier* (Santa Fe: Press of the Territorian, 1966).

164 **The third writer:** For material on this influential friend of the Hunts and the Bibos, regional promoter, tourism booster, champion of Hispano and Indian rights and arts, and energetic master of purple-prose journalism, see Mark Thomson, *American Character: The Curious Life of Charles Fletcher Lummis and the Rediscovery of the Southwest* (New York: Arcade Publishing, 2001); Sherry L. Smith, "Charles Fletcher Lummis and the Fight for the Multicultural Southwest," in her *Reimagining Indians: Native Americans Through Anglo Eyes, 1880–1940* (New York: Oxford University Press, 2000); Martin Padgett, "Travel, Exoticism, and the Writing of Region: Charles Fletcher Lummis and the 'Cre-

ation' of the Southwest," chapter 4 in his *Indian Country: Travels in the American Southwest, 1840–1935* (Albuquerque: University of New Mexico Press, 2004); and Ramón A. Gutiérrez's critique of Lummis's sensationalistic recording of Penitente practices in "Crucifixion, Slavery and Death: The Hermanos Penitentes of the Southwest," in *Over the Edge: Remapping the American West*, ed. Valerie J. Matsumoto and Blake Allmendinger (Berkeley: University of California Press, 1999). Along with Lummis's own prolific and often recycled writings, for his New Mexico associations, see *Letters from the Southwest*, ed. James Byrkit (Tucson: University of Arizona Press, 1989), and Edwin R. Bingham, *Charles F. Lummis: Editor of the Southwest* (San Marino, CA: Huntington Library, 1955). One of Lummis's early visits to Acoma mesa in the company of Solomon Bibo, Laguna notable John M. Gunn, photographer Ben Wittick, and others (possibly Edward Hunt as well) was in mid-June 1898 (Lummis Journals, Braun Research Library, Autry National Center, Los Angeles), which may have also been when this book's cover photo was taken. His notebooks testify that he remained friends with Solomon and Juana Bibo for the rest of his life and visited them in San Francisco and they him in Los Angeles.

168 **In the indigenous Southwest:** Peter M. Whiteley, "The Southwest," in *Native American Religions: North America*, ed. Lawrence E. Sullivan (New York: Macmillan, 1987), pp. 62–63.

Chapter 23: With Divided Heart (1887)

169 **"Now it is true":** William Forrest Howard, quoted in Jo Ann Ruckman, "Indian Schooling in New Mexico in the 1890s: Letters of a Teacher in the Indian Service," *New Mexico Historical Review* 56, no. 1 (1981): 58.

170 **Now that he was home:** From comments in EPH-1, EPH-2.

171 **Other ceremonies, even if Catholicized:** See endnotes for chapter 21.

171 **Outside were lit:** While attending the Haskell Institute at Lawrence, Kansas, Edward's son Ervin wrote "Christmas Among the Pueblos" for the school journal, based on Acoma memories like these; reprinted in *The Weewish Tree: A Magazine of Indian America for Young People* 2, no. 3 (November 1973) (San Francisco: American Indian Historical Society), pp. 3–5.

173 **Then the oldest:** James Miller's account "The Story of a 'Civilized' Indian" is in George Wharton James, *A Little Journey to Some Strange Places and Peoples in Our Southwestern Land* (Chicago: A. Flanagan Co., 1991), pp. 118–22.

Chapter 24: The Last Hunt (1887)

176 **"These people had abilities":** Quoted in Peter Whiteley, *Deliberate Acts: Changing Hopi Culture Through the Oraibi Split* (Tucson: University of Arizona Press, 1988), pp. 203–4.

176 **Seizing any opportunity:** Overview on American Indian "surround and drive" forms of collective hunting: Bengt Anell, *Running Down and Driving of Game in North America* (Studia Ethnographica Upsaliensia XXX, 1969). Thanks to Larry Loendorf for rock art in the Dinetah area related to animal drives; also to Kurt F. Anschuetz and Gregson Schachner for information on possible animal drive

representations in rock art nearer Acoma, plus illustrations in Karl F. Kumli's report, III, *Cebolleta Historic District: A Survey of the History of Cebolleta, New Mexico Until 1900* (New Mexico Historic Preservation Division, August 2009). Also helpful on Pueblo subsistence practices is Ernest Beaglehole, *Hopi Hunting and Hunting Ritual* (New Haven, CT: Yale University Publications in Anthropology 4, 1937), and Ruth Underhill, *Workaday Life of the Pueblos* (Department of the Interior, Bureau of Indian Affairs, Indian Life and Customs #4, 1954).

177 **When he was around:** As part of Hunt family lore told and retold for over a century, it is sometimes hard to reconcile the multiple versions of these hunting expeditions. I have discerned three separate experiences, primarily based on information in EPH-1 and EPH-2, an undated account remembered by his daughter-in-law Vedna, and numerous interviews by myself and others with Wilbert Hunt that are all part of the Hunt Family–Peter Nabokov Collection at the Center for Southwest Research in Zimmerman Library at the University of New Mexico. The first expedition is in EPH-2, the third antelope hunt and killing the bear incident are in EPH-1. On bears in Pueblo culture: Hamilton A. Tyler, chapter 8, of *Pueblo Animals and Myths* (Norman: University of Oklahoma Press, 1975), and in a Cochiti ceremony, Edith Hart Wilson, "Enemy Bear," *Masterkey* 22, no. 3 (May 1948). Accounts of the origins of hunting, the Acoma Hunters Society and the proper treatment of slain animals are in Edward Hunt's version of the creation myth, EPH-3 as well as Paytiamo 1932. For Acoma Pueblo's Docket 266, Indian Claims Commission submissions, Florence Hawley Ellis, provided summations of her ethnographic interviews concerning "Acoma and Laguna Hunting Structures, Storage Structures, Windbreak Shelters, and Sweathouses" and "Acoma and Laguna Gathering and Hunting Areas," which were graciously copied by the University of New Mexico's Maxwell Museum. Also helpful was B. A. Reuter's manuscript "Acoma Pueblo: Rabbit Hunt," one of the numerous Reuter pieces on Acoma written for the WPA and archived in the Chavez Library, Palace of the Governors; and Andrew Leis's brief account "Hunting," in Wick R. Miller, *Acoma Grammar and Texts* (Berkeley: University of California Press, 1965). Many hunting songs were recorded during the Hunt's Smithsonian sojourn in 1928; Frances Densmore's *Music of Acoma, Isleta, Cochiti and Zuni Pueblo,* Bureau of American Ethnology, Bulletin 165 (Washington DC: Smithsonian Institution, 1957) included others; Paytiamo 1932 and Simon Ortiz's *Song, Poetry and Language: Expression and Perception* (Tsaile, AZ: Navajo Community College Press, 1977) discuss their importance.

Chapter 25: Becoming a Delight Maker (1888)

For material in this chapter: EPH-1; EPH-2; EPH-3; WH—4/11/94; White 1932; Curtis 1926.

183 **"The leader who":** Emory Sekaquaptewa, "One More Smile for a Hopi Clown," in *I Become Part of It: Sacred Dimensions in Native American Life,* ed. D. M. Dooling and Paul Jordan-Smith (San Francisco: Harper San Francisco, 1989), p. 151. For Edward Hunt, his initiation into this society, at the behest of his dying father we are told, was momentous. He described it and the connected ceremo-

nial activities, especially the "scalp" and "battle with the Katsina" enactments, numerous times: for Edward S. Curtis, Leslie A. White, and for EPH-2. He also spoke of it while on tour, when Wolf Robe billed his father as "last of the delight makers," and began advertising himself as one as well.

185 **Given Pueblo Indian:** Among essays I reviewed on this favored academic topic: Louis A. Hieb, "The Ritual Clown: Humor and Ethics," in *Forms of Play of Native North Americans,* ed. Edward Norbeck and Claire R. Farrer (St. Paul, MN: West Publishing Co., 1977); Barbara Babcock, "The Clown's Way," in *Teachings from the American Earth,* ed. Barbara and Dennis Tedlock (New York: Liveright, 1975); Jill D. Sweet, "Burlesquing 'the Other' in Pueblo Performance," *Annals of Tourism Research* 16, no. 1 (1989); Eric Knight, "The Funny Men," *New Mexico Magazine* 19, no. 6 (June 1941); and Barbara Babcock, "Arrange Me into Disorder: Fragments and Reflections on Ritual Clowning," in *Rite, Drama, Festival, Spectacle: Rehearsals Towards a Theory of Cultural Performance,* ed. John MacAloon (Philadelphia: Institute for the Study of Human Issues, 1984).

186 **But as a Hopi:** Don C. Talayesva and Leo W. Simmons, *Sun Chief: The Autobiography of a Hopi Indian* (New Haven, CT: Yale University Press, 1963), p. 53.

188 **Bandelier cribbed its title:** See Hulda Hobbs, "The Story of *The Delight Makers* from Bandelier's Own Journals," *El Palacio* 49, no. 6 (1942), and her "Addenda to *The Delight Makers,*" *El Palacio* 49, no. 8 (1942); Russell S. Saxton "The Truth About the Pueblo Indians: Bandelier's Delight Makers," *New Mexico Historical Review* 56, no. 3 (1981); and Barbara A. Babcock, "Ritual Undress and the Comedy of Self and Other: Bandelier's *The Delight Makers,*" in *A Crack in the Mirror,* ed. Jay Ruby (Philadelphia: University of Pennsylvania Press, 1982).

188 **The Pueblo scholar:** This account is in the Alfonso Ortiz memoir entitled "Becoming a Sacred Clown" (Princeton University Library, Special Collections, Alfonso Ortiz papers, Collection #WC126).

Chapter 26: Love and Marriage (1889)

For material in this chapter: WH—7/4/93; WH—4/7–8/94; WH—7/20–21/98.

190 **"When I got married":** Quoted in Richard Spivey, *The Legacy of Maria Poveka Martinez* (Santa Fe: Museum of New Mexico Press, 2003), p. 172.

192 **Edward's only recorded memory:** In EPH-1.

194 **The blackened outback:** Aside from dates in EPH-2 for his marriage to Marie Valle, the couple's three years of banishment on the eastern rim of the Malpais volcanic area went unrecorded. When Wilbert Hunt, Eddie Hunt, and I tried to locate his parents' cave the current landowner denied us access. Data on Zuni, Navajo, and Acoma accounts of the mythic creation of the Malpais is scattered through their folklore, and guidebooks on El Malpais, such as Ken Mabery, compiler, *Natural History of El Malpais National Monument* (Socorro: New Mexico Bureau of Mines & Natural Resources, 1997); Sherry Robinson, *El Malpais, Mt. Taylor, and the Zuni Mountains* (Albuquerque: University of New Mexico Press, 1994); and the report Neil C. Mangum, *In the Land of Frozen Fires: A History of Occupation in El Malpais Country* (Santa Fe: Southwest Cultural Resources Center, Paper no. 32, 1990). This chapter is largely surmised out of information on

Western Pueblo foraging, plant use, and survival skills in Swank 1932; Matilda Coxe Stevenson, *The Zuni Indians and Their Uses of Plants* (Mineola: NY: Dover Publications, 1993 [1915]); and Florence Hawley Ellis, "The Woman's Page: Laguna Pueblo," *El Palacio*, February 1959. Still today the Malpais remains a mysterious and primordial zone, replete with tales of hidden treasure, oversize rattlesnakes, lost prospectors, and unexplored native ruins.

196 **Still older is:** From interview with Mrs. Audrey Dittert, Phoenix, Arizona (5/8/2008). I am grateful for her comments on her husband's work, which were reported in Reynold J. Ruppe and Alfred E. Dittert, "The Archaeology of Cebolleta Mesa and Acoma Pueblo," *El Palacio* 59 (1952), and his dissertation, "Culture Change in the Cebolleta Mesa Region, Central Western New Mexico" (Dept. of Anthropology, University of Arizona, 1959).

Chapter 27: Brother Bibo Steps Up (1889–1910)

198 **"One day Solomon":** San Mateo historian and author Abe Peña shared this anecdote at his home in Grants, New Mexico (6/25/2007).

200 **But the role:** I am grateful to UCLA Anderson School professor John Hughes for his conjectures (5/5/2011) about frontier economics of the complex, fiscally rudimentary but culturally blended sort, as practiced by Edward Hunt and the Bibos, and to Tomas Jaehn of the New Mexico History Museum for citations (4/27/2011), including his chapter on economics in *Germans of the Southwest* (Albuquerque: University of New Mexico Press, 2004). On the earlier Indian economic customs that infiltrated these practices: Richard I. Ford, "Inter-Indian Exchange in the Southwest," in Alfonzo Ortiz, ed., *Southwest*, vol. 10 of *Handbook of the North American Indians* (Washington, DC: Smithsonian Institution, 1983). For general background I delved into Frank McNitt's *The Indian Traders* (Norman: University of Oklahoma Press, 1962) (and then McNitt's papers at the New Mexico State Archives and Records Center), and Josiah Gregg's classic *The Commerce of the Prairies* (Lincoln: University of Nebraska Press, 1967 [1831]). For New Mexico material: the marvelously intimate look provided in Jane Lenz Elder and David J. Weber, ed., *Trading in Santa Fe: John M. Kingsbury's Correspondence with James Josiah Webb, 1853–1861* (Dallas: Southern Methodist University Press, 1996); Daniel T. Kelly, *The Buffalo Head: A Century of Mercantile Pioneering in the Southwest* (Santa Fe: Vergara Publishing Co., 1972); and William J. Parish, "The German Jew and the Commercial Revolution in Territorial New Mexico, 1850–1900," *New Mexico Quarterly* 29 (1959) (and references in the literature about the region's Jewish pioneers and residents cited in chapters 14 and 19). Most writing on this topic has concerned the world of Navajo traders and debates over their business practices, leaving bicultural economics in Pueblo country largely understudied, with the exception of newspaper articles about Fred Thompson's colorful trading post at Santo Domingo Pueblo.

201 **As critical as:** Conviviality, recreation, and mutual understanding, as fostered by store life such as surrounded the Bibo and Hunt establishments, often gets short shrift in historical chronicles. But Weigle and White 1988 underscore it nicely in their section (pp. 364–82) on "Passing Time: Occasional Encounters and Gatherings." An outlet like Edward's offered a rare opportunity for Hispanos, Pueblos,

Navajos, and others to informally and personally interact. Otherwise, so isolated and self-protective were many western New Mexico Hispano hamlets that after one reads such local histories as Abe Peña's San Mateo–centered *Memories of Cibola: Stories from New Mexico Villages* (Albuquerque: University of New Mexico Press, 1997), Nasario Garcia's *Mas Antes: Hispanic Folklore of the Rio Puerco Valley* (Santa Fe: Museum of New Mexico Press, 1997), or Oracio Elijio Molinas's self-published *Aldea Escondida (Hidden Village): Marquez, New Mexico* (2008), it can seem as if their Pueblo neighbors didn't even exist.

204 **Upon moving to San Francisco:** Glimpses of Solomon and Juana's life in California are Sandra Lea Rollins, "Solomon Bibo, Jewish Indian Chief," *Western States Jewish History* 1, no. 4 (July 1969); Gordon Bronitsky, "Solomon Bibo: Jew and Indian at Acoma Pueblo," Southwest Jewish Archives, University of Arizona; and Joyce R. Starr, "Solomon Bibo: Jewish Indian Chief" (book proposal, 1992).

Chapter 28: New Merchant in Town (1900–10)

For material in this chapter: WH—7/20–21/98; WH—2/8/94; WH—6/21/98; WH—7/6/98.

205 **Cultural intermediaries have:** See the important anthology by Margaret Connell Szasz, ed., *Between Indian and White Worlds: The Cultural Broker* (Norman: University of Oklahoma Press, 1994), p. 21.

207 **As one entered:** These final three chapters of part 2 benefit from Wilbert Hunt's precise memories of his childhood around his father's Acomita home and store (WH—6/21/98; WH—7/20/98). He accompanied them by having me draw maps of the place and the Acomita-Alaska area showing his father's San Jose bottom fields, his second store at the mesa, the bridge Edward built, and other local sights.

Chapter 29: Around the House (1911–15)

For material in this chapter: WH—7/4/93; WH—12/29/95.

212 **"The dinner was":** From the novel by Bobette Gugliotta, *Katzimo, Mysterious Mesa* (New York: Dodd, Mead & Co., 1974), p. 110. Written by a direct descendant of the Bibo family, her story, while set in 1925 after the Hunts had actually left for Santa Ana, is based on the author's tape-recorded interviews in 1970 and thereafter with Arthur Bibo, Carl Bibo, Harold Bibo, Helen Vallo (a.k.a. Valle) Keith Lummis, and Leo Bibo. It nicely conveys the region's early-twentieth-century period and the mutually cooperative spirit that Wilbert often talked about of the Bibo-Valle-Hunt interfamily group, and features Wilbert Hunt by name—who attended such Shabbat dinners.

213 **Aside from the pleasure:** Thanks to Barbara Larsen of the National Archives and Records Administration, Central Plains Region (11/4/2008), for assistance in obtaining Haskell Institute school records and correspondence for five of the Hunt children, Alfred, Allen, Cecelia, Evelyn, and Ervin, covering the years 1911–15. As described in general in Myriam Vučković's *Voices from Haskell: Indian Students Between Two Worlds, 1884–1928* (Lawrence: University Press of

Kansas, 2008), health and sanitary conditions at the school were bad; the experience was especially harsh for the Hunts. While the boys enjoyed playing in the Haskell band, Cecelia returned home with a full-blown case of tuberculosis. Edward had to quarantine her in a shack away from the house where food was left in a plate outside the door; she died in 1917 and is buried in the Acomita cemetery with her headstone carved by Edward. Allen was also found to have signs of the disease in his left lung and was sent home (he survived). Although the family's oldest girl, Evelyn, wanted to stay, fearing for her survival, Edward had her come home as well. See postscript for more on Hunt family members.

Chapter 30: The Noose Tightens (1917–18)

For material in this chapter: WH—4/8–11/94; WH—12/29/95; WH—5/10/97; WH—2/8/94, WH—7/21/98.

219 **"One whose eyes":** Charles F. Lummis, *Pueblo Indian Folk-Stories* (New York: The Century Co., 1910) p. 146.

221 **Edward, like everyone:** (WH—4/8/94). See chapter 5, "Pueblo Witchcraft," in Marc Simmons's *Witchcraft in the Southwest: Spanish and Indian Supernaturalism on the Rio Grande* (Lincoln: University of Nebraska Press, 1980), pp. 80–81, which contains the story of the bewitched Albuquerque schoolboy from Acoma. Edward's nephew's account, "A Witch's Tale," is in Paytiamo 1932, pp. 135–42. Also Florence Hawley, "The Mechanics of Perpetuation in Pueblo Witchcraft," in *For the Dean: Essays in Anthropology in Honor of Byron Cummings* (Tucson: Hohokam Museums Assn., 1950).

226 **Taking a first step:** In Patricia Fogelman Lange, Louis A. Hieb, and Thomas J. Steele, S.J., ed., *The Indians of Arizona and New Mexico: Nineteenth Century Ethnographic Notes of Archbishop John Baptist Salpointe* (Los Ranchos, NM: Rio Grande Books, 2010), p. 157.

Chapter 31: A Second Chance (1918)

For material in this chapter: WH—5/9/97.

231 **"This village is":** Adolph F. Bandelier and Edgar L. Hewett, *Indians of the Rio Grande* (Albuquerque: University of New Mexico Press, 1937), p. 111.

232 **Pressed between the:** For key sources on this village that initially harbored the exiled Hunts: Pauline Turner Strong, "Santa Ana," in Alfonso Ortiz, ed., *Southwest,* vol. 9 of *Handbook of the North American Indians* (Washington, DC: Smithsonian Institution, 1979); Leslie A. White, *The Pueblo of Santa Ana, New Mexico,* Memoirs of the American Anthropological Association, no. 60, 1942; Laura Bayer with Floyd Montoya and the Pueblo of Santa Ana, *Santa Ana: The People, the Pueblo, and the History of Tamaya* (Albuquerque: University of New Mexico Press, 1994). It is a measure of Leslie White's negative reputation in this village that there is not a single mention of his writing or very existence in this 1994 self-portrait.

236 **Four days before:** White 1942, "Opening the Irrigation Ditch," pp. 237–41.

237 **"To your Paternal Reverence's health":** Quoted in White 1942, p. 25.

Chapter 32: Storms Far and Near (1918–21)

For material in this chapter: WH—7/16/98.

238 **"They have also"**: Quote from George Parker Winship, review of Mrs. William T. Sedgewick, *Acoma, the Sky City*, in *Saturday Review of Literature*, May 8, 1926, p. 769.

238 **Much of America:** "New Mexico in the Great War," *New Mexico Historical Review*, nos. 1 (January 1926), 2 (April 1926), 3 (July 1926).

239 **With Pershing and Patton:** Quote in EPH-2.

239 **Of the well:** Edward and Agent Lonergan sought to recruit locally, with limited success—EPH-2. See Thomas A. Britten, *American Indians in World War I: At War and at Home* (Albuquerque: University of New Mexico Press, 1997); Russel Lawrence Barsh, "American Indians in the Great War," *Ethnohistory* 38, no. 3 (Summer 1991); and *The American Indian in the World War* (Washington, DC: Department of the Interior, Office of Indian Affairs, Bulletin 15, 1927).

239 **During Pershing's stand:** Material on Pueblo Indians who did serve, from Acoma in particular, is from the U.S. National Archives, Pueblo Indian Agency, Southern Pueblos, Index #610, Denver. Thanks to archivist Marlene Baker.

242 **By the time Mabel Dodge:** Aside from Mabel Dodge Luhan's own three-volume autobiography, see Lois Palken Rudnick, *Mabel Dodge Luhan: New Woman, New Worlds* (Albuquerque: University of New Mexico Press, 1984), especially part 6, "Choice: Indian Policy Through World War II."

Chapter 33: Threats to Pueblo Lands (1922)

246 **"The Acomas held":** Quoted in Alida Sims Malkus, "What Is to Become of the Pueblo Indian?," *McClure's Magazine* 55, no. 2 (April 1923): 90.

246 **After his close friend:** The story of the Acoma shepherd Francisco Salvador is from S. C. Hamilton to Margaret McKittrick, April 14, 1931, and accompanying papers, New Mexico Association on Indian Affairs Collection, Santa Fe: New Mexico State Records Center and Archives; it is also in "Report of Adelina Otero-Warren, Inspector, February 15, 1924," Santa Fe: New Mexico State Records Center and Archives. In its Southwestern Association of Indian Affairs collection is also the useful 1922 typescript survey "Provisional Data on the Economic Condition of Five of the Northern Pueblos," which provides a grim overview of the times.

247 **But land surveys:** Quote from William Brophy interviews on Espirito Santo Grant, from Zia, Jemez, and Santa Ana tribal members, May 1949. Sophie D. Aberle Collection, Center for Southwest Research, Zimmerman Library, University of New Mexico, Mss. 509 BC, p. 18.

248 **In 1876 the Pueblo Indian's anomalous status:** See Gerald Torres, "Who Is an Indian?: The Story of United States v. Sandoval," in *Indian Law Stories*, ed. Carole Goldberg et al. (New York: Foundation Press, 2011).

250 **John Collier caught:** Kenneth R. Philp, *John Collier's Crusade for Indian Reform* (Tucson: University of Arizona Press, 1973); Lawrence C. Kelly, *The Assault on Assimilation: John Collier and the Origins of Indian Reform* (Albuquerque:

University of New Mexico Press, 1983), especially chapter 7, "The Bursum Bill,"
pp. 213–254); *Indian Self-Rule: First-Hand Accounts of Indian-White Relations
from Roosevelt to Reagan,* ed. Kenneth R. Philp (Salt Lake City: Howe Brothers,
1986). Excellent on local politics and factions during the 1920s in Santa Fe is Tisa
Wenger's "Land, Culture and Sovereignty in the Pueblo Dance Controversy,"
Journal of the Southwest 16, no. 2 (Fall 2004). Much material on the Bursum Bill
and the coalition it inspired is scattered throughout the Southwestern Association of Indian Affairs collection at the New Mexico State Records Center and
Archives in Santa Fe, at the Laboratory of Anthropology archives, Santa Fe, and
in the Albert B. Fall collection at the Huntington Library, San Marino, California.

253 **Ever the ringmaster:** Collier to Acoma, November 22, 1922, Southwestern Association of Indian Affairs Papers, New Mexico State Records Center and Archives,
Serial 9683, Folder 25. At the same time Collier could adamantly deny such ma-
nipulations: "But the suggestion which was made last year by the Indian Bureau,
that the dances and bonnets are in the nature of show properties adopted for
present publicity purposes can only be made in great ignorance of the life of the
Rio Grande Pueblos. The so-called 'pleasure dances' of the Rio Grand Pueblos
have partaken of the Plains Indian dance system, for unknown age.... I would
never assume to tell the Pueblos what they should or should not wear, or how
they should or should not dance, whether in their plazas or eastern cities." John
Collier to Frederick S. Dallanbaugh, March 12, 1924, Laboratory of Anthropology Archives, Santa Fe, Collection 891SC.012.

Chapter 34: Children of the Railroad (1922)

254 **"It was like":** Mary Toya, "Laguna Exile," in *A Route 66 Companion,* ed. David
King Dunaway (Austin: University of Texas Press, 2012), p. 106.

255 **Wilbert's brothers' disappearance:** Thanks to Professor Kurt M. Peters for his
interview (5/20/2008). For background on labor issues, see Colin J. Davis, *Power at
Odds: The 1922 National Railroad Shopmen's Strike* (Urbana: University of Illinois
Press, 1997). I am indebted to Dr. Peters's doctoral research over 1991–93 that
yielded "Boxcar Babies: The Santa Fe Railroad Indian Villages at Richmond, Cali-
fornia, 1940–1945," in *Native American Perspectives on Literature and History,* ed.
Alan R. Velie (Norman: University of Oklahoma Press, 1995), pp. 407–20; "Santa
Fe Indian Camp, House 21, Richmond, California: Persistence of Identity Among
Laguna Pueblo Railroad Laborers, 1945–1982," *American Indian Culture and Research Journal* 19, no. 3 (1995): 33–70; "Continuing Identity: Pueblo Railroaders in
Richmond, California," *American Indian Culture and Research Journal* 22, no. 4
(1998): 187–98; and "Watering the Flower: Laguna Pueblo and the Santa Fe Railroad, 1880–1943," in *Native Americans and Wage Labor,* ed. Alice Littlefield and
Martha C. Knack (Norman: University of Oklahoma Press, 1996). More details on
the Richmond Indian village came from Edward's grandson John Johnson, who
recalled visits to the Richmond village as a boy, my own look at the site, articles in
the Richmond City Library from the *Richmond Independent* (March 11, 1954, and
November 10, 1961, when the village, located at 1st and Nevada streets, was to be
torn down), "Native People of Richmond, CA, Talk of Santa Fe Indian Village,"

Callie Shanafelt, November 26, 2009, http://teachingthevaluesofpeace.blogspot
.com/2009_11_01_archive.html, and the Toya 2012 reminiscence.

Chapter 35: Entrepreneurs in the Making (1902–24)

262 **"Clearly the west":** Nancy Peake, "'If It Came from Wright's, You Bought It
Right': Charles A Wright, Proprietor, Wright's Trading Post," *New Mexico Historical Review* 66, no. 3 (July 1991): 262–63.

262 **Henry Wayne, the fifth:** Material on Wolf Robe's upbringing, arts, travels, and
family life is from his "A Wild Injun" column for the *Tulsa Daily World* (biweekly, 1937), and the following interviews: Cheryl Dobbins, "Wolf Robe Hunt,
Delight Maker," *Tulsa Magazine,* July 11, 1974; "Song of the Delight Maker," interview by editor Francine Ringold for *NIMROD*, a University of Tulsa literary
review, *NIMROD* 20, no. 2 (Spring/Summer 1976).

264 **Over these decades:** On the professionalization of cultural studies in the Southwest, see "New Institutions, New Directions," chapter 29 of Don D. Fowler's *A
Laboratory for Anthropology: Science and Romanticism in the American Southwest, 1846-1930* (Albuquerque: University of New Mexico Press, 2000).

268 **She was Nina Otero-Warren:** See Charlotte Whaley on this remarkable, bicultural woman who seemed to navigate gracefully between Santa Fe's mutually
feuding constituencies in *Nina Otero-Warren of Santa Fe* (Santa Fe: Sunstone
Press, 2007) and Kenneth Darber, "Pueblo Pottery and the Politics of Regional
Identity," *Journal of the Southwest* 32 (1990).

Chapter 36: Troubles at Santa Ana (1922–25)

For material in this chapter: EPH-1; WH—5/9/97.

269 **"If all of":** Leslie A. White, *The Pueblo of Santa Ana, New Mexico,* Memoirs of
the American Anthropological Association, no. 60, 1942, p. 190.

270 **After clearing, plowing:** In May 2012 a Hunt family relative showed me the
eroding remains of Edward and Marie's Ranchitos barn and house and "Gaire's
Field" so I could appreciate its cramped location between Indian and Hispano
mother ditches. In White 1942 he focuses on the Hunt family crisis here (pp.
188–89), and Hunt may have provided some of his other information on the
pueblo as well.

270 **Well before the Spanish:** On comparative irrigation practices: Sylvia Rodriguez,
Acequia: Water Sharing, Sanctity and Place (Santa Fe: School of Advanced Research, 2006); Jose A. Rivera, *Acequia Culture: Water, Land and Community in
the Southwest* (Albuquerque: University of New Mexico Press, 1998); Fred M.
Philips, G. Emlen Hall, and Mary E. Black, *Reining in the Rio Grande: People,
Land and Water* (Albuquerque: University of New Mexico Press, 2011); and Timothy D. Maxwell and Eric Blinman, "2000 Years of Water Woes," *El Palacio* 108,
no. 2 (2013).

271 **Projecting this theory:** Although now largely discredited, still see Karl A. Wittfogel and Esther S. Goldfrank, "Some Aspects of Pueblo Mythology and Society,"
Journal of American Folklore 56, no. 219 (1943): 17–30.

273 **Over the next couple:** Material on Hunt's back-and-forth with Santa Ana Pueblo over his duties to the community's irrigation ditch comes from the March 14 (H. P. Marble to Frank Livingston), November 17 (Edward Hunt to R. E. Twitchell), and November 19 (R. E. Twitchell to Hon. Charles Burke) communiqués for 1923 (Records of the Special Attorney for the Pueblos, Miscellaneous Correspondence 1908–1935, Records of the Bureau of Indian Affairs, RG 75, National Archives and Records Administration, Denver). Transcripts for the April 10, 1924, hearing, where Hunt and Santa Ana Pueblo officials were interviewed in Santa Fe about his problems with Santa Ana elders over his irrigation responsibilities, and over the terms of his eventual departure, by a seven-member commission chaired by Navajo commissioner Herbert Hagerman, are in Records of the Special Attorney for the Pueblos, Miscellaneous Correspondence 1908–1935, Records of the Bureau of Indian Affairs, RG 75. Copies of the series of interviews, hearings, and testimonies that intermix the Hunts' personal issues at Santa Ana with the larger debate over Pueblo religious rights and compilation of the "secret file" are found in the National Archives and Records Administration, Denver; the Indian Pueblo Cultural Center Archives in Albuquerque; the New Mexico Records Center and Archives in Santa Fe; the E. S. Curtis Collection, #C 1–3, Braun Research Library, Southwest Museum, Los Angeles; and the Indian Rights Association papers. Details of the meetings of reformers and the Council of Progressive Pueblo Indians that were hosted by Edward Hunt at Santa Ana Pueblo over May 1–3, 1924, are in Central Classified Files, 1907–1939, Northern Pueblo Records; and Records of the Bureau of Indian Affairs, RG 75, File 150, National Archives and Records Administration, Washington, D.C.

275 **As he entered downtown:** Eight years after the Morley, Colorado, store and warehouse of the Colorado Supply Company was built in 1908, with towers and horizontal extension inspired by Acoma's San Estevan and convent, the Santa Fe architectural firm Rapp and Rapp designed the New Mexico building for San Diego's Panama-California Exposition, also after that Pueblo church. A year later came Santa Fe's Art Museum, of which Paul Horgan wrote, "In its over-all idiom recalled the Pueblo massing of walls, terraces, and recessions; while the museum auditorium by itself was derived largely from the church of Saint Stephen at Acoma, which was as much Spanish Franciscan as it was Pueblo Indian. The modern statement of such architecture was accepted with admiration by residents and visitors alike, and became the necessary mode of almost all new construction at Santa Fe in the twentieth century." Horgan, *The Centuries of Santa Fe* (New York: E. P. Dutton, 1956), p. 312.

Chapter 37: Threats to Pueblo Spirits (1922–25)

For material in this chapter: WH—5/9/97.

278 **"Much has been written":** Matthew K. Sniffen correspondence, E. S. Curtis Collection, #A 1–10, Braun Research Library, Southwest Museum, Los Angeles. For more on Sniffen and his organization: William T. Hagen, *The Indian Rights Association: The Herbert Welsh Years, 1882–1904* (Tucson: University of Arizona Press, 1985). This followed the association's deeper and contradictory prejudice

toward Indians who attempted to "progress," as J. B. Harrison, an Indian Rights Association member, wrote in 1887: "Education for Indians should consist of instruction and training adapted to prepare them for the life of laborers.... Most Indians who try to live by their wits are likely to be worthless idlers. The competition of white men will be too intense for many Indians to succeed in the learned professions. They are, as a race, distinctly inferior to white men in intellectual vitality and capability, and their wise friends will advise them to look forward to the life of toilers." *The Critic* (New York), December 24, 1887.

278 **By now every:** For background on the predicament of Pueblo progressives like the Hunts, mostly consisting of a minority of boarding school graduates, during these tense years, I found pamphlets, letters to the editor, correspondence, and other primary materials in Santa Fe's Southwestern Association of Indian Affairs Collection at the New Mexico State Records Center and Archives; the National Archives materials on the Hunt case (Record Group RG 75, Ralph Twitchell, "Investigation into the Hunt Case," April 10, 1924, Records of Special Attorney for the Pueblos); the Laboratory of Anthropology archives; and the previously cited E. S. Curtis Collection, which underscores Curtis's almost schizophrenic attitude toward native traditions.

279 **On the national stage:** Launched with its first conference in October 1911, the Society of American Indians created a journal, the *American Indian Magazine,* and lobbied on a host of issues for American Indian rights and respect. During its short life span, it engaged a generation (also mostly boarding school graduates) of Indian intellectuals, activists, and artists with varying perspectives who debated and promoted a range of Indian interests. Its final meeting was in 1923. See the classic, prescient book on the society by Hazel W. Hertzberg, *The Search for an American Indian Identity: Modern Pan-Indian Movements* (Syracuse, NY: Syracuse University Press, 1971), and its follow-up by Lucy Maddox, *Citizen Indians: Native American Intellectuals, Race and Reform* (Ithaca, NY: Cornell University Press, 2005).

280 **Then Indian Commissioner:** Background on U.S. government's attempted suppression of American Indian social and religious practices in the nineteenth century: Jacqueline Shea Murphy, *The People Have Never Stopped Dancing: Native American Modern Dance Histories* (Minneapolis: University of Minnesota Press, 2007), and Clyde Ellis, *A Dancing People: Powwow Culture on the Southern Plains* (Lawrence: University Press of Kansas, 2003). For a close-up look: Margo Liberty, "Suppression and Survival of the Northern Cheyenne Sun Dance," *Minnesota Archaeologist* 27, no. 4 (1965). For great coverage of the similar government campaign in the early-twentieth-century Southwest: Tisa Wenger, *We Have a Religion: The 1920s Pueblo Indian Dance Controversy and American Indian Religious Freedom* (Chapel Hill: University of North Carolina Press, 2009). On the role of activist women in both the Bursum Bill and religious freedom issues, as old-style assimilationists and antiassimilationists alike, see Margaret D. Jacobs, *Engendered Encounters: Feminism and Pueblo Cultures, 1879–1934* (Lincoln: University of Nebraska Press, 1999). Both of these excellently researched works cover the role of the Hunts, the Indian Rights Association, and Anglo supporters of both the Bursum Bill and the antireligion crusade.

281 **This time around:** A lively debate ensued: the old East Coast–based reformer's Indian Rights Association was pitted against the new reformer's Southwest-based Indian Defense Association; *The Forum,* a respected journal, set Flora Warren Seymour's lengthy, impassioned "The Delusion of the Sentimentalists" against Mary Austin's equally strong "The Folly of the Officials" (vol. 3, March 1924); and Clara True, the experienced Indian Bureau teacher and administrator who lived near Santa Clara Pueblo in the Española Valley, was scathing in her contempt for the likes of Collier, Luhan, and their Taos–Santa Fe set. Resolving conflicts among Indians "can't be done at dude ranches," she wrote, "not at teas in the art colonies [nor by] boy scoutish persons from the Atlantic seaboard who have been successful in inducing Greek bootblacks to use tooth brushes [or] rich women who graduated from Birth Control and the Soviet to find a thrill in Native Art." Quoted in Margaret D. Jacobs, "Clara True and Female Moral Authority," in *The Human Tradition in the American West,* ed. Benson Tong and Regan A. Lutz (Wilmington, DE: Scholarly Resources, Inc., 2002), p. 313.

Chapter 38: Indians as Global Icons (1927)

For material in this chapter: EPH-1; WH—7/3/93; WH—9/3/94; WH—4/1/98; WH—12/29/95; WH—4/5/01.

287 **"How can we save":** Chauncey Yellow Robe, "The Menace of the Wild West Show," *Quarterly Journal* 2 (1914): 224–25.

288 **There had been one lapse:** Wilbert Hunt's earlier, November 10, 1926, experience as a "deserter" from Albuquerque Indian School is recorded in Albuquerque School File #823, Albuquerque Indian School student case files, 1877–1989; thanks to archivist Eric Bittner, National Archives and Records Administration, Denver.

288 **The Hunts had landed:** Thanks to University of Oklahoma, Western History Collection, for sending materials from their "Miller Brothers 101 Ranch and Wild West Show Collection" files that also helped with Ponca origins of the Hunt's Big Snake and Blue Sky Eagle stage names. Background on the Miller Brothers 101 Ranch: Michael Wallis, *The Real Wild West: The 101 Ranch and the Creation of the American West* (New York: St. Martin's, 1999); Ellsworth Collings and Alma Miller England, *The 101 Ranch* (Norman: University of Oklahoma Press, 1971 [1937]); and Paul Reddin, "'An Empire within Itself': The 101 Ranch and Its Wild West Show," chapter 6 in *Wild West Shows* (Urbana: University of Illinois Press, 1999). On Indian imagery: John C. Ewers, "The Plains Indian as Symbol," *Southwestern Art* 1, no. 2 (Summer 1966). On Wild West shows in general and the Buffalo Bill enterprise that started it all: L. G. Moses, *Wild West Shows and the Images of American Indians, 1883–1933* (Albuquerque: University of New Mexico Press, 1996); Joy S. Kasson, *Buffalo Bill's Wild West: Celebrity, Memory, and Popular History* (New York: Hill & Wang, 2000); Louis S. Warren, *Buffalo Bill's America: William Cody and the Wild West Show* (New York: Vintage, 2006); Phyllis Rogers, "'Buffalo Bill' and the Siouan Image," *American Indian Culture and Research Journal* 7, no. 3 (1983); Robert W. Rydell and Rob Kroes, *Buffalo Bill in Bologna: The Americanization of the World, 1869–1922* (Chicago: University of Chicago Press, 2005); and the Amon Carter Museum of

Western Art catalog, *The Wild West* (Fort Worth, TX: Amon Carter Museum of Western Art, 1970).

290 **Some, like Iroquois:** Arthur C. Parker maintained that Show Indians like the Hunts "misrepresent their people, libel the work of patient teachers and devoted missionaries, and defraud the public. . . . This causes humiliation to the better class of Indians." As quoted in Maddox, *Citizen Indians*, p. 50. Both Parker and his colleague Chauncey Yellow Robe were key figures in the Society of American Indians; their opinions suggest a class division within American Indian "progressives": local strugglers on the white man's road, such as Hunt and his regional Pueblo compatriots, contrasted with the high achievers who occupied professional roles and secured national profiles in white society. However, commentators as diverse as Commissioner of Indian Affairs John Collier and author Vine Deloria Jr. held an alternative opinion. "The Wild West [shows]," wrote Deloria, "served to give them confidence by emphasizing the nobility of their most cherished exploits and memories." "The Indians," in *Buffalo Bill and the West: An Exhibition of the Museum of Art, Carnegie Institute, and the Buffalo Bill Historical Center* (catalog, 1991), p. 53.

291 **One, detested by progressives:** John P. Clum, "Apaches as Thespians in 1876," *New Mexico Historical Review* (1930).

292 **The chief's refusal:** The saga of Chief Standing Bear's resistance to Ponca removal, with mentions of his brother Big Snake, has been told in books and movies; see David J. Wishart, *An Unspeakable Sadness: The Dispossession of the Nebraska Indians* (Lincoln: University of Nebraska Press, 1995), and Valerie Sherer Mathes and Richard Lowitt, *The Standing Bear Controversy: Prelude to Indian Reform* (Urbana: University of Illinois Press, 2003).

Chapter 39: Joining the Circus (1927)

For material in this chapter: WH—7/3/93; WH—4/1/98; WH—6/5/93; WH—4/2/94; WH—7/23–25/98.

296 **"Suffice to say":** Hartmut Lutz, "'Okay, I'll Be Their Annual Indian for Next Year'—Thoughts on the Marketing of a Canadian Indian Icon in Germany," in *Imaginary (Re-)Locations: Tradition, Modernity, and the Market in Contemporary American Literature and Culture,* ed. Helbrecht Breinig (Tübingen: Stauffenberg Verlag, 2003), p. 219.

296 **Dresden was long famed:** Special thanks to official Sarrasani historian, Dresden resident Ernst Günther, for showing me around the city, introducing me to Sarrasani's great-grandson, Andres Sarrasani, who still performs, giving me a copy of his book about the circus, *Sarrasani: Geschichte und Geschichten* (Dresden: edition Sächsische Zeitung, 2005), and indulging my subsequent questions by mail. Marline Otte has also focused on the Sarrasani enterprise in "Sarrasani's Theater of the World: Monumental Circus Entertainment in Dresden, from Kaiserreich to Third Reich," *German History* 17, no. 4 (1999). More material on German and Indians, Wild West shows in Germany, and Karl May is in the magnificently illustrated exhibition catalog *I Like America: Fictions of the Wild West,* ed. Pamela Kort and Max Hollein (Munich: Prested, 2007); also Eric Ames's similarly

well-illustrated *Carl Hagenbeck's Empire of Entertainments* (Seattle: University of Washington Press, 2009). A creative approach to discussing and critiquing Indian Medicine shows in general and overseas performances as well is Norman K. Denzin's *Indians on Display: Global Commodification of Native America in Performance, Art and Museums* (Walnut Creek, CA: Left Coast Press, 2013), while Linda Scarangella McNenly's *Native Performers in Wild West Shows: From Buffalo Bill to Euro Disney* (Norman: University of Oklahoma Press, 2012) starts the process of looking at these experiences through Indian eyes.

298 **Whether caught and coerced:** Gratitude to Hartmut Lutz, who answered queries and sent materials from Germany. For background: Carolyn Thomas Foreman, *Indians Abroad, 1493–1938* (Norman: University of Oklahoma Press, 1943). For a marvelous investigation of a delegation of possibly Creek Indian notables visiting Dresden in the early eighteenth century: John Jeremiah Sullivan, "The Princes: A Reconstruction," *Paris Review* (Spring 2012): 35–88. I also delved into Christian F. Feest, ed., *Indians and Europe: An Interdisciplinary Collection of Essays* (Lincoln: University of Nebraska Press, 1989); Colin G. Calloway, ed., *Germans and Indians: Fantasies, Encounters, Projections* (Lincoln: University of Nebraska Press, 2002); and Dagmar Wernitznig, *Europe's Indians, Indians in Europe: European Perceptions and Appropriations of Native American Cultures from Pocahontas to the Present* (Lanham, MD: University Press of America, 2007), which was especially helpful on Karl May.

Chapter 40: Another Greatest Story Ever Told (1928)

304 **"The old myths":** Quoted in Richard B. Carter, "Dionysus: The Therapeutic Mask," *St. John's Review* 54, no. 2 (Spring 2013): 35.

306 **For American Indians:** On the tradition of Indians visiting the nation's capital, see Kathryn C. Turner, *Red Men Calling on the Great White Father* (Norman: University of Oklahoma Press, 1951), and Herman J. Viola, *Diplomats in Buckskins: A History of Indian Delegations in Washington City* (Washington, DC: Smithsonian Institution, 1981), especially its epilogue, "Delegations in the Twentieth Century," in which the issue of Indians being asked to dress traditionally for positive lobbying impact is discussed by Indian delegates themselves.

309 **Of the stripe today:** For a splendid roundup of brief biographies of native consultants like Hunt, sometimes described as "organic intellectuals," see Margot Liberty, ed. *American Indian Intellectuals* (St. Paul, MN: West Publishing Co., 1978).

309 **By now the Smithsonian:** An overview of the bureau's body of work to which the Hunts were contributing is Neil M. Judd, *The Bureau of American Ethnology: A Partial History* (Norman: University of Oklahoma Press, 1967); also special issue, *Journal of the Southwest,* with nine articles on the bureau, 41, no. 3 (Autumn 1999). From J. W. Powell, "Sketch of the Mythology of the North American Indians," in the bureau's first annual report (1881), one can see its abiding focus on American Indian narrative traditions like the Acoma origin narrative. Publishing work by such nineteenth-century field scholars as Erminie A. Smith (on Iroquois), Rev. J. Owen Dorsey (on Omaha and Osage), Frank H. Cushing (on Zuni), Washington Matthews (on Navajo), W. J. Hoffman (on Ojibwa), James Mooney (on Cherokee), John G. Bourke (on Apaches), and others, hardly a year

went by that the bureau, in its annual reports, and then "in cheaper form," according to Director Powell, in a bulletin series launched in 1886, did not add to the corpus of mythological and ritual accounts that eventually covered much of Native America. After the death of John Wesley Powell, his successor, William Henry Holmes, inserted into Powell's official eulogy, "The series of volumes published by the Bureau, which are more completely Powell's own than the world can ever know, are a splendid monument to his memory, and will stand, not only for himself but for the nation, among the most important contributions to human history ever made by an individual, an institution, or a state." Quoted in Wallace Stegner, *Beyond the Hundredth Meridian: John Wesley Powell and the Second Opening of the West* (New York: Penguin, 1992 [1954]), p. 259.

310 **To compile such narratives:** On the literary production behind such totalizing myths for peoples, tribes, or nations, as are collected in Charles H. Long, *Alpha: The Myths of Creation* (Atlanta: Scholars Press, 1963), and excellently introduced in Karen Armstrong, *A Short History of Myth* (New York: Canongate, 2005), I consulted Harvey J. Graff, *The Legacies of Literacy: Continuities and Contradictions in Western Culture and Society* (Bloomington: Indiana University Press, 1986); Jack Goody, ed., *Literacy in Traditional Societies* (Cambridge: Cambridge University Press, 1968), and V. Philips Long, *The Art of Biblical History* (Grand Rapids, MI: Zondervan, 1994). For a useful typology, see Ana Birgitta Rooth, "The Creation Myths of the North American Indians," *Anthropos* 52 (1957); for analyses of key characters and themes in Pueblo myths: Jay Miller, "Deified Mind Among the Keresan Pueblos" in *General and Amerindian Linguistics*, ed. Mary Ritchie Key and Henry M. Hoenigswald (Berlin: Mouton de Gruyter, 1989); Sandra Prewitt Edelman, "Ascension Motifs and Reversals in Tewa Narratives," *Journal of Anthropological Research* 30, no. 1 (Spring 1974); and Donald M. Bahr, "On the Complexity of Southwest Emergence Myths," *Journal of Anthropological Research* 33, no. 3 (Autumn 1977).

310 **Sometimes the old values:** Before and after Edward spliced together his various oral narratives into this monomyth, other whole or partial versions of the Acoma/Keresan creation story became available. Among them are a shorter version by Edward's fellow Progressive, boarding school alumni, and former Acoma governor James H. Miller, sent in a letter to engineer William Boone Douglass (Center for Southwest Research, Zimmerman Library, University of New Mexico, Collection #MSS 39 SC, July 4, 1923), and a more recent, undated typed account by Brian Vallo (New Mexico State Records Center and Archives). A section of the tribe's postemergence migration experience was narrated by famed Acoma poet Simon Ortiz and incorporated as "What We See: A Perspective on Chaco Canyon and its Ancestry" into Mary Peck et al., ed., *Chaco Canyon: A Center and its World* (Santa Fe: Museum of New Mexico Press, 1994). In his 1932 ethnography of Acoma, anthropologist Leslie White included a brief account—probably narrated by Edward. And Edward most likely contributed the version in one of Edward S. Curtis's two volumes on the Southwest, vol. 16 (1926), from his twenty-volume *The North American Indian* life's work. In part one of Franz Boas's *Keresan Texts* (American Ethnological Society, 1928) there are Laguna-inflected origin accounts, and among the Florence Hawley Ellis papers at the University of New Mexico's Hibben Center there is an "Acoma Origin Legend"

given to the Acoma Tribal Council and Dr. Ellis by elder Syme Sanchez during a May 7, 1957, meeting, which she recorded and annotated. (And included in the F. H. Ellis papers at the Maxwell Musem, University of New Mexico, is her detailed analysis of Edward's version, which had appeared by that time.) In her *American Indian Creation Myths,* San Juan and Nambe Pueblo resident Teresa Pijoan includes a brief Acoma creation story (Santa Fe: Sunstone Press, 2005). For the time being, however, the Edward Hunt version remains the lengthiest and most detailed in print, which, as reviewer Richard Long wrote in *MAN* (July–August 1945), "is not only an account of the origin of the people but is the authority for ritual practices, and the relevant parts of it are repeated before undertaking the performance of the rituals. . . . Altogether this is an excellent piece of work." In this regard, however, it may be useful to quote internationally recognized scholar of world myth and religion Karen Armstrong: "There is never a single, orthodox version of a myth. As our circumstances change, we need to tell our stories differently in order to bring out their timeless truths." *A Short History of Myth* (Edinburgh: Canongate, 2005), p. 11. And scholar of American Indian mythologies of both North and South America Claude Lévi-Strauss, concurs: "There isn't a good version [of a myth], or an authentic or primitive one. All versions must be taken seriously." Didier Eribon, *Conversations with Claude Lévi-Strauss* (Chicago: University of Chicago Press, 1991), p. 141. Ethnographer Paul Radin, who devoted an entire monograph to make the case against any single "historically primary" or "correct" or "original" version of a myth and for the equal importance to native peoples of multiple, variable versions, has traced this inevitable variability to "the influence of different types of plot elaboration, which in turn is due to the artistic individuality [and, I would argue, breadth of exposure to diverse aspects of his/her own tradition] of the raconteur." *Literary Aspects of North American Mythology* (Canada Geological Survey Museum Bulletin no. 16, Anthropological Series no. 6, 1915, p. 26). I touch on the question of many versions versus monomyths in "Multiple Accounts of Indian Pasts," in my *A Forest of Time: American Indian Ways of History* (New York: Cambridge University Press, 2002).

Chapter 41: Telling the Myth I: Iatiku's World (1928)

313 **"Edward Hunt insisted":** Among the Elsie Clews Parsons Papers at the American Philosophical Society in Philadelphia I found her pencil-edited version of Stirling's handwritten preamble to the 1942 publication, from which she excised all mention of Hunt. This followed her common practice for protecting informants and securing their continued availability.

313 **Having been only:** See introduction endnotes for background material on Matthew W. Stirling, who led the Bureau of American Ethnology from 1928 through 1953.

314 **Even by the standards:** Among the many writings on current protocols and standards for the professional recording and representation of oral narratives and scholarly attempts to retain their oral and cultural storytelling contexts and atmospheres, I reviewed Richard Bauman, *Verbal Arts as Performance* (Prospect Heights, IL: Waveland Press, 1977); Dennis Tedlock, *The Spoken Word and the Work of Interpretation* (Philadelphia: University of Pennsylvania Press, 1983);

and all of Brian Swann's anthologies of interpretive essays and examples, including his latest, *Sky Loom: Native American Myth, Story and Song* (Lincoln: University of Nebraska Press, 2014). An excellent critique of popular compendia of Indian narratives is William M. Clements, "The Anthology as Museum of Verbal Art," chapter 9 in his *Native American Verbal Art: Texts and Contexts* (Tucson: University of Arizona Press, 1996), for which the persistent lack of contextualization for excerptions of Edward's version of the Acoma origin story becomes a case in point.

315 **Apparently a rental:** Despite repeated queries to the Smithsonian Institution's historians and archivists, to date no one has been able to locate any paper trail for any logistics of the Hunt family sojourn in Washington. In the absence of more information I surmise their residence from dates (November–December 1928) and return address (312 S. 3rd St., Richmond, Virginia) in handwritten letters by Marie Hunt to a California Indian friend, Phoebe Maddux, whom she met at the Smithsonian while Ms. Maddux was helping linguist John P. Harrington (John Peabody Harrington Papers, National Anthropological Archives).

316 **"In the beginning":** The inserted sections from Edward's myth in chapters 41, 43, and 45 are from the most recent edition: Edward Proctor Hunt, *The Origin Myth of Acoma Pueblo,* introduction and notes by Peter Nabokov (New York: Penguin Classics, 2015).

319 **Stirling let this section:** The opening portion was published separately by visiting British anthropologist C. Daryll Forde: "A Creation Myth from Acoma," *Folklore* 41 (1930).

Chapter 42: Creation's Sights and Sounds (1928)

321 **"In nearly every Indian myth":** From Natalie Curtis, *The Indians' Book: Authentic Native American Legends, Lore and Music* (New York: Harper & Brothers, 1907), p. xxx.

321 **Makeshift though it was:** Surely the Smithsonian scholars were aware of the decade's popular interest in American Indian song, poetry, and art. As with many of its bureau's early transcriptions of American Indian ritual litanies, incantations, prayers, chants, and songs of all kinds, Indian supporters and artistic popularizers of the period were soon to edit and even rephrase from its publications. For many this was their "American Orient," and subject to similar romantic projections as were foisted on the Middle East, abetted by richly atmospheric Indian pictures by painters and photographers alike. The 1920s and '30s were a time of remarkable popularity for Indian and Indianesque visual, verbal, and musical arts. A decade after Natalie Curtis's 1907 call to "let us pause in the stress of modern life to listen to the ancient lore of our own land" in *The Indians' Book,* there appeared George Cronyn's *The Path of the Rainbow: An Anthology of Songs and Chants from the Indians of North America,* the first anthology that launched, according to Oliver La Farge, "the beginning of the union between art and anthropology." It was followed by such compilations as Mary Austin's 1930 *The American Rhythm: Studies and Reexpressions of Amerindian Songs* and Julia Buttree Seton's 1937 *The Rhythm of the Redman: In Song, Dance and Decoration.* Riding this wave of popularity, the Hunts were able to find work and audiences

over the middle decades of the twentieth century. On Natalie Curtis and these (mostly women) colleagues, see Helen Addison Howard, "Literary Translators and Interpreters of Indian Songs," *Journal of the West* 12, no. 2 (April 1973), and "A Survey of the Densmore Collection of American Indian Music," *Journal of the West* 13, no. 2 (April 1974), in which she covers the prolific scholar's sixty-four-year career that produced books, articles, and albums based upon twenty-six field studies.

321 **When Iatiku first:** Edward's myth recitation was punctuated with the songs that energized and brought life to the creative actions of the narrative's sacred sister, Iatiku, the "mother of all Indians." They were verbally narrated by Edward, then sung by Philip Sanchez for recording by Stirling's assistant, Anthony Wilding, on wax cylinders. At the same time, the Smithsonian's official photographer, De Lancey Gill, made studio portraits of the family in their performing clothes and Sanchez and Wilbert in street clothes with musical instruments. In April 1929, Frances Densmore was the first to listen to these recordings and conduct a musical analysis, which ultimately constituted the Acoma portion of the 1957 Smithsonian Institution Bureau of American Ethnology Bulletin 165, *Music of Acoma, Isleta, Cochiti and Zuni Pueblos,* together with their poetic translations. Although no genre analysis was conducted, the corpus included creation songs, hunters' songs, sacred clown songs, medicine men's songs, corn-grinding songs, Katsina songs, animal dance songs, and others. While the Hunts had their own drums and rattles, a Smithsonian carpenter improvised a *morache,* or rasping stick, with a gourd resonator.

323 **Since the 1880s:** Although largely unaware of it, the Hunts would be making their living as musical performers in the midst of a complex interplay between Indians struggling to maintain or revitalize tribal music and dance traditions, itinerant performers like themselves appealing to older Wild West show fans and younger Indian Lore aficionados, ethnographers documenting native musical cultures, Indians carving their own place in white popular musical traditions, and non-Indians developing Indian-themed musical genres at high and mass culture levels. This multirepresentational context is well covered in John W. Troutman, *Indian Blues: American Indians and the Politics of Music, 1870–1934* (Norman: University of Oklahoma Press, 2009).

324 **In his later anthology:** William Brandon, *The Magic World: American Indian Songs and Poems* (New York: William Morrow, 1971), p. xiv.

325 **When he began:** By encouraging Wolf Robe to illustrate the entire company of Acoma Katsina masks, altarpieces, and other pictures to accompany his father's recitation of the myth, Stirling was following the practice inaugurated by his predecessor, J. Walter Fewkes (*Hopi Kachinas, Drawn by Native Artists* [Washington, DC: Bureau of American Ethnology, Annual Report 21, 1903], a famous work often termed the *Codex Hopiensis*). Ruth Bunzel would elicit a similar visual record for 129 Zuni Kachinas (1929–30); Esther Goldfrank would collect a wider visual representation of religious activities at Isleta Pueblo from a native artist (1962). More artistically competent is Duane Dista's magnificent gallery from Zuni in Barton Wright's *Kachinas of the Zuni* (Flagstaff, AZ: Northland Press, 1985) and Fred Kabotie's depictions in *Fred Kabotie: Hopi Indian Artist, an Autobiography Told with Bill Belknap* (Flagstaff: Museum of Northern Ari-

zona Press, 1977). Community criticism often attended this representations and caused problems for their artists.

327 **The Isleta artist's life:** From Esther S. Goldfrank's memoir of anthropological work, primarily in the Southwest: *Notes on an Unexpected Life: As One Anthropologist Tells It* (Queens College Publications in Anthropology, no. 3, 1977), p. 218.

Chapter 43: Telling the Myth II: The War Gods' World (1928)

328 **"Those two fellows":** Quoted in Albert Yava and Harold Courlander, *Big Falling Snow: A Tewa-Hopi Indian's Life and Times and the Traditions of His People* (Albuquerque: University of New Mexico Press, 1982), pp. 46–47.

329 **The boys' magical birth:** Although it was published as an addendum to Edward's recitation of the myth, I am presuming that Edward told the story of the War Twins' birth in some sort of chronological sequence, making their role in the final sections more understandable. But for some reason, perhaps because it seemed out of tune with the rest or it was too risqué, the editors put it into the back matter. Although other, more human individuals appear as noble protagonists in Acoma folktales, the War Twins embody the characteristics and follow at least a portion of the storyline we associate with classic Hero narratives. Although they are not the children of kingly parents, as in most European Hero myths, here their semidivine conception and magical birth, rapid maturation, maternal assistance (in the form of a grandmother/Spider/female deity), complementary quest for paternal approval, subsequent tests and ordeals, ultimate acceptance by the father, receipt of supernatural powers and magical accessories (whether dress or weapons), and then clearing the world of monsters and rendering it acceptable for human habitation, are ubiquitous in Pueblo oral tradition. For a discussion of the Zuni equivalent, where the Twins help the people to finally settle in their "Center Place," see M. Jane Young, "Morning Star, Evening Star," in *Earth and Sky: Visions of the Cosmos in Native American Folklore,* ed. Ray A. Williamson and Claire R. Farrer (Albuquerque: University of New Mexico Press, 1992). For another analysis, see southwestern anthropologist Clyde Kluckhohn, "Recurrent Themes in Myths and Mythmaking," *DAEDALUS,* special issue, *Myths and Mythmaking* 88, no. 2 (Spring 1959), while for an example of how this Hero pattern played out in the Navajo traditions studied by Kluckhohn, see Maud Oakes and Joseph Campbell, *Where the Two Came to Their Father: A Navajo War Ceremonial Given by Jeff King* (Princeton, NJ: Princeton University Press/Bollingen Paperbacks, 1969).

Chapter 44: Explaining the Pueblos (1928)

336 **"Benedict deemphasized the role":** *The Pueblo Indians of North America,* an excellent synthesis by the Santa Clara Pueblo anthropologist Edward P. Dozier (New York: Holt, Rinehart & Winston, 1970), p. 203.

339 **Another of Boas's disciples:** For background on Ruth Benedict, see Margaret Mead, *Ruth Benedict: A Humanist in Anthropology* (New York: Columbia University Press, 1975); Margaret M. Caffey, *Ruth Benedict: Stranger in This Land* (Austin: University of Texas Press, 1989); and Mead's collection of Benedict's

published and unpublished writings, *An Anthropologist at Work* (New York: Avon, 1973). After her *Patterns of Culture* appeared (Boston: Houghton Mifflin, 1934), its popularity and promotion of anthropology as an exciting discipline initially insulated it from criticism. Eventually her academic recycling of the simplistic dichotomy between Plains and Pueblo cultural "patterns," borrowing the Nietzschean paradigm, came under attack. One example came from architectural historian Vincent Scully amid his praise for Adolph Bandelier's 1890 ethnographic novel *The Delight Makers*: "A gothic tale of most Un-Apollonian romance, intrigue and warfare between Keres and Tewa. Probably closer to the reality than Benedict's famous, brilliant generalizations about the moderation of Pueblo behavior with their misleading Nietzschean terminology." In *Pueblo, Mountain, Village, Dance* (New York: Viking, 1975), p. 394. Among the volumes of commentary on Benedict's career and most famous work see Sidney Mintz, "Ruth Benedict," in *Totems and Teachers: Perspectives on the History of Anthropology,* ed. Sydel Silverman (New York: Columbia University Press, 1986).

For reviews of anthropological scholarship in the Southwest: Fowler 2000; Keith H. Basso, "History of Ethnological Research," in Alfonso Ortiz, ed. *Southwest,* vol. 9 of *Handbook of the North American Indians* (Washington, DC: Smithsonian Institution, 1979); William Willard, "Towards an Anthropology of Anthropology: Cultural Heroes, Origin Myths, and Mythological Places of Southwestern Anthropology," in *New Voices in Native American Literary Criticism,* ed. Arnold Krupat (Washington, DC: Smithsonian Institution, 1993); and, on the preponderance of women investigators, Nancy J. Parezo, ed., *Hidden Scholars: Women Anthropologists and the Native American Southwest* (Albuquerque: University of New Mexico Press, 1993), as well as mentions throughout Regna Darnell, *Invisible Genealogies: A History of Americanist Anthropology* (Lincoln: University of Nebraska Press, 2001).

Chapter 45: Telling the Myth III: Into This World (1928)

343 **"After mankind had":** Hamilton A. Tyler, *Pueblo Gods and Myths* (Norman: University of Oklahoma Press, 1964), p. 115.

344 **No sooner had:** Edward's description of this devastating war between humans and spirits would seem unique in southwestern mythology, as well as in wider American Indian sacred narratives. The closest parallel, apparently, comes in a Zuni ritual enactment, held every four years, that dramatizes their battle with an enemy group known as the Ky'anakwe—who are not Katsinas. Again the War Twins are involved; they use magic rabbit sticks given them by the Sun, their father; and the dramatization also concludes with a scalp ceremony to purge the participants of being haunted by the ghosts of their victims (see Parsons 1996, vol. 2, pp. 761–64; also Wright, *Kachinas of the Zuni,* pp. 74–77).

As Henry R. Schoolcraft wrote of his collection of Great Lakes Indian stories in 1856, "It is in these legends that we obtain their true views of life and death, their religion, their theory of the state of the dead, their mythology, their cosmogony, their notions of astrology, and often of their biography and history—for the boundaries between history and fiction are vaguely defined." *The Myth of Hiawatha and Other Oral Legends, Mythologic and Allegoric, of the North Amer-*

ican Indians (Philadelphia: J. B. Lippincott, 1956), p. xxiii. Many of the characters and elements in Edward's version of the Acoma origin myth can be explored in the motif index accompanying Stith Thompson's *Tales of the North American Indians* (Bloomington: Indiana University Press, 1966 [1929]), and entries in Sam D. Gill and Irene F. Sullivan, ed., *Dictionary of Native American Mythology* (Oxford: Oxford University Press, 1992). An interesting use of Edward's myth is Marta Weigle's "feminist reflections on mythologies of cosmogony and parturition," in her *Creation and Procreation* (Philadelphia: University of Pennsylvania Press, 1989). One is tempted to ponder Edward's relationships to his myth, and motivations for piecing it together into this single version. Given his uncertain parentage, might the Twins' search for their father and his eventual approval, for instance, have held special meaning?

Chapter 46: Back to the Present (1928–30)

For material in this chapter: WH—6/5/93; WH—7/3/93.

353 **"Being an Indian"**: David Martinez, *Dakota Philosopher: Charles Eastman and American Indian Thought* (Minneapolis: Minnesota Historical Society Press, 2009), p. ix.

353 **What the Hunts found:** Try as I might I was unable to find corroboration for Wilbert Hunt's repeated and definite memories of his family traveling up and down the East Coast immediately following their return to the United States (roughly January–August 1928) under the sponsorship of the Keith-Albee-Orpheum Circuit and accompanying such stars of late vaudeville as Fanny Brice, Edgar Bergen and Charlie McCarthy, and Al Jolson.

354 **The new turnaround:** This document was Lewis Meriam et al., *The Problem of Indian Administration,* produced for the Institute for Government Research, Studies in Administration (Baltimore: Johns Hopkins University Press, 1928). Anthropologist Nancy Lurie critiqued the Meriam Report in terms that are pertinent today: "While recognizing a widespread sense of grievance and pleading for justice, it failed to see that to Indian people the fundamental injustice was in being treated and considered as 'wards' on an individual basis rather than as mature people organized in viable communities desiring to manage their own affairs on lands guaranteed to them as communities in various treaties and agreements." From "An American Indian Renascence?," afterword in *The American Indian Today,* ed. Stuart Levine and Nancy O. Lurie (Baltimore: Pelican Books, 1970). For an inner look at the Meriam crew's progress, see Donald L. Parman and Lewis Meriam, "Lewis Meriam's Letters During the Survey of Indian Affairs, 1926–1927," Part I, *Arizona and the West* 24, no. 3 (Autumn 1982), and Part II, *Arizona and the West* 24, no. 4 (Winter 1982). I also consulted Donald T. Critchlow, "Lewis Meriam, Expertise, and Indian Reform," *Historian* 43, no. 3 (May 1981).

355 **When geographer-geologist:** A partial roster of American-era surveys of Indian life during the late nineteenth and early twentieth centuries includes: Henry R. Schoolcraft, *Historical and Statistical Information Respecting the History, Condition and Prospects of the Indian Tribes of the United States,* 6 vols. (Philadelphia: J. B. Lippincott, 1851–57); Hubert Howe Bancroft, *The Native Races of*

the Pacific States of North America, 5 vols. (San Francisco: History Company, 1874–76); James R. Dolittle et. al, *Conditions of the Indian Tribes,* Senate Report no. 156, 39th Congress, 2nd sess. (Washington, DC: Government Printing Office, 1867); George W. Manypenny, *Our Indian Wards* (Cincinnati: R. Clark, 1880) (in which the Indian commissioner perfunctorily dismisses the Pueblos as democratic, lawmaking, self-supporting, and docile "as a woman's school"); Helen Hunt Jackson, *A Century of Dishonor,* 1881 (which was excoriated by Theodore Roosevelt in his *The Winning of the West*); and Alice C. Fletcher, *Indian Education and Civilization: A Report Prepared in Answer to Senate Resolution of February 23, 1885,* 48th Congress, 2nd sess, Senate Exec. Doc. 95 (Serial no. 22649) (Washington, DC: Government Printing Office, 1888). The survey to which John Collier so objected is: G. E. E. Lindquist, *The Red Man in the United States: An Intimate Study of the Social, Economic and Religious Life of the American Indian* (New York: George H. Doran Co., 1923). And the practice of compiling summarizing reports on Indian conditions would continue. See, among others, William A. Brophy and Sophie D. Aberle, compilers, *The Indian America's Unfinished Business: A Report of the Commission on the Rights, Liberties and Responsibilities of The American Indian* (Norman: University of Oklahoma Press, 1966).

357 **"We are puzzled":** Clark Wissler, *Red Man Reservations* (New York: Collier, 1971 [1938]), p. 140.

360 **Life wasn't easy:** Gene Weltfish, "When the Indian Comes to the City," *The American Indian* 1, no. 2 (Winter 1944): 6–10. On the belated recognition of the unique predicament of urban Indians, Howard M. Bahr, Bruce A. Chadwick, and Robert C. Day, *Native Americans Today: Sociological Perspectives* (New York: Harper & Row, 1972); Jack O. Waddell and O. Michael Watson, ed., *The American Indian in Urban Society* (Boston: Little, Brown, 1971); and Donald L. Fixico, *The Urban Indian Experience in America* (Albuquerque: University of New Mexico Press, 2000). More to the Southwest is Myla Vicenti Carpio, *Indigenous Albuquerque* (Lubbock: Texas Tech University Press, 2011). Yet these works mostly deal with the post-1950, relocation/termination era, leaving the experiences of late-nineteenth-and early-twentieth-century Indian urban pioneers like the Hunts yet untold.

Chapter 47: Some Indians Survive (1929–32)

361 **"Some of you":** From Alfonso Ortiz, "The Twenties at San Juan," in *Indian Self-Rule: First-Hand Accounts of Indian–White Relations from Roosevelt to Reagan,* ed. Kenneth R. Philp (Salt Lake City: Howe Brothers, 1986), p. 64.

363 **However Wolf Robe:** To reconstruct Wolf Robe's career over the following chapters I am indebted to the hospitality of Mrs. Zelta Davis of Catoosa, Oklahoma, for escorting Wilbert and Eddie Hunt and me around Wolf Robe's old trading post on one side of old Route 66 and her late husband's Blue Whale center on the other side (which has since undergone a facelift)—and for an interview (4/23/ 1995). I also utilized the 9.8 linear feet of boxed materials (1930–78) in the Wolf Robe Papers at the National Anthropological Archives, Smithsonian Institution, donated in 1979 by his widow, Glenal Davis Hunt, containing personal letters, official endorsements, Indian Lore notes, autobiographical fragments, daybooks,

itineraries, financial papers, handbills, newspaper clippings, and photographs covering his New Mexico and Oklahoma years and travels to Europe in the 1960s (finding aid prepared by Jill Watson, 1980, and completed by Judith S. Engelberg, 1992). In addition I researched the sizable Wolf Robe Hunt collections (finding aid by Jeanne S. King, 1988) in Tulsa's Gilcrease Museum's Art Department and Library for the correspondence, copies of his thirty newspaper columns, "A Wild Injun" (*Tulsa Daily World,* May 21, 1938, through January 16, 1938), photographs, collected sheet music, newspaper articles, miscellaneous papers, and sketches and paintings, including illustrations for his coauthored book, *The Dancing Horses of Acoma.* Finally there are the Wolf Robe papers that Mrs. Davis donated as part of the Hunt Family–Peter Nabokov Collection at the Center for Southwest Research in Zimmerman Library at the University of New Mexico.

363 **In New Mexico:** On the Depression and Dust Bowl generally, I consulted T. H. Watkins, *The Great Depression in the 1930s* (Boston: Little, Brown, 1993), and Timothy Egan, *The Worst Hard Time* (Boston: Houghton Mifflin, 2006). For New Mexico, Simmons 1982 and Charles D. Biebel, *Making the Most of it: Public Works in Albuquerque During the Great Depression* (Albuquerque: Albuquerque Museum, 1986).

Chapter 48: A Family of Freelancers (1930–40)

For material in this chapter: WH—7/4/93; WH—7/16–24/98.

369 **"The Indian is the":** Charles A. Eastman, *Indian Scout Talks: A Guide for Boy Scouts and Campfire Girls* (Boston: Little, Brown, 1914), pp. 189–90.

369 **That was the number:** On Boy Scouting and its female counterpart, the Camp Fire Girls, I drew from William D. Murray, *The History of the Boy Scouts of America* (New York: Boy Scouts of America, 1937); Jay Mechling, "'Playing Indian' and the Search for Authenticity in Modern White America," *Prospects* 5 (1980); his subsequent book *On My Honor: Boy Scouts and the Making of American Youth* (Chicago: University of Chicago Press, 2001); and Polly Turner Strong, "'To Light the Fire of Our Desire': Primitivism in the Camp Fire Girls," in *New Perspectives on Native North America: Cultures, Histories, and Representations,* ed. Sergei A. Kan and Pauline Turner Strong (Lincoln: University of Nebraska Press, 2006). Among the many news clippings in various Wolf Robe Hunt archives are numerous references to their Boy Scout appearances, such as the *St. Louis Times* report of March 14, 1931, where Edward's photo accompanies that of such top-level scouting executives as Dr. James E. West.

369 **Unlike with other forms:** For background on Indians in the white imaginary I began with Robert Berkhofer, *The White Man's Indian* (New York: Alfred A. Knopf, 1978), and then Philip J. Deloria, *Playing Indian* (New Haven, CT: Yale University Press, 1998). For further guidance on the Indian Lore movement, Indian hobbyism in the United States, and Boy Scouting, including its Order of the Arrow and Koshare Indian offshoots, I am extremely grateful to Dr. Clyde Ellis of Elon University. On Scouting's main promoter of Indian activities and philosophy and his own organization, the Woodcraft Indians (later the Woodcraft League), Ernest Thompson Seton, I consulted H. Allen Anderson, *The Chief:*

Ernest Thompson Seton and the Changing West (College Station: Texas A&M University Press, 1986), David L. Witt, *Ernest Thompson Seton: The Life and Legacy of an Artist and Conservationist* (Layton, UT: Gibbs Smith, 2010), H. Allen Anderson, "Ernest Thompson Seton's First Visit to New Mexico, 1893–1894," *New Mexico Historical Review* 56, no. 4 (1981), and Ernest Thompson Seton, *The Book of Woodcraft and Indian Lore* (Garden City, NY: Doubleday, 1921). On Indian Lore: William K. Powers, "The Indian Hobbyist Movement in North America," in Wilcomb E. Washburn, ed., *History of Indian-White Relations,* vol. 4 of *Handbook of the North American Indians* (Washington, DC: Smithsonian Institution, 1989).

373 **Based in La Junta:** It has intrigued me whether Edward Hunt did inspire scoutmaster James "Buck" Burshears's Koshare Indians operation (as suggested by Wilbert Hunt), since the two probably met in the early 1930s at various Boy Scout jamborees where Edward was heralded as the last Acoma Koshare, or "delight maker," and talked openly about his experiences. Again thanks to Clyde Ellis for materials on this offshoot of La Junta, Colorado, Scout Troop 230 and Koshare founder Burshears. This documentation included the group's own *The Story of the Koshare Indians* and *Koshare Indian Dancers* (n.d.) publications, Jack Kelly's *Koshare* (Boulder, CO: Pruett Publishing Co., 1975), articles in *Boys' Life* magazine (esp. May 1947), and assorted news clippings. Their organization then copyrighted the term "Koshare" and logo of a sacred Pueblo clown, created a kiva dance hall modeled after the ancient "great kiva" structure at Aztec, New Mexico, and built its own museum in 1949. In 1954, the La Junta organization, in a culture clash similar to that experienced by the white "Smoki" Snake Dancers of Prescott, Arizona, were criticized by the Zuni tribe over their exactingly accurate appropriation of a highly sacred Zuni ceremony, the annual Shalako Festival, and thereafter agreed to discontinue the performance (*New York Times,* February 21, 1954). On both German and American Indian Lore practitioners, see Rayna D. Green, "The Tribe Called Wannabee: Playing Indian in America and Europe," *Folklore* 99, no. 1 (1988).

376 **Following in the mold:** See Margaret D. Jacobs, "The Eastmans and the Luhans: Interracial Marriage Between White Women and Native American Men, 1875–1935," *Frontiers: A Journal of Women's Studies* 23, no. 3 (2002).

Chapter 49: Do Individuals Exist? (1930–40)

For material in this chapter: WH—12/15/95.

377 **"If I seem to say":** Quoted in Harold Courlander, *Big Falling Snow: A Tewa-Hopi Indian's Life and Times and the History and Traditions of His People* (New York: Crown, 1978), p. 4.

377 **White's scholarly career:** Thanks to William J. Peace, author of the intellectual biography *Leslie A. White: Evolution and Revolution in Anthropology* (Lincoln: University of Nebraska Press, 2004), for guiding me to correspondence between White and E. C. Parsons, which contains Parsons's sometimes dismissive references to Edward Hunt and family, and other Leslie White sources. My characterization of White's ethnographic practice is colored by my late friend Alfonso Ortiz's strong views, White's own journal entries in the Special Collections,

Bentley Historical Library, University of Michigan, and archaeologist Reynold J. Ruppe's discovery, when he was permitted in 1951 to conduct a highly controlled and brief excavation on the mesa, that "the Acoma people were aware of the subterfuge practices by Leslie White when he posed as a collector of old pottery for the purpose of gathering ethnological information." *The Acoma Culture Province: An Archaeological Concept* (New York: Garland, 1990), p. 213. White's clearest critique of Franz Boas is *The Ethnography and Ethnology of Franz Boas,* Bulletin no. 6, Texas Memorial Museum (Austin: Museum of the University of Texas, April 1963). After his first field trip to Acoma in 1926, White wrote that he found its people "second to none in surliness and secrecy"—from "Summary Report of Fieldwork at Acoma," *American Anthropologist* 30, no. 4 (October–December 1928): 568. More sophisticated and positive assessments of White's contributions to anthropological theory and his students are in obituary responses by Elman R. Service and Richard K. Beardsley, *American Anthropologist* 78 (1976).

381 **In searching for a database:** Regarding White's impetus for conducting a life history, on July 22, 1932, Parsons wrote him, "[Morris Edward] Opler has just sent me an Apache autobiography of a schoolbred Apache who brings out a large number of acculturation points. If you are short on material on anybody and if any school bred Hopi is available you might consider autobiography" (American Philosophical Society, Elsie Clews Parsons correspondence). As to White's prior interest in the impact of society on the individual, see his "Personality and Culture," *Open Court,* Issue #3, (1925): 146. For a useful overview of the life history in anthropological science, see L. L. Langness and Gelya Frank, *Lives: An Anthropological Approach to Biography* (Novato, CA: Chandler & Sharp, 1981). When anthropologist Paul Radin first championed this approach he argued that autobiographies might provide "an inside view of the Indian's emotional life" that could add flesh to "skeleton and bones" ethnographic profiles. For examples that preceded and followed Radin's breakthrough studies in the early twentieth century, see H. David Brumble III's summaries in *An Annotated Bibliography on American Indian and Eskimo Autobiographies* (Lincoln: University of Nebraska Press, 1981) and his subsequent analysis of such material, *American Indian Autobiography* (Lincoln: University of Nebraska Press, 2008). Specifically for native women, see Gretchen M. Bataille and Kathleen Mullen Sands, *American Indian Women: Telling Their Lives* (Lincoln: University of Nebraska Press, 1984). Of more recent practitioners, the sophisticated work of Julie Cruikshank in the far Northwest (*Life Lived Like a Story* [Lincoln: University of Nebraska Press, 1998] and other publications) and Theodore Rios and Kathleen Mullen Sands (*Telling a Good One: The Process of Native American Collaborative Biography* [Lincoln: University of Nebraska Press, 2000]) stand out.

Among critiques of this autobiographical approach, see Susan Berry Brill de Ramirez, *Native American Life-History Narratives: Colonial and Postcolonial Navajo Ethnography* (Albuquerque: University of New Mexico Press, 2007). Leslie White and others felt the Pueblos unfertile ground for life histories, and anthropologist Triloki Pandey, working with the Zuni, agreed: "The Pueblo traditions do not provide any model for such confessional introspection, as people hardly remember individuals after their death. After all, traditionally an individual is not that important in Pueblo culture." However, the intimate, first-person accounts in Leo Simmons's *Sun Chief* (1942), Helen Sekaquaptewa's *Me and Mine* (1969), Virgil Wyaco's *A Zuni Life: A Pueblo Indian in Two Worlds* (1998), Pablita Velarde's *Painting Her People* (2001), Irving Pabanale's *Standing Flower: The Life of Irving Pabanale, an Arizona Tewa Indian* (2002), and Esther Martinez's *My Life in San Juan Pueblo* (2004), among others, belie that opinion.

Chapter 50: Another Native World (1936–45)

For material in this chapter: WH—7/3/93; WH—5/9/97.

384 **"One day in Memphis":** "Chief Wolf Robe Hunt" newspaper column, "A Wild Injun," *Tulsa Daily World,* March 3, 1936.

385 **For most Indians:** Special thanks to highway historian Quinta Scott, author of *Along Route 66* (Norman: University of Oklahoma Press, 2000), for copies of her interviews with members of the Hunt-Davis family. On Oklahoma's native peoples, Muriel H. Wright, *A Guide to the Indian Tribes of Oklahoma* (Norman: University of Oklahoma Press, 1957), and its update, Blue Clark, *Indian Tribes of Oklahoma: A Guide* (Norman: University of Oklahoma Press, 2009), which emphasizes contemporary economics; also Angie Debo, *Oklahoma: A History of Five Centuries* (Norman: University of Oklahoma Press, 1980), and *Oklahoma: Footloose and Fancy Free* (Norman: University of Oklahoma Press, 1987).

386 **After they returned:** On car culture and highways: John B. Rae, *The Road and the Car in American Life* (Cambridge, MA: MIT Press, 1971), especially chapter 50; William A. Tydeman, "A New Deal for Tourists: Route 66 and Promotion of New Mexico," *New Mexico Historical Review* 66, no. 2 (April 1991).

389 **He renamed their troupe:** On Wolf Robe's Oklahoma years I am grateful to the archives and citations above (see sources and notes for chapter 47). In April 1995, Wilbert, Eddie, and Shirley Hunt and I visited the site of Wolf Robe's trading post in Catoosa, visited with Mrs. Hugh Davis, and surveyed the Wolf Robe materials at the Gilcrease Museum archives. In addition, Wolf Robe was interviewed for the Doris Duke Oral History Project by Mike Weber (Tape #134, n.d., transcript in Center for Southwest Research, Zimmerman Library at the University of New Mexico). His thumbnail biographies are in Patrick D. Lester and Jeanne Snodgrass, *The Biographical Dictionary of Native American Painters* (Norman: University of Oklahoma Press, 1995); multiple editions of Marion E. Gridley's *Indians of Today* (Sponsored by the Indian Council Fire of Chicago); and the *Dictionary of Indians of North America* (St. Clair Shores, MI: Scholarly Press, 1978). Also, personal thanks to Jeanne O. Snodgrass for sharing her notes on Wolf Robe Hunt for his entry in her *American Indian Painters* (New York: Museum of the American Indian, 1968); also Roger Matuz, ed., *St. James Guide to Native North American Artists* (Detroit: St. James Press, 1997). Among magazine and newspaper features that I consulted on Wolf Robe's life: C. L. Packer, "Silver Pounder," *Tulsa Sunday World Magazine,* June 7, 1953; "Indian Saves the Show," *Charlotte Observer,* October 29, 1965; Cheryl Dobbins, "Wolf Robe Hunt, Delight Maker," *Tulsa Magazine,* July 11, 1974; Charles L. Van Buskirk, "Song of the Delight Maker: Wolf Robe Hunt," *NIMROD* 20, no. 2 (Spring/Summer 1976); and Keith Buell, "Touching the

Spirit of Wolf Robe Hunt," *Tulsa Magazine,* May 1977. Wolf Robe may not have been the properly initiated Acoma Koshare, or "Delight Maker," that he always claimed, inheriting his father's mantle. But perhaps even more than the family's designated jokester, Clyde "Sunny Skies" Hunt of Carlsbad, he was clearly its Trickster, always ready to step into any Indianesque role or function he was asked to perform, regardless of its tribal origin or his own "authenticity."

Chapter 51: Wilbert's War (1942–45)

For material in this chapter: Thelma Johnson—3/10/97; WH—4/2/94; WH—7/16/98; WH—4/11/94; WH—7/24-25/98.

390 **"Men of all ages":** May 23, 1943, from the wartime letters of Wilbert Hunt to Vedna Eckerman Hunt (Hunt Family–Peter Nabokov Collection, Center for Southwest Research, Zimmerman Library, University of New Mexico).

391 **As soon as:** This chapter derives from interviews with Wilbert Hunt and the over 350 letters he wrote his wife, Vedna, over 1942–45, which she saved, Wilbert kept in shoeboxes in his closet, and Eddie Hunt turned over to the Hunt Family–Peter Nabokov Collection, Center for Southwest Research. None of her letters to him have survived.

392 **Although Indian Commissioner:** For background on Indians and this war: Alison R. Bernstein, *American Indians and World War II* (Norman: University of Oklahoma Press, 1991), and Kenneth William Townsend, *World War II and the American Indian* (Albuquerque: University of New Mexico Press, 2000), in which an undated memo in the U.S. National Archives drafted by University of Chicago anthropologist Donald Collier is cited for this anecdote: "In 1938 Berlin granted Aryan status to the grandson of a Sioux woman and a German immigrant to the United States. Officials soon afterwards extended that recognition to embrace all Sioux Indians" (pp. 32–33); also Jere Bishop Franco, *Crossing the Pond: The Native American Effort in World War II* (Denton: University of North Texas Press, 1999), which describes "Indian support on the home front," and adds to the Sioux-as-Aryan story by citing its mention in *Congressional Record,* 77th Congress, 2nd Session, A4385. During my visits to Germany the prominence of Sioux Indians as epitomizing Indians in general remained strong; as for Pueblo Indians representing Indians, I found disdain for their bobbed haircuts and traditional embroidered kilts—"real" Indians had braids, wore beaded, fringed buckskin shirts, and donned war bonnets.

393 **At Desert Training Center:** On General George S. Patton Jr. and his Desert Training Center, I consulted Stanley P. Hirschson, *General Patton: A Soldier's Life* (New York: HarperCollins, 2002), and Martin Blumenson, *Patton: The Man Behind the Legend, 1885-1945* (New York: William Morrow, 1985). On the creation of the Alcan Highway, I used Gerald D. Nash, *World War II and the West: Reshaping the Economy* (Lincoln: University of Nebraska Press, 1990).

397 **"Taking a scalp":** Even though Wolf Robe Hunt wasn't in the war, in an interview with his friend Herman Viola, former National Anthropological Archives director at the Smithsonian, he described the proper care for tokens taken in

warfare in Viola, *Warriors in Uniform: The Legacy of American Indian Heroism* (Washington, DC: National Geographic Society, 2008) p. 13.

Chapter 52: What Place for Indians? (1945–50)

For material in this chapter: WH—7/24/98.

398 **"In stimulating traditionalism":** Gerald D. Nash, *The American West Transformed: The Impact of the Second World War* (Bloomington: Indiana University Press, 1985), p. 147.

398 **But a longer-lasting:** John Adair and Evon Vogt, "Navajo and Zuni Veterans: A Study of Contrasting Modes of Culture Change," *American Anthropologist,* New Series 51, no. 4 (December 1949). They quote one Navajo veteran, whose comments might have been echoed by many a Pueblo soldier as well: "The ceremony was arranged by my grandfather. He said we needed it because we seen lots of dead Germans. Not only see them, but step on them and smell some dead German bodies. He was afraid that later on we might go loco if we don't have this ceremony" (p. 553).

402 **One place where:** On Gallup the town, see Frank Waters's colorful "The Trading Capital," in *A Frank Waters Reader: A Southwestern Life in Writing,* ed. Thomas J. Lyon (Athens: Ohio University Press, 2000), pp. 43–46. On the Gallup Inter-Tribal Ceremonial: JoAllyn Archambault, "Indian Imagery and the Development of Tourism in the Southwest," in *Anthropology, History, and American Indians: Essays in Honor of William Curtis Sturtevant,* ed. William L. Merrill and Ives Goddard (Washington, DC: Smithsonian Institution Press, 2002), drawn from her "The Gallup Ceremonial" (PhD dissertation, University of California, 1984). Also Terry Lee Carroll, "Gallup and Her Ceremonials" (PhD dissertation, University of New Mexico, 1971). Thanks to Gallup historian Ernie Bulow for tours around town, to the old and new Ceremonial grounds, for historical information on the Inter-Tribal Ceremonial and related imagery, and for showing me the street mural with Wilbert Hunt portrayed beating a hand drum.

405 **After all Edward:** Wars in which Indians fought and died resurrected the obvious justification for their rights to full citizenship. After the Great War, as the United States headed for the Paris Peace Conference, progressive Indian writer and Society of American Indians intellectual Gertrude Bonnin editorialized in the society's official organ, "The Red man asks for a very simple thing—citizenship in the land that was once his own—America. Who shall represent his cause at the World's Peace Conference? The American Indian, too, made the supreme sacrifice for liberty's sake. He loves democratic ideals. What shall world democracy mean to his race? There never was a time more opportune than now for America to enfranchise the Red Man." *American Indian Magazine* 6, no. 4 (Winter 1919). Or as a young Sioux veteran retorted after being complimented for his loyalty in World War I, "Why shouldn't we be loyal. This was our country before it was yours." *American Legion Monthly,* July 1928. Now, nearly thirty years later, veterans and their parents felt much the same. On Miguel Trujillo of Isleta Pueblo and the long struggle for Pueblo voting rights, see Gordon Bronitsky, "Isleta's Unsung Hero," *New Mexico Magazine,* August 1989; and Joe S. Sando,

Pueblo Profiles: Cultural Identity Through Centuries of Change (Santa Fe: Clear Light, 1998), pp. 56–62.

Chapter 53: Legacy of a Narrative (1948–70)

406 **"I can hardly describe":** Claude Lévi-Strauss, "Anthropology: Its Achievements and Future," *Current Anthropology* 7, no. 2 (April 1966): 124.

408 **"It enables us:** White's review was in *Journal of American Folklore* 56, no. 219 (January–March 1943); two years later came the Richard Long review in *MAN* 45 (July–August 1945).

408 **The instigator was:** Background material on the interpersonally fraught and ultimately unfinished Bernhard Reuter/Helen Roberts Acoma project is in the archives of the Laboratory of Anthropology, Santa Fe. It presumably produced 473 Ediphone records, and over six hundred pages of half-finished transcriptions and songs, which, in the estimation of a scholar who perused the materials in 1937, "have in their present condition little or no scientific value."

411 **As the 1960s and '70s:** Among the popular anthologies that excerpted from Edward's version was Richard Erdoes and Alfonso Ortiz, *American Indian Myths and Legends* (New York: Pantheon, 1984), but see Brian Swann, *Sky Loom: Native American Myth, Story and Song* (Lincoln: University of Nebraska Press, 2014), especially pp. xvi–xvii, for critiques of this and other anthologies assembled for the mass market.

412 **One appropriation of:** Ramón A. Gutiérrez relied on Edward's version of the Acoma origin myth for the foundational early chapter in his controversial *When Jesus Came, the Corn Mothers Went Away: Marriage, Sexuality, and Power in New Mexico, 1500–1946* (Stanford, CA: Stanford University Press, 1991). Although the book received initial acclaim, the united hand of Pueblo academia fell hard on him, as evidenced by the special issue of *American Indian Culture and Research Journal* 17, no. 3 (1993), which included strong critiques by Ted Jojola of Isleta Pueblo, Simon J. Ortiz of Acoma Pueblo, Joe Sando of Jemez Pueblo, Rina Swentzell of Santa Clara Pueblo, Penny Bird of Santo Domingo Pueblo, Glenabah Martinez of Taos Pueblo, and others. The best summation of the entire controversy is Sylvia Rodriguez, "Subaltern Historiography on the Rio Grande: On Gutiérrez's *When Jesus Came, the Corn Mothers Went Away,*" *American Ethnologist* 21, no. 4 (1994). At the same time it is notable that Leslie Marmon Silko and Paula Gunn Allen, famous novelists and poets to emerge from Laguna Pueblo, draw upon characters and features of their Keresan origin myth; see special issue of *Studies in American Indian Literature* (SAIL) 5, no. 1 (Spring 1993).

412 **By the time:** I am grateful to Dr. Lévi-Strauss for answering my queries about Lucien Sebag, whom he clearly cherished. For background I relied on Patrick Wilcken's insightful interpretive biography, *Claude Lévi-Strauss: The Poet in the Laboratory* (New York: Penguin Press, 2010). The French scholar would discuss his research into Pueblo mythology in *Anthropology and Myth* (London: Blackwell, 1987) and (with Didier Eribon) *Conversations with Claude Lévi-Strauss* (Chicago: University of Chicago Press, 1991). Lévi-Strauss wrote the short obituary upon the suicide of Sebag, who was one of his favorite students (*Journal de la Société des Américanistes* 53, 1964). One gets the sense that the abundance of

dualities, inversions, oppositions, and mediators in Pueblo mythology were so evident on the surface that a scholar-detective of Lévi-Strauss's skills was left with little to uncover. Yet from 1951 to 1954, while teaching at the École pratique des hautes études, Lévi-Strauss began his analyses of various Hopi, Zuni, and Eastern Pueblo myths, and during his seminars of 1961–62 returned to the Pueblo material, adding Keresan examples and engaging a shifting team of four or five top students, among whom was the brilliant Tunisian Sebag. Of Edward Hunt's version of the origin myth, Lévi-Strauss/Sebag would write, "The text forms an homogenous whole which begins with the creation of the world and finishes with the settlement of the Acomas at the center of the world; its coherence is total, and one does not note contradictions between the diverse parts of the myth. This is the greatest Keresan myth that has reached us, and it will constitute the focus ('centre') of our research." From Sebag's *L'invention du monde chez les Indiens pueblos* (Paris: François Maspero, 1971), p. 23. Thereafter Sebag conducted fieldwork among the natives of Bolivia and Paraguay, and wrote *Marxism and Structuralism* (1964), while also working on these Keresan Pueblo texts. After his death, Lévi-Strauss found the manuscript on his desk, titled it, and arranged for its publication.

413 **"The day will come":** Lévi-Strauss 1966, p. 124.

Chapter 54: Acoma and Its Inheritance (1920–70)

414 **"It was five years ago":** Wick R. Miller, "When I Was a Guide at Acoma," in *Acoma Grammar and Texts* (Berkeley: University of California Press, 1965), p. 213.

415 **"Yet here is Acoma":** In Agnes C. Laut, *Through Our Unknown Southwest* (New York: Robert M. McBride & Co., 1915), p. 83.

416 **In the spring of 1928:** Correspondence and telegrams documenting the struggle between documentary filmmaker Robert Flaherty and novelist and producer Elizabeth Pickett over rights to film on Acoma mesa in 1927 is in Miscellaneous Correspondence 1908–1935, Records of the Bureau of Indian Affairs, RG 75, National Archives and Records Administration, Denver, and was brought to my attention courtesy of archivists Christopher Baker and Marlene Baker. Among dramatic films shot on top of Acoma mesa are *Redskin,* released by Paramount in 1929, and featuring Richard Dix; *Sundown,* made around 1940, featuring Gene Tierney and George Sanders, in which Acoma village was recast as an African desert outpost; and Sergio Leone's *My Name Is Nobody,* made in 1971 with Terence Hill and Henry Fonda, in which gunplay takes place in the middle of San Estevan del Rey cemetery.

418 **To answer them:** See Thomas Le Duc, "The Work of the Indian Land Claims Commission Under the Act of 1946," *Pacific Historical Review* 26, no. 1 (February 1957). Other evaluations of the ICC include the range of opinions in Imre Sutton, ed., *Irredeemable America: The Indians' Estate and Land Claims* (Albuquerque: University of New Mexico Press, 1985), and the thoughtful assessment by anthropologist Nancy O. Lurie, "The Indian Claims Commission Act," *Annals of the Academy of Political and Social Science* 311 (May 1957). Along with Ward Minge, Robert Rands, and the Acoma Pueblo advisory team, ethnohisto-

rian and consultant for both the Laguna and Acoma dockets, Florence Hawley Ellis, kept detailed notes of her interviews with tribal members and travels to early Acoma sites and shrines with tribal committeeman Syme Sanchez, an Antelope Clan member. It bears mentioning that an enthusiastic early participant in Acoma's ICC effort was rancher Arthur G. Bibo, Emil's son and Solomon's nephew, who ran cattle along the Acoma boundary, created the Kowina Foundation cultural center, field school, and library for the study of Acoma culture, and willed his land and research materials to the tribe. The results of the land claims work is ably reported for general readers in Minge 2002. On the concept of an "Acoma Cultural Province" that largely resulted from these reassessments, see Reynold Ruppe's 1953 Harvard University dissertation *The Acoma Cultural Province: An Archaeological Concept* (New York: Garland, 1990).

Chapter 55: By Whose Hand (1960–80)

For material in this chapter: WH—8/31/94; WH—5/10/97.

422 **"And the fact is":** Witter Bynner, "Navajo Silversmithing: The Collector's Viewpoint," *New Mexico Association on Indian Affairs,* Indian Art Series no. 7, Santa Fe, 1936.

422 **Like craftspeople:** WH—8/31/94 described Clyde's silverwork, Wolf Robe's craftsmanship, and his own silverwork both at home, in his own short-lived downtown shop, and as a long-term employee of Bell Trading Company in Albuquerque. For background on curio shops, trading posts, cottage industries, and assembly lines for producing and marketing Indian arts and crafts, thanks to Jonathan Batkin of the Wheelright Museum, and for his exhaustive *The Native American Curio Trade in New Mexico* (Santa Fe: Wheelright Museum of the American Indian, 2008). I also drew from Erika Marie Bsumek, *Indian-Made: Navajo Culture in the Marketplace, 1868–1940* (Lawrence: University Press of Kansas, 2008); Molly H. Mullin's insightful *Culture in the Marketplace: Gender, Art and Value in the American Southwest* (Durham, NC: Duke University Press, 2001); Kathleen L. Howard's "'A Most Remarkable Success': Herman Schweizer and the Fred Harvey Indian Department," in the collection, *The Great Southwest of the Fred Harvey Company and the Santa Fe Railway,* ed. Marta Weigle and Barbara A. Babcock (Phoenix: Heard Museum, 1996); and Nancy Peake's "If It Came from Wright's, You Bought It Right," *New Mexico Historical Review* 66, no. 3 (July 1991). A pioneering study is John Adair, *The Navajo and Pueblo Silversmiths* (Norman: University of Oklahoma Press, 1945). For official efforts to regulate Indian handiwork and assure its "authenticity," see Robert Fay Schrader, *The Indian Arts and Crafts Board: An Aspect of New Deal Policy* (Albuquerque: University of New Mexico Press, 1983).

427 **Before long Wolf Robe:** Wolf Robe was in the thick of the rise in public awareness of Indian art, especially centered in the New Mexico–Oklahoma axis that was his regular commute by that time. For background on this entire art scene I consulted the breakthrough work on the New Mexican Indian art world, J. J. Brody, *Indian Painters and White Patrons* (Albuquerque: University of New Mexico Press, 1971), followed by his *Pueblo Indian Painting: Tradition and*

Modernism in New Mexico 1900–1930 (Santa Fe: School of American Research Press, 1997). In his first book Brody is direct: "The year after Medina won the Grand Award [at Tulsa's Philbrook Art Center, in 1966], this prize went to an equally inept painting by Wolf Robe Hunt. Obviously, some of the sponsors of Indian painting, as well as some of the painters, were concerned about the shape of Indian painting for the sixties but had not the slightest idea how to bring it into the mainstream" (p. 172). Other insightful pieces on the much-analyzed New Mexico native art world include Kay A. Reeve, "Pueblos, Poets, and Painters: The Role of the Pueblo Indians in the Development of the Santa Fe–Taos Region as an American Cultural Center," *American Indian Culture and Research Journal* 5, no. 4 (1981); Edwin L. Wade, Straddling the Cultural Fence: The Conflict for Ethnic Artists Within Pueblo Societies," in *The Arts of the North American Indian*, ed. Edwin L. Wade (Tulsa: Philbrook Art Center, 1986); David W. Penney and Lisa Roberts, "America's Pueblo Artists: Encounters on the Borderlands," in *Native American Art in the Twentieth Century: Makers, Meanings, Histories*, ed. W. Jackson Rushing III (New York: Routledge, 1999); Cary C. Collins, "Art Crafted in the Red Man's Image: Hazel Pete, the Indian New Deal, and the Indian Arts and Crafts Program at Santa Fe Indian School, 1932–1935," *New Mexico Historical Review* 78, (2003); and Elizabeth Hutchinson, *The Indian Craze: Primitivism, Modernism, and Transculturation in American Art, 1890–1915* (Durham, NC: Duke University Press, 2009).

Whereas these regional art traditions are sometimes conflated—"The Oklahoma and Southwest painters of the 1920s created the foundation of what would become institutionalized in the 1930s as 'traditional' American Indian Painting," writes David W. Penney in *North American Indian Art* (London: Thames & Hudson, 2004), p. 198—my impression is that their social contexts (and consequent social pressures) were somewhat different. On the Oklahoma Indian art scene my gratitude to W. Richard West for an interview (5/30/2014) regarding personal memories of his father, the renowned Southern Cheyenne painter Dick West, and his Tulsa-based circle of artist friends, especially Wolf Robe Hunt and the role of his shop as a gathering place. Additionally I drew upon J. J. Brody's short section "Oklahoma Regionalism" in his 1971 book; special issue, "Plains Indian Painting," *Oklahoma Today* 8, no. 3 (Summer 1958); chapter 13, "Where Can One See Some Indians," in Angie Debo's *Oklahoma* (Norman: University of Oklahoma Press, 1980); "Acee Blue Eagle: An Artistic Pathfinder," *Native Peoples*, September/October 2010; Bill Anthes, "'Why Injun Artist Me': Acee Blue Eagle's Diasporic Performance," in *Native Diasporas: Indigenous Identities and Settler Colonialism in the Americas*, ed. Gregory D. Smithers and Brooke N. Newman (Lincoln: University of Nebraska Press, 2014); and Jason Baird Jackson, "Picturing Traditional Culture: Heritage as Subject and Motivation in the Work of Three Muscogee (Creek) Painters," on the emergence of the Traditional Oklahoma Flatstyle, *American Indian Art* 37, no. 1 (Winter 2011). But it has been left largely to prolific Oklahoma scholar (on law, film, and the visual arts) Rennard Strickland to explore it, in "The Changing World of Indian Painting and Philbrook Art Center," in *Native American Art at Philbrook* (Tulsa: Philbrook Art Center, 1980); but especially Rennard Strickland and Edwin L. Wade, "Native American Painting: Schools, Styles and Movements," in *The James T. Bialac Na-*

tive American Art Collection, Selected Works, ed. Mark Andrew White (Norman: University of Oklahoma Press, 2012), in which they suggest the looser ambience of the Oklahoma scene, and identify Wolf Robe Hunt as a "master shape shifter . . . dancing in, out of, and between the emerging regional conventions coming to be known as Native American painting" (p. 75).

430 **Worst of all:** With Wolf Robe playing loose with tribal traditions—apparently inventing the Shooting the Final Arrow rite for the memorial rites of his friends Acee Blue Eagle and part Creek Indian W. Thomas Gilcrease, and his snake dance performances—it is interesting no one called him out. Living in Oklahoma rather than New Mexico probably shielded him from criticism. Wolf Robe's conduct of Blue Eagle's ceremony in 1959 was filmed; a copy is in the Human Studies Film Archives of the Smithsonian Institution (#87.17.2). In its factsheet on Thomas Gilcrease (n.d.), the Oklahoma Historical Society solemnly recorded his ritual without commentary: "Upon Gilcrease's death in Tulsa on May 6, 1962, his funeral was conducted by Chief Wolf Robe Hunt, a Delight Maker from the Acoma Indian Reservation in New Mexico. After a prayer, corn meal was sprinkled to provide food for Gilcrease's journey, and arrows were shot into the air to seal his spirit against evil on the way to She-Pap-Po, the happy hunting ground. Gilcrease was buried in a private mausoleum on his Tulsa home and museum property."

But unlike true Indian imposters, such as Buffalo Child Long Lance and others—as profiled in James A. Clifton's anthologies, *Being and Becoming Indian: Biographical Studies of North American Frontiers* (Chicago: Dorsey Press, 1989), and *The Invented Indian: Cultural Fictions and Government Policies* (New Brunswick, NJ: Transaction, 1990)—or the background of Wolf Robe's good friend, the Estes Park, Colorado, trading post proprietor and Indian Lore lecturer Charlie Eagle Plume (see *"Joy": The Life of Charlie Eagle Plume, an American Legend,* by Henry F. Pedersen Jr., self-published, Estes Park, Colorado, 1991), Wolf Robe *was* an Indian. Marion E. Gridley of the Chicago-based Indian Council Fire organization even wrote Wolf Robe about her challenge to Eagle Plume's ethnic legitimacy (October 16, 1934), and the following February forwarded him the wording of a proposed congressional bill making it unlawful "for any person other than an Indian to represent himself to be Indian for the purpose of obtaining employment" (n.d.). More recently, Ojibwe writer David Treuer has plumbed the whys and wherefores of such self-misrepresentation ("Going Native: Why Do Writers Pretend to be Indians?," *Slate,* March 7, 2008).

Chapter 56: Yet Another Conversion (1964)

For material in this chapter: WH—7/4/93; WH—8/31/94; WH—9/4/94; WH—7/20/98.

430 **"'The Lamanites, while'":** Quoted in Evon Z. Vogt and Ethel M. Albert, ed., *People of Rimrock: A Study in Value in Five Cultures.* (Cambridge, MA: Harvard University Press, 1966), p. 69.

433 **Like everyone in:** Wilbert and Vedna's adoption of Mormonism is from various sources: WH—7/20/98; and the couple's lengthy interviews with D. Corydon

Hamilton for the Doris Duke–supported American Indian History Project, and filed with the Western History Center, University of Utah (Vedna on 8/19/1967, Duke Number 71; Wilbert on 8/19/1967, Duke Number 72). In addition, Wilbert wrote a five-page "My Testimony" summary of the religious experiences that led to his conversion (n.d.). Vedna wrote an insightful three-page "Our Testimony: Wilbert and Vedna E. Hunt" account (n.d.). Lois and Nevelyn Eckerman added an illustrated, four-page tribute to Vedna and Wilbert with numerous references to their church (n.d.). I am thankful to the Eckerman sisters for donating this material to the Hunt Family–Peter Nabokov Collection, Center for Southwest Research, Zimmerman Library University of New Mexico.

For background on the Church of Jesus Christ of Latter-day Saints, see Claudia Lauper Bushman and Richard Lyman Bushman, *Building a Kingdom: A History of Mormons in America* (New York: Oxford University Press, 1999), and Armand L. Mauss, *All Abraham's Children: Changing Mormon Conceptions of Race and Lineage* (Urbana: University of Illinois Press, 2003). More specifically on Mormons and native peoples: John A. Price, "Mormon Missions to the Indians," in Wilcomb E. Washburn, ed., *History of Indian-White Relations*, vol. 4 of *Handbook of the North American Indians* (Washington, DC: Smithsonian Institution, 1988); Hokulani K. Aikau, *A Chosen People, a Promised Land: Mormonism and Race in Hawai'i* (Minneapolis: University of Minnesota Press, 2012). For Mormonism's impact upon the greater Southwest, see Richard V. Francaviglia, *The Mormon Landscape: Existence, Creation, and Perception of a Unique Image in the American West* (New York: AMS Press, 1978); Jared Farmer, *On Zion's Mount: Mormons, Indians, and the American Landscape* (Cambridge, MA: Harvard University Press, 2008); Lawrence G. Coates, "Brigham Young and Mormon Indian Policies: The Formative Period," *BYU Studies* 18, no. 3 (Spring 1978); Leonard J. Arrington, "Mormons in Twentieth-Century New Mexico," in *Religion in Modern New Mexico*, ed. Ferenc M. Szasz and Richard Etulain (Albuquerque: University of New Mexico Press, 1997). Another Pueblo account of conversion to Mormonism is in Helen Sekaquaptewa's autobiography, *Me and Mine* (Tucson: University of Arizona Press, 1969). With his good looks, colorful regalia, and theatrical experience, Wilbert Hunt was frequently asked to provide an Indian face for Mormon-funded multiethnic presentations and films.

Chapter 57: Return to Europe (1965–70)

For material in this chapter: WH—6/5/93.

437 **"A simple explanation":** Christian F. Feest, "Indians and Europe? Editor's Postcript," in *Indians and Europe: An Interdisciplinary Collection of Essays,* ed. Christian F. Feest (Lincoln: University of Nebraska Press, 1989), p. 509.

437 **The same year:** The Clyde Warrior column was reprinted in Stan Steiner, *The New Indians* (New York: Harper & Row, 1968), appendix F.

438 **By recruiting "Chief":** News clippings, correspondence, and photographs on the Hunts' various European business trips of the 1960s are in the National Anthropological Archives, the Wolf Robe Hunt Collection, and I added more material, courtesy of Zelta Davis and Wilbert Hunt, for the Hunt Family–Peter

Nabokov Collection, Center for Southwest Research, Zimmerman Library, University of New Mexico. Delving further into the Karl May story and his influence, I used Tomas Jaehn, "Karl May and His Wild West," *El Palacio* 117, no. 3 (Fall 2002), which itemizes German sources. On the annual Bad Segeberg Karl May Festival, see essays in Pamela Kort and Max Hollein, ed., *I Like America Fictions of the Wild West* (Munich: Prestel, 2007). Hartmut Lutz's *Approaches: Essays in Native American Studies and Literature* (Augsburg: Wissner, 2002) continues his analytical forays into European and European-American "approaches to First Nations cultures," as does H. Glenn Penny, *Kindred by Choice: Germans and American Indians Since 1800* (Chapel Hill: University of North Carolina Press, 2013); Katrin Sieg, "Winnetou's Grandchildren: Indian Identification, Ethnic Expertise, White Embodiment," chapter 3 in her *Ethnic Drag: Performing Race, Nation, Sexuality in West Germany* (Ann Arbor: University of Michigan Press, 2002); and Wilcomb E. Washburn, ed., *History of Indian-White Relations,* vol. 4 of *Handbook of the North American Indians* (Washington, DC: Smithsonian Institution, 1988). One of the earliest American scholars to address the Karl May influence was U.S. Army veteran and eminent High Plains archaeologist W. Raymond Wood, "The Role of the Romantic West in Shaping the Third Reich," *Plains Anthropologist* 35, no. 132 (1990).

Chapter 58: Changes on the Mesa (1980–2004)

For material in this chapter: WH—4/11/94; WH—7/21/98.

443 **"Po'pay's name was":** Quote in Joe S. Sando and Herman Agoyo, *Po'pay: Leader of the First American Revolution* (Santa Fe: Clear Light, 2005), p. xiv.

443 **"The truth is":** Fray Angelico Chavez, in *Santa Fe New Mexican,* Centennial Fiesta Edition, 1949, as quoted in Wilson 1997, p. 222.

444 **But Wilbert was taken aback:** My personal coverage in August 1980 of this Pueblo Indian–created riposte to the Santa Fe Fiesta and other celebrations of the Spanish and Catholic triumphalism is *Indian Running* (Santa Barbara, CA: Capra Press, 1981). Thanks to Emmett Hunt Jr. (9/8/2012) for sharing his experiences in the All-Pueblo Run of August 1980 that honored the three hundredth anniversary of the All-Pueblo Revolt of 1680.

446 **One by one, communities:** With the gaming era, economic change for New Mexico tribes went into high gear. My chronicle of the growth of Acoma's tourism and gaming industries is from Wilbert Hunt's personal collection of Gallup, Grants, Albuquerque, and Santa Fe newspaper clippings, Acoma Business Enterprises newsletters, *Southwest Indian Tourism and Gaming News* issues, tribal notifications, and other periodic handouts (now deposited in the Hunt Family–Peter Nabokov Collection, Center for Southwest Research, Zimmerman Library, University of New Mexico). For background on this fiscal phenomenon I consulted anthropologist Jessica R. Cattelino's writings: "Gaming," in Garrick A. Bailey, ed., *Indians in Contemporary Society,* vol. 2 of *Handbook of the North American Indians* (Washington, DC: Smithsonian Institution Press, 2008); "Casino Roots: The Cultural Production of Twentieth Century Seminole Economic Development," in *Native Pathways: Economic Development and American Indian*

Culture in the Twentieth Century, ed. Brian Hosmer and C. O'Neill (Boulder: University of Colorado Press, 2004); and her major treatment, *High Stakes: Florida Seminole Gaming and Sovereignty* (Durham, NC: Duke University Press, 2008). Also Joseph G. Jorgenson, "Gaming and Recent American Indian Economic Development," in *American Nations: Encounters in Indian Country, 1850 to the Present,* ed. Frederick E. Hoxie, Peter C. Mancall, and James H. Merrell (New York: Routledge, 2001); and for a good review of stereotypes and misunderstandings (of Osages and other American Indians) in the country's economic history, Alexandra Harmon, *Rich Indians: Native People and the Problem of Wealth in American History* (Chapel Hill: University of North Carolina Press, 2010).

448 **With these opportunities:** For background on tourism I reviewed a number of government-funded professional evaluations of Acoma's economic future and self-promoting opportunities over the years: Anne M. Smith, *New Mexico Indians: Economic, Educational and Social Problems* (Santa Fe: Museum of New Mexico, 1966) (for Acoma, pp. 93–98); Checchi and Company, *The Potential Power of Tourism-Acoma Reservation* (Washington, DC, 1963); Kirschner Associates, *Development of Tourist Potential Acoma Indian Reservation, New Mexico* (Albuquerque, November 1965), which featured renowned architectural scholar Bainbridge Bunting's detailed report on the preservation of Acoma village, especially its domestic architecture; and Ward Alan Minge's draft of a possible guided tour; and Yguado Association's *Acoma Pueblo: Historical Preservation and Design Plan* (October 1973).

449 **Housing all her people:** For material on the People of Acoma Housing Authority (PAHA), new housing projects at Acomita, and Hunt family activities during this waiting interval, Wilbert turned over such documents as meeting agendas with housing participants, the pueblo of Acoma's application for housing rehabilitation work in 1982 on the mesa and Acomita, McCartys, and Anzac (under the Department of Housing and Urban Development [HUD] program for Indian tribes and Alaskan Natives), and daily entries he meticulously kept in his wall calendar.

Chapter 59: One Came Home (2004)

For material in this chapter: WH—7/21/98.

451 **"The Pueblo of Acoma":** Quote from Ward Alan Minge, *Acoma: Pueblo in the Sky,* rev. ed. (Albuquerque: University of New Mexico Press, 2002), p. 146.

452 **Governor Chino's encouragement:** On his parents' earlier unsuccessful return to Acoma: WH—6/21/1998. Thanks to Eddie Hunt for the interview (4/16/2014) revisiting the family's experience with the Skyline One and Skyline Two housing projects, Wilbert's application process for a unit, and their interactions with Acoma authorities.

Chapter 60: Moving On (2007)

458 **"I go back":** James Paytiamo, *Flaming Arrow's People* (New York: Duffield & Green, 1932), p. 112.

I am grateful to Wilbert Hunt's nephews Eddie Hunt (5/25–27/2014) and Johnny and Nancy Johnson of Phoenix (6/20/2014) for information on Wilbert's final days. I relied on them and my own observations around Wilbert's memorial service in Grants, his wake at his Acomita home, and his interment at the Santa Fe National Cemetery. Two months toward the end Wilbert was fairly noncommunicative. But Eddie still encouraged me to talk to him. So I put my mouth to his ear to double-check the name of the steamship that returned his family to America in 1928. Without hesitation he barked back, "SS *Deutschland*," then shot me a look that said, "Do your job."

ILLUSTRATION CREDITS

Albuquerque Museum: pp. 113, 132, 424, 426

Braun Research Library Collection, Autry National Center, Los Angeles: pp. 5, 11, 34, 47, 68, 108, 142, 165, 172, 174, 200, 248, 271, 318

Hunt Family–Peter Nabokov Collection, Center for Southwest Research, University Libraries, University of New Mexico: pp. 37, 74, 77, 101, 103, 115, 118, 140, 187, 189, 194, 203, 209, 210, 214, 217, 220, 223, 229, 252, 257, 258, 264, 265, 267, 280, 284, 297, 298, 306, 326, 338, 341, 351, 355, 362, 365, 367, 370, 378, 383, 387, 389, 392, 393, 396, 399, 404, 409, 411, 416, 429, 432, 435, 440, 442, 449, 453, 461, 465

Wolf Robe Hunt paintings from *The Dancing Horses of Acoma*: pp. 29, 324, 332

Huntington Library, Pierce Collection, San Marino, California: pp. 82, 177, 243

Kansas State Historical Society: p. 128

Karl Kernberger Collection: pp. 445, 447

Lester S. Levy Collection of Sheet Music, Sheridan Libraries, Johns Hopkins University Library: p. 358

Margretta S. Dietrich Photograph Collections; courtesy of New Mexico State Records Center and Archives, Santa Fe: p. 233

Maxwell Museum of Anthropology, University of New Mexico: p. 88

Karl-May-Museum, Radebeul, Germany: p. 302

National Anthropological Archives, Smithsonian Institution: pp. 162, 311, 322, 438

National Geographic Society: p. 314

National Statuary Gallery, Washington, D.C.: p. 38

Palace of the Governors Photo Archives: pp. 9, 14, 17, 23, 26, 30, 50, 51, 52, 84, 90, 94, 97, 122, 126, 134, 146, 148, 154, 157, 158, 168, 206, 225, 235, 276, 345, 348, 374, 456

Shirin Raban: pp. 19, 43, 58–59, 70, 329, 420

A.E. "Bob" Roland Collection: p. 193

Sky City Casino: p. 455

Ruth Underhill, *Workaday Life of the Pueblos*, Department of the Interior, Bureau of Indian Affairs, Phoenix Indian School Print Shop: pp. 179, 195

U.S. Government Printing Office, Washington, 1942: p. 407

U.S. National Archives: p. 240

Western History Collections, University of Oklahoma: pp. 289, 293

INDEX

Page numbers in *Italics* refer to Illustrations.